OFFICE OF POPULATION CENSUSES AND SURVEYS

1991 Census

County report

Laid before Parliament pursuant to Section 4(1)
Census Act 1920

Cumbria

part 1

London: HMSO

First published 1992

ISBN 0 11 691376 2

HMSO
Standing order service

Placing a standing order with HMSO BOOKS enables a customer to receive future titles in this series automatically as published. This saves the time, trouble and expense of placing individual orders and avoids the problem of knowing when to do so. For details please write to HMSO BOOKS (PC 13A/1), Publications Centre, PO Box 276, London SW8 5DT quoting reference 02 02 009. The standing order service also enables customers to recieve automatically as published all material of their choice which additionally saves extensive catalogue research. The scope and selectivity of the service has been extended by new techniques, and there are more than 3,500 classifications to choose from. A special leaflet describing the service in detail may be obtained on request.

Cover illustration by Guy Eves

Contents

Page

1	**Introduction**	1
2	**The 1991 Census**	2
3	**Local results from the Census**	2
4	**The range of information in the Report**	2
5	**Finding information in the Report**	3
6	**The populations covered in the Report**	4
7	**Definitions and explanatory notes**	6
8	**The '10 per cent' sample**	6
9	**Evaluation of the results**	6
10	**Comparisons of results with those of earlier censuses**	7
11	**Further results from the 1991 Census**	8
12	**Copyright and reproduction of material from this Report**	8
13	**Further information**	9
14	**Reference map**	9
15	**Summary of the 1991 Census results for Cumbria**	11
	Tables A - L	
16	**Indexes and main tables**	
	Tables by key word title (Parts 1 and 2)	27
	Topic and key word index (Part 1)	29
	Full table titles (Parts 1 and 2)	35
	Tables 1 - 66	
	Annexes	
	A 1981-91 boundary changes (if applicable)	397
	B How to obtain 1991 Census results	399
	C Explanatory notes - Tables A - L - Tables 1 - 66	403

1 Introduction

1.1 This volume is the first part of the Report for Cumbria from the Census of Great Britain which took place on 21 April 1991. It is published and laid before Parliament under the authority of, and to meet the requirements of, section 4(1) of the Census Act 1920.

1.2 The 1991 Census was the nineteenth in a series begun in 1801, and carried out every tenth year except 1941, and the ninth in which there have been reports for each county.

1.3 The Report contains statistical tables on all topics covered by the 1991 Census. Part 1 includes the results based on processing all Census returns, prefaced by a summary of the main results. Part 2 includes results based on the subsequent processing of a one in ten sample of the returns, and is published separately and later. Each of the main tables is presented for the county as a whole and for each local authority district within the county.

1.4 A similar Report is being made for each county in England and Wales, and for each Region and Islands Area in Scotland. These are being published in a series during 1992 and 1993. To complete the series, there will be a Report for Great Britain as a whole, including figures for Scotland as a whole, Wales as a whole, and for each of the standard statistical regions in England.

1.5 The contents of the Reports were designed, after extensive consultations, to meet needs for statistical facts in consistent form over the whole country on population, housing, employment, health, education, and transport. The series of Reports will serve: local and health authorities; the elected representatives of the community; business and commerce; academic research; education and teaching; local community groups; and, taking the series of Reports as a whole, central government and other national organisations.

1.6 In addition, the forms of table included in this Report were designed to be the basis of standard sets of *statistical abstracts* available, under the terms of section 4(2) of the Census Act 1920, for areas such as wards which are smaller than a local authority. Thus the results of the Census can be analysed for counties, for local authority areas, and for still smaller local areas with comparability throughout Great Britain.

1.7 The text of this Report gives brief background information on the 1991 Census, an introduction to the detailed content of the report, and guidance to assist the user. It also includes a summary of the complete programme of reports and other results from the Census. There is guidance on how to obtain further information.

1.8 This Report was made possible by the co-operation of the households and other members of the public in Cumbria in responding to the Census, by the hard work of the many members of the temporary Census field staff who delivered and collected the Census forms, and by other help given locally. The Registrar General is most grateful for all these contributions. They will be repaid by the value of the results of the Census both to people and organisations in Cumbria and more widely.

2 The 1991 Census

2.1 The Census was held on Sunday 21 April 1991, when every household in Great Britain was required by law to complete a census form. In England there were five questions on housing and 19 questions on each person, while in Wales there was one additional question, and in Scotland two further questions. People in communal establishments such as hospitals, hotels, and prisons were also included. The forms were delivered shortly before Census day by some 118,000 'enumerators', each responsible for a precisely defined area, and then collected in the following days. Enumeration went well over Britain as a whole, although some households, mainly in inner city areas, proved difficult to contact.

2.2 The first results of the Census were published in July 1991 in *Preliminary Reports* for England and Wales and for Scotland. These results were derived from summary records made by the field staff. The main processing of the Census began in June 1991. The publication of County and Region Reports is scheduled to be completed during 1993.

2.3 Preparations for the Census began well in advance, and included trials in the field. Consultation on the topics to be included took place in 1987/8 and the Government issued its plans in a Parliamentary White Paper in July 1988[1]. Parliament debated and approved plans for the Census at the end of 1989 and they became law shortly afterwards. Consultation on the form of statistical output began in August 1988, and, for the County Reports, was completed by mid 1990.

*The 1991 Census Reports to Parliament will be concluded by a **General Report** covering all aspects of the conduct of the Census; in the meantime more information may be obtained from the addresses given in section 13.*

3 Local results from the Census

3.1 Results have been published for local areas of Great Britain from every census since the first in 1801. Reports for each county have been published from censuses in this century. These reports have covered most of the questions asked in each successive census, but there were innovations in the way the 1991 Census County Reports were prepared.

3.2 The Census Offices planned from the outset that the 1991 County Reports should provide results from *all* the topics covered by the Census, and that there should be a single base of standard statistical tables for the Reports and for the associated statistical abstracts which would be made available for smaller areas. It was therefore possible, for the first time, to consult with users of local statistics with a focus on one main objective.

3.3 The Census Offices prepared initial proposals for the local statistics based on those produced from the 1981 Census, and invited comment from advisory groups representing government departments and local and health authorities. Meetings, which were open to all those with an interest, were also held in various parts of the country to discuss the proposals, and written comments were invited. The form of the local statistics was then developed and refined through two further rounds of consultations.

3.4 It was decided to produce two tiers of local statistics. The upper tier is the set of main tables appearing in this Report - they are also known as the 'Local Base Statistics'. This upper tier is also available as statistical abstracts for wards in England and Wales and for postcode sectors in Scotland, provided that the wards or sectors are above a minimum population size. The lower tier - known as the 'Small Area Statistics' (SAS) - is a set of some 80 tables which, for comparability, are either whole or abbreviated versions of the upper tier tables. The SAS are available as statistical abstracts for smaller areas. More information is given in Annex B.

4 The range of information in the Report

4.1 This Report gives Census results for Cumbria, and for the local authority districts within it, *as constituted on 21 April 1991*. The county and district boundaries are shown on the map which forms section 14. There have been changes in the boundaries of Allerdale, Carlisle, Eden and South Lakeland districts since the Census on 5 April 1981.

4.2 The starting point of the topics covered in this Report is the Census form itself. There are facsimiles of the forms used in the Census in the volume of *1991 Census Definitions* - see section 7. All the topics in the 1981 Census were included in the 1991 Census, with the exception of a separate question on outside WCs. However, the answer categories in questions like tenure and economic position (whether in work, etc) were updated. There were also new questions on ethnic group, limiting long-term illness, term-time address of students and schoolchildren, and central heating; a question on weekly hours worked was reintroduced; and information was collected to give a count of dwellings and building types. As in the 1981 and previous censuses, a number of 'hard to code' questions, such as occupation, name and business of employer, and workplace, have been processed only for a 10 per cent sample of households - see section 8.2.

[1] *1991 Census of Population* (Cm 430). HMSO, 1988 ISBN 010 104302 3

4.3 The Census questions for all people, whether they were in households or in communal establishments like hospitals and hotels, were:

age (date of birth)
sex
marital status
relationship to head of household*/position in establishment
whereabouts on Census night - asked in households only
usual address
term-time address of students and schoolchildren
usual address one year ago (migration)
country of birth
ethnic group
long-term illness;

and for all those aged 16 or over:

economic activity in preceding week and employment status (self-employed, employee, etc)
hours worked weekly*
occupation*
industry of employment (name and business of employer)*
address of work-place*
means of daily journey to work*
higher qualifications*.

* Analysed for a 10 per cent sample of the population - see section 8.

In Wales there was a question on the Welsh language and in Scotland a question on Gaelic.

4.4 In addition, the person filling in the form in each household was asked about:

number of rooms
'shared' accommodation
tenure
amenities (WC, bath, central heating)
number of cars and vans available
lowest floor of accommodation - Scotland only.

The name and address of the household was recorded on the form, but, apart from the postcode of the address, this information was not included in the processing operation.

4.5 If a household was absent, or no contact was made with a household which appeared to be present on Census day, the census enumerators recorded the type of accommodation and an estimate of the number of rooms and the number of residents. Absent households were asked to complete a census form voluntarily on return. Where they did so, the data from the forms have been included in the results; where they did not, data about such households have been imputed.

4.6 Each topic on the Census form is covered by tables in this Report. But one of the strengths of the Census is the facility to derive additional variables from a number of questions asked at one time. Examples of derived variables for individuals are 'socio-economic group' and 'social class' (based on occupation) and, for households, an example is the type of household by composition.

5 Finding information in the Report

The tables

5.1 Each Report contains the following tables:

Summary tables in (Part 1)

A to L	All parts of Great Britain
M	Areas in Wales or Scotland only (Welsh or Gaelic language)

Main tables in (Part 1)

1 to 66	All parts of Great Britain
67	Areas in Wales or Scotland only (Welsh or Gaelic language)
68-70	Areas in Scotland only (special housing tables)

Main tables in (Part 2)

71-99	All parts of Great Britain

The *main tables* are either *cross-tabulations*, that is where each element in the population is counted only once in the matrix of table *cells*, or groupings of two or more cross-tabulations of related statistics. Some additional counts are given in *single cells* which do not form part of the matrix of a cross-tabulation.

5.2 Each of the main tables has a short *key word title* which appears at the head of each page and indicates the main feature of the table, but not necessarily every aspect included. These key word titles are listed in table number order in section 16. The tables are grouped into six main subject areas:

in part 1 of the Report:

1-18	Demographic and economic characteristics
19-27	Housing
28-53	Households and household composition
54-66	Household spaces and dwellings
67-70	Scotland and Wales only tables;

and, in part 2 of the Report:

71-99 Socio-economic characteristics (tables based on the 10 per cent sample)

The *Topic and key word index* in section 16 shows where topics and cross-tabulations of topics are found.

Table conventions

5.3 In each table, the figures for the county as a whole are given first, with the local authority areas following in alphabetical order. In the larger tables, the margins are repeated for each area. To make the table content clear, the wording in the table margins is as comprehensive as possible, and abbreviations have been kept to a minimum. There are also a number of standard conventions used in the tables.

Margins (row and column headings)

The *population base* or *bases* for each table - see section 6, are shown in the banner heading over the column headings; when the table contains two or more bases, these are separated by semi-colons.

Indentation in row headings indicates that counts in that row are *sub-totals* of counts in the previous non-indented rows (equivalent to the sub-divisions of column headings).

Text set in italics signifies either that no counts will appear for that row/column, or that counts in that row/column are a *sub-set* of a previous row/column and should not be added to other rows/columns when totalling.

Total rows/columns are indicated by text in capital letters.

Counts

Counts based on full processing (Tables 1 to 70) are given without modification; a cell where the count is zero, but where a non-zero count was possible, is shown with a dash, whereas a cell for which a non-zero count is impossible is left blank. Some cells obviously duplicating others are also left blank.

Counts based on the one in ten sample of returns (Tables 71 to 99) are given as the count obtained in the sample without modification; the count must be multiplied by ten to provide an estimated figure for the enumerated population as a whole; a cell with no member of the sample population is shown with a dash, but this is not necessarily an estimate of a nil value in the population as a whole. (part 2 of the Report gives fuller guidance.)

Cross-tabulations, that is where an element of the population is counted only once, are separated by *ruled lines* within tables, as are single cell counts; where a table has a total row or column common to a number of cross-tabulations, it is usually shown only for the first cross-tabulation.

6 The populations covered in the Report

6.1 Each cross-tabulation in this Report has a *population base*, that is the total population distributed among the tabulation cells - using the term 'population' in the wider statistical sense of the items being counted. Most of the bases count people or households, but some count other items, and many tabulations have bases which are sub-sets of populations as a whole.

6.2 The tabulations count people in an area in one of two basic ways - those who were *present* on Census night, and those who were *resident* whether or not they were present. The method of counting people present is unchanged from previous censuses; the method of enumerating people resident was revised for the 1991 Census to provide a more complete count.

6.3 The Census placed a legal obligation on every household in which someone was present on Census night, and on every person present in a communal establishment, to complete a census form whether they were resident there or a visitor resident elsewhere in Great Britain or outside Britain. Additionally in 1991, for the first time in a British census, there was an arrangement to enumerate, on a voluntary basis, households where nobody was present on Census night - 'wholly absent households'. Census forms and reply paid envelopes were left for completion on the return of such households. (This part of the enumeration was on a voluntary basis because members of the absent households either would have fulfilled their legal obligation by filling in forms if they were elsewhere in Britain, or, if they were outside Britain, had no such obligation.)

6.4 In all cases of wholly absent households, or where no contact was made with a household which appeared to have been present on Census day, the census enumerator recorded the type of accommodation and an estimate of the number of rooms and residents. Where a wholly absent household did not subsequently return a form or where no contact was made with a household, values for the fully processed parts of the Census form were imputed during computer processing using the basic information returned and data on households nearby. The number of people in an area, included either on the basis of voluntary returns or by imputation, is shown in Table 1, with more detail in Table 18; the number of households included by imputation is shown in Table 19.

6.5 The addition of data from wholly absent households and non-contacted households is an improvement compared with the 1981 Census, when people from absent households were only enumerated where they were present on Census night (if in Britain). In 1981, people in wholly absent households, although included in the counts of people present, were excluded from the tables with a base of residents in the 1981 County Reports. The change to the base does, however, slightly affect comparisons between 1981 and 1991 - see section 10.

Population bases

6.6 The main population bases used in cross-tabulations in this Report are defined in full in the volume *1991 Census Definitions* - see section 7. In summary they are as follows:

Persons present in the area on the night of 21 April 1991.

Residents of the area, who are:

- people both present and resident in a household or communal establishment;
- people resident in, but absent on the night of 21 April 1991, from a household in which one or more other people were present (people resident in communal establishments but absent on Census night are *not* included since the Census forms for communal establishments covered only those people present on Census night);
- people resident in wholly absent households who returned a census form; and
- people imputed as resident in wholly absent households and in households where no contact was made (Tables A to M and 1 to 70 only).

Households with residents.

Households with people present but no residents.

Household spaces occupied by a household, or unoccupied.

Dwellings - structurally separate premises (a building or part of one) designed for occupation by a single household.

Figure 1 below shows the relationship between the elements in the population bases of *persons present* and *residents.*

6.7 In addition, there are bases of: *families* of resident persons; units of *non-permanent accommodation*; units of *converted or shared accommodation*; *rooms*; *cars in* (available to) *households*; and *communal establishments.*

6.8 Many tabulations count sub-sets of the main bases, for example, residents in households (that is, excluding those in communal establishments). Two tabulations - Tables 10 and 26 - combine more than one sub-set by including both students who were residents and those whose usual addresses were elsewhere. *Bases should therefore be checked before making comparisons between tabulations.*

Fig 1 Inter-relationship of population bases

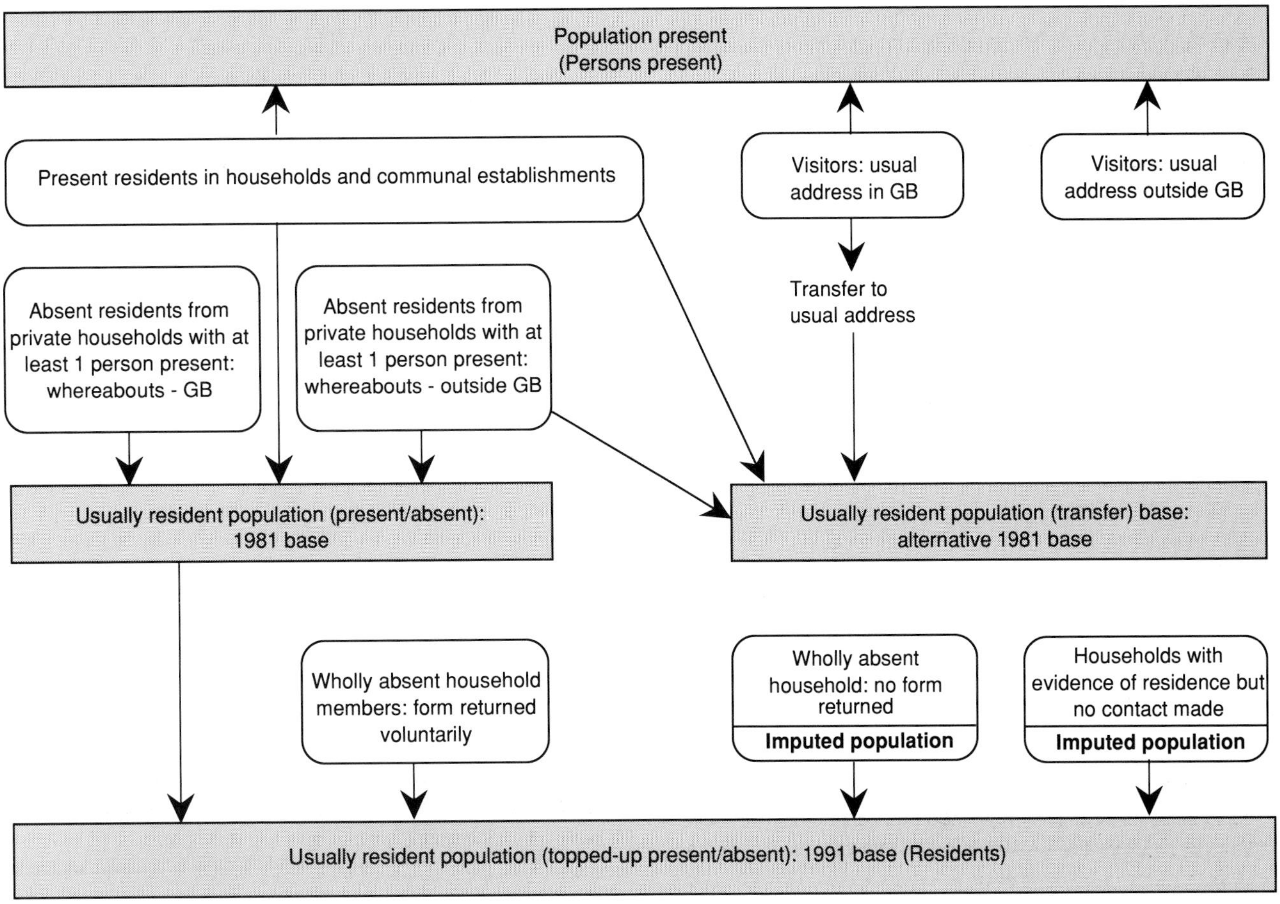

7 Definitions and explanatory notes

7.1 Definitions of all the terms used in the tables in this Report are given in *1991 Census Definitions* published by HMSO[2]. There are too many such definitions for them to be included in the text of this Report, although the terms used in the summary tables in section 15 are defined in Annex C after the main tables.

7.2 The margins of tables in this Report have been made as self-explanatory as possible, with as few abbreviations as possible. But they do not provide a complete definition of the statistics tabulated, and reference should also be made to the *1991 Census Definitions*. Reference may also need to be made to the volumes of *Definitions* for previous censuses if comparisons are being made, or to the appropriate definitions of terms in non-census sources.

7.3 Explanatory notes for the main tables, where they are necessary, are given in Annex C after the main tables.

8 The '10 per cent' sample
(Tables 71-99 in part 2 of the Report)

8.1 The answers to certain census questions, mainly those which are difficult to code because of a wide range of written responses, have been processed for a sample of a nominal one in ten returns. The questions are identified in the list in section 4. The sample is drawn from the edited records prepared during the processing of all the returns. Thus the processing of the sample follows after the full processing, and the results are published somewhat later.

8.2 The sample is drawn by randomly selecting one complete enumerated (but not imputed) household from each 'stratum' of ten sequentially numbered forms, together with one person randomly selected from each stratum of ten sequentially numbered individual forms in communal establishments. This method of sampling avoids the types of bias that can occur in field sampling, and the stratification improves the geographical spread of households included in the sample. However, the clustering of people within households tends to reduce the precision of estimates for variables such as migration or mode of travel to work where the characteristics of individuals within the same household tend to be inter-dependent. Data are not imputed for the sampled topics. *Imputed wholly absent households - see section 6 - are therefore not included in the '10 per cent' tables and the sample is therefore slightly fewer than 10 per cent* of the households included in the '100 per cent' tables. The 'sampling fraction' varies slightly from one area to another according to the proportion of imputed wholly absent households in the area.

[2]OPCS/GRO(S). *1991 Census Definitions, Great Britain.* HMSO, 1992

9 Evaluation of the results

9.1 The results presented in this Report will inevitably contain some inaccuracies arising from deficiencies and errors in coverage or response. The main causes are:

(a) failure to identify all residential accommodation;

(b) failure to identify all households and household spaces within accommodation;

(c) failure to enumerate all persons present or resident within households or communal establishments;

(d) errors in the estimates of numbers of persons in wholly absent households or where no contact was made;

(e) mis-classification of accommodation, for example, classifying wholly absent households as vacant, or vice versa;

(f) errors of double counting persons recorded as resident at more than one address;

(g) incorrect information supplied by filling in the forms, including missing responses; and

(h) errors introduced when processing the forms, including the imputation of data.

Steps are taken to assess the prevalence of these inaccuracies; but, because of the impracticability of conducting a very large number of one-to-one checks, the results are fairly broad estimates. These provide the basis of allowances for inaccuracies in the Census when the Registrar General's mid-year population estimates are made, and provide users of the Census with indications of the degree of confidence that may be placed in the Census results. The figures in Census Reports themselves are *not* adjusted.

9.2 The main check on the completeness and quality of response to the 1991 Census is provided by a Census Validation Survey (CVS). This was a voluntary sample survey conducted soon after the Census in 1,200 Census Enumeration Districts by interviewers employed in the Social Survey by the Office of Population Censuses and Surveys (OPCS). The sampling fraction for the CVS was higher in Inner and Outer London, and in the Metropolitan Counties and Glasgow.

9.3 The checks on *coverage* assessed whether:

(a) any household spaces in accommodation in the sampled areas had been missed;

(b) any of a sample of unoccupied household spaces had been mis-classified;

(c) any household in a sample of multi-occupied buildings had been missed; and whether

(d) anyone was present on Census night in a sample of households reported to have been wholly absent.

A sample of households where no contact had been made was also checked. On the basis of the coverage checks, estimates of under- or over-enumeration are being made for Inner London, Outer London, Glasgow, other Metropolitan Counties as a whole, the remaining parts of England and Wales as a whole, and the remaining parts of Scotland as a whole.

9.4 The check on the *quality* of response is provided by a further sample of households taken in the sampled Enumeration Districts. As well as checking whether everybody in the household had been included on the Census form (as part of the coverage check), the interviewer checked the accuracy of responses on the form by asking further questions, noting any explanations for differences. Analyses of gross and net differences will be prepared.

9.5 All estimates from the CVS will, of course, be subject to sampling error. Also, the CVS cannot provide a complete check on coverage and quality, even for the households included in the sample, because of changes in the circumstances of respondents between the Census and the CVS and because of incomplete response to the CVS. Despite these inherent limitations, the CVS is expected to provide much valuable information about the coverage and quality of the Census.

9.6 Results of the CVS are published as they become available, starting in summer 1992 with the first results on coverage. The full report on the CVS is scheduled to be published early in 1994. The *Census Newsletter* - see section 13, will include summaries of the main findings.

9.7 The Registrar General's mid-year estimates for local authorities in 1991 and subsequent years will take the Census counts of usual residents given in the County Reports as the starting point. The Census counts will be adjusted as necessary, the main adjustments being as follows:

(a) allowances for any estimated under- (or over-) enumeration indicated by the CVS and any other appropriate evidence;

(b) allowances for differences in the definition of 'residents' between the Census and the estimates; in particular, students are included in the estimates at term-time addresses (an extra question was included in the 1991 Census to provide a better basis for this adjustment);

(c) allowances in respect of armed forces personnel and their dependants; and

(d) the lapse of time between the Census and mid-year 1991.

The counts of residents in this Report and the 1991 mid-year population estimates will therefore not be identical. Differences should be interpreted in the light of the adjustments described above.

10 Comparisons of results with those of earlier censuses

10.1 The population of Cumbria at successive censuses from 1891 to 1991 is given in summary Table A in section 15. Comparisons between 1981 and 1991 are also given for selected variables in other tables in section 15.

10.2 Further comparisons between censuses are affected by changes in: the geographic base; the topics included in the censuses; and the definition of counts presented in the tables. The detail of changes over the long series of censuses is complex, and there is no single guide for users. Reports since the 1901 Census have listed intercensal boundary changes - on the lines of Annex A in this Report, and the *Guide to Census Reports*[3] describes the general changes in censuses up to 1966.

10.3 A guide to the detailed comparability of the 1971 and 1981 Census Small Area Statistics was issued after the 1981 Census (OPCS *1981 User Guide 84*[4]), but it does not cover comparison between 1971 and 1981 County Reports where they differ from the Small Area Statistics for those years. There is a similar guide on the detailed comparability of 1981 Small Area Statistics and 1991 Local and Small Area Statistics (OPCS/GRO(S) *1991 User Guide 28*[5]), and, although the Guide is not specific to the 1981 County Reports - the content of which differed somewhat from the Small Area Statistics, OPCS *1981 User Guide 86*[6] gives the link between 1981 SAS and 1981 County Report tables. It is therefore possible to determine where comparisons can be made between figures in the 1981 and 1991 County Report tables, and where comparisons must be qualified.

---

[3]OPCS/GRO(S). *Guide to Census reports, Great Britain 1801-1966.* HMSO, 1977. ISBN 0 11 690638 3

[4]OPCS. *Guide to Statistical Comparability 1971-81: England and Wales.* User Guide 84, OPCS Census Customer Services, 1984

[5]OPCS. *Guide to Statistical Comparability of 1981 Small Area Statistics and 1991 Local Base and Small Area Statistics - Prospectus.* User Guide 28, OPCS Census Customer Services, 1992

[6]OPCS. *1981 Small Area Statistics/County Reports. A guide to comparison. User Guide 86,* OPCS Census Customer Services, 1982

11 Further results from the 1991 Census

11.1 The results of the Census are made available in two ways:

(a) in printed reports made to Parliament and sold by HMSO bookshops (or, in a few cases, directly from the Census Offices); or

(b) in statistical abstracts available, on request and for a charge, from the Census Offices.

11.2 The results also tend to fall into two broad types: local statistics which cover the full range of census topics - such as this Report - or a summary selection of all topics; and topic statistics which focus on a particular census topic in more detail, mainly at national and regional level. There are also other products which provide further information from the Census. All the main results and products are described in *Prospectuses* in the OPCS/GRO(S) 1991 *User Guide* series, available from the addresses given in section 13. A brief guide to sources of comparable local statistics for other areas, and to sources of more detailed results on particular census topics, together with relevant *Prospectuses,* is included at Annex B.

12 Copyright and reproduction of material from this Report

12.1 All text, statistical and other material in this Report and information of any kind derived from the statistics or other material in the Report is CROWN COPYRIGHT and may be reproduced only with the permission of the Office of Population Censuses and Surveys (OPCS).

12.2 OPCS is prepared to allow extracts of statistics or other material from this Report to be reproduced without a licence provided that these form part of a larger work not primarily designed to reproduce the extracts *and* provided that any extract of statistics represents only a limited part of a table or tables *and* provided that Crown Copyright and the source are prominently acknowledged. OPCS reserves its rights in all circumstances and should be consulted in any case of uncertainty. Enquiries about the reproduction of material should be directed to OPCS at the address given in section 13, and reproduction may require a licence and payment of fees.

13 Further information

13.1 Any *queries* about the content of this Report or on the interpretation of the results in the Report should be made to:

Census Division
OPCS
St Catherine's House
10 Kingsway
London WC2B 6JP

telephone 071 396 2008

13.2 All *Prospectuses/User Guides* mentioned in this Report may be obtained (by those in England and Wales, or outside Great Britain) from:

Census Customer Services
OPCS
Segensworth Road
Titchfield
Fareham
Hants PO15 5RR

telephone 0329 81 3800

or (by those in Scotland) from:

Census Customer Services
General Register Office for Scotland
Ladywell House
Ladywell Road
Edinburgh EH12 7TF

telephone 031 314 4254

Census Customer Services will also arrange the supply of any statistical abstracts required.

Request to reproduce material from this Report - see section 12, should be made to Census Customer Services at OPCS.

Reports published by HMSO may be purchased from the addresses shown on the back cover of this Report.

Census Newsletter

News on all aspects of the Census, including the availability of results, is provided by the ***Census Newsletter*** *issued several times a year by the Census Offices and distributed without charge. Names may be added to the mailing list by contacting Census Customer Services. It is also possible to register with Census Customer Services as a user of the Census to obtain details of relevant products automatically and to ensure inclusion in consultation over future developments.*

14 Reference map

14.1 The map on the following page shows the boundaries of districts covered by this Report, and the boundaries of neighbouring counties. The map is reproduced from the Ordnance Survey 1:250,000 map with the permission of the Controller of Her Majesty's Stationery Office, Crown Copyright reserved.

14.2 The highlighted county/county district boundary lines were drawn by OPCS and reflect, as accurately as possible, the boundaries as constituted at 21 April 1991. As the base maps supplied by Ordnance Survey may not always reflect the latest boundary changes, the county boundary lines on the base map and the highlighted boundaries will not always correspond exactly.

SCOTLAND
NORTHUMBERLAND
CARLISLE
ALLERDALE
CUMBRIA
EDEN
DURHAM
COPELAND
SOUTH LAKELAND
BARROW-IN-FURNESS
NORTH YORKSHIRE
LANCASHIRE
Kilometres 10 0 10
© Crown copyright

15 Summary of 1991 Census results for Cumbria

The Tables A to L in this section were first published in 1992: Cumbria, County Monitor in July 1992.

15.1 This section of the Report contains a summary of the final figures of the population and housing in Cumbria and its districts. The statistics in the summary tables are derived largely from the main tables in the Report, and there is a short commentary on each summary table. In addition, the section contains: population counts from 1891 to 1991; selected measures of changes between 1981 to 1991; and a size in hectares and population density figures.

Comparisons between 1981 and 1991; terms and abbreviations

15.2 Section 6 explains the differences between the population bases used in the 1981 and 1991 Reports. The difference has necessitated the use of particular population bases in the parts of the summary tables showing change, and these are explained in Annex C after the main tables. Annex C also explains the terms and conventions used in the summary tables.

Population present on Census night (Tables A and B)

15.3 The figures of population *present* in an area include visitors to a household on Census night and exclude any residents who were away from the area on Census night. The 1991 Census showed that the population present on Census night in Cumbria was 489,354, an increase of about 4,900 compared with the rounded figure for 1981 - see Annex C. This represents an increase of 0.10 per cent per year in the population of the county during the decade, compared with virtually no change for England and Wales as a whole (based on preliminary figures), and with an increase of 0.17 per cent per year for the county over the period 1971-81.

15.4 The period in which there was the greatest rate of change in the county over the last century was 1939-1951, with an increase of 0.68 per cent per year. The changing size of the population present from 1891 to 1991 is illustrated by the diagram below.

Resident population (Tables C and D)

15.5 The number of people *resident* in Cumbria on Census night (that is, excluding visitors but including residents who were recorded as absent on Census night) was 483,163 (Table D). There was an increase of 0.4 per cent since 1981 (using the 1981 population base in each year - see Annex C). This change results principally from a net gain due to migration, despite there being more deaths than births in the county.

Population present 1891-1991 Cumbria

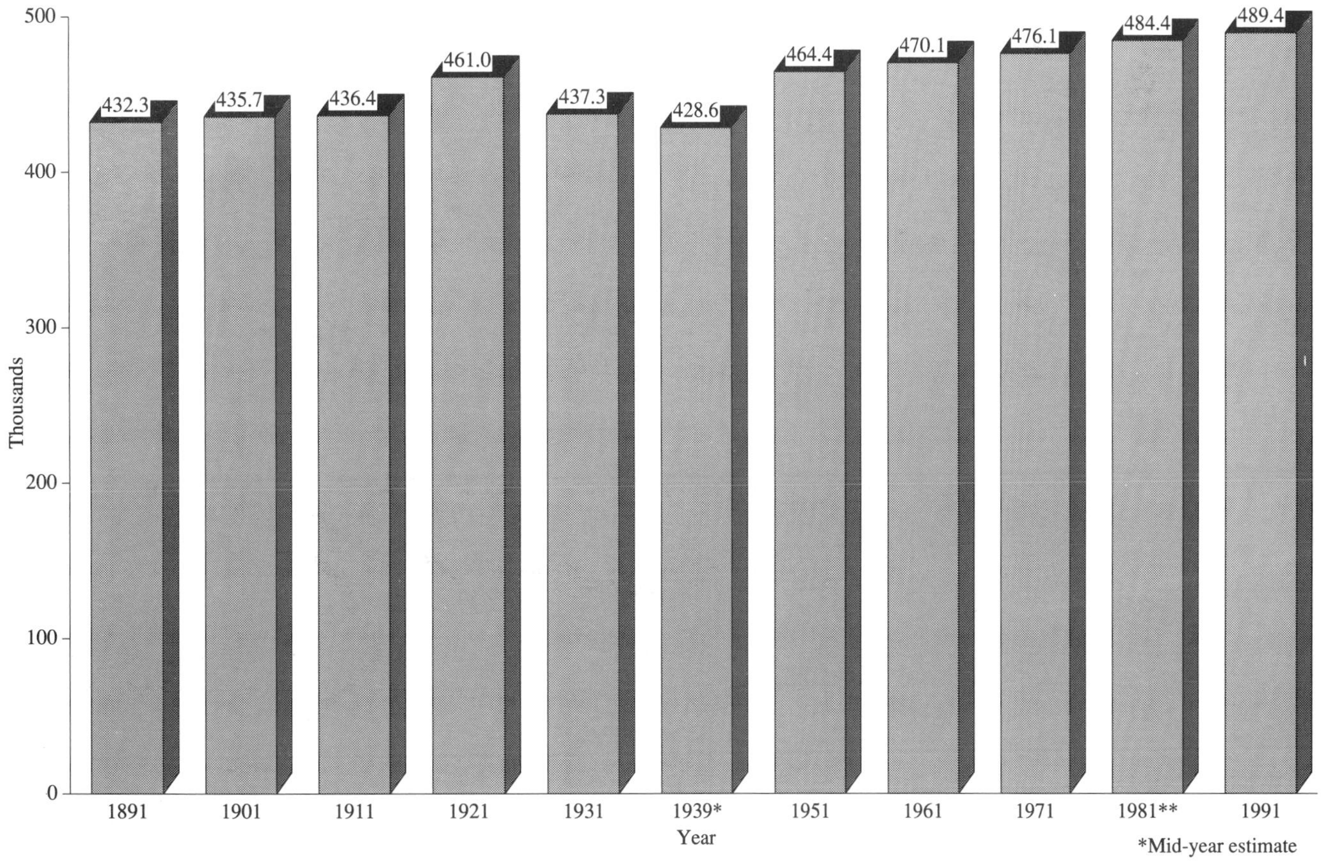

*Mid-year estimate
**Preliminary count

Percentage change in resident population (1981 population base) 1981-91: districts in Cumbria

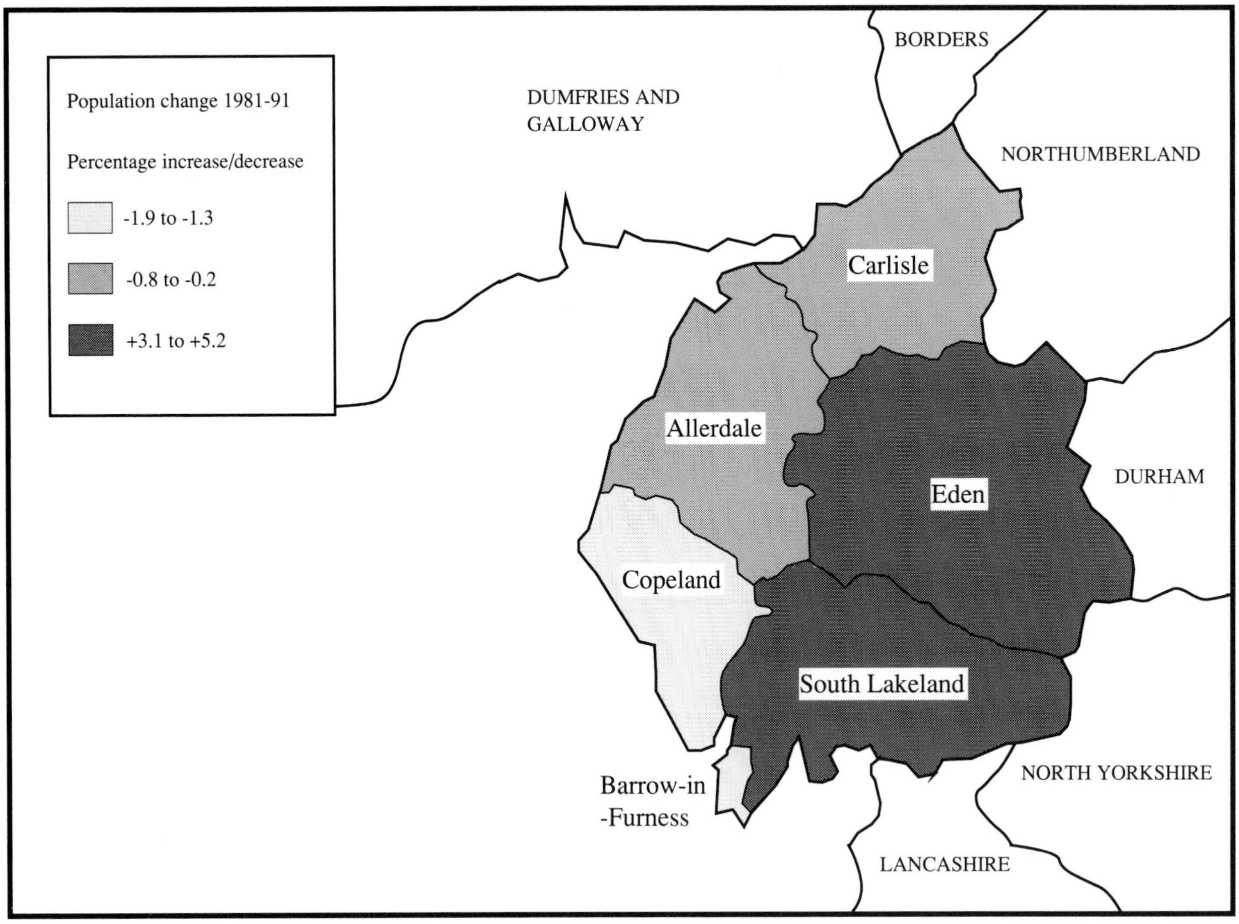

15.6 The changes between 1981 and 1991 in the resident population of the districts in Cumbria varied from an increase of 5.2 per cent in Eden to a decrease of 1.9 per cent in Copeland. These changes are illustrated by the map above. The shading classes in the map have been chosen to highlight the pattern of population change in Cumbria, and will not necessarily be in the same as those used for other counties.

15.7 The district with the largest proportion of people resident in communal establishments was South Lakeland, with a figure of 3.0 per cent; this compares with 1.7 per cent for Cumbria as a whole.

Density of population (Table D)

15.8 People in Cumbria were living at an average density of 0.7 persons per hectare on Census night, compared with a provisional figure of 3.2 for England and Wales as a whole. Barrow-in-Furness was the most densely populated district (9.4 persons per hectare) and Eden the least densely populated (0.2).

15.9 OPCS acknowledges the use of hectare figures supplied by Ordnance Survey in this table.

Children and young adults (Tables E and K)

15.10 At the 1991 Census, children (people aged under 16) made up 18.9 per cent of the population resident in Cumbria. The proportion was highest in Copeland (20.6 per cent) and lowest in South Lakeland (16.8 per cent).

15.11 The proportion of the total population in households who were young adults (people aged 16-24) was highest in Barrow-in-Furness (13.3 per cent) and lowest in South Lakeland (11.3 per cent). The proportion of young adults in households who were lone parents in 1991 was highest in Barrow-in-Furness (2.8 per cent).

15.12 South Lakeland had the highest proportion of people aged 16-24 resident in households who were full-time students, 28.5 per cent, compared with 22.0 per cent for the county as a whole. Copeland was the district with the highest proportion of young adults who were unemployed, 11.5 per cent, compared with the county figure of 8.9 per cent.

Pensioners (Tables E and L)

15.13 People of pensionable age (that is, 65 years and over for men and 60 years and over for women) made up 20.3 per cent of the population of Cumbria in 1991, an increase of 1.1 percentage points since 1981 (using the 1981 population base in each year - see Annex C). The proportion of men and women who were aged 75 years and over increased, respectively, by 0.5 percentage points and 0.8 percentage points between 1981 and 1991. The proportion who were aged 85 years and over increased by 0.5 percentage points in the intercensal period.

15.14 The proportion of people of pensionable age in 1991 was highest in South Lakeland (24.0 per cent) and lowest in Copeland (17.4 per cent).

15.15 In 1991, the total number of households containing at least one pensioner in Cumbria was 70,058. This was 36.1 per cent of all households in the county, a decrease of 1.3 percentage points from the figure in 1981. South Lakeland, with 40.4 per cent, was the district with the highest proportion of such households in 1991.

15.16 Of all households in Cumbria in 1991, 26.6 per cent consisted only of pensioners; an increase of 0.8 percentage points since 1981. The district with the highest proportion of households with at least one pensioner and which either lacked or shared basic amenities (bath/shower; inside WC) was Eden, with 2.5 per cent.

Economic characteristics (Table F)

15.17 In Cumbria, 80.7 per cent of men aged 16-64 and 65.6 per cent of women aged 16-59 were in employment (full-time or part-time employees, self-employed, or on a Government scheme) at some time in the week before the Census. This was a fall of 2.1 percentage points for men and a rise of 10.0 percentage points for women since 1981 (using the 1981 population base, and the 1981 definition of students, in each year - see Annex C). At the 1991 Census 7.0 per cent of men and 3.8 per cent of women were unemployed (that is, seeking work, prevented by temporary sickness from seeking work, or waiting to take up a job already accepted). The remaining 12.3 per cent of men and 30.6 per cent of women were economically inactive. (See Annex C for further definitions.)

15.18 The proportion of men aged 16-64 who were economically active but unemployed in the week before the Census in 1991 was highest in Copeland (9.1 per cent) and lowest in South Lakeland (3.8 per cent). The corresponding figures for women were 5.0 per cent in Barrow-in-Furness and 2.2 per cent in South Lakeland.

Tenure (Table G)

15.19 The 1991 Census showed that 70.0 per cent of households in Cumbria were living in owner occupied accommodation (either owned outright or buying) and 16.5 per cent in accommodation that was rented from a local authority or new town association. This represents a rise of 12.6 percentage points and a fall of 9.8 percentage points respectively since 1981 (using the 1981 population base in each year - see Annex C). The proportion in owner occupied accommodation ranged from 65.4 per cent in Copeland to 78.4 per cent in Barrow-in-Furness.

Amenities (Table G)

15.20 In the county as a whole, 1.3 per cent of households lacked, or had to share with another household, the use of either a bath/shower or an inside WC. This represented an improvement since 1981 when the figure was 3.3 percentage points higher (using the 1981 population base in each year - see Annex C). The district with the highest proportion of such households was Eden (1.9 per cent). The lowest proportion was in South Lakeland, with 1.0 per cent.

15.21 The 1991 Census showed that 26.1 per cent of households in Cumbria had no central heating in any rooms though over nine-tenths of these had exclusive use of bath/shower and WC. The district with the highest proportion of accommodation without central heating was Barrow-in-Furness (41.8 per cent) and the lowest was in Copeland with 20.6 per cent.

15.22 Barrow-in-Furness had the highest proportion of households with no car available in 1991 (39.5 per cent). Eden had the highest proportion with two or more cars (30.2 per cent). These compare with respective figures of 30.8 per cent and 21.5 per cent for Cumbria as a whole in 1991. Car availability had generally increased since the 1981 Census when the proportion of households with no car was 6.2 percentage points higher, and that with two or more cars 7.3 percentage points lower, than in 1991.

Overcrowding (Table G)

15.23 In 1991, 1.2 per cent of households in the county were living at a density of more than one person per room. This represents a decrease of 1.4 percentage points since 1981 (using the 1981 population base in each year - see Annex C). This figure varied throughout the county from a high of 1.6 per cent in Barrow-in-Furness and Copeland to 0.8 per cent in South Lakeland.

Dwellings (Table H)

15.24 There were 209,377 dwellings in Cumbria in 1991. Of these, 22.9 per cent were detached household spaces, 30.6 per cent semi-detached, and 35.9 per cent terraced housing. 0.1 per cent of dwellings were shared - see Annex C. The percentage of shared dwellings was virtually the same in each district of the county.

Household composition (Table I)

15.25 There were 193,893 households in Cumbria at the 1991 Census. Of these, 11.6 per cent had at least one child aged under 5, 3.9 per cent had three or more children aged under 16, and 26.4 per cent had one person living alone. Compared with the 1981 Census, the proportion of households with a young family had decreased by 0.3 percentage points; the proportion with large families decreased 1.1 percentage points; and the proportion of single person households increased by 4.1 percentage points (using the 1981 population base in each year - see Annex C). Barrow-in-Furness was the district with the highest proportion of households with a young family, while Copeland had the greatest proportion with large families, and South Lakeland the largest proportion of single person households.

Limiting long-term illness (Tables E and I)

15.26 A question on long-term illness was asked in the 1991 Census for the first time. Barrow-in-Furness had the highest proportion of households containing at least one person with a long-term illness (27.1 per cent) while Eden, with 22.6 per cent, had the lowest. These figures compare with 24.9 per cent for the county as a whole.

15.27 In Cumbria, 13.1 per cent of people had a long-term illness. This figure ranged from 14.1 per cent of persons in Barrow-in-Furness, the district with the highest proportion, to 11.8 per cent in Eden, the district with the lowest.

Ethnic group (Table J)

15.28 The 1991 Census included, for the first time, a question on ethnic group. In Cumbria the White group formed 99.6 per cent of the population.

Summary Tables

Explanatory notes for the tables begin on the first page of Annex C, after the main tables

Table A Population present 1891 - 1991

Notes: (1) The figures relate to the County as constituted at 21 April 1991.
(2) § Based on preliminary counts (rounded to the nearest hundred) - see notes.

Date of census	Population present	Intercensal increase or decrease (–)	
		Amount	Per cent per year
1891, April 5/6	432,335		
1901, March 31/April 1	435,654	3,319	0.08
1911, April 2/3	436,392	738	0.02
1921, June 19/20	461,034	24,642	0.54
1931, April 26/27	437,268	– 23,766	– 0.54
1939, Mid-year estimate	*428,570*	*– 8,698*	*– 0.25*
1951, April 8/9	464,396	35,826	0.68
1961, April 23/24	470,128	5,732	0.12
1971, April 25/26	476,131	6,003	0.13
1981, April 5/6	484,400 §	8,300 §	0.17
1991, April 21/22	489,354	4,900 §	0.10

Table B Population present 1971 - 91

Notes: (1) All figures relate to the areas as constituted at 21 April 1991.
(2) Changes since 1981 are denoted by:
* boundary
† name
# denotes that the district has been granted borough status.
(3) § Based on preliminary counts (rounded to the nearest hundred) - see notes.

Area	Population present							Intercensal increase or decrease (–)		
	1971	1981 §			1991			Amount §	Per cent per year	
	Total persons	Total persons	Males	Females	Total persons	Males	Females	1981 - 1991	1971 - 1981	1981 - 1991
CUMBRIA *	**476,131**	**484,400**	**235,800**	**248,600**	**489,354**	**238,001**	**251,353**	**4,900**	**0.17**	**0.10**
Districts										
Allerdale *	94,943	96,700	47,000	49,600	96,715	47,143	49,572	100	0.18	0.01
Barrow-in-Furness	75,269	72,600	35,500	37,100	72,192	35,240	36,952	– 400	– 0.36	– 0.06
Carlisle *	100,850	100,700	48,400	52,300	100,039	48,164	51,875	– 700	– 0.02	– 0.07
Copeland	71,794	72,800	36,300	36,500	71,405	35,536	35,869	– 1,400	0.14	– 0.19
Eden *	41,945	44,000	21,900	22,100	46,413	22,876	23,537	2,400	0.48	0.54
South Lakeland *	91,330	97,700	46,600	51,000	102,590	49,042	53,548	4,900	0.68	0.49

Table C Resident population - 1981 base

Note: The 1981 population base excludes households wholly absent on Census night.

Area	Residents (1981 population base)		Percentage increase or decrease (-) 1981 - 91		
	1981	1991	Total	By births and deaths	Migration and other changes
CUMBRIA	**471,694**	**473,447**	**0.4**	**- 0.9**	**1.2**
Districts					
Allerdale	94,244	94,064	- 0.2	- 1.2	1.0
Barrow-in-Furness	72,647	71,695	- 1.3	0.8	- 2.1
Carlisle	99,507	98,692	- 0.8	- 0.5	- 0.3
Copeland	71,457	70,088	- 1.9	1.9	- 3.8
Eden	42,425	44,645	5.2	- 2.2	7.4
South Lakeland	91,414	94,263	3.1	- 3.8	7.0

Table D Resident population and area

Note: A hectare is equivalent to 2.471 acres.

Area	Area (hectares)	Persons per hectare	Residents					
			Total persons = 100 per cent	Males	Females	In households	In communal establishments	
							Number	Percentage of total
CUMBRIA	**681,675**	**0.7**	**483,163**	**234,841**	**248,322**	**474,787**	**8,376**	**1.7**
Districts								
Allerdale	125,054	0.8	95,702	46,617	49,085	93,935	1,767	1.8
Barrow-in-Furness	7,786	9.4	73,125	35,714	37,411	72,564	561	0.8
Carlisle	104,010	1.0	100,562	48,480	52,082	99,059	1,503	1.5
Copeland	74,149	1.0	71,296	35,195	36,101	70,485	811	1.1
Eden	215,645	0.2	45,581	22,451	23,130	44,711	870	1.9
South Lakeland	155,030	0.6	96,897	46,384	50,513	94,033	2,864	3.0

Table E Residents by age

Note: The 1981 population base excludes households wholly absent on Census night.

Area	Total persons = 100 per cent	Percentage aged:											Percentage of all persons with limiting long-term illness
		0 - 4	5 - 15	16 - 17	18 - 29	30 - 44	45 up to pensionable age	Pensionable age to 74	75 - 84	85 and over	75 and over		
											Males	Females	
Residents - 1991 population base													
CUMBRIA	**483,163**	**6.0**	**12.9**	**2.5**	**16.9**	**20.9**	**20.3**	**12.9**	**5.8**	**1.6**	**2.6**	**4.9**	**13.1**
Districts													
Allerdale	95,702	5.8	13.3	2.6	16.6	21.2	20.5	13.0	5.5	1.5	2.4	4.6	13.5
Barrow-in-Furness	73,125	6.9	13.1	2.6	18.6	20.5	19.7	12.2	5.2	1.2	2.2	4.2	14.1
Carlisle	100,562	6.1	13.1	2.5	17.1	21.2	19.8	12.7	5.9	1.6	2.5	4.9	13.3
Copeland	71,296	6.6	14.0	2.6	17.8	21.4	20.0	11.7	4.6	1.1	2.0	3.8	12.8
Eden	45,581	5.5	12.6	2.5	16.2	21.3	21.2	13.0	6.1	1.7	2.8	5.0	11.8
South Lakeland	96,897	5.1	11.7	2.4	15.6	20.2	21.1	14.3	7.4	2.3	3.3	6.4	12.8
Residents - 1981 population base													
Cumbria													
1981	471,694	5.6	16.1	3.4	16.2	19.3	20.5	12.9	5.0	1.1	2.0	4.0	
1991	473,447	6.0	13.1	2.6	17.0	21.0	20.3	12.7	5.8	1.6	2.5	4.8	13.1

Table F Economic characteristics

Notes: (1) * 1991 base counts include students who were also in employment, or seeking work, in the week before the Census. 1981 base counts categorise all students as economically inactive.
(2) The 1981 population base excludes households wholly absent on Census night.

Area	Total males aged 16 - 64 = 100 per cent	Percentage of males aged 16 - 64							
		Economically active*						Economically inactive	Students (economically active or inactive)
		Total	Employees		Self-employed	On a Government scheme	Unemployed		
			Full-time	Part-time					
Residents - 1991 population base									
CUMBRIA	**154,250**	**87.7**	**62.8**	**1.9**	**14.6**	**1.3**	**7.0**	**12.3**	**4.2**
Districts									
Allerdale	30,557	86.9	60.7	1.7	14.2	1.8	8.6	13.1	4.3
Barrow-in-Furness	23,550	88.4	70.2	1.2	7.4	1.3	8.3	11.6	3.4
Carlisle	31,764	88.4	63.9	2.5	13.1	1.2	7.7	11.6	3.8
Copeland	23,338	86.8	66.4	1.3	8.6	1.5	9.1	13.2	3.9
Eden	14,897	88.5	54.2	2.0	27.5	1.0	3.9	11.5	4.6
South Lakeland	30,144	87.6	59.8	2.6	20.7	0.8	3.8	12.4	5.2
Residents - 1981 population base									
Cumbria									
1981	147,382	91.0	68.4	1.5	12.7		8.5	9.0	4.3
1991	151,202	87.4	62.9	1.6	14.6	1.3	7.0	12.6	4.2

Total females aged 16 - 59 = 100 per cent	Percentage of females aged 16 - 59								Area
	Economically active*						Economically inactive	Students (economically active or inactive)	
	Total	Employees		Self-employed	On a Government scheme	Unemployed			
		Full-time	Part-time						
139,366	**69.4**	**32.8**	**26.0**	**5.8**	**1.0**	**3.8**	**30.6**	**5.2**	**CUMBRIA**
									Districts
27,674	66.9	31.2	23.8	6.0	1.4	4.5	33.1	5.4	Allerdale
21,326	66.7	29.9	27.1	3.5	1.3	5.0	33.3	4.3	Barrow-in-Furness
29,240	72.3	34.7	28.6	4.2	1.0	3.8	27.7	4.9	Carlisle
20,772	65.7	32.0	24.1	3.9	1.1	4.6	34.3	5.4	Copeland
13,007	70.2	31.6	25.5	10.0	0.7	2.3	29.8	5.1	Eden
27,347	73.5	35.6	26.3	8.7	0.7	2.2	26.5	6.2	South Lakeland
132,892	59.6	29.5	21.6	3.9		4.7	40.4	4.9	1981
136,896	68.7	32.6	25.4	5.8	1.0	3.8	31.3	5.3	1991

Table G Tenure and amenities: selected categories

Note: The 1981 population base excludes households wholly absent on Census night.

Area	Total households = 100 per cent	Percentage of households									
		Owner occupied (owned outright or buying)	Rented privately, from a housing association, or with a job	Rented from a local authority or new town	Over 1.0 person per room	Lacking or sharing use of bath/ shower and/or inside WC		Exclusive use of bath/shower and inside WC		No car	2 or more cars
						With central heating	No central heating	With central heating	No central heating		
Households with residents - 1991 population base											
CUMBRIA	**193,893**	**70.0**	**13.5**	**16.5**	**1.2**	**0.4**	**0.9**	**73.5**	**25.2**	**30.8**	**21.5**
Districts											
Allerdale	37,867	66.2	16.1	17.7	1.0	0.4	0.8	76.4	22.4	30.8	22.3
Barrow-in-Furness	29,627	78.4	8.6	13.0	1.6	0.2	1.2	58.1	40.6	39.5	12.9
Carlisle	40,883	67.2	10.6	22.2	1.4	0.4	1.0	73.4	25.2	34.2	19.8
Copeland	27,752	65.4	14.1	20.5	1.6	0.2	0.9	79.1	19.7	34.2	19.2
Eden	18,017	70.1	18.8	11.1	1.1	0.6	1.2	76.7	21.5	20.3	30.2
South Lakeland	39,747	73.7	14.6	11.7	0.8	0.4	0.6	77.0	21.9	23.0	26.7
Households with residents - 1981 population base											
Cumbria											
1981	171,964	57.4	16.0	26.5	2.7	4.5		95.5		36.9	14.4
1991	188,050	70.0	13.3	16.7	1.3	0.3	0.9	73.4	25.3	30.7	21.7

Table H Dwellings

Note: No comparable statistics available for 1981.

Area	Total dwellings = 100 per cent	Percentage of dwellings					
		Unshared dwellings					Shared dwellings
		Detached house	Semi-detached house	Terraced house	Purpose-built flat	In converted or partly converted accommodation	
CUMBRIA	**209,377**	**22.9**	**30.6**	**35.9**	**7.7**	**2.7**	**0.1**
Districts							
Allerdale	40,868	22.9	31.5	36.3	7.1	2.1	0.1
Barrow-in-Furness	30,727	8.8	26.5	53.6	9.3	1.5	0.1
Carlisle	42,649	20.2	34.4	34.7	8.9	1.6	0.2
Copeland	29,272	18.2	35.7	38.2	6.0	1.8	0.1
Eden	20,313	38.3	27.7	25.1	6.4	2.3	0.1
South Lakeland	45,548	31.3	26.8	28.0	7.9	5.9	0.1

Table I Household composition: selected categories

Notes: (1) * See introductory notes for the definition of a 'dependant'.
(2) The 1981 population base excludes households wholly absent on Census night.

Area	Total households = 100 per cent	Percentage of households with:					
		Child(ren) aged under 5	3 or more children aged under 16	Only 1 person aged 16 or over with child(ren) aged 0 - 15	1 person living alone	1 or more person(s) with limiting long-term illness	Only 'dependants' *
	Households with residents - 1991 population base						
CUMBRIA	**193,893**	**11.6**	**3.9**	**3.0**	**26.4**	**24.9**	**8.5**
Districts							
Allerdale	37,867	11.5	3.8	3.1	25.5	25.8	8.6
Barrow-in-Furness	29,627	13.5	4.4	3.8	27.0	27.1	9.9
Carlisle	40,883	11.8	3.9	3.5	27.3	24.7	9.1
Copeland	27,752	13.4	4.8	3.5	24.9	25.3	8.0
Eden	18,017	10.6	3.7	1.9	25.0	22.6	6.6
South Lakeland	39,747	9.5	3.2	2.1	27.5	23.2	8.1
	Households with residents - 1981 population base						
Cumbria							
1981	171,964	12.1	5.1	1.8	21.5		
1991	188,050	11.8	4.0	3.1	25.6	24.9	8.4

Table J Ethnic group of residents

Note: No comparable statistics available for 1981.

Area	Total persons = 100 per cent	Ethnic group - percentage									
		White	Black Carib-bean	Black African	Black other	Indian	Pakis-tani	Bangla-deshi	Chinese	Other groups	
										Asian	Other
CUMBRIA	**483,163**	**99.6**	**0.0**	**0.0**	**0.1**	**0.1**	**0.0**	**0.0**	**0.1**	**0.0**	**0.1**
Districts											
Allerdale	95,702	99.7	0.0	0.0	0.0	0.0	0.0	0.0	0.1	0.0	0.1
Barrow-in-Furness	73,125	99.5	0.0	0.0	0.1	0.1	0.0	0.0	0.1	0.0	0.2
Carlisle	100,562	99.4	0.0	0.0	0.1	0.1	0.0	0.1	0.1	0.0	0.1
Copeland	71,296	99.6	0.0	0.0	0.1	0.1	0.0	0.0	0.1	0.1	0.1
Eden	45,581	99.8	0.0	0.0	0.0	0.0	-	0.0	0.0	0.0	0.1
South Lakeland	96,897	99.6	0.0	0.0	0.1	0.1	0.0	0.0	0.1	0.0	0.1

Table K Young adults: selected categories

Notes: (1) * 1991 base counts include students who were also in employment, or seeking work, in the week before the Census. 1981 base counts categorise all students as economically inactive.
(2) The 1981 population base excludes households wholly absent on Census night.

Area	Total persons aged 16 - 24 in households = 100 per cent	Percentage of persons aged 16 - 24 in households who are:					
		Married	The only adult in household with child(ren) aged 0 - 15	Students (economically active or inactive)	Economically active*	On a Government scheme	Unemployed*
		Residents - 1991 population base					
CUMBRIA	**58,082**	**11.7**	**1.9**	**22.0**	**74.2**	**4.0**	**8.9**
Districts							
Allerdale	11,487	13.0	1.9	22.2	73.3	5.1	10.3
Barrow-in-Furness	9,647	13.2	2.8	16.5	76.5	4.3	10.4
Carlisle	12,217	11.4	2.3	20.4	75.9	3.5	9.7
Copeland	8,786	12.6	2.2	21.0	73.2	4.9	11.5
Eden	5,338	10.2	0.7	23.5	74.8	3.0	4.7
South Lakeland	10,607	9.1	0.9	28.5	71.6	2.7	4.8
		Residents - 1981 population base					
Cumbria							
1981	61,650	20.5		19.9	72.3		10.7
1991	57,264	11.6	1.9	22.0	71.4	4.0	8.8

Table L Pensioners: selected categories

Note: The 1981 population base excludes households wholly absent on Census night.

Area	All households			Households with pensioners				
	Total households = 100 per cent	Percentage with: 1 pensioner living alone	Percentage with: 2 or more pensioners and no other person(s)	Total households = 100 per cent	Total pensioners	Percentage of households which: Lack or share use of bath/ shower and/or inside WC	Percentage of households which: Have no central heating	Percentage of households which: Have no car
Households and residents - 1991 population base								
CUMBRIA	**193,893**	**16.2**	**10.4**	**70,058**	**93,802**	**1.9**	**30.4**	**49.6**
Districts								
Allerdale	37,867	16.3	10.1	13,694	18,290	1.8	27.4	51.4
Barrow-in-Furness	29,627	15.9	9.5	9,991	13,221	2.3	47.3	59.8
Carlisle	40,883	16.4	9.8	14,533	19,277	1.9	32.3	53.3
Copeland	27,752	14.7	8.5	9,164	12,042	1.7	25.2	55.4
Eden	18,017	15.4	10.9	6,602	8,957	2.5	27.3	38.4
South Lakeland	39,747	17.8	13.1	16,074	22,015	1.6	25.1	39.5
Households and residents - 1981 population base								
Cumbria								
1981	171,964	15.0	10.5	64,031	86,106	7.1		56.7
1991	188,050	15.9	10.4	67,447	90,471	1.9	30.7	49.7

16 Indexes and main tables

Tables by key word title

Summary tables

A Population present 1891-1991
B Population present 1971-91
C Resident population 1981 base
D Resident population and area
E Residents by age
F Economic characteristics
G Tenure and amenities: selected categories
H Dwellings
I Household composition: selected categories
J Ethnic group of residents
K Young adults: selected categories
L Pensioners: selected categories
M Born in Wales/Welsh speakers (Wales only)

Main tables (Part 1)

I Demographic and Economic characteristics

1 Population bases
2 Age and marital status
3 Communal establishments
4 Medical and care establishments
5 Hotels and other establishments

6 Ethnic group
7 Country of birth
8 Economic position
9 Economic position and ethnic group
10 Term-time address

11 Persons present
12 Long-term illness in households
13 Long-term illness in communal establishments
14 Long-term illness and economic position

15 Migrants
16 Wholly moving households
17 Ethnic group of migrants
18 Imputed residents

II Housing

19 Imputed households
20 Tenure and amenities
21 Car availability
22 Rooms and household size
23 Persons per room

24 Residents 18 and over
25 Visitor households
26 Students in households
27 Households: 1971/81/91 bases

III Households and household composition

28 Dependants in households
29 Dependants and long-term illness
30 'Carers'
31 Dependent children in households
32 Children aged 0-15 in households

33 Women in 'couples': economic position
34 Economic position of household residents
35 Age and marital status of household residents
36 'Earners' and dependent children
37 Young adults

38 Single years of age
39 Headship
40 Lone 'parents'
41 Shared accommodation
42 Household composition and housing

43 Household composition and ethnic group
44 Household composition and long-term illness
45 Migrant household heads
46 Households with dependent children: housing
47 Households with pensioners: housing

48 Households with dependants: housing
49 Ethnic group: housing
50 Country of birth: household heads and residents
51 Country of birth and ethnic group
52 Language indicators
53 'Lifestages'

IV Household spaces and dwellings

54 Occupancy (occupied, vacant and other accommodation)
55 Household spaces and occupancy
56 Household space type and occupancy
57 Household space type: rooms and household size
58 Household space type: tenure and amenities

59 Household space type: household composition
60 Dwellings and household spaces
61 Dwelling type and occupancy
62 Occupancy and tenure of dwellings

63 Dwelling type and tenure
64 Tenure of dwellings and household spaces
65 Occupancy of dwellings and household spaces
66 Shared dwellings

V Scotland and Wales only tables

67 Welsh language
67 Gaelic language
68 Floor level of accommodation
69 Occupancy norm: households
70 Occupancy norm: residents

Main tables (Part 2)

VI 10 per cent topics

71 Comparison of 100% and 10% counts
72 Economic and employment status (10% sample)
73 Industry (10% sample)
74 Occupation (10% sample)
75 Hours worked (10% sample)

76 Occupation and industry (10% sample)
77 Industry and hours worked (10% sample)
78 Occupation and hours worked (10% sample)
79 Industry and employment status (10% sample)
80 Working parents: hours worked (10% sample)

81 Occupation and employment status (10% sample)
82 Travel to work and SEG (10% sample)
83 Travel to work and car availability (10% sample)
84 Qualified manpower (10% sample)
85 Ethnic group of qualified manpower (10% sample)

86 SEG of households and families (10% sample)
87 Family type and tenure (10% sample)
88 'Concealed' families (10% sample)
89 Family composition (10% sample)
90 Social class of households (10% sample)

91 Social class and economic position (10% sample)
92 SEG and economic position (10% sample)
93 SEG, social class and ethnic group (10% sample)
94 Former industry of unemployed (10% sample)
95 Former occupation of unemployed (10% sample)

96 Armed forces (10% sample)
97 Armed forces: households (10% sample)
98 Occupation orders: 1980 classification (10% sample)
99 Occupation: Standard Occupational Classification (10% sample)

Topic and key word index (Part 1)

The numerical and alpha references in this index refer to county report and summary tables respectively

Absent residents
- in households *1*
- students *10*
- imputed *18, 19*

Absent households *19*

Adults
- amenities in households *42*
- economically active *36, 37*
- ethnic group of head of household *43*
- in employment *36*
- in household with long-term illness *44*
- tenure of household *46*
- unemployed *37*
- with/without (dependent) children *31, 36, 37, 42, 43, 46, 59*

Age
- all residents *2, 52, (E)*
- 'carers' *30*
- children aged 0-15 *32, 40*
- country of birth *50, 52*
- dependants *28-30, 48*
- dependent children *31, 46, 68*
- economic position *8, 14*
- ethnic group *6, 43*
- head of household *39, 45, 53*
- headship *39*
- imputed residents *18*
- in communal establishments (not in households) *4, 5, 11, 13*
- lifestage *53*
- long-term illness *12-14, 44, (E)*
- marital status *2, 35, 37, 39*
- migrants *15, 45*
- non-dependants *30*
- not in households *4, 5, 11, 13, 67*
- pensioners *47, (E)*
- persons present *11, 13*
- single years of age *38*
- students *10*
- Welsh speakers (Wales only) *67*
- young adults *37*
- 1981/1991 population base *(E)*

Amenities
- ethnic group of head of household *49*
- household composition *42*
- household space type *58*
- households with dependants *48*
- households with dependent children *46*
- households with pensioners *47, (L)*
- imputed households *19*
- no car *20*
- non permanent accommodation *20*
- selected categories *(G)*

Amenities - *continued*
- shared accommodation *41*
- student households *26*
- tenure *20*
- visitor households *25*
- 1981/1991 population base *(G)*

Area (hectares) *(D)*

Availability of cars - see *Car availability*

Bath/shower - see *Amenities*

Bedsit - see *Household space type*

Born
- in Ireland *6, 7, 9, 17, 43, 50, 51*
- in New Commonwealth *7, 50-52*
- in Scotland *7, 50, 51, (M)*
- in UK *6, 7, 50, 51*
- in Wales *7, 50, 51, 67, (M)*
- outside UK *7, 10, 50, 51*

Campers *3, 5*

Car availability
- no car
  - amenities *20*
  - ethnic group of head of household *49*
  - household composition *42*
  - households with dependants *48*
  - households with dependent children *46*
  - household with pensioners *47, (L)*
  - imputed households *19*
  - number of persons aged 17 and over in household *21*
  - shared accommodation *41*
  - tenure *20*
- number of cars *21*
- total cars *21, 25, 26*
- two or more cars *42, (G)*
- 1981/1991 population base *(G)*

'Carers' *30*

Central heating - see *Amenities*

Communal establishments *3-5, 13*

Converted flat - see *Household space type*

Converted/shared accommodation - see *Dwelling type*

Country of birth
all residents *7, 50-52*
born in Ireland *6, 7, 9, 17, 43, 49-51*
born in Scotland *7, 50, 51, (M)*
born in UK *6, 7, 50, 51*
born in Wales *7, 50, 51, 67, (M)*
born outside UK *7, 10, 50*
ethnic group *51*
household heads *49-52*

Couples
household heads *53*
women in 'couples' *33*

Density (persons per hectare) *(D)*

Dependants
age *28-30, 48*
age of non-dependants *30*
amenities *48*
household composition *29*

Dependent children/Children aged 0-15
age *31-33, 35, 40, 42, 46, 53, 59*
amenities *42, 46*
availability of car *42, 46*
economic activity of adults *36, 40*
ethnic group of head of household *43*
household composition *42, 43*
household space type *59*
in households with long-term illness *44*
non-permanent accommodation *59*
not self-contained accommodation *42, 46, 59*
persons per room *42, 46*
tenure *42, 46*

Different address one year before the Census - see *Migrants*

Dwellings
converted/shared accommodation *60, 66*
household space type *61, 63, (H)*
number of household spaces *55, 60*
occupancy type *61, 62, 65*
tenure *62-64*
type of dwelling *60, 61, 63*

'Earners' *36*

Economic activity
age 8
ethnic group *9*
households with dependent children *31, 32, 36*
imputed residents *18*
in communal establishments *5*
lifestage *53*
lone 'parents' *40*
long-term illness *14, 44*
marital status *8, 34*
migrant heads of household *45*

Economic activity - *continued*
non-dependants *28*
women in 'couples' *33*
young adults *37, (K)*
1981/1991 population base *(F), (K)*

Economically inactive - see *Economic activity*

Economic position
age *8*
ethnic group *9*
lone 'parents' *40*
long-term illness *14*
marital status *8, 34*
women in 'couples' *33*
1981/1991 population base *(F)*

Employees - see *Economic position*

Establishments - see *Communal establishments*

Ethnic group
age *6*
country of birth *51*
economic position *9*
head of household *43, 49, 51*
household composition *43*
housing characteristics *49*
imputed residents *18*
in communal establishments *4, 5*
long-term illness *6*
migrants *17*
percentage distribution *(J)*

Exclusive use of amenities - see *Amenities*

Full-time/part-time employees - see *Economic position*

Government scheme, on a *8, 9, 14, 34, 37, (F), (K)*

Head of household
age *39, 45, 53*
age of residents in household *50*
birthplace of residents in household *50, 51*
country of birth *50, 51*
ethnic group *43, 49, 51*
lifestage *53*
marital status *39*
migrants *45, 57, 59*
tenure *45*

Headship *39*

Hectares *(D)*

Holiday accommodation *54, 55, 61, 64, 65*

Hotels and boarding houses *3, 5*

Household composition
- amenities *42, 46-48*
- car availability/no car *21, 42, 46-48*
- children aged 0-15 *32, 33, 46*
- dependants *28-30, 48*
- dependent children *31, 36, 42, 44, 46, 59*
- ethnic group of head of household *43*
- household size *24*
- household space type *59*
- lifestage *53*
- lone 'parents' *40*
- migrant heads of household *59*
- not in self-contained accommodation *46-48*
- persons of pensionable age *43, 47, 59*
- persons per room *42, 46, 48*
- persons with long-term illness *29, 44, 47*
- students *25, 26*
- tenure *42, 46, 47*
- wholly moving households *16*
- 1981/1991 population base *(I)*

Households
- age of dependants/non-dependants *28-30*
- age of head *45*
- age of residents *39*
- amenities *20, 41, 42, 46-49, 58*
- car availability/no car *20, 21, 41, 42, 46-48*
- economic activity/position *33, 34, 36, 44, 45*
- ethnic group of head of household *43, 49*
- household size (number of persons) *19, 22, 24, 26, 29, 31, 32, 36, 41-43, 57*
- household space type *57-59*
- imputed *19*
- in not self-contained/shared accommodation *41, 42, 46-49, 57*
- lone 'parent' *40*
- migrant heads *45, 57, 59*
- number of dependants/non-dependants *28-30, 48*
- number of rooms *22, 57*
- persons per room *23, 41, 42, 46-49, 57*
- tenure *19, 20, 22, 23, 25, 26, 42, 45-47, 49, 58*
- wholly moving *16*
- with long-term illness *29, 44, 47, 49, (I)*
- with no children aged 0-15 *32, 33*
- with no residents *25*
- with one person living alone *(I)*
- with persons of pensionable age *43, 47, 48, 59, (L)*
- with students *25, 26*
- with/without children aged 0-15 *32, 33, (I)*
- with/without dependants *28-30, 48, (I)*
- with/without dependent children *31, 36, 42-44, 46, 59*
- 1971/81/91 bases *27*

Household size - see *Number of persons in household*

Household spaces
- in dwellings *55, 60, 64-66*
- occupancy type *54-56, 65*
- tenure *64*

Household space type *56-61, 63, 66*

Imputed absent households *19*

Imputed absent residents *1, 18*

In employment - see *Economic activity*

Intercensal change in population
- present *(A), (B)*
- resident *(C)*

Irish (born in Ireland) - see *Ethnic group*

Language indicator *52*

Lifestage *53*

(Limiting) Long-term illness
- age *12-14*
- dependants *29*
- economic position *14*
- ethnic group of head of household *49*
- household composition *44*
- housing characteristics *47*
- imputed residents *18*
- in communal establishments *4, 13*
- in households *12*
- pensioners *47*
- percentage of households *(I)*
- percentage of residents *(E)*

Living alone *(I), (L)*

Lone 'parent(s)'
- age *37, 48*
- amenities *42, 46, 48*
- economic activity *40*
- ethnic group *43*
- household space type *59*
- imputed *19*
- long-term illness *44*
- migrant head of household *59*
- tenure *42, 46*

Marital status
- age *2, 35, 37, 39*
- economic position *8, 34*
- imputed residents *18*

Medical and care establishments *3, 4, 13*

Migrants
- age *15*
- ethnic group *17*
- heads of household *45, 57, 59*
- in communal establishments *4, 5*
- type of move *15, 16*
- wholly moving households *16*

New Commonwealth head of household *49-52*

No car - see *Car availability*

No central heating - see *Amenities*

Non-dependants *28-30, 48*

Non-permanent accommodation
- amenities *20, 58*
- household composition *59*
- household size *57*
- number of rooms *57*
- occupancy type *56, 61*
- persons per room *23, 57*
- tenure *58, 63*

Not in households
- age *4, 5, 11*
- economic activity *5*
- ethnic group *4, 5*
- long-term illness *4, 13*
- migrants *4, 5*
- non-staff *4, 5*
- persons of pensionable age *4, 5*
- persons present *3, 11*
- residents *1, 4, 5, (D)*
- staff *11*
- students *10*
- type of establishment *3-5*
- visitors (not resident) *1, 3*
- Welsh language (Wales only) *67*

Not self-contained/shared accommodation
- amenities *58*
- dependants *48*
- dwelling type *60*
- ethnic group of head of household *49*
- household composition *42, 47, 59*
- household size *41, 57*
- household spaces in shared dwellings *66*
- households with dependent children *46, 59*
- no car *41*
- number of rooms *41, 57*
- occupancy type *56, 61, 65*
- pensioners *47, 59*
- persons per room *41, 57*
- students *26*
- tenure *58, 63, 64*
- visitor households *25*

Number of persons in household (household size)
- amenities *41, 42, 48*
- ethnic group of head of household *43*
- household space type *57*
- imputed households *19*
- in employment *28, 36, 44*
- in shared accommodation *41*
- number of dependants/non-dependants *29, 30*
- number of persons aged 18 and over *24*
- number of rooms *22*
- number of students *26*
- tenure *22, 42*

Number of persons in household (household size) - *continued*
- with migrant head *57*
- 1971/81/91 population bases *27*

Occupancy type
- dwellings *61, 62, 64, 65*
- household spaces *54-56, 65*
- household space type *56, 61*
- rooms *54*
- tenure *62, 64*

On a Government scheme - see *Government scheme, on a*

Owner occupied - see *Tenure*

Part-time employees - see *Economic position*

Permanently sick *8, 9, 14, 34*

Persons aged
- 17 and over *21*
- 18 and over *24*

Persons of pensionable age
- age *43, 47, 50, 53, 59, (E)*
- 'carers' *30*
- country of birth *50, 52*
- dependants *28, 30*
- ethnic group of head of household *43*
- household space type *59*
- housing characteristics *47, 48, (L)*
- imputed residents *18*
- migrant head of household *59*
- no car *47, 48*
- with long-term illness *14, 47*
- 1981/1991 population base *(E), (L)*

Persons per hectare *(D)*

Persons per room
- ethnic group of head of household *49*
- household composition *42, 46-48*
- household size *41*
- household space type *57*
- households with migrant head *57*
- non-permanent accommodation *23*
- not self-contained accommodation *41*
- tenure *23*
- 1981/1991 population base *(G)*

Persons present
- in households *1, 11, 25-27*
- not in households *1, 3, 11, 13*
- 1891-1991 *(A)*
- 1971-1991 *(B)*

Persons sleeping rough *3, 5*

Population bases *1, 27*

Present residents *1, 3-5, 11, 13*

Purpose built flat - see *Household space type*

Rented accommodation - see *Tenure*

Resident outside UK *1*

Residents
- absent *1, 10, 18, 19*
- aged 1 and over *17*
- aged 16-24 *37*
- aged 16 and over *8, 9, 14, 34*
- aged 17 and over *21*
- aged 18 and over *24*
- imputed *18, 19*
- in communal establishments (not in households) *3-5, 13, (D)*
- present *1, 3-5, 11, 13*
- students *10, 26*
- with different address one year before Census - see *Migrants*
- 1981 base *(C)*

Rooms (number of)
- dwelling type *60*
- hotels and boarding houses *54*
- household size *22*
- household space type *57*
- in households with migrant head *57*
- occupancy type *54*
- shared accommodation *41*
- student households *26*
- tenure *22*
- visitor households *25*
- 1971/81/91 population bases *27*

Second residences *54, 55, 61, 64, 65*

Self-employed - see *Economic position*

Shared accommodation/dwellings - see *Not self-contained/ shared accommodation*

Shared/lacking use of amenities - see *Amenities*

Ships *3, 5*

Single years of age *38*

Student accommodation *54, 55, 61, 64, 65*

Students
- economically active - see *Economic activity*
- in households *10, 25, 26, 37*
- not in households *10*
- term-time address *10*

Tenure
- amenities *20*
- dependent children *42*

Tenure - *continued*
- dwellings *62-64*
- economic activity of head of household *45*
- ethnic group of head of household *49*
- household composition *42, 46, 47*
- household size *22*
- household space type *58*
- imputed households *19*
- migrant heads of household *45*
- number of persons per room *23*
- number of rooms *22*
- occupancy type *62, 64*
- pensioner households *47*
- student households *26*
- visitor households *25*
- 1981/1991 population base *(G)*

Term-time address *10*

Type of move *15, 16*

Unattached household spaces *55, 60*

Unemployed - see *Economic activity*

Unshared dwellings
- amenities *58*
- household composition *59*
- household size *57*
- household space type *60*
- number of rooms *57*
- occupancy type *56, 61, 63, 65*
- percentage of dwellings *(H)*
- persons per room *57*
- tenure *58, 63, 64*

Usual residents - see *Residents*

Use of amenities - see *Amenities*

Vacant accommodation *54-56, 61, 64, 65*

Visitors (not resident) *1, 3, 25, 26*

WC - see *Amenities*

Welsh language (Wales only) *67, (M)*

Wholly moving households *16*

Women in 'couples' *33*

Young adults *37, (K)*

1971 population base *1, 27*

1981 population base *1, 27, (B), (C), (E-G), (I), (K-M)*

Full table titles

The following notes describe how to interpret the titles, which are constructed in standard forms. Titles of simple tables which are generally a *cross-tabulation* with a single variable in the rows, but possibly have more than one variable in the columns, follow the form:

(row variable) "by" (column variable(s))

Table 7 is an example.

Titles of tables with more than one variable in the rows have the general form:

(row variables) "all by" (column variable(s))

Where cross-tabulations share a common set of total counts, this 'concatenation' is separated by a comma. Different tabulations *within* a table are separated by a semi-colon (for example, where a set of counts shares only the same population base but no common variables). Table 47 illustrates these features:

An example of a complex table illustrates these features.

(key word title)

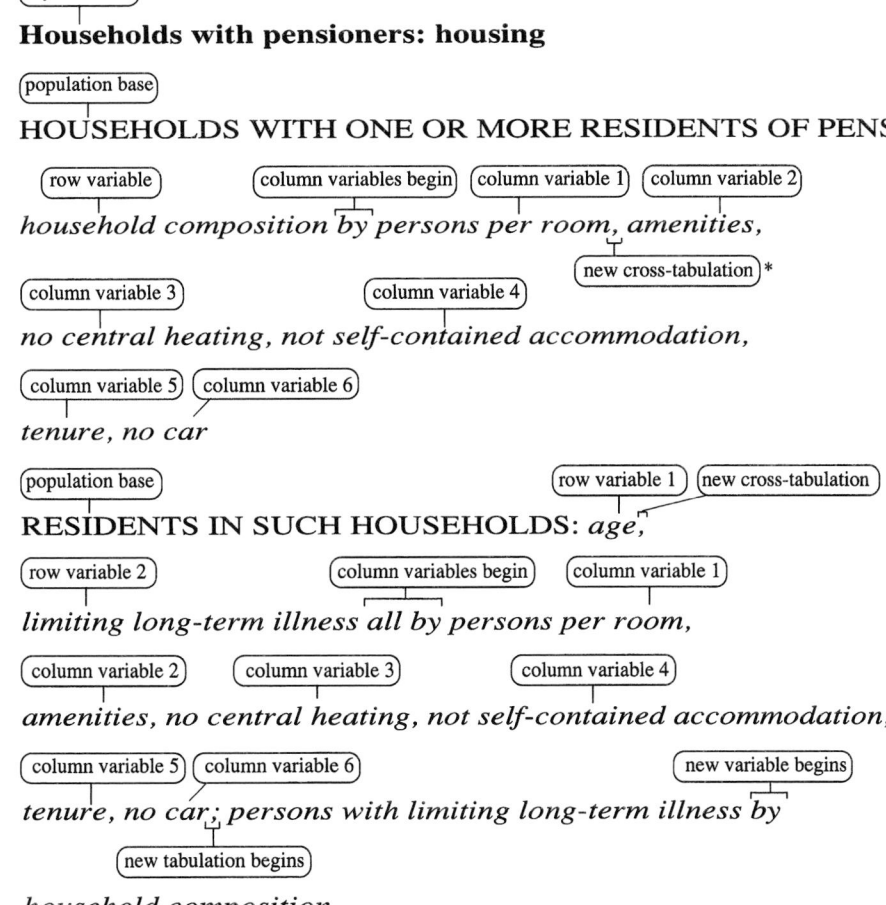

47 **Households with pensioners: housing**

(population base)

HOUSEHOLDS WITH ONE OR MORE RESIDENTS OF PENSIONABLE AGE:

(row variable) (column variables begin) (column variable 1) (column variable 2)

household composition by persons per room, amenities,

(new cross-tabulation)*

(column variable 3) (column variable 4)

no central heating, not self-contained accommodation,

(column variable 5) (column variable 6)

tenure, no car

(population base) (row variable 1) (new cross-tabulation)

RESIDENTS IN SUCH HOUSEHOLDS: *age,*

(row variable 2) (column variables begin) (column variable 1)

limiting long-term illness all by persons per room,

(column variable 2) (column variable 3) (column variable 4)

amenities, no central heating, not self-contained accommodation,

(column variable 5) (column variable 6) (new variable begins)

tenure, no car; persons with limiting long-term illness by

(new tabulation begins)

household composition

*** refers to all commas**

Where row or column variables are 'nested', that is where one variable is broken down by another along one axis of a table, they are separated by the word "by". Where this 'nesting' occurs in the rows axis, the 'nested' variables will be followed by "all by". Table 73 illustrates these features:

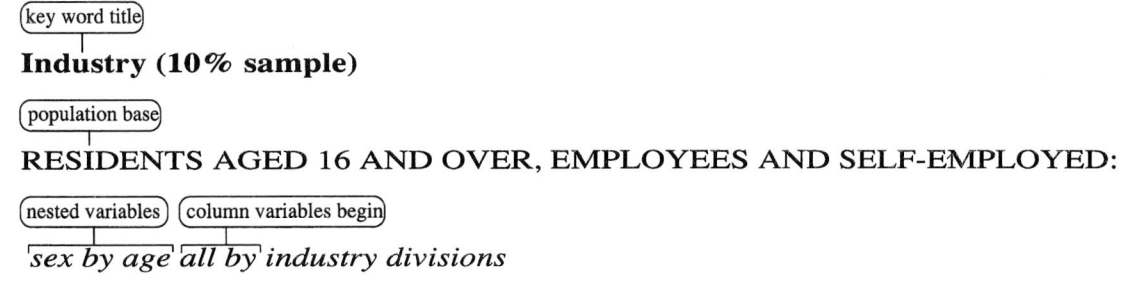

(key word title)

73 **Industry (10% sample)**

(population base)

RESIDENTS AGED 16 AND OVER, EMPLOYEES AND SELF-EMPLOYED:

(nested variables) (column variables begin)

sex by age all by industry divisions

Main tables (Part 1)

Page

I Demographic and Economic characteristics

1 **Population bases** 49

PERSONS PRESENT PLUS ABSENT RESIDENTS IN HOUSEHOLDS: *whether present or absent residents or visitors, 1971, 1981 and 1991 population base counts by whether in a household by sex*

2 **Age and marital status** 51

RESIDENTS: *age by sex by marital status*

3 **Communal establishments** 55

ESTABLISHMENTS: *number of establishments by type*
PERSONS PRESENT NOT IN HOUSEHOLDS: *type of establishment by status in establishment by sex*

4 **Medical and care establishments** 62

RESIDENTS (NON-STAFF) PRESENT NOT IN HOUSEHOLDS: *type of establishment by age by sex, migrants, limiting long-term illness, ethnic group*

5 **Hotels and other establishments** 66

RESIDENTS (NON-STAFF) PRESENT NOT IN HOUSEHOLDS: *type of establishment by age by sex, economic position, migrants, ethnic group*

6 **Ethnic group** 70

RESIDENTS: *age by sex, born in UK, limiting long-term illness by sex all by ethnic group, born in Ireland*

7 **Country of birth** 77

RESIDENTS: *country of birth by sex*

8 **Economic position** 84

RESIDENTS AGED 16 AND OVER: *sex by marital status for females by economic position all by age*

9 **Economic position and ethnic group** 108

RESIDENTS AGED 16 AND OVER: *sex by economic position all by ethnic group, born in Ireland*

10 **Term-time address** 115

STUDENTS (16 AND OVER) PRESENT PLUS ABSENT RESIDENT STUDENTS (16 AND OVER): *residence status by term-time address all by age, born outside UK*

11 **Persons present** 119

PERSONS PRESENT: *age by whether enumerated in a household or not by sex, status if not in a household by sex*

12 **Long-term illness in households** 123

RESIDENTS IN HOUSEHOLDS WITH LIMITING LONG-TERM ILLNESS: *age by sex*

Main tables (Part 1) - *continued*

Page

13 **Long-term illness in communal establishments** 124

PERSONS PRESENT NOT IN HOUSEHOLDS WITH LIMITING LONG-TERM ILLNESS: *age by type of establishment by sex, status in establishment by sex for residents*

14 **Long-term illness and economic position** 126

RESIDENTS AGED 16 AND OVER WITH LIMITING LONG-TERM ILLNESS: *economic position by age*

15 **Migrants** 130

RESIDENTS WITH DIFFERENT ADDRESS ONE YEAR BEFORE CENSUS: *all migrants by age, migrants in households by age, all by type of move by sex*

16 **Wholly moving households** 144

WHOLLY MOVING HOUSEHOLDS: *type of household by type of move*
RESIDENTS IN SUCH HOUSEHOLDS: *type of household by type of move*

17 **Ethnic group of migrants** 148

RESIDENTS AGED 1 AND OVER: *total persons, migrants all by ethnic group, born in Ireland*

18 **Imputed residents** 149

IMPUTED RESIDENTS OF WHOLLY ABSENT HOUSEHOLDS: *age, marital status, limiting long-term illness, economic position, ethnic group all by sex*

II Housing

19 **Imputed households** 151

WHOLLY ABSENT HOUSEHOLDS WITH IMPUTED RESIDENTS: *tenure, amenities, no central heating, no car, lone 'parent' households all by number of persons in household*
IMPUTED RESIDENTS IN SUCH HOUSEHOLDS: *tenure, amenities, central heating, no car, lone 'parent' households*

20 **Tenure and amenities** 154

HOUSEHOLDS WITH RESIDENTS: *amenities, no car all by tenure of households in permanent accommodation, non-permanent accommodation, no car*
RESIDENTS IN HOUSEHOLDS: *amenities, no car all by tenure of households in permanent accommodation, non-permanent accommodation, no car*

21 **Car availability** 168

HOUSEHOLDS WITH RESIDENTS: *household composition, by number of cars available*
RESIDENTS IN HOUSEHOLDS: *household composition; all persons and persons aged 17 and over all by number of cars available*
CARS IN HOUSEHOLDS: *household composition*

22 **Rooms and household size** 170

HOUSEHOLDS WITH RESIDENTS: *tenure by number of persons all by number of rooms*
RESIDENTS IN HOUSEHOLDS: *tenure by number of rooms*
ROOMS IN HOUSEHOLD SPACES: *tenure by number of persons*

23 **Persons per room** 182

HOUSEHOLDS WITH RESIDENTS: *tenure of households in permanent buildings, non-permanent accommodation all by number of persons per room*
RESIDENTS IN HOUSEHOLDS: *tenure of households in permanent buildings, non-permanent accommodation all by number of persons per room*

24 **Residents 18 and over** 186

HOUSEHOLDS WITH RESIDENTS: *number of persons by number of persons aged 18 and over*
RESIDENTS IN HOUSEHOLDS: *total persons by number of persons aged 18 and over; total persons aged 18 and over by number of persons*

25 **Visitor households** 188

HOUSEHOLDS WITH PERSONS PRESENT BUT NO RESIDENTS: *household composition by amenities, no central heating, not self-contained accommodation, tenure*
PERSONS PRESENT IN SUCH HOUSEHOLDS: *total persons, total students all by amenities, no central heating, not self-contained accommodation, tenure; total students by household composition*
CARS IN SUCH HOUSEHOLDS: *household composition*
ROOMS IN SUCH HOUSEHOLDS: *household composition*

26 **Students in households** 190

HOUSEHOLDS WITH RESIDENTS: *household composition, number of students in household all by amenities, no central heating, not self-contained accommodation, tenure, number of persons present or resident*
RESIDENTS IN HOUSEHOLDS, PERSONS PRESENT IN HOUSEHOLDS: *total persons present or resident, total students present or resident all by amenities, no central heating, not self-contained accommodation, tenure, number of persons present or resident, household composition, number of students in household all by total student visitors, total student residents*
ROOMS IN HOUSEHOLD SPACES: *household composition, number of students in household*
CARS IN HOUSEHOLDS: *household composition, number of students in household*

27 **Households: 1971/81/91 bases** 196

HOUSEHOLDS WITH PERSONS PRESENT (1971 POPULATION BASE): *number of persons*
HOUSEHOLDS (1981 POPULATION BASE): *number of persons*
HOUSEHOLDS ENUMERATED OR ABSENT (1991 POPULATION BASE): *number of persons*
PRESENT RESIDENTS AND VISITORS (1971 POPULATION BASE): *total*
PRESENT AND ABSENT RESIDENTS (1981 POPULATION BASE): *total*
PRESENT AND ABSENT RESIDENTS AND IMPUTED MEMBERS OF WHOLLY ABSENT HOUSEHOLDS (1991 POPULATION BASE): *total*
ROOMS: *in 1971, 1981, and 1991 population base households*

Main tables (Part 1) - *continued*

Page

III Households and household composition

28 **Dependants in households** 198

HOUSEHOLDS WITH RESIDENTS: *household composition by economic position of non-dependants*
RESIDENTS IN HOUSEHOLDS: *non-dependants, dependants all by economic position of non-dependants*

29 **Dependants and long-term illness** 212

HOUSEHOLDS WITH RESIDENTS: *household composition*
DEPENDANTS IN HOUSEHOLDS: *household composition by dependency type*

30 **'Carers'** 214

HOUSEHOLDS WITH RESIDENTS: *number of non-dependants by sex by age all by ages in combination of dependants*
RESIDENTS IN HOUSEHOLDS WITH DEPENDANTS: non-dependants, dependants all by number, age and sex of non-dependants

31 **Dependent children in households** 218

HOUSEHOLDS WITH RESIDENTS: *number of adults by sex all by number of dependent children by age*
RESIDENTS IN HOUSEHOLDS: *number of adults in household by sex all by whether dependent children in household by economic activity*

32 **Children aged 0-15 in households** 221

HOUSEHOLDS WITH RESIDENTS: *number of persons aged 16 and over by sex all by number of persons aged 0-15 by age*
RESIDENTS IN HOUSEHOLDS: *number of persons aged 16 and over in household by sex all by whether persons aged 0-15 in household by economic activity*

33 **Women in 'couples': economic position** 224

FEMALES RESIDENT IN HOUSEHOLDS OF ONE MALE AGED 16 OR OVER AND ONE FEMALE AGED 16 OR OVER WITH OR WITHOUT PERSONS AGED 0-15: *ages in combination of persons aged under 16 by economic activity*
PERSONS AGED 0-15 IN SUCH HOUSEHOLDS: *age by economic position of female aged 16 or over*

34 **Economic position of household residents** 226

RESIDENTS AGED 16 AND OVER IN HOUSEHOLDS: *economic position by sex by marital status*

35 **Age and marital status of household residents** 229

RESIDENTS IN HOUSEHOLDS: *age by sex by marital status*

36 **'Earners' and dependent children** 233

HOUSEHOLDS WITH RESIDENTS: *number and economic position of adults all by number of dependent children*
RESIDENT ADULTS: *economic position by number of dependent children in household*
RESIDENT DEPENDENT CHILDREN: *number and economic position of adults in household*

37 **Young adults** 236

RESIDENTS AGED 16-24 IN HOUSEHOLDS: *age by marital status, lone 'parents' with children aged 0-15, economic position*

38 **Single years of age** 238

RESIDENTS IN HOUSEHOLDS: *age by sex*

39 **Headship** 245

RESIDENTS IN HOUSEHOLDS: *age by sex by marital status; persons by household head's age, sex and marital status*

40 **Lone 'parents'** 249

LONE 'PARENTS' AGED 16 AND OVER IN HOUSEHOLDS OF ONE PERSON AGED 16 AND OVER WITH PERSON(S) AGED 0-15: *ages of children in combination by sex by economic position*
PERSONS AGED 0-15 IN SUCH HOUSEHOLDS: *age by sex by economic position of lone 'parent'*

41 **Shared accommodation** 252

HOUSEHOLDS WITH RESIDENTS NOT IN SELF-CONTAINED ACCOMMODATION: *number of persons by persons per room, amenities, central heating, no car*
ROOMS IN SUCH HOUSEHOLDS: *number of persons*

42 **Household composition and housing** 254

HOUSEHOLDS WITH RESIDENTS: *household composition by persons per room, amenities, no central heating, not self-contained accommodation, tenure, car availability*
DEPENDENT CHILDREN IN HOUSEHOLDS: *age by persons per room, amenities, no central heating, not self-contained accommodation, tenure, car availability*

43 **Household composition and ethnic group** 260

HOUSEHOLDS WITH RESIDENTS: *household composition, pensioner households all by ethnic group of head of household, household head born in Ireland*
RESIDENTS IN HOUSEHOLDS: *age by ethnic group of head of household, household head born in Ireland*

44 **Household composition and long-term illness** 268

HOUSEHOLDS CONTAINING PERSONS WITH LIMITING LONG-TERM ILLNESS: *household composition, economic position of household members*
RESIDENTS IN SUCH HOUSEHOLDS: *household composition, economic position of household members, economic position all by limiting long-term illness by age by sex*

45 **Migrant household heads** 276

HOUSEHOLDS WITH RESIDENTS: *tenure by household heads, economic activity all by age by sex of migrant heads, age by sex of all household heads*

Main tables (Part 1) - *continued*

Page

46 **Households with dependent children: housing** 284

HOUSEHOLDS WITH DEPENDENT CHILDREN: *household composition by persons per room, amenities, no central heating, not self-contained accommodation, tenure, no car*
RESIDENTS IN SUCH HOUSEHOLDS: *household composition by age all by persons per room, amenities, no central heating, not self-contained accommodation, tenure, no car; household composition*

47 **Households with pensioners: housing** 292

HOUSEHOLDS WITH ONE OR MORE RESIDENTS OF PENSIONABLE AGE: *household composition by persons per room, amenities, no central heating, not self-contained accommodation, tenure, no car*
RESIDENTS IN SUCH HOUSEHOLDS: *age, limiting long-term illness all by persons per room, amenities, no central heating, not self-contained accommodation, tenure, no car; persons with limiting long-term illness by household composition*

48 **Households with dependants: housing** 300

HOUSEHOLDS WITH RESIDENTS: *non-dependants and dependants by age of youngest and oldest dependants in combination all by persons per room, amenities, no central heating, not self-contained accommodation, no car*

49 **Ethnic group: housing** 307

HOUSEHOLDS WITH RESIDENTS: *persons per room, tenure, amenities, no central heating, not self-contained accommodation, no car, containing person(s) with limiting long-term illness all by ethnic group of household head, country of birth of household head*
RESIDENTS IN HOUSEHOLDS: persons per room, amenities, no central heating, not self-contained accommodation, no car all by ethnic group of household head, country of birth of household head

50 **Country of birth: household heads and residents** 314

RESIDENTS IN HOUSEHOLDS: *country of birth of household head by age, by country of birth of persons*
HOUSEHOLD HEADS: *country of birth*

51 **Country of birth and ethnic group** 322

RESIDENTS IN HOUSEHOLDS: *country of birth by ethnic group; country of birth of household heads by ethnic group of persons*
HOUSEHOLD HEADS: *country of birth by ethnic group*

52 **Language indicators** 333

RESIDENTS: *whether in a household by age all by country of birth, country of birth of household head*

53 **'Lifestages'** 335

RESIDENTS AGED 16 AND OVER IN HOUSEHOLDS: *age and household composition (lifestage category) all by whether in a 'couple' household*

Main tables (Part 1) - *continued*

Page

IV Household spaces and dwellings

54 **Occupancy (occupied, vacant, and other accommodation)** 338

HOUSEHOLD SPACES: *occupancy type*
ROOMS IN HOUSEHOLD SPACES: *occupancy type*
ROOMS IN HOTELS AND BOARDING HOUSES: *total*

55 **Household spaces and occupancy** 340

HOUSEHOLD SPACES IN PERMANENT BUILDINGS: *occupancy type by number of household spaces in dwelling, unattached household spaces (not in a dwelling)*
DWELLINGS: *number of household spaces in dwelling*

56 **Household space type and occupancy** 344

HOUSEHOLD SPACES: *occupancy type by household space type in permanent buildings, non-permanent accommodation*

57 **Household space type: rooms and household size** 348

HOUSEHOLDS WITH RESIDENTS: *number of rooms, number of persons, persons per room all by household space type in permanent buildings, non-permanent accommodation, with migrant head*
RESIDENTS IN HOUSEHOLDS: *household space type in permanent buildings, non-permanent accommodation, with migrant head*
ROOMS IN HOUSEHOLD SPACES: *household space type in permanent buildings, non-permanent accommodation, with migrant head*

58 **Household space type: tenure and amenities** 355

HOUSEHOLDS WITH RESIDENTS: *tenure, amenities all by household space type in permanent buildings, non-permanent accommodation*

59 **Household space type: household composition** 362

HOUSEHOLDS WITH RESIDENTS: *household composition, pensioner households all by household space type in permanent buildings, non-permanent accommodation, with migrant head*
RESIDENTS IN HOUSEHOLDS: *age by household space type in permanent buildings, non-permanent accommodation, with migrant head; persons in households with migrant head by household composition, pensioner households*

60 **Dwellings and household spaces** 370

CONVERTED OR SHARED ACCOMMODATION (MULTI-OCCUPIED BUILDINGS): *number and type of dwellings*
DWELLINGS: *number and type in building by number of household spaces*
HOUSEHOLD SPACES: *number and type of dwellings in building by unattached household spaces, household space type*
ROOMS IN SUCH ACCOMMODATION: *number and type of dwellings in building*

61 **Dwelling type and occupancy** 374

DWELLINGS: *occupancy type by type of dwelling*
NON-PERMANENT ACCOMMODATION: *occupancy type*

Main tables (Part 1) - *continued* **Page**

62 **Occupancy and tenure of dwellings** 378

DWELLINGS WITH PERSONS PRESENT OR RESIDENT: *occupancy type by tenure*

63 **Dwelling type and tenure** 380

DWELLINGS WITH RESIDENTS: *tenure by type of dwelling*
NON-PERMANENT ACCOMMODATION: *tenure*

64 **Tenure of dwellings and household spaces** 383

DWELLINGS: *tenure or occupancy type by type of dwelling*
HOUSEHOLD SPACES IN DWELLINGS: *tenure or occupancy type of dwelling by tenure or occupancy type of household spaces*

65 **Occupancy of dwellings and household spaces** 387

DWELLINGS: *occupancy type by type of dwelling*
HOUSEHOLD SPACES IN DWELLINGS: *occupancy type of dwelling by occupancy type of household spaces*

66 **Shared dwellings** 394

SHARED DWELLINGS: *number of household spaces within dwelling*
HOUSEHOLD SPACES IN SHARED DWELLINGS: *number of household spaces in dwelling by type of household spaces*

V Wales only tables

67 **Welsh language**

RESIDENTS: *age, not in households, born in Wales all by speaking, reading, writing Welsh, sex*

Main Tables (Part 2)

VI 10 per cent topics

Page numbers for tables are given in Part 2 of the report published separately and later.

71 **Comparison of 100% and 10% counts**

RESIDENTS: *100% and 10% sample counts all by whether in households, whether imputed residents in a wholly absent household*
HOUSEHOLDS WITH RESIDENTS: *100% and 10% counts all by whether imputed wholly absent households*

72 **Economic and employment status (10% sample)**

RESIDENTS AGED 16 AND OVER: *economic position and employment status all by sex, students (economically active or inactive)*

73 **Industry (10% sample)**

RESIDENTS AGED 16 AND OVER, EMPLOYEES AND SELF-EMPLOYED: *sex, by age all by industry divisions*

74 **Occupation (10% sample)**

RESIDENTS AGED 16 AND OVER, EMPLOYEES AND SELF-EMPLOYED: *Standard Occupational Classification sub-major groups by sex, by age*

75 **Hours worked (10% sample)**

RESIDENTS AGED 16 AND OVER, EMPLOYEES AND SELF-EMPLOYED: *sex, by age, sex by marital status, limiting long-term illness by sex all by hours worked weekly*

76 **Occupation and industry (10% sample)**

RESIDENTS AGED 16 AND OVER, EMPLOYEES AND SELF-EMPLOYED: *Standard Occupational Classification sub-major groups, working outside district of usual residence all by industry divisions, working outside district of usual residence*

77 **Industry and hours worked (10% sample)**

RESIDENTS AGED 16 AND OVER, EMPLOYEES AND SELF-EMPLOYED: *hours worked weekly by industry divisions*

78 **Occupation and hours worked (10% sample)**

RESIDENTS AGED 16 AND OVER, EMPLOYEES AND SELF-EMPLOYED: *Standard Occupational Classification sub-major groups, working outside district of usual residence all by hours worked weekly*

79 **Industry and employment status (10% sample)**

RESIDENTS AGED 16 AND OVER, EMPLOYEES AND SELF-EMPLOYED: *sex, by employment status all by industry divisions*

80 **Working parents: hours worked (10% sample)**

WOMEN IN COUPLE FAMILIES AND LONE PARENTS IN EMPLOYMENT: *family composition by hours worked weekly*

81 **Occupation and employment status (10% sample)**

RESIDENTS AGED 16 AND OVER, EMPLOYEES AND SELF-EMPLOYED: *sex, by employment status all by Standard Occupational Classification major groups*

82 **Travel to work and SEG (10% sample)**

RESIDENTS AGED 16 AND OVER, EMPLOYEES AND SELF-EMPLOYED: *socio-economic group, working outside district of usual residence, car availability by means of transport to work, working outside district of usual residence*

83 **Travel to work and car availability (10% sample)**

HOUSEHOLDS WITH RESIDENTS AGED 16 AND OVER, EMPLOYEES AND SELF-EMPLOYED: *car availability by number of resident employees or self-employed aged 16 and over by means of transport to work*

84 **Qualified manpower (10% sample)**

RESIDENTS AGED 18 AND OVER: *level of highest qualification, by age, economic position all by sex*

Main tables (Part 2) - *continued*

85 **Ethnic group of qualified manpower (10% sample)**

RESIDENTS AGED 16 AND OVER: *whether qualified, by age, economic position all by ethnic group, born in Ireland*

86 **SEG of households and families (10% sample)**

HOUSEHOLDS WITH RESIDENTS: *socio-economic group by tenure, migrant head of household, no car*
RESIDENTS IN HOUSEHOLDS: *total, economically active, dependent children all by tenure, migrant head of household, no car, in families, in lone parent with dependent child(ren) families; socio-economic group by economically active, dependent children, adults with limiting long-term illness*
FAMILIES OF RESIDENT PERSONS: *socio-economic group by total, lone parent families with dependent child(ren) by socio-economic group*

87 **Family type and tenure (10% sample)**

HOUSEHOLDS WITH RESIDENTS: *household and family composition by tenure, migrant head of household, car availability*
RESIDENTS IN HOUSEHOLDS: *dependent children aged 0-17 in lone parent families by tenure, migrant head of household, car availability; household and family composition by total, dependent children*

88 **'Concealed' families (10% sample)**

FAMILIES OF RESIDENT PERSONS: *family composition by age of head of household; composition of concealed families by age of head of family*

89 **Family composition (10% sample)**

FAMILIES OF RESIDENT PERSONS: *family composition, in households with two or more families by type of family*

90 **Social class of households (10% sample)**

HOUSEHOLDS WITH RESIDENTS: *social class based on occupation of household head, household head on a Government scheme, economic position of economically inactive heads*
RESIDENTS IN HOUSEHOLDS: *social class based on occupation of household head, household head on a Government scheme, economic position of economically inactive heads all by age, females in couples*

91 **Social class and economic position (10% sample)**

RESIDENTS AGED 16 AND OVER IN HOUSEHOLDS: *social class based on occupation, on a Government scheme, economic position of the economically inactive all by economic position, by sex, females in a couple*

92 **SEG and economic position (10% sample)**

ECONOMICALLY ACTIVE RESIDENTS: *socio-economic group, on a Government scheme all by economic position by sex , migrants, by sex*

93 **SEG, social class and ethnic group (10% sample)**

RESIDENTS AGED 16 AND OVER, EMPLOYEES AND SELF-EMPLOYED: *socio-economic group, social class based on occupation all by ethnic group, born in Ireland*

94 **Former industry of unemployed (10% sample)**

RESIDENTS ON A GOVERNMENT SCHEME OR UNEMPLOYED: *sex, by industry division of most recent job in last 10 years*

95 **Former occupation of unemployed (10% sample)**

RESIDENTS ON A GOVERNMENT SCHEME OR UNEMPLOYED: *sex by Standard Occupational Classification major group of most recent job in last 10 years*

96 **Armed forces (10% sample)**

RESIDENT ARMED FORCES, IN EMPLOYMENT: *age by whether in households by sex; age of migrants by type of move by whether in households*

97 **Armed forces: households (10% sample)**

RESIDENTS IN HOUSEHOLDS WITH HEAD IN EMPLOYMENT IN ARMED FORCES: *household heads: age, migrants all by marital status by sex; all persons: age, migrants all by marital status, by sex*

98 **Occupation orders: 1980 classification (10% sample)**

RESIDENTS AGED 16 AND OVER, EMPLOYEES AND SELF-EMPLOYED: *1980 occupation orders by sex*

99 **Occupation: Standard Occupational Classification (10% sample)**

RESIDENTS AGED 16 AND OVER, EMPLOYEES AND SELF EMPLOYED: *Standard Occupational Classification minor groups by sex*

Main Tables

Explanatory notes for tables appear in Annex C, after the tables. Notes are in the numerical order of the tables.

Note: * All tables for residents on 100% topics are on this population base

1. Persons present plus absent residents, in households

	TOTAL PERSONS	In households			Not in households		
		Total	Males	Females	Total	Males	Females
a	b	c	d	e	f	g	h
CUMBRIA							
1 Present residents	464,702	456,326	222,123	234,203	8,376	3,250	5,126
2 Absent residents (part of household present)	8,745	8,745	4,899	3,846			
3 Absent residents (wholly absent household - enumerated)	5,855	5,855	2,732	3,123			
4 Absent residents (wholly absent household - imputed)	3,861	3,861	1,837	2,024			
5 Visitors	24,652	13,505	6,684	6,821	11,147	5,944	5,203
Resident in UK	22,866	12,577	6,176	6,401	10,289	5,490	4,799
Resident outside UK	1,786	928	508	420	858	454	404
PERSONS PRESENT 1991: 1971 BASE (1+5)	489,354	469,831	228,807	241,024	19,523	9,194	10,329
RESIDENTS 1991: 1981 BASE (1+2)	473,447	465,071	227,022	238,049	8,376	3,250	5,126
RESIDENTS 1991: 1991 BASE (1+2+3+4)*	483,163	474,787	231,591	243,196	8,376	3,250	5,126
Allerdale							
1 Present residents	92,560	90,793	44,361	46,432	1,767	668	1,099
2 Absent residents (part of household present)	1,504	1,504	836	668			
3 Absent residents (wholly absent household - enumerated)	1,026	1,026	471	555			
4 Absent residents (wholly absent household - imputed)	612	612	281	331			
5 Visitors	4,155	2,530	1,268	1,262	1,625	846	779
Resident in UK	3,850	2,369	1,187	1,182	1,481	760	721
Resident outside UK	305	161	81	80	144	86	58
PERSONS PRESENT 1991: 1971 BASE (1+5)	96,715	93,323	45,629	47,694	3,392	1,514	1,878
RESIDENTS 1991: 1981 BASE (1+2)	94,064	92,297	45,197	47,100	1,767	668	1,099
RESIDENTS 1991: 1991 BASE (1+2+3+4)*	95,702	93,935	45,949	47,986	1,767	668	1,099
Barrow-in-Furness							
1 Present residents	70,597	70,036	34,137	35,899	561	216	345
2 Absent residents (part of household present)	1,098	1,098	673	425			
3 Absent residents (wholly absent household - enumerated)	666	666	319	347			
4 Absent residents (wholly absent household - imputed)	764	764	369	395			
5 Visitors	1,595	1,007	558	449	588	329	259
Resident in UK	1,467	927	509	418	540	284	256
Resident outside UK	128	80	49	31	48	45	3
PERSONS PRESENT 1991: 1971 BASE (1+5)	72,192	71,043	34,695	36,348	1,149	545	604
RESIDENTS 1991: 1981 BASE (1+2)	71,695	71,134	34,810	36,324	561	216	345
RESIDENTS 1991: 1991 BASE (1+2+3+4)*	73,125	72,564	35,498	37,066	561	216	345
Carlisle							
1 Present residents	96,946	95,443	46,004	49,439	1,503	576	927
2 Absent residents (part of household present)	1,746	1,746	972	774			
3 Absent residents (wholly absent household - enumerated)	1,162	1,162	570	592			
4 Absent residents (wholly absent household - imputed)	708	708	358	350			
5 Visitors	3,093	1,720	838	882	1,373	746	627
Resident in UK	2,813	1,556	739	817	1,257	666	591
Resident outside UK	280	164	99	65	116	80	36
PERSONS PRESENT 1991: 1971 BASE (1+5)	100,039	97,163	46,842	50,321	2,876	1,322	1,554
RESIDENTS 1991: 1981 BASE (1+2)	98,692	97,189	46,976	50,213	1,503	576	927
RESIDENTS 1991: 1991 BASE (1+2+3+4)*	100,562	99,059	47,904	51,155	1,503	576	927

Note: * All tables for residents on 100% topics are on this population base

1. Persons present plus absent residents, in households

	TOTAL PERSONS	In households			Not in households		
		Total	Males	Females	Total	Males	Females
a	b	c	d	e	f	g	h
		Copeland					
1 Present residents	68,901	68,090	33,615	34,475	811	330	481
2 Absent residents (part of household present)	1,187	1,187	663	524			
3 Absent residents (wholly absent household - enumerated)	717	717	343	374			
4 Absent residents (wholly absent household - imputed)	491	491	244	247			
5 Visitors	2,504	1,209	680	529	1,295	911	384
Resident in UK	2,375	1,133	634	499	1,242	875	367
Resident outside UK	129	76	46	30	53	36	17
PERSONS PRESENT 1991: 1971 BASE (1+5)	71,405	69,299	34,295	35,004	2,106	1,241	865
RESIDENTS 1991: 1981 BASE (1+2)	70,088	69,277	34,278	34,999	811	330	481
RESIDENTS 1991: 1991 BASE (1+2+3+4)*	71,296	70,485	34,865	35,620	811	330	481
		Eden					
1 Present residents	43,791	42,921	21,190	21,731	870	349	521
2 Absent residents (part of household present)	854	854	469	385			
3 Absent residents (wholly absent household - enumerated)	578	578	273	305			
4 Absent residents (wholly absent household - imputed)	358	358	170	188			
5 Visitors	2,622	1,709	825	884	913	512	401
Resident in UK	2,495	1,619	771	848	876	489	387
Resident outside UK	127	90	54	36	37	23	14
PERSONS PRESENT 1991: 1971 BASE (1+5)	46,413	44,630	22,015	22,615	1,783	861	922
RESIDENTS 1991: 1981 BASE (1+2)	44,645	43,775	21,659	22,116	870	349	521
RESIDENTS 1991: 1991 BASE (1+2+3+4)*	45,581	44,711	22,102	22,609	870	349	521
		South Lakeland					
1 Present residents	91,907	89,043	42,816	46,227	2,864	1,111	1,753
2 Absent residents (part of household present)	2,356	2,356	1,286	1,070			
3 Absent residents (wholly absent household - enumerated)	1,706	1,706	756	950			
4 Absent residents (wholly absent household - imputed)	928	928	415	513			
5 Visitors	10,683	5,330	2,515	2,815	5,353	2,600	2,753
Resident in UK	9,866	4,973	2,336	2,637	4,893	2,416	2,477
Resident outside UK	817	357	179	178	460	184	276
PERSONS PRESENT 1991: 1971 BASE (1+5)	102,590	94,373	45,331	49,042	8,217	3,711	4,506
RESIDENTS 1991: 1981 BASE (1+2)	94,263	91,399	44,102	47,297	2,864	1,111	1,753
RESIDENTS 1991: 1991 BASE (1+2+3+4)*	96,897	94,033	45,273	48,760	2,864	1,111	1,753

2. Residents

Age	TOTAL PERSONS	Males					Females				
		Total	Single	Married	Widowed	Divorced	Total	Single	Married	Widowed	Divorced
a	b	c	d	e	f	g	h	i	j	k	l
CUMBRIA											
ALL AGES	**483,163**	**234,841**	**98,811**	**118,174**	**7,937**	**9,919**	**248,322**	**86,243**	**118,774**	**30,827**	**12,478**
0 - 4	28,904	14,706	14,706				14,198	14,198			
5 - 9	28,967	14,959	14,959				14,008	14,008			
10 - 14	27,991	14,422	14,422				13,569	13,569			
15	5,592	2,843	2,843				2,749	2,749			
16 - 17	12,276	6,301	6,287	11	1	2	5,975	5,951	18	4	2
18 - 19	13,226	6,687	6,636	46	1	4	6,539	6,357	172	-	10
20 - 24	33,903	16,982	14,764	2,116	3	99	16,921	12,136	4,449	15	321
25 - 29	34,740	17,593	8,509	8,310	12	762	17,147	5,259	10,622	40	1,226
30 - 34	33,442	16,822	4,205	11,288	19	1,310	16,620	2,182	12,635	87	1,716
35 - 39	31,305	15,716	2,338	11,989	37	1,352	15,589	1,219	12,518	132	1,720
40 - 44	36,403	18,387	1,920	14,681	104	1,682	18,016	879	14,921	256	1,960
45 - 49	30,395	15,371	1,313	12,579	151	1,328	15,024	597	12,460	443	1,524
50 - 54	28,091	13,951	1,142	11,493	187	1,129	14,140	583	11,634	765	1,158
55 - 59	26,652	13,256	1,008	11,033	397	818	13,396	689	10,394	1,437	876
60 - 64	27,484	13,184	1,127	10,758	694	605	14,300	923	9,863	2,835	679
65 - 69	26,205	11,991	970	9,412	1,206	403	14,214	1,043	8,292	4,309	570
70 - 74	21,746	9,349	722	6,995	1,409	223	12,397	1,016	5,650	5,385	346
75 - 79	17,049	6,708	503	4,545	1,530	130	10,341	1,032	3,250	5,842	217
80 - 84	11,167	3,738	282	2,137	1,262	57	7,429	959	1,387	4,981	102
85 - 89	5,600	1,504	131	682	678	13	4,096	612	431	3,012	41
90 and over	2,025	371	24	99	246	2	1,654	282	78	1,284	10
Allerdale											
ALL AGES	**95,702**	**46,617**	**19,403**	**23,733**	**1,640**	**1,841**	**49,085**	**16,749**	**23,817**	**6,176**	**2,343**
0 - 4	5,551	2,796	2,796				2,755	2,755			
5 - 9	5,801	3,044	3,044				2,757	2,757			
10 - 14	5,817	3,070	3,070				2,747	2,747			
15	1,143	578	578				565	565			
16 - 17	2,459	1,269	1,266	2	-	1	1,190	1,183	4	3	-
18 - 19	2,640	1,334	1,326	8	-	-	1,306	1,260	42	-	4
20 - 24	6,626	3,302	2,801	481	-	20	3,324	2,299	960	2	63
25 - 29	6,587	3,327	1,497	1,693	1	136	3,260	900	2,096	10	254
30 - 34	6,508	3,251	727	2,247	10	267	3,257	391	2,506	23	337
35 - 39	6,277	3,107	422	2,430	6	249	3,170	228	2,564	29	349
40 - 44	7,529	3,785	392	3,073	23	297	3,744	183	3,152	52	357
45 - 49	6,082	3,110	246	2,589	33	242	2,972	127	2,515	78	252
50 - 54	5,559	2,786	251	2,269	42	224	2,773	97	2,321	158	197
55 - 59	5,342	2,664	190	2,220	89	165	2,678	132	2,080	279	187
60 - 64	5,490	2,622	225	2,135	152	110	2,868	181	1,970	595	122
65 - 69	5,259	2,398	218	1,865	249	66	2,861	212	1,648	895	106
70 - 74	4,345	1,881	160	1,379	310	32	2,464	210	1,082	1,118	54
75 - 79	3,181	1,284	105	849	312	18	1,897	197	535	1,125	40
80 - 84	2,086	670	51	363	245	11	1,416	161	255	988	12
85 - 89	1,078	281	33	115	131	2	797	114	71	604	8
90 and over	342	58	5	15	37	1	284	50	16	217	1

2. Residents

Age	TOTAL PERSONS	Males					Females				
		Total	Single	Married	Widowed	Divorced	Total	Single	Married	Widowed	Divorced
a	b	c	d	e	f	g	h	i	j	k	l
					Barrow-in-Furness						
ALL AGES	**73,125**	**35,714**	**15,341**	**17,315**	**1,192**	**1,866**	**37,411**	**13,298**	**17,408**	**4,477**	**2,228**
0 - 4	5,063	2,602	2,602				2,461	2,461			
5 - 9	4,580	2,334	2,334				2,246	2,246			
10 - 14	4,134	2,098	2,098				2,036	2,036			
15	883	458	458				425	425			
16 - 17	1,920	982	979	3	-	-	938	935	3	-	-
18 - 19	2,116	1,060	1,053	7	-	-	1,056	1,033	22	-	1
20 - 24	5,663	2,811	2,377	420	-	14	2,852	1,976	820	1	55
25 - 29	5,788	2,920	1,316	1,450	5	149	2,868	776	1,842	4	246
30 - 34	5,089	2,601	596	1,781	-	224	2,488	309	1,881	11	287
35 - 39	4,599	2,307	321	1,746	2	238	2,292	151	1,810	16	315
40 - 44	5,328	2,698	240	2,132	17	309	2,630	108	2,135	32	355
45 - 49	4,634	2,372	181	1,877	32	282	2,262	84	1,815	65	298
50 - 54	4,238	2,127	149	1,720	38	220	2,111	68	1,707	108	228
55 - 59	3,715	1,886	138	1,533	63	152	1,829	93	1,370	229	137
60 - 64	3,717	1,786	140	1,424	96	126	1,931	93	1,333	408	97
65 - 69	3,598	1,640	139	1,229	195	77	1,958	112	1,115	639	92
70 - 74	3,366	1,388	99	1,029	217	43	1,978	113	897	912	56
75 - 79	2,389	933	76	619	221	17	1,456	114	425	888	29
80 - 84	1,442	489	29	270	177	13	953	82	176	672	23
85 - 89	636	174	11	67	94	2	462	57	49	350	6
90 and over	227	48	5	8	35	-	179	26	8	142	3
					Carlisle						
ALL AGES	**100,562**	**48,480**	**20,629**	**24,021**	**1,656**	**2,174**	**52,082**	**18,541**	**24,181**	**6,475**	**2,885**
0 - 4	6,164	3,152	3,152				3,012	3,012			
5 - 9	6,176	3,137	3,137				3,039	3,039			
10 - 14	5,828	2,946	2,946				2,882	2,882			
15	1,155	583	583				572	572			
16 - 17	2,511	1,260	1,258	1	1	-	1,251	1,246	5	-	-
18 - 19	2,867	1,449	1,432	13	1	3	1,418	1,377	37	-	4
20 - 24	6,999	3,450	2,978	440	1	31	3,549	2,567	901	4	77
25 - 29	7,366	3,688	1,769	1,737	3	179	3,678	1,194	2,201	8	275
30 - 34	7,330	3,675	929	2,428	3	315	3,655	505	2,731	20	399
35 - 39	6,637	3,327	500	2,510	6	311	3,310	285	2,590	26	409
40 - 44	7,351	3,718	409	2,937	29	343	3,633	196	2,950	55	432
45 - 49	6,010	2,986	259	2,423	30	274	3,024	132	2,455	108	329
50 - 54	5,635	2,752	229	2,271	34	218	2,883	142	2,310	159	272
55 - 59	5,570	2,731	222	2,237	87	185	2,839	174	2,154	302	209
60 - 64	5,685	2,728	284	2,177	143	124	2,957	214	1,965	608	170
65 - 69	5,557	2,531	205	1,992	244	90	3,026	227	1,727	929	143
70 - 74	4,250	1,808	139	1,357	256	56	2,442	199	1,076	1,080	87
75 - 79	3,577	1,403	106	905	360	32	2,174	228	698	1,195	53
80 - 84	2,326	792	60	452	270	10	1,534	187	294	1,034	19
85 - 89	1,128	282	27	123	129	3	846	105	79	655	7
90 and over	440	82	5	18	59	-	358	58	8	292	-

2. Residents

Age	TOTAL PERSONS	Males					Females				
		Total	Single	Married	Widowed	Divorced	Total	Single	Married	Widowed	Divorced
a	b	c	d	e	f	g	h	i	j	k	l
					Copeland						
ALL AGES	**71,296**	**35,195**	**15,550**	**17,078**	**1,123**	**1,444**	**36,101**	**12,967**	**17,136**	**4,252**	**1,746**
0 - 4	4,738	2,390	2,390				2,348	2,348			
5 - 9	4,740	2,508	2,508				2,232	2,232			
10 - 14	4,381	2,264	2,264				2,117	2,117			
15	858	438	438				420	420			
16 - 17	1,883	940	938	2	-	-	943	940	3	-	-
18 - 19	1,886	935	930	5	-	-	951	923	27	-	1
20 - 24	5,156	2,613	2,248	348	1	16	2,543	1,752	725	3	63
25 - 29	5,667	2,906	1,380	1,399	2	125	2,761	750	1,805	6	200
30 - 34	5,278	2,699	661	1,834	1	203	2,579	306	1,976	12	285
35 - 39	4,679	2,385	366	1,808	5	206	2,294	168	1,856	19	251
40 - 44	5,275	2,736	306	2,152	11	267	2,539	117	2,109	44	269
45 - 49	4,317	2,193	200	1,807	28	158	2,124	62	1,797	66	199
50 - 54	4,149	2,065	191	1,682	31	161	2,084	90	1,714	136	144
55 - 59	3,933	1,979	144	1,657	70	108	1,954	75	1,521	253	105
60 - 64	3,870	1,887	179	1,515	115	78	1,983	101	1,349	447	86
65 - 69	3,506	1,639	173	1,212	189	65	1,867	119	1,061	621	66
70 - 74	2,882	1,223	111	855	226	31	1,659	143	681	787	48
75 - 79	2,001	764	69	494	182	19	1,237	100	341	775	21
80 - 84	1,288	439	41	229	162	7	849	101	130	613	5
85 - 89	588	153	11	70	72	-	435	76	32	326	1
90 and over	221	39	2	9	28	-	182	27	9	144	2
					Eden						
ALL AGES	**45,581**	**22,451**	**9,398**	**11,534**	**722**	**797**	**23,130**	**7,796**	**11,585**	**2,814**	**935**
0 - 4	2,491	1,257	1,257				1,234	1,234			
5 - 9	2,590	1,300	1,300				1,290	1,290			
10 - 14	2,640	1,355	1,355				1,285	1,285			
15	494	259	259				235	235			
16 - 17	1,130	606	605	1	-	-	524	523	1	-	-
18 - 19	1,219	616	611	4	-	1	603	585	18	-	-
20 - 24	3,107	1,643	1,486	153	-	4	1,464	1,069	367	1	27
25 - 29	3,045	1,569	827	685	-	57	1,476	468	932	1	75
30 - 34	3,114	1,563	420	1,037	3	103	1,551	214	1,193	6	138
35 - 39	3,064	1,553	249	1,189	3	112	1,511	109	1,272	13	117
40 - 44	3,545	1,807	192	1,471	7	137	1,738	81	1,472	18	167
45 - 49	2,993	1,523	173	1,242	8	100	1,470	65	1,255	45	105
50 - 54	2,721	1,363	125	1,129	16	93	1,358	46	1,151	73	88
55 - 59	2,604	1,292	115	1,088	30	59	1,312	51	1,058	137	66
60 - 64	2,760	1,362	121	1,131	58	52	1,398	101	1,017	233	47
65 - 69	2,491	1,180	102	941	104	33	1,311	74	804	388	45
70 - 74	2,039	930	92	690	128	20	1,109	98	517	469	25
75 - 79	1,629	668	53	457	141	17	961	93	325	523	20
80 - 84	1,140	404	32	230	135	7	736	102	147	476	11
85 - 89	557	160	22	75	61	2	397	51	44	300	2
90 and over	208	41	2	11	28	-	167	22	12	131	2

2. Residents

Age	TOTAL PERSONS	Males					Females				
		Total	Single	Married	Widowed	Divorced	Total	Single	Married	Widowed	Divorced
a	b	c	d	e	f	g	h	i	j	k	l
South Lakeland											
ALL AGES	**96,897**	**46,384**	**18,490**	**24,493**	**1,604**	**1,797**	**50,513**	**16,892**	**24,647**	**6,633**	**2,341**
0 - 4	4,897	2,509	2,509				2,388	2,388			
5 - 9	5,080	2,636	2,636				2,444	2,444			
10 - 14	5,191	2,689	2,689				2,502	2,502			
15	1,059	527	527				532	532			
16 - 17	2,373	1,244	1,241	2	-	1	1,129	1,124	2	1	2
18 - 19	2,498	1,293	1,284	9	-	-	1,205	1,179	26	-	-
20 - 24	6,352	3,163	2,874	274	1	14	3,189	2,473	676	4	36
25 - 29	6,287	3,183	1,720	1,346	1	116	3,104	1,171	1,746	11	176
30 - 34	6,123	3,033	872	1,961	2	198	3,090	457	2,348	15	270
35 - 39	6,049	3,037	480	2,306	15	236	3,012	278	2,426	29	279
40 - 44	7,375	3,643	381	2,916	17	329	3,732	194	3,103	55	380
45 - 49	6,359	3,187	254	2,641	20	272	3,172	127	2,623	81	341
50 - 54	5,789	2,858	197	2,422	26	213	2,931	140	2,431	131	229
55 - 59	5,488	2,704	199	2,298	58	149	2,784	164	2,211	237	172
60 - 64	5,962	2,799	178	2,376	130	115	3,163	233	2,229	544	157
65 - 69	5,794	2,603	133	2,173	225	72	3,191	299	1,937	837	118
70 - 74	4,864	2,119	121	1,685	272	41	2,745	253	1,397	1,019	76
75 - 79	4,272	1,656	94	1,221	314	27	2,616	300	926	1,336	54
80 - 84	2,885	944	69	593	273	9	1,941	326	385	1,198	32
85 - 89	1,613	454	27	232	191	4	1,159	209	156	777	17
90 and over	587	103	5	38	59	1	484	99	25	358	2

3. Establishments: persons present not in households

Type of establishment	Number of establish-ments	TOTAL PERSONS	Total males	Total females	Not resident			Residents					
								Staff			Other residents		
					Total	Males	Females	Total	Males	Females	Total	Males	Females
a	b	c	d	e	f	g	h	i	j	k	l	m	n
					CUMBRIA								
ALL ESTABLISHMENTS	**1,080**	**19,523**	**9,194**	**10,329**	**11,147**	**5,944**	**5,203**	**2,911**	**1,505**	**1,406**	**5,465**	**1,745**	**3,720**
Medical and care sector	**281**	**7,500**	**2,516**	**4,984**	**2,377**	**1,077**	**1,300**	**323**	**149**	**174**	**4,800**	**1,290**	**3,510**
NHS hospitals/homes - psychiatric	1	177	82	95	159	70	89	18	12	6	-	-	-
NHS hospitals/homes - other	22	2,297	877	1,420	1,473	572	901	104	49	55	720	256	464
Non-NHS hospitals - psychiatric	-	-	-	-	-	-	-	-	-	-	-	-	-
Non-NHS hospitals - other	5	115	33	82	57	12	45	-	-	-	58	21	37
Local authority homes	65	1,716	629	1,087	371	258	113	18	8	10	1,327	363	964
Housing association homes and hostels	16	199	93	106	10	8	2	9	5	4	180	80	100
Nursing homes (non-NHS/LA/HA)	55	1,020	275	745	113	44	69	54	20	34	853	211	642
Residential homes (non-NHS/LA/HA)	104	1,856	462	1,394	170	97	73	102	45	57	1,584	320	1,264
Children's homes	13	120	65	55	24	16	8	18	10	8	78	39	39
Detention, defence and education	**35**	**2,577**	**1,506**	**1,071**	**2,336**	**1,354**	**982**	**136**	**62**	**74**	**105**	**90**	**15**
Prison service establishments	1	327	327	-	308	308	-	-	-	-	19	19	-
Defence establishments	5	58	58	-	9	9	-				49	49	-
Educational establishments	29	2,192	1,121	1,071	2,019	1,037	982	136	62	74	37	22	15
Other groups	**764**	**9,446**	**5,172**	**4,274**	**6,434**	**3,513**	**2,921**	**2,452**	**1,294**	**1,158**	**560**	**365**	**195**
Hotels, boarding houses etc	722	8,748	4,661	4,087	6,022	3,183	2,839	2,382	1,260	1,122	344	218	126
Hostels and common lodging houses (non-HA)	7	68	47	21	20	15	5	11	4	7	37	28	9
Other miscellaneous establishments	26	521	365	156	292	225	67	59	30	29	170	110	60
Persons sleeping rough		3	3	-	-	-	-				3	3	-
Campers		16	7	9	16	7	9				-	-	-
Civilian ships, boats and barges	9	90	89	1	84	83	1				6	6	-

Table 3 Communal establishments – continued

3. Establishments: persons present not in households

Type of establishment	Number of establishments	TOTAL PERSONS	Total males	Total females	Not resident			Residents					
								Staff			Other residents		
					Total	Males	Females	Total	Males	Females	Total	Males	Females
a	b	c	d	e	f	g	h	i	j	k	l	m	n
Allerdale													
ALL ESTABLISHMENTS	**222**	**3,392**	**1,514**	**1,878**	**1,625**	**846**	**779**	**670**	**330**	**340**	**1,097**	**338**	**759**
Medical and care sector	**55**	**1,208**	**377**	**831**	**136**	**54**	**82**	**48**	**26**	**22**	**1,024**	**297**	**727**
NHS hospitals/homes - psychiatric	-	-	-	-	-	-	-	-	-	-	-	-	-
NHS hospitals/homes - other	6	365	149	216	45	22	23	7	4	3	313	123	190
Non-NHS hospitals - psychiatric	-	-	-	-	-	-	-	-	-	-	-	-	-
Non-NHS hospitals - other	1	1	1	-	1	1	-	-	-	-	-	-	-
Local authority homes	13	305	95	210	31	8	23	3	1	2	271	86	185
Housing association homes and hostels	2	58	19	39	2	2	-	-	-	-	56	17	39
Nursing homes (non-NHS/LA/HA)	7	78	15	63	11	3	8	-	-	-	67	12	55
Residential homes (non-NHS/LA/HA)	23	375	86	289	46	18	28	29	17	12	300	51	249
Children's homes	3	26	12	14	-	-	-	9	4	5	17	8	9
Detention, defence and education	**2**	**150**	**76**	**74**	**135**	**71**	**64**	**15**	**5**	**10**	**-**	**-**	**-**
Prison service establishments	-	-	-	-	-	-	-	-	-	-	-	-	-
Defence establishments	-	-	-	-	-	-	-				-	-	-
Educational establishments	2	150	76	74	135	71	64	15	5	10	-	-	-
Other groups	**165**	**2,034**	**1,061**	**973**	**1,354**	**721**	**633**	**607**	**299**	**308**	**73**	**41**	**32**
Hotels, boarding houses etc	157	1,955	1,021	934	1,305	691	614	592	293	299	58	37	21
Hostels and common lodging houses (non-HA)	1	15	9	6	10	7	3	5	2	3	-	-	-
Other miscellaneous establishments	6	46	18	28	25	14	11	10	4	6	11	-	11
Persons sleeping rough		3	3	-	-	-	-				3	3	-
Campers		10	5	5	10	5	5				-	-	-
Civilian ships, boats and barges	1	5	5	-	4	4	-				1	1	-

Table 3 Communal establishments – **continued**

3. Establishments: persons present not in households

Type of establishment	Number of establish-ments	TOTAL PERSONS	Total males	Total females	Not resident			Residents					
								Staff			Other residents		
					Total	Males	Females	Total	Males	Females	Total	Males	Females
a	b	c	d	e	f	g	h	i	j	k	l	m	n
Barrow-in-Furness													
ALL ESTABLISHMENTS	**60**	**1,149**	**545**	**604**	**588**	**329**	**259**	**97**	**46**	**51**	**464**	**170**	**294**
Medical and care sector	**25**	**856**	**304**	**552**	**410**	**161**	**249**	**38**	**17**	**21**	**408**	**126**	**282**
NHS hospitals/homes - psychiatric	-	-	-	-	-	-	-	-	-	-	-	-	-
NHS hospitals/homes - other	2	461	178	283	381	148	233	32	14	18	48	16	32
Non-NHS hospitals - psychiatric	-	-	-	-	-	-	-	-	-	-	-	-	-
Non-NHS hospitals - other	1	5	2	3	5	2	3	-	-	-	-	-	-
Local authority homes	9	194	69	125	19	8	11	2	1	1	173	60	113
Housing association homes and hostels	-	-	-	-	-	-	-	-	-	-	-	-	-
Nursing homes (non-NHS/LA/HA)	6	59	22	37	2	1	1	4	2	2	53	19	34
Residential homes (non-NHS/LA/HA)	7	137	33	104	3	2	1	-	-	-	134	31	103
Children's homes	-	-	-	-	-	-	-	-	-	-	-	-	-
Detention, defence and education	-	-	-	-	-	-	-	-	-	-	-	-	-
Prison service establishments	-	-	-	-	-	-	-	-	-	-	-	-	-
Defence establishments	-	-	-	-	-	-	-				-	-	-
Educational establishments	-	-	-	-	-	-	-	-	-	-	-	-	-
Other groups	**35**	**293**	**241**	**52**	**178**	**168**	**10**	**59**	**29**	**30**	**56**	**44**	**12**
Hotels, boarding houses etc	30	225	174	51	113	104	9	59	29	30	53	41	12
Hostels and common lodging houses (non-HA)	-	-	-	-	-	-	-	-	-	-	-	-	-
Other miscellaneous establishments	-	-	-	-	-	-	-	-	-	-	-	-	-
Persons sleeping rough		-	-	-	-	-	-				-	-	-
Campers		-	-	-	-	-	-				-	-	-
Civilian ships, boats and barges	5	68	67	1	65	64	1				3	3	-

Table 3 Communal establishments – continued

3. Establishments: persons present not in households

Type of establishment	Number of establish-ments	TOTAL PERSONS	Total males	Total females	Not resident			Residents					
								Staff			Other residents		
					Total	Males	Females	Total	Males	Females	Total	Males	Females
a	b	c	d	e	f	g	h	i	j	k	l	m	n
Carlisle													
ALL ESTABLISHMENTS	**118**	**2,876**	**1,322**	**1,554**	**1,373**	**746**	**627**	**172**	**96**	**76**	**1,331**	**480**	**851**
Medical and care sector	**61**	**1,851**	**654**	**1,197**	**567**	**227**	**340**	**68**	**35**	**33**	**1,216**	**392**	**824**
NHS hospitals/homes - psychiatric	-	-	-	-	-	-	-	-	-	-	-	-	-
NHS hospitals/homes - other	5	848	332	516	501	205	296	42	25	17	305	102	203
Non-NHS hospitals - psychiatric	-	-	-	-	-	-	-	-	-	-	-	-	-
Non-NHS hospitals - other	1	4	2	2	4	2	2	-	-	-	-	-	-
Local authority homes	11	314	95	219	31	10	21	-	-	-	283	85	198
Housing association homes and hostels	7	62	53	9	6	6	-	-	-	-	56	47	9
Nursing homes (non-NHS/LA/HA)	7	152	54	98	5	1	4	5	2	3	142	51	91
Residential homes (non-NHS/LA/HA)	24	423	96	327	17	2	15	18	6	12	388	88	300
Children's homes	6	48	22	26	3	1	2	3	2	1	42	19	23
Detention, defence and education	**7**	**359**	**274**	**85**	**293**	**215**	**78**	**9**	**7**	**2**	**57**	**52**	**5**
Prison service establishments	-	-	-	-	-	-	-	-	-	-	-	-	-
Defence establishments	4	57	57	-	9	9	-				48	48	-
Educational establishments	3	302	217	85	284	206	78	9	7	2	9	4	5
Other groups	**50**	**666**	**394**	**272**	**513**	**304**	**209**	**95**	**54**	**41**	**58**	**36**	**22**
Hotels, boarding houses etc	44	611	357	254	500	294	206	93	53	40	18	10	8
Hostels and common lodging houses (non-HA)	4	42	30	12	9	7	2	2	1	1	31	22	9
Other miscellaneous establishments	2	13	7	6	4	3	1	-	-	-	9	4	5
Persons sleeping rough		-	-	-	-	-	-				-	-	-
Campers		-	-	-	-	-	-				-	-	-
Civilian ships, boats and barges	-	-	-	-	-	-	-				-	-	-

3. Establishments: persons present not in households

Type of establishment	Number of establish-ments	TOTAL PERSONS	Total males	Total females	Not resident			Residents					
								Staff			Other residents		
					Total	Males	Females	Total	Males	Females	Total	Males	Females
a	b	c	d	e	f	g	h	i	j	k	l	m	n
					Copeland								
ALL ESTABLISHMENTS	**92**	**2,106**	**1,241**	**865**	**1,295**	**911**	**384**	**194**	**97**	**97**	**617**	**233**	**384**
Medical and care sector	**29**	**899**	**272**	**627**	**391**	**149**	**242**	**40**	**14**	**26**	**468**	**109**	**359**
NHS hospitals/homes - psychiatric	-	-	-	-	-	-	-	-	-	-	-	-	-
NHS hospitals/homes - other	2	416	154	262	375	141	234	23	6	17	18	7	11
Non-NHS hospitals - psychiatric	-	-	-	-	-	-	-	-	-	-	-	-	-
Non-NHS hospitals - other	-	-	-	-	-	-	-	-	-	-	-	-	-
Local authority homes	7	182	43	139	12	7	5	-	-	-	170	36	134
Housing association homes and hostels	4	50	15	35	1	-	1	5	3	2	44	12	32
Nursing homes (non-NHS/LA/HA)	3	72	21	51	2	1	1	-	-	-	70	20	50
Residential homes (non-NHS/LA/HA)	12	175	38	137	1	-	1	12	5	7	162	33	129
Children's homes	1	4	1	3	-	-	-	-	-	-	4	1	3
Detention, defence and education	**3**	**504**	**422**	**82**	**469**	**395**	**74**	**13**	**7**	**6**	**22**	**20**	**2**
Prison service establishments	1	327	327	-	308	308	-	-	-	-	19	19	-
Defence establishments	-	-	-	-	-	-	-				-	-	-
Educational establishments	2	177	95	82	161	87	74	13	7	6	3	1	2
Other groups	**60**	**703**	**547**	**156**	**435**	**367**	**68**	**141**	**76**	**65**	**127**	**104**	**23**
Hotels, boarding houses etc	52	397	279	118	254	196	58	114	65	49	29	18	11
Hostels and common lodging houses (non-HA)	1	5	2	3	1	1	-	4	1	3	-	-	-
Other miscellaneous establishments	4	284	249	35	165	155	10	23	10	13	96	84	12
Persons sleeping rough		-	-	-	-	-	-				-	-	-
Campers		-	-	-	-	-	-				-	-	-
Civilian ships, boats and barges	3	17	17	-	15	15	-				2	2	-

Table 3 Communal establishments - **continued**

3. Establishments: persons present not in households

Type of establishment	Number of establish-ments	TOTAL PERSONS	Total males	Total females	Not resident			Residents					
								Staff			Other residents		
					Total	Males	Females	Total	Males	Females	Total	Males	Females
a	b	c	d	e	f	g	h	i	j	k	l	m	n
Eden													
ALL ESTABLISHMENTS	**131**	**1,783**	**861**	**922**	**913**	**512**	**401**	**327**	**185**	**142**	**543**	**164**	**379**
Medical and care sector	**25**	**812**	**304**	**508**	**282**	**157**	**125**	**33**	**20**	**13**	**497**	**127**	**370**
NHS hospitals/homes - psychiatric	1	177	82	95	159	70	89	18	12	6	-	-	-
NHS hospitals/homes - other	1	14	4	10	7	3	4	-	-	-	7	1	6
Non-NHS hospitals - psychiatric	-	-	-	-	-	-	-	-	-	-	-	-	-
Non-NHS hospitals - other	1	70	23	47	26	4	22	-	-	-	44	19	25
Local authority homes	7	141	51	90	26	23	3	2	1	1	113	27	86
Housing association homes and hostels	1	8	3	5	-	-	-	2	1	1	6	2	4
Nursing homes (non-NHS/LA/HA)	6	206	52	154	10	6	4	2	2	-	194	44	150
Residential homes (non-NHS/LA/HA)	8	196	89	107	54	51	3	9	4	5	133	34	99
Children's homes	-	-	-	-	-	-	-	-	-	-	-	-	-
Detention, defence and education	**4**	**56**	**53**	**3**	**45**	**43**	**2**	**2**	**2**	**-**	**9**	**8**	**1**
Prison service establishments	-	-	-	-	-	-	-	-	-	-	-	-	-
Defence establishments	1	1	1	-	-	-	-				1	1	-
Educational establishments	3	55	52	3	45	43	2	2	2	-	8	7	1
Other groups	**102**	**915**	**504**	**411**	**586**	**312**	**274**	**292**	**163**	**129**	**37**	**29**	**8**
Hotels, boarding houses etc	98	902	496	406	574	304	270	291	163	128	37	29	8
Hostels and common lodging houses (non-HA)	-	-	-	-	-	-	-	-	-	-	-	-	-
Other miscellaneous establishments	4	13	8	5	12	8	4	1	-	1	-	-	-
Persons sleeping rough		-	-	-	-	-	-				-	-	-
Campers		-	-	-	-	-	-				-	-	-
Civilian ships, boats and barges	-	-	-	-	-	-	-				-	-	-

3. Establishments: persons present not in households

Type of establishment	Number of establish-ments	TOTAL PERSONS	Total males	Total females	Not resident			Residents					
								Staff			Other residents		
					Total	Males	Females	Total	Males	Females	Total	Males	Females
a	b	c	d	e	f	g	h	i	j	k	l	m	n
				South Lakeland									
ALL ESTABLISHMENTS	**457**	**8,217**	**3,711**	**4,506**	**5,353**	**2,600**	**2,753**	**1,451**	**751**	**700**	**1,413**	**360**	**1,053**
Medical and care sector	**86**	**1,874**	**605**	**1,269**	**591**	**329**	**262**	**96**	**37**	**59**	**1,187**	**239**	**948**
NHS hospitals/homes - psychiatric	-	-	-	-	-	-	-	-	-	-	-	-	-
NHS hospitals/homes - other	6	193	60	133	164	53	111	-	-	-	29	7	22
Non-NHS hospitals - psychiatric	-	-	-	-	-	-	-	-	-	-	-	-	-
Non-NHS hospitals - other	1	35	5	30	21	3	18	-	-	-	14	2	12
Local authority homes	18	580	276	304	252	202	50	11	5	6	317	69	248
Housing association homes and hostels	2	21	3	18	1	-	1	2	1	1	18	2	16
Nursing homes (non-NHS/LA/HA)	26	453	111	342	83	32	51	43	14	29	327	65	262
Residential homes (non-NHS/LA/HA)	30	550	120	430	49	24	25	34	13	21	467	83	384
Children's homes	3	42	30	12	21	15	6	6	4	2	15	11	4
Detention, defence and education	**19**	**1,508**	**681**	**827**	**1,394**	**630**	**764**	**97**	**41**	**56**	**17**	**10**	**7**
Prison service establishments	-	-	-	-	-	-	-	-	-	-	-	-	-
Defence establishments	-	-	-	-	-	-	-				-	-	-
Educational establishments	19	1,508	681	827	1,394	630	764	97	41	56	17	10	7
Other groups	**352**	**4,835**	**2,425**	**2,410**	**3,368**	**1,641**	**1,727**	**1,258**	**673**	**585**	**209**	**111**	**98**
Hotels, boarding houses etc	341	4,658	2,334	2,324	3,276	1,594	1,682	1,233	657	576	149	83	66
Hostels and common lodging houses (non-HA)	1	6	6	-	-	-	-	-	-	-	6	6	-
Other miscellaneous establishments	10	165	83	82	86	45	41	25	16	9	54	22	32
Persons sleeping rough		-	-	-	-	-	-				-	-	-
Campers		6	2	4	6	2	4				-	-	-
Civilian ships, boats and barges	-	-	-	-	-	-	-				-	-	-

Table 4 Medical and care establishments

4. Residents (non-staff) present not in households

Type of establishment	TOTAL PERSONS	Total males	Total females	Age 0 - 15		16 - 44		45 up to pensionable age		Pensionable age - 74	
				Males	Females	Males	Females	Males	Females	Males	Females
a	b	c	d	e	f	g	h	i	j	k	l
CUMBRIA											
ALL MEDICAL AND CARE ESTABLISHMENTS	**4,722**	**1,251**	**3,471**	**24**	**21**	**160**	**147**	**144**	**85**	**237**	**411**
NHS hospitals/homes - psychiatric	-	-	-	-	-	-	-	-	-	-	-
NHS hospitals/homes - other	720	256	464	1	1	61	75	49	32	49	83
Non-NHS hospitals - psychiatric	-	-	-	-	-	-	-	-	-	-	-
Non-NHS hospitals - other	58	21	37	-	-	-	-	-	-	6	5
Local authority homes	1,327	363	964	3	-	25	23	34	12	93	112
Housing association homes and hostels	180	80	100	14	9	33	24	11	4	9	8
Nursing homes (non-NHS/LA/HA)	853	211	642	4	11	9	4	20	6	38	65
Residential homes (non-NHS/LA/HA)	1,584	320	1,264	2	-	32	21	30	31	42	138
Allerdale											
ALL MEDICAL AND CARE ESTABLISHMENTS	**1,007**	**289**	**718**	**7**	**3**	**56**	**41**	**41**	**29**	**47**	**91**
NHS hospitals/homes - psychiatric	-	-	-	-	-	-	-	-	-	-	-
NHS hospitals/homes - other	313	123	190	1	-	39	25	25	21	16	37
Non-NHS hospitals - psychiatric	-	-	-	-	-	-	-	-	-	-	-
Non-NHS hospitals - other	-	-	-	-	-	-	-	-	-	-	-
Local authority homes	271	86	185	-	-	7	7	12	4	23	24
Housing association homes and hostels	56	17	39	6	3	3	6	-	-	1	3
Nursing homes (non-NHS/LA/HA)	67	12	55	-	-	-	1	1	-	2	6
Residential homes (non-NHS/LA/HA)	300	51	249	-	-	7	2	3	4	5	21
Barrow-in-Furness											
ALL MEDICAL AND CARE ESTABLISHMENTS	**408**	**126**	**282**	**-**	**1**	**12**	**15**	**16**	**9**	**27**	**35**
NHS hospitals/homes - psychiatric	-	-	-	-	-	-	-	-	-	-	-
NHS hospitals/homes - other	48	16	32	-	1	1	1	1	-	3	7
Non-NHS hospitals - psychiatric	-	-	-	-	-	-	-	-	-	-	-
Non-NHS hospitals - other	-	-	-	-	-	-	-	-	-	-	-
Local authority homes	173	60	113	-	-	7	4	4	4	17	12
Housing association homes and hostels	-	-	-	-	-	-	-	-	-	-	-
Nursing homes (non-NHS/LA/HA)	53	19	34	-	-	1	1	7	2	2	6
Residential homes (non-NHS/LA/HA)	134	31	103	-	-	3	9	4	3	5	10
Carlisle											
ALL MEDICAL AND CARE ESTABLISHMENTS	**1,174**	**373**	**801**	**2**	**1**	**77**	**69**	**60**	**31**	**78**	**98**
NHS hospitals/homes - psychiatric	-	-	-	-	-	-	-	-	-	-	-
NHS hospitals/homes - other	305	102	203	-	-	20	42	21	11	27	34
Non-NHS hospitals - psychiatric	-	-	-	-	-	-	-	-	-	-	-
Non-NHS hospitals - other	-	-	-	-	-	-	-	-	-	-	-
Local authority homes	283	85	198	-	-	8	8	11	1	19	14
Housing association homes and hostels	56	47	9	2	1	28	8	10	-	5	-
Nursing homes (non-NHS/LA/HA)	142	51	91	-	-	6	2	7	2	11	12
Residential homes (non-NHS/LA/HA)	388	88	300	-	-	15	9	11	17	16	38

Age				Migrants	With limiting long-term illness	Ethnic group				Type of establishment
75 - 84		85 and over				White	Black groups	Indian, Pakistani and Bangladeshi	Chinese and other groups	
Males	Females	Males	Females							
m	n	o	p	q	r	s	t	u	v	a
425	**1,216**	**261**	**1,591**	**1,285**	**4,288**	**4,706**	**9**	**5**	**2**	**ALL MEDICAL AND CARE ESTABLISHMENTS**
-	-	-	-	-	-	-	-	-	-	NHS hospitals/homes - psychiatric
68	129	28	144	95	661	713	1	4	2	NHS hospitals/homes - other
-	-	-	-	-	-	-	-	-	-	Non-NHS hospitals - psychiatric
10	18	5	14	21	58	58	-	-	-	Non-NHS hospitals - other
133	374	75	443	384	1,265	1,327	-	-	-	Local authority homes
10	26	3	29	101	96	180	-	-	-	Housing association homes and hostels
84	242	56	314	272	742	853	-	-	-	Nursing homes (non-NHS/LA/HA)
120	427	94	647	412	1,466	1,575	8	1	-	Residential homes (non-NHS/LA/HA)
92	**237**	**46**	**317**	**311**	**931**	**1,007**	**-**	**-**	**-**	**ALL MEDICAL AND CARE ESTABLISHMENTS**
-	-	-	-	-	-	-	-	-	-	NHS hospitals/homes - psychiatric
29	50	13	57	49	311	313	-	-	-	NHS hospitals/homes - other
-	-	-	-	-	-	-	-	-	-	Non-NHS hospitals - psychiatric
-	-	-	-	-	-	-	-	-	-	Non-NHS hospitals - other
30	69	14	81	94	257	271	-	-	-	Local authority homes
6	12	1	15	51	35	56	-	-	-	Housing association homes and hostels
3	16	6	32	20	66	67	-	-	-	Nursing homes (non-NHS/LA/HA)
24	90	12	132	97	262	300	-	-	-	Residential homes (non-NHS/LA/HA)
45	**92**	**26**	**130**	**68**	**391**	**407**	**1**	**-**	**-**	**ALL MEDICAL AND CARE ESTABLISHMENTS**
-	-	-	-	-	-	-	-	-	-	NHS hospitals/homes - psychiatric
9	9	2	14	2	45	47	1	-	-	NHS hospitals/homes - other
-	-	-	-	-	-	-	-	-	-	Non-NHS hospitals - psychiatric
-	-	-	-	-	-	-	-	-	-	Non-NHS hospitals - other
22	43	10	50	42	169	173	-	-	-	Local authority homes
-	-	-	-	-	-	-	-	-	-	Housing association homes and hostels
6	12	3	13	9	45	53	-	-	-	Nursing homes (non-NHS/LA/HA)
8	28	11	53	15	132	134	-	-	-	Residential homes (non-NHS/LA/HA)
94	**276**	**62**	**326**	**320**	**1,062**	**1,168**	**1**	**4**	**1**	**ALL MEDICAL AND CARE ESTABLISHMENTS**
-	-	-	-	-	-	-	-	-	-	NHS hospitals/homes - psychiatric
24	59	10	57	35	260	300	-	4	1	NHS hospitals/homes - other
-	-	-	-	-	-	-	-	-	-	Non-NHS hospitals - psychiatric
-	-	-	-	-	-	-	-	-	-	Non-NHS hospitals - other
27	79	20	96	93	268	283	-	-	-	Local authority homes
2	-	-	-	30	25	56	-	-	-	Housing association homes and hostels
15	44	12	31	75	140	142	-	-	-	Nursing homes (non-NHS/LA/HA)
26	94	20	142	87	369	387	1	-	-	Residential homes (non-NHS/LA/HA)

Table 4 Medical and care establishments - continued

4. Residents (non-staff) present not in households

Type of establishment	TOTAL PERSONS	Total males	Total females	Age: 0 - 15		Age: 16 - 44		Age: 45 up to pensionable age		Age: Pensionable age - 74	
				Males	Females	Males	Females	Males	Females	Males	Females
a	b	c	d	e	f	g	h	i	j	k	l
Copeland											
ALL MEDICAL AND CARE ESTABLISHMENTS	**464**	**108**	**356**	**6**	**5**	**5**	**11**	**9**	**5**	**28**	**47**
NHS hospitals/homes - psychiatric	-	-	-	-	-	-	-	-	-	-	-
NHS hospitals/homes - other	18	7	11	-	-	-	1	2	-	1	2
Non-NHS hospitals - psychiatric	-	-	-	-	-	-	-	-	-	-	-
Non-NHS hospitals - other	-	-	-	-	-	-	-	-	-	-	-
Local authority homes	170	36	134	-	-	-	-	1	-	9	24
Housing association homes and hostels	44	12	32	6	5	2	10	1	4	2	4
Nursing homes (non-NHS/LA/HA)	70	20	50	-	-	-	-	2	-	10	5
Residential homes (non-NHS/LA/HA)	162	33	129	-	-	3	-	3	1	6	12
Eden											
ALL MEDICAL AND CARE ESTABLISHMENTS	**497**	**127**	**370**	**4**	**-**	**1**	**-**	**2**	**-**	**23**	**36**
NHS hospitals/homes - psychiatric	-	-	-	-	-	-	-	-	-	-	-
NHS hospitals/homes - other	7	1	6	-	-	-	-	-	-	-	-
Non-NHS hospitals - psychiatric	-	-	-	-	-	-	-	-	-	-	-
Non-NHS hospitals - other	44	19	25	-	-	-	-	-	-	6	4
Local authority homes	113	27	86	2	-	1	-	-	-	7	8
Housing association homes and hostels	6	2	4	-	-	-	-	-	-	-	1
Nursing homes (non-NHS/LA/HA)	194	44	150	-	-	-	-	2	-	9	11
Residential homes (non-NHS/LA/HA)	133	34	99	2	-	-	-	-	-	1	12
South Lakeland											
ALL MEDICAL AND CARE ESTABLISHMENTS	**1,172**	**228**	**944**	**5**	**11**	**9**	**11**	**16**	**11**	**34**	**104**
NHS hospitals/homes - psychiatric	-	-	-	-	-	-	-	-	-	-	-
NHS hospitals/homes - other	29	7	22	-	-	1	6	-	-	2	3
Non-NHS hospitals - psychiatric	-	-	-	-	-	-	-	-	-	-	-
Non-NHS hospitals - other	14	2	12	-	-	-	-	-	-	-	1
Local authority homes	317	69	248	1	-	2	4	6	3	18	30
Housing association homes and hostels	18	2	16	-	-	-	-	-	-	1	-
Nursing homes (non-NHS/LA/HA)	327	65	262	4	11	2	-	1	2	4	25
Residential homes (non-NHS/LA/HA)	467	83	384	-	-	4	1	9	6	9	45

Age				Migrants	With limiting long-term illness	Ethnic group				Type of establishment
75 - 84		85 and over				White	Black groups	Indian, Pakistani and Bangladeshi	Chinese and other groups	
Males	Females	Males	Females							
m	n	o	p	q	r	s	t	u	v	a
40	**127**	**20**	**161**	**113**	**415**	**462**	**-**	**1**	**1**	**ALL MEDICAL AND CARE ESTABLISHMENTS**
-	-	-	-	-	-	-	-	-	-	NHS hospitals/homes - psychiatric
4	2	-	6	4	16	17	-	-	1	NHS hospitals/homes - other
-	-	-	-	-	-	-	-	-	-	Non-NHS hospitals - psychiatric
-	-	-	-	-	-	-	-	-	-	Non-NHS hospitals - other
19	54	7	56	32	156	170	-	-	-	Local authority homes
-	3	1	6	16	21	44	-	-	-	Housing association homes and hostels
6	19	2	26	18	65	70	-	-	-	Nursing homes (non-NHS/LA/HA)
11	49	10	67	43	157	161	-	1	-	Residential homes (non-NHS/LA/HA)

m	n	o	p	q	r	s	t	u	v	a
57	**139**	**40**	**195**	**155**	**432**	**497**	**-**	**-**	**-**	**ALL MEDICAL AND CARE ESTABLISHMENTS**
-	-	-	-	-	-	-	-	-	-	NHS hospitals/homes - psychiatric
-	3	1	3	-	7	7	-	-	-	NHS hospitals/homes - other
-	-	-	-	-	-	-	-	-	-	Non-NHS hospitals - psychiatric
10	13	3	8	21	44	44	-	-	-	Non-NHS hospitals - other
9	33	8	45	35	105	113	-	-	-	Local authority homes
1	-	1	3	1	5	6	-	-	-	Housing association homes and hostels
18	59	15	80	54	156	194	-	-	-	Nursing homes (non-NHS/LA/HA)
19	31	12	56	44	115	133	-	-	-	Residential homes (non-NHS/LA/HA)

m	n	o	p	q	r	s	t	u	v	a
97	**345**	**67**	**462**	**318**	**1,057**	**1,165**	**7**	**-**	**-**	**ALL MEDICAL AND CARE ESTABLISHMENTS**
-	-	-	-	-	-	-	-	-	-	NHS hospitals/homes - psychiatric
2	6	2	7	5	22	29	-	-	-	NHS hospitals/homes - other
-	-	-	-	-	-	-	-	-	-	Non-NHS hospitals - psychiatric
-	5	2	6	-	14	14	-	-	-	Non-NHS hospitals - other
26	96	16	115	88	310	317	-	-	-	Local authority homes
1	11	-	5	3	10	18	-	-	-	Housing association homes and hostels
36	92	18	132	96	270	327	-	-	-	Nursing homes (non-NHS/LA/HA)
32	135	29	197	126	431	460	7	-	-	Residential homes (non-NHS/LA/HA)

Table 5 Hotels and other establishments

5. Residents (non-staff) present not in households

TOTAL PERSONS	Total males	Total females	Age 0 - 15 Males	0 - 15 Females	16 - 17 Males	16 - 17 Females	18 - 29 Males	18 - 29 Females	30 - 44 Males	30 - 44 Females	45 up to pensionable age Males	45 up to pensionable age Females	Pensionable age and over Males	Pensionable age and over Females
a	b	c	d	e	f	g	h	i	j	k	l	m	n	o
							CUMBRIA							
743	**494**	**249**	**61**	**51**	**10**	**6**	**216**	**83**	**96**	**36**	**84**	**30**	**27**	**43**
78	39	39	39	39	-	-	-	-	-	-	-	-	-	-
19	19	-	-	-	-	-	7	-	8	-	4	-	-	-
49	49	-	-	-	-	-	42	-	7	-	-	-	-	-
37	22	15	5	1	2	-	9	6	2	3	3	-	1	5
344	218	126	11	6	4	6	86	49	42	26	55	19	20	20
37	28	9	3	2	4	-	4	2	8	-	5	-	4	5
170	110	60	3	3	-	-	64	26	28	7	13	11	2	13
3	3	-	-	-	-	-	2	-	-	-	1	-	-	-
-	-	-	-	-	-	-	-	-	-	-	-	-	-	-
6	6	-	-	-	-	-	2	-	1	-	3	-	-	-
							Allerdale							
90	**49**	**41**	**12**	**10**	**-**	**-**	**16**	**6**	**6**	**8**	**11**	**6**	**4**	**11**
17	8	9	8	9	-	-	-	-	-	-	-	-	-	-
-	-	-	-	-	-	-	-	-	-	-	-	-	-	-
-	-	-	-	-	-	-	-	-	-	-	-	-	-	-
-	-	-	-	-	-	-	-	-	-	-	-	-	-	-
58	37	21	4	1	-	-	14	6	6	8	9	4	4	2
-	-	-	-	-	-	-	-	-	-	-	-	-	-	-
11	-	11	-	-	-	-	-	-	-	-	-	2	-	9
3	3	-	-	-	-	-	2	-	-	-	1	-	-	-
-	-	-	-	-	-	-	-	-	-	-	-	-	-	-
1	1	-	-	-	-	-	-	-	-	-	1	-	-	-
							Barrow-in-Furness							
56	**44**	**12**	**-**	**-**	**1**	**2**	**14**	**3**	**11**	**2**	**11**	**2**	**7**	**3**
-	-	-	-	-	-	-	-	-	-	-	-	-	-	-
-	-	-	-	-	-	-	-	-	-	-	-	-	-	-
-	-	-	-	-	-	-	-	-	-	-	-	-	-	-
-	-	-	-	-	-	-	-	-	-	-	-	-	-	-
53	41	12	-	-	1	2	14	3	10	2	9	2	7	3
-	-	-	-	-	-	-	-	-	-	-	-	-	-	-
-	-	-	-	-	-	-	-	-	-	-	-	-	-	-
-	-	-	-	-	-	-	-	-	-	-	-	-	-	-
-	-	-	-	-	-	-	-	-	-	-	-	-	-	-
3	3	-	-	-	-	-	-	-	1	-	2	-	-	-
							Carlisle							
157	**107**	**50**	**25**	**28**	**3**	**-**	**50**	**8**	**13**	**1**	**11**	**1**	**5**	**12**
42	19	23	19	23	-	-	-	-	-	-	-	-	-	-
-	-	-	-	-	-	-	-	-	-	-	-	-	-	-
48	48	-	-	-	-	-	42	-	6	-	-	-	-	-
9	4	5	-	-	-	-	-	-	-	-	3	-	1	5
18	10	8	-	-	-	-	5	5	-	-	4	1	1	2
31	22	9	3	2	3	-	3	2	6	-	4	-	3	5
9	4	5	3	3	-	-	-	1	1	1	-	-	-	-
-	-	-	-	-	-	-	-	-	-	-	-	-	-	-
-	-	-	-	-	-	-	-	-	-	-	-	-	-	-
-	-	-	-	-	-	-	-	-	-	-	-	-	-	-

Type of establishment	In employment	Un-employed	Econ-omically inactive	Econ-omically active students	Migrants	Ethnic group: White	Black groups	Indian, Pakistani and Bangla-deshi	Chinese and other groups
p	q	r	s	t	u	v	w	x	y
ALL HOTELS AND OTHER ESTABLISHMENTS	**332**	**110**	**189**	**6**	**358**	**736**	**1**	**5**	**1**
Children's homes	-	-	-	-	54	77	-	1	-
Prison service establishments	-	-	19	-	6	18	-	1	-
Defence establishments	49	-	-	-	28	49	-	-	-
Educational establishments	2	-	29	2	15	37	-	-	-
Hotels, boarding houses etc	141	81	105	3	131	341	1	1	1
Hostels and common lodging houses (non-HA)	5	15	12	-	26	37	-	-	-
Other miscellaneous establishments	129	13	22	1	95	168	-	2	-
Persons sleeping rough	-	1	2	-	3	3	-	-	-
Campers	-	-	-	-	-	-	-	-	-
Civilian ships, boats and barges	6	-	-	-	-	6	-	-	-

Type of establishment	In employment	Un-employed	Econ-omically inactive	Econ-omically active students	Migrants	Ethnic group: White	Black groups	Indian, Pakistani and Bangla-deshi	Chinese and other groups
ALL HOTELS AND OTHER ESTABLISHMENTS	**26**	**16**	**26**	**1**	**35**	**89**	**-**	**1**	**-**
Children's homes	-	-	-	-	11	17	-	-	-
Prison service establishments	-	-	-	-	-	-	-	-	-
Defence establishments	-	-	-	-	-	-	-	-	-
Educational establishments	-	-	-	-	-	-	-	-	-
Hotels, boarding houses etc	22	15	16	1	20	57	-	1	-
Hostels and common lodging houses (non-HA)	-	-	-	-	-	-	-	-	-
Other miscellaneous establishments	3	-	8	-	1	11	-	-	-
Persons sleeping rough	-	1	2	-	3	3	-	-	-
Campers	-	-	-	-	-	-	-	-	-
Civilian ships, boats and barges	1	-	-	-	-	1	-	-	-

Type of establishment	In employment	Un-employed	Econ-omically inactive	Econ-omically active students	Migrants	Ethnic group: White	Black groups	Indian, Pakistani and Bangla-deshi	Chinese and other groups
ALL HOTELS AND OTHER ESTABLISHMENTS	**18**	**20**	**18**	**-**	**20**	**56**	**-**	**-**	**-**
Children's homes	-	-	-	-	-	-	-	-	-
Prison service establishments	-	-	-	-	-	-	-	-	-
Defence establishments	-	-	-	-	-	-	-	-	-
Educational establishments	-	-	-	-	-	-	-	-	-
Hotels, boarding houses etc	15	20	18	-	20	53	-	-	-
Hostels and common lodging houses (non-HA)	-	-	-	-	-	-	-	-	-
Other miscellaneous establishments	-	-	-	-	-	-	-	-	-
Persons sleeping rough	-	-	-	-	-	-	-	-	-
Campers	-	-	-	-	-	-	-	-	-
Civilian ships, boats and barges	3	-	-	-	-	3	-	-	-

Type of establishment	In employment	Un-employed	Econ-omically inactive	Econ-omically active students	Migrants	Ethnic group: White	Black groups	Indian, Pakistani and Bangla-deshi	Chinese and other groups
ALL HOTELS AND OTHER ESTABLISHMENTS	**61**	**16**	**27**	**-**	**98**	**157**	**-**	**-**	**-**
Children's homes	-	-	-	-	35	42	-	-	-
Prison service establishments	-	-	-	-	-	-	-	-	-
Defence establishments	48	-	-	-	27	48	-	-	-
Educational establishments	-	-	9	-	-	9	-	-	-
Hotels, boarding houses etc	9	3	6	-	4	18	-	-	-
Hostels and common lodging houses (non-HA)	4	11	11	-	24	31	-	-	-
Other miscellaneous establishments	-	2	1	-	8	9	-	-	-
Persons sleeping rough	-	-	-	-	-	-	-	-	-
Campers	-	-	-	-	-	-	-	-	-
Civilian ships, boats and barges	-	-	-	-	-	-	-	-	-

Table 5 Hotels and other establishments - **continued**

5. Residents (non-staff) present not in households

TOTAL PERSONS	Total males	Total females	Age											
			0 - 15		16 - 17		18 - 29		30 - 44		45 up to pensionable age		Pensionable age and over	
			Males	Females	Males	Females	Males	Females	Males	Females	Males	Females	Males	Females
a	b	c	d	e	f	g	h	i	j	k	l	m	n	o
Copeland														
153	**125**	**28**	**2**	**4**	**1**	**-**	**72**	**16**	**29**	**4**	**20**	**2**	**1**	**2**
4	1	3	1	3	-	-	-	-	-	-	-	-	-	-
19	19	-	-	-	-	-	7	-	8	-	4	-	-	-
-	-	-	-	-	-	-	-	-	-	-	-	-	-	-
3	1	2	-	-	1	-	-	-	-	2	-	-	-	-
29	18	11	1	1	-	-	7	4	3	2	6	2	1	2
-	-	-	-	-	-	-	-	-	-	-	-	-	-	-
96	84	12	-	-	-	-	56	12	18	-	10	-	-	-
-	-	-	-	-	-	-	-	-	-	-	-	-	-	-
-	-	-	-	-	-	-	-	-	-	-	-	-	-	-
2	2	-	-	-	-	-	2	-	-	-	-	-	-	-
Eden														
46	**37**	**9**	**5**	**1**	**-**	**1**	**12**	**5**	**9**	**-**	**8**	**2**	**3**	**-**
-	-	-	-	-	-	-	-	-	-	-	-	-	-	-
-	-	-	-	-	-	-	-	-	-	-	-	-	-	-
1	1	-	-	-	-	-	-	-	1	-	-	-	-	-
8	7	1	4	-	-	-	2	1	1	-	-	-	-	-
37	29	8	1	1	-	1	10	4	7	-	8	2	3	-
-	-	-	-	-	-	-	-	-	-	-	-	-	-	-
-	-	-	-	-	-	-	-	-	-	-	-	-	-	-
-	-	-	-	-	-	-	-	-	-	-	-	-	-	-
-	-	-	-	-	-	-	-	-	-	-	-	-	-	-
-	-	-	-	-	-	-	-	-	-	-	-	-	-	-
South Lakeland														
241	**132**	**109**	**17**	**8**	**5**	**3**	**52**	**45**	**28**	**21**	**23**	**17**	**7**	**15**
15	11	4	11	4	-	-	-	-	-	-	-	-	-	-
-	-	-	-	-	-	-	-	-	-	-	-	-	-	-
-	-	-	-	-	-	-	-	-	-	-	-	-	-	-
17	10	7	1	1	1	-	7	5	1	1	-	-	-	-
149	83	66	5	3	3	3	36	27	16	14	19	8	4	11
6	6	-	-	-	1	-	1	-	2	-	1	-	1	-
54	22	32	-	-	-	-	8	13	9	6	3	9	2	4
-	-	-	-	-	-	-	-	-	-	-	-	-	-	-
-	-	-	-	-	-	-	-	-	-	-	-	-	-	-
-	-	-	-	-	-	-	-	-	-	-	-	-	-	-

Type of establishment	In employment	Un-employed	Econ-omically inactive	Econ-omically active students	Migrants	Ethnic group: White	Ethnic group: Black groups	Ethnic group: Indian, Pakistani and Bangla-deshi	Ethnic group: Chinese and other groups
p	q	r	s	t	u	v	w	x	y
ALL HOTELS AND OTHER ESTABLISHMENTS	**112**	**8**	**27**	**1**	**84**	**150**	**-**	**3**	**-**
Children's homes	-	-	-	-	4	4	-	-	-
Prison service establishments	-	-	19	-	6	18	-	1	-
Defence establishments	-	-	-	-	-	-	-	-	-
Educational establishments	-	-	3	-	-	3	-	-	-
Hotels, boarding houses etc	15	7	5	-	6	29	-	-	-
Hostels and common lodging houses (non-HA)	-	-	-	-	-	-	-	-	-
Other miscellaneous establishments	95	1	-	1	68	94	-	2	-
Persons sleeping rough	-	-	-	-	-	-	-	-	-
Campers	-	-	-	-	-	-	-	-	-
Civilian ships, boats and barges	2	-	-	-	-	2	-	-	-
ALL HOTELS AND OTHER ESTABLISHMENTS	**21**	**2**	**17**	**-**	**23**	**45**	**-**	**-**	**1**
Children's homes	-	-	-	-	-	-	-	-	-
Prison service establishments	-	-	-	-	-	-	-	-	-
Defence establishments	1	-	-	-	1	1	-	-	-
Educational establishments	-	-	4	-	7	8	-	-	-
Hotels, boarding houses etc	20	2	13	-	15	36	-	-	1
Hostels and common lodging houses (non-HA)	-	-	-	-	-	-	-	-	-
Other miscellaneous establishments	-	-	-	-	-	-	-	-	-
Persons sleeping rough	-	-	-	-	-	-	-	-	-
Campers	-	-	-	-	-	-	-	-	-
Civilian ships, boats and barges	-	-	-	-	-	-	-	-	-
ALL HOTELS AND OTHER ESTABLISHMENTS	**94**	**48**	**74**	**4**	**98**	**239**	**1**	**1**	**-**
Children's homes	-	-	-	-	4	14	-	1	-
Prison service establishments	-	-	-	-	-	-	-	-	-
Defence establishments	-	-	-	-	-	-	-	-	-
Educational establishments	2	-	13	2	8	17	-	-	-
Hotels, boarding houses etc	60	34	47	2	66	148	1	-	-
Hostels and common lodging houses (non-HA)	1	4	1	-	2	6	-	-	-
Other miscellaneous establishments	31	10	13	-	18	54	-	-	-
Persons sleeping rough	-	-	-	-	-	-	-	-	-
Campers	-	-	-	-	-	-	-	-	-
Civilian ships, boats and barges	-	-	-	-	-	-	-	-	-

6. Residents

Age	TOTAL PERSONS	Ethnic group: White	Black Caribbean	Black African	Black other	Indian	Pakistani	Bangla-deshi	Chinese	Other groups: Asian	Other groups: Other	Persons born in Ireland
a	b	c	d	e	f	g	h	i	j	k	l	m
					CUMBRIA							
TOTAL PERSONS	**483,163**	**481,052**	**109**	**81**	**260**	**269**	**94**	**137**	**453**	**171**	**537**	**3,760**
Males, all ages	**234,841**	**233,743**	**56**	**50**	**144**	**129**	**54**	**100**	**225**	**61**	**279**	**1,839**
0 - 4	14,706	14,590	3	4	20	3	5	13	26	3	39	12
5 - 9	14,959	14,849	3	11	11	12	3	11	18	3	38	35
10 - 14	14,422	14,342	1	3	14	9	3	3	14	5	28	39
15	2,843	2,818	1	1	-	3	-	4	9	1	6	6
16 - 17	6,301	6,271	-	1	3	1	1	9	6	2	7	17
18 - 19	6,687	6,650	2	2	6	4	1	3	12	1	6	26
20 - 24	16,982	16,867	8	3	21	6	5	26	22	7	17	88
25 - 29	17,593	17,498	8	5	13	12	4	4	24	6	19	93
30 - 34	16,822	16,726	1	4	8	12	12	7	20	6	26	97
35 - 39	15,716	15,624	4	7	11	10	5	6	18	5	26	138
40 - 44	18,387	18,298	8	2	8	16	7	2	16	7	23	168
45 - 49	15,371	15,301	4	2	11	13	1	3	11	3	22	160
50 - 54	13,951	13,909	2	4	6	7	4	1	6	4	8	182
55 - 59	13,256	13,218	2	-	2	8	1	1	10	5	9	179
60 - 64	13,184	13,153	4	-	3	8	1	2	8	2	3	152
65 - 69	11,991	11,972	2	1	3	3	-	5	3	-	2	171
70 - 74	9,349	9,343	2	-	1	1	-	-	1	1	-	140
75 - 79	6,708	6,705	-	-	1	1	-	-	1	-	-	82
80 - 84	3,738	3,736	-	-	2	-	-	-	-	-	-	43
85 and over	1,875	1,873	1	-	-	-	1	-	-	-	-	11
Females, all ages	**248,322**	**247,309**	**53**	**31**	**116**	**140**	**40**	**37**	**228**	**110**	**258**	**1,921**
0 - 4	14,198	14,098	3	2	22	7	6	7	20	5	28	19
5 - 9	14,008	13,915	6	2	9	9	1	5	22	2	37	31
10 - 14	13,569	13,493	4	3	8	8	5	5	15	4	24	27
15	2,749	2,731	-	-	4	3	-	1	3	-	7	6
16 - 17	5,975	5,941	3	1	4	5	2	1	11	2	5	15
18 - 19	6,539	6,505	3	1	3	4	1	1	3	4	14	23
20 - 24	16,921	16,831	2	3	9	13	7	4	23	10	19	96
25 - 29	17,147	17,026	5	6	9	18	8	5	23	14	33	102
30 - 34	16,620	16,501	6	4	10	15	3	4	35	18	24	112
35 - 39	15,589	15,503	2	3	11	17	3	1	17	20	12	145
40 - 44	18,016	17,939	2	2	7	11	-	-	21	16	18	168
45 - 49	15,024	14,974	1	1	6	7	1	1	7	9	17	157
50 - 54	14,140	14,105	2	1	5	8	1	1	9	5	3	162
55 - 59	13,396	13,374	1	-	2	4	-	-	9	1	5	150
60 - 64	14,300	14,280	5	2	1	2	1	1	5	-	3	181
65 - 69	14,214	14,197	1	-	2	5	1	-	3	-	5	168
70 - 74	12,397	12,390	3	-	1	1	-	-	1	-	1	138
75 - 79	10,341	10,335	2	-	2	1	-	-	1	-	-	113
80 - 84	7,429	7,425	1	-	1	-	-	-	-	-	2	65
85 and over	5,750	5,746	1	-	-	2	-	-	-	-	1	43
Born in UK	473,621	472,615	70	37	222	75	44	51	158	26	323	2,336
With limiting long-term illness	**63,520**	**63,373**	**21**	**7**	**26**	**12**	**6**	**6**	**23**	**12**	**34**	**731**
Males	29,020	28,940	8	5	15	5	4	4	15	6	18	368
Females	34,500	34,433	13	2	11	7	2	2	8	6	16	363

6. Residents

Age	TOTAL PERSONS	Ethnic group								Other groups		Persons born in Ireland
		White	Black Caribbean	Black African	Black other	Indian	Pakistani	Bangla-deshi	Chinese	Asian	Other	
a	b	c	d	e	f	g	h	i	j	k	l	m
					Allerdale							
TOTAL PERSONS	**95,702**	**95,382**	**12**	**7**	**41**	**31**	**17**	**13**	**85**	**19**	**95**	**471**
Males, all ages	**46,617**	**46,452**	**7**	**4**	**23**	**16**	**11**	**12**	**41**	**5**	**46**	**225**
0 - 4	2,796	2,774	-	1	5	1	1	-	6	-	8	-
5 - 9	3,044	3,027	-	1	1	1	1	1	5	1	6	2
10 - 14	3,070	3,057	1	-	2	1	1	1	3	-	4	5
15	578	577	-	-	-	-	-	-	-	-	1	1
16 - 17	1,269	1,265	-	-	-	-	-	2	1	-	1	1
18 - 19	1,334	1,330	-	-	1	-	-	-	1	-	2	5
20 - 24	3,302	3,286	1	-	3	-	1	4	6	-	1	12
25 - 29	3,327	3,311	1	1	2	2	1	1	2	-	6	12
30 - 34	3,251	3,239	-	-	1	1	2	2	3	1	2	11
35 - 39	3,107	3,092	1	-	1	1	2	1	5	-	4	16
40 - 44	3,785	3,772	2	-	1	2	2	-	1	1	4	24
45 - 49	3,110	3,098	1	-	3	1	-	-	2	-	5	18
50 - 54	2,786	2,781	-	1	1	1	-	-	1	1	-	30
55 - 59	2,664	2,657	-	-	1	2	-	-	3	1	-	25
60 - 64	2,622	2,615	-	-	1	3	-	-	2	-	1	14
65 - 69	2,398	2,397	-	-	-	-	-	-	-	-	1	18
70 - 74	1,881	1,881	-	-	-	-	-	-	-	-	-	21
75 - 79	1,284	1,284	-	-	-	-	-	-	-	-	-	6
80 - 84	670	670	-	-	-	-	-	-	-	-	-	4
85 and over	339	339	-	-	-	-	-	-	-	-	-	-
Females, all ages	**49,085**	**48,930**	**5**	**3**	**18**	**15**	**6**	**1**	**44**	**14**	**49**	**246**
0 - 4	2,755	2,739	-	-	4	1	-	-	5	1	5	1
5 - 9	2,757	2,739	-	-	1	1	-	-	6	-	10	5
10 - 14	2,747	2,739	-	-	-	-	3	-	1	-	4	8
15	565	562	-	-	1	-	-	-	-	-	2	-
16 - 17	1,190	1,183	1	-	-	-	-	-	5	-	1	2
18 - 19	1,306	1,299	-	-	1	1	-	-	-	1	4	5
20 - 24	3,324	3,314	-	-	1	1	1	-	3	1	3	14
25 - 29	3,260	3,247	-	1	-	-	-	-	3	3	6	10
30 - 34	3,257	3,238	-	-	-	2	1	1	8	4	3	13
35 - 39	3,170	3,159	1	-	2	3	1	-	1	2	1	21
40 - 44	3,744	3,734	-	1	-	2	-	-	3	-	4	20
45 - 49	2,972	2,959	-	1	4	1	-	-	1	2	4	16
50 - 54	2,773	2,765	-	-	2	1	-	-	4	-	1	20
55 - 59	2,678	2,672	1	-	2	1	-	-	2	-	-	21
60 - 64	2,868	2,866	1	-	-	-	-	-	1	-	-	15
65 - 69	2,861	2,859	-	-	-	1	-	-	-	-	1	33
70 - 74	2,464	2,462	1	-	-	-	-	-	1	-	-	21
75 - 79	1,897	1,897	-	-	-	-	-	-	-	-	-	10
80 - 84	1,416	1,416	-	-	-	-	-	-	-	-	-	10
85 and over	1,081	1,081	-	-	-	-	-	-	-	-	-	1
Born in UK	94,274	94,117	4	2	33	8	12	-	34	4	60	280
With limiting long-term illness	**12,916**	**12,897**	**2**	**1**	**4**	**2**	**-**	**-**	**2**	**1**	**7**	**73**
Males	6,013	6,004	1	1	-	1	-	-	2	1	3	36
Females	6,903	6,893	1	-	4	1	-	-	-	-	4	37

6. Residents

Age	TOTAL PERSONS	Ethnic group: White	Black Caribbean	Black African	Black other	Indian	Pakistani	Bangla-deshi	Chinese	Other groups: Asian	Other groups: Other	Persons born in Ireland
a	b	c	d	e	f	g	h	i	j	k	l	m
					Barrow-in-Furness							
TOTAL PERSONS	**73,125**	**72,725**	**12**	**13**	**43**	**46**	**17**	**13**	**108**	**35**	**113**	**887**
Males, all ages	**35,714**	**35,510**	**5**	**8**	**26**	**22**	**10**	**7**	**55**	**11**	**60**	**454**
0 - 4	2,602	2,582	-	-	4	-	-	-	7	-	9	2
5 - 9	2,334	2,314	-	1	2	1	-	1	3	-	12	7
10 - 14	2,098	2,084	-	-	2	2	-	-	4	1	5	4
15	458	451	-	1	-	-	-	1	4	-	1	2
16 - 17	982	978	-	-	-	-	1	1	1	-	1	2
18 - 19	1,060	1,054	-	-	-	1	1	-	3	-	1	1
20 - 24	2,811	2,791	1	1	4	-	1	-	7	3	3	9
25 - 29	2,920	2,909	-	-	1	-	1	1	4	1	3	14
30 - 34	2,601	2,591	-	1	1	3	3	-	1	1	-	24
35 - 39	2,307	2,288	-	3	5	1	-	1	4	-	5	28
40 - 44	2,698	2,671	1	1	2	9	1	1	4	3	5	31
45 - 49	2,372	2,354	-	-	2	1	1	-	4	1	9	25
50 - 54	2,127	2,119	-	-	1	1	-	1	2	-	3	60
55 - 59	1,886	1,880	-	-	-	-	-	-	3	1	2	57
60 - 64	1,786	1,779	1	-	1	2	1	-	2	-	-	48
65 - 69	1,640	1,635	2	-	1	1	-	-	-	-	1	57
70 - 74	1,388	1,387	-	-	-	-	-	-	1	-	-	34
75 - 79	933	932	-	-	-	-	-	-	1	-	-	31
80 - 84	489	489	-	-	-	-	-	-	-	-	-	15
85 and over	222	222	-	-	-	-	-	-	-	-	-	3
Females, all ages	**37,411**	**37,215**	**7**	**5**	**17**	**24**	**7**	**6**	**53**	**24**	**53**	**433**
0 - 4	2,461	2,446	-	-	1	1	2	1	3	2	5	2
5 - 9	2,246	2,222	3	1	3	4	-	1	1	-	11	2
10 - 14	2,036	2,020	-	1	2	3	-	1	5	-	4	3
15	425	423	-	-	1	-	-	-	1	-	-	1
16 - 17	938	932	-	-	1	1	-	-	1	1	2	2
18 - 19	1,056	1,051	-	1	1	-	-	1	-	-	2	5
20 - 24	2,852	2,830	1	-	1	1	-	-	11	5	3	12
25 - 29	2,868	2,851	-	-	-	2	3	-	3	3	6	18
30 - 34	2,488	2,465	2	-	2	1	-	1	8	1	8	18
35 - 39	2,292	2,274	-	-	3	4	2	1	3	4	1	30
40 - 44	2,630	2,611	-	1	1	1	-	-	6	5	5	39
45 - 49	2,262	2,256	-	-	-	1	-	-	2	1	2	32
50 - 54	2,111	2,105	-	-	-	3	-	-	1	2	-	32
55 - 59	1,829	1,823	-	-	-	-	-	-	5	-	1	45
60 - 64	1,931	1,927	1	1	-	1	-	-	1	-	-	45
65 - 69	1,958	1,955	-	-	1	-	-	-	1	-	1	49
70 - 74	1,978	1,977	-	-	-	-	-	-	-	-	1	35
75 - 79	1,456	1,454	-	-	-	1	-	-	1	-	-	34
80 - 84	953	952	-	-	-	-	-	-	-	-	1	15
85 and over	641	641	-	-	-	-	-	-	-	-	-	14
Born in UK	71,622	71,460	9	4	40	11	5	5	27	5	56	625
With limiting long-term illness	**10,326**	**10,300**	**1**	**1**	**3**	**2**	**-**	**-**	**8**	**2**	**9**	**226**
Males	4,597	4,585	-	-	2	1	-	-	4	-	5	118
Females	5,729	5,715	1	1	1	1	-	-	4	2	4	108

6. Residents

Age	TOTAL PERSONS	Ethnic group: White	Black Caribbean	Black African	Black other	Indian	Pakistani	Bangla-deshi	Chinese	Other groups: Asian	Other groups: Other	Persons born in Ireland
a	b	c	d	e	f	g	h	i	j	k	l	m
					Carlisle							
TOTAL PERSONS	**100,562**	**99,957**	**25**	**22**	**68**	**100**	**21**	**82**	**124**	**41**	**122**	**950**
Males, all ages	**48,480**	**48,142**	**19**	**13**	**37**	**45**	**14**	**63**	**62**	**20**	**65**	**449**
0 - 4	3,152	3,125	-	-	6	1	2	9	3	-	6	3
5 - 9	3,137	3,101	2	3	4	4	1	7	7	2	6	11
10 - 14	2,946	2,925	-	3	2	2	-	2	4	1	7	12
15	583	574	-	-	-	3	-	2	2	-	2	1
16 - 17	1,260	1,253	-	-	-	-	-	5	1	-	1	3
18 - 19	1,449	1,436	2	2	1	1	-	2	1	1	3	7
20 - 24	3,450	3,407	-	-	7	2	-	21	4	2	7	23
25 - 29	3,688	3,658	3	-	7	3	1	1	8	2	5	25
30 - 34	3,675	3,644	1	-	1	4	4	3	8	1	9	18
35 - 39	3,327	3,301	1	-	2	4	1	1	6	2	9	38
40 - 44	3,718	3,693	5	1	2	3	1	1	7	2	3	47
45 - 49	2,986	2,968	2	2	-	7	-	2	2	1	2	50
50 - 54	2,752	2,734	1	2	1	5	3	-	1	3	2	35
55 - 59	2,731	2,720	-	-	1	3	-	1	3	1	2	36
60 - 64	2,728	2,719	1	-	-	2	-	1	2	2	1	35
65 - 69	2,531	2,521	-	-	1	1	-	5	3	-	-	42
70 - 74	1,808	1,806	1	-	1	-	-	-	-	-	-	26
75 - 79	1,403	1,402	-	-	1	-	-	-	-	-	-	19
80 - 84	792	792	-	-	-	-	-	-	-	-	-	15
85 and over	364	363	-	-	-	-	1	-	-	-	-	3
Females, all ages	**52,082**	**51,815**	**6**	**9**	**31**	**55**	**7**	**19**	**62**	**21**	**57**	**501**
0 - 4	3,012	2,980	3	1	7	1	1	3	7	2	7	7
5 - 9	3,039	3,014	-	-	2	4	1	2	4	1	11	12
10 - 14	2,882	2,868	-	-	-	2	-	2	6	2	2	2
15	572	562	-	-	2	3	-	1	2	-	2	2
16 - 17	1,251	1,240	-	1	3	2	-	1	3	-	1	3
18 - 19	1,418	1,410	1	-	-	3	-	-	3	-	1	9
20 - 24	3,549	3,523	-	2	3	5	3	4	2	2	5	22
25 - 29	3,678	3,645	-	2	3	9	2	3	4	1	9	37
30 - 34	3,655	3,627	-	2	4	7	-	1	9	2	3	36
35 - 39	3,310	3,294	1	-	1	1	-	-	6	3	4	39
40 - 44	3,633	3,614	-	-	1	5	-	-	6	5	2	51
45 - 49	3,024	3,008	1	-	-	4	-	1	3	1	6	36
50 - 54	2,883	2,872	-	-	2	3	-	1	2	1	2	43
55 - 59	2,839	2,835	-	-	-	1	-	-	1	1	1	38
60 - 64	2,957	2,953	-	1	-	1	-	-	2	-	-	45
65 - 69	3,026	3,021	-	-	-	2	-	-	2	-	1	35
70 - 74	2,442	2,440	-	-	1	1	-	-	-	-	-	29
75 - 79	2,174	2,173	-	-	1	-	-	-	-	-	-	29
80 - 84	1,534	1,533	-	-	1	-	-	-	-	-	-	14
85 and over	1,204	1,203	-	-	-	1	-	-	-	-	-	12
Born in UK	98,235	97,961	17	11	52	25	8	31	47	10	73	595
With limiting long-term illness	**13,405**	**13,362**	**3**	**2**	**9**	**2**	**3**	**5**	**7**	**5**	**7**	**163**
Males	6,103	6,077	3	1	6	-	2	3	5	3	3	82
Females	7,302	7,285	-	1	3	2	1	2	2	2	4	81

6. Residents

Age	TOTAL PERSONS	Ethnic group: White	Ethnic group: Black Caribbean	Ethnic group: Black African	Ethnic group: Black other	Ethnic group: Indian	Ethnic group: Pakistani	Ethnic group: Bangla-deshi	Ethnic group: Chinese	Ethnic group: Other groups: Asian	Ethnic group: Other groups: Other	Persons born in Ireland
a	b	c	d	e	f	g	h	i	j	k	l	m
					Copeland							
TOTAL PERSONS	**71,296**	**71,020**	**24**	**10**	**42**	**37**	**19**	**7**	**49**	**39**	**49**	**479**
Males, all ages	**35,195**	**35,035**	**14**	**6**	**26**	**21**	**10**	**4**	**23**	**18**	**38**	**264**
0 - 4	2,390	2,369	3	1	2	1	1	1	5	1	6	2
5 - 9	2,508	2,496	1	1	2	4	1	-	1	-	2	6
10 - 14	2,264	2,249	-	-	3	2	-	-	2	3	5	7
15	438	435	1	-	-	-	-	-	-	1	1	1
16 - 17	940	933	-	-	2	-	-	-	1	1	3	3
18 - 19	935	930	-	-	3	1	-	-	1	-	-	4
20 - 24	2,613	2,598	2	-	3	3	2	-	2	2	1	21
25 - 29	2,906	2,893	1	1	2	3	1	-	2	3	-	17
30 - 34	2,699	2,681	-	2	2	1	2	1	2	2	6	20
35 - 39	2,385	2,370	2	1	1	3	1	1	1	1	4	22
40 - 44	2,736	2,724	-	-	1	1	2	-	3	1	4	23
45 - 49	2,193	2,182	1	-	3	1	-	1	1	1	3	21
50 - 54	2,065	2,063	-	-	-	-	-	-	1	-	1	19
55 - 59	1,979	1,973	2	-	-	1	-	-	1	1	1	19
60 - 64	1,887	1,884	1	-	1	-	-	-	-	-	1	20
65 - 69	1,639	1,639	-	-	-	-	-	-	-	-	-	23
70 - 74	1,223	1,222	-	-	-	-	-	-	-	1	-	23
75 - 79	764	764	-	-	-	-	-	-	-	-	-	10
80 - 84	439	438	-	-	1	-	-	-	-	-	-	2
85 and over	192	192	-	-	-	-	-	-	-	-	-	1
Females, all ages	**36,101**	**35,985**	**10**	**4**	**16**	**16**	**9**	**3**	**26**	**21**	**11**	**215**
0 - 4	2,348	2,339	-	-	2	-	2	2	3	-	-	3
5 - 9	2,232	2,220	2	-	1	-	-	-	7	1	1	3
10 - 14	2,117	2,106	2	1	2	3	-	-	1	1	1	5
15	420	420	-	-	-	-	-	-	-	-	-	-
16 - 17	943	941	1	-	-	-	-	-	-	1	-	4
18 - 19	951	947	2	-	-	-	-	-	-	-	2	2
20 - 24	2,543	2,529	1	-	2	3	2	-	2	2	2	15
25 - 29	2,761	2,745	-	2	-	3	2	1	5	3	-	12
30 - 34	2,579	2,562	1	-	1	2	1	-	4	5	3	14
35 - 39	2,294	2,284	-	-	3	3	-	-	1	3	-	14
40 - 44	2,539	2,529	-	-	3	1	-	-	2	4	-	16
45 - 49	2,124	2,122	-	-	-	-	-	-	-	1	1	24
50 - 54	2,084	2,081	-	1	1	-	-	-	1	-	-	15
55 - 59	1,954	1,953	-	-	-	-	-	-	-	-	1	13
60 - 64	1,983	1,981	-	-	1	-	1	-	-	-	-	21
65 - 69	1,867	1,866	-	-	-	-	1	-	-	-	-	20
70 - 74	1,659	1,658	1	-	-	-	-	-	-	-	-	12
75 - 79	1,237	1,237	-	-	-	-	-	-	-	-	-	9
80 - 84	849	849	-	-	-	-	-	-	-	-	-	8
85 and over	617	616	-	-	-	1	-	-	-	-	-	5
Born in UK	70,114	69,973	17	5	39	12	8	4	21	3	32	302
With limiting long-term illness	**9,095**	**9,077**	**2**	**-**	**4**	**1**	**-**	**1**	**3**	**3**	**4**	**99**
Males	4,344	4,329	2	-	3	-	-	1	3	2	4	58
Females	4,751	4,748	-	-	1	1	-	-	-	1	-	41

6. Residents

Age	TOTAL PERSONS	Ethnic group: White	Black Caribbean	Black African	Black other	Indian	Pakistani	Bangla-deshi	Chinese	Other groups: Asian	Other groups: Other	Persons born in Ireland
a	b	c	d	e	f	g	h	i	j	k	l	m
					Eden							
TOTAL PERSONS	**45,581**	**45,468**	**5**	**7**	**14**	**4**	**-**	**12**	**22**	**8**	**41**	**267**
Males, all ages	**22,451**	**22,392**	**2**	**5**	**7**	**3**	**-**	**9**	**11**	**2**	**20**	**144**
0 - 4	1,257	1,248	-	-	-	-	-	3	-	1	5	4
5 - 9	1,300	1,291	-	3	1	1	-	2	-	-	2	4
10 - 14	1,355	1,353	-	-	2	-	-	-	-	-	-	6
15	259	256	-	-	-	-	-	-	2	-	1	-
16 - 17	606	604	-	-	-	-	-	-	2	-	-	-
18 - 19	616	615	-	-	-	-	-	-	1	-	-	5
20 - 24	1,643	1,638	1	1	1	-	-	1	-	-	1	10
25 - 29	1,569	1,564	1	-	-	-	-	1	2	-	1	12
30 - 34	1,563	1,555	-	-	1	-	-	-	-	1	6	5
35 - 39	1,553	1,551	-	-	1	-	-	1	-	-	-	10
40 - 44	1,807	1,804	-	-	-	-	-	-	-	-	3	14
45 - 49	1,523	1,522	-	-	-	-	-	-	1	-	-	10
50 - 54	1,363	1,359	-	1	1	-	-	-	1	-	1	11
55 - 59	1,292	1,291	-	-	-	1	-	-	-	-	-	13
60 - 64	1,362	1,359	-	-	-	-	-	1	2	-	-	13
65 - 69	1,180	1,179	-	-	-	1	-	-	-	-	-	6
70 - 74	930	930	-	-	-	-	-	-	-	-	-	11
75 - 79	668	668	-	-	-	-	-	-	-	-	-	6
80 - 84	404	404	-	-	-	-	-	-	-	-	-	3
85 and over	201	201	-	-	-	-	-	-	-	-	-	1
Females, all ages	**23,130**	**23,076**	**3**	**2**	**7**	**1**	**-**	**3**	**11**	**6**	**21**	**123**
0 - 4	1,234	1,230	-	-	1	-	-	1	-	-	2	3
5 - 9	1,290	1,288	-	1	1	-	-	-	-	-	-	4
10 - 14	1,285	1,281	-	-	2	-	-	-	1	-	1	4
15	235	234	-	-	-	-	-	-	-	-	1	1
16 - 17	524	523	-	-	-	-	-	-	1	-	-	2
18 - 19	603	602	-	-	-	-	-	-	-	-	1	1
20 - 24	1,464	1,462	-	-	-	-	-	-	2	-	-	6
25 - 29	1,476	1,466	-	-	-	1	-	1	2	2	4	11
30 - 34	1,551	1,543	-	1	1	-	-	-	1	2	3	6
35 - 39	1,511	1,507	-	-	1	-	-	-	2	-	1	10
40 - 44	1,738	1,733	1	-	1	-	-	-	2	-	1	11
45 - 49	1,470	1,466	-	-	-	-	-	-	-	2	2	13
50 - 54	1,358	1,357	1	-	-	-	-	-	-	-	-	15
55 - 59	1,312	1,310	-	-	-	-	-	-	-	-	2	6
60 - 64	1,398	1,396	-	-	-	-	-	1	-	-	1	11
65 - 69	1,311	1,311	-	-	-	-	-	-	-	-	-	3
70 - 74	1,109	1,109	-	-	-	-	-	-	-	-	-	9
75 - 79	961	961	-	-	-	-	-	-	-	-	-	3
80 - 84	736	735	-	-	-	-	-	-	-	-	1	3
85 and over	564	562	1	-	-	-	-	-	-	-	1	1
Born in UK	44,790	44,728	2	5	14	2	-	7	7	-	25	174
With limiting long-term illness	**5,401**	**5,392**	**2**	**1**	**1**	**1**	**-**	**-**	**2**	**1**	**1**	**40**
Males	2,567	2,564	-	1	1	1	-	-	-	-	-	20
Females	2,834	2,828	2	-	-	-	-	-	2	1	1	20

6. Residents

Age	TOTAL PERSONS	Ethnic group: White	Black Caribbean	Black African	Black other	Indian	Pakistani	Bangla-deshi	Chinese	Other groups: Asian	Other groups: Other	Persons born in Ireland
a	b	c	d	e	f	g	h	i	j	k	l	m
					South Lakeland							
TOTAL PERSONS	**96,897**	**96,500**	**31**	**22**	**52**	**51**	**20**	**10**	**65**	**29**	**117**	**706**
Males, all ages	**46,384**	**46,212**	**9**	**14**	**25**	**22**	**9**	**5**	**33**	**5**	**50**	**303**
0 - 4	2,509	2,492	-	2	3	-	1	-	5	1	5	1
5 - 9	2,636	2,620	-	2	1	1	-	-	2	-	10	5
10 - 14	2,689	2,674	-	-	3	2	2	-	1	-	7	5
15	527	525	-	-	-	-	-	1	1	-	-	1
16 - 17	1,244	1,238	-	1	1	1	-	1	-	1	1	8
18 - 19	1,293	1,285	-	-	1	1	-	1	5	-	-	4
20 - 24	3,163	3,147	3	1	3	1	1	-	3	-	4	13
25 - 29	3,183	3,163	2	3	1	4	-	-	6	-	4	13
30 - 34	3,033	3,016	-	1	2	3	1	1	6	-	3	19
35 - 39	3,037	3,022	-	3	1	1	1	1	2	2	4	24
40 - 44	3,643	3,634	-	-	2	1	1	-	1	-	4	29
45 - 49	3,187	3,177	-	-	3	3	-	-	1	-	3	36
50 - 54	2,858	2,853	1	-	2	-	1	-	-	-	1	27
55 - 59	2,704	2,697	-	-	-	1	1	-	-	1	4	29
60 - 64	2,799	2,797	1	-	-	1	-	-	-	-	-	22
65 - 69	2,603	2,601	-	1	1	-	-	-	-	-	-	25
70 - 74	2,119	2,117	1	-	-	1	-	-	-	-	-	25
75 - 79	1,656	1,655	-	-	-	1	-	-	-	-	-	10
80 - 84	944	943	-	-	1	-	-	-	-	-	-	4
85 and over	557	556	1	-	-	-	-	-	-	-	-	3
Females, all ages	**50,513**	**50,288**	**22**	**8**	**27**	**29**	**11**	**5**	**32**	**24**	**67**	**403**
0 - 4	2,388	2,364	-	1	7	4	1	-	2	-	9	3
5 - 9	2,444	2,432	1	-	1	-	-	2	4	-	4	5
10 - 14	2,502	2,479	2	1	2	-	2	2	1	1	12	5
15	532	530	-	-	-	-	-	-	-	-	2	2
16 - 17	1,129	1,122	1	-	-	2	2	-	1	-	1	2
18 - 19	1,205	1,196	-	-	1	-	1	-	-	3	4	1
20 - 24	3,189	3,173	-	1	2	3	1	-	3	-	6	27
25 - 29	3,104	3,072	5	1	6	3	1	-	6	2	8	14
30 - 34	3,090	3,066	3	1	2	3	1	1	5	4	4	25
35 - 39	3,012	2,985	-	3	1	6	-	-	4	8	5	31
40 - 44	3,732	3,718	1	-	1	2	-	-	2	2	6	31
45 - 49	3,172	3,163	-	-	2	1	1	-	1	2	2	36
50 - 54	2,931	2,925	1	-	-	1	1	-	1	2	-	37
55 - 59	2,784	2,781	-	-	-	2	-	-	1	-	-	27
60 - 64	3,163	3,157	3	-	-	-	-	-	1	-	2	44
65 - 69	3,191	3,185	1	-	1	2	-	-	-	-	2	28
70 - 74	2,745	2,744	1	-	-	-	-	-	-	-	-	32
75 - 79	2,616	2,613	2	-	1	-	-	-	-	-	-	28
80 - 84	1,941	1,940	1	-	-	-	-	-	-	-	-	15
85 and over	1,643	1,643	-	-	-	-	-	-	-	-	-	10
Born in UK	94,586	94,376	21	10	44	17	11	4	22	4	77	360
With limiting long-term illness	**12,377**	**12,345**	**11**	**2**	**5**	**4**	**3**	**-**	**1**	**-**	**6**	**130**
Males	5,396	5,381	2	2	3	2	2	-	1	-	3	54
Females	6,981	6,964	9	-	2	2	1	-	-	-	3	76

7. Residents

Country of birth	TOTAL PERSONS	Males	Females
a	b	c	d
CUMBRIA			
ALL COUNTRIES OF BIRTH	**483,163**	**234,841**	**248,322**
Europe	478,048	232,381	245,667
European Community	477,131	231,904	245,227
United Kingdom	**473,621**	**230,297**	**243,324**
England	451,519	219,401	232,118
Scotland	16,897	8,317	8,580
Wales	2,857	1,422	1,435
Northern Ireland	2,336	1,148	1,188
United Kingdom (part not stated)	12	9	3
Outside United Kingdom	**9,542**	**4,544**	**4,998**
Channel Islands	65	32	33
Isle of Man	221	98	123
Irish Republic	1,420	688	732
Ireland (part not stated)	4	3	1
Old Commonwealth	**1,117**	**505**	**612**
Australia	431	184	247
Canada	462	205	257
New Zealand	224	116	108
New Commonwealth	**2,278**	**1,118**	**1,160**
Africa	497	255	242
Eastern Africa	306	161	145
Kenya	102	50	52
Malawi	23	15	8
Tanzania	46	27	19
Uganda	36	20	16
Zambia	99	49	50
Southern Africa	136	64	72
Zimbabwe	122	58	64
Botswana, Lesotho and Swaziland	14	6	8
Western Africa	55	30	25
Gambia	1	-	1
Ghana	10	5	5
Nigeria	38	23	15
Sierra Leone	6	2	4
Caribbean	147	67	80
Barbados	8	5	3
Jamaica	33	15	18
Trinidad and Tobago	28	10	18
Other Independent States	32	18	14
Caribbean Dependent Territories	12	5	7
West Indies (so stated)	7	6	1
Belize	8	1	7
Guyana	19	7	12
Asia	1,254	625	629
South Asia	718	385	333
Bangladesh	115	79	36
India	458	231	227
Pakistan	98	51	47
Sri Lanka	47	24	23
South East Asia	536	240	296
Hong Kong	301	143	158
Malaysia	94	47	47
Singapore	141	50	91

Country of birth	TOTAL PERSONS	Males	Females
a	b	c	d
CUMBRIA - *continued*			
Remainder of New Commonwealth	380	171	209
Cyprus	147	73	74
Gibraltar	46	22	24
Malta and Gozo	129	51	78
Mauritius	16	8	8
Seychelles	8	2	6
Other New Commonwealth	34	15	19
European Community	**2,086**	**916**	**1,170**
Belgium	65	26	39
Denmark	61	25	36
France	129	57	72
Germany	1,315	561	754
Greece	18	6	12
Italy	254	134	120
Luxembourg	-	-	-
Netherlands	129	52	77
Portugal	25	11	14
Spain	90	44	46
Remainder of Europe	**631**	**347**	**284**
Albania	-	-	-
Austria	105	32	73
Bulgaria	1	-	1
Czechoslovakia	40	22	18
Finland	14	2	12
Hungary	38	25	13
Norway	48	17	31
Poland	269	196	73
Romania	16	12	4
Sweden	39	10	29
Switzerland	44	21	23
Yugoslavia	15	9	6
Other Europe	2	1	1
Turkey	**23**	**17**	**6**
U.S.S.R.	**121**	**96**	**25**
Africa	**522**	**248**	**274**
Algeria	12	6	6
Egypt	70	40	30
Libya	23	15	8
Morocco	8	3	5
Tunisia	8	7	1
South Africa, Republic of	369	159	210
Other Africa	32	18	14
America	**609**	**273**	**336**
United States of America	482	217	265
Caribbean	2	1	1
Central America	20	8	12
South America	105	47	58
Asia	**439**	**197**	**242**
Middle East	191	116	75
Iran	51	38	13
Israel	18	8	10
Other Middle East	122	70	52
Remainder of Asia	248	81	167
Burma (Myanmar, Union of)	46	23	23
China, Peoples Republic of	78	36	42
Japan	13	2	11
Philippines	46	3	43
Vietnam	14	8	6
Other Asia	51	9	42
Rest of the world and at sea/in the air	**6**	**6**	**-**

7. Residents

Country of birth	TOTAL PERSONS	Males	Females
a	b	c	d
Allerdale			
ALL COUNTRIES OF BIRTH	**95,702**	**46,617**	**49,085**
Europe	94,922	46,256	48,666
European Community	94,787	46,188	48,599
United Kingdom	**94,274**	**45,949**	**48,325**
England	90,989	44,326	46,663
Scotland	2,511	1,225	1,286
Wales	494	261	233
Northern Ireland	280	137	143
United Kingdom (part not stated)	-	-	-
Outside United Kingdom	**1,428**	**668**	**760**
Channel Islands	7	2	5
Isle of Man	38	14	24
Irish Republic	191	88	103
Ireland (part not stated)	-	-	-
Old Commonwealth	**188**	**83**	**105**
Australia	69	32	37
Canada	76	35	41
New Zealand	43	16	27
New Commonwealth	**338**	**168**	**170**
Africa	77	43	34
Eastern Africa	55	31	24
Kenya	23	11	12
Malawi	1	1	-
Tanzania	11	8	3
Uganda	5	4	1
Zambia	15	7	8
Southern Africa	14	9	5
Zimbabwe	11	8	3
Botswana, Lesotho and Swaziland	3	1	2
Western Africa	8	3	5
Gambia	-	-	-
Ghana	1	-	1
Nigeria	5	3	2
Sierra Leone	2	-	2
Caribbean	24	7	17
Barbados	1	1	-
Jamaica	4	1	3
Trinidad and Tobago	2	-	2
Other Independent States	8	1	7
Caribbean Dependent Territories	1	-	1
West Indies (so stated)	3	2	1
Belize	1	-	1
Guyana	4	2	2
Asia	183	96	87
South Asia	96	55	41
Bangladesh	13	12	1
India	70	35	35
Pakistan	10	6	4
Sri Lanka	3	2	1
South East Asia	87	41	46
Hong Kong	49	23	26
Malaysia	11	7	4
Singapore	27	11	16

Country of birth	TOTAL PERSONS	Males	Females
a	b	c	d
Allerdale - *continued*			
Remainder of New Commonwealth	54	22	32
Cyprus	23	11	12
Gibraltar	5	1	4
Malta and Gozo	16	6	10
Mauritius	1	1	-
Seychelles	2	1	1
Other New Commonwealth	7	2	5
European Community	**322**	**151**	**171**
Belgium	20	10	10
Denmark	8	2	6
France	30	17	13
Germany	181	79	102
Greece	1	-	1
Italy	37	18	19
Luxembourg	-	-	-
Netherlands	28	16	12
Portugal	2	1	1
Spain	15	8	7
Remainder of Europe	**90**	**52**	**38**
Albania	-	-	-
Austria	12	6	6
Bulgaria	1	-	1
Czechoslovakia	9	5	4
Finland	1	-	1
Hungary	5	4	1
Norway	15	9	6
Poland	16	14	2
Romania	1	1	-
Sweden	14	6	8
Switzerland	11	5	6
Yugoslavia	4	2	2
Other Europe	1	-	1
Turkey	**6**	**5**	**1**
U.S.S.R.	**10**	**9**	**1**
Africa	**79**	**27**	**52**
Algeria	3	1	2
Egypt	13	7	6
Libya	2	2	-
Morocco	2	-	2
Tunisia	1	1	-
South Africa, Republic of	53	13	40
Other Africa	5	3	2
America	**80**	**33**	**47**
United States of America	57	21	36
Caribbean	-	-	-
Central America	6	3	3
South America	17	9	8
Asia	**79**	**36**	**43**
Middle East	34	22	12
Iran	11	5	6
Israel	2	2	-
Other Middle East	21	15	6
Remainder of Asia	45	14	31
Burma (Myanmar, Union of)	5	2	3
China, Peoples Republic of	22	9	13
Japan	-	-	-
Philippines	7	-	7
Vietnam	3	1	2
Other Asia	8	2	6
Rest of the world and at sea/in the air	-	-	-

7. Residents

Country of birth	TOTAL PERSONS	Males	Females
a	b	c	d
Barrow-in-Furness			
ALL COUNTRIES OF BIRTH	**73,125**	**35,714**	**37,411**
Europe	72,277	35,307	36,970
European Community	72,142	35,228	36,914
United Kingdom	**71,622**	**35,001**	**36,621**
England	68,187	33,181	35,006
Scotland	2,386	1,275	1,111
Wales	423	218	205
Northern Ireland	625	326	299
United Kingdom (part not stated)	1	1	-
Outside United Kingdom	**1,503**	**713**	**790**
Channel Islands	6	4	2
Isle of Man	61	31	30
Irish Republic	261	127	134
Ireland (part not stated)	1	1	-
Old Commonwealth	**169**	**79**	**90**
Australia	71	30	41
Canada	78	39	39
New Zealand	20	10	10
New Commonwealth	**364**	**181**	**183**
Africa	64	37	27
Eastern Africa	39	22	17
Kenya	10	4	6
Malawi	9	6	3
Tanzania	3	3	-
Uganda	-	-	-
Zambia	17	9	8
Southern Africa	19	10	9
Zimbabwe	18	9	9
Botswana, Lesotho and Swaziland	1	1	-
Western Africa	6	5	1
Gambia	-	-	-
Ghana	3	2	1
Nigeria	3	3	-
Sierra Leone	-	-	-
Caribbean	17	7	10
Barbados	2	1	1
Jamaica	2	1	1
Trinidad and Tobago	3	1	2
Other Independent States	2	1	1
Caribbean Dependent Territories	2	-	2
West Indies (so stated)	2	2	-
Belize	-	-	-
Guyana	4	1	3
Asia	206	103	103
South Asia	94	49	45
Bangladesh	8	4	4
India	62	34	28
Pakistan	13	8	5
Sri Lanka	11	3	8
South East Asia	112	54	58
Hong Kong	71	36	35
Malaysia	15	10	5
Singapore	26	8	18
Barrow-in-Furness - *continued*			
Remainder of New Commonwealth	77	34	43
Cyprus	27	12	15
Gibraltar	13	7	6
Malta and Gozo	33	14	19
Mauritius	2	-	2
Seychelles	1	-	1
Other New Commonwealth	1	1	-
European Community	**258**	**99**	**159**
Belgium	11	4	7
Denmark	5	2	3
France	12	6	6
Germany	180	62	118
Greece	2	1	1
Italy	21	13	8
Luxembourg	-	-	-
Netherlands	15	6	9
Portugal	2	-	2
Spain	10	5	5
Remainder of Europe	**68**	**44**	**24**
Albania	-	-	-
Austria	9	2	7
Bulgaria	-	-	-
Czechoslovakia	1	-	1
Finland	1	-	1
Hungary	8	7	1
Norway	4	2	2
Poland	31	26	5
Romania	2	-	2
Sweden	3	1	2
Switzerland	9	6	3
Yugoslavia	-	-	-
Other Europe	-	-	-
Turkey	**4**	**2**	**2**
U.S.S.R.	**4**	**3**	**1**
Africa	**92**	**46**	**46**
Algeria	1	1	-
Egypt	15	9	6
Libya	7	4	3
Morocco	1	-	1
Tunisia	-	-	-
South Africa, Republic of	64	28	36
Other Africa	4	4	-
America	**139**	**61**	**78**
United States of America	117	53	64
Caribbean	-	-	-
Central America	2	1	1
South America	20	7	13
Asia	**72**	**31**	**41**
Middle East	34	23	11
Iran	19	16	3
Israel	4	1	3
Other Middle East	11	6	5
Remainder of Asia	38	8	30
Burma (Myanmar, Union of)	1	1	-
China, Peoples Republic of	14	5	9
Japan	2	-	2
Philippines	6	-	6
Vietnam	2	1	1
Other Asia	13	1	12
Rest of the world and at sea/in the air	**4**	**4**	**-**

7. Residents

Country of birth	TOTAL PERSONS	Males	Females
a	b	c	d
Carlisle			
ALL COUNTRIES OF BIRTH	**100,562**	**48,480**	**52,082**
Europe	99,380	47,866	51,514
European Community	99,176	47,758	51,418
United Kingdom	**98,235**	**47,322**	**50,913**
England	90,551	43,617	46,934
Scotland	6,578	3,192	3,386
Wales	509	234	275
Northern Ireland	595	277	318
United Kingdom (part not stated)	2	2	-
Outside United Kingdom	**2,327**	**1,158**	**1,169**
Channel Islands	18	10	8
Isle of Man	26	12	14
Irish Republic	353	171	182
Ireland (part not stated)	2	1	1
Old Commonwealth	**208**	**90**	**118**
Australia	62	25	37
Canada	100	38	62
New Zealand	46	27	19
New Commonwealth	**628**	**320**	**308**
Africa	103	51	52
Eastern Africa	67	35	32
Kenya	22	14	8
Malawi	5	2	3
Tanzania	11	4	7
Uganda	9	6	3
Zambia	20	9	11
Southern Africa	24	9	15
Zimbabwe	22	8	14
Botswana, Lesotho and Swaziland	2	1	1
Western Africa	12	7	5
Gambia	1	-	1
Ghana	2	2	-
Nigeria	9	5	4
Sierra Leone	-	-	-
Caribbean	30	20	10
Barbados	1	1	-
Jamaica	12	7	5
Trinidad and Tobago	5	2	3
Other Independent States	6	6	-
Caribbean Dependent Territories	1	-	1
West Indies (so stated)	-	-	-
Belize	1	1	-
Guyana	4	3	1
Asia	371	194	177
South Asia	234	133	101
Bangladesh	59	42	17
India	134	70	64
Pakistan	31	17	14
Sri Lanka	10	4	6
South East Asia	137	61	76
Hong Kong	82	40	42
Malaysia	25	9	16
Singapore	30	12	18
Carlisle – *continued*			
Remainder of New Commonwealth	124	55	69
Cyprus	61	30	31
Gibraltar	13	4	9
Malta and Gozo	34	12	22
Mauritius	6	4	2
Seychelles	-	-	-
Other New Commonwealth	10	5	5
European Community	**586**	**264**	**322**
Belgium	9	3	6
Denmark	9	3	6
France	27	11	16
Germany	407	181	226
Greece	6	1	5
Italy	75	41	34
Luxembourg	-	-	-
Netherlands	24	7	17
Portugal	7	5	2
Spain	22	12	10
Remainder of Europe	**160**	**86**	**74**
Albania	-	-	-
Austria	26	4	22
Bulgaria	-	-	-
Czechoslovakia	11	8	3
Finland	1	-	1
Hungary	9	6	3
Norway	6	2	4
Poland	93	57	36
Romania	2	2	-
Sweden	1	-	1
Switzerland	6	4	2
Yugoslavia	5	3	2
Other Europe	-	-	-
Turkey	**5**	**4**	**1**
U.S.S.R.	**63**	**53**	**10**
Africa	**101**	**51**	**50**
Algeria	2	-	2
Egypt	14	9	5
Libya	3	2	1
Morocco	2	1	1
Tunisia	5	4	1
South Africa, Republic of	73	34	39
Other Africa	2	1	1
America	**82**	**41**	**41**
United States of America	61	31	30
Caribbean	-	-	-
Central America	5	2	3
South America	16	8	8
Asia	**93**	**53**	**40**
Middle East	36	24	12
Iran	7	7	-
Israel	4	2	2
Other Middle East	25	15	10
Remainder of Asia	57	29	28
Burma (Myanmar, Union of)	18	11	7
China, Peoples Republic of	19	12	7
Japan	2	1	1
Philippines	7	-	7
Vietnam	6	4	2
Other Asia	5	1	4
Rest of the world and at sea/in the air	**2**	**2**	**-**

7. Residents

Country of birth	TOTAL PERSONS	Males	Females
a	b	c	d
Copeland			
ALL COUNTRIES OF BIRTH	**71,296**	**35,195**	**36,101**
Europe	70,737	34,924	35,813
European Community	70,585	34,843	35,742
United Kingdom	**70,114**	**34,608**	**35,506**
England	67,736	33,378	34,358
Scotland	1,721	873	848
Wales	353	194	159
Northern Ireland	302	162	140
United Kingdom (part not stated)	2	1	1
Outside United Kingdom	**1,182**	**587**	**595**
Channel Islands	10	6	4
Isle of Man	43	19	24
Irish Republic	177	102	75
Ireland (part not stated)	-	-	-
Old Commonwealth	**104**	**49**	**55**
Australia	35	18	17
Canada	53	25	28
New Zealand	16	6	10
New Commonwealth	**259**	**129**	**130**
Africa	56	32	24
Eastern Africa	32	18	14
Kenya	8	3	5
Malawi	-	-	-
Tanzania	8	5	3
Uganda	2	2	-
Zambia	14	8	6
Southern Africa	18	10	8
Zimbabwe	18	10	8
Botswana, Lesotho and Swaziland	-	-	-
Western Africa	6	4	2
Gambia	-	-	-
Ghana	-	-	-
Nigeria	6	4	2
Sierra Leone	-	-	-
Caribbean	13	8	5
Barbados	1	-	1
Jamaica	3	2	1
Trinidad and Tobago	1	-	1
Other Independent States	5	4	1
Caribbean Dependent Territories	1	1	-
West Indies (so stated)	1	1	-
Belize	-	-	-
Guyana	1	-	1
Asia	146	69	77
South Asia	89	45	44
Bangladesh	19	12	7
India	44	18	26
Pakistan	16	8	8
Sri Lanka	10	7	3
South East Asia	57	24	33
Hong Kong	33	15	18
Malaysia	9	3	6
Singapore	15	6	9

Country of birth	TOTAL PERSONS	Males	Females
a	b	c	d
Copeland - *continued*			
Remainder of New Commonwealth	44	20	24
Cyprus	13	6	7
Gibraltar	7	4	3
Malta and Gozo	20	8	12
Mauritius	-	-	-
Seychelles	3	1	2
Other New Commonwealth	1	1	-
European Community	**294**	**133**	**161**
Belgium	6	2	4
Denmark	15	11	4
France	15	5	10
Germany	182	78	104
Greece	2	-	2
Italy	46	23	23
Luxembourg	-	-	-
Netherlands	12	5	7
Portugal	5	3	2
Spain	11	6	5
Remainder of Europe	**99**	**56**	**43**
Albania	-	-	-
Austria	19	6	13
Bulgaria	-	-	-
Czechoslovakia	3	1	2
Finland	3	-	3
Hungary	8	5	3
Norway	3	-	3
Poland	50	38	12
Romania	1	-	1
Sweden	4	1	3
Switzerland	2	1	1
Yugoslavia	5	3	2
Other Europe	1	1	-
Turkey	**3**	**3**	**-**
U.S.S.R.	**10**	**7**	**3**
Africa	**84**	**43**	**41**
Algeria	1	1	-
Egypt	11	4	7
Libya	7	5	2
Morocco	-	-	-
Tunisia	1	1	-
South Africa, Republic of	60	29	31
Other Africa	4	3	1
America	**54**	**22**	**32**
United States of America	46	18	28
Caribbean	-	-	-
Central America	-	-	-
South America	8	4	4
Asia	**45**	**18**	**27**
Middle East	20	14	6
Iran	5	4	1
Israel	1	1	-
Other Middle East	14	9	5
Remainder of Asia	25	4	21
Burma (Myanmar, Union of)	1	-	1
China, Peoples Republic of	7	2	5
Japan	-	-	-
Philippines	9	1	8
Vietnam	-	-	-
Other Asia	8	1	7
Rest of the world and at sea/in the air	**-**	**-**	**-**

7. Residents

Country of birth	TOTAL PERSONS	Males	Females
a	b	c	d
Eden			
ALL COUNTRIES OF BIRTH	**45,581**	**22,451**	**23,130**
Europe	45,144	22,231	22,913
European Community	45,065	22,192	22,873
United Kingdom	**44,790**	**22,052**	**22,738**
England	43,013	21,199	21,814
Scotland	1,338	644	694
Wales	262	119	143
Northern Ireland	174	88	86
United Kingdom (part not stated)	3	2	1
Outside United Kingdom	**791**	**399**	**392**
Channel Islands	9	4	5
Isle of Man	14	7	7
Irish Republic	93	56	37
Ireland (part not stated)	-	-	-
Old Commonwealth	**109**	**53**	**56**
Australia	39	18	21
Canada	39	17	22
New Zealand	31	18	13
New Commonwealth	**164**	**80**	**84**
Africa	38	17	21
Eastern Africa	19	9	10
Kenya	10	4	6
Malawi	2	2	-
Tanzania	1	-	1
Uganda	1	1	-
Zambia	5	2	3
Southern Africa	14	6	8
Zimbabwe	12	5	7
Botswana, Lesotho and Swaziland	2	1	1
Western Africa	5	2	3
Gambia	-	-	-
Ghana	1	-	1
Nigeria	3	2	1
Sierra Leone	1	-	1
Caribbean	14	6	8
Barbados	2	1	1
Jamaica	3	1	2
Trinidad and Tobago	1	1	-
Other Independent States	4	3	1
Caribbean Dependent Territories	1	-	1
West Indies (so stated)	-	-	-
Belize	1	-	1
Guyana	2	-	2
Asia	88	43	45
South Asia	54	31	23
Bangladesh	5	4	1
India	36	21	15
Pakistan	8	3	5
Sri Lanka	5	3	2
South East Asia	34	12	22
Hong Kong	19	7	12
Malaysia	9	5	4
Singapore	6	-	6
Eden - *continued*			
Remainder of New Commonwealth	24	14	10
Cyprus	8	7	1
Gibraltar	2	2	-
Malta and Gozo	6	4	2
Mauritius	-	-	-
Seychelles	1	-	1
Other New Commonwealth	7	1	6
European Community	**182**	**84**	**98**
Belgium	7	3	4
Denmark	8	1	7
France	15	5	10
Germany	119	61	58
Greece	4	2	2
Italy	15	8	7
Luxembourg	-	-	-
Netherlands	8	1	7
Portugal	1	-	1
Spain	5	3	2
Remainder of Europe	**56**	**28**	**28**
Albania	-	-	-
Austria	11	2	9
Bulgaria	-	-	-
Czechoslovakia	3	2	1
Finland	-	-	-
Hungary	3	1	2
Norway	3	-	3
Poland	28	21	7
Romania	-	-	-
Sweden	3	-	3
Switzerland	4	1	3
Yugoslavia	1	1	-
Other Europe	-	-	-
Turkey	**-**	**-**	**-**
U.S.S.R.	**17**	**15**	**2**
Africa	**37**	**24**	**13**
Algeria	1	1	-
Egypt	5	5	-
Libya	1	1	-
Morocco	-	-	-
Tunisia	-	-	-
South Africa, Republic of	27	14	13
Other Africa	3	3	-
America	**65**	**28**	**37**
United States of America	52	23	29
Caribbean	-	-	-
Central America	-	-	-
South America	13	5	8
Asia	**45**	**20**	**25**
Middle East	26	15	11
Iran	3	2	1
Israel	2	1	1
Other Middle East	21	12	9
Remainder of Asia	19	5	14
Burma (Myanmar, Union of)	2	1	1
China, Peoples Republic of	6	3	3
Japan	2	-	2
Philippines	5	-	5
Vietnam	-	-	-
Other Asia	4	1	3
Rest of the world and at sea/in the air	**-**	**-**	**-**

7. Residents

Country of birth	TOTAL PERSONS	Males	Females
a	b	c	d
South Lakeland			
ALL COUNTRIES OF BIRTH	**96,897**	**46,384**	**50,513**
Europe	95,588	45,797	49,791
European Community	95,376	45,695	49,681
United Kingdom	**94,586**	**45,365**	**49,221**
England	91,043	43,700	47,343
Scotland	2,363	1,108	1,255
Wales	816	396	420
Northern Ireland	360	158	202
United Kingdom (part not stated)	4	3	1
Outside United Kingdom	**2,311**	**1,019**	**1,292**
Channel Islands	15	6	9
Isle of Man	39	15	24
Irish Republic	345	144	201
Ireland (part not stated)	1	1	-
Old Commonwealth	**339**	**151**	**188**
Australia	155	61	94
Canada	116	51	65
New Zealand	68	39	29
New Commonwealth	**525**	**240**	**285**
Africa	159	75	84
Eastern Africa	94	46	48
Kenya	29	14	15
Malawi	6	4	2
Tanzania	12	7	5
Uganda	19	7	12
Zambia	28	14	14
Southern Africa	47	20	27
Zimbabwe	41	18	23
Botswana, Lesotho and Swaziland	6	2	4
Western Africa	18	9	9
Gambia	-	-	-
Ghana	3	1	2
Nigeria	12	6	6
Sierra Leone	3	2	1
Caribbean	49	19	30
Barbados	1	1	-
Jamaica	9	3	6
Trinidad and Tobago	16	6	10
Other Independent States	7	3	4
Caribbean Dependent Territories	6	4	2
West Indies (so stated)	1	1	-
Belize	5	-	5
Guyana	4	1	3
Asia	260	120	140
South Asia	151	72	79
Bangladesh	11	5	6
India	112	53	59
Pakistan	20	9	11
Sri Lanka	8	5	3
South East Asia	109	48	61
Hong Kong	47	22	25
Malaysia	25	13	12
Singapore	37	13	24
South Lakeland - *continued*			
Remainder of New Commonwealth	57	26	31
Cyprus	15	7	8
Gibraltar	6	4	2
Malta and Gozo	20	7	13
Mauritius	7	3	4
Seychelles	1	-	1
Other New Commonwealth	8	5	3
European Community	**444**	**185**	**259**
Belgium	12	4	8
Denmark	16	6	10
France	30	13	17
Germany	246	100	146
Greece	3	2	1
Italy	60	31	29
Luxembourg	-	-	-
Netherlands	42	17	25
Portugal	8	2	6
Spain	27	10	17
Remainder of Europe	**158**	**81**	**77**
Albania	-	-	-
Austria	28	12	16
Bulgaria	-	-	-
Czechoslovakia	13	6	7
Finland	8	2	6
Hungary	5	2	3
Norway	17	4	13
Poland	51	40	11
Romania	10	9	1
Sweden	14	2	12
Switzerland	12	4	8
Yugoslavia	-	-	-
Other Europe	-	-	-
Turkey	**5**	**3**	**2**
U.S.S.R.	**17**	**9**	**8**
Africa	**129**	**57**	**72**
Algeria	4	2	2
Egypt	12	6	6
Libya	3	1	2
Morocco	3	2	1
Tunisia	1	1	-
South Africa, Republic of	92	41	51
Other Africa	14	4	10
America	**189**	**88**	**101**
United States of America	149	71	78
Caribbean	2	1	1
Central America	7	2	5
South America	31	14	17
Asia	**105**	**39**	**66**
Middle East	41	18	23
Iran	6	4	2
Israel	5	1	4
Other Middle East	30	13	17
Remainder of Asia	64	21	43
Burma (Myanmar, Union of)	19	8	11
China, Peoples Republic of	10	5	5
Japan	7	1	6
Philippines	12	2	10
Vietnam	3	2	1
Other Asia	13	3	10
Rest of the world and at sea/in the air	**-**	**-**	**-**

Table 8 Economic position

8. Residents aged 16 and over

Sex, marital status and economic position	TOTAL AGED 16 AND OVER	Age 16	17	18	19	20	21 - 24	25 - 29	30 - 34	35 - 39
a	b	c	d	e	f	g	h	i	j	k
CUMBRIA										
TOTAL PERSONS	**391,709**	**6,050**	**6,226**	**6,477**	**6,749**	**6,980**	**26,923**	**34,740**	**33,442**	**31,305**
Economically active	**238,954**	**2,009**	**4,072**	**4,792**	**5,292**	**5,574**	**22,547**	**28,994**	**27,804**	**26,774**
Employees - full time	143,762	676	2,010	3,028	3,912	4,244	16,961	19,779	16,668	15,557
- part time	42,529	587	674	594	408	364	1,730	3,843	5,510	5,735
Self-employed - with employees	13,005	2	2	7	6	13	210	725	1,399	1,604
- without employees	19,997	12	21	45	86	154	990	2,006	2,325	2,376
On a Government scheme	3,449	414	975	475	156	82	229	275	194	188
Unemployed	16,212	318	390	643	724	717	2,427	2,366	1,708	1,314
Economically active students (included above)	*1,754*	*482*	*478*	*343*	*119*	*89*	*159*	*29*	*17*	*15*
Economically inactive	**152,755**	**4,041**	**2,154**	**1,685**	**1,457**	**1,406**	**4,376**	**5,746**	**5,638**	**4,531**
Students	12,029	4,007	2,036	1,468	1,116	961	1,609	312	172	135
Permanently sick	14,968	7	21	29	57	68	340	552	643	752
Retired	78,461	1	2	1	-	3	6	8	10	21
Other inactive	47,297	26	95	187	284	374	2,421	4,874	4,813	3,623
Total males	**187,911**	**3,151**	**3,150**	**3,295**	**3,392**	**3,512**	**13,470**	**17,593**	**16,822**	**15,716**
Economically active	**137,941**	**1,092**	**2,243**	**2,624**	**2,836**	**2,987**	**12,383**	**17,054**	**16,333**	**15,161**
Employees - full time	97,336	438	1,258	1,735	2,126	2,296	9,470	12,948	12,160	11,167
- part time	3,836	192	205	185	117	79	214	238	194	170
Self-employed - with employees	9,171	2	1	6	4	11	145	528	976	1,131
- without employees	14,728	10	17	39	69	117	790	1,597	1,735	1,702
On a Government scheme	1,995	242	549	282	90	48	138	197	107	98
Unemployed	10,875	208	213	377	430	436	1,626	1,546	1,161	893
Economically active students (included above)	*636*	*155*	*159*	*124*	*52*	*36*	*74*	*12*	*4*	*8*
Economically inactive	**49,970**	**2,059**	**907**	**671**	**556**	**525**	**1,087**	**539**	**489**	**555**
Students	5,823	2,052	889	653	514	482	849	181	64	49
Permanently sick	8,757	4	11	10	31	34	182	291	332	392
Retired	34,479	-	1	1	-	1	4	4	3	8
Other inactive	911	3	6	7	11	8	52	63	90	106
Total females	**203,798**	**2,899**	**3,076**	**3,182**	**3,357**	**3,468**	**13,453**	**17,147**	**16,620**	**15,589**
Economically active	**101,013**	**917**	**1,829**	**2,168**	**2,456**	**2,587**	**10,164**	**11,940**	**11,471**	**11,613**
Employees - full time	46,426	238	752	1,293	1,786	1,948	7,491	6,831	4,508	4,390
- part time	38,693	395	469	409	291	285	1,516	3,605	5,316	5,565
Self-employed - with employees	3,834	-	1	1	2	2	65	197	423	473
- without employees	5,269	2	4	6	17	37	200	409	590	674
On a Government scheme	1,454	172	426	193	66	34	91	78	87	90
Unemployed	5,337	110	177	266	294	281	801	820	547	421
Economically active students (included above)	*1,118*	*327*	*319*	*219*	*67*	*53*	*85*	*17*	*13*	*7*
Economically inactive	**102,785**	**1,982**	**1,247**	**1,014**	**901**	**881**	**3,289**	**5,207**	**5,149**	**3,976**
Students	6,206	1,955	1,147	815	602	479	760	131	108	86
Permanently sick	6,211	3	10	19	26	34	158	261	311	360
Retired	43,982	1	1	-	-	2	2	4	7	13
Other inactive	46,386	23	89	180	273	366	2,369	4,811	4,723	3,517

Age 40 - 44	45 - 49	50 - 54	55 - 59	60 - 64	65 - 69	70 - 74	75 and over	Students (economically active or inactive)	Sex, marital status and economic position
l	m	n	o	p	q	r	s	t	a
36,403	**30,395**	**28,091**	**26,652**	**27,484**	**26,205**	**21,746**	**35,841**	**13,783**	**TOTAL PERSONS**
31,797	**25,948**	**22,053**	**17,355**	**9,795**	**2,353**	**1,067**	**728**	**1,754**	**Economically active**
18,585	15,098	12,635	9,342	4,672	327	115	153	189	Employees - full time
6,423	5,031	4,363	3,518	2,054	1,035	470	190	1,511	- part time
2,405	2,158	1,661	1,304	828	332	178	171	5	Self-employed - with employees
2,834	2,440	2,182	1,979	1,420	633	294	200	4	- without employees
173	107	92	68	12	3	1	5		On a Government scheme
1,377	1,114	1,120	1,144	809	23	9	9	45	Unemployed
16	*5*	-	*1*	*1*	-	-	-		*Economically active students (included above)*
4,606	**4,447**	**6,038**	**9,297**	**17,689**	**23,852**	**20,679**	**35,113**	**12,029**	**Economically inactive**
120	45	26	3	5	4	1	9	12,029	Students
1,129	1,362	1,844	2,706	3,173	975	379	931		Permanently sick
52	124	611	2,326	10,666	19,309	17,006	28,315		Retired
3,305	2,916	3,557	4,262	3,845	3,564	3,293	5,858		Other inactive
18,387	**15,371**	**13,951**	**13,256**	**13,184**	**11,991**	**9,349**	**12,321**	**6,459**	**Total males**
17,632	**14,575**	**12,714**	**10,640**	**7,046**	**1,453**	**696**	**472**	**636**	**Economically active**
12,790	10,435	8,973	7,030	4,120	232	72	86	104	Employees - full time
198	169	239	335	420	498	268	115	498	- part time
1,635	1,476	1,170	949	629	248	133	127	4	Self-employed - with employees
2,016	1,712	1,544	1,472	1,094	460	216	138	3	- without employees
75	51	62	42	10	1	-	3		On a Government scheme
918	732	726	812	773	14	7	3	27	Unemployed
9	*2*	-	-	*1*	-	-	-		*Economically active students (included above)*
755	**796**	**1,237**	**2,616**	**6,138**	**10,538**	**8,653**	**11,849**	**5,823**	**Economically inactive**
47	19	12	2	3	2	-	5	5,823	Students
587	650	954	1,608	2,603	693	175	200		Permanently sick
28	54	204	938	3,453	9,799	8,436	11,545		Retired
93	73	67	68	79	44	42	99		Other inactive
18,016	**15,024**	**14,140**	**13,396**	**14,300**	**14,214**	**12,397**	**23,520**	**7,324**	**Total females**
14,165	**11,373**	**9,339**	**6,715**	**2,749**	**900**	**371**	**256**	**1,118**	**Economically active**
5,795	4,663	3,662	2,312	552	95	43	67	85	Employees - full time
6,225	4,862	4,124	3,183	1,634	537	202	75	1,013	- part time
770	682	491	355	199	84	45	44	1	Self-employed - with employees
818	728	638	507	326	173	78	62	1	- without employees
98	56	30	26	2	2	1	2		On a Government scheme
459	382	394	332	36	9	2	6	18	Unemployed
7	*3*	-	*1*	-	-	-	-		*Economically active students (included above)*
3,851	**3,651**	**4,801**	**6,681**	**11,551**	**13,314**	**12,026**	**23,264**	**6,206**	**Economically inactive**
73	26	14	1	2	2	1	4	6,206	Students
542	712	890	1,098	570	282	204	731		Permanently sick
24	70	407	1,388	7,213	9,510	8,570	16,770		Retired
3,212	2,843	3,490	4,194	3,766	3,520	3,251	5,759		Other inactive

Table 8 Economic position - continued

8. Residents aged 16 and over

Sex, marital status and economic position	TOTAL AGED 16 AND OVER	Age								
		16	17	18	19	20	21 - 24	25 - 29	30 - 34	35 - 39
a	b	c	d	e	f	g	h	i	j	k
			CUMBRIA - *continued*							
Married females	**118,774**	**5**	**13**	**41**	**131**	**298**	**4,151**	**10,622**	**12,635**	**12,518**
Economically active	**64,217**	**1**	**3**	**17**	**79**	**175**	**2,851**	**6,858**	**8,516**	**9,238**
Employees - full time	23,350	1	-	6	48	99	1,834	3,160	2,683	2,972
- part time	31,179	-	-	6	18	45	729	2,880	4,663	4,979
Self-employed - with employees	3,231	-	-	-	-	1	24	140	365	405
- without employees	4,112	-	-	-	1	5	70	262	448	588
On a Government scheme	252	-	1	-	-	2	9	23	41	58
Unemployed	2,093	-	2	5	12	23	185	393	316	236
Economically active students (included above)	*26*	-	-	-	-	-	-	*6*	*10*	*3*
Economically inactive	**54,557**	**4**	**10**	**24**	**52**	**123**	**1,300**	**3,764**	**4,119**	**3,280**
Students	289	4	3	-	-	5	19	46	68	60
Permanently sick	3,041	-	1	1	-	4	37	99	137	206
Retired	18,093	-	-	-	-	-	1	1	6	10
Other inactive	33,134	-	6	23	52	114	1,243	3,618	3,908	3,004
Single, widowed or divorced females	**85,024**	**2,894**	**3,063**	**3,141**	**3,226**	**3,170**	**9,302**	**6,525**	**3,985**	**3,071**
Economically active	**36,796**	**916**	**1,826**	**2,151**	**2,377**	**2,412**	**7,313**	**5,082**	**2,955**	**2,375**
Employees - full time	23,076	237	752	1,287	1,738	1,849	5,657	3,671	1,825	1,418
- part time	7,514	395	469	403	273	240	787	725	653	586
Self-employed - with employees	603	-	1	1	2	1	41	57	58	68
- without employees	1,157	2	4	6	16	32	130	147	142	86
On a Government scheme	1,202	172	425	193	66	32	82	55	46	32
Unemployed	3,244	110	175	261	282	258	616	427	231	185
Economically active students (included above)	*1,092*	*327*	*319*	*219*	*67*	*53*	*85*	*11*	*3*	*4*
Economically inactive	**48,228**	**1,978**	**1,237**	**990**	**849**	**758**	**1,989**	**1,443**	**1,030**	**696**
Students	5,917	1,951	1,144	815	602	474	741	85	40	26
Permanently sick	3,170	3	9	18	26	30	121	162	174	154
Retired	25,889	1	1	-	-	2	1	3	1	3
Other inactive	13,252	23	83	157	221	252	1,126	1,193	815	513
			Allerdale							
TOTAL PERSONS	**77,390**	**1,201**	**1,258**	**1,335**	**1,305**	**1,393**	**5,233**	**6,587**	**6,508**	**6,277**
Economically active	**46,245**	**366**	**818**	**954**	**1,011**	**1,094**	**4,380**	**5,340**	**5,286**	**5,257**
Employees - full time	27,396	101	362	577	719	792	3,233	3,651	3,157	3,068
- part time	7,601	93	119	103	66	72	340	638	945	1,061
Self-employed - with employees	2,734	1	-	1	3	5	47	134	269	303
- without employees	3,696	3	1	8	18	23	155	334	438	457
On a Government scheme	919	94	232	127	47	27	62	82	61	51
Unemployed	3,899	74	104	138	158	175	543	501	416	317
Economically active students (included above)	*278*	*76*	*79*	*51*	*21*	*17*	*29*	*3*	*1*	*1*
Economically inactive	**31,145**	**835**	**440**	**381**	**294**	**299**	**853**	**1,247**	**1,222**	**1,020**
Students	2,538	829	422	331	216	218	281	71	46	52
Permanently sick	3,406	-	6	5	17	19	87	139	154	168
Retired	15,310	-	1	-	-	-	-	4	-	2
Other inactive	9,891	6	11	45	61	62	485	1,033	1,022	798

Age 40 - 44	45 - 49	50 - 54	55 - 59	60 - 64	65 - 69	70 - 74	75 and over	Students (economically active or inactive)	Sex, marital status and economic position
l	m	n	o	p	q	r	s	t	a
14,921	**12,460**	**11,634**	**10,394**	**9,863**	**8,292**	**5,650**	**5,146**	**315**	**Married females**
11,673	**9,410**	**7,621**	**5,079**	**1,917**	**531**	**178**	**70**	**26**	**Economically active**
4,337	3,503	2,714	1,574	340	48	18	13	4	Employees - full time
5,627	4,426	3,640	2,609	1,141	304	89	23	17	- part time
688	617	446	299	156	50	24	16	1	Self-employed - with employees
699	612	565	410	259	128	47	18	1	- without employees
60	28	15	14	1	-	-	-		On a Government scheme
262	224	241	173	20	1	-	-	3	Unemployed
4	*2*	-	*1*	-	-	-	-		*Economically active students (included above)*
3,248	**3,050**	**4,013**	**5,315**	**7,946**	**7,761**	**5,472**	**5,076**	**289**	**Economically inactive**
55	20	7	-	2	-	-	-	289	Students
317	388	519	674	339	137	73	109		Permanently sick
12	58	316	1,009	4,581	5,233	3,627	3,239		Retired
2,864	2,584	3,171	3,632	3,024	2,391	1,772	1,728		Other inactive
3,095	**2,564**	**2,506**	**3,002**	**4,437**	**5,922**	**6,747**	**18,374**	**7,009**	**Single, widowed or divorced females**
2,492	**1,963**	**1,718**	**1,636**	**832**	**369**	**193**	**186**	**1,092**	**Economically active**
1,458	1,160	948	738	212	47	25	54	81	Employees - full time
598	436	484	574	493	233	113	52	996	- part time
82	65	45	56	43	34	21	28	-	Self-employed - with employees
119	116	73	97	67	45	31	44	-	- without employees
38	28	15	12	1	2	1	2		On a Government scheme
197	158	153	159	16	8	2	6	15	Unemployed
3	*1*	-	-	-	-	-	-		*Economically active students (included above)*
603	**601**	**788**	**1,366**	**3,605**	**5,553**	**6,554**	**18,188**	**5,917**	**Economically inactive**
18	6	7	1	-	2	1	4	5,917	Students
225	324	371	424	231	145	131	622		Permanently sick
12	12	91	379	2,632	4,277	4,943	13,531		Retired
348	259	319	562	742	1,129	1,479	4,031		Other inactive
7,529	**6,082**	**5,559**	**5,342**	**5,490**	**5,259**	**4,345**	**6,687**	**2,816**	**TOTAL PERSONS**
6,492	**5,112**	**4,248**	**3,343**	**1,836**	**393**	**188**	**127**	**278**	**Economically active**
3,750	2,946	2,433	1,731	770	61	18	27	29	Employees - full time
1,261	933	779	595	353	148	74	21	238	- part time
519	488	345	278	191	72	38	40	1	Self-employed - with employees
545	463	396	387	274	105	56	33	1	- without employees
60	24	25	20	4	1	-	2		On a Government scheme
357	258	270	332	244	6	2	4	9	Unemployed
-	-	-	-	-	-	-	-		*Economically active students (included above)*
1,037	**970**	**1,311**	**1,999**	**3,654**	**4,866**	**4,157**	**6,560**	**2,538**	**Economically inactive**
38	19	10	1	1	1	-	2	2,538	Students
226	298	409	632	744	220	85	197		Permanently sick
10	19	119	466	2,105	3,912	3,413	5,259		Retired
763	634	773	900	804	733	659	1,102		Other inactive

Table 8 Economic position - continued

8. Residents aged 16 and over

Sex, marital status and economic position	TOTAL AGED 16 AND OVER	Age								
		16	17	18	19	20	21 - 24	25 - 29	30 - 34	35 - 39
a	b	c	d	e	f	g	h	i	j	k
				Allerdale - *continued*						
Total males	**37,129**	**607**	**662**	**685**	**649**	**697**	**2,605**	**3,327**	**3,251**	**3,107**
Economically active	**27,010**	**187**	**464**	**526**	**539**	**581**	**2,418**	**3,200**	**3,134**	**2,982**
Employees - full time	18,630	63	243	328	396	422	1,814	2,443	2,275	2,174
- part time	631	23	34	30	15	17	37	29	28	29
Self-employed - with employees	1,938	1	-	1	1	3	35	99	197	221
- without employees	2,643	1	-	8	14	18	117	243	305	331
On a Government scheme	542	52	131	80	25	17	38	60	36	28
Unemployed	2,626	47	56	79	88	104	377	326	293	199
Economically active students (included above)	*101*	*19*	*29*	*21*	*7*	*8*	*15*	*1*	-	*1*
Economically inactive	**10,119**	**420**	**198**	**159**	**110**	**116**	**187**	**127**	**117**	**125**
Students	1,211	419	193	153	99	106	133	37	19	18
Permanently sick	2,024	-	5	3	8	8	45	80	81	89
Retired	6,710	-	-	-	-	-	-	2	-	1
Other inactive	174	1	-	3	3	2	9	8	17	17
Total females	**40,261**	**594**	**596**	**650**	**656**	**696**	**2,628**	**3,260**	**3,257**	**3,170**
Economically active	**19,235**	**179**	**354**	**428**	**472**	**513**	**1,962**	**2,140**	**2,152**	**2,275**
Employees - full time	8,766	38	119	249	323	370	1,419	1,208	882	894
- part time	6,970	70	85	73	51	55	303	609	917	1,032
Self-employed - with employees	796	-	-	-	2	2	12	35	72	82
- without employees	1,053	2	1	-	4	5	38	91	133	126
On a Government scheme	377	42	101	47	22	10	24	22	25	23
Unemployed	1,273	27	48	59	70	71	166	175	123	118
Economically active students (included above)	*177*	*57*	*50*	*30*	*14*	*9*	*14*	*2*	*1*	-
Economically inactive	**21,026**	**415**	**242**	**222**	**184**	**183**	**666**	**1,120**	**1,105**	**895**
Students	1,327	410	229	178	117	112	148	34	27	34
Permanently sick	1,382	-	1	2	9	11	42	59	73	79
Retired	8,600	-	1	-	-	-	-	2	-	1
Other inactive	9,717	5	11	42	58	60	476	1,025	1,005	781
Married females	**23,817**	**1**	**3**	**7**	**35**	**66**	**894**	**2,096**	**2,506**	**2,564**
Economically active	**12,489**	**-**	**2**	**3**	**19**	**39**	**596**	**1,274**	**1,619**	**1,835**
Employees - full time	4,654	-	-	1	11	20	381	584	547	628
- part time	5,690	-	-	1	4	10	147	494	816	928
Self-employed - with employees	678	-	-	-	-	1	7	22	63	73
- without employees	837	-	-	-	-	2	16	69	103	112
On a Government scheme	81	-	1	-	-	1	3	7	14	21
Unemployed	549	-	1	1	4	5	42	98	76	73
Economically active students (included above)	*2*	-	-	-	-	-	-	*1*	*1*	-
Economically inactive	**11,328**	**1**	**1**	**4**	**16**	**27**	**298**	**822**	**887**	**729**
Students	94	1	-	-	-	2	7	13	19	25
Permanently sick	685	-	-	-	-	1	11	23	32	50
Retired	3,536	-	-	-	-	-	-	-	-	1
Other inactive	7,013	-	1	4	16	24	280	786	836	653

Age 40 - 44	45 - 49	50 - 54	55 - 59	60 - 64	65 - 69	70 - 74	75 and over	Students (economically active or inactive)	Sex, marital status and economic position
l	m	n	o	p	q	r	s	t	a
3,785	**3,110**	**2,786**	**2,664**	**2,622**	**2,398**	**1,881**	**2,293**	**1,312**	**Total males**
3,629	**2,926**	**2,507**	**2,101**	**1,360**	**251**	**125**	**80**	**101**	**Economically active**
2,598	2,071	1,750	1,306	679	42	11	15	14	Employees - full time
34	31	48	71	79	70	42	14	79	- part time
343	333	243	201	148	59	28	25	1	Self-employed - with employees
382	315	275	276	215	78	42	23	1	- without employees
25	10	22	13	4	-	-	1		On a Government scheme
247	166	169	234	235	2	2	2	6	Unemployed
-	-	-	-	-	-	-	-		*Economically active students (included above)*
156	**184**	**279**	**563**	**1,262**	**2,147**	**1,756**	**2,213**	**1,211**	**Economically inactive**
13	13	6	1	1	-	-	-	1,211	Students
119	147	219	384	603	151	34	48		Permanently sick
5	8	39	167	640	1,989	1,715	2,144		Retired
19	16	15	11	18	7	7	21		Other inactive
3,744	**2,972**	**2,773**	**2,678**	**2,868**	**2,861**	**2,464**	**4,394**	**1,504**	**Total females**
2,863	**2,186**	**1,741**	**1,242**	**476**	**142**	**63**	**47**	**177**	**Economically active**
1,152	875	683	425	91	19	7	12	15	Employees - full time
1,227	902	731	524	274	78	32	7	159	- part time
176	155	102	77	43	13	10	15	-	Self-employed - with employees
163	148	121	111	59	27	14	10	-	- without employees
35	14	3	7	-	1	-	1		On a Government scheme
110	92	101	98	9	4	-	2	3	Unemployed
-	-	-	-	-	-	-	-		*Economically active students (included above)*
881	**786**	**1,032**	**1,436**	**2,392**	**2,719**	**2,401**	**4,347**	**1,327**	**Economically inactive**
25	6	4	-	-	1	-	2	1,327	Students
107	151	190	248	141	69	51	149		Permanently sick
5	11	80	299	1,465	1,923	1,698	3,115		Retired
744	618	758	889	786	726	652	1,081		Other inactive
3,152	**2,515**	**2,321**	**2,080**	**1,970**	**1,648**	**1,082**	**877**	**96**	**Married females**
2,399	**1,850**	**1,460**	**941**	**328**	**84**	**27**	**13**	**2**	**Economically active**
902	677	527	298	61	9	5	3	-	Employees - full time
1,119	839	660	431	186	42	10	3	1	- part time
158	145	98	64	30	8	5	4	-	Self-employed - with employees
136	124	103	92	46	24	7	3	-	- without employees
20	11	-	3	-	-	-	-		On a Government scheme
64	54	72	53	5	1	-	-	1	Unemployed
-	-	-	-	-	-	-	-		*Economically active students (included above)*
753	**665**	**861**	**1,139**	**1,642**	**1,564**	**1,055**	**864**	**94**	**Economically inactive**
20	5	2	-	-	-	-	-	94	Students
65	85	108	160	82	25	20	23		Permanently sick
3	8	66	215	939	1,058	694	552		Retired
665	567	685	764	621	481	341	289		Other inactive

Table 8 Economic position - continued

8. Residents aged 16 and over

Sex, marital status and economic position	TOTAL AGED 16 AND OVER	Age								
		16	17	18	19	20	21 - 24	25 - 29	30 - 34	35 - 39
a	b	c	d	e	f	g	h	i	j	k
Allerdale - *continued*										
Single, widowed or divorced females	**16,444**	**593**	**593**	**643**	**621**	**630**	**1,734**	**1,164**	**751**	**606**
Economically active	**6,746**	**179**	**352**	**425**	**453**	**474**	**1,366**	**866**	**533**	**440**
Employees - full time	4,112	38	119	248	312	350	1,038	624	335	266
- part time	1,280	70	85	72	47	45	156	115	101	104
Self-employed - with employees	118	-	-	-	2	1	5	13	9	9
- without employees	216	2	1	-	4	3	22	22	30	14
On a Government scheme	296	42	100	47	22	9	21	15	11	2
Unemployed	724	27	47	58	66	66	124	77	47	45
Economically active students (included above)	*175*	*57*	*50*	*30*	*14*	*9*	*14*	*1*	-	-
Economically inactive	**9,698**	**414**	**241**	**218**	**168**	**156**	**368**	**298**	**218**	**166**
Students	1,233	409	229	178	117	110	141	21	8	9
Permanently sick	697	-	1	2	9	10	31	36	41	29
Retired	5,064	-	1	-	-	-	-	2	-	-
Other inactive	2,704	5	10	38	42	36	196	239	169	128
Barrow-in-Furness										
TOTAL PERSONS	**58,465**	**955**	**965**	**1,027**	**1,089**	**1,153**	**4,510**	**5,788**	**5,089**	**4,599**
Economically active	**35,695**	**308**	**696**	**831**	**920**	**944**	**3,723**	**4,698**	**4,118**	**3,887**
Employees - full time	23,020	114	345	514	671	715	2,782	3,241	2,600	2,379
- part time	6,443	73	93	105	73	60	308	676	873	904
Self-employed - with employees	1,029	-	-	-	-	1	20	68	119	145
- without employees	1,586	1	1	2	7	12	96	210	195	182
On a Government scheme	589	75	188	82	25	11	39	48	26	33
Unemployed	3,028	45	69	128	144	145	478	455	305	244
Economically active students (included above)	*226*	*56*	*65*	*51*	*11*	*6*	*21*	*4*	*2*	*6*
Economically inactive	**22,770**	**647**	**269**	**196**	**169**	**209**	**787**	**1,090**	**971**	**712**
Students	1,488	642	232	152	102	97	164	47	24	13
Permanently sick	2,644	2	6	7	13	13	61	109	125	140
Retired	11,128	-	-	-	-	1	-	2	-	4
Other inactive	7,510	3	31	37	54	98	562	932	822	555
Total males	**28,222**	**496**	**486**	**521**	**539**	**580**	**2,231**	**2,920**	**2,601**	**2,307**
Economically active	**21,051**	**175**	**373**	**459**	**483**	**526**	**2,081**	**2,837**	**2,518**	**2,228**
Employees - full time	16,580	78	241	320	377	419	1,640	2,266	2,077	1,810
- part time	398	26	20	30	11	9	27	25	11	17
Self-employed - with employees	662	-	-	-	-	1	14	46	76	83
- without employees	1,149	1	1	2	5	7	67	158	137	140
On a Government scheme	307	38	80	39	13	5	25	40	13	18
Unemployed	1,955	32	31	68	77	85	308	302	204	160
Economically active students (included above)	*72*	*22*	*12*	*17*	*2*	*2*	*10*	*1*	-	*3*
Economically inactive	**7,171**	**321**	**113**	**62**	**56**	**54**	**150**	**83**	**83**	**79**
Students	719	319	108	59	43	46	105	25	6	4
Permanently sick	1,429	2	3	2	10	5	36	44	61	65
Retired	4,881	-	-	-	-	-	-	-	-	-
Other inactive	142	-	2	1	3	3	9	14	16	10

Age 40 - 44	45 - 49	50 - 54	55 - 59	60 - 64	65 - 69	70 - 74	75 and over	Students (economically active or inactive)	Sex, marital status and economic position
l	m	n	o	p	q	r	s	t	a
592	**457**	**452**	**598**	**898**	**1,213**	**1,382**	**3,517**	**1,408**	**Single, widowed or divorced females**
464	**336**	**281**	**301**	**148**	**58**	**36**	**34**	**175**	**Economically active**
250	198	156	127	30	10	2	9	15	Employees - full time
108	63	71	93	88	36	22	4	158	- part time
18	10	4	13	13	5	5	11	-	Self-employed - with employees
27	24	18	19	13	3	7	7	-	- without employees
15	3	3	4	-	1	-	1		On a Government scheme
46	38	29	45	4	3	-	2	2	Unemployed
-	-	-	-	-	-	-	-		*Economically active students (included above)*
128	**121**	**171**	**297**	**750**	**1,155**	**1,346**	**3,483**	**1,233**	**Economically inactive**
5	1	2	-	-	1	-	2	1,233	Students
42	66	82	88	59	44	31	126		Permanently sick
2	3	14	84	526	865	1,004	2,563		Retired
79	51	73	125	165	245	311	792		Other inactive
5,328	**4,634**	**4,238**	**3,715**	**3,717**	**3,598**	**3,366**	**4,694**	**1,714**	**TOTAL PERSONS**
4,572	**3,892**	**3,217**	**2,343**	**1,162**	**201**	**105**	**78**	**226**	**Economically active**
2,864	2,501	2,050	1,490	684	35	18	17	21	Employees - full time
965	799	663	436	211	119	59	26	199	- part time
211	163	112	87	54	16	16	17	-	Self-employed - with employees
270	189	170	135	63	25	11	17	-	- without employees
19	17	13	12	-	1	-	-		On a Government scheme
243	223	209	183	150	5	1	1	6	Unemployed
3	*1*	-	-	-	-	-	-		*Economically active students (included above)*
756	**742**	**1,021**	**1,372**	**2,555**	**3,397**	**3,261**	**4,616**	**1,488**	**Economically inactive**
11	-	3	-	-	-	-	1	1,488	Students
250	281	370	460	505	142	49	111		Permanently sick
3	13	76	296	1,569	2,770	2,683	3,711		Retired
492	448	572	616	481	485	529	793		Other inactive
2,698	**2,372**	**2,127**	**1,886**	**1,786**	**1,640**	**1,388**	**1,644**	**791**	**Total males**
2,569	**2,220**	**1,913**	**1,535**	**899**	**111**	**70**	**54**	**72**	**Economically active**
2,073	1,824	1,563	1,206	634	24	15	13	11	Employees - full time
18	16	17	29	31	54	38	19	56	- part time
127	101	75	62	45	9	10	13	-	Self-employed - with employees
186	136	127	104	43	19	7	9	-	- without employees
11	10	6	8	-	1	-	-		On a Government scheme
154	133	125	126	146	4	-	-	5	Unemployed
2	*1*	-	-	-	-	-	-		*Economically active students (included above)*
129	**152**	**214**	**351**	**887**	**1,529**	**1,318**	**1,590**	**719**	**Economically inactive**
3	-	-	-	-	-	-	1	719	Students
112	132	176	229	403	103	18	28		Permanently sick
2	8	21	112	470	1,419	1,293	1,556		Retired
12	12	17	10	14	7	7	5		Other inactive

Table 8 Economic position – continued

8. Residents aged 16 and over

Sex, marital status and economic position	TOTAL AGED 16 AND OVER	Age 16	17	18	19	20	21 - 24	25 - 29	30 - 34	35 - 39
a	b	c	d	e	f	g	h	i	j	k
				Barrow-in-Furness – *continued*						
Total females	**30,243**	**459**	**479**	**506**	**550**	**573**	**2,279**	**2,868**	**2,488**	**2,292**
Economically active	**14,644**	**133**	**323**	**372**	**437**	**418**	**1,642**	**1,861**	**1,600**	**1,659**
Employees - full time	6,440	36	104	194	294	296	1,142	975	523	569
- part time	6,045	47	73	75	62	51	281	651	862	887
Self-employed - with employees	367	-	-	-	-	-	6	22	43	62
- without employees	437	-	-	-	2	5	29	52	58	42
On a Government scheme	282	37	108	43	12	6	14	8	13	15
Unemployed	1,073	13	38	60	67	60	170	153	101	84
Economically active students (included above)	*154*	*34*	*53*	*34*	*9*	*4*	*11*	*3*	*2*	*3*
Economically inactive	**15,599**	**326**	**156**	**134**	**113**	**155**	**637**	**1,007**	**888**	**633**
Students	769	323	124	93	59	51	59	22	18	9
Permanently sick	1,215	-	3	5	3	8	25	65	64	75
Retired	6,247	-	-	-	-	1	-	2	-	4
Other inactive	7,368	3	29	36	51	95	553	918	806	545
Married females	**17,408**	**2**	**1**	**10**	**12**	**62**	**758**	**1,842**	**1,881**	**1,810**
Economically active	**9,076**	**-**	**-**	**1**	**5**	**26**	**480**	**1,166**	**1,198**	**1,306**
Employees - full time	3,161	-	-	1	3	14	300	509	295	376
- part time	4,818	-	-	-	1	5	129	521	757	778
Self-employed - with employees	298	-	-	-	-	-	5	15	32	53
- without employees	329	-	-	-	-	-	9	35	43	39
On a Government scheme	37	-	-	-	-	-	-	3	9	9
Unemployed	433	-	-	-	1	7	37	83	62	51
Economically active students (included above)	*6*	-	-	-	-	-	-	*2*	*2*	*2*
Economically inactive	**8,332**	**2**	**1**	**9**	**7**	**36**	**278**	**676**	**683**	**504**
Students	40	2	-	-	-	2	1	8	11	6
Permanently sick	626	-	-	1	-	1	5	26	37	43
Retired	2,685	-	-	-	-	-	-	1	-	3
Other inactive	4,981	-	1	8	7	33	272	641	635	452
Single, widowed or divorced females	**12,835**	**457**	**478**	**496**	**538**	**511**	**1,521**	**1,026**	**607**	**482**
Economically active	**5,568**	**133**	**323**	**371**	**432**	**392**	**1,162**	**695**	**402**	**353**
Employees - full time	3,279	36	104	193	291	282	842	466	228	193
- part time	1,227	47	73	75	61	46	152	130	105	109
Self-employed - with employees	69	-	-	-	-	-	1	7	11	9
- without employees	108	-	-	-	2	5	20	17	15	3
On a Government scheme	245	37	108	43	12	6	14	5	4	6
Unemployed	640	13	38	60	66	53	133	70	39	33
Economically active students (included above)	*148*	*34*	*53*	*34*	*9*	*4*	*11*	*1*	-	*1*
Economically inactive	**7,267**	**324**	**155**	**125**	**106**	**119**	**359**	**331**	**205**	**129**
Students	729	321	124	93	59	49	58	14	7	3
Permanently sick	589	-	3	4	3	7	20	39	27	32
Retired	3,562	-	-	-	-	1	-	1	-	1
Other inactive	2,387	3	28	28	44	62	281	277	171	93

Age: 40 - 44	45 - 49	50 - 54	55 - 59	60 - 64	65 - 69	70 - 74	75 and over	Students (economically active or inactive)	Sex, marital status and economic position
l	m	n	o	p	q	r	s	t	a
2,630	**2,262**	**2,111**	**1,829**	**1,931**	**1,958**	**1,978**	**3,050**	**923**	**Total females**
2,003	**1,672**	**1,304**	**808**	**263**	**90**	**35**	**24**	**154**	**Economically active**
791	677	487	284	50	11	3	4	10	Employees - full time
947	783	646	407	180	65	21	7	143	- part time
84	62	37	25	9	7	6	4	-	Self-employed - with employees
84	53	43	31	20	6	4	8	-	- without employees
8	7	7	4	-	-	-	-		On a Government scheme
89	90	84	57	4	1	1	1	1	Unemployed
1	-	-	-	-	-	-	-		*Economically active students (included above)*
627	**590**	**807**	**1,021**	**1,668**	**1,868**	**1,943**	**3,026**	**769**	**Economically inactive**
8	-	3	-	-	-	-	-	769	Students
138	149	194	231	102	39	31	83		Permanently sick
1	5	55	184	1,099	1,351	1,390	2,155		Retired
480	436	555	606	467	478	522	788		Other inactive
2,135	**1,815**	**1,707**	**1,370**	**1,333**	**1,115**	**897**	**658**	**46**	**Married females**
1,633	**1,360**	**1,045**	**601**	**176**	**50**	**21**	**8**	**6**	**Economically active**
581	511	348	181	33	4	2	3	1	Employees - full time
853	701	564	335	121	39	10	4	4	- part time
70	51	34	21	6	5	5	1	-	Self-employed - with employees
71	45	40	27	14	2	4	-	-	- without employees
6	2	6	2	-	-	-	-		On a Government scheme
52	50	53	35	2	-	-	-	1	Unemployed
-	-	-	-	-	-	-	-		*Economically active students (included above)*
502	**455**	**662**	**769**	**1,157**	**1,065**	**876**	**650**	**40**	**Economically inactive**
7	-	3	-	-	-	-	-	40	Students
79	76	110	142	64	17	12	13		Permanently sick
1	4	43	124	725	748	605	431		Retired
415	375	506	503	368	300	259	206		Other inactive
495	**447**	**404**	**459**	**598**	**843**	**1,081**	**2,392**	**877**	**Single, widowed or divorced females**
370	**312**	**259**	**207**	**87**	**40**	**14**	**16**	**148**	**Economically active**
210	166	139	103	17	7	1	1	9	Employees - full time
94	82	82	72	59	26	11	3	139	- part time
14	11	3	4	3	2	1	3	-	Self-employed - with employees
13	8	3	4	6	4	-	8	-	- without employees
2	5	1	2	-	-	-	-		On a Government scheme
37	40	31	22	2	1	1	1	-	Unemployed
1	-	-	-	-	-	-	-		*Economically active students (included above)*
125	**135**	**145**	**252**	**511**	**803**	**1,067**	**2,376**	**729**	**Economically inactive**
1	-	-	-	-	-	-	-	729	Students
59	73	84	89	38	22	19	70		Permanently sick
-	1	12	60	374	603	785	1,724		Retired
65	61	49	103	99	178	263	582		Other inactive

Table 8 Economic position - **continued**

8. Residents aged 16 and over

Sex, marital status and economic position	TOTAL AGED 16 AND OVER	Age 16	17	18	19	20	21 - 24	25 - 29	30 - 34	35 - 39
a	b	c	d	e	f	g	h	i	j	k
				Carlisle						
TOTAL PERSONS	**81,239**	**1,256**	**1,255**	**1,369**	**1,498**	**1,438**	**5,561**	**7,366**	**7,330**	**6,637**
Economically active	**50,668**	**481**	**863**	**1,070**	**1,150**	**1,146**	**4,706**	**6,260**	**6,191**	**5,742**
Employees - full time	30,732	167	414	661	833	866	3,510	4,194	3,717	3,343
- part time	9,897	137	183	151	101	85	391	989	1,362	1,333
Self-employed - with employees	2,250	1	-	1	2	2	34	136	267	317
- without employees	3,534	2	2	7	13	28	189	355	427	422
On a Government scheme	683	81	160	78	29	17	63	57	36	44
Unemployed	3,572	93	104	172	172	148	519	529	382	283
Economically active students (included above)	*396*	*105*	*121*	*85*	*26*	*18*	*22*	*11*	*4*	*2*
Economically inactive	**30,571**	**775**	**392**	**299**	**348**	**292**	**855**	**1,106**	**1,139**	**895**
Students	2,229	768	363	245	261	184	300	61	18	11
Permanently sick	3,320	1	4	12	12	16	63	101	149	179
Retired	16,257	-	-	1	-	1	1	2	2	5
Other inactive	8,765	6	25	41	75	91	491	942	970	700
Total males	**38,662**	**659**	**601**	**691**	**758**	**726**	**2,724**	**3,688**	**3,675**	**3,327**
Economically active	**28,631**	**269**	**452**	**579**	**626**	**628**	**2,530**	**3,582**	**3,563**	**3,203**
Employees - full time	20,378	109	229	362	441	480	1,883	2,713	2,681	2,385
- part time	995	49	59	52	36	23	60	95	74	47
Self-employed - with employees	1,648	1	-	1	2	2	19	104	187	236
- without employees	2,769	2	2	4	11	23	164	294	341	309
On a Government scheme	394	49	101	44	17	10	37	40	20	20
Unemployed	2,447	59	61	116	119	90	367	336	260	206
Economically active students (included above)	*147*	*35*	*41*	*35*	*14*	*7*	*6*	*6*	*1*	*1*
Economically inactive	**10,031**	**390**	**149**	**112**	**132**	**98**	**194**	**106**	**112**	**124**
Students	1,054	390	147	105	123	88	152	32	8	4
Permanently sick	1,894	-	2	4	7	10	32	56	73	90
Retired	6,890	-	-	1	-	-	-	2	1	2
Other inactive	193	-	-	2	2	-	10	16	30	28
Total females	**42,577**	**597**	**654**	**678**	**740**	**712**	**2,837**	**3,678**	**3,655**	**3,310**
Economically active	**22,037**	**212**	**411**	**491**	**524**	**518**	**2,176**	**2,678**	**2,628**	**2,539**
Employees - full time	10,354	58	185	299	392	386	1,627	1,481	1,036	958
- part time	8,902	88	124	99	65	62	331	894	1,288	1,286
Self-employed - with employees	602	-	-	-	-	-	15	32	80	81
- without employees	765	-	-	3	2	5	25	61	86	113
On a Government scheme	289	32	59	34	12	7	26	17	16	24
Unemployed	1,125	34	43	56	53	58	152	193	122	77
Economically active students (included above)	*249*	*70*	*80*	*50*	*12*	*11*	*16*	*5*	*3*	*1*
Economically inactive	**20,540**	**385**	**243**	**187**	**216**	**194**	**661**	**1,000**	**1,027**	**771**
Students	1,175	378	216	140	138	96	148	29	10	7
Permanently sick	1,426	1	2	8	5	6	31	45	76	89
Retired	9,367	-	-	-	-	1	1	-	1	3
Other inactive	8,572	6	25	39	73	91	481	926	940	672

Age								Students (economically active or inactive)	Sex, marital status and economic position
40 - 44	45 - 49	50 - 54	55 - 59	60 - 64	65 - 69	70 - 74	75 and over		
l	m	n	o	p	q	r	s	t	a
7,351	**6,010**	**5,635**	**5,570**	**5,685**	**5,557**	**4,250**	**7,471**	**2,625**	**TOTAL PERSONS**
6,527	**5,179**	**4,557**	**3,811**	**2,150**	**483**	**178**	**174**	**396**	**Economically active**
3,903	3,095	2,614	2,115	1,145	80	23	52	38	Employees - full time
1,379	1,068	1,017	865	488	232	80	36	345	- part time
401	316	292	236	138	43	23	41	1	Self-employed - with employees
501	443	360	348	223	123	50	41	-	- without employees
40	26	32	15	3	1	-	1		On a Government scheme
303	231	242	232	153	4	2	3	12	Unemployed
1	*1*	-	-	-	-	-	-		*Economically active students (included above)*
824	**831**	**1,078**	**1,759**	**3,535**	**5,074**	**4,072**	**7,297**	**2,229**	**Economically inactive**
10	4	-	-	2	-	1	1	2,229	Students
224	293	379	585	663	242	100	297		Permanently sick
11	23	93	405	2,172	4,173	3,434	5,934		Retired
579	511	606	769	698	659	537	1,065		Other inactive
3,718	**2,986**	**2,752**	**2,731**	**2,728**	**2,531**	**1,808**	**2,559**	**1,201**	**Total males**
3,556	**2,830**	**2,520**	**2,216**	**1,541**	**309**	**118**	**109**	**147**	**Economically active**
2,633	2,060	1,790	1,512	1,005	58	12	25	20	Employees - full time
43	37	53	73	98	127	46	23	121	- part time
297	221	211	179	104	33	20	31	1	Self-employed - with employees
378	343	283	273	185	89	38	30	-	- without employees
14	12	20	7	3	-	-	-		On a Government scheme
191	157	163	172	146	2	2	-	5	Unemployed
1	-	-	-	-	-	-	-		*Economically active students (included above)*
162	**156**	**232**	**515**	**1,187**	**2,222**	**1,690**	**2,450**	**1,054**	**Economically inactive**
3	-	-	-	1	-	-	1	1,054	Students
132	135	189	335	552	172	51	54		Permanently sick
7	7	35	169	619	2,037	1,633	2,377		Retired
20	14	8	11	15	13	6	18		Other inactive
3,633	**3,024**	**2,883**	**2,839**	**2,957**	**3,026**	**2,442**	**4,912**	**1,424**	**Total females**
2,971	**2,349**	**2,037**	**1,595**	**609**	**174**	**60**	**65**	**249**	**Economically active**
1,270	1,035	824	603	140	22	11	27	18	Employees - full time
1,336	1,031	964	792	390	105	34	13	224	- part time
104	95	81	57	34	10	3	10	-	Self-employed - with employees
123	100	77	75	38	34	12	11	-	- without employees
26	14	12	8	-	1	-	1		On a Government scheme
112	74	79	60	7	2	-	3	7	Unemployed
-	*1*	-	-	-	-	-	-		*Economically active students (included above)*
662	**675**	**846**	**1,244**	**2,348**	**2,852**	**2,382**	**4,847**	**1,175**	**Economically inactive**
7	4	-	-	1	-	1	-	1,175	Students
92	158	190	250	111	70	49	243		Permanently sick
4	16	58	236	1,553	2,136	1,801	3,557		Retired
559	497	598	758	683	646	531	1,047		Other inactive

Table 8 Economic position - continued

8. Residents aged 16 and over

Sex, marital status and economic position	TOTAL AGED 16 AND OVER	Age								
		16	17	18	19	20	21 - 24	25 - 29	30 - 34	35 - 39
a	b	c	d	e	f	g	h	i	j	k
			Carlisle - *continued*							
Married females	**24,181**	**1**	**4**	**6**	**31**	**67**	**834**	**2,201**	**2,731**	**2,590**
Economically active	**13,827**	**-**	**-**	**4**	**20**	**43**	**604**	**1,533**	**1,930**	**1,969**
Employees - full time	5,052	-	-	2	13	30	391	658	579	613
- part time	7,199	-	-	1	4	8	163	726	1,132	1,142
Self-employed - with employees	505	-	-	-	-	-	3	22	70	71
- without employees	593	-	-	-	-	-	6	41	71	94
On a Government scheme	50	-	-	-	-	-	2	4	6	12
Unemployed	428	-	-	1	3	5	39	82	72	37
Economically active students (included above)	*5*	-	-	-	-	-	-	*1*	*3*	-
Economically inactive	**10,354**	**1**	**4**	**2**	**11**	**24**	**230**	**668**	**801**	**621**
Students	33	1	1	-	-	-	3	7	5	6
Permanently sick	631	-	-	-	-	-	8	16	32	48
Retired	3,709	-	-	-	-	-	-	-	1	3
Other inactive	5,981	-	3	2	11	24	219	645	763	564
Single, widowed or divorced females	**18,396**	**596**	**650**	**672**	**709**	**645**	**2,003**	**1,477**	**924**	**720**
Economically active	**8,210**	**212**	**411**	**487**	**504**	**475**	**1,572**	**1,145**	**698**	**570**
Employees - full time	5,302	58	185	297	379	356	1,236	823	457	345
- part time	1,703	88	124	98	61	54	168	168	156	144
Self-employed - with employees	97	-	-	-	-	-	12	10	10	10
- without employees	172	-	-	3	2	5	19	20	15	19
On a Government scheme	239	32	59	34	12	7	24	13	10	12
Unemployed	697	34	43	55	50	53	113	111	50	40
Economically active students (included above)	*244*	*70*	*80*	*50*	*12*	*11*	*16*	*4*	-	*1*
Economically inactive	**10,186**	**384**	**239**	**185**	**205**	**170**	**431**	**332**	**226**	**150**
Students	1,142	377	215	140	138	96	145	22	5	1
Permanently sick	795	1	2	8	5	6	23	29	44	41
Retired	5,658	-	-	-	-	1	1	-	-	-
Other inactive	2,591	6	22	37	62	67	262	281	177	108
			Copeland							
TOTAL PERSONS	**56,579**	**904**	**979**	**941**	**945**	**1,038**	**4,118**	**5,667**	**5,278**	**4,679**
Economically active	**34,604**	**267**	**661**	**676**	**743**	**815**	**3,391**	**4,636**	**4,320**	**3,883**
Employees - full time	22,280	93	329	413	536	593	2,507	3,226	2,747	2,464
- part time	5,625	60	66	54	46	58	229	588	803	790
Self-employed - with employees	1,294	-	1	-	-	1	21	89	159	146
- without employees	1,746	-	1	5	4	9	79	186	229	211
On a Government scheme	577	72	200	91	21	15	31	48	27	25
Unemployed	3,082	42	64	113	136	139	524	499	355	247
Economically active students (included above)	*192*	*54*	*54*	*35*	*12*	*9*	*16*	*4*	*3*	-
Economically inactive	**21,975**	**637**	**318**	**265**	**202**	**223**	**727**	**1,031**	**958**	**796**
Students	1,831	630	299	231	148	136	232	48	41	22
Permanently sick	2,434	3	3	1	4	11	47	86	100	131
Retired	10,076	-	1	-	-	-	-	-	-	2
Other inactive	7,634	4	15	33	50	76	448	897	817	641

Age								Students (economically active or inactive)	Sex, marital status and economic position
40 - 44	45 - 49	50 - 54	55 - 59	60 - 64	65 - 69	70 - 74	75 and over		
l	m	n	o	p	q	r	s	t	a
2,950	**2,455**	**2,310**	**2,154**	**1,965**	**1,727**	**1,076**	**1,079**	**38**	**Married females**
2,404	**1,899**	**1,645**	**1,201**	**427**	**103**	**31**	**14**	**5**	**Economically active**
903	754	604	398	90	11	4	2	-	Employees - full time
1,212	934	853	664	272	66	19	3	4	- part time
97	82	75	47	28	5	1	4	-	Self-employed - with employees
106	81	69	59	33	21	7	5	-	- without employees
14	4	4	4	-	-	-	-	-	On a Government scheme
72	44	40	29	4	-	-	-	1	Unemployed
-	*1*	-	-	-	-	-	-		*Economically active students (included above)*
546	**556**	**665**	**953**	**1,538**	**1,624**	**1,045**	**1,065**	**33**	**Economically inactive**
7	2	-	-	1	-	-	-	33	Students
52	89	97	146	64	36	12	31		Permanently sick
1	13	36	158	913	1,146	742	696		Retired
486	452	532	649	560	442	291	338		Other inactive
683	**569**	**573**	**685**	**992**	**1,299**	**1,366**	**3,833**	**1,386**	**Single, widowed or divorced females**
567	**450**	**392**	**394**	**182**	**71**	**29**	**51**	**244**	**Economically active**
367	281	220	205	50	11	7	25	18	Employees - full time
124	97	111	128	118	39	15	10	220	- part time
7	13	6	10	6	5	2	6	-	Self-employed - with employees
17	19	8	16	5	13	5	6	-	- without employees
12	10	8	4	-	1	-	1		On a Government scheme
40	30	39	31	3	2	-	3	6	Unemployed
-	-	-	-	-	-	-	-		*Economically active students (included above)*
116	**119**	**181**	**291**	**810**	**1,228**	**1,337**	**3,782**	**1,142**	**Economically inactive**
-	2	-	-	-	-	1	-	1,142	Students
40	69	93	104	47	34	37	212		Permanently sick
3	3	22	78	640	990	1,059	2,861		Retired
73	45	66	109	123	204	240	709		Other inactive
5,275	**4,317**	**4,149**	**3,933**	**3,870**	**3,506**	**2,882**	**4,098**	**2,023**	**TOTAL PERSONS**
4,500	**3,584**	**3,130**	**2,409**	**1,193**	**229**	**93**	**74**	**192**	**Economically active**
2,894	2,316	2,014	1,452	639	29	14	14	23	Employees - full time
875	664	567	450	233	92	32	18	161	- part time
228	197	172	126	75	44	20	15	2	Self-employed - with employees
237	207	188	157	122	61	25	25	-	- without employees
21	12	4	8	1	-	-	1		On a Government scheme
245	188	185	216	123	3	2	1	6	Unemployed
4	-	-	-	*1*	-	-	-		*Economically active students (included above)*
775	**733**	**1,019**	**1,524**	**2,677**	**3,277**	**2,789**	**4,024**	**1,831**	**Economically inactive**
24	10	5	2	-	3	-	-	1,831	Students
200	237	347	467	519	147	51	80		Permanently sick
6	15	82	387	1,570	2,608	2,253	3,152		Retired
545	471	585	668	588	519	485	792		Other inactive

Table 8 Economic position - **continued**

8. Residents aged 16 and over

Sex, marital status and economic position	TOTAL AGED 16 AND OVER	Age								
		16	17	18	19	20	21 - 24	25 - 29	30 - 34	35 - 39
a	b	c	d	e	f	g	h	i	j	k
			Copeland - *continued*							
Total males	**27,595**	**466**	**474**	**477**	**458**	**509**	**2,104**	**2,906**	**2,699**	**2,385**
Economically active	**20,500**	**146**	**353**	**392**	**400**	**431**	**1,945**	**2,819**	**2,621**	**2,273**
Employees - full time	15,530	63	191	254	292	318	1,494	2,190	2,050	1,818
- part time	365	12	16	15	11	9	17	27	24	16
Self-employed - with employees	890	-	1	-	-	1	15	58	117	103
- without employees	1,240	-	-	3	3	5	56	152	172	138
On a Government scheme	351	46	110	52	17	9	21	33	17	16
Unemployed	2,124	25	35	68	77	89	342	359	241	182
Economically active students (included above)	*57*	*14*	*13*	*8*	*7*	*3*	*8*	-	*1*	-
Economically inactive	**7,095**	**320**	**121**	**85**	**58**	**78**	**159**	**87**	**78**	**112**
Students	844	319	118	85	58	69	126	27	14	8
Permanently sick	1,474	1	-	-	-	6	22	48	53	81
Retired	4,616	-	1	-	-	-	-	-	-	1
Other inactive	161	-	2	-	-	3	11	12	11	22
Total females	**28,984**	**438**	**505**	**464**	**487**	**529**	**2,014**	**2,761**	**2,579**	**2,294**
Economically active	**14,104**	**121**	**308**	**284**	**343**	**384**	**1,446**	**1,817**	**1,699**	**1,610**
Employees - full time	6,750	30	138	159	244	275	1,013	1,036	697	646
- part time	5,260	48	50	39	35	49	212	561	779	774
Self-employed - with employees	404	-	-	-	-	-	6	31	42	43
- without employees	506	-	1	2	1	4	23	34	57	73
On a Government scheme	226	26	90	39	4	6	10	15	10	9
Unemployed	958	17	29	45	59	50	182	140	114	65
Economically active students (included above)	*135*	*40*	*41*	*27*	*5*	*6*	*8*	*4*	*2*	-
Economically inactive	**14,880**	**317**	**197**	**180**	**144**	**145**	**568**	**944**	**880**	**684**
Students	987	311	181	146	90	67	106	21	27	14
Permanently sick	960	2	3	1	4	5	25	38	47	50
Retired	5,460	-	-	-	-	-	-	-	-	1
Other inactive	7,473	4	13	33	50	73	437	885	806	619
Married females	**17,136**	**-**	**3**	**8**	**19**	**51**	**674**	**1,805**	**1,976**	**1,856**
Economically active	**9,097**	**-**	**1**	**4**	**13**	**30**	**447**	**1,110**	**1,288**	**1,297**
Employees - full time	3,661	-	-	2	6	15	277	525	454	458
- part time	4,323	-	-	1	3	11	107	458	690	699
Self-employed - with employees	334	-	-	-	-	-	2	26	35	37
- without employees	393	-	-	-	-	-	7	23	43	67
On a Government scheme	25	-	-	-	-	1	3	3	3	5
Unemployed	361	-	1	1	4	3	51	75	63	31
Economically active students (included above)	*3*	-	-	-	-	-	-	*1*	-	-
Economically inactive	**8,039**	**-**	**2**	**4**	**6**	**21**	**227**	**695**	**688**	**559**
Students	59	-	1	-	-	-	2	11	20	10
Permanently sick	522	-	1	-	-	2	7	18	16	29
Retired	2,242	-	-	-	-	-	-	-	-	1
Other inactive	5,216	-	-	4	6	19	218	666	652	519

Age								Students (economically active or inactive)	Sex, marital status and economic position
40 - 44	45 - 49	50 - 54	55 - 59	60 - 64	65 - 69	70 - 74	75 and over		
l	m	n	o	p	q	r	s	t	a
2,736	**2,193**	**2,065**	**1,979**	**1,887**	**1,639**	**1,223**	**1,395**	**901**	**Total males**
2,599	**2,046**	**1,849**	**1,504**	**875**	**142**	**52**	**53**	**57**	**Economically active**
2,057	1,633	1,460	1,113	558	20	7	12	17	Employees - full time
25	16	19	33	53	46	16	10	35	- part time
162	117	120	87	55	29	13	12	1	Self-employed - with employees
167	139	118	118	92	46	14	17	-	- without employees
13	6	3	6	1	-	-	1		On a Government scheme
175	135	129	147	116	1	2	1	4	Unemployed
2	-	-	-	*1*	-	-	-		*Economically active students (included above)*
137	**147**	**216**	**475**	**1,012**	**1,497**	**1,171**	**1,342**	**844**	**Economically inactive**
10	5	2	1	-	2	-	-	844	Students
105	121	179	293	418	109	25	13		Permanently sick
5	5	24	165	589	1,375	1,139	1,312		Retired
17	16	11	16	5	11	7	17		Other inactive
2,539	**2,124**	**2,084**	**1,954**	**1,983**	**1,867**	**1,659**	**2,703**	**1,122**	**Total females**
1,901	**1,538**	**1,281**	**905**	**318**	**87**	**41**	**21**	**135**	**Economically active**
837	683	554	339	81	9	7	2	6	Employees - full time
850	648	548	417	180	46	16	8	126	- part time
66	80	52	39	20	15	7	3	1	Self-employed - with employees
70	68	70	39	30	15	11	8	-	- without employees
8	6	1	2	-	-	-	-		On a Government scheme
70	53	56	69	7	2	-	-	2	Unemployed
2	-	-	-	-	-	-	-		*Economically active students (included above)*
638	**586**	**803**	**1,049**	**1,665**	**1,780**	**1,618**	**2,682**	**987**	**Economically inactive**
14	5	3	1	-	1	-	-	987	Students
95	116	168	174	101	38	26	67		Permanently sick
1	10	58	222	981	1,233	1,114	1,840		Retired
528	455	574	652	583	508	478	775		Other inactive
2,109	**1,797**	**1,714**	**1,521**	**1,349**	**1,061**	**681**	**512**	**62**	**Married females**
1,582	**1,300**	**1,050**	**679**	**211**	**58**	**18**	**9**	**3**	**Economically active**
647	536	434	248	49	6	3	1	-	Employees - full time
778	598	485	330	123	31	6	3	2	- part time
55	75	44	34	15	8	1	2	1	Self-employed - with employees
62	55	60	33	19	13	8	3	-	- without employees
5	3	1	1	-	-	-	-		On a Government scheme
35	33	26	33	5	-	-	-	-	Unemployed
2	-	-	-	-	-	-	-		*Economically active students (included above)*
527	**497**	**664**	**842**	**1,138**	**1,003**	**663**	**503**	**59**	**Economically inactive**
10	4	1	-	-	-	-	-	59	Students
63	70	108	108	60	22	11	7		Permanently sick
1	8	46	176	624	651	427	308		Retired
453	415	509	558	454	330	225	188		Other inactive

Table 8 Economic position - **continued**

8. Residents aged 16 and over

Sex, marital status and economic position	TOTAL AGED 16 AND OVER	Age								
		16	17	18	19	20	21 - 24	25 - 29	30 - 34	35 - 39
a	b	c	d	e	f	g	h	i	j	k
				Copeland - *continued*						
Single, widowed or divorced females	**11,848**	**438**	**502**	**456**	**468**	**478**	**1,340**	**956**	**603**	**438**
Economically active	**5,007**	**121**	**307**	**280**	**330**	**354**	**999**	**707**	**411**	**313**
Employees - full time	3,089	30	138	157	238	260	736	511	243	188
- part time	937	48	50	38	32	38	105	103	89	75
Self-employed - with employees	70	-	-	-	-	-	4	5	7	6
- without employees	113	-	1	2	1	4	16	11	14	6
On a Government scheme	201	26	90	39	4	5	7	12	7	4
Unemployed	597	17	28	44	55	47	131	65	51	34
Economically active students (included above)	*132*	*40*	*41*	*27*	*5*	*6*	*8*	*3*	*2*	-
Economically inactive	**6,841**	**317**	**195**	**176**	**138**	**124**	**341**	**249**	**192**	**125**
Students	928	311	180	146	90	67	104	10	7	4
Permanently sick	438	2	2	1	4	3	18	20	31	21
Retired	3,218	-	-	-	-	-	-	-	-	-
Other inactive	2,257	4	13	29	44	54	219	219	154	100
				Eden						
TOTAL PERSONS	**37,366**	**572**	**558**	**623**	**596**	**627**	**2,480**	**3,045**	**3,114**	**3,064**
Economically active	**23,286**	**201**	**342**	**454**	**467**	**516**	**2,119**	**2,589**	**2,644**	**2,657**
Employees - full time	12,293	76	195	320	360	419	1,607	1,679	1,407	1,306
- part time	4,000	65	56	60	32	24	146	292	515	555
Self-employed - with employees	2,156	-	-	2	1	4	31	121	204	251
- without employees	3,714	3	13	13	20	34	201	366	408	458
On a Government scheme	245	32	65	32	20	5	8	15	19	13
Unemployed	878	25	13	27	34	30	126	116	91	74
Economically active students (included above)	*176*	*53*	*38*	*45*	*13*	*9*	*14*	*1*	*1*	*1*
Economically inactive	**14,080**	**371**	**216**	**169**	**129**	**111**	**361**	**456**	**470**	**407**
Students	1,162	370	214	155	104	94	162	17	15	10
Permanently sick	972	-	1	2	6	2	25	31	34	37
Retired	7,079	-	-	-	-	-	1	-	2	3
Other inactive	4,867	1	1	12	19	15	173	408	419	357
Total males	**18,280**	**311**	**295**	**319**	**297**	**338**	**1,305**	**1,569**	**1,563**	**1,553**
Economically active	**13,618**	**110**	**208**	**245**	**236**	**279**	**1,181**	**1,534**	**1,535**	**1,517**
Employees - full time	8,104	45	118	176	177	220	888	1,049	991	913
- part time	412	22	23	17	9	5	21	16	14	26
Self-employed - with employees	1,572	-	-	2	1	4	22	95	142	182
- without employees	2,807	3	11	13	16	31	165	303	319	341
On a Government scheme	147	21	47	22	13	2	7	8	7	5
Unemployed	576	19	9	15	20	17	78	63	62	50
Economically active students (included above)	*69*	*17*	*20*	*13*	*6*	*5*	*6*	-	*1*	*1*
Economically inactive	**4,662**	**201**	**87**	**74**	**61**	**59**	**124**	**35**	**28**	**36**
Students	609	201	87	74	58	57	102	12	4	3
Permanently sick	608	-	-	-	1	2	16	18	19	19
Retired	3,356	-	-	-	-	-	1	-	-	-
Other inactive	89	-	-	-	2	-	5	5	5	14

40 - 44	45 - 49	50 - 54	55 - 59	60 - 64	65 - 69	70 - 74	75 and over	Students (economically active or inactive)	Sex, marital status and economic position
				Age					
l	m	n	o	p	q	r	s	t	a
430	**327**	**370**	**433**	**634**	**806**	**978**	**2,191**	**1,060**	**Single, widowed or divorced females**
319	**238**	**231**	**226**	**107**	**29**	**23**	**12**	**132**	**Economically active**
190	147	120	91	32	3	4	1	6	Employees - full time
72	50	63	87	57	15	10	5	124	- part time
11	5	8	5	5	7	6	1	-	Self-employed - with employees
8	13	10	6	11	2	3	5	-	- without employees
3	3	-	1	-	-	-	-		On a Government scheme
35	20	30	36	2	2	-	-	2	Unemployed
-	-	-	-	-	-	-	-		*Economically active students (included above)*
111	**89**	**139**	**207**	**527**	**777**	**955**	**2,179**	**928**	**Economically inactive**
4	1	2	1	-	1	-	-	928	Students
32	46	60	66	41	16	15	60		Permanently sick
-	2	12	46	357	582	687	1,532		Retired
75	40	65	94	129	178	253	587		Other inactive
3,545	**2,993**	**2,721**	**2,604**	**2,760**	**2,491**	**2,039**	**3,534**	**1,338**	**TOTAL PERSONS**
3,119	**2,542**	**2,147**	**1,718**	**1,124**	**346**	**187**	**114**	**176**	**Economically active**
1,532	1,190	992	698	454	32	13	13	19	Employees - full time
594	465	407	368	203	122	62	34	155	- part time
404	385	273	212	129	66	40	33	-	Self-employed - with employees
491	430	395	369	284	125	71	33	-	- without employees
15	10	4	4	1	-	1	1		On a Government scheme
83	62	76	67	53	1	-	-	2	Unemployed
1	-	-	-	-	-	-	-		*Economically active students (included above)*
426	**451**	**574**	**886**	**1,636**	**2,145**	**1,852**	**3,420**	**1,162**	**Economically inactive**
13	3	5	-	-	-	-	-	1,162	Students
64	89	107	174	227	67	31	75		Permanently sick
8	15	73	229	937	1,680	1,449	2,682		Retired
341	344	389	483	472	398	372	663		Other inactive
1,807	**1,523**	**1,363**	**1,292**	**1,362**	**1,180**	**930**	**1,273**	**678**	**Total males**
1,760	**1,470**	**1,266**	**1,047**	**798**	**224**	**134**	**74**	**69**	**Economically active**
1,025	839	708	522	396	23	10	4	9	Employees - full time
22	18	32	32	38	60	37	20	59	- part time
283	275	192	163	99	54	32	26	-	Self-employed - with employees
371	300	280	276	214	86	55	23	-	- without employees
4	5	2	2	1	-	-	1		On a Government scheme
55	33	52	52	50	1	-	-	1	Unemployed
-	-	-	-	-	-	-	-		*Economically active students (included above)*
47	**53**	**97**	**245**	**564**	**956**	**796**	**1,199**	**609**	**Economically inactive**
7	1	3	-	-	-	-	-	609	Students
28	42	58	129	195	46	16	19		Permanently sick
4	6	31	107	356	910	775	1,166		Retired
8	4	5	9	13	-	5	14		Other inactive

8. Residents aged 16 and over

Sex, marital status and economic position	TOTAL AGED 16 AND OVER	Age								
		16	17	18	19	20	21 - 24	25 - 29	30 - 34	35 - 39
a	b	c	d	e	f	g	h	i	j	k
			Eden - *continued*							
Total females	**19,086**	**261**	**263**	**304**	**299**	**289**	**1,175**	**1,476**	**1,551**	**1,511**
Economically active	**9,668**	**91**	**134**	**209**	**231**	**237**	**938**	**1,055**	**1,109**	**1,140**
Employees - full time	4,189	31	77	144	183	199	719	630	416	393
- part time	3,588	43	33	43	23	19	125	276	501	529
Self-employed - with employees	584	-	-	-	-	-	9	26	62	69
- without employees	907	-	2	-	4	3	36	63	89	117
On a Government scheme	98	11	18	10	7	3	1	7	12	8
Unemployed	302	6	4	12	14	13	48	53	29	24
Economically active students (included above)	*107*	*36*	*18*	*32*	*7*	*4*	*8*	*1*	-	-
Economically inactive	**9,418**	**170**	**129**	**95**	**68**	**52**	**237**	**421**	**442**	**371**
Students	553	169	127	81	46	37	60	5	11	7
Permanently sick	364	-	1	2	5	-	9	13	15	18
Retired	3,723	-	-	-	-	-	-	-	2	3
Other inactive	4,778	1	1	12	17	15	168	403	414	343
Married females	**11,585**	**1**	**-**	**3**	**15**	**11**	**356**	**932**	**1,193**	**1,272**
Economically active	**6,222**	**1**	**-**	**1**	**10**	**6**	**242**	**577**	**814**	**947**
Employees - full time	2,010	1	-	-	7	3	165	289	241	281
- part time	2,867	-	-	1	2	2	57	209	432	485
Self-employed - with employees	496	-	-	-	-	-	1	16	56	59
- without employees	718	-	-	-	1	-	14	42	65	103
On a Government scheme	25	-	-	-	-	-	-	2	3	5
Unemployed	106	-	-	-	-	1	5	19	17	14
Economically active students (included above)	*2*	-	-	-	-	-	-	*1*	-	-
Economically inactive	**5,363**	**-**	**-**	**2**	**5**	**5**	**114**	**355**	**379**	**325**
Students	18	-	-	-	-	-	-	2	6	5
Permanently sick	166	-	-	-	-	-	2	5	8	12
Retired	1,525	-	-	-	-	-	-	-	2	2
Other inactive	3,654	-	-	2	5	5	112	348	363	306
Single, widowed or divorced females	**7,501**	**260**	**263**	**301**	**284**	**278**	**819**	**544**	**358**	**239**
Economically active	**3,446**	**90**	**134**	**208**	**221**	**231**	**696**	**478**	**295**	**193**
Employees - full time	2,179	30	77	144	176	196	554	341	175	112
- part time	721	43	33	42	21	17	68	67	69	44
Self-employed - with employees	88	-	-	-	-	-	8	10	6	10
- without employees	189	-	2	-	3	3	22	21	24	14
On a Government scheme	73	11	18	10	7	3	1	5	9	3
Unemployed	196	6	4	12	14	12	43	34	12	10
Economically active students (included above)	*105*	*36*	*18*	*32*	*7*	*4*	*8*	-	-	-
Economically inactive	**4,055**	**170**	**129**	**93**	**63**	**47**	**123**	**66**	**63**	**46**
Students	535	169	127	81	46	37	60	3	5	2
Permanently sick	198	-	1	2	5	-	7	8	7	6
Retired	2,198	-	-	-	-	-	-	-	-	1
Other inactive	1,124	1	1	10	12	10	56	55	51	37

Age 40 - 44	45 - 49	50 - 54	55 - 59	60 - 64	65 - 69	70 - 74	75 and over	Students (economically active or inactive)	Sex, marital status and economic position
l	m	n	o	p	q	r	s	t	a
1,738	**1,470**	**1,358**	**1,312**	**1,398**	**1,311**	**1,109**	**2,261**	**660**	**Total females**
1,359	**1,072**	**881**	**671**	**326**	**122**	**53**	**40**	**107**	**Economically active**
507	351	284	176	58	9	3	9	10	Employees - full time
572	447	375	336	165	62	25	14	96	- part time
121	110	81	49	30	12	8	7	-	Self-employed - with employees
120	130	115	93	70	39	16	10	-	- without employees
11	5	2	2	-	-	1	-		On a Government scheme
28	29	24	15	3	-	-	-	1	Unemployed
1	-	-	-	-	-	-	-		*Economically active students (included above)*
379	**398**	**477**	**641**	**1,072**	**1,189**	**1,056**	**2,221**	**553**	**Economically inactive**
6	2	2	-	-	-	-	-	553	Students
36	47	49	45	32	21	15	56		Permanently sick
4	9	42	122	581	770	674	1,516		Retired
333	340	384	474	459	398	367	649		Other inactive
1,472	**1,255**	**1,151**	**1,058**	**1,017**	**804**	**517**	**528**	**20**	**Married females**
1,132	**897**	**733**	**524**	**229**	**73**	**23**	**13**	**2**	**Economically active**
390	256	217	125	30	4	-	1	-	Employees - full time
511	409	324	273	116	32	9	5	2	- part time
111	100	70	42	23	8	6	4	-	Self-employed - with employees
98	115	104	78	58	29	8	3	-	- without employees
9	4	1	1	-	-	-	-		On a Government scheme
13	13	17	5	2	-	-	-	-	Unemployed
1	-	-	-	-	-	-	-		*Economically active students (included above)*
340	**358**	**418**	**534**	**788**	**731**	**494**	**515**	**18**	**Economically inactive**
4	-	1	-	-	-	-	-	18	Students
17	23	28	24	21	15	5	6		Permanently sick
2	9	37	88	388	437	264	296		Retired
317	326	352	422	379	279	225	213		Other inactive
266	**215**	**207**	**254**	**381**	**507**	**592**	**1,733**	**640**	**Single, widowed or divorced females**
227	**175**	**148**	**147**	**97**	**49**	**30**	**27**	**105**	**Economically active**
117	95	67	51	28	5	3	8	10	Employees - full time
61	38	51	63	49	30	16	9	94	- part time
10	10	11	7	7	4	2	3	-	Self-employed - with employees
22	15	11	15	12	10	8	7	-	- without employees
2	1	1	1	-	-	1	-		On a Government scheme
15	16	7	10	1	-	-	-	1	Unemployed
-	-	-	-	-	-	-	-		*Economically active students (included above)*
39	**40**	**59**	**107**	**284**	**458**	**562**	**1,706**	**535**	**Economically inactive**
2	2	1	-	-	-	-	-	535	Students
19	24	21	21	11	6	10	50		Permanently sick
2	-	5	34	193	333	410	1,220		Retired
16	14	32	52	80	119	142	436		Other inactive

Table 8 Economic position - continued

8. Residents aged 16 and over

Sex, marital status and economic position	TOTAL AGED 16 AND OVER	Age								
		16	17	18	19	20	21 - 24	25 - 29	30 - 34	35 - 39
a	b	c	d	e	f	g	h	i	j	k
				South Lakeland						
TOTAL PERSONS	**80,670**	**1,162**	**1,211**	**1,182**	**1,316**	**1,331**	**5,021**	**6,287**	**6,123**	**6,049**
Economically active	**48,456**	**386**	**692**	**807**	**1,001**	**1,059**	**4,228**	**5,471**	**5,245**	**5,348**
Employees - full time	28,041	125	365	543	793	859	3,322	3,788	3,040	2,997
- part time	8,963	159	157	121	90	65	316	660	1,012	1,092
Self-employed - with employees	3,542	-	1	3	-	-	57	177	381	442
- without employees	5,721	3	3	10	24	48	270	555	628	646
On a Government scheme	436	60	130	65	14	7	26	25	25	22
Unemployed	1,753	39	36	65	80	80	237	266	159	149
Economically active students (included above)	*486*	*138*	*121*	*76*	*36*	*30*	*57*	*6*	*6*	*5*
Economically inactive	**32,214**	**776**	**519**	**375**	**315**	**272**	**793**	**816**	**878**	**701**
Students	2,781	768	506	354	285	232	470	68	28	27
Permanently sick	2,192	1	1	2	5	7	57	86	81	97
Retired	18,611	1	-	-	-	1	4	-	6	5
Other inactive	8,630	6	12	19	25	32	262	662	763	572
Total males	**38,023**	**612**	**632**	**602**	**691**	**662**	**2,501**	**3,183**	**3,033**	**3,037**
Economically active	**27,131**	**205**	**393**	**423**	**552**	**542**	**2,228**	**3,082**	**2,962**	**2,958**
Employees - full time	18,114	80	236	295	443	437	1,751	2,287	2,086	2,067
- part time	1,035	60	53	41	35	16	52	46	43	35
Self-employed - with employees	2,461	-	-	2	-	-	40	126	257	306
- without employees	4,120	3	3	9	20	33	221	447	461	443
On a Government scheme	254	36	80	45	5	5	10	16	14	11
Unemployed	1,147	26	21	31	49	51	154	160	101	96
Economically active students (included above)	*190*	*48*	*44*	*30*	*16*	*11*	*29*	*4*	*1*	*2*
Economically inactive	**10,892**	**407**	**239**	**179**	**139**	**120**	**273**	**101**	**71**	**79**
Students	1,386	404	236	177	133	116	231	48	13	12
Permanently sick	1,328	1	1	1	5	3	31	45	45	48
Retired	8,026	-	-	-	-	1	3	-	2	4
Other inactive	152	2	2	1	1	-	8	8	11	15
Total females	**42,647**	**550**	**579**	**580**	**625**	**669**	**2,520**	**3,104**	**3,090**	**3,012**
Economically active	**21,325**	**181**	**299**	**384**	**449**	**517**	**2,000**	**2,389**	**2,283**	**2,390**
Employees - full time	9,927	45	129	248	350	422	1,571	1,501	954	930
- part time	7,928	99	104	80	55	49	264	614	969	1,057
Self-employed - with employees	1,081	-	1	1	-	-	17	51	124	136
- without employees	1,601	-	-	1	4	15	49	108	167	203
On a Government scheme	182	24	50	20	9	2	16	9	11	11
Unemployed	606	13	15	34	31	29	83	106	58	53
Economically active students (included above)	*296*	*90*	*77*	*46*	*20*	*19*	*28*	*2*	*5*	*3*
Economically inactive	**21,322**	**369**	**280**	**196**	**176**	**152**	**520**	**715**	**807**	**622**
Students	1,395	364	270	177	152	116	239	20	15	15
Permanently sick	864	-	-	1	-	4	26	41	36	49
Retired	10,585	1	-	-	-	-	1	-	4	1
Other inactive	8,478	4	10	18	24	32	254	654	752	557

Age								Students (economically active or inactive)	Sex, marital status and economic position
40 - 44	45 - 49	50 - 54	55 - 59	60 - 64	65 - 69	70 - 74	75 and over		
l	m	n	o	p	q	r	s	t	a
7,375	**6,359**	**5,789**	**5,488**	**5,962**	**5,794**	**4,864**	**9,357**	**3,267**	**TOTAL PERSONS**
6,587	**5,639**	**4,754**	**3,731**	**2,330**	**701**	**316**	**161**	**486**	**Economically active**
3,642	3,050	2,532	1,856	980	90	29	30	59	Employees - full time
1,349	1,102	930	804	566	322	163	55	413	- part time
642	609	467	365	241	91	41	25	1	Self-employed - with employees
790	708	673	583	454	194	81	51	3	- without employees
18	18	14	9	3	-	-	-		On a Government scheme
146	152	138	114	86	4	2	-	10	Unemployed
7	*3*	-	*1*	-	-	-	-		*Economically active students (included above)*
788	**720**	**1,035**	**1,757**	**3,632**	**5,093**	**4,548**	**9,196**	**2,781**	**Economically inactive**
24	9	3	-	2	-	-	5	2,781	Students
165	164	232	388	515	157	63	171		Permanently sick
14	39	168	543	2,313	4,166	3,774	7,577		Retired
585	508	632	826	802	770	711	1,443		Other inactive
3,643	**3,187**	**2,858**	**2,704**	**2,799**	**2,603**	**2,119**	**3,157**	**1,576**	**Total males**
3,519	**3,083**	**2,659**	**2,237**	**1,573**	**416**	**197**	**102**	**190**	**Economically active**
2,404	2,008	1,702	1,371	848	65	17	17	33	Employees - full time
56	51	70	97	121	141	89	29	148	- part time
423	429	329	257	178	64	30	20	1	Self-employed - with employees
532	479	461	425	345	142	60	36	2	- without employees
8	8	9	6	1	-	-	-		On a Government scheme
96	108	88	81	80	4	1	-	6	Unemployed
4	*1*	-	-	-	-	-	-		*Economically active students (included above)*
124	**104**	**199**	**467**	**1,226**	**2,187**	**1,922**	**3,055**	**1,386**	**Economically inactive**
11	-	1	-	1	-	-	3	1,386	Students
91	73	133	238	432	112	31	38		Permanently sick
5	20	54	218	779	2,069	1,881	2,990		Retired
17	11	11	11	14	6	10	24		Other inactive
3,732	**3,172**	**2,931**	**2,784**	**3,163**	**3,191**	**2,745**	**6,200**	**1,691**	**Total females**
3,068	**2,556**	**2,095**	**1,494**	**757**	**285**	**119**	**59**	**296**	**Economically active**
1,238	1,042	830	485	132	25	12	13	26	Employees - full time
1,293	1,051	860	707	445	181	74	26	265	- part time
219	180	138	108	63	27	11	5	-	Self-employed - with employees
258	229	212	158	109	52	21	15	1	- without employees
10	10	5	3	2	-	-	-		On a Government scheme
50	44	50	33	6	-	1	-	4	Unemployed
3	*2*	-	*1*	-	-	-	-		*Economically active students (included above)*
664	**616**	**836**	**1,290**	**2,406**	**2,906**	**2,626**	**6,141**	**1,395**	**Economically inactive**
13	9	2	-	1	-	-	2	1,395	Students
74	91	99	150	83	45	32	133		Permanently sick
9	19	114	325	1,534	2,097	1,893	4,587		Retired
568	497	621	815	788	764	701	1,419		Other inactive

Table 8 Economic position - continued

8. Residents aged 16 and over

Sex, marital status and economic position	TOTAL AGED 16 AND OVER	Age								
		16	17	18	19	20	21 - 24	25 - 29	30 - 34	35 - 39
a	b	c	d	e	f	g	h	i	j	k
					South Lakeland - *continued*					
Married females	**24,647**	**-**	**2**	**7**	**19**	**41**	**635**	**1,746**	**2,348**	**2,426**
Economically active	**13,506**	**-**	**-**	**4**	**12**	**31**	**482**	**1,198**	**1,667**	**1,884**
Employees - full time	4,812	-	-	-	8	17	320	595	567	616
- part time	6,282	-	-	2	4	9	126	472	836	947
Self-employed - with employees	920	-	-	-	-	-	6	39	109	112
- without employees	1,242	-	-	-	-	3	18	52	123	173
On a Government scheme	34	-	-	-	-	-	1	4	6	6
Unemployed	216	-	-	2	-	2	11	36	26	30
Economically active students (included above)	*8*	-	-	-	-	-	-	-	*4*	*1*
Economically inactive	**11,141**	**-**	**2**	**3**	**7**	**10**	**153**	**548**	**681**	**542**
Students	45	-	1	-	-	1	6	5	7	8
Permanently sick	411	-	-	-	-	-	4	11	12	24
Retired	4,396	-	-	-	-	-	1	-	3	-
Other inactive	6,289	-	1	3	7	9	142	532	659	510
Single, widowed or divorced females	**18,000**	**550**	**577**	**573**	**606**	**628**	**1,885**	**1,358**	**742**	**586**
Economically active	**7,819**	**181**	**299**	**380**	**437**	**486**	**1,518**	**1,191**	**616**	**506**
Employees - full time	5,115	45	129	248	342	405	1,251	906	387	314
- part time	1,646	99	104	78	51	40	138	142	133	110
Self-employed - with employees	161	-	1	1	-	-	11	12	15	24
- without employees	359	-	-	1	4	12	31	56	44	30
On a Government scheme	148	24	50	20	9	2	15	5	5	5
Unemployed	390	13	15	32	31	27	72	70	32	23
Economically active students (included above)	*288*	*90*	*77*	*46*	*20*	*19*	*28*	*2*	*1*	*2*
Economically inactive	**10,181**	**369**	**278**	**193**	**169**	**142**	**367**	**167**	**126**	**80**
Students	1,350	364	269	177	152	115	233	15	8	7
Permanently sick	453	-	-	1	-	4	22	30	24	25
Retired	6,189	1	-	-	-	-	-	-	1	1
Other inactive	2,189	4	9	15	17	23	112	122	93	47

Age 40 - 44	45 - 49	50 - 54	55 - 59	60 - 64	65 - 69	70 - 74	75 and over	Students (economically active or inactive)	Sex, marital status and economic position
l	m	n	o	p	q	r	s	t	a
3,103	**2,623**	**2,431**	**2,211**	**2,229**	**1,937**	**1,397**	**1,492**	**53**	**Married females**
2,523	**2,104**	**1,688**	**1,133**	**546**	**163**	**58**	**13**	**8**	**Economically active**
914	769	584	324	77	14	4	3	3	Employees - full time
1,154	945	754	576	323	94	35	5	4	- part time
197	164	125	91	54	16	6	1	-	Self-employed - with employees
226	192	189	121	89	39	13	4	1	- without employees
6	4	3	3	1	-	-	-		On a Government scheme
26	30	33	18	2	-	-	-	-	Unemployed
1	*1*	-	*1*	-	-	-	-		*Economically active students (included above)*
580	**519**	**743**	**1,078**	**1,683**	**1,774**	**1,339**	**1,479**	**45**	**Economically inactive**
7	9	-	-	1	-	-	-	45	Students
41	45	68	94	48	22	13	29		Permanently sick
4	16	88	248	992	1,193	895	956		Retired
528	449	587	736	642	559	431	494		Other inactive
629	**549**	**500**	**573**	**934**	**1,254**	**1,348**	**4,708**	**1,638**	**Single, widowed or divorced females**
545	**452**	**407**	**361**	**211**	**122**	**61**	**46**	**288**	**Economically active**
324	273	246	161	55	11	8	10	23	Employees - full time
139	106	106	131	122	87	39	21	261	- part time
22	16	13	17	9	11	5	4	-	Self-employed - with employees
32	37	23	37	20	13	8	11	-	- without employees
4	6	2	-	1	-	-	-		On a Government scheme
24	14	17	15	4	-	1	-	4	Unemployed
2	*1*	-	-	-	-	-	-		*Economically active students (included above)*
84	**97**	**93**	**212**	**723**	**1,132**	**1,287**	**4,662**	**1,350**	**Economically inactive**
6	-	2	-	-	-	-	2	1,350	Students
33	46	31	56	35	23	19	104		Permanently sick
5	3	26	77	542	904	998	3,631		Retired
40	48	34	79	146	205	270	925		Other inactive

Table 9 Economic position and ethnic group

9. Residents aged 16 and over

Economic position	TOTAL PERSONS	Ethnic group										Persons born in Ireland
		White	Black Caribbean	Black African	Black other	Indian	Pakistani	Bangladeshi	Chinese	Other groups		
										Asian	Other	
a	b	c	d	e	f	g	h	i	j	k	l	m
CUMBRIA												
TOTAL PERSONS	**391,709**	**390,216**	**88**	**55**	**172**	**215**	**71**	**88**	**326**	**148**	**330**	**3,585**
Males 16 and over	**187,911**	**187,144**	**48**	**31**	**99**	**102**	**43**	**69**	**158**	**49**	**168**	**1,747**
Economically active	**137,941**	**137,280**	**38**	**29**	**87**	**88**	**35**	**62**	**131**	**44**	**147**	**1,150**
of which, aged under 25	*24,165*	*24,022*	*9*	*5*	*27*	*9*	*3*	*37*	*28*	*6*	*19*	*108*
Employees - full time	97,336	96,916	29	19	51	60	20	47	60	33	101	816
- part time	3,836	3,815	1	2	1	1	-	-	9	-	7	33
Self-employed - with employees	9,171	9,074	1	3	6	15	8	7	44	2	11	73
- without employees	14,728	14,677	2	-	9	4	2	4	9	4	17	114
On a Government scheme	1,995	1,977	-	1	5	5	2	-	2	2	1	10
Unemployed	10,875	10,821	5	4	15	3	3	4	7	3	10	104
of which, aged under 25	*3,290*	*3,273*	*1*	-	*7*	*2*	-	*2*	*1*	*1*	*3*	*16*
Economically active students (included above)	*636*	*634*	-	-	-	-	-	-	*2*	-	-	*3*
Economically inactive	**49,970**	**49,864**	**10**	**2**	**12**	**14**	**8**	**7**	**27**	**5**	**21**	**597**
Students	5,823	5,781	1	1	3	2	3	1	15	4	12	24
Permanently sick	8,757	8,741	4	-	2	2	-	1	3	-	4	109
Retired	34,479	34,435	5	1	7	9	3	5	9	1	4	446
Other inactive	911	907	-	-	-	1	2	-	-	-	1	18
Females 16 and over	**203,798**	**203,072**	**40**	**24**	**73**	**113**	**28**	**19**	**168**	**99**	**162**	**1,838**
Economically active	**101,013**	**100,615**	**19**	**16**	**48**	**60**	**12**	**5**	**105**	**46**	**87**	**849**
of which, aged under 25	*20,121*	*20,033*	*5*	*3*	*11*	*13*	*4*	*2*	*21*	*7*	*22*	*109*
Employees - full time	46,426	46,247	9	3	22	30	7	-	34	27	47	406
- part time	38,693	38,584	5	9	12	20	1	2	32	10	18	336
Self-employed - with employees	3,834	3,800	1	1	4	4	2	-	20	1	1	33
- without employees	5,269	5,241	1	-	3	-	1	-	12	3	8	25
On a Government scheme	1,454	1,445	1	1	2	2	-	-	-	1	2	7
Unemployed	5,337	5,298	2	2	5	4	1	3	7	4	11	42
of which, aged under 25	*1,929*	*1,916*	*1*	-	*3*	*1*	-	*2*	*3*	*1*	*2*	*9*
Economically active students (included above)	*1,118*	*1,109*	-	*1*	*1*	*2*	-	*1*	-	-	*4*	*5*
Economically inactive	**102,785**	**102,457**	**21**	**8**	**25**	**53**	**16**	**14**	**63**	**53**	**75**	**989**
Students	6,206	6,155	2	2	1	9	2	-	14	8	13	19
Permanently sick	6,211	6,193	-	-	4	1	2	-	2	2	7	79
Retired	43,982	43,939	8	1	3	10	1	-	9	-	11	481
Other inactive	46,386	46,170	11	5	17	33	11	14	38	43	44	410

9. Residents aged 16 and over

Economic position	TOTAL PERSONS	Ethnic group										Persons born in Ireland
		White	Black Caribbean	Black African	Black other	Indian	Pakistani	Bangladeshi	Chinese	Other groups		
										Asian	Other	
a	b	c	d	e	f	g	h	i	j	k	l	m
Allerdale												
TOTAL PERSONS	**77,390**	**77,168**	**11**	**5**	**27**	**26**	**11**	**11**	**59**	**17**	**55**	**449**
Males 16 and over	**37,129**	**37,017**	**6**	**2**	**15**	**13**	**8**	**10**	**27**	**4**	**27**	**217**
Economically active	**27,010**	**26,911**	**5**	**2**	**15**	**11**	**8**	**10**	**21**	**4**	**23**	**155**
of which, aged under 25	*4,715*	*4,697*	*1*	-	*4*	-	*1*	*6*	*4*	-	*2*	*16*
Employees - full time	18,630	18,573	4	1	9	5	4	10	4	3	17	114
- part time	631	629	-	-	-	1	-	-	-	-	1	3
Self-employed - with employees	1,938	1,916	-	1	2	4	3	-	12	-	-	8
- without employees	2,643	2,632	1	-	2	1	1	-	2	1	3	14
On a Government scheme	542	541	-	-	1	-	-	-	-	-	-	3
Unemployed	2,626	2,620	-	-	1	-	-	-	3	-	2	13
of which, aged under 25	*751*	*749*	-	-	*1*	-	-	-	*1*	-	-	*2*
Economically active students (included above)	*101*	*101*	-	-	-	-	-	-	-	-	-	-
Economically inactive	**10,119**	**10,106**	**1**	-	-	**2**	-	-	**6**	-	**4**	**62**
Students	1,211	1,204	-	-	-	-	-	-	4	-	3	2
Permanently sick	2,024	2,023	1	-	-	-	-	-	-	-	-	11
Retired	6,710	6,705	-	-	-	2	-	-	2	-	1	47
Other inactive	174	174	-	-	-	-	-	-	-	-	-	2
Females 16 and over	**40,261**	**40,151**	**5**	**3**	**12**	**13**	**3**	**1**	**32**	**13**	**28**	**232**
Economically active	**19,235**	**19,168**	**2**	**3**	**9**	**7**	-	-	**21**	**6**	**19**	**103**
of which, aged under 25	*3,908*	*3,893*	-	-	*2*	*1*	-	-	*4*	*1*	*7*	*17*
Employees - full time	8,766	8,733	-	1	5	4	-	-	6	4	13	55
- part time	6,970	6,953	1	2	-	3	-	-	9	1	1	32
Self-employed - with employees	796	794	1	-	-	-	-	-	1	-	-	5
- without employees	1,053	1,048	-	-	1	-	-	-	2	1	1	5
On a Government scheme	377	375	-	-	1	-	-	-	-	-	1	1
Unemployed	1,273	1,265	-	-	2	-	-	-	3	-	3	5
of which, aged under 25	*441*	*439*	-	-	*1*	-	-	-	-	-	*1*	*4*
Economically active students (included above)	*177*	*177*	-	-	-	-	-	-	-	-	-	*1*
Economically inactive	**21,026**	**20,983**	**3**	-	**3**	**6**	**3**	**1**	**11**	**7**	**9**	**129**
Students	1,327	1,320	1	-	-	1	-	-	4	1	-	2
Permanently sick	1,382	1,381	-	-	-	-	-	-	-	-	1	9
Retired	8,600	8,597	-	-	-	2	-	-	1	-	-	66
Other inactive	9,717	9,685	2	-	3	3	3	1	6	6	8	52

Table 9 Economic position and ethnic group – **continued**

9. Residents aged 16 and over

Economic position	TOTAL PERSONS	Ethnic group: White	Black Caribbean	Black African	Black other	Indian	Pakistani	Bangladeshi	Chinese	Other groups: Asian	Other groups: Other	Persons born in Ireland
a	b	c	d	e	f	g	h	i	j	k	l	m
Barrow-in-Furness												
TOTAL PERSONS	**58,465**	**58,183**	**9**	**9**	**28**	**35**	**15**	**8**	**80**	**32**	**66**	**864**
Males 16 and over	**28,222**	**28,079**	**5**	**6**	**18**	**19**	**10**	**5**	**37**	**10**	**33**	**439**
Economically active	**21,051**	**20,929**	**3**	**5**	**17**	**15**	**7**	**4**	**31**	**9**	**31**	**260**
of which, aged under 25	*4,097*	*4,076*	*1*	-	*4*	-	*1*	-	*9*	*2*	*4*	*10*
Employees - full time	16,580	16,507	2	4	13	8	3	1	13	7	22	200
- part time	398	392	-	-	-	-	-	-	6	-	-	8
Self-employed - with employees	662	644	-	-	-	5	2	-	9	-	2	9
- without employees	1,149	1,136	-	-	1	2	1	2	2	1	4	9
On a Government scheme	307	306	-	-	-	-	-	-	-	-	1	1
Unemployed	1,955	1,944	1	1	3	-	1	1	1	1	2	33
of which, aged under 25	*601*	*599*	-	-	-	-	-	-	-	-	*2*	*2*
Economically active students (included above)	*72*	*71*	-	-	-	-	-	-	*1*	-	-	-
Economically inactive	**7,171**	**7,150**	**2**	**1**	**1**	**4**	**3**	**1**	**6**	**1**	**2**	**179**
Students	719	710	-	1	-	1	2	1	2	1	1	2
Permanently sick	1,429	1,427	-	-	-	1	-	-	1	-	-	34
Retired	4,881	4,871	2	-	1	2	1	-	3	-	1	142
Other inactive	142	142	-	-	-	-	-	-	-	-	-	1
Females 16 and over	**30,243**	**30,104**	**4**	**3**	**10**	**16**	**5**	**3**	**43**	**22**	**33**	**425**
Economically active	**14,644**	**14,577**	**1**	**1**	**4**	**9**	**3**	**-**	**22**	**11**	**16**	**165**
of which, aged under 25	*3,325*	*3,307*	*1*	-	*2*	*2*	-	-	*8*	*2*	*3*	*14*
Employees - full time	6,440	6,414	1	-	2	4	2	-	6	6	5	62
- part time	6,045	6,016	-	1	2	5	-	-	9	4	8	78
Self-employed - with employees	367	362	-	-	-	-	1	-	3	1	-	7
- without employees	437	434	-	-	-	-	-	-	2	-	1	2
On a Government scheme	282	281	-	-	-	-	-	-	-	-	1	-
Unemployed	1,073	1,070	-	-	-	-	-	-	2	-	1	16
of which, aged under 25	*408*	*406*	-	-	-	-	-	-	*2*	-	-	*2*
Economically active students (included above)	*154*	*151*	-	-	-	*1*	-	-	-	-	*2*	-
Economically inactive	**15,599**	**15,527**	**3**	**2**	**6**	**7**	**2**	**3**	**21**	**11**	**17**	**260**
Students	769	761	-	-	-	-	-	-	2	3	3	2
Permanently sick	1,215	1,209	-	-	1	-	-	-	1	1	3	30
Retired	6,247	6,237	-	1	1	1	-	-	4	-	3	133
Other inactive	7,368	7,320	3	1	4	6	2	3	14	7	8	95

Table 9 Economic position and ethnic group – **continued**

9. Residents aged 16 and over

Economic position	TOTAL PERSONS	Ethnic group										Persons born in Ireland
		White	Black Caribbean	Black African	Black other	Indian	Pakistani	Bangladeshi	Chinese	Other groups		
										Asian	Other	
a	b	c	d	e	f	g	h	i	j	k	l	m
Carlisle												
TOTAL PERSONS	**81,239**	**80,808**	**20**	**15**	**45**	**80**	**16**	**54**	**89**	**33**	**79**	**900**
Males 16 and over	**38,662**	**38,417**	**17**	**7**	**25**	**35**	**11**	**43**	**46**	**17**	**44**	**422**
Economically active	**28,631**	**28,419**	**14**	**7**	**20**	**33**	**9**	**38**	**38**	**15**	**38**	**283**
of which, aged under 25	*5,084*	*5,030*	*1*	*2*	*7*	*3*	-	*28*	*4*	*1*	*8*	*27*
Employees - full time	20,378	20,236	8	3	10	24	6	30	22	12	27	197
- part time	995	988	1	1	1	-	-	-	-	-	4	10
Self-employed - with employees	1,648	1,622	1	2	1	3	1	3	12	1	2	10
- without employees	2,769	2,761	-	-	1	1	-	2	2	-	2	34
On a Government scheme	394	386	-	-	3	3	1	-	1	-	-	2
Unemployed	2,447	2,426	4	1	4	2	1	3	1	2	3	30
of which, aged under 25	*812*	*803*	*1*	-	*2*	*2*	-	*2*	-	*1*	*1*	*6*
Economically active students (included above)	*147*	*147*	-	-	-	-	-	-	-	-	-	-
Economically inactive	**10,031**	**9,998**	**3**	**-**	**5**	**2**	**2**	**5**	**8**	**2**	**6**	**139**
Students	1,054	1,043	1	-	1	-	-	-	4	2	3	7
Permanently sick	1,894	1,889	1	-	1	-	-	-	1	-	2	25
Retired	6,890	6,874	1	-	3	2	1	5	3	-	1	100
Other inactive	193	192	-	-	-	-	1	-	-	-	-	7
Females 16 and over	**42,577**	**42,391**	**3**	**8**	**20**	**45**	**5**	**11**	**43**	**16**	**35**	**478**
Economically active	**22,037**	**21,946**	**1**	**5**	**9**	**21**	**2**	**4**	**25**	**6**	**18**	**249**
of which, aged under 25	*4,332*	*4,316*	-	*2*	*3*	*4*	*1*	*2*	*1*	*1*	*2*	*26*
Employees - full time	10,354	10,315	-	1	1	11	-	-	12	2	12	120
- part time	8,902	8,876	1	3	5	5	-	2	6	2	2	107
Self-employed - with employees	602	593	-	1	-	1	1	-	6	-	-	4
- without employees	765	760	-	-	-	-	1	-	1	1	2	4
On a Government scheme	289	286	-	-	1	2	-	-	-	-	-	3
Unemployed	1,125	1,116	-	-	2	2	-	2	-	1	2	11
of which, aged under 25	*396*	*391*	-	-	*1*	-	-	*2*	-	*1*	*1*	-
Economically active students (included above)	*249*	*247*	-	-	-	*1*	-	*1*	-	-	-	*2*
Economically inactive	**20,540**	**20,445**	**2**	**3**	**11**	**24**	**3**	**7**	**18**	**10**	**17**	**229**
Students	1,175	1,151	1	2	1	7	-	-	7	2	4	8
Permanently sick	1,426	1,420	-	-	2	-	1	-	1	1	1	18
Retired	9,367	9,357	-	-	2	4	-	-	2	-	2	106
Other inactive	8,572	8,517	1	1	6	13	2	7	8	7	10	97

Table 9 Economic position and ethnic group – **continued**

9. Residents aged 16 and over

Economic position	TOTAL PERSONS	Ethnic group										Persons born in Ireland
		White	Black Caribbean	Black African	Black other	Indian	Pakistani	Bangladeshi	Chinese	Other groups		
										Asian	Other	
a	b	c	d	e	f	g	h	i	j	k	l	m
Copeland												
TOTAL PERSONS	**56,579**	**56,386**	**15**	**7**	**30**	**27**	**15**	**4**	**30**	**32**	**33**	**452**
Males 16 and over	**27,595**	**27,486**	**9**	**4**	**19**	**14**	**8**	**3**	**15**	**13**	**24**	**248**
Economically active	**20,500**	**20,409**	**7**	**4**	**15**	**14**	**7**	**2**	**12**	**12**	**18**	**165**
of which, aged under 25	*3,667*	*3,648*	*2*	-	*6*	*4*	*1*	-	*2*	*3*	*1*	*26*
Employees - full time	15,530	15,471	7	3	9	11	4	1	5	8	11	119
- part time	365	361	-	-	-	-	-	-	2	-	2	5
Self-employed - with employees	890	879	-	-	-	2	2	1	1	1	4	12
- without employees	1,240	1,237	-	-	-	-	-	-	2	1	-	12
On a Government scheme	351	347	-	-	1	-	1	-	-	2	-	2
Unemployed	2,124	2,114	-	1	5	1	-	-	2	-	1	15
of which, aged under 25	*636*	*633*	-	-	*3*	-	-	-	-	-	-	*5*
Economically active students (included above)	*57*	*57*	-	-	-	-	-	-	-	-	-	*1*
Economically inactive	**7,095**	**7,077**	**2**	**-**	**4**	**-**	**1**	**1**	**3**	**1**	**6**	**83**
Students	844	837	-	-	2	-	-	-	2	-	3	2
Permanently sick	1,474	1,468	2	-	-	-	-	1	1	-	2	23
Retired	4,616	4,612	-	-	2	-	-	-	-	1	1	57
Other inactive	161	160	-	-	-	-	1	-	-	-	-	1
Females 16 and over	**28,984**	**28,900**	**6**	**3**	**11**	**13**	**7**	**1**	**15**	**19**	**9**	**204**
Economically active	**14,104**	**14,055**	**3**	**2**	**8**	**7**	**2**	**-**	**13**	**10**	**4**	**91**
of which, aged under 25	*2,886*	*2,874*	*3*	-	*1*	*2*	*1*	-	*2*	*2*	*1*	*16*
Employees - full time	6,750	6,727	2	-	5	3	1	-	4	7	1	48
- part time	5,260	5,254	-	-	1	-	-	-	1	1	3	36
Self-employed - with employees	404	398	-	-	-	3	-	-	3	-	-	1
- without employees	506	500	-	-	1	-	-	-	5	-	-	1
On a Government scheme	226	225	-	-	-	-	-	-	-	1	-	2
Unemployed	958	951	1	2	1	1	1	-	-	1	-	3
of which, aged under 25	*382*	*379*	*1*	-	*1*	*1*	-	-	-	-	-	*1*
Economically active students (included above)	*135*	*134*	-	-	-	-	-	-	-	-	*1*	*1*
Economically inactive	**14,880**	**14,845**	**3**	**1**	**3**	**6**	**5**	**1**	**2**	**9**	**5**	**113**
Students	987	985	-	-	-	-	-	-	-	-	2	5
Permanently sick	960	960	-	-	-	-	-	-	-	-	-	9
Retired	5,460	5,457	1	-	-	1	1	-	-	-	-	47
Other inactive	7,473	7,443	2	1	3	5	4	1	2	9	3	52

9. Residents aged 16 and over

Economic position	TOTAL PERSONS	Ethnic group: White	Black Caribbean	Black African	Black other	Indian	Pakistani	Bangladeshi	Chinese	Other groups: Asian	Other groups: Other	Persons born in Ireland
a	b	c	d	e	f	g	h	i	j	k	l	m
Eden												
TOTAL PERSONS	**37,366**	**37,287**	**5**	**3**	**7**	**3**	**-**	**6**	**19**	**7**	**29**	**241**
Males 16 and over	**18,280**	**18,244**	**2**	**2**	**4**	**2**	**-**	**4**	**9**	**1**	**12**	**130**
Economically active	**13,618**	**13,587**	**2**	**2**	**4**	**-**	**-**	**4**	**6**	**1**	**12**	**89**
of which, aged under 25	*2,259*	*2,253*	*1*	*1*	*1*	-	-	*1*	*1*	-	*1*	*10*
Employees - full time	8,104	8,086	2	1	1	-	-	2	3	1	8	52
- part time	412	410	-	1	-	-	-	-	1	-	-	3
Self-employed - with employees	1,572	1,567	-	-	2	-	-	2	1	-	-	11
- without employees	2,807	2,804	-	-	-	-	-	-	1	-	2	17
On a Government scheme	147	147	-	-	-	-	-	-	-	-	-	1
Unemployed	576	573	-	-	1	-	-	-	-	-	2	5
of which, aged under 25	*158*	*158*	-	-	-	-	-	-	-	-	-	*1*
Economically active students (included above)	*69*	*68*	-	-	-	-	-	-	*1*	-	-	-
Economically inactive	**4,662**	**4,657**	**-**	**-**	**-**	**2**	**-**	**-**	**3**	**-**	**-**	**41**
Students	609	607	-	-	-	-	-	-	2	-	-	5
Permanently sick	608	608	-	-	-	-	-	-	-	-	-	2
Retired	3,356	3,354	-	-	-	1	-	-	1	-	-	30
Other inactive	89	88	-	-	-	1	-	-	-	-	-	4
Females 16 and over	**19,086**	**19,043**	**3**	**1**	**3**	**1**	**-**	**2**	**10**	**6**	**17**	**111**
Economically active	**9,668**	**9,646**	**1**	**1**	**3**	**1**	**-**	**1**	**7**	**2**	**6**	**52**
of which, aged under 25	*1,840*	*1,838*	-	-	-	-	-	-	*2*	-	-	*8*
Employees - full time	4,189	4,184	-	-	1	-	-	-	1	1	2	22
- part time	3,588	3,581	1	-	-	1	-	-	4	-	1	20
Self-employed - with employees	584	581	-	-	2	-	-	-	1	-	-	6
- without employees	907	906	-	-	-	-	-	-	1	-	-	3
On a Government scheme	98	97	-	1	-	-	-	-	-	-	-	-
Unemployed	302	297	-	-	-	-	-	1	-	1	3	1
of which, aged under 25	*97*	*97*	-	-	-	-	-	-	-	-	-	*1*
Economically active students (included above)	*107*	*107*	-	-	-	-	-	-	-	-	-	-
Economically inactive	**9,418**	**9,397**	**2**	**-**	**-**	**-**	**-**	**1**	**3**	**4**	**11**	**59**
Students	553	551	-	-	-	-	-	-	1	-	1	1
Permanently sick	364	364	-	-	-	-	-	-	-	-	-	4
Retired	3,723	3,718	1	-	-	-	-	-	1	-	3	18
Other inactive	4,778	4,764	1	-	-	-	-	1	1	4	7	36

Table 9 Economic position and ethnic group – **continued**

9. Residents aged 16 and over

Economic position	TOTAL PERSONS	Ethnic group										Persons born in Ireland
		White	Black Caribbean	Black African	Black other	Indian	Pakistani	Bangladeshi	Chinese	Other groups		
										Asian	Other	
a	b	c	d	e	f	g	h	i	j	k	l	m
South Lakeland												
TOTAL PERSONS	**80,670**	**80,384**	**28**	**16**	**35**	**44**	**14**	**5**	**49**	**27**	**68**	**679**
Males 16 and over	**38,023**	**37,901**	**9**	**10**	**18**	**19**	**6**	**4**	**24**	**4**	**28**	**291**
Economically active	**27,131**	**27,025**	**7**	**9**	**16**	**15**	**4**	**4**	**23**	**3**	**25**	**198**
of which, aged under 25	*4,343*	*4,318*	*3*	*2*	*5*	*2*	-	*2*	*8*	-	*3*	*19*
Employees - full time	18,114	18,043	6	7	9	12	3	3	13	2	16	134
- part time	1,035	1,035	-	-	-	-	-	-	-	-	-	4
Self-employed - with employees	2,461	2,446	-	-	1	1	-	1	9	-	3	23
- without employees	4,120	4,107	1	-	5	-	-	-	-	1	6	28
On a Government scheme	254	250	-	1	-	2	-	-	1	-	-	1
Unemployed	1,147	1,144	-	1	1	-	1	-	-	-	-	8
of which, aged under 25	*332*	*331*	-	-	*1*	-	-	-	-	-	-	-
Economically active students (included above)	*190*	*190*	-	-	-	-	-	-	-	-	-	*2*
Economically inactive	**10,892**	**10,876**	**2**	**1**	**2**	**4**	**2**	**-**	**1**	**1**	**3**	**93**
Students	1,386	1,380	-	-	-	1	1	-	1	1	2	6
Permanently sick	1,328	1,326	-	-	1	1	-	-	-	-	-	14
Retired	8,026	8,019	2	1	1	2	1	-	-	-	-	70
Other inactive	152	151	-	-	-	-	-	-	-	-	1	3
Females 16 and over	**42,647**	**42,483**	**19**	**6**	**17**	**25**	**8**	**1**	**25**	**23**	**40**	**388**
Economically active	**21,325**	**21,223**	**11**	**4**	**15**	**15**	**5**	**-**	**17**	**11**	**24**	**189**
of which, aged under 25	*3,830*	*3,805*	*1*	*1*	*3*	*4*	*2*	-	*4*	*1*	*9*	*28*
Employees - full time	9,927	9,874	6	1	8	8	4	-	5	7	14	99
- part time	7,928	7,904	2	3	4	6	1	-	3	2	3	63
Self-employed - with employees	1,081	1,072	-	-	2	-	-	-	6	-	1	10
- without employees	1,601	1,593	1	-	1	-	-	-	1	1	4	10
On a Government scheme	182	181	1	-	-	-	-	-	-	-	-	1
Unemployed	606	599	1	-	-	1	-	-	2	1	2	6
of which, aged under 25	*205*	*204*	-	-	-	-	-	-	*1*	-	-	*1*
Economically active students (included above)	*296*	*293*	-	*1*	*1*	-	-	-	-	-	*1*	*1*
Economically inactive	**21,322**	**21,260**	**8**	**2**	**2**	**10**	**3**	**1**	**8**	**12**	**16**	**199**
Students	1,395	1,387	-	-	-	1	2	-	-	2	3	1
Permanently sick	864	859	-	-	1	1	1	-	-	-	2	9
Retired	10,585	10,573	6	-	-	2	-	-	1	-	3	111
Other inactive	8,478	8,441	2	2	1	6	-	1	7	10	8	78

10. Students (16 and over) present plus absent resident students (16 and over)

	TOTAL STUDENTS	Age											Born outside UK
		16	17	18	19	20	21	22	23	24	25 - 34	35 and over	
a	b	c	d	e	f	g	h	i	j	k	l	m	n
CUMBRIA													
TOTAL STUDENTS	**16,334**	**4,898**	**2,946**	**2,164**	**1,552**	**1,360**	**1,040**	**698**	**362**	**200**	**668**	**446**	**688**
Students in households	**14,730**	**4,516**	**2,538**	**1,902**	**1,379**	**1,247**	**979**	**641**	**323**	**182**	**614**	**409**	**414**
Present residents	10,249	4,301	2,335	1,468	504	360	244	151	103	57	388	338	228
Term-time address - this address	9,533	4,279	2,307	1,401	360	195	125	90	78	45	349	304	205
- elsewhere	716	22	28	67	144	165	119	61	25	12	39	34	23
Absent residents	3,425	165	158	323	725	683	586	353	160	93	137	42	110
Term-time address - this address	492	83	50	58	78	75	50	36	13	13	27	9	28
- elsewhere	2,933	82	108	265	647	608	536	317	147	80	110	33	82
Non-residents	1,056	50	45	111	150	204	149	137	60	32	89	29	76
Term-time address - this address	598	19	24	67	102	99	88	91	30	17	52	9	36
- elsewhere	458	31	21	44	48	105	61	46	30	15	37	20	40
Students not in households	**1,604**	**382**	**408**	**262**	**173**	**113**	**61**	**57**	**39**	**18**	**54**	**37**	**274**
Present residents	109	23	21	20	6	7	8	8	3	2	5	6	6
Term-time address - this address	82	22	18	16	3	3	5	4	-	2	5	4	3
- elsewhere	27	1	3	4	3	4	3	4	3	-	-	2	3
Non-residents	1,495	359	387	242	167	106	53	49	36	16	49	31	268
Term-time address - this address	1,021	297	266	192	97	61	26	27	21	8	17	9	156
- elsewhere	474	62	121	50	70	45	27	22	15	8	32	22	112
Allerdale													
TOTAL STUDENTS	**3,116**	**950**	**558**	**411**	**288**	**271**	**176**	**83**	**57**	**40**	**150**	**132**	**107**
Students in households	**2,904**	**911**	**502**	**386**	**249**	**260**	**168**	**79**	**52**	**36**	**136**	**125**	**59**
Present residents	2,153	876	470	327	86	79	47	29	17	12	93	117	34
Term-time address - this address	2,010	869	465	318	62	43	22	13	13	11	83	111	32
- elsewhere	143	7	5	9	24	36	25	16	4	1	10	6	2
Absent residents	641	25	26	50	150	154	107	43	30	22	27	7	14
Term-time address - this address	98	13	9	5	23	21	13	4	3	4	2	1	2
- elsewhere	543	12	17	45	127	133	94	39	27	18	25	6	12
Non-residents	110	10	6	9	13	27	14	7	5	2	16	1	11
Term-time address - this address	45	4	4	5	4	11	4	-	1	1	10	1	4
- elsewhere	65	6	2	4	9	16	10	7	4	1	6	-	7
Students not in households	**212**	**39**	**56**	**25**	**39**	**11**	**8**	**4**	**5**	**4**	**14**	**7**	**48**
Present residents	22	4	5	5	1	2	2	-	1	-	1	1	2
Term-time address - this address	15	4	4	3	-	1	1	-	-	-	1	1	1
- elsewhere	7	-	1	2	1	1	1	-	1	-	-	-	1
Non-residents	190	35	51	20	38	9	6	4	4	4	13	6	46
Term-time address - this address	51	16	14	5	4	-	1	-	3	2	4	2	11
- elsewhere	139	19	37	15	34	9	5	4	1	2	9	4	35

Table 10 Term-time address – **continued**

10. Students (16 and over) present plus absent resident students (16 and over)

	TOTAL STUDENTS	Age											Born outside UK
		16	17	18	19	20	21	22	23	24	25 - 34	35 and over	
a	b	c	d	e	f	g	h	i	j	k	l	m	n
Barrow-in-Furness													
TOTAL STUDENTS	**1,782**	**706**	**300**	**208**	**118**	**114**	**84**	**57**	**38**	**30**	**85**	**42**	**59**
Students in households	**1,759**	**701**	**297**	**207**	**116**	**113**	**82**	**55**	**38**	**28**	**82**	**40**	**56**
Present residents	1,384	679	282	170	53	41	28	16	14	10	57	34	37
Term-time address - this address	1,296	678	280	163	36	21	15	9	9	7	50	28	35
- elsewhere	88	1	2	7	17	20	13	7	5	3	7	6	2
Absent residents	323	17	13	33	59	62	49	33	17	16	20	4	15
Term-time address - this address	44	13	3	6	5	5	2	3	-	2	5	-	6
- elsewhere	279	4	10	27	54	57	47	30	17	14	15	4	9
Non-residents	52	5	2	4	4	10	5	6	7	2	5	2	4
Term-time address - this address	10	2	-	1	2	-	-	3	2	-	-	-	2
- elsewhere	42	3	2	3	2	10	5	3	5	2	5	2	2
Students not in households	**23**	**5**	**3**	**1**	**2**	**1**	**2**	**2**	**-**	**2**	**3**	**2**	**3**
Present residents	7	2	2	-	1	-	1	-	-	1	-	-	1
Term-time address - this address	7	2	2	-	1	-	1	-	-	1	-	-	1
- elsewhere	-	-	-	-	-	-	-	-	-	-	-	-	-
Non-residents	16	3	1	1	1	1	1	2	-	1	3	2	2
Term-time address - this address	6	1	-	1	-	1	-	2	-	-	1	-	-
- elsewhere	10	2	1	-	1	-	1	-	-	1	2	2	2
Carlisle													
TOTAL STUDENTS	**3,062**	**928**	**517**	**405**	**396**	**267**	**192**	**116**	**57**	**34**	**110**	**40**	**145**
Students in households	**2,932**	**879**	**494**	**384**	**382**	**264**	**188**	**109**	**54**	**33**	**106**	**39**	**99**
Present residents	1,968	844	457	264	136	81	44	28	18	9	60	27	59
Term-time address - this address	1,864	839	454	258	109	53	29	21	14	7	55	25	54
- elsewhere	104	5	3	6	27	28	15	7	4	2	5	2	5
Absent residents	651	29	26	64	151	121	116	66	22	17	33	6	25
Term-time address - this address	97	16	9	12	20	14	7	5	2	4	7	1	5
- elsewhere	554	13	17	52	131	107	109	61	20	13	26	5	20
Non-residents	313	6	11	56	95	62	28	15	14	7	13	6	15
Term-time address - this address	234	3	8	43	83	54	20	9	9	1	4	-	9
- elsewhere	79	3	3	13	12	8	8	6	5	6	9	6	6
Students not in households	**130**	**49**	**23**	**21**	**14**	**3**	**4**	**7**	**3**	**1**	**4**	**1**	**46**
Present residents	6	-	1	2	-	-	-	1	-	1	1	-	-
Term-time address - this address	4	-	1	1	-	-	-	-	-	1	1	-	-
- elsewhere	2	-	-	1	-	-	-	1	-	-	-	-	-
Non-residents	124	49	22	19	14	3	4	6	3	-	3	1	46
Term-time address - this address	102	48	21	18	6	2	3	2	1	-	1	-	39
- elsewhere	22	1	1	1	8	1	1	4	2	-	2	1	7

10. Students (16 and over) present plus absent resident students (16 and over)

	TOTAL STUDENTS	Age											Born outside UK
		16	17	18	19	20	21	22	23	24	25 - 34	35 and over	
a	b	c	d	e	f	g	h	i	j	k	l	m	n
Copeland													
TOTAL STUDENTS	**2,235**	**723**	**399**	**292**	**175**	**165**	**138**	**89**	**48**	**21**	**106**	**79**	**73**
Students in households	**2,087**	**688**	**356**	**268**	**170**	**156**	**130**	**83**	**42**	**19**	**104**	**71**	**41**
Present residents	1,531	663	337	227	57	47	36	17	11	3	74	59	21
Term-time address - this address	1,427	662	331	218	39	21	15	8	8	2	69	54	20
- elsewhere	104	1	6	9	18	26	21	9	3	1	5	5	1
Absent residents	483	19	15	38	103	98	78	60	25	15	22	10	15
Term-time address - this address	62	7	5	8	10	12	5	6	1	-	5	3	2
- elsewhere	421	12	10	30	93	86	73	54	24	15	17	7	13
Non-residents	73	6	4	3	10	11	16	6	6	1	8	2	5
Term-time address - this address	24	2	2	1	6	1	6	1	2	1	2	-	1
- elsewhere	49	4	2	2	4	10	10	5	4	-	6	2	4
Students not in households	**148**	**35**	**43**	**24**	**5**	**9**	**8**	**6**	**6**	**2**	**2**	**8**	**32**
Present residents	9	2	1	1	-	-	1	2	-	-	-	2	-
Term-time address - this address	6	2	1	1	-	-	-	-	-	-	-	2	-
- elsewhere	3	-	-	-	-	-	1	2	-	-	-	-	-
Non-residents	139	33	42	23	5	9	7	4	6	2	2	6	32
Term-time address - this address	94	27	33	22	3	-	2	1	3	1	-	2	26
- elsewhere	45	6	9	1	2	9	5	3	3	1	2	4	6
Eden													
TOTAL STUDENTS	**1,491**	**439**	**260**	**226**	**139**	**127**	**95**	**71**	**27**	**17**	**51**	**39**	**44**
Students in households	**1,404**	**430**	**252**	**208**	**126**	**114**	**92**	**64**	**26**	**15**	**40**	**37**	**39**
Present residents	971	401	225	161	44	32	21	15	8	6	30	28	21
Term-time address - this address	893	399	222	149	30	16	8	7	5	5	27	25	16
- elsewhere	78	2	3	12	14	16	13	8	3	1	3	3	5
Absent residents	351	21	22	37	72	70	66	37	14	5	2	5	11
Term-time address - this address	53	11	5	9	8	5	7	2	2	1	1	2	4
- elsewhere	298	10	17	28	64	65	59	35	12	4	1	3	7
Non-residents	82	8	5	10	10	12	5	12	4	4	8	4	7
Term-time address - this address	38	6	5	6	3	4	-	6	-	3	5	-	2
- elsewhere	44	2	-	4	7	8	5	6	4	1	3	4	5
Students not in households	**87**	**9**	**8**	**18**	**13**	**13**	**3**	**7**	**1**	**2**	**11**	**2**	**5**
Present residents	16	1	5	2	1	1	2	2	-	-	2	-	-
Term-time address - this address	13	1	4	2	-	-	2	2	-	-	2	-	-
- elsewhere	3	-	1	-	1	1	-	-	-	-	-	-	-
Non-residents	71	8	3	16	12	12	1	5	1	2	9	2	5
Term-time address - this address	34	7	3	4	3	10	1	2	-	2	2	-	2
- elsewhere	37	1	-	12	9	2	-	3	1	-	7	2	3

Table 10 Term-time address - **continued**

10. Students (16 and over) present plus absent resident students (16 and over)

	TOTAL STUDENTS	Age											Born outside UK
		16	17	18	19	20	21	22	23	24	25 - 34	35 and over	
a	b	c	d	e	f	g	h	i	j	k	l	m	n
South Lakeland													
TOTAL STUDENTS	**4,648**	**1,152**	**912**	**622**	**436**	**416**	**355**	**282**	**135**	**58**	**166**	**114**	**260**
Students in households	**3,644**	**907**	**637**	**449**	**336**	**340**	**319**	**251**	**111**	**51**	**146**	**97**	**120**
Present residents	2,242	838	564	319	128	80	68	46	35	17	74	73	56
Term-time address - this address	2,043	832	555	295	84	41	36	32	29	13	65	61	48
- elsewhere	199	6	9	24	44	39	32	14	6	4	9	12	8
Absent residents	976	54	56	101	190	178	170	114	52	18	33	10	30
Term-time address - this address	138	23	19	18	12	18	16	16	5	2	7	2	9
- elsewhere	838	31	37	83	178	160	154	98	47	16	26	8	21
Non-residents	426	15	17	29	18	82	81	91	24	16	39	14	34
Term-time address - this address	247	2	5	11	4	29	58	72	16	11	31	8	18
- elsewhere	179	13	12	18	14	53	23	19	8	5	8	6	16
Students not in households	**1,004**	**245**	**275**	**173**	**100**	**76**	**36**	**31**	**24**	**7**	**20**	**17**	**140**
Present residents	49	14	7	10	3	4	2	3	2	-	1	3	3
Term-time address - this address	37	13	6	9	2	2	1	2	-	-	1	1	1
- elsewhere	12	1	1	1	1	2	1	1	2	-	-	2	2
Non-residents	955	231	268	163	97	72	34	28	22	7	19	14	137
Term-time address - this address	734	198	195	142	81	48	19	20	14	3	9	5	78
- elsewhere	221	33	73	21	16	24	15	8	8	4	10	9	59

11. Persons present

Age	TOTAL PERSONS	In households			Not in households						
					Persons present			Residents			
								Staff		Other	
		Total	Males	Females	Total	Males	Females	Males	Females	Males	Females
a	b	c	d	e	f	g	h	i	j	k	l
CUMBRIA											
ALL AGES	**489,354**	**469,831**	**228,807**	**241,024**	**19,523**	**9,194**	**10,329**	**1,505**	**1,406**	**1,745**	**3,720**
0 - 4	29,221	28,931	14,725	14,206	290	152	138	31	37	23	18
5 - 9	28,992	28,751	14,855	13,896	241	137	104	41	44	17	7
10 - 14	28,866	27,482	14,120	13,362	1,384	783	601	42	42	29	32
15	5,898	5,452	2,749	2,703	446	285	161	15	6	16	15
16 - 17	12,857	11,907	6,143	5,764	950	514	436	45	48	13	11
18 - 19	13,039	12,192	6,181	6,011	847	446	401	105	116	26	25
20 - 24	33,610	31,736	15,807	15,929	1,874	977	897	320	367	144	102
25 - 29	35,531	34,216	17,206	17,010	1,315	800	515	209	159	109	32
30 - 34	33,863	32,961	16,500	16,461	902	559	343	139	82	67	34
35 - 39	31,583	30,866	15,378	15,488	717	462	255	105	77	64	33
40 - 44	36,582	35,788	17,981	17,807	794	474	320	110	109	59	35
45 - 49	30,673	29,846	15,045	14,801	827	467	360	100	100	76	41
50 - 54	28,383	27,581	13,658	13,923	802	417	385	94	85	46	37
55 - 59	27,048	26,284	13,066	13,218	764	394	370	96	72	33	37
60 - 64	28,038	27,158	13,020	14,138	880	424	456	36	27	73	76
65 - 69	26,578	25,637	11,787	13,850	941	431	510	6	12	102	139
70 - 74	22,089	21,164	9,118	12,046	925	401	524	8	5	152	220
75 - 79	17,275	16,149	6,406	9,743	1,126	393	733	2	10	212	465
80 - 84	11,403	10,059	3,475	6,584	1,344	346	998	1	3	221	762
85 - 89	5,742	4,390	1,303	3,087	1,352	245	1,107	-	1	189	957
90 and over	2,083	1,281	284	997	802	87	715	-	4	74	642
Allerdale											
ALL AGES	**96,715**	**93,323**	**45,629**	**47,694**	**3,392**	**1,514**	**1,878**	**330**	**340**	**338**	**759**
0 - 4	5,585	5,529	2,784	2,745	56	24	32	7	11	9	6
5 - 9	5,799	5,752	3,015	2,737	47	27	20	16	11	4	1
10 - 14	5,895	5,742	3,031	2,711	153	76	77	12	16	4	4
15	1,163	1,128	567	561	35	20	15	1	1	2	2
16 - 17	2,524	2,411	1,247	1,164	113	52	61	6	12	-	1
18 - 19	2,553	2,413	1,226	1,187	140	71	69	18	32	2	1
20 - 24	6,485	6,180	3,068	3,112	305	148	157	67	77	13	9
25 - 29	6,751	6,480	3,257	3,223	271	151	120	49	46	23	10
30 - 34	6,615	6,433	3,209	3,224	182	103	79	23	18	16	18
35 - 39	6,369	6,212	3,070	3,142	157	101	56	29	17	13	10
40 - 44	7,578	7,416	3,714	3,702	162	93	69	30	27	11	6
45 - 49	6,182	6,002	3,047	2,955	180	96	84	17	23	21	10
50 - 54	5,652	5,491	2,765	2,726	161	73	88	22	18	6	13
55 - 59	5,438	5,270	2,626	2,644	168	77	91	18	14	8	12
60 - 64	5,609	5,445	2,600	2,845	164	85	79	8	5	17	22
65 - 69	5,402	5,253	2,416	2,837	149	75	74	3	4	16	25
70 - 74	4,383	4,241	1,848	2,393	142	62	80	2	1	33	52
75 - 79	3,184	2,998	1,225	1,773	186	62	124	1	5	46	93
80 - 84	2,098	1,877	625	1,252	221	56	165	1	2	47	147
85 - 89	1,102	850	246	604	252	47	205	-	-	35	189
90 and over	348	200	43	157	148	15	133	-	-	12	128

11. Persons present

Age	TOTAL PERSONS	In households			Not in households						
					Persons present			Residents			
								Staff		Other	
		Total	Males	Females	Total	Males	Females	Males	Females	Males	Females
a	b	c	d	e	f	g	h	i	j	k	l
				Barrow-in-Furness							
ALL AGES	**72,192**	**71,043**	**34,695**	**36,348**	**1,149**	**545**	**604**	**46**	**51**	**170**	**294**
0 - 4	5,071	5,034	2,594	2,440	37	25	12	2	2	-	1
5 - 9	4,562	4,558	2,321	2,237	4	2	2	-	1	-	-
10 - 14	4,102	4,086	2,068	2,018	16	12	4	2	-	-	-
15	883	875	451	424	8	6	2	-	1	-	-
16 - 17	1,895	1,880	968	912	15	5	10	2	2	1	2
18 - 19	2,049	2,028	1,030	998	21	11	10	3	4	4	2
20 - 24	5,467	5,395	2,664	2,731	72	35	37	5	17	9	1
25 - 29	5,755	5,675	2,828	2,847	80	55	25	7	5	8	5
30 - 34	5,049	5,000	2,555	2,445	49	32	17	6	2	4	2
35 - 39	4,538	4,499	2,242	2,257	39	24	15	3	2	5	5
40 - 44	5,264	5,209	2,626	2,583	55	37	18	6	5	7	5
45 - 49	4,541	4,491	2,291	2,200	50	35	15	2	3	11	4
50 - 54	4,185	4,137	2,064	2,073	48	31	17	2	4	7	3
55 - 59	3,649	3,619	1,840	1,779	30	21	9	5	1	1	4
60 - 64	3,623	3,598	1,733	1,865	25	15	10	-	2	8	3
65 - 69	3,497	3,429	1,557	1,872	68	33	35	-	-	14	13
70 - 74	3,319	3,237	1,330	1,907	82	41	41	1	-	18	20
75 - 79	2,381	2,271	888	1,383	110	43	67	-	-	24	38
80 - 84	1,463	1,327	449	878	136	45	91	-	-	23	56
85 - 89	656	531	156	375	125	24	101	-	-	17	81
90 and over	243	164	40	124	79	13	66	-	-	9	49
				Carlisle							
ALL AGES	**100,039**	**97,163**	**46,842**	**50,321**	**2,876**	**1,322**	**1,554**	**96**	**76**	**480**	**851**
0 - 4	6,157	6,117	3,125	2,992	40	25	15	-	1	5	5
5 - 9	6,159	6,114	3,105	3,009	45	28	17	3	1	7	5
10 - 14	5,873	5,712	2,875	2,837	161	107	54	3	2	9	13
15	1,167	1,120	563	557	47	29	18	-	1	6	6
16 - 17	2,546	2,456	1,245	1,211	90	68	22	2	3	4	4
18 - 19	2,841	2,770	1,367	1,403	71	51	20	8	4	8	3
20 - 24	6,771	6,590	3,254	3,336	181	85	96	19	21	40	44
25 - 29	7,341	7,192	3,585	3,607	149	90	59	21	12	34	6
30 - 34	7,273	7,176	3,581	3,595	97	63	34	10	3	18	6
35 - 39	6,583	6,481	3,198	3,283	102	66	36	10	5	22	6
40 - 44	7,270	7,175	3,600	3,575	95	59	36	2	3	17	9
45 - 49	5,959	5,863	2,899	2,964	96	58	38	4	5	20	12
50 - 54	5,557	5,468	2,658	2,810	89	47	42	6	3	15	9
55 - 59	5,512	5,412	2,648	2,764	100	52	48	5	6	10	11
60 - 64	5,644	5,489	2,628	2,861	155	77	78	2	2	26	23
65 - 69	5,518	5,328	2,422	2,906	190	88	102	-	2	41	40
70 - 74	4,288	4,106	1,735	2,371	182	91	91	1	-	40	41
75 - 79	3,611	3,373	1,327	2,046	238	94	144	-	1	53	112
80 - 84	2,361	2,076	736	1,340	285	67	218	-	-	43	168
85 - 89	1,162	869	236	633	293	57	236	-	-	43	196
90 and over	446	276	55	221	170	20	150	-	1	19	132

11. Persons present

Age	TOTAL PERSONS	In households: Total	In households: Males	In households: Females	Not in households: Persons present: Total	Not in households: Persons present: Males	Not in households: Persons present: Females	Residents: Staff: Males	Residents: Staff: Females	Residents: Other: Males	Residents: Other: Females
a	b	c	d	e	f	g	h	i	j	k	l
					Copeland						
ALL AGES	**71,405**	**69,299**	**34,295**	**35,004**	**2,106**	**1,241**	**865**	**97**	**97**	**233**	**384**
0 - 4	4,758	4,706	2,377	2,329	52	27	25	3	5	6	5
5 - 9	4,733	4,721	2,502	2,219	12	10	2	4	1	-	-
10 - 14	4,384	4,317	2,229	2,088	67	37	30	3	4	2	3
15	871	847	430	417	24	13	11	2	-	-	1
16 - 17	1,927	1,843	925	918	84	46	38	2	1	1	-
18 - 19	1,816	1,750	874	876	66	38	28	7	8	3	3
20 - 24	5,146	4,805	2,429	2,376	341	252	89	14	34	48	18
25 - 29	5,770	5,559	2,830	2,729	211	177	34	15	9	21	2
30 - 34	5,326	5,197	2,644	2,553	129	104	25	9	5	13	3
35 - 39	4,740	4,652	2,363	2,289	88	68	20	5	5	10	1
40 - 44	5,296	5,185	2,682	2,503	111	85	26	12	10	11	4
45 - 49	4,349	4,257	2,165	2,092	92	67	25	9	7	9	1
50 - 54	4,126	4,047	2,004	2,043	79	56	23	6	4	8	2
55 - 59	3,911	3,842	1,943	1,899	69	49	20	3	3	5	4
60 - 64	3,814	3,761	1,834	1,927	53	34	19	3	1	7	2
65 - 69	3,448	3,381	1,583	1,798	67	37	30	-	-	10	14
70 - 74	2,860	2,762	1,184	1,578	98	37	61	-	-	18	33
75 - 79	1,986	1,875	722	1,153	111	39	72	-	-	20	53
80 - 84	1,315	1,178	410	768	137	36	101	-	-	21	74
85 - 89	605	466	137	329	139	18	121	-	-	11	101
90 and over	224	148	28	120	76	11	65	-	-	9	60
					Eden						
ALL AGES	**46,413**	**44,630**	**22,015**	**22,615**	**1,783**	**861**	**922**	**185**	**142**	**164**	**379**
0 - 4	2,568	2,544	1,280	1,264	24	14	10	6	2	-	-
5 - 9	2,587	2,576	1,300	1,276	11	5	6	2	4	-	-
10 - 14	2,644	2,584	1,322	1,262	60	51	9	6	4	5	1
15	508	475	241	234	33	33	-	6	-	4	-
16 - 17	1,115	1,086	590	496	29	20	9	4	5	1	1
18 - 19	1,179	1,095	554	541	84	54	30	14	15	1	1
20 - 24	3,073	2,931	1,529	1,402	142	84	58	35	30	8	3
25 - 29	3,201	3,099	1,597	1,502	102	64	38	23	9	3	1
30 - 34	3,147	3,078	1,523	1,555	69	46	23	20	10	3	-
35 - 39	3,117	3,045	1,529	1,516	72	50	22	13	10	4	-
40 - 44	3,591	3,537	1,790	1,747	54	34	20	7	9	2	-
45 - 49	3,035	2,965	1,511	1,454	70	38	32	15	14	1	1
50 - 54	2,750	2,677	1,332	1,345	73	48	25	15	12	4	-
55 - 59	2,670	2,604	1,286	1,318	66	34	32	12	9	2	1
60 - 64	2,876	2,782	1,386	1,396	94	40	54	4	4	3	4
65 - 69	2,585	2,455	1,160	1,295	130	64	66	2	2	11	10
70 - 74	2,130	2,005	914	1,091	125	51	74	1	1	15	22
75 - 79	1,667	1,549	643	906	118	37	81	-	-	20	44
80 - 84	1,186	1,013	369	644	173	48	125	-	1	37	95
85 - 89	571	410	126	284	161	36	125	-	-	31	114
90 and over	213	120	33	87	93	10	83	-	1	9	81

11. Persons present

Age	TOTAL PERSONS	In households			Not in households						
					Persons present			Residents			
								Staff		Other	
		Total	Males	Females	Total	Males	Females	Males	Females	Males	Females
a	b	c	d	e	f	g	h	i	j	k	l
					South Lakeland						
ALL AGES	**102,590**	**94,373**	**45,331**	**49,042**	**8,217**	**3,711**	**4,506**	**751**	**700**	**360**	**1,053**
0 - 4	5,082	5,001	2,565	2,436	81	37	44	13	16	3	1
5 - 9	5,152	5,030	2,612	2,418	122	65	57	16	26	6	1
10 - 14	5,968	5,041	2,595	2,446	927	500	427	16	16	9	11
15	1,306	1,007	497	510	299	184	115	6	3	4	6
16 - 17	2,850	2,231	1,168	1,063	619	323	296	29	25	6	3
18 - 19	2,601	2,136	1,130	1,006	465	221	244	55	53	8	15
20 - 24	6,668	5,835	2,863	2,972	833	373	460	180	188	26	27
25 - 29	6,713	6,211	3,109	3,102	502	263	239	94	78	20	8
30 - 34	6,453	6,077	2,988	3,089	376	211	165	71	44	13	5
35 - 39	6,236	5,977	2,976	3,001	259	153	106	45	38	10	11
40 - 44	7,583	7,266	3,569	3,697	317	166	151	53	55	11	11
45 - 49	6,607	6,268	3,132	3,136	339	173	166	53	48	14	13
50 - 54	6,113	5,761	2,835	2,926	352	162	190	43	44	6	10
55 - 59	5,868	5,537	2,723	2,814	331	161	170	53	39	7	5
60 - 64	6,472	6,083	2,839	3,244	389	173	216	19	13	12	22
65 - 69	6,128	5,791	2,649	3,142	337	134	203	1	4	10	37
70 - 74	5,109	4,813	2,107	2,706	296	119	177	3	3	28	52
75 - 79	4,446	4,083	1,601	2,482	363	118	245	1	4	49	125
80 - 84	2,980	2,588	886	1,702	392	94	298	-	-	50	222
85 - 89	1,646	1,264	402	862	382	63	319	-	1	52	276
90 and over	609	373	85	288	236	18	218	-	2	16	192

12. Residents in households with limiting long-term illness

Age	TOTAL PERSONS	Males	Females	Age	TOTAL PERSONS	Males	Females
a	b	c	d	a	b	c	d
	CUMBRIA				**Copeland**		
ALL AGES	**58,975**	**27,740**	**31,235**	**ALL AGES**	**8,663**	**4,235**	**4,428**
0 - 4	461	269	192	0 - 4	77	41	36
5 - 15	1,353	782	571	5 - 15	225	139	86
16 - 17	301	174	127	16 - 17	51	30	21
18 - 29	2,723	1,407	1,316	18 - 29	397	206	191
30 - 44	5,357	2,821	2,536	30 - 44	853	472	381
45 - 54	6,318	3,116	3,202	45 - 54	1,057	536	521
55 - 59	5,087	2,726	2,361	55 - 59	857	475	382
60 - 64	7,183	4,147	3,036	60 - 64	1,129	659	470
65 - 74	14,785	7,079	7,706	65 - 74	2,171	1,053	1,118
75 - 84	11,868	4,300	7,568	75 - 84	1,439	525	914
85 and over	3,539	919	2,620	85 and over	407	99	308
	Allerdale				**Eden**		
ALL AGES	**11,930**	**5,715**	**6,215**	**ALL AGES**	**4,945**	**2,439**	**2,506**
0 - 4	85	47	38	0 - 4	29	20	9
5 - 15	286	173	113	5 - 15	100	56	44
16 - 17	53	34	19	16 - 17	21	11	10
18 - 29	544	270	274	18 - 29	206	125	81
30 - 44	1,085	581	504	30 - 44	418	214	204
45 - 54	1,292	650	642	45 - 54	518	267	251
55 - 59	1,115	596	519	55 - 59	411	238	173
60 - 64	1,548	905	643	60 - 64	600	362	238
65 - 74	3,059	1,480	1,579	65 - 74	1,291	667	624
75 - 84	2,224	815	1,409	75 - 84	1,053	391	662
85 and over	639	164	475	85 and over	298	88	210
	Barrow-in-Furness				**South Lakeland**		
ALL AGES	**9,915**	**4,466**	**5,449**	**ALL AGES**	**11,201**	**5,125**	**6,076**
0 - 4	98	59	39	0 - 4	71	43	28
5 - 15	255	142	113	5 - 15	193	116	77
16 - 17	59	35	24	16 - 17	64	37	27
18 - 29	506	251	255	18 - 29	479	246	233
30 - 44	996	490	506	30 - 44	836	445	391
45 - 54	1,154	538	616	45 - 54	995	500	495
55 - 59	857	420	437	55 - 59	813	441	372
60 - 64	1,216	674	542	60 - 64	1,269	717	552
65 - 74	2,472	1,105	1,367	65 - 74	2,754	1,322	1,432
75 - 84	1,837	631	1,206	75 - 84	2,729	988	1,741
85 and over	465	121	344	85 and over	998	270	728
	Carlisle						
ALL AGES	**12,321**	**5,760**	**6,561**				
0 - 4	101	59	42				
5 - 15	294	156	138				
16 - 17	53	27	26				
18 - 29	591	309	282				
30 - 44	1,169	619	550				
45 - 54	1,302	625	677				
55 - 59	1,034	556	478				
60 - 64	1,421	830	591				
65 - 74	3,038	1,452	1,586				
75 - 84	2,586	950	1,636				
85 and over	732	177	555				

13. Persons present not in households with limiting long-term illness

Age	Medical and care establishments				Other			
	Total persons	Non-residents	Residents		Total persons	Non-residents	Residents	
			Males	Females			Males	Females
a	b	c	d	e	f	g	h	i
				CUMBRIA				
ALL AGES	**5,606**	**1,285**	**1,153**	**3,168**	**818**	**594**	**127**	**97**
0 - 4	4	3	1	-	6	2	-	4
5 - 15	83	64	10	9	39	34	3	2
16 - 17	16	15	1	-	24	22	1	1
18 - 29	127	60	46	21	105	60	26	19
30 - 44	206	63	84	59	102	57	29	16
45 - 54	184	71	59	54	96	54	28	14
55 - 59	102	46	23	33	63	44	13	6
60 - 64	189	69	62	58	93	73	10	10
65 - 74	815	264	224	327	168	147	15	6
75 - 84	1,926	398	399	1,129	102	91	2	9
85 and over	1,954	232	244	1,478	20	10	-	10
				Allerdale				
ALL AGES	**1,033**	**92**	**273**	**668**	**141**	**96**	**25**	**20**
0 - 4	-	-	-	-	2	-	-	2
5 - 15	5	-	-	5	8	6	1	1
16 - 17	-	-	-	-	2	2	-	-
18 - 29	46	11	22	13	14	8	3	3
30 - 44	62	4	34	24	17	7	6	4
45 - 54	48	9	21	18	21	13	6	2
55 - 59	19	2	6	11	18	13	3	2
60 - 64	34	1	16	17	21	16	1	4
65 - 74	128	14	45	69	25	20	5	-
75 - 84	337	26	86	225	11	9	-	2
85 and over	354	25	43	286	2	2	-	-
				Barrow-in-Furness				
ALL AGES	**638**	**247**	**117**	**274**	**24**	**4**	**14**	**6**
0 - 4	1	1	-	-	-	-	-	-
5 - 15	-	-	-	-	-	-	-	-
16 - 17	2	2	-	-	-	-	-	-
18 - 29	15	6	6	3	3	-	3	-
30 - 44	24	9	5	10	5	-	4	1
45 - 54	31	15	10	6	4	-	3	1
55 - 59	10	6	1	3	3	1	1	1
60 - 64	14	6	5	3	1	-	1	-
65 - 74	119	62	25	32	4	2	1	1
75 - 84	225	97	40	88	4	1	1	2
85 and over	197	43	25	129	-	-	-	-
				Carlisle				
ALL AGES	**1,423**	**358**	**331**	**734**	**91**	**72**	**12**	**7**
0 - 4	-	-	-	-	2	-	-	2
5 - 15	2	1	-	1	3	3	-	-
16 - 17	-	-	-	-	1	1	-	-
18 - 29	35	14	17	4	4	3	1	-
30 - 44	86	35	34	17	7	3	3	1
45 - 54	62	22	21	19	12	6	6	-
55 - 59	39	20	8	11	3	2	1	-
60 - 64	77	32	25	20	15	15	-	-
65 - 74	223	71	76	76	31	30	1	-
75 - 84	462	99	92	271	10	8	-	2
85 and over	437	64	58	315	3	1	-	2

13. Persons present not in households with limiting long-term illness

Age	Medical and care establishments				Other			
	Total persons	Non-residents	Residents		Total persons	Non-residents	Residents	
			Males	Females			Males	Females
a	b	c	d	e	f	g	h	i
			Copeland					
ALL AGES	**640**	**224**	**98**	**318**	**78**	**62**	**11**	**5**
0 - 4	3	2	1	-	-	-	-	-
5 - 15	5	5	-	-	1	1	-	-
16 - 17	-	-	-	-	3	3	-	-
18 - 29	9	8	-	1	29	23	5	1
30 - 44	21	14	5	2	23	20	2	1
45 - 54	20	16	2	2	9	7	2	-
55 - 59	18	14	1	3	6	3	2	1
60 - 64	21	14	6	1	3	2	-	1
65 - 74	128	57	26	45	3	2	-	1
75 - 84	214	64	39	111	1	1	-	-
85 and over	201	30	18	153	-	-	-	-
			Eden					
ALL AGES	**549**	**115**	**113**	**321**	**89**	**67**	**15**	**7**
0 - 4	-	-	-	-	-	-	-	-
5 - 15	48	44	4	-	2	2	-	-
16 - 17	5	4	1	-	2	2	-	-
18 - 29	-	-	-	-	9	3	5	1
30 - 44	-	-	-	-	8	8	-	-
45 - 54	1	1	-	-	15	7	4	4
55 - 59	3	2	1	-	3	2	1	-
60 - 64	13	7	2	4	5	4	1	-
65 - 74	75	25	20	30	31	26	4	1
75 - 84	193	21	50	122	11	11	-	-
85 and over	211	11	35	165	3	2	-	1
			South Lakeland					
ALL AGES	**1,323**	**249**	**221**	**853**	**395**	**293**	**50**	**52**
0 - 4	-	-	-	-	2	2	-	-
5 - 15	23	14	6	3	25	22	2	1
16 - 17	9	9	-	-	16	14	1	1
18 - 29	22	21	1	-	46	23	9	14
30 - 44	13	1	6	6	42	19	14	9
45 - 54	22	8	5	9	35	21	7	7
55 - 59	13	2	6	5	30	23	5	2
60 - 64	30	9	8	13	48	36	7	5
65 - 74	142	35	32	75	74	67	4	3
75 - 84	495	91	92	312	65	61	1	3
85 and over	554	59	65	430	12	5	-	7

14. Residents aged 16 and over with limiting long-term illness

Economic position	TOTAL AGED 16 AND OVER	Age: 16 - 17	Age: 18 - 19	Age: 20 - 29	Age: 30 - 44	Age: 45 up to pensionable age	Age: Pensionable age and over	Students (economically active or inactive)
a	b	c	d	e	f	g	h	i
CUMBRIA								
TOTAL PERSONS	**61,677**	**304**	**360**	**2,475**	**5,545**	**15,854**	**37,139**	**345**
Economically active	**9,802**	**118**	**209**	**1,258**	**2,508**	**4,711**	**998**	**31**
Employees - full time	4,654	33	114	732	1,316	2,276	183	7
Employees - part time	1,683	25	16	115	409	756	362	21
Self-employed - with employees	718	-	1	18	131	394	174	-
Self-employed - without employees	1,089	1	3	57	212	566	250	-
On a Government scheme	300	41	28	73	94	61	3	
Unemployed	1,358	18	47	263	346	658	26	3
Economically active students (included above)	*31*	*18*	*5*	*4*	*4*	-	-	
Economically inactive	**51,875**	**186**	**151**	**1,217**	**3,037**	**11,143**	**36,141**	**314**
Students	314	152	56	67	27	8	4	314
Permanently sick	14,968	28	86	960	2,524	8,515	2,855	
Retired	29,475	1	1	4	24	1,346	28,099	
Other inactive	7,118	5	8	186	462	1,274	5,183	
Allerdale								
TOTAL PERSONS	**12,536**	**53**	**68**	**517**	**1,153**	**3,398**	**7,347**	**73**
Economically active	**1,824**	**16**	**37**	**218**	**488**	**893**	**172**	**5**
Employees - full time	836	4	19	127	251	399	36	-
Employees - part time	256	3	5	14	60	125	49	4
Self-employed - with employees	138	-	-	3	26	71	38	-
Self-employed - without employees	211	-	-	8	44	118	41	-
On a Government scheme	67	5	4	16	27	15	-	
Unemployed	316	4	9	50	80	165	8	1
Economically active students (included above)	*5*	*3*	*2*	-	-	-	-	
Economically inactive	**10,712**	**37**	**31**	**299**	**665**	**2,505**	**7,175**	**68**
Students	68	31	9	15	9	3	1	68
Permanently sick	3,406	6	22	245	548	1,942	643	
Retired	5,799	-	-	2	5	267	5,525	
Other inactive	1,439	-	-	37	103	293	1,006	
Barrow-in-Furness								
TOTAL PERSONS	**9,973**	**59**	**72**	**446**	**1,016**	**2,717**	**5,663**	**49**
Economically active	**1,516**	**22**	**41**	**215**	**395**	**742**	**101**	**5**
Employees - full time	835	5	23	126	231	430	20	2
Employees - part time	244	2	2	20	55	111	54	2
Self-employed - with employees	59	-	-	1	13	33	12	-
Self-employed - without employees	76	-	-	7	28	31	10	-
On a Government scheme	49	12	7	10	9	10	1	
Unemployed	253	3	9	51	59	127	4	1
Economically active students (included above)	*5*	*2*	-	*1*	*2*	-	-	
Economically inactive	**8,457**	**37**	**31**	**231**	**621**	**1,975**	**5,562**	**44**
Students	44	28	8	5	3	-	-	44
Permanently sick	2,644	8	20	183	515	1,514	404	
Retired	4,523	-	-	-	2	215	4,306	
Other inactive	1,246	1	3	43	101	246	852	

14. Residents aged 16 and over with limiting long-term illness

Economic position	TOTAL AGED 16 AND OVER	Age						Students (economically active or inactive)
		16 - 17	18 - 19	20 - 29	30 - 44	45 up to pensionable age	Pensionable age and over	
a	b	c	d	e	f	g	h	i
Carlisle								
TOTAL PERSONS	**13,007**	**53**	**83**	**530**	**1,224**	**3,257**	**7,860**	**53**
Economically active	**2,110**	**26**	**44**	**298**	**563**	**967**	**212**	**6**
Employees - full time	999	8	20	147	293	467	64	2
- part time	373	6	5	30	97	172	63	4
Self-employed - with employees	132	-	1	5	22	71	33	-
- without employees	182	-	-	12	32	94	44	-
On a Government scheme	88	6	6	24	27	24	1	
Unemployed	336	6	12	80	92	139	7	-
Economically active students (included above)	*6*	*4*	*1*	*1*	-	-	-	
Economically inactive	**10,897**	**27**	**39**	**232**	**661**	**2,290**	**7,648**	**47**
Students	47	21	11	13	1	1	-	47
Permanently sick	3,320	5	24	180	552	1,809	750	
Retired	6,231	-	1	-	6	265	5,959	
Other inactive	1,299	1	3	39	102	215	939	
Copeland								
TOTAL PERSONS	**8,792**	**51**	**42**	**362**	**863**	**2,592**	**4,882**	**58**
Economically active	**1,322**	**17**	**28**	**176**	**351**	**651**	**99**	**3**
Employees - full time	700	3	14	106	209	350	18	-
- part time	193	2	1	14	54	88	34	2
Self-employed - with employees	76	-	-	2	14	42	18	-
- without employees	103	-	1	4	15	57	26	-
On a Government scheme	34	8	4	10	10	2	-	
Unemployed	216	4	8	40	49	112	3	1
Economically active students (included above)	*3*	*2*	*1*	-	-	-	-	
Economically inactive	**7,470**	**34**	**14**	**186**	**512**	**1,941**	**4,783**	**55**
Students	55	25	9	9	9	2	1	55
Permanently sick	2,434	6	5	144	431	1,469	379	
Retired	3,849	1	-	-	2	255	3,591	
Other inactive	1,132	2	-	33	70	215	812	
Eden								
TOTAL PERSONS	**5,268**	**22**	**33**	**179**	**418**	**1,304**	**3,312**	**32**
Economically active	**1,030**	**8**	**18**	**107**	**239**	**499**	**159**	**4**
Employees - full time	369	4	9	66	96	177	17	2
- part time	189	3	1	6	45	89	45	2
Self-employed - with employees	132	-	-	2	17	76	37	-
- without employees	226	-	2	15	43	107	59	-
On a Government scheme	26	-	3	8	10	4	1	
Unemployed	88	1	3	10	28	46	-	-
Economically active students (included above)	*4*	*2*	-	*1*	*1*	-	-	
Economically inactive	**4,238**	**14**	**15**	**72**	**179**	**805**	**3,153**	**28**
Students	28	13	6	6	1	2	-	28
Permanently sick	972	1	8	58	135	565	205	
Retired	2,534	-	-	-	4	115	2,415	
Other inactive	704	-	1	8	39	123	533	

14. Residents aged 16 and over with limiting long-term illness

Economic position	TOTAL AGED 16 AND OVER	Age						Students (economically active or inactive)
		16 - 17	18 - 19	20 - 29	30 - 44	45 up to pensionable age	Pensionable age and over	
a	b	c	d	e	f	g	h	i
			South Lakeland					
TOTAL PERSONS	**12,101**	**66**	**62**	**441**	**871**	**2,586**	**8,075**	**80**
Economically active	**2,000**	**29**	**41**	**244**	**472**	**959**	**255**	**8**
Employees - full time	915	9	29	160	236	453	28	1
- part time	428	9	2	31	98	171	117	7
Self-employed - with employees	181	-	-	5	39	101	36	-
- without employees	291	1	-	11	50	159	70	-
On a Government scheme	36	10	4	5	11	6	-	
Unemployed	149	-	6	32	38	69	4	-
Economically active students (included above)	*8*	*5*	*1*	*1*	*1*	-	-	
Economically inactive	**10,101**	**37**	**21**	**197**	**399**	**1,627**	**7,820**	**72**
Students	72	34	13	19	4	-	2	72
Permanently sick	2,192	2	7	150	343	1,216	474	
Retired	6,539	-	-	2	5	229	6,303	
Other inactive	1,298	1	1	26	47	182	1,041	

Table 15 Migrants

15. Residents with different address one year before census

Age	TOTAL PERSONS	Total males	Total females	Moved within wards		Between wards but within district		Between districts but within county	
				Males	Females	Males	Females	Males	Females
a	b	c	d	e	f	g	h	i	j
				CUMBRIA					
All migrants									
ALL AGES 1 AND OVER	**44,448**	**21,826**	**22,622**	**5,812**	**5,917**	**9,319**	**9,936**	**1,691**	**1,771**
1 - 4	3,290	1,701	1,589	516	459	727	725	114	96
5 - 9	2,661	1,400	1,261	414	393	582	502	102	75
10 - 14	1,935	981	954	313	298	425	407	56	58
15	328	165	163	46	49	77	78	16	15
16	405	203	202	63	50	84	93	13	19
17	508	220	288	59	66	100	155	17	28
18 - 19	1,850	687	1,163	165	279	307	557	61	99
20 - 24	8,001	3,623	4,378	846	964	1,619	2,111	266	341
25 - 28	5,718	3,013	2,705	813	634	1,342	1,216	232	229
29	1,105	581	524	143	133	251	244	49	40
30 - 34	4,323	2,326	1,997	584	516	1,001	830	191	161
35 - 39	2,883	1,549	1,334	393	329	649	560	131	94
40 - 44	2,430	1,358	1,072	357	287	561	437	108	83
45 - 49	1,707	886	821	204	205	358	322	74	79
50 - 54	1,340	696	644	186	163	272	239	49	47
55 - 59	1,039	540	499	152	139	196	188	38	30
60 - 64	1,123	518	605	159	195	188	210	39	46
65 - 69	1,000	466	534	131	192	187	213	31	35
70 - 74	794	336	458	95	154	156	186	36	28
75 - 84	1,328	453	875	132	259	189	401	50	89
85 and over	680	124	556	41	153	48	262	18	79
Migrants in households									
All ages 1 and over	**41,764**	**20,681**	**21,083**	**5,655**	**5,620**	**8,987**	**9,334**	**1,526**	**1,548**
1 - 4	3,261	1,690	1,571	514	455	724	721	112	91
5 - 9	2,639	1,387	1,252	412	392	577	499	99	74
10 - 14	1,899	962	937	312	297	413	400	53	54
15	309	154	155	46	49	70	75	14	14
16	384	193	191	62	49	84	89	11	17
17	466	201	265	58	63	96	150	15	22
18 - 19	1,665	610	1,055	158	267	289	534	49	88
20 - 24	7,517	3,374	4,143	822	940	1,593	2,078	243	323
25 - 28	5,504	2,880	2,624	794	622	1,318	1,204	221	221
29	1,077	561	516	142	132	250	241	48	40
30 - 34	4,207	2,241	1,966	574	509	992	825	182	158
35 - 39	2,803	1,487	1,316	383	328	633	553	124	92
40 - 44	2,378	1,320	1,058	354	287	551	435	102	82
45 - 49	1,653	850	803	200	205	347	313	71	76
50 - 54	1,315	684	631	186	160	267	235	48	46
55 - 59	1,017	528	489	150	138	193	183	36	28
60 - 64	1,083	497	586	156	193	176	201	33	39
65 - 69	936	441	495	129	180	168	196	28	27
70 - 74	666	277	389	87	137	123	146	18	19
75 - 84	816	295	521	100	184	109	203	15	30
85 and over	169	49	120	16	33	14	53	4	7

Between counties but within region		Between regions or from Scotland		From outside GB		Between neighbouring districts		Between neighbouring counties/Scottish Regions		Age
Males	Females	Males	Females	Males	Females	Males	Females	Males	Females	
k	l	m	n	o	p	q	r	s	t	a
										All migrants
454	**479**	**3,914**	**3,861**	**636**	**658**	**1,776**	**1,904**	**1,002**	**1,073**	**ALL AGES 1 AND OVER**
31	32	283	225	30	52	120	112	68	76	1 - 4
29	34	224	219	49	38	117	88	65	57	5 - 9
12	18	149	146	26	27	57	55	34	42	10 - 14
1	4	24	15	1	2	17	15	6	7	15
3	5	36	31	4	4	14	19	10	7	16
4	2	31	30	9	7	17	28	8	10	17
21	36	120	158	13	34	56	91	40	55	18 - 19
105	98	666	723	121	141	268	369	155	182	20 - 24
56	54	478	466	92	106	237	247	115	122	25 - 28
15	16	105	78	18	13	50	46	25	26	29
41	43	435	389	74	58	209	174	96	94	30 - 34
35	30	286	268	55	53	141	112	82	73	35 - 39
21	19	270	212	41	34	113	85	73	60	40 - 44
18	17	203	174	29	24	77	81	62	59	45 - 49
14	13	152	162	23	20	48	49	41	41	50 - 54
9	7	126	118	19	17	41	40	32	28	55 - 59
12	15	107	128	13	11	48	50	25	31	60 - 64
11	10	97	77	9	7	34	36	24	21	65 - 69
4	8	39	78	6	4	37	31	11	19	70 - 74
12	11	66	109	4	6	57	93	26	44	75 - 84
-	7	17	55	-	-	18	83	4	19	85 and over
										Migrants in households
398	**419**	**3,543**	**3,560**	**572**	**602**	**1,605**	**1,675**	**911**	**981**	**All ages 1 and over**
31	32	279	220	30	52	118	109	68	76	1 - 4
29	34	221	216	49	37	115	86	64	56	5 - 9
12	17	146	142	26	27	54	54	33	40	10 - 14
-	2	23	13	1	2	16	14	6	5	15
2	3	30	29	4	4	12	18	10	7	16
4	1	21	23	7	6	14	22	6	9	17
13	21	92	119	9	26	44	80	30	41	18 - 19
81	79	537	612	98	111	243	348	123	158	20 - 24
47	47	426	434	74	96	225	239	101	113	25 - 28
13	15	92	75	16	13	49	46	23	26	29
37	42	386	375	70	57	198	170	89	89	30 - 34
34	30	265	261	48	52	132	111	77	72	35 - 39
19	17	254	204	40	33	108	83	68	53	40 - 44
16	17	188	170	28	22	74	78	59	57	45 - 49
14	13	148	157	21	20	47	48	38	41	50 - 54
9	7	121	117	19	16	39	38	31	28	55 - 59
12	14	107	128	13	11	42	43	25	30	60 - 64
11	10	96	75	9	7	32	27	24	20	65 - 69
4	8	39	75	6	4	19	22	11	19	70 - 74
10	10	57	88	4	6	20	36	21	36	75 - 84
-	-	15	27	-	-	4	3	4	5	85 and over

Table 15 Migrants - continued

15. Residents with different address one year before census

Age	TOTAL PERSONS	Total males	Total females	Moved within wards		Between wards but within district		Between districts but within county	
				Males	Females	Males	Females	Males	Females
a	b	c	d	e	f	g	h	i	j
				Allerdale					
All migrants									
ALL AGES 1 AND OVER	**8,353**	**4,061**	**4,292**	**1,327**	**1,445**	**1,557**	**1,659**	**381**	**396**
1 - 4	646	308	338	105	140	112	125	27	24
5 - 9	522	282	240	105	97	98	92	31	13
10 - 14	433	234	199	88	74	94	81	19	13
15	59	32	27	11	12	14	10	5	3
16	82	40	42	13	12	19	17	3	7
17	82	33	49	15	17	11	20	1	7
18 - 19	320	110	210	40	74	39	84	11	18
20 - 24	1,411	638	773	193	206	257	331	47	80
25 - 28	995	509	486	167	142	213	195	54	54
29	211	107	104	37	33	34	34	12	17
30 - 34	788	414	374	130	134	157	147	45	27
35 - 39	542	291	251	84	72	112	97	36	20
40 - 44	469	270	199	81	71	101	68	18	17
45 - 49	315	170	145	55	43	63	48	12	14
50 - 54	243	117	126	41	40	39	36	11	20
55 - 59	215	105	110	34	37	32	44	13	3
60 - 64	210	95	115	33	45	34	31	4	7
65 - 69	212	96	116	29	45	33	46	6	4
70 - 74	162	71	91	18	38	40	34	8	9
75 - 84	278	111	167	35	60	48	70	14	20
85 and over	158	28	130	13	53	7	49	4	19
Migrants in households									
All ages 1 and over	**7,775**	**3,843**	**3,932**	**1,286**	**1,348**	**1,482**	**1,531**	**346**	**338**
1 - 4	633	301	332	103	139	112	124	25	23
5 - 9	516	278	238	103	97	96	91	31	13
10 - 14	425	230	195	88	73	90	80	19	11
15	56	30	26	11	12	12	10	5	2
16	77	39	38	13	11	19	16	2	5
17	77	31	46	15	17	9	19	1	6
18 - 19	284	100	184	39	71	35	80	9	15
20 - 24	1,335	603	732	191	200	253	325	44	78
25 - 28	950	487	463	162	138	210	189	53	52
29	204	102	102	37	33	33	33	12	17
30 - 34	768	403	365	129	131	155	145	44	27
35 - 39	527	280	247	81	72	108	94	35	20
40 - 44	460	264	196	80	71	99	68	17	16
45 - 49	306	164	142	54	43	61	47	12	12
50 - 54	237	116	121	41	39	39	34	10	19
55 - 59	209	103	106	33	36	32	41	12	3
60 - 64	206	93	113	33	45	33	30	3	7
65 - 69	201	91	110	28	43	29	44	6	2
70 - 74	125	56	69	16	31	32	23	3	5
75 - 84	149	60	89	24	38	21	31	3	5
85 and over	30	12	18	5	8	4	7	-	-

Between counties but within region		Between regions or from Scotland		From outside GB		Between neighbouring districts		Between neighbouring counties/Scottish Regions		Age
Males	Females	Males	Females	Males	Females	Males	Females	Males	Females	
k	l	m	n	o	p	q	r	s	t	a
										All migrants
95	**82**	**608**	**609**	**93**	**101**	**367**	**388**	**139**	**130**	**ALL AGES 1 AND OVER**
4	3	51	39	9	7	25	24	7	10	1 - 4
8	3	31	26	9	9	28	13	9	5	5 - 9
2	2	28	24	3	5	18	12	9	7	10 - 14
-	1	2	1	-	-	5	3	1	1	15
-	1	3	4	2	1	2	6	1	1	16
2	-	2	5	2	-	1	7	1	1	17
3	6	17	24	-	4	11	18	6	8	18 - 19
18	18	102	111	21	27	46	80	25	13	20 - 24
14	6	56	71	5	18	51	54	9	11	25 - 28
2	5	18	14	4	1	12	16	1	5	29
9	8	61	51	12	7	45	27	11	10	30 - 34
8	5	40	48	11	9	34	19	15	15	35 - 39
6	8	58	31	6	4	17	16	14	7	40 - 44
6	3	32	36	2	1	12	14	10	8	45 - 49
4	2	22	28	-	-	11	18	7	5	50 - 54
-	2	23	21	3	3	13	3	3	3	55 - 59
4	4	20	27	-	1	4	7	-	7	60 - 64
3	1	23	18	2	2	6	4	5	2	65 - 69
-	-	4	9	1	1	8	9	2	1	70 - 74
2	2	11	14	1	1	14	19	3	8	75 - 84
-	2	4	7	-	-	4	19	-	2	85 and over
										Migrants in households
86	**72**	**556**	**554**	**87**	**89**	**332**	**332**	**129**	**116**	**All ages 1 and over**
4	3	48	36	9	7	23	23	7	10	1 - 4
8	3	31	26	9	8	28	13	9	5	5 - 9
2	2	28	24	3	5	18	11	9	7	10 - 14
-	1	2	1	-	-	5	2	1	1	15
-	1	3	4	2	1	1	5	1	1	16
2	-	2	4	2	-	1	6	1	1	17
3	3	14	12	-	3	9	15	5	4	18 - 19
14	15	83	95	18	19	43	78	21	10	20 - 24
12	6	47	61	3	17	50	52	6	9	25 - 28
2	4	14	14	4	1	12	16	1	5	29
8	8	55	47	12	7	44	27	10	9	30 - 34
8	5	38	47	10	9	33	19	15	15	35 - 39
6	8	56	30	6	3	16	15	14	7	40 - 44
6	3	29	36	2	1	12	12	10	8	45 - 49
4	2	22	27	-	-	10	17	7	5	50 - 54
-	2	23	21	3	3	12	3	3	3	55 - 59
4	3	20	27	-	1	3	7	-	6	60 - 64
3	1	23	18	2	2	6	2	5	2	65 - 69
-	-	4	9	1	1	3	5	2	1	70 - 74
-	2	11	12	1	1	3	4	2	7	75 - 84
-	-	3	3	-	-	-	-	-	-	85 and over

15. Residents with different address one year before census

Age	TOTAL PERSONS	Total males	Total females	Moved within wards		Between wards but within district		Between districts but within county	
				Males	Females	Males	Females	Males	Females
a	b	c	d	e	f	g	h	i	j
				Barrow-in-Furness					
All migrants									
ALL AGES 1 AND OVER	**6,360**	**3,202**	**3,158**	**857**	**845**	**1,614**	**1,648**	**204**	**198**
1 - 4	538	295	243	89	68	149	130	14	8
5 - 9	373	179	194	47	63	96	87	9	8
10 - 14	283	146	137	50	41	68	71	2	5
15	45	20	25	6	5	10	17	1	2
16	64	32	32	10	5	16	20	2	2
17	82	27	55	5	10	21	35	1	5
18 - 19	286	102	184	30	51	53	106	8	15
20 - 24	1,279	580	699	139	175	309	390	52	55
25 - 28	900	487	413	127	97	252	223	35	25
29	174	97	77	18	23	56	37	4	1
30 - 34	586	347	239	90	61	164	118	21	17
35 - 39	393	219	174	56	46	110	85	18	14
40 - 44	347	191	156	58	42	86	82	10	6
45 - 49	251	122	129	27	39	61	60	9	11
50 - 54	202	115	87	27	17	56	46	4	4
55 - 59	126	63	63	23	16	26	30	2	3
60 - 64	113	64	49	19	18	30	21	5	2
65 - 69	109	46	63	14	24	17	22	2	2
70 - 74	71	32	39	10	10	15	18	-	2
75 - 84	93	31	62	11	22	15	27	4	8
85 and over	45	7	38	1	12	4	23	1	3
Migrants in households									
All ages 1 and over	**6,233**	**3,144**	**3,089**	**848**	**827**	**1,597**	**1,615**	**201**	**190**
1 - 4	537	294	243	89	68	149	130	14	8
5 - 9	372	179	193	47	63	96	87	9	8
10 - 14	283	146	137	50	41	68	71	2	5
15	45	20	25	6	5	10	17	1	2
16	63	31	32	10	5	16	20	2	2
17	80	27	53	5	10	21	33	1	5
18 - 19	280	100	180	30	49	52	105	8	14
20 - 24	1,265	574	691	137	173	308	389	52	54
25 - 28	891	481	410	125	97	251	223	35	24
29	173	96	77	18	23	56	37	4	1
30 - 34	575	338	237	89	60	164	118	20	17
35 - 39	387	216	171	56	46	110	85	18	12
40 - 44	342	186	156	58	42	86	82	10	6
45 - 49	246	119	127	27	39	61	58	8	11
50 - 54	199	112	87	27	17	55	46	4	4
55 - 59	124	62	62	22	16	26	30	2	2
60 - 64	112	63	49	19	18	29	21	5	2
65 - 69	105	45	60	14	23	16	20	2	2
70 - 74	65	27	38	9	10	11	17	-	2
75 - 84	70	22	48	9	18	9	19	3	7
85 and over	19	6	13	1	4	3	7	1	2

Between counties but within region		Between regions or from Scotland		From outside GB		Between neighbouring districts		Between neighbouring counties/Scottish Regions		Age
Males	Females	Males	Females	Males	Females	Males	Females	Males	Females	
k	l	m	n	o	p	q	r	s	t	a
										All migrants
25	**17**	**404**	**353**	**98**	**97**	**166**	**168**	**73**	**80**	**ALL AGES 1 AND OVER**
4	2	35	24	4	11	11	7	7	5	1 - 4
1	1	19	28	7	7	9	7	4	7	5 - 9
2	-	17	17	7	3	2	3	6	1	10 - 14
-	-	2	1	1	-	1	1	-	1	15
-	-	4	5	-	-	2	2	-	2	16
-	-	-	4	-	1	1	5	-	2	17
1	-	8	8	2	4	5	9	2	2	18 - 19
7	4	62	63	11	12	44	51	8	14	20 - 24
1	2	55	55	17	11	29	21	4	9	25 - 28
1	1	14	12	4	3	3	-	4	3	29
-	2	59	29	13	12	17	14	8	8	30 - 34
1	-	26	19	8	10	11	12	5	3	35 - 39
1	-	29	21	7	5	9	5	6	7	40 - 44
1	-	21	15	3	4	8	10	5	4	45 - 49
2	4	20	12	6	4	3	3	6	5	50 - 54
2	-	8	11	2	3	1	3	1	1	55 - 59
-	-	7	5	3	3	5	1	2	-	60 - 64
1	-	11	14	1	1	1	1	3	3	65 - 69
-	-	5	7	2	2	-	2	2	2	70 - 74
-	1	1	3	-	1	4	8	-	1	75 - 84
-	-	1	-	-	-	-	3	-	-	85 and over
										Migrants in households
25	**17**	**381**	**345**	**92**	**95**	**163**	**162**	**71**	**79**	**All ages 1 and over**
4	2	34	24	4	11	11	7	7	5	1 - 4
1	1	19	27	7	7	9	7	4	7	5 - 9
2	-	17	17	7	3	2	3	6	1	10 - 14
-	-	2	1	1	-	1	1	-	1	15
-	-	3	5	-	-	2	2	-	2	16
-	-	-	4	-	1	1	5	-	2	17
1	-	8	8	1	4	5	9	2	2	18 - 19
7	4	59	59	11	12	44	50	8	14	20 - 24
1	2	52	54	17	10	29	20	4	9	25 - 28
1	1	13	12	4	3	3	-	4	3	29
-	2	53	29	12	11	16	14	8	8	30 - 34
1	-	24	18	7	10	11	11	5	3	35 - 39
1	-	25	21	6	5	9	5	5	7	40 - 44
1	-	20	15	2	4	7	10	5	4	45 - 49
2	4	19	12	5	4	3	3	5	5	50 - 54
2	-	8	11	2	3	1	2	1	1	55 - 59
-	-	7	5	3	3	5	1	2	-	60 - 64
1	-	11	14	1	1	1	1	3	3	65 - 69
-	-	5	7	2	2	-	2	2	2	70 - 74
-	1	1	2	-	1	3	7	-	-	75 - 84
-	-	1	-	-	-	-	2	-	-	85 and over

15. Residents with different address one year before census

Age	TOTAL PERSONS	Total males	Total females	Moved within wards		Between wards but within district		Between districts but within county	
				Males	Females	Males	Females	Males	Females
a	b	c	d	e	f	g	h	i	j
				Carlisle					
All migrants									
ALL AGES 1 AND OVER	**9,806**	**4,781**	**5,025**	**1,119**	**1,176**	**2,266**	**2,469**	**357**	**345**
1 - 4	728	356	372	94	72	167	192	25	22
5 - 9	624	335	289	92	74	141	123	18	15
10 - 14	461	223	238	64	79	103	107	7	7
15	79	36	43	8	9	23	21	2	1
16	86	42	44	12	14	16	19	3	6
17	115	43	72	8	8	21	53	6	3
18 - 19	458	171	287	36	46	86	155	16	30
20 - 24	1,783	813	970	162	182	409	540	58	75
25 - 28	1,217	667	550	144	110	329	273	51	46
29	217	103	114	23	24	53	58	9	5
30 - 34	952	513	439	109	107	241	199	38	29
35 - 39	640	336	304	77	71	156	147	19	14
40 - 44	500	275	225	60	48	127	96	24	17
45 - 49	351	186	165	40	50	78	62	19	17
50 - 54	268	143	125	36	35	64	44	14	7
55 - 59	215	107	108	25	30	47	50	10	7
60 - 64	233	112	121	35	35	47	51	10	12
65 - 69	229	110	119	26	41	59	55	7	10
70 - 74	194	73	121	27	46	33	50	7	6
75 - 84	311	103	208	28	62	50	114	10	9
85 and over	145	34	111	13	33	16	60	4	7
Migrants in households									
All ages 1 and over	**9,276**	**4,529**	**4,747**	**1,086**	**1,120**	**2,150**	**2,312**	**325**	**318**
1 - 4	723	355	368	94	71	166	191	25	20
5 - 9	614	328	286	92	74	138	121	15	14
10 - 14	443	216	227	64	79	97	101	6	6
15	67	30	37	8	9	19	19	-	1
16	83	40	43	12	14	16	18	2	6
17	108	40	68	8	7	20	52	6	1
18 - 19	440	157	283	32	46	83	153	14	29
20 - 24	1,724	778	946	156	178	401	532	55	73
25 - 28	1,179	636	543	141	110	323	271	51	45
29	211	99	112	23	24	53	57	9	5
30 - 34	938	501	437	109	107	239	198	35	28
35 - 39	620	317	303	74	71	150	146	15	14
40 - 44	490	266	224	59	48	122	96	22	17
45 - 49	341	177	164	39	50	72	61	18	17
50 - 54	264	140	124	36	35	62	43	14	7
55 - 59	211	104	107	25	30	45	50	10	7
60 - 64	210	100	110	33	33	38	45	9	9
65 - 69	204	97	107	25	38	48	48	7	8
70 - 74	166	57	109	25	43	20	41	6	6
75 - 84	200	78	122	24	46	34	56	5	3
85 and over	40	13	27	7	7	4	13	1	2

Between counties but within region		Between regions or from Scotland		From outside GB		Between neighbouring districts		Between neighbouring counties/Scottish Regions		Age
Males	Females	Males	Females	Males	Females	Males	Females	Males	Females	
k	l	m	n	o	p	q	r	s	t	a
										All migrants
115	**146**	**784**	**763**	**140**	**126**	**366**	**373**	**242**	**262**	**ALL AGES 1 AND OVER**
10	12	57	57	3	17	24	26	18	27	1 - 4
7	14	65	56	12	7	25	24	22	15	5 - 9
2	6	41	32	6	7	10	9	9	13	10 - 14
-	3	3	7	-	2	2	2	2	4	15
1	-	9	5	1	-	4	5	2	1	16
2	-	5	5	1	3	5	3	3	3	17
5	9	25	40	3	7	12	25	8	15	18 - 19
20	28	141	123	23	22	61	79	34	41	20 - 24
15	14	104	88	24	19	51	46	36	30	25 - 28
2	9	11	15	5	3	8	8	2	7	29
17	14	91	84	17	6	38	33	30	27	30 - 34
9	6	65	59	10	7	19	22	18	15	35 - 39
5	4	48	49	11	11	25	16	15	12	40 - 44
4	6	38	28	7	2	21	17	16	12	45 - 49
2	4	20	28	7	7	12	7	4	9	50 - 54
2	2	17	16	6	3	9	9	6	3	55 - 59
5	3	14	18	1	2	12	12	4	5	60 - 64
2	4	14	9	2	-	7	8	5	4	65 - 69
-	4	6	15	-	-	5	5	-	5	70 - 74
5	1	9	21	1	1	12	11	7	9	75 - 84
-	3	1	8	-	-	4	6	1	5	85 and over
										Migrants in households
110	**138**	**732**	**735**	**126**	**124**	**339**	**348**	**230**	**249**	**All ages 1 and over**
10	12	57	57	3	17	24	26	18	27	1 - 4
7	14	64	56	12	7	24	23	22	15	5 - 9
2	5	41	29	6	7	9	9	9	11	10 - 14
-	1	3	5	-	2	1	2	2	2	15
1	-	8	5	1	-	3	5	2	1	16
2	-	4	5	-	3	5	1	3	3	17
4	9	22	39	2	7	10	24	5	14	18 - 19
19	26	125	117	22	20	57	77	31	40	20 - 24
14	14	89	84	18	19	51	45	32	29	25 - 28
2	9	9	14	3	3	8	8	2	7	29
16	14	85	84	17	6	36	32	29	27	30 - 34
9	6	61	59	8	7	16	22	17	15	35 - 39
4	4	48	48	11	11	24	16	15	12	40 - 44
4	6	37	28	7	2	20	17	16	12	45 - 49
2	4	20	28	6	7	12	7	4	9	50 - 54
2	2	16	15	6	3	9	9	6	3	55 - 59
5	3	14	18	1	2	11	9	4	5	60 - 64
2	4	13	9	2	-	7	6	5	4	65 - 69
-	4	6	15	-	-	4	5	-	5	70 - 74
5	1	9	15	1	1	7	5	7	7	75 - 84
-	-	1	5	-	-	1	-	1	1	85 and over

15. Residents with different address one year before census

Age	TOTAL PERSONS	Total males	Total females	Moved within wards		Between wards but within district		Between districts but within county	
				Males	Females	Males	Females	Males	Females
a	b	c	d	e	f	g	h	i	j
				Copeland					
All migrants									
ALL AGES 1 AND OVER	**5,978**	**3,029**	**2,949**	**913**	**859**	**1,387**	**1,454**	**188**	**214**
1 - 4	525	280	245	111	82	128	131	13	9
5 - 9	429	238	191	72	65	115	94	11	8
10 - 14	273	131	142	54	46	51	59	4	12
15	47	20	27	8	9	7	14	3	4
16	42	21	21	5	6	12	12	2	1
17	80	39	41	14	12	19	20	2	4
18 - 19	214	80	134	24	38	42	76	5	9
20 - 24	1,117	538	579	117	137	251	294	35	51
25 - 28	831	452	379	146	94	210	200	19	28
29	163	82	81	23	23	37	42	10	10
30 - 34	609	343	266	99	88	152	117	34	19
35 - 39	386	205	181	67	53	95	87	8	8
40 - 44	326	175	151	51	49	84	71	15	13
45 - 49	184	95	89	21	24	46	45	5	4
50 - 54	148	76	72	25	25	21	29	4	2
55 - 59	102	62	40	14	12	30	14	3	6
60 - 64	121	53	68	18	23	20	30	5	3
65 - 69	109	51	58	23	26	22	23	2	5
70 - 74	98	44	54	7	22	26	25	5	2
75 - 84	114	34	80	13	14	14	45	3	12
85 and over	60	10	50	1	11	5	26	-	4
Migrants in households									
All ages 1 and over	**5,730**	**2,917**	**2,813**	**907**	**843**	**1,367**	**1,387**	**177**	**196**
1 - 4	518	278	240	111	82	126	129	13	7
5 - 9	429	238	191	72	65	115	94	11	8
10 - 14	270	129	141	54	46	50	59	4	11
15	46	20	26	8	9	7	13	3	4
16	42	21	21	5	6	12	12	2	1
17	79	39	40	14	12	19	20	2	4
18 - 19	207	78	129	24	37	41	73	5	9
20 - 24	1,047	495	552	117	137	250	287	32	49
25 - 28	810	438	372	145	93	209	199	18	28
29	159	78	81	23	23	37	42	9	10
30 - 34	589	329	260	98	87	152	117	33	17
35 - 39	383	203	180	67	53	95	87	8	8
40 - 44	323	173	150	51	49	84	70	15	13
45 - 49	183	94	89	21	24	46	45	5	4
50 - 54	146	74	72	25	25	20	29	4	2
55 - 59	99	59	40	14	12	30	14	2	6
60 - 64	119	51	68	18	23	19	30	4	3
65 - 69	104	49	55	23	25	21	22	1	4
70 - 74	84	41	43	7	18	24	19	4	1
75 - 84	74	26	48	10	12	10	23	2	5
85 and over	19	4	15	-	5	-	3	-	2

Between counties but within region: Males	Between counties but within region: Females	Between regions or from Scotland: Males	Between regions or from Scotland: Females	From outside GB: Males	From outside GB: Females	Between neighbouring districts: Males	Between neighbouring districts: Females	Between neighbouring counties/Scottish Regions: Males	Between neighbouring counties/Scottish Regions: Females	Age
k	l	m	n	o	p	q	r	s	t	a
										All migrants
53	**42**	**414**	**310**	**74**	**70**	**167**	**193**	**57**	**44**	**ALL AGES 1 AND OVER**
2	1	21	15	5	7	13	9	2	1	1 - 4
2	3	27	17	11	4	10	7	2	2	5 - 9
-	1	16	22	6	2	1	11	2	4	10 - 14
-	-	2	-	-	-	3	4	-	-	15
-	1	2	-	-	1	2	1	-	-	16
-	1	1	2	3	2	2	4	-	-	17
2	1	7	8	-	2	4	7	4	1	18 - 19
22	11	104	72	9	14	30	44	15	12	20 - 24
9	9	60	37	8	11	16	28	5	4	25 - 28
3	1	7	5	2	-	9	10	2	2	29
2	2	46	33	10	7	34	18	5	3	30 - 34
3	1	28	25	4	7	8	8	4	-	35 - 39
2	2	22	14	1	2	13	12	2	3	40 - 44
3	1	15	8	5	7	4	3	4	1	45 - 49
-	1	22	14	4	1	3	2	2	4	50 - 54
1	-	12	6	2	2	3	6	5	-	55 - 59
-	2	8	10	2	-	4	2	-	1	60 - 64
-	-	4	3	-	1	1	4	1	1	65 - 69
1	1	4	4	1	-	5	2	-	1	70 - 74
1	2	2	7	1	-	2	9	-	3	75 - 84
-	1	4	8	-	-	-	2	2	1	85 and over
										Migrants in households
42	**36**	**352**	**283**	**72**	**68**	**157**	**178**	**47**	**38**	**All ages 1 and over**
2	1	21	14	5	7	13	7	2	1	1 - 4
2	3	27	17	11	4	10	7	2	2	5 - 9
-	1	15	22	6	2	1	11	2	4	10 - 14
-	-	2	-	-	-	3	4	-	-	15
-	1	2	-	-	1	2	1	-	-	16
-	1	1	2	3	1	2	4	-	-	17
1	1	7	7	-	2	4	7	4	1	18 - 19
15	8	73	58	8	13	27	43	9	9	20 - 24
8	8	51	33	7	11	15	28	5	2	25 - 28
2	1	5	5	2	-	8	10	1	2	29
2	2	34	30	10	7	33	16	5	3	30 - 34
3	1	26	24	4	7	8	8	4	-	35 - 39
1	2	21	14	1	2	13	12	1	3	40 - 44
3	1	14	8	5	7	4	3	4	1	45 - 49
-	1	21	14	4	1	3	2	1	4	50 - 54
1	-	10	6	2	2	2	6	4	-	55 - 59
-	2	8	10	2	-	3	2	-	1	60 - 64
-	-	4	3	-	1	1	3	1	1	65 - 69
1	1	4	4	1	-	4	1	-	1	70 - 74
1	1	2	7	1	-	1	3	-	3	75 - 84
-	-	4	5	-	-	-	-	2	-	85 and over

15. Residents with different address one year before census

Age	TOTAL PERSONS	Total males	Total females	Moved within wards		Between wards but within district		Between districts but within county	
				Males	Females	Males	Females	Males	Females
a	b	c	d	e	f	g	h	i	j
				Eden					
All migrants									
ALL AGES 1 AND OVER	**4,335**	**2,134**	**2,201**	**577**	**549**	**776**	**805**	**210**	**244**
1 - 4	315	167	148	42	38	67	51	15	14
5 - 9	248	118	130	32	37	45	38	12	15
10 - 14	175	92	83	24	20	40	35	10	7
15	37	24	13	4	5	10	5	2	1
16	46	22	24	9	8	6	9	2	2
17	45	27	18	6	6	14	8	3	1
18 - 19	156	55	101	12	23	18	39	4	8
20 - 24	689	317	372	87	94	109	157	27	29
25 - 28	529	260	269	86	62	92	93	26	33
29	103	62	41	14	9	24	19	5	2
30 - 34	466	235	231	62	46	100	85	19	25
35 - 39	278	152	126	36	23	63	48	14	17
40 - 44	241	147	94	33	27	54	30	14	14
45 - 49	199	99	100	21	22	31	32	14	17
50 - 54	154	81	73	23	13	23	25	10	8
55 - 59	100	53	47	16	13	12	16	4	4
60 - 64	140	65	75	22	25	20	24	8	8
65 - 69	110	52	58	17	26	16	14	7	10
70 - 74	73	33	40	13	8	5	17	5	2
75 - 84	148	55	93	16	26	18	34	5	16
85 and over	83	18	65	2	18	9	26	4	11
Migrants in households									
All ages 1 and over	**4,063**	**2,018**	**2,045**	**561**	**516**	**747**	**749**	**190**	**214**
1 - 4	315	167	148	42	38	67	51	15	14
5 - 9	248	118	130	32	37	45	38	12	15
10 - 14	174	91	83	24	20	40	35	10	7
15	35	22	13	4	5	10	5	2	1
16	45	22	23	9	8	6	8	2	2
17	43	26	17	6	6	13	8	3	1
18 - 19	132	46	86	12	22	15	37	3	8
20 - 24	646	290	356	84	92	107	155	23	27
25 - 28	516	253	263	86	59	91	93	24	32
29	103	62	41	14	9	24	19	5	2
30 - 34	453	223	230	59	46	100	85	18	25
35 - 39	275	149	126	36	23	63	48	14	17
40 - 44	238	145	93	33	27	54	30	14	14
45 - 49	195	96	99	20	22	31	32	14	17
50 - 54	152	79	73	23	13	22	25	10	8
55 - 59	99	52	47	16	13	12	16	4	4
60 - 64	138	64	74	22	25	20	23	7	8
65 - 69	102	51	51	17	25	16	11	6	7
70 - 74	58	27	31	11	7	3	11	3	1
75 - 84	80	30	50	11	16	6	15	-	4
85 and over	16	5	11	-	3	2	4	1	-

Between counties but within region		Between regions or from Scotland		From outside GB		Between neighbouring districts		Between neighbouring counties/Scottish Regions		Age
Males	Females	Males	Females	Males	Females	Males	Females	Males	Females	
k	l	m	n	o	p	q	r	s	t	a
										All migrants
81	**92**	**433**	**453**	**57**	**58**	**217**	**256**	**105**	**132**	**ALL AGES 1 AND OVER**
7	9	34	33	2	3	14	19	9	14	1 - 4
2	6	26	30	1	4	13	15	8	6	5 - 9
4	4	14	15	-	2	9	6	2	8	10 - 14
1	-	7	2	-	-	2	1	1	1	15
1	1	4	4	-	-	2	2	2	1	16
-	-	4	3	-	-	3	1	-	1	17
7	9	13	16	1	6	3	10	4	9	18 - 19
14	15	64	71	16	6	28	32	13	20	20 - 24
7	8	41	59	8	14	27	35	12	16	25 - 28
3	-	14	8	2	3	6	2	6	3	29
5	9	43	57	6	9	20	24	7	14	30 - 34
5	10	29	24	5	4	16	20	9	9	35 - 39
5	1	35	18	6	4	16	14	11	3	40 - 44
2	4	26	25	5	-	14	17	5	10	45 - 49
4	1	18	24	3	2	9	6	7	3	50 - 54
3	2	17	12	1	-	4	6	2	2	55 - 59
1	2	13	16	1	-	8	7	1	3	60 - 64
3	4	9	4	-	-	8	11	1	2	65 - 69
3	2	7	11	-	-	6	2	2	2	70 - 74
4	4	12	12	-	1	5	14	3	3	75 - 84
-	1	3	9	-	-	4	12	-	2	85 and over
										Migrants in households
72	**84**	**398**	**427**	**50**	**55**	**199**	**227**	**98**	**122**	**All ages 1 and over**
7	9	34	33	2	3	14	19	9	14	1 - 4
2	6	26	30	1	4	13	15	8	6	5 - 9
4	4	13	15	-	2	9	6	2	8	10 - 14
-	-	6	2	-	-	2	1	1	1	15
1	1	4	4	-	-	2	2	2	1	16
-	-	4	2	-	-	3	1	-	1	17
3	4	12	11	1	4	2	9	3	5	18 - 19
12	14	51	63	13	5	26	31	12	19	20 - 24
7	8	38	57	7	14	25	34	11	16	25 - 28
3	-	14	8	2	3	6	2	6	3	29
4	8	38	57	4	9	19	24	5	13	30 - 34
5	10	27	24	4	4	16	20	9	9	35 - 39
5	1	33	17	6	4	16	14	10	2	40 - 44
1	4	25	24	5	-	14	17	5	9	45 - 49
4	1	17	24	3	2	9	6	6	3	50 - 54
3	2	16	12	1	-	4	6	2	2	55 - 59
1	2	13	16	1	-	7	7	1	3	60 - 64
3	4	9	4	-	-	7	8	1	2	65 - 69
3	2	7	10	-	-	4	1	2	2	70 - 74
4	4	9	10	-	1	-	4	3	2	75 - 84
-	-	2	4	-	-	1	-	-	1	85 and over

Table 15 Migrants - continued

15. Residents with different address one year before census

Age	TOTAL PERSONS	Total males	Total females	Moved within wards		Between wards but within district		Between districts but within county	
				Males	Females	Males	Females	Males	Females
a	b	c	d	e	f	g	h	i	j
South Lakeland									
All migrants									
ALL AGES 1 AND OVER	**9,616**	**4,619**	**4,997**	**1,019**	**1,043**	**1,719**	**1,901**	**351**	**374**
1 - 4	538	295	243	75	59	104	96	20	19
5 - 9	465	248	217	66	57	87	68	21	16
10 - 14	310	155	155	33	38	69	54	14	14
15	61	33	28	9	9	13	11	3	4
16	85	46	39	14	5	15	16	1	1
17	104	51	53	11	13	14	19	4	8
18 - 19	416	169	247	23	47	69	97	17	19
20 - 24	1,722	737	985	148	170	284	399	47	51
25 - 28	1,246	638	608	143	129	246	232	47	43
29	237	130	107	28	21	47	54	9	5
30 - 34	922	474	448	94	80	187	164	34	44
35 - 39	644	346	298	73	64	113	96	36	21
40 - 44	547	300	247	74	50	109	90	27	16
45 - 49	407	214	193	40	27	79	75	15	16
50 - 54	325	164	161	34	33	69	59	6	6
55 - 59	281	150	131	40	31	49	34	6	7
60 - 64	306	129	177	32	49	37	53	7	14
65 - 69	231	111	120	22	30	40	53	7	4
70 - 74	196	83	113	20	30	37	42	11	7
75 - 84	384	119	265	29	75	44	111	14	24
85 and over	189	27	162	11	26	7	78	5	35
Migrants in households									
All ages 1 and over	**8,687**	**4,230**	**4,457**	**967**	**966**	**1,644**	**1,740**	**287**	**292**
1 - 4	535	295	240	75	57	104	96	20	19
5 - 9	460	246	214	66	56	87	68	21	16
10 - 14	304	150	154	32	38	68	54	12	14
15	60	32	28	9	9	12	11	3	4
16	74	40	34	13	5	15	15	1	1
17	79	38	41	10	11	14	18	2	5
18 - 19	322	129	193	21	42	63	86	10	13
20 - 24	1,500	634	866	137	160	274	390	37	42
25 - 28	1,158	585	573	135	125	234	229	40	40
29	227	124	103	27	20	47	53	9	5
30 - 34	884	447	437	90	78	182	162	32	44
35 - 39	611	322	289	69	63	107	93	34	21
40 - 44	525	286	239	73	50	106	89	24	16
45 - 49	382	200	182	39	27	76	70	14	15
50 - 54	317	163	154	34	31	69	58	6	6
55 - 59	275	148	127	40	31	48	32	6	6
60 - 64	298	126	172	31	49	37	52	5	10
65 - 69	220	108	112	22	26	38	51	6	4
70 - 74	168	69	99	19	28	33	35	2	4
75 - 84	243	79	164	22	54	29	59	2	6
85 and over	45	9	36	3	6	1	19	1	1

Between counties but within region		Between regions or from Scotland		From outside GB		Between neighbouring districts		Between neighbouring counties/Scottish Regions		Age
Males	Females	Males	Females	Males	Females	Males	Females	Males	Females	
k	l	m	n	o	p	q	r	s	t	a
										All migrants
85	**100**	**1,271**	**1,373**	**174**	**206**	**493**	**526**	**386**	**425**	**ALL AGES 1 AND OVER**
4	5	85	57	7	7	33	27	25	19	1 - 4
9	7	56	62	9	7	32	22	20	22	5 - 9
2	5	33	36	4	8	17	14	6	9	10 - 14
-	-	8	4	-	-	4	4	2	-	15
1	2	14	13	1	2	2	3	5	2	16
-	1	19	11	3	1	5	8	4	3	17
3	11	50	62	7	11	21	22	16	20	18 - 19
24	22	193	283	41	60	59	83	60	82	20 - 24
10	15	162	156	30	33	63	63	49	52	25 - 28
4	-	41	24	1	3	12	10	10	6	29
8	8	135	135	16	17	55	58	35	32	30 - 34
9	8	98	93	17	16	53	31	31	31	35 - 39
2	4	78	79	10	8	33	22	25	28	40 - 44
2	3	71	62	7	10	18	20	22	24	45 - 49
2	1	50	56	3	6	10	13	15	15	50 - 54
1	1	49	52	5	6	11	13	15	19	55 - 59
2	4	45	52	6	5	15	21	18	15	60 - 64
2	1	36	29	4	3	11	8	9	9	65 - 69
-	1	13	32	2	1	13	11	5	8	70 - 74
-	1	31	52	1	2	20	32	13	20	75 - 84
-	-	4	23	-	-	6	41	1	9	85 and over
										Migrants in households
63	**72**	**1,124**	**1,216**	**145**	**171**	**415**	**428**	**336**	**377**	**All ages 1 and over**
4	5	85	56	7	7	33	27	25	19	1 - 4
9	7	54	60	9	7	31	21	19	21	5 - 9
2	5	32	35	4	8	15	14	5	9	10 - 14
-	-	8	4	-	-	4	4	2	-	15
-	-	10	11	1	2	2	3	5	2	16
-	-	10	6	2	1	2	5	2	2	17
1	4	29	42	5	6	14	16	11	15	18 - 19
14	12	146	220	26	42	46	69	42	66	20 - 24
5	9	149	145	22	25	55	60	43	48	25 - 28
3	-	37	22	1	3	12	10	9	6	29
7	8	121	128	15	17	50	57	32	29	30 - 34
8	8	89	89	15	15	48	31	27	30	35 - 39
2	2	71	74	10	8	30	21	23	22	40 - 44
1	3	63	59	7	8	17	19	19	23	45 - 49
2	1	49	52	3	6	10	13	15	15	50 - 54
1	1	48	52	5	5	11	12	15	19	55 - 59
2	4	45	52	6	5	13	17	18	15	60 - 64
2	1	36	27	4	3	10	7	9	8	65 - 69
-	1	13	30	2	1	4	8	5	8	70 - 74
-	1	25	42	1	2	6	13	9	17	75 - 84
-	-	4	10	-	-	2	1	1	3	85 and over

Note: * May include a small number of households with no adults

16. Wholly moving households; residents in such households

Household composition and number of residents	ALL TYPES OF MOVE	Moved within wards	Between wards but within district	Between districts but within county	Between counties but within region	Between regions or from Scotland	From outside GB	Between neigh-bouring districts	Between neigh-bouring counties/ Scottish Regions
a	b	c	d	e	f	g	h	i	j
CUMBRIA									
TOTAL WHOLLY MOVING HOUSEHOLDS	**12,705**	**3,345**	**5,781**	**909**	**229**	**2,149**	**292**	**970**	**579**
TOTAL PERSONS IN WHOLLY MOVING HOUSEHOLDS	**28,775**	**7,848**	**12,925**	**1,960**	**524**	**4,815**	**703**	**2,114**	**1,289**
*Wholly moving households with dependent children**									
Persons	16,103	4,669	7,233	963	289	2,531	418	1,059	677
All households	4,525	1,312	2,086	266	74	678	109	291	183
Wholly moving households, no dependent children, no person aged 60 or over									
Persons	9,080	2,020	4,245	791	164	1,634	226	823	427
All households	5,903	1,274	2,773	516	111	1,081	148	536	279
Single person households	3,249	679	1,570	278	63	578	81	290	146
Wholly moving households, no dependent children, no person aged under 60									
Persons	2,586	827	1,047	154	50	473	35	169	132
All households	1,838	618	753	103	34	307	23	114	91
Single person households	1,100	413	463	53	18	142	11	60	50
Other wholly moving households									
Persons	1,006	332	400	52	21	177	24	63	53
All households	439	141	169	24	10	83	12	29	26
Allerdale									
TOTAL WHOLLY MOVING HOUSEHOLDS	**2,395**	**783**	**977**	**197**	**51**	**342**	**45**	**191**	**74**
TOTAL PERSONS IN WHOLLY MOVING HOUSEHOLDS	**5,516**	**1,906**	**2,186**	**434**	**113**	**769**	**108**	**418**	**175**
*Wholly moving households with dependent children**									
Persons	3,212	1,212	1,266	217	54	388	75	204	98
All households	913	342	372	62	14	104	19	59	26
Wholly moving households, no dependent children, no person aged 60 or over									
Persons	1,628	448	655	188	43	269	25	186	55
All households	1,051	277	436	115	27	175	21	113	34
Single person households	575	144	261	52	14	87	17	50	15
Wholly moving households, no dependent children, no person aged under 60									
Persons	479	172	179	24	9	87	8	23	17
All households	344	130	132	18	7	52	5	17	12
Single person households	212	89	87	12	5	17	2	11	7
Other wholly moving households									
Persons	197	74	86	5	7	25	-	5	5
All households	87	34	37	2	3	11	-	2	2

Note: * May include a small number of households with no adults

16. Wholly moving households; residents in such households

Household composition and number of residents	ALL TYPES OF MOVE	Moved within wards	Between wards but within district	Between districts but within county	Between counties but within region	Between regions or from Scotland	From outside GB	Between neigh-bouring districts	Between neigh-bouring counties/ Scottish Regions
a	b	c	d	e	f	g	h	i	j
			Barrow-in-Furness						
TOTAL WHOLLY MOVING HOUSEHOLDS	**1,855**	**475**	**996**	**104**	**11**	**218**	**51**	**86**	**46**
TOTAL PERSONS IN WHOLLY MOVING HOUSEHOLDS	**4,222**	**1,118**	**2,246**	**210**	**29**	**493**	**126**	**175**	**108**
*Wholly moving households with dependent children**									
Persons	2,436	655	1,308	100	20	289	64	87	64
All households	699	190	384	27	5	77	16	23	18
Wholly moving households, no dependent children, no person aged 60 or over									
Persons	1,435	347	782	88	7	160	51	69	34
All households	937	213	515	62	5	113	29	50	23
Single person households	528	113	291	39	3	70	12	33	13
Wholly moving households, no dependent children, no person aged under 60									
Persons	231	79	97	16	-	32	7	13	6
All households	169	59	72	12	-	22	4	10	3
Single person households	108	40	47	8	-	12	1	7	-
Other wholly moving households									
Persons	120	37	59	6	2	12	4	6	4
All households	50	13	25	3	1	6	2	3	2
			Carlisle						
TOTAL WHOLLY MOVING HOUSEHOLDS	**2,843**	**676**	**1,406**	**207**	**62**	**432**	**60**	**219**	**142**
TOTAL PERSONS IN WHOLLY MOVING HOUSEHOLDS	**6,285**	**1,515**	**3,046**	**424**	**145**	**992**	**163**	**463**	**330**
*Wholly moving households with dependent children**									
Persons	3,587	889	1,718	183	81	597	119	232	200
All households	1,014	254	499	51	20	159	31	65	52
Wholly moving households, no dependent children, no person aged 60 or over									
Persons	1,902	345	981	192	46	303	35	184	92
All households	1,299	229	675	129	31	212	23	128	64
Single person households	787	132	414	80	18	129	14	85	38
Wholly moving households, no dependent children, no person aged under 60									
Persons	622	216	275	41	12	77	1	36	24
All households	455	167	202	24	8	53	1	22	19
Single person households	291	119	130	8	4	29	1	9	14
Other wholly moving households									
Persons	174	65	72	8	6	15	8	11	14
All households	75	26	30	3	3	8	5	4	7

Note: * May include a small number of households with no adults

16. Wholly moving households; residents in such households

Household composition and number of residents	ALL TYPES OF MOVE	Moved within wards	Between wards but within district	Between districts but within county	Between counties but within region	Between regions or from Scotland	From outside GB	Between neigh-bouring districts	Between neigh-bouring counties/ Scottish Regions
a	b	c	d	e	f	g	h	i	j
			Copeland						
TOTAL WHOLLY MOVING HOUSEHOLDS	**1,675**	**518**	**824**	**101**	**19**	**180**	**33**	**94**	**27**
TOTAL PERSONS IN WHOLLY MOVING HOUSEHOLDS	**3,968**	**1,276**	**1,950**	**216**	**37**	**403**	**86**	**204**	**53**
*Wholly moving households with dependent children**									
Persons	2,436	839	1,193	104	20	224	56	101	27
All households	678	230	341	29	6	57	15	28	7
Wholly moving households, no dependent children, no person aged 60 or over									
Persons	1,152	304	581	90	13	140	24	86	20
All households	747	198	367	58	10	98	16	55	15
Single person households	417	112	204	29	7	56	9	27	10
Wholly moving households, no dependent children, no person aged under 60									
Persons	282	94	144	15	4	24	1	10	6
All households	207	71	104	10	3	18	1	7	5
Single person households	133	49	64	5	2	12	1	4	4
Other wholly moving households									
Persons	98	39	32	7	-	15	5	7	-
All households	43	19	12	4	-	7	1	4	-
			Eden						
TOTAL WHOLLY MOVING HOUSEHOLDS	**1,236**	**312**	**465**	**131**	**49**	**251**	**28**	**132**	**59**
TOTAL PERSONS IN WHOLLY MOVING HOUSEHOLDS	**2,874**	**724**	**1,100**	**297**	**109**	**587**	**57**	**304**	**141**
*Wholly moving households with dependent children**									
Persons	1,552	373	621	148	56	325	29	152	88
All households	422	102	168	40	14	89	9	40	25
Wholly moving households, no dependent children, no person aged 60 or over									
Persons	925	230	342	104	33	189	27	107	43
All households	583	139	221	65	23	117	18	66	28
Single person households	290	63	119	30	13	56	9	29	14
Wholly moving households, no dependent children, no person aged under 60									
Persons	263	87	71	27	17	60	1	27	8
All households	173	57	48	18	11	38	1	18	5
Single person households	83	27	25	9	5	16	1	9	2
Other wholly moving households									
Persons	134	34	66	18	3	13	-	18	2
All households	58	14	28	8	1	7	-	8	1

Note: * May include a small number of households with no adults

16. Wholly moving households; residents in such households

Household composition and number of residents	ALL TYPES OF MOVE	Moved within wards	Between wards but within district	Between districts but within county	Between counties but within region	Between regions or from Scotland	From outside GB	Between neigh-bouring districts	Between neigh-bouring counties/ Scottish Regions
a	b	c	d	e	f	g	h	i	j
			South Lakeland						
TOTAL WHOLLY MOVING HOUSEHOLDS	**2,701**	**581**	**1,113**	**169**	**37**	**726**	**75**	**248**	**231**
TOTAL PERSONS IN WHOLLY MOVING HOUSEHOLDS	**5,910**	**1,309**	**2,397**	**379**	**91**	**1,571**	**163**	**550**	**482**
*Wholly moving households with dependent children**									
Persons	2,880	701	1,127	211	58	708	75	283	200
All households	799	194	322	57	15	192	19	76	55
Wholly moving households, no dependent children, no person aged 60 or over									
Persons	2,038	346	904	129	22	573	64	191	183
All households	1,286	218	559	87	15	366	41	124	115
Single person households	652	115	281	48	8	180	20	66	56
Wholly moving households, no dependent children, no person aged under 60									
Persons	709	179	281	31	8	193	17	60	71
All households	490	134	195	21	5	124	11	40	47
Single person households	273	89	110	11	2	56	5	20	23
Other wholly moving households									
Persons	283	83	85	8	3	97	7	16	28
All households	126	35	37	4	2	44	4	8	14

Table 17 Ethnic group of migrants

17. Residents aged 1 and over

	TOTAL PERSONS	Ethnic group										Persons born in Ireland
		White	Black Caribbean	Black African	Black other	Indian	Pakistani	Bangladeshi	Chinese	Other groups		
										Asian	Other	
a	b	c	d	e	f	g	h	i	j	k	l	m
CUMBRIA												
TOTAL PERSONS	**477,264**	**475,188**	**107**	**80**	**254**	**268**	**92**	**133**	**445**	**168**	**529**	**3,758**
With different address one year before census (migrants)	44,448	43,990	22	25	41	67	17	36	85	52	113	409
Allerdale												
TOTAL PERSONS	**94,564**	**94,250**	**12**	**7**	**39**	**31**	**17**	**13**	**85**	**18**	**92**	**471**
With different address one year before census (migrants)	8,353	8,268	3	2	3	4	6	4	35	5	23	54
Barrow-in-Furness												
TOTAL PERSONS	**72,080**	**71,683**	**12**	**13**	**43**	**46**	**17**	**13**	**107**	**34**	**112**	**887**
With different address one year before census (migrants)	6,360	6,292	3	3	7	5	3	2	16	9	20	73
Carlisle												
TOTAL PERSONS	**99,248**	**98,657**	**23**	**22**	**65**	**99**	**20**	**81**	**121**	**40**	**120**	**950**
With different address one year before census (migrants)	9,806	9,674	2	7	12	24	3	29	20	10	25	108
Copeland												
TOTAL PERSONS	**70,377**	**70,105**	**24**	**10**	**42**	**37**	**18**	**6**	**48**	**39**	**48**	**479**
With different address one year before census (migrants)	5,978	5,912	5	3	3	16	5	-	3	16	15	56
Eden												
TOTAL PERSONS	**45,064**	**44,954**	**5**	**7**	**14**	**4**	**-**	**10**	**22**	**8**	**40**	**265**
With different address one year before census (migrants)	4,335	4,315	3	1	1	-	-	-	-	5	10	36
South Lakeland												
TOTAL PERSONS	**95,931**	**95,539**	**31**	**21**	**51**	**51**	**20**	**10**	**62**	**29**	**117**	**706**
With different address one year before census (migrants)	9,616	9,529	6	9	15	18	-	1	11	7	20	82

18. Imputed residents of wholly absent households

Age, marital status, long-term illness, economic position and ethnic group	TOTAL PERSONS	Males	Females	Age, marital status, long-term illness, economic position and ethnic group	TOTAL PERSONS	Males	Females
a	b	c	d	a	b	c	d
	CUMBRIA				**Barrow-in-Furness**		
TOTAL PERSONS	**3,861**	**1,837**	**2,024**	**TOTAL PERSONS**	**764**	**369**	**395**
0 - 15	372	200	172	0 - 15	83	44	39
16 - 17	61	27	34	16 - 17	17	9	8
18 - 29	656	369	287	18 - 29	129	72	57
30 - 44	755	417	338	30 - 44	147	82	65
45 up to pensionable age	812	450	362	45 up to pensionable age	149	82	67
Pensionable age and over	1,205	374	831	Pensionable age and over	239	80	159
Single	1,288	708	580	Single	266	145	121
Married	1,674	855	819	Married	298	154	144
Widowed or divorced	899	274	625	Widowed or divorced	200	70	130
With limiting long-term illness	643	291	352	With limiting long-term illness	163	76	87
In employment	1,686	982	704	In employment	316	189	127
Unemployed	158	98	60	Unemployed	33	22	11
Economically inactive	1,645	557	1,088	Economically inactive	332	114	218
White	3,821	1,805	2,016	White	762	369	393
Other ethnic group	40	32	8	Other ethnic group	2	-	2
	Allerdale				**Carlisle**		
TOTAL PERSONS	**612**	**281**	**331**	**TOTAL PERSONS**	**708**	**358**	**350**
0 - 15	55	30	25	0 - 15	75	41	34
16 - 17	6	3	3	16 - 17	12	2	10
18 - 29	137	85	52	18 - 29	118	67	51
30 - 44	113	54	59	30 - 44	141	89	52
45 up to pensionable age	115	63	52	45 up to pensionable age	154	86	68
Pensionable age and over	186	46	140	Pensionable age and over	208	73	135
Single	229	128	101	Single	260	150	110
Married	240	125	115	Married	288	151	137
Widowed or divorced	143	28	115	Widowed or divorced	160	57	103
With limiting long-term illness	86	38	48	With limiting long-term illness	136	64	72
In employment	263	139	124	In employment	319	201	118
Unemployed	36	25	11	Unemployed	24	12	12
Economically inactive	258	87	171	Economically inactive	290	104	186
White	610	279	331	White	685	335	350
Other ethnic group	2	2	-	Other ethnic group	23	23	-

18. Imputed residents of wholly absent households

Age, marital status, long-term illness, economic position and ethnic group	TOTAL PERSONS	Males	Females
a	b	c	d
	Copeland		
TOTAL PERSONS	**491**	**244**	**247**
0 - 15	60	34	26
16 - 17	5	1	4
18 - 29	77	40	37
30 - 44	99	59	40
45 up to pensionable age	97	58	39
Pensionable age and over	153	52	101
Single	152	90	62
Married	217	110	107
Widowed or divorced	122	44	78
With limiting long-term illness	71	33	38
In employment	212	127	85
Unemployed	22	15	7
Economically inactive	197	68	129
White	486	241	245
Other ethnic group	5	3	2
	Eden		
TOTAL PERSONS	**358**	**170**	**188**
0 - 15	27	14	13
16 - 17	8	5	3
18 - 29	44	21	23
30 - 44	74	43	31
45 up to pensionable age	93	52	41
Pensionable age and over	112	35	77
Single	102	52	50
Married	181	89	92
Widowed or divorced	75	29	46
With limiting long-term illness	47	28	19
In employment	159	92	67
Unemployed	17	10	7
Economically inactive	155	54	101
White	354	167	187
Other ethnic group	4	3	1

Age, marital status, long-term illness, economic position and ethnic group	TOTAL PERSONS	Males	Females
a	b	c	d
	South Lakeland		
TOTAL PERSONS	**928**	**415**	**513**
0 - 15	72	37	35
16 - 17	13	7	6
18 - 29	151	84	67
30 - 44	181	90	91
45 up to pensionable age	204	109	95
Pensionable age and over	307	88	219
Single	279	143	136
Married	450	226	224
Widowed or divorced	199	46	153
With limiting long-term illness	140	52	88
In employment	417	234	183
Unemployed	26	14	12
Economically inactive	413	130	283
White	924	414	510
Other ethnic group	4	1	3

19. Wholly absent households with imputed residents; imputed residents in such households

	TOTAL HOUSEHOLDS	Households with the following persons			TOTAL RESIDENTS
		1	2	3 or more	
a	b	c	d	e	f
CUMBRIA					
ALL HOUSEHOLDS	**2,328**	**1,340**	**659**	**329**	**3,861**
Owner occupied	1,578	827	513	238	2,728
Rented privately	322	205	71	46	509
Rented from a housing association	102	78	17	7	136
Rented from a local authority or new town	276	201	46	29	398
Lacking or sharing use of a bath/shower and/or inside WC	88	82	4	2	98
No central heating	608	396	136	76	937
No car	889	732	110	47	1,122
1 person aged 16 and over with child(ren) aged 0 - 15	37		21	16	92
Allerdale					
ALL HOUSEHOLDS	**388**	**238**	**103**	**47**	**612**
Owner occupied	234	130	76	28	385
Rented privately	57	37	10	10	89
Rented from a housing association	29	22	5	2	41
Rented from a local authority or new town	54	39	9	6	78
Lacking or sharing use of a bath/shower and/or inside WC	20	18	2	-	22
No central heating	68	44	14	10	105
No car	139	119	15	5	166
1 person aged 16 and over with child(ren) aged 0 - 15	5		3	2	12
Barrow-in-Furness					
ALL HOUSEHOLDS	**458**	**274**	**104**	**80**	**764**
Owner occupied	307	171	78	58	537
Rented privately	58	36	12	10	92
Rented from a housing association	24	19	4	1	30
Rented from a local authority or new town	64	44	9	11	99
Lacking or sharing use of a bath/shower and/or inside WC	29	29	-	-	29
No central heating	177	113	36	28	283
No car	240	191	28	21	317
1 person aged 16 and over with child(ren) aged 0 - 15	7		3	4	18

19. Wholly absent households with imputed residents; imputed residents in such households

	TOTAL HOUSEHOLDS	Households with the following persons			TOTAL RESIDENTS
		1	2	3 or more	
a	b	c	d	e	f
Carlisle					
ALL HOUSEHOLDS	**425**	**257**	**105**	**63**	**708**
Owner occupied	286	159	84	43	489
Rented privately	54	36	9	9	89
Rented from a housing association	11	9	1	1	14
Rented from a local authority or new town	69	51	9	9	105
Lacking or sharing use of a bath/shower and/or inside WC	16	14	1	1	21
No central heating	130	92	21	17	199
No car	190	158	19	13	250
1 person aged 16 and over with child(ren) aged 0 - 15	6		3	3	16
Copeland					
ALL HOUSEHOLDS	**294**	**166**	**85**	**43**	**491**
Owner occupied	202	101	67	34	359
Rented privately	26	15	5	6	46
Rented from a housing association	26	20	5	1	33
Rented from a local authority or new town	34	26	7	1	44
Lacking or sharing use of a bath/shower and/or inside WC	5	4	-	1	7
No central heating	73	49	18	6	107
No car	111	89	19	3	137
1 person aged 16 and over with child(ren) aged 0 - 15	10		6	4	25
Eden					
ALL HOUSEHOLDS	**212**	**116**	**66**	**30**	**358**
Owner occupied	156	76	54	26	278
Rented privately	31	23	5	3	46
Rented from a housing association	4	3	1	-	5
Rented from a local authority or new town	15	11	4	-	19
Lacking or sharing use of a bath/shower and/or inside WC	6	5	1	-	7
No central heating	49	32	8	9	79
No car	55	49	5	1	62
1 person aged 16 and over with child(ren) aged 0 - 15	1		1	-	2

19. Wholly absent households with imputed residents; imputed residents in such households

	TOTAL HOUSEHOLDS	Households with the following persons			TOTAL RESIDENTS
		1	2	3 or more	
a	b	c	d	e	f
	South Lakeland				
ALL HOUSEHOLDS	**551**	**289**	**196**	**66**	**928**
Owner occupied	393	190	154	49	680
Rented privately	96	58	30	8	147
Rented from a housing association	8	5	1	2	13
Rented from a local authority or new town	40	30	8	2	53
Lacking or sharing use of a bath/shower and/or inside WC	12	12	-	-	12
No central heating	111	66	39	6	164
No car	154	126	24	4	190
1 person aged 16 and over with child(ren) aged 0 - 15	8		5	3	19

20. Households with residents; residents in households

Amenities	All permanent	Tenure of households in permanent buildings: Owner occupied: Owned outright	Owner occupied: Buying	Rented privately: Furnished	Rented privately: Un-furnished	Rented with a job or business	Rented from a housing association	Rented from a local authority or new town	Non-permanent accommodation	No car
a	b	c	d	e	f	g	h	i	j	k
				CUMBRIA						
TOTAL HOUSEHOLDS	**192,689**	**55,995**	**79,000**	**5,084**	**8,413**	**4,887**	**7,352**	**31,958**	**1,204**	**59,653**
Exclusive use of bath/shower	**191,023**	**55,550**	**78,921**	**4,615**	**8,083**	**4,851**	**7,282**	**31,721**	**990**	**58,279**
Exclusive use of inside WC	**190,452**	**55,255**	**78,856**	**4,594**	**7,992**	**4,829**	**7,277**	**31,649**	**947**	**57,938**
With central heating - all rooms	110,467	30,879	51,968	2,141	2,336	2,334	4,711	16,098	519	26,641
- some rooms	31,494	10,174	12,023	720	1,404	1,052	983	5,138	80	9,014
No central heating	48,491	14,202	14,865	1,733	4,252	1,443	1,583	10,413	348	22,283
Shared use of inside WC	**16**	**2**	**-**	**5**	**3**	**1**	**1**	**4**	**1**	**14**
With central heating - all rooms	7	1	-	1	1	-	1	3	1	7
- some rooms	2	-	-	1	-	1	-	-	-	2
No central heating	7	1	-	3	2	-	-	1	-	5
No inside WC	**555**	**293**	**65**	**16**	**88**	**21**	**4**	**68**	**42**	**327**
With central heating - all rooms	54	21	11	2	4	3	1	12	10	17
- some rooms	61	33	12	1	4	4	1	6	5	27
No central heating	440	239	42	13	80	14	2	50	27	283
Shared use of bath/shower	**813**	**17**	**17**	**435**	**62**	**19**	**52**	**211**	**69**	**681**
Exclusive use of inside WC	**224**	**1**	**3**	**14**	**4**	**2**	**11**	**189**	**24**	**222**
With central heating - all rooms	206	-	3	6	2	2	10	183	6	197
- some rooms	7	-	-	1	-	-	1	5	1	7
No central heating	11	1	-	7	2	-	-	1	17	18
Shared use of inside WC	**587**	**16**	**14**	**420**	**57**	**17**	**41**	**22**	**19**	**449**
With central heating - all rooms	195	8	6	112	9	7	35	18	5	150
- some rooms	37	2	4	24	3	3	-	1	1	20
No central heating	355	6	4	284	45	7	6	3	13	279
No inside WC	**2**	**-**	**-**	**1**	**1**	**-**	**-**	**-**	**26**	**10**
With central heating - all rooms	-	-	-	-	-	-	-	-	3	-
- some rooms	-	-	-	-	-	-	-	-	-	-
No central heating	2	-	-	1	1	-	-	-	23	10
No bath/shower	**853**	**428**	**62**	**34**	**268**	**17**	**18**	**26**	**145**	**693**
Exclusive use of inside WC	**244**	**118**	**28**	**8**	**58**	**4**	**12**	**16**	**40**	**202**
With central heating - all rooms	38	13	4	-	4	1	7	9	1	25
- some rooms	24	10	6	2	4	-	1	1	-	17
No central heating	182	95	18	6	50	3	4	6	39	160
Shared use of inside WC	**1**	**-**	**-**	**-**	**1**	**-**	**-**	**-**	**1**	**-**
With central heating - all rooms	1	-	-	-	1	-	-	-	-	-
- some rooms	-	-	-	-	-	-	-	-	-	-
No central heating	-	-	-	-	-	-	-	-	1	-
No inside WC	**608**	**310**	**34**	**26**	**209**	**13**	**6**	**10**	**104**	**491**
With central heating - all rooms	11	5	-	-	2	-	2	2	2	10
- some rooms	19	11	-	2	5	1	-	-	3	16
No central heating	578	294	34	24	202	12	4	8	99	465
No car	59,277	16,290	9,810	2,287	3,360	824	4,799	21,907	376	

20. Households with residents; residents in households

Amenities	All permanent	Tenure of households in permanent buildings: Owner occupied: Owned outright	Owner occupied: Buying	Rented privately: Furnished	Rented privately: Unfurnished	Rented with a job or business	Rented from a housing association	Rented from a local authority or new town	Non-permanent accommodation	No car
a	b	c	d	e	f	g	h	i	j	k
				CUMBRIA - *continued*						
TOTAL PERSONS IN HOUSEHOLDS	**472,505**	**112,580**	**232,063**	**8,986**	**17,371**	**13,524**	**15,010**	**72,971**	**2,282**	**108,592**
Exclusive use of bath/shower	**470,322**	**111,943**	**231,902**	**8,439**	**16,955**	**13,459**	**14,921**	**72,703**	**1,914**	**106,953**
Exclusive use of inside WC	**469,284**	**111,440**	**231,760**	**8,403**	**16,797**	**13,406**	**14,913**	**72,565**	**1,817**	**106,438**
With central heating - all rooms	279,111	63,903	155,627	4,029	5,140	6,463	8,852	35,097	962	47,827
- some rooms	79,222	20,827	35,782	1,404	3,184	3,111	2,306	12,608	169	17,147
No central heating	110,951	26,710	40,351	2,970	8,473	3,832	3,755	24,860	686	41,464
Shared use of inside WC	**23**	**2**	**-**	**7**	**3**	**5**	**1**	**5**	**2**	**21**
With central heating - all rooms	9	1	-	2	1	-	1	4	2	9
- some rooms	6	-	-	1	-	5	-	-	-	6
No central heating	8	1	-	4	2	-	-	1	-	6
No inside WC	**1,015**	**501**	**142**	**29**	**155**	**48**	**7**	**133**	**95**	**494**
With central heating - all rooms	119	46	30	3	13	5	2	20	26	26
- some rooms	134	61	30	2	11	11	1	18	11	42
No central heating	762	394	82	24	131	32	4	95	58	426
Shared use of bath/shower	**978**	**39**	**37**	**497**	**76**	**38**	**63**	**228**	**100**	**748**
Exclusive use of inside WC	**231**	**1**	**7**	**14**	**4**	**2**	**11**	**192**	**32**	**227**
With central heating - all rooms	213	-	7	6	2	2	10	186	6	200
- some rooms	7	-	-	1	-	-	1	5	1	7
No central heating	11	1	-	7	2	-	-	1	25	20
Shared use of inside WC	**745**	**38**	**30**	**482**	**71**	**36**	**52**	**36**	**24**	**510**
With central heating - all rooms	247	14	12	129	10	14	41	27	5	178
- some rooms	63	5	11	35	7	3	-	2	1	23
No central heating	435	19	7	318	54	19	11	7	18	309
No inside WC	**2**	**-**	**-**	**1**	**1**	**-**	**-**	**-**	**44**	**11**
With central heating - all rooms	-	-	-	-	-	-	-	-	4	-
- some rooms	-	-	-	-	-	-	-	-	-	-
No central heating	2	-	-	1	1	-	-	-	40	11
No bath/shower	**1,205**	**598**	**124**	**50**	**340**	**27**	**26**	**40**	**268**	**891**
Exclusive use of inside WC	**343**	**155**	**61**	**8**	**69**	**8**	**18**	**24**	**62**	**257**
With central heating - all rooms	59	17	11	-	7	1	10	13	1	33
- some rooms	36	13	14	2	5	-	1	1	-	26
No central heating	248	125	36	6	57	7	7	10	61	198
Shared use of inside WC	**1**	**-**	**-**	**-**	**1**	**-**	**-**	**-**	**2**	**-**
With central heating - all rooms	1	-	-	-	1	-	-	-	-	-
- some rooms	-	-	-	-	-	-	-	-	-	-
No central heating	-	-	-	-	-	-	-	-	2	-
No inside WC	**861**	**443**	**63**	**42**	**270**	**19**	**8**	**16**	**204**	**634**
With central heating - all rooms	18	8	-	-	3	-	3	4	3	15
- some rooms	21	12	-	2	6	1	-	-	4	17
No central heating	822	423	63	40	261	18	5	12	197	602
No car	108,037	22,725	23,215	3,450	5,134	1,574	8,331	43,608	555	

20. Households with residents; residents in households

Amenities	All permanent	Tenure of households in permanent buildings: Owner occupied: Owned outright	Owner occupied: Buying	Rented privately: Furnished	Rented privately: Un-furnished	Rented with a job or business	Rented from a housing associa-tion	Rented from a local authority or new town	Non-permanent accomm-odation	No car
a	b	c	d	e	f	g	h	i	j	k
				Allerdale						
TOTAL HOUSEHOLDS	**37,644**	**10,768**	**14,126**	**838**	**1,406**	**806**	**2,994**	**6,706**	**223**	**11,668**
Exclusive use of bath/shower	**37,340**	**10,689**	**14,108**	**765**	**1,335**	**802**	**2,964**	**6,677**	**192**	**11,427**
Exclusive use of inside WC	**37,223**	**10,616**	**14,097**	**760**	**1,314**	**800**	**2,963**	**6,673**	**184**	**11,366**
With central heating - all rooms	23,454	6,005	9,816	397	450	403	1,890	4,493	99	6,401
- some rooms	5,358	1,879	2,102	115	204	161	318	579	20	1,356
No central heating	8,411	2,732	2,179	248	660	236	755	1,601	65	3,609
Shared use of inside WC	**3**	**1**	**-**	**1**	**1**	**-**	**-**	**-**	**1**	**3**
With central heating - all rooms	2	1	-	-	1	-	-	-	1	2
- some rooms	-	-	-	-	-	-	-	-	-	-
No central heating	1	-	-	1	-	-	-	-	-	1
No inside WC	**114**	**72**	**11**	**4**	**20**	**2**	**1**	**4**	**7**	**58**
With central heating - all rooms	16	6	3	1	2	1	1	2	1	2
- some rooms	7	4	2	-	1	-	-	-	2	2
No central heating	91	62	6	3	17	1	-	2	4	54
Shared use of bath/shower	**135**	**1**	**8**	**60**	**18**	**1**	**21**	**26**	**12**	**113**
Exclusive use of inside WC	**41**	**-**	**2**	**4**	**3**	**1**	**8**	**23**	**2**	**38**
With central heating - all rooms	38	-	2	3	1	1	8	23	1	35
- some rooms	-	-	-	-	-	-	-	-	-	-
No central heating	3	-	-	1	2	-	-	-	1	3
Shared use of inside WC	**94**	**1**	**6**	**56**	**15**	**-**	**13**	**3**	**8**	**74**
With central heating - all rooms	53	1	2	28	6	-	13	3	3	42
- some rooms	3	-	-	3	-	-	-	-	-	3
No central heating	38	-	4	25	9	-	-	-	5	29
No inside WC	**-**	**-**	**-**	**-**	**-**	**-**	**-**	**-**	**2**	**1**
With central heating - all rooms	-	-	-	-	-	-	-	-	-	-
- some rooms	-	-	-	-	-	-	-	-	-	-
No central heating	-	-	-	-	-	-	-	-	2	1
No bath/shower	**169**	**78**	**10**	**13**	**53**	**3**	**9**	**3**	**19**	**128**
Exclusive use of inside WC	**57**	**26**	**5**	**2**	**14**	**1**	**7**	**2**	**6**	**42**
With central heating - all rooms	8	1	1	-	1	-	4	1	-	6
- some rooms	7	2	2	-	2	-	-	1	-	5
No central heating	42	23	2	2	11	1	3	-	6	31
Shared use of inside WC	**-**	**-**	**-**	**-**	**-**	**-**	**-**	**-**	**-**	**-**
With central heating - all rooms	-	-	-	-	-	-	-	-	-	-
- some rooms	-	-	-	-	-	-	-	-	-	-
No central heating	-	-	-	-	-	-	-	-	-	-
No inside WC	**112**	**52**	**5**	**11**	**39**	**2**	**2**	**1**	**13**	**86**
With central heating - all rooms	1	1	-	-	-	-	-	-	1	2
- some rooms	3	2	-	1	-	-	-	-	-	2
No central heating	108	49	5	10	39	2	2	1	12	82
No car	11,605	2,974	1,284	370	587	134	1,838	4,418	63	

20. Households with residents; residents in households

Amenities	All permanent	Tenure of households in permanent buildings: Owner occupied		Rented privately		Rented with a job or business	Rented from a housing association	Rented from a local authority or new town	Non-permanent accommodation	No car
		Owned outright	Buying	Furnished	Un-furnished					
a	b	c	d	e	f	g	h	i	j	k
				Allerdale - *continued*						
TOTAL PERSONS IN HOUSEHOLDS	**93,507**	**22,478**	**42,430**	**1,434**	**2,887**	**2,187**	**6,608**	**15,483**	**428**	**21,073**
Exclusive use of bath/shower	**93,140**	**22,373**	**42,402**	**1,352**	**2,806**	**2,181**	**6,573**	**15,453**	**374**	**20,796**
Exclusive use of inside WC	**92,928**	**22,253**	**42,376**	**1,344**	**2,761**	**2,178**	**6,571**	**15,445**	**356**	**20,711**
With central heating - all rooms	59,492	12,878	29,940	722	990	1,092	3,876	9,994	185	11,464
- some rooms	13,736	4,022	6,312	209	479	466	764	1,484	36	2,526
No central heating	19,700	5,353	6,124	413	1,292	620	1,931	3,967	135	6,721
Shared use of inside WC	**3**	**1**	**-**	**1**	**1**	**-**	**-**	**-**	**2**	**3**
With central heating - all rooms	2	1	-	-	1	-	-	-	2	2
- some rooms	-	-	-	-	-	-	-	-	-	-
No central heating	1	-	-	1	-	-	-	-	-	1
No inside WC	**209**	**119**	**26**	**7**	**44**	**3**	**2**	**8**	**16**	**82**
With central heating - all rooms	34	13	6	2	7	1	2	3	1	3
- some rooms	20	10	7	-	3	-	-	-	4	3
No central heating	155	96	13	5	34	2	-	5	11	76
Shared use of bath/shower	**146**	**2**	**12**	**65**	**19**	**1**	**21**	**26**	**13**	**118**
Exclusive use of inside WC	**42**	**-**	**3**	**4**	**3**	**1**	**8**	**23**	**2**	**38**
With central heating - all rooms	39	-	3	3	1	1	8	23	1	35
- some rooms	-	-	-	-	-	-	-	-	-	-
No central heating	3	-	-	1	2	-	-	-	1	3
Shared use of inside WC	**104**	**2**	**9**	**61**	**16**	**-**	**13**	**3**	**9**	**79**
With central heating - all rooms	58	2	2	32	6	-	13	3	3	44
- some rooms	3	-	-	3	-	-	-	-	-	3
No central heating	43	-	7	26	10	-	-	-	6	32
No inside WC	**-**	**-**	**-**	**-**	**-**	**-**	**-**	**-**	**2**	**1**
With central heating - all rooms	-	-	-	-	-	-	-	-	-	-
- some rooms	-	-	-	-	-	-	-	-	-	-
No central heating	-	-	-	-	-	-	-	-	2	1
No bath/shower	**221**	**103**	**16**	**17**	**62**	**5**	**14**	**4**	**41**	**159**
Exclusive use of inside WC	**75**	**33**	**7**	**2**	**15**	**3**	**12**	**3**	**8**	**53**
With central heating - all rooms	12	1	1	-	2	-	6	2	-	9
- some rooms	8	2	3	-	2	-	-	1	-	6
No central heating	55	30	3	2	11	3	6	-	8	38
Shared use of inside WC	**-**	**-**	**-**	**-**	**-**	**-**	**-**	**-**	**-**	**-**
With central heating - all rooms	-	-	-	-	-	-	-	-	-	-
- some rooms	-	-	-	-	-	-	-	-	-	-
No central heating	-	-	-	-	-	-	-	-	-	-
No inside WC	**146**	**70**	**9**	**15**	**47**	**2**	**2**	**1**	**33**	**106**
With central heating - all rooms	2	2	-	-	-	-	-	-	1	3
- some rooms	3	2	-	1	-	-	-	-	-	2
No central heating	141	66	9	14	47	2	2	1	32	101
No car	20,977	4,228	3,003	528	879	249	3,379	8,711	96	

20. Households with residents; residents in households

Amenities	All permanent	Tenure of households in permanent buildings							Non-permanent accomm-odation	No car
		Owner occupied		Rented privately		Rented with a job or business	Rented from a housing associa-tion	Rented from a local authority or new town		
		Owned outright	Buying	Furnished	Un-furnished					
a	b	c	d	e	f	g	h	i	j	k
				Barrow-in-Furness						
TOTAL HOUSEHOLDS	**29,342**	**9,005**	**13,967**	**815**	**1,100**	**269**	**348**	**3,838**	**285**	**11,705**
Exclusive use of bath/shower	**29,059**	**8,896**	**13,948**	**740**	**1,044**	**269**	**330**	**3,832**	**278**	**11,467**
Exclusive use of inside WC	**28,960**	**8,824**	**13,936**	**737**	**1,038**	**268**	**330**	**3,827**	**273**	**11,387**
With central heating - all rooms	12,785	3,668	7,400	212	85	151	223	1,046	225	3,067
- some rooms	4,193	1,253	1,776	60	56	33	32	983	10	1,768
No central heating	11,982	3,903	4,760	465	897	84	75	1,798	38	6,552
Shared use of inside WC	**1**	**1**	**-**	**-**	**-**	**-**	**-**	**-**	**-**	**-**
With central heating - all rooms	-	-	-	-	-	-	-	-	-	-
- some rooms	-	-	-	-	-	-	-	-	-	-
No central heating	1	1	-	-	-	-	-	-	-	-
No inside WC	**98**	**71**	**12**	**3**	**6**	**1**	**-**	**5**	**5**	**80**
With central heating - all rooms	6	3	1	-	-	-	-	2	-	3
- some rooms	5	4	1	-	-	-	-	-	1	3
No central heating	87	64	10	3	6	1	-	3	4	74
Shared use of bath/shower	**105**	**-**	**3**	**68**	**16**	**-**	**17**	**1**	**5**	**89**
Exclusive use of inside WC	**4**	**-**	**-**	**4**	**-**	**-**	**-**	**-**	**-**	**3**
With central heating - all rooms	-	-	-	-	-	-	-	-	-	-
- some rooms	-	-	-	-	-	-	-	-	-	-
No central heating	4	-	-	4	-	-	-	-	-	3
Shared use of inside WC	**100**	**-**	**3**	**64**	**15**	**-**	**17**	**1**	**2**	**83**
With central heating - all rooms	20	-	1	6	1	-	12	-	-	18
- some rooms	3	-	2	1	-	-	-	-	-	-
No central heating	77	-	-	57	14	-	5	1	2	65
No inside WC	**1**	**-**	**-**	**-**	**1**	**-**	**-**	**-**	**3**	**3**
With central heating - all rooms	-	-	-	-	-	-	-	-	-	-
- some rooms	-	-	-	-	-	-	-	-	-	-
No central heating	1	-	-	-	1	-	-	-	3	3
No bath/shower	**178**	**109**	**16**	**7**	**40**	**-**	**1**	**5**	**2**	**149**
Exclusive use of inside WC	**28**	**20**	**1**	**-**	**4**	**-**	**1**	**2**	**-**	**22**
With central heating - all rooms	3	1	-	-	-	-	1	1	-	1
- some rooms	2	2	-	-	-	-	-	-	-	2
No central heating	23	17	1	-	4	-	-	1	-	19
Shared use of inside WC	**-**	**-**	**-**	**-**	**-**	**-**	**-**	**-**	**-**	**-**
With central heating - all rooms	-	-	-	-	-	-	-	-	-	-
- some rooms	-	-	-	-	-	-	-	-	-	-
No central heating	-	-	-	-	-	-	-	-	-	-
No inside WC	**150**	**89**	**15**	**7**	**36**	**-**	**-**	**3**	**2**	**127**
With central heating - all rooms	-	-	-	-	-	-	-	-	-	-
- some rooms	7	6	-	-	1	-	-	-	-	5
No central heating	143	83	15	7	35	-	-	3	2	122
No car	11,590	3,971	3,011	476	767	90	283	2,992	115	

20. Households with residents; residents in households

Amenities	All permanent	Tenure of households in permanent buildings							Non-permanent accommodation	No car
		Owner occupied		Rented privately		Rented with a job or business	Rented from a housing association	Rented from a local authority or new town		
		Owned outright	Buying	Furnished	Unfurnished					
a	b	c	d	e	f	g	h	i	j	k
				Barrow-in-Furness – *continued*						
TOTAL PERSONS IN HOUSEHOLDS	**72,056**	**17,325**	**41,080**	**1,466**	**1,980**	**688**	**558**	**8,959**	**508**	**22,612**
Exclusive use of bath/shower	**71,655**	**17,158**	**41,048**	**1,373**	**1,907**	**688**	**530**	**8,951**	**496**	**22,298**
Exclusive use of inside WC	**71,494**	**17,050**	**41,021**	**1,366**	**1,896**	**686**	**530**	**8,945**	**488**	**22,178**
With central heating - all rooms	33,545	7,607	22,675	422	178	413	319	1,931	404	5,753
- some rooms	10,489	2,384	5,302	127	107	75	66	2,428	16	3,626
No central heating	27,460	7,059	13,044	817	1,611	198	145	4,586	68	12,799
Shared use of inside WC	**1**	**1**	**-**	**-**	**-**	**-**	**-**	**-**	**-**	**-**
With central heating - all rooms	-	-	-	-	-	-	-	-	-	-
- some rooms	-	-	-	-	-	-	-	-	-	-
No central heating	1	1	-	-	-	-	-	-	-	-
No inside WC	**160**	**107**	**27**	**7**	**11**	**2**	**-**	**6**	**8**	**120**
With central heating - all rooms	11	5	4	-	-	-	-	2	-	4
- some rooms	8	5	3	-	-	-	-	-	1	3
No central heating	141	97	20	7	11	2	-	4	7	113
Shared use of bath/shower	**131**	**-**	**8**	**77**	**18**	**-**	**26**	**2**	**9**	**104**
Exclusive use of inside WC	**4**	**-**	**-**	**4**	**-**	**-**	**-**	**-**	**-**	**3**
With central heating - all rooms	-	-	-	-	-	-	-	-	-	-
- some rooms	-	-	-	-	-	-	-	-	-	-
No central heating	4	-	-	4	-	-	-	-	-	3
Shared use of inside WC	**126**	**-**	**8**	**73**	**17**	**-**	**26**	**2**	**5**	**98**
With central heating - all rooms	26	-	2	7	1	-	16	-	-	22
- some rooms	9	-	6	3	-	-	-	-	-	-
No central heating	91	-	-	63	16	-	10	2	5	76
No inside WC	**1**	**-**	**-**	**-**	**1**	**-**	**-**	**-**	**4**	**3**
With central heating - all rooms	-	-	-	-	-	-	-	-	-	-
- some rooms	-	-	-	-	-	-	-	-	-	-
No central heating	1	-	-	-	1	-	-	-	4	3
No bath/shower	**270**	**167**	**24**	**16**	**55**	**-**	**2**	**6**	**3**	**210**
Exclusive use of inside WC	**39**	**25**	**4**	**-**	**5**	**-**	**2**	**3**	**-**	**26**
With central heating - all rooms	6	2	-	-	-	-	2	2	-	2
- some rooms	2	2	-	-	-	-	-	-	-	2
No central heating	31	21	4	-	5	-	-	1	-	22
Shared use of inside WC	**-**	**-**	**-**	**-**	**-**	**-**	**-**	**-**	**-**	**-**
With central heating - all rooms	-	-	-	-	-	-	-	-	-	-
- some rooms	-	-	-	-	-	-	-	-	-	-
No central heating	-	-	-	-	-	-	-	-	-	-
No inside WC	**231**	**142**	**20**	**16**	**50**	**-**	**-**	**3**	**3**	**184**
With central heating - all rooms	-	-	-	-	-	-	-	-	-	-
- some rooms	9	7	-	-	2	-	-	-	-	6
No central heating	222	135	20	16	48	-	-	3	3	178
No car	22,432	5,877	7,508	777	1,285	187	436	6,362	180	

20. Households with residents; residents in households

Amenities	All permanent	Tenure of households in permanent buildings							Non-permanent accomm-odation	No car
		Owner occupied		Rented privately		Rented with a job or business	Rented from a housing associa-tion	Rented from a local authority or new town		
		Owned outright	Buying	Furnished	Un-furnished					
a	b	c	d	e	f	g	h	i	j	k
					Carlisle					
TOTAL HOUSEHOLDS	**40,740**	**9,856**	**17,526**	**1,119**	**1,405**	**907**	**838**	**9,089**	**143**	**13,976**
Exclusive use of bath/shower	**40,372**	**9,795**	**17,514**	**954**	**1,350**	**902**	**827**	**9,030**	**95**	**13,643**
Exclusive use of inside WC	**40,227**	**9,755**	**17,499**	**951**	**1,318**	**896**	**827**	**8,981**	**81**	**13,532**
With central heating - all rooms	23,518	5,847	11,942	488	438	472	572	3,759	42	6,129
- some rooms	6,460	1,680	2,408	135	216	181	89	1,751	4	2,260
No central heating	10,249	2,228	3,149	328	664	243	166	3,471	35	5,143
Shared use of inside WC	**3**	**-**	**-**	**2**	**-**	**-**	**-**	**1**	**-**	**3**
With central heating - all rooms	-	-	-	-	-	-	-	-	-	-
- some rooms	1	-	-	1	-	-	-	-	-	1
No central heating	2	-	-	1	-	-	-	1	-	2
No inside WC	**142**	**40**	**15**	**1**	**32**	**6**	**-**	**48**	**14**	**108**
With central heating - all rooms	10	2	2	-	1	-	-	5	3	6
- some rooms	13	7	1	-	-	1	-	4	1	11
No central heating	119	31	12	1	31	5	-	39	10	91
Shared use of bath/shower	**248**	**2**	**2**	**163**	**14**	**3**	**11**	**53**	**14**	**220**
Exclusive use of inside WC	**59**	**1**	**1**	**3**	**-**	**1**	**1**	**52**	**5**	**57**
With central heating - all rooms	53	-	1	2	-	1	-	49	2	50
- some rooms	3	-	-	-	-	-	1	2	-	3
No central heating	3	1	-	1	-	-	-	1	3	4
Shared use of inside WC	**189**	**1**	**1**	**160**	**14**	**2**	**10**	**1**	**2**	**159**
With central heating - all rooms	56	-	-	45	1	-	10	-	1	52
- some rooms	7	-	1	5	1	-	-	-	-	3
No central heating	126	1	-	110	12	2	-	1	1	104
No inside WC	**-**	**-**	**-**	**-**	**-**	**-**	**-**	**-**	**7**	**4**
With central heating - all rooms	-	-	-	-	-	-	-	-	-	-
- some rooms	-	-	-	-	-	-	-	-	-	-
No central heating	-	-	-	-	-	-	-	-	7	4
No bath/shower	**120**	**59**	**10**	**2**	**41**	**2**	**-**	**6**	**34**	**113**
Exclusive use of inside WC	**36**	**22**	**5**	**-**	**5**	**-**	**-**	**4**	**3**	**31**
With central heating - all rooms	7	4	1	-	-	-	-	2	1	5
- some rooms	1	-	1	-	-	-	-	-	-	1
No central heating	28	18	3	-	5	-	-	2	2	25
Shared use of inside WC	**-**	**-**	**-**	**-**	**-**	**-**	**-**	**-**	**-**	**-**
With central heating - all rooms	-	-	-	-	-	-	-	-	-	-
- some rooms	-	-	-	-	-	-	-	-	-	-
No central heating	-	-	-	-	-	-	-	-	-	-
No inside WC	**84**	**37**	**5**	**2**	**36**	**2**	**-**	**2**	**31**	**82**
With central heating - all rooms	4	2	-	-	1	-	-	1	-	4
- some rooms	4	-	-	1	2	1	-	-	1	2
No central heating	76	35	5	1	33	1	-	1	30	76
No car	13,924	2,951	2,404	613	589	198	612	6,557	52	

20. Households with residents; residents in households

Amenities	All permanent	Tenure of households in permanent buildings: Owner occupied: Owned outright	Owner occupied: Buying	Rented privately: Furnished	Rented privately: Un-furnished	Rented with a job or business	Rented from a housing association	Rented from a local authority or new town	Non-permanent accommodation	No car
a	b	c	d	e	f	g	h	i	j	k
				Carlisle - *continued*						
TOTAL PERSONS IN HOUSEHOLDS	**98,771**	**19,539**	**50,524**	**1,874**	**2,963**	**2,524**	**1,364**	**19,983**	**288**	**25,555**
Exclusive use of bath/shower	**98,338**	**19,465**	**50,494**	**1,690**	**2,897**	**2,518**	**1,351**	**19,923**	**207**	**25,181**
Exclusive use of inside WC	**98,084**	**19,404**	**50,461**	**1,682**	**2,851**	**2,509**	**1,351**	**19,826**	**160**	**25,002**
With central heating - all rooms	59,275	11,960	35,201	888	985	1,352	849	8,040	73	11,109
- some rooms	16,053	3,456	7,160	244	477	518	172	4,026	15	4,313
No central heating	22,756	3,988	8,100	550	1,389	639	330	7,760	72	9,580
Shared use of inside WC	**4**	**-**	**-**	**3**	**-**	**-**	**-**	**1**	**-**	**4**
With central heating - all rooms	-	-	-	-	-	-	-	-	-	-
- some rooms	1	-	-	1	-	-	-	-	-	1
No central heating	3	-	-	2	-	-	-	1	-	3
No inside WC	**250**	**61**	**33**	**5**	**46**	**9**	**-**	**96**	**47**	**175**
With central heating - all rooms	22	4	6	-	1	-	-	11	17	12
- some rooms	23	9	1	-	-	1	-	12	2	18
No central heating	205	48	26	5	45	8	-	73	28	145
Shared use of bath/shower	**277**	**3**	**7**	**182**	**15**	**4**	**13**	**53**	**17**	**238**
Exclusive use of inside WC	**62**	**1**	**4**	**3**	**-**	**1**	**1**	**52**	**7**	**57**
With central heating - all rooms	56	-	4	2	-	1	-	49	2	50
- some rooms	3	-	-	-	-	-	1	2	-	3
No central heating	3	1	-	1	-	-	-	1	5	4
Shared use of inside WC	**215**	**2**	**3**	**179**	**15**	**3**	**12**	**1**	**2**	**176**
With central heating - all rooms	65	-	-	52	1	-	12	-	1	60
- some rooms	12	-	3	7	2	-	-	-	-	3
No central heating	138	2	-	120	12	3	-	1	1	113
No inside WC	**-**	**-**	**-**	**-**	**-**	**-**	**-**	**-**	**8**	**5**
With central heating - all rooms	-	-	-	-	-	-	-	-	-	-
- some rooms	-	-	-	-	-	-	-	-	-	-
No central heating	-	-	-	-	-	-	-	-	8	5
No bath/shower	**156**	**71**	**23**	**2**	**51**	**2**	**-**	**7**	**64**	**136**
Exclusive use of inside WC	**50**	**26**	**13**	**-**	**6**	**-**	**-**	**5**	**3**	**37**
With central heating - all rooms	12	5	4	-	-	-	-	3	1	6
- some rooms	1	-	1	-	-	-	-	-	-	1
No central heating	37	21	8	-	6	-	-	2	2	30
Shared use of inside WC	**-**	**-**	**-**	**-**	**-**	**-**	**-**	**-**	**-**	**-**
With central heating - all rooms	-	-	-	-	-	-	-	-	-	-
- some rooms	-	-	-	-	-	-	-	-	-	-
No central heating	-	-	-	-	-	-	-	-	-	-
No inside WC	**106**	**45**	**10**	**2**	**45**	**2**	**-**	**2**	**61**	**99**
With central heating - all rooms	5	3	-	-	1	-	-	1	-	5
- some rooms	4	-	-	1	2	1	-	-	2	2
No central heating	97	42	10	1	42	1	-	1	59	92
No car	25,483	4,056	5,492	924	922	389	863	12,837	72	

20. Households with residents; residents in households

Amenities	All permanent	Tenure of households in permanent buildings							Non-permanent accommodation	No car
		Owner occupied		Rented privately		Rented with a job or business	Rented from a housing association	Rented from a local authority or new town		
		Owned outright	Buying	Furnished	Unfurnished					
a	b	c	d	e	f	g	h	i	j	k
				Copeland						
TOTAL HOUSEHOLDS	**27,551**	**6,284**	**11,731**	**489**	**636**	**546**	**2,167**	**5,698**	**201**	**9,492**
Exclusive use of bath/shower	**27,335**	**6,203**	**11,718**	**426**	**598**	**541**	**2,161**	**5,688**	**168**	**9,309**
Exclusive use of inside WC	**27,262**	**6,162**	**11,706**	**422**	**587**	**540**	**2,159**	**5,686**	**165**	**9,274**
With central heating - all rooms	17,454	3,166	7,987	188	205	313	1,320	4,275	72	5,573
- some rooms	4,401	1,271	1,910	71	106	97	400	546	21	1,286
No central heating	5,407	1,725	1,809	163	276	130	439	865	72	2,415
Shared use of inside WC	**3**	**-**	**-**	**1**	**1**	**-**	**-**	**1**	**-**	**2**
With central heating - all rooms	1	-	-	-	-	-	-	1	-	1
- some rooms	-	-	-	-	-	-	-	-	-	-
No central heating	2	-	-	1	1	-	-	-	-	1
No inside WC	**70**	**41**	**12**	**3**	**10**	**1**	**2**	**1**	**3**	**33**
With central heating - all rooms	6	1	3	1	-	-	-	1	1	1
- some rooms	7	3	2	-	1	-	1	-	-	2
No central heating	57	37	7	2	9	1	1	-	2	30
Shared use of bath/shower	**83**	**6**	**1**	**60**	**7**	**2**	**1**	**6**	**17**	**70**
Exclusive use of inside WC	**3**	**-**	**-**	**2**	**-**	**-**	**-**	**1**	**13**	**12**
With central heating - all rooms	1	-	-	-	-	-	-	1	2	3
- some rooms	1	-	-	1	-	-	-	-	1	1
No central heating	1	-	-	1	-	-	-	-	10	8
Shared use of inside WC	**80**	**6**	**1**	**58**	**7**	**2**	**1**	**5**	**1**	**57**
With central heating - all rooms	16	3	1	6	-	1	-	5	1	12
- some rooms	12	2	-	9	1	-	-	-	-	7
No central heating	52	1	-	43	6	1	1	-	-	38
No inside WC	**-**	**-**	**-**	**-**	**-**	**-**	**-**	**-**	**3**	**1**
With central heating - all rooms	-	-	-	-	-	-	-	-	-	-
- some rooms	-	-	-	-	-	-	-	-	-	-
No central heating	-	-	-	-	-	-	-	-	3	1
No bath/shower	**133**	**75**	**12**	**3**	**31**	**3**	**5**	**4**	**16**	**113**
Exclusive use of inside WC	**42**	**21**	**8**	**2**	**6**	**1**	**2**	**2**	**11**	**43**
With central heating - all rooms	9	4	1	-	1	1	1	1	-	6
- some rooms	5	1	2	1	-	-	1	-	-	3
No central heating	28	16	5	1	5	-	-	1	11	34
Shared use of inside WC	**-**	**-**	**-**	**-**	**-**	**-**	**-**	**-**	**-**	**-**
With central heating - all rooms	-	-	-	-	-	-	-	-	-	-
- some rooms	-	-	-	-	-	-	-	-	-	-
No central heating	-	-	-	-	-	-	-	-	-	-
No inside WC	**91**	**54**	**4**	**1**	**25**	**2**	**3**	**2**	**5**	**70**
With central heating - all rooms	1	-	-	-	-	-	1	-	-	1
- some rooms	-	-	-	-	-	-	-	-	-	-
No central heating	90	54	4	1	25	2	2	2	5	69
No car	9,425	1,797	1,467	209	268	132	1,511	4,041	67	

20. Households with residents; residents in households

Amenities	All permanent	Tenure of households in permanent buildings							Non-permanent accommodation	No car
		Owner occupied		Rented privately		Rented with a job or business	Rented from a housing association	Rented from a local authority or new town		
		Owned outright	Buying	Furnished	Unfurnished					
a	b	c	d	e	f	g	h	i	j	k
			Copeland - *continued*							
TOTAL PERSONS IN HOUSEHOLDS	**70,111**	**13,307**	**34,915**	**844**	**1,322**	**1,499**	**4,668**	**13,556**	**374**	**18,844**
Exclusive use of bath/shower	**69,785**	**13,185**	**34,887**	**767**	**1,266**	**1,484**	**4,660**	**13,536**	**321**	**18,605**
Exclusive use of inside WC	**69,652**	**13,113**	**34,859**	**763**	**1,247**	**1,480**	**4,656**	**13,534**	**317**	**18,557**
With central heating - all rooms	45,388	6,962	23,974	354	456	842	2,598	10,202	131	11,248
- some rooms	11,448	2,743	5,778	133	221	286	997	1,290	44	2,670
No central heating	12,816	3,408	5,107	276	570	352	1,061	2,042	142	4,639
Shared use of inside WC	**3**	**-**	**-**	**1**	**1**	**-**	**-**	**1**	**-**	**2**
With central heating - all rooms	1	-	-	-	-	-	-	1	-	1
- some rooms	-	-	-	-	-	-	-	-	-	-
No central heating	2	-	-	1	1	-	-	-	-	1
No inside WC	**130**	**72**	**28**	**3**	**18**	**4**	**4**	**1**	**4**	**46**
With central heating - all rooms	16	3	11	1	-	-	-	1	1	1
- some rooms	14	4	6	-	3	-	1	-	-	2
No central heating	100	65	11	2	15	4	3	-	3	43
Shared use of bath/shower	**127**	**15**	**2**	**74**	**13**	**11**	**1**	**11**	**27**	**82**
Exclusive use of inside WC	**3**	**-**	**-**	**2**	**-**	**-**	**-**	**1**	**17**	**14**
With central heating - all rooms	1	-	-	-	-	-	-	1	2	3
- some rooms	1	-	-	1	-	-	-	-	1	1
No central heating	1	-	-	1	-	-	-	-	14	10
Shared use of inside WC	**124**	**15**	**2**	**72**	**13**	**11**	**1**	**10**	**1**	**67**
With central heating - all rooms	28	4	2	9	-	3	-	10	1	20
- some rooms	18	5	-	11	2	-	-	-	-	7
No central heating	78	6	-	52	11	8	1	-	-	40
No inside WC	**-**	**-**	**-**	**-**	**-**	**-**	**-**	**-**	**9**	**1**
With central heating - all rooms	-	-	-	-	-	-	-	-	-	-
- some rooms	-	-	-	-	-	-	-	-	-	-
No central heating	-	-	-	-	-	-	-	-	9	1
No bath/shower	**199**	**107**	**26**	**3**	**43**	**4**	**7**	**9**	**26**	**157**
Exclusive use of inside WC	**67**	**32**	**19**	**2**	**8**	**1**	**2**	**3**	**16**	**62**
With central heating - all rooms	13	5	2	-	2	1	1	2	-	9
- some rooms	12	1	9	1	-	-	1	-	-	10
No central heating	42	26	8	1	6	-	-	1	16	43
Shared use of inside WC	**-**	**-**	**-**	**-**	**-**	**-**	**-**	**-**	**-**	**-**
With central heating - all rooms	-	-	-	-	-	-	-	-	-	-
- some rooms	-	-	-	-	-	-	-	-	-	-
No central heating	-	-	-	-	-	-	-	-	-	-
No inside WC	**132**	**75**	**7**	**1**	**35**	**3**	**5**	**6**	**10**	**95**
With central heating - all rooms	2	-	-	-	-	-	2	-	-	2
- some rooms	-	-	-	-	-	-	-	-	-	-
No central heating	130	75	7	1	35	3	3	6	10	93
No car	18,752	2,632	3,634	300	423	269	2,896	8,598	92	

20. Households with residents; residents in households

Amenities	All permanent	Tenure of households in permanent buildings							Non-permanent accommodation	No car
		Owner occupied		Rented privately		Rented with a job or business	Rented from a housing association	Rented from a local authority or new town		
		Owned outright	Buying	Furnished	Unfurnished					
a	b	c	d	e	f	g	h	i	j	k
					Eden					
TOTAL HOUSEHOLDS	**17,827**	**6,224**	**6,290**	**454**	**1,429**	**1,045**	**410**	**1,975**	**190**	**3,660**
Exclusive use of bath/shower	**17,630**	**6,177**	**6,280**	**426**	**1,385**	**1,036**	**408**	**1,918**	**123**	**3,503**
Exclusive use of inside WC	**17,570**	**6,143**	**6,275**	**425**	**1,375**	**1,029**	**406**	**1,917**	**116**	**3,481**
With central heating - all rooms	9,561	3,449	4,046	184	328	390	301	863	46	1,569
- some rooms	4,196	1,462	1,431	105	331	269	46	552	17	759
No central heating	3,813	1,232	798	136	716	370	59	502	53	1,153
Shared use of inside WC	**3**	**-**	**-**	**1**	**-**	**1**	**1**	**-**	**-**	**3**
With central heating - all rooms	2	-	-	1	-	-	1	-	-	2
- some rooms	1	-	-	-	-	1	-	-	-	1
No central heating	-	-	-	-	-	-	-	-	-	-
No inside WC	**57**	**34**	**5**	**-**	**10**	**6**	**1**	**1**	**7**	**19**
With central heating - all rooms	8	5	-	-	1	2	-	-	3	2
- some rooms	14	8	4	-	1	-	-	1	1	3
No central heating	35	21	1	-	8	4	1	-	3	14
Shared use of bath/shower	**95**	**4**	**3**	**24**	**4**	**4**	**1**	**55**	**9**	**72**
Exclusive use of inside WC	**50**	**-**	**-**	**-**	**1**	**-**	**1**	**48**	**1**	**48**
With central heating - all rooms	49	-	-	-	1	-	1	47	-	47
- some rooms	1	-	-	-	-	-	-	1	-	1
No central heating	-	-	-	-	-	-	-	-	1	-
Shared use of inside WC	**44**	**4**	**3**	**23**	**3**	**4**	**-**	**7**	**3**	**23**
With central heating - all rooms	15	1	2	5	-	1	-	6	-	5
- some rooms	4	-	1	3	-	-	-	-	1	2
No central heating	25	3	-	15	3	3	-	1	2	16
No inside WC	**1**	**-**	**-**	**1**	**-**	**-**	**-**	**-**	**5**	**1**
With central heating - all rooms	-	-	-	-	-	-	-	-	2	-
- some rooms	-	-	-	-	-	-	-	-	-	-
No central heating	1	-	-	1	-	-	-	-	3	1
No bath/shower	**102**	**43**	**7**	**4**	**40**	**5**	**1**	**2**	**58**	**85**
Exclusive use of inside WC	**27**	**7**	**5**	**2**	**9**	**1**	**1**	**2**	**15**	**23**
With central heating - all rooms	6	2	-	-	1	-	1	2	-	3
- some rooms	1	-	-	-	1	-	-	-	-	1
No central heating	20	5	5	2	7	1	-	-	15	19
Shared use of inside WC	**1**	**-**	**-**	**-**	**1**	**-**	**-**	**-**	**1**	**-**
With central heating - all rooms	1	-	-	-	1	-	-	-	-	-
- some rooms	-	-	-	-	-	-	-	-	-	-
No central heating	-	-	-	-	-	-	-	-	1	-
No inside WC	**74**	**36**	**2**	**2**	**30**	**4**	**-**	**-**	**42**	**62**
With central heating - all rooms	2	2	-	-	-	-	-	-	-	1
- some rooms	3	1	-	-	2	-	-	-	2	5
No central heating	69	33	2	2	28	4	-	-	40	56
No car	3,612	1,259	436	151	355	79	247	1,085	48	

20. Households with residents; residents in households

Amenities	All permanent	Tenure of households in permanent buildings: Owner occupied: Owned outright	Owner occupied: Buying	Rented privately: Furnished	Rented privately: Un-furnished	Rented with a job or business	Rented from a housing association	Rented from a local authority or new town	Non-permanent accommodation	No car
a	b	c	d	e	f	g	h	i	j	k
				***Eden** – continued*						
TOTAL PERSONS IN HOUSEHOLDS	**44,322**	**13,216**	**18,656**	**847**	**3,227**	**3,058**	**740**	**4,578**	**389**	**5,810**
Exclusive use of bath/shower	**44,059**	**13,147**	**18,631**	**811**	**3,175**	**3,039**	**738**	**4,518**	**258**	**5,632**
Exclusive use of inside WC	**43,921**	**13,069**	**18,621**	**809**	**3,155**	**3,017**	**736**	**4,514**	**246**	**5,593**
With central heating - all rooms	24,094	7,415	12,131	342	753	1,142	540	1,771	103	2,385
- some rooms	11,012	3,190	4,275	214	832	844	83	1,574	43	1,400
No central heating	8,815	2,464	2,215	253	1,570	1,031	113	1,169	100	1,808
Shared use of inside WC	**8**	**-**	**-**	**2**	**-**	**5**	**1**	**-**	**-**	**8**
With central heating - all rooms	3	-	-	2	-	-	1	-	-	3
- some rooms	5	-	-	-	-	5	-	-	-	5
No central heating	-	-	-	-	-	-	-	-	-	-
No inside WC	**130**	**78**	**10**	**-**	**20**	**17**	**1**	**4**	**12**	**31**
With central heating - all rooms	22	13	-	-	5	4	-	-	4	2
- some rooms	38	22	9	-	3	-	-	4	4	7
No central heating	70	43	1	-	12	13	1	-	4	22
Shared use of bath/shower	**120**	**9**	**8**	**30**	**5**	**9**	**1**	**58**	**18**	**76**
Exclusive use of inside WC	**50**	**-**	**-**	**-**	**1**	**-**	**1**	**48**	**2**	**48**
With central heating - all rooms	49	-	-	-	1	-	1	47	-	47
- some rooms	1	-	-	-	-	-	-	1	-	1
No central heating	-	-	-	-	-	-	-	-	2	-
Shared use of inside WC	**69**	**9**	**8**	**29**	**4**	**9**	**-**	**10**	**3**	**27**
With central heating - all rooms	21	1	6	6	-	2	-	6	-	6
- some rooms	7	-	2	5	-	-	-	-	1	3
No central heating	41	8	-	18	4	7	-	4	2	18
No inside WC	**1**	**-**	**-**	**1**	**-**	**-**	**-**	**-**	**13**	**1**
With central heating - all rooms	-	-	-	-	-	-	-	-	3	-
- some rooms	-	-	-	-	-	-	-	-	-	-
No central heating	1	-	-	1	-	-	-	-	10	1
No bath/shower	**143**	**60**	**17**	**6**	**47**	**10**	**1**	**2**	**113**	**102**
Exclusive use of inside WC	**40**	**11**	**11**	**2**	**10**	**3**	**1**	**2**	**28**	**31**
With central heating - all rooms	8	3	-	-	2	-	1	2	-	3
- some rooms	1	-	-	-	1	-	-	-	-	1
No central heating	31	8	11	2	7	3	-	-	28	27
Shared use of inside WC	**1**	**-**	**-**	**-**	**1**	**-**	**-**	**-**	**2**	**-**
With central heating - all rooms	1	-	-	-	1	-	-	-	-	-
- some rooms	-	-	-	-	-	-	-	-	-	-
No central heating	-	-	-	-	-	-	-	-	2	-
No inside WC	**102**	**49**	**6**	**4**	**36**	**7**	**-**	**-**	**83**	**71**
With central heating - all rooms	3	3	-	-	-	-	-	-	-	1
- some rooms	3	1	-	-	2	-	-	-	2	5
No central heating	96	45	6	4	34	7	-	-	81	65
No car	5,734	1,617	980	225	492	144	350	1,926	76	

20. Households with residents; residents in households

Amenities	All permanent	Tenure of households in permanent buildings: Owner occupied: Owned outright	Owner occupied: Buying	Rented privately: Furnished	Rented privately: Un-furnished	Rented with a job or business	Rented from a housing associa-tion	Rented from a local authority or new town	Non-permanent accomm-odation	No car
a	b	c	d	e	f	g	h	i	j	k
				South Lakeland						
TOTAL HOUSEHOLDS	**39,585**	**13,858**	**15,360**	**1,369**	**2,437**	**1,314**	**595**	**4,652**	**162**	**9,152**
Exclusive use of bath/shower	**39,287**	**13,790**	**15,353**	**1,304**	**2,371**	**1,301**	**592**	**4,576**	**134**	**8,930**
Exclusive use of inside WC	**39,210**	**13,755**	**15,343**	**1,299**	**2,360**	**1,296**	**592**	**4,565**	**128**	**8,898**
With central heating - all rooms	23,695	8,744	10,777	672	830	605	405	1,662	35	3,902
- some rooms	6,886	2,629	2,396	234	491	311	98	727	8	1,585
No central heating	8,629	2,382	2,170	393	1,039	380	89	2,176	85	3,411
Shared use of inside WC	**3**	**-**	**-**	**-**	**1**	**-**	**-**	**2**	**-**	**3**
With central heating - all rooms	2	-	-	-	-	-	-	2	-	2
- some rooms	-	-	-	-	-	-	-	-	-	-
No central heating	1	-	-	-	1	-	-	-	-	1
No inside WC	**74**	**35**	**10**	**5**	**10**	**5**	**-**	**9**	**6**	**29**
With central heating - all rooms	8	4	2	-	-	-	-	2	2	3
- some rooms	15	7	2	1	1	3	-	1	-	6
No central heating	51	24	6	4	9	2	-	6	4	20
Shared use of bath/shower	**147**	**4**	**-**	**60**	**3**	**9**	**1**	**70**	**12**	**117**
Exclusive use of inside WC	**67**	**-**	**-**	**1**	**-**	**-**	**1**	**65**	**3**	**64**
With central heating - all rooms	65	-	-	1	-	-	1	63	1	62
- some rooms	2	-	-	-	-	-	-	2	-	2
No central heating	-	-	-	-	-	-	-	-	2	-
Shared use of inside WC	**80**	**4**	**-**	**59**	**3**	**9**	**-**	**5**	**3**	**53**
With central heating - all rooms	35	3	-	22	1	5	-	4	-	21
- some rooms	8	-	-	3	1	3	-	1	-	5
No central heating	37	1	-	34	1	1	-	-	3	27
No inside WC	**-**	**-**	**-**	**-**	**-**	**-**	**-**	**-**	**6**	**-**
With central heating - all rooms	-	-	-	-	-	-	-	-	1	-
- some rooms	-	-	-	-	-	-	-	-	-	-
No central heating	-	-	-	-	-	-	-	-	5	-
No bath/shower	**151**	**64**	**7**	**5**	**63**	**4**	**2**	**6**	**16**	**105**
Exclusive use of inside WC	**54**	**22**	**4**	**2**	**20**	**1**	**1**	**4**	**5**	**41**
With central heating - all rooms	5	1	1	-	1	-	-	2	-	4
- some rooms	8	5	1	1	1	-	-	-	-	5
No central heating	41	16	2	1	18	1	1	2	5	32
Shared use of inside WC	**-**	**-**	**-**	**-**	**-**	**-**	**-**	**-**	**-**	**-**
With central heating - all rooms	-	-	-	-	-	-	-	-	-	-
- some rooms	-	-	-	-	-	-	-	-	-	-
No central heating	-	-	-	-	-	-	-	-	-	-
No inside WC	**97**	**42**	**3**	**3**	**43**	**3**	**1**	**2**	**11**	**64**
With central heating - all rooms	3	-	-	-	1	-	1	1	1	2
- some rooms	2	2	-	-	-	-	-	-	-	2
No central heating	92	40	3	3	42	3	-	1	10	60
No car	9,121	3,338	1,208	468	794	191	308	2,814	31	

20. Households with residents; residents in households

Amenities	All permanent	Tenure of households in permanent buildings							Non-permanent accommodation	No car
		Owner occupied		Rented privately		Rented with a job or business	Rented from a housing association	Rented from a local authority or new town		
		Owned outright	Buying	Furnished	Unfurnished					
a	b	c	d	e	f	g	h	i	j	k
				South Lakeland – *continued*						
TOTAL PERSONS IN HOUSEHOLDS	**93,738**	**26,715**	**44,458**	**2,521**	**4,992**	**3,568**	**1,072**	**10,412**	**295**	**14,698**
Exclusive use of bath/shower	**93,345**	**26,615**	**44,440**	**2,446**	**4,904**	**3,549**	**1,069**	**10,322**	**258**	**14,441**
Exclusive use of inside WC	**93,205**	**26,551**	**44,422**	**2,439**	**4,887**	**3,536**	**1,069**	**10,301**	**250**	**14,397**
With central heating - all rooms	57,317	17,081	31,706	1,301	1,778	1,622	670	3,159	66	5,868
- some rooms	16,484	5,032	6,955	477	1,068	922	224	1,806	15	2,612
No central heating	19,404	4,438	5,761	661	2,041	992	175	5,336	169	5,917
Shared use of inside WC	**4**	**-**	**-**	**-**	**1**	**-**	**-**	**3**	**-**	**4**
With central heating - all rooms	3	-	-	-	-	-	-	3	-	3
- some rooms	-	-	-	-	-	-	-	-	-	-
No central heating	1	-	-	-	1	-	-	-	-	1
No inside WC	**136**	**64**	**18**	**7**	**16**	**13**	**-**	**18**	**8**	**40**
With central heating - all rooms	14	8	3	-	-	-	-	3	3	4
- some rooms	31	11	4	2	2	10	-	2	-	9
No central heating	91	45	11	5	14	3	-	13	5	27
Shared use of bath/shower	**177**	**10**	**-**	**69**	**6**	**13**	**1**	**78**	**16**	**130**
Exclusive use of inside WC	**70**	**-**	**-**	**1**	**-**	**-**	**1**	**68**	**4**	**67**
With central heating - all rooms	68	-	-	1	-	-	1	66	1	65
- some rooms	2	-	-	-	-	-	-	2	-	2
No central heating	-	-	-	-	-	-	-	-	3	-
Shared use of inside WC	**107**	**10**	**-**	**68**	**6**	**13**	**-**	**10**	**4**	**63**
With central heating - all rooms	49	7	-	23	2	9	-	8	-	26
- some rooms	14	-	-	6	3	3	-	2	-	7
No central heating	44	3	-	39	1	1	-	-	4	30
No inside WC	**-**	**-**	**-**	**-**	**-**	**-**	**-**	**-**	**8**	**-**
With central heating - all rooms	-	-	-	-	-	-	-	-	1	-
- some rooms	-	-	-	-	-	-	-	-	-	-
No central heating	-	-	-	-	-	-	-	-	7	-
No bath/shower	**216**	**90**	**18**	**6**	**82**	**6**	**2**	**12**	**21**	**127**
Exclusive use of inside WC	**72**	**28**	**7**	**2**	**25**	**1**	**1**	**8**	**7**	**48**
With central heating - all rooms	8	1	4	-	1	-	-	2	-	4
- some rooms	12	8	1	1	2	-	-	-	-	6
No central heating	52	19	2	1	22	1	1	6	7	38
Shared use of inside WC	**-**	**-**	**-**	**-**	**-**	**-**	**-**	**-**	**-**	**-**
With central heating - all rooms	-	-	-	-	-	-	-	-	-	-
- some rooms	-	-	-	-	-	-	-	-	-	-
No central heating	-	-	-	-	-	-	-	-	-	-
No inside WC	**144**	**62**	**11**	**4**	**57**	**5**	**1**	**4**	**14**	**79**
With central heating - all rooms	6	-	-	-	2	-	1	3	2	4
- some rooms	2	2	-	-	-	-	-	-	-	2
No central heating	136	60	11	4	55	5	-	1	12	73
No car	14,659	4,315	2,598	696	1,133	336	407	5,174	39	

Notes: (1) * Households with three or more cars are counted as having 3 cars
(2) ** May include a small number of households with no persons aged 17 and over

21. Households with residents; residents in households; cars in households

Number of persons aged 17 and over (with or without others)	TOTAL PERSONS (ALL AGES)	TOTAL HOUSEHOLDS	Households with:				TOTAL CARS*
			No car	1 car	2 cars	3 or more cars	
a	b	c	d	e	f	g	h
		CUMBRIA					
ALL HOUSEHOLDS**	**474,787**	**193,893**	**59,653**	**92,498**	**34,465**	**7,277**	**183,259**
1 male aged 17 and over	20,632	19,733	8,554	10,337	686	156	12,177
1 female aged 17 and over	47,737	37,775	27,404	10,043	280	48	10,747
2 (1 male and 1 female) aged 17 and over	261,591	95,679	17,072	56,640	20,440	1,527	102,101
2 (same sex) aged 17 and over	12,118	5,443	2,138	2,396	826	83	4,297
3 or more aged 17 and over	132,679	35,244	4,477	13,074	12,232	5,461	53,921
TOTAL PERSONS (ALL AGES)		**474,787**	**108,592**	**230,859**	**108,615**	**26,721**	
Persons aged 17 and over		377,742	89,108	181,022	84,168	23,444	
		Allerdale					
ALL HOUSEHOLDS**	**93,935**	**37,867**	**11,668**	**17,772**	**6,923**	**1,504**	**36,130**
1 male aged 17 and over	3,851	3,677	1,645	1,892	109	31	2,203
1 female aged 17 and over	9,177	7,247	5,405	1,786	50	6	1,904
2 (1 male and 1 female) aged 17 and over	51,576	18,764	3,376	11,009	4,062	317	20,084
2 (same sex) aged 17 and over	2,147	951	366	448	119	18	740
3 or more aged 17 and over	27,182	7,226	876	2,636	2,583	1,131	11,195
TOTAL PERSONS (ALL AGES)		**93,935**	**21,073**	**45,086**	**22,239**	**5,537**	
Persons aged 17 and over		74,537	17,395	35,196	17,121	4,825	
		Barrow-in-Furness					
ALL HOUSEHOLDS**	**72,564**	**29,627**	**11,705**	**14,092**	**3,260**	**570**	**22,322**
1 male aged 17 and over	3,465	3,313	1,840	1,379	78	16	1,583
1 female aged 17 and over	7,867	5,901	4,804	1,073	21	3	1,124
2 (1 male and 1 female) aged 17 and over	39,644	14,336	3,690	8,933	1,608	105	12,464
2 (same sex) aged 17 and over	1,927	853	388	362	94	9	577
3 or more aged 17 and over	19,660	5,223	982	2,345	1,459	437	6,574
TOTAL PERSONS (ALL AGES)		**72,564**	**22,612**	**37,364**	**10,524**	**2,064**	
Persons aged 17 and over		56,960	18,018	28,708	8,401	1,833	
		Carlisle					
ALL HOUSEHOLDS**	**99,059**	**40,883**	**13,976**	**18,810**	**6,795**	**1,302**	**36,306**
1 male aged 17 and over	4,455	4,263	2,012	2,086	136	29	2,445
1 female aged 17 and over	10,860	8,428	6,405	1,968	47	8	2,086
2 (1 male and 1 female) aged 17 and over	54,225	19,797	3,955	11,532	4,034	276	20,428
2 (same sex) aged 17 and over	2,820	1,260	557	545	148	10	871
3 or more aged 17 and over	26,695	7,132	1,044	2,679	2,430	979	10,476
TOTAL PERSONS (ALL AGES)		**99,059**	**25,555**	**47,120**	**21,603**	**4,781**	
Persons aged 17 and over		78,551	20,885	36,893	16,586	4,187	
		Copeland					
ALL HOUSEHOLDS**	**70,485**	**27,752**	**9,492**	**12,936**	**4,436**	**888**	**24,472**
1 male aged 17 and over	3,076	2,939	1,364	1,482	74	19	1,687
1 female aged 17 and over	6,754	5,031	3,957	1,043	27	4	1,109
2 (1 male and 1 female) aged 17 and over	38,090	13,546	2,891	7,960	2,497	198	13,548
2 (same sex) aged 17 and over	1,747	781	359	292	120	10	562
3 or more aged 17 and over	20,817	5,454	920	2,159	1,718	657	7,566
TOTAL PERSONS (ALL AGES)		**70,485**	**18,844**	**34,119**	**14,228**	**3,294**	
Persons aged 17 and over		54,905	14,870	26,080	11,076	2,879	

Notes: (1) * Households with three or more cars are counted as having 3 cars
(2) ** May include a small number of households with no persons aged 17 and over

21. Households with residents; residents in households; cars in households

Number of persons aged 17 and over (with or without others)	TOTAL PERSONS (ALL AGES)	TOTAL HOUSEHOLDS	Households with:				TOTAL CARS*
			No car	1 car	2 cars	3 or more cars	
a	b	c	d	e	f	g	h
		Eden					
ALL HOUSEHOLDS**	**44,711**	**18,017**	**3,660**	**8,922**	**4,301**	**1,134**	**20,926**
1 male aged 17 and over	1,869	1,779	539	1,112	102	26	1,394
1 female aged 17 and over	3,664	3,099	1,936	1,113	43	7	1,220
2 (1 male and 1 female) aged 17 and over	24,996	9,179	865	5,420	2,683	211	11,419
2 (same sex) aged 17 and over	1,086	488	133	237	110	8	481
3 or more aged 17 and over	13,079	3,464	185	1,035	1,362	882	6,405
TOTAL PERSONS (ALL AGES)		**44,711**	**5,810**	**21,289**	**13,409**	**4,203**	
Persons aged 17 and over		35,966	5,074	16,904	10,262	3,726	
		South Lakeland					
ALL HOUSEHOLDS**	**94,033**	**39,747**	**9,152**	**19,966**	**8,750**	**1,879**	**43,103**
1 male aged 17 and over	3,916	3,762	1,154	2,386	187	35	2,865
1 female aged 17 and over	9,415	8,069	4,897	3,060	92	20	3,304
2 (1 male and 1 female) aged 17 and over	53,060	20,057	2,295	11,786	5,556	420	24,158
2 (same sex) aged 17 and over	2,391	1,110	335	512	235	28	1,066
3 or more aged 17 and over	25,246	6,745	470	2,220	2,680	1,375	11,705
TOTAL PERSONS (ALL AGES)		**94,033**	**14,698**	**45,881**	**26,612**	**6,842**	
Persons aged 17 and over		76,823	12,866	37,241	20,722	5,994	

22. Households with residents; residents in households; rooms in household spaces

Households with the following tenure and persons	TOTAL HOUSE-HOLDS	Households with the following rooms							TOTAL ROOMS
		1	2	3	4	5	6	7 or more	
a	b	c	d	e	f	g	h	i	j
				CUMBRIA					
ALL TENURES	**193,893**	**1,881**	**4,553**	**11,248**	**40,472**	**62,406**	**41,934**	**31,399**	**1,020,955**
1	51,169	1,675	3,461	6,817	15,751	12,981	7,068	3,416	226,367
2	66,033	160	983	3,305	16,584	21,819	14,050	9,132	344,007
3	32,487	27	77	765	5,078	12,228	8,305	6,007	181,411
4	31,000	7	25	304	2,462	11,250	8,908	8,044	184,723
5	10,038	10	4	43	489	3,249	2,765	3,478	63,332
6	2,514	-	2	12	93	725	646	1,036	16,685
7 or more	652	2	1	2	15	154	192	286	4,430
TOTAL PERSONS	**474,787**	**2,169**	**5,801**	**17,239**	**77,113**	**160,013**	**114,825**	**97,627**	
Owner occupied - owned outright	**56,657**	**74**	**433**	**1,874**	**12,426**	**17,306**	**13,749**	**10,795**	**311,951**
1	19,262	43	295	1,135	5,869	5,920	3,885	2,115	97,126
2	25,000	20	105	602	5,409	8,007	6,312	4,545	137,787
3	6,958	3	21	93	841	2,131	1,993	1,876	41,304
4	3,905	1	10	39	254	992	1,172	1,437	24,853
5	1,171	7	1	3	46	211	312	591	8,081
6	308	-	-	2	7	38	64	197	2,378
7 or more	53	-	1	-	-	7	11	34	422
Total persons	**113,859**	**131**	**624**	**2,801**	**20,498**	**33,631**	**29,202**	**26,972**	
Owner occupied - buying	**79,159**	**56**	**411**	**2,091**	**12,926**	**26,685**	**20,437**	**16,553**	**446,237**
1	9,909	35	258	843	3,287	3,035	1,693	758	47,433
2	23,611	11	127	801	5,489	8,190	5,482	3,511	125,991
3	17,248	6	15	284	2,478	6,408	4,719	3,338	97,401
4	20,517	3	8	139	1,379	6,959	6,336	5,693	123,722
5	6,214	-	2	21	243	1,755	1,785	2,408	40,078
6	1,343	-	1	2	44	284	340	672	9,329
7 or more	317	1	-	1	6	54	82	173	2,283
Total persons	**232,402**	**95**	**605**	**3,977**	**28,737**	**77,344**	**63,720**	**57,924**	
Rented privately - furnished	**5,294**	**820**	**513**	**791**	**1,269**	**986**	**547**	**368**	**20,403**
1	2,743	719	360	450	582	355	180	97	8,751
2	1,607	84	136	272	496	348	170	101	6,683
3	548	14	13	50	126	168	107	70	2,733
4	283	2	2	12	50	91	64	62	1,557
5	85	1	1	3	14	15	20	31	528
6	25	-	1	4	1	8	5	6	133
7 or more	3	-	-	-	-	1	1	1	18
Total persons	**9,331**	**942**	**690**	**1,231**	**2,228**	**2,049**	**1,236**	**955**	
Rented privately - unfurnished	**8,487**	**134**	**470**	**1,000**	**2,313**	**2,190**	**1,360**	**1,020**	**40,639**
1	3,358	117	325	589	1,054	735	376	162	13,981
2	2,921	15	129	296	844	821	487	329	14,158
3	1,021	-	15	84	247	281	209	185	5,440
4	815	-	1	23	140	266	185	200	4,692
5	277	1	-	7	22	65	83	99	1,735
6	79	-	-	1	6	22	15	35	519
7 or more	16	1	-	-	-	-	5	10	114
Total persons	**17,509**	**159**	**632**	**1,566**	**4,189**	**4,741**	**3,262**	**2,960**	

22. Households with residents; residents in households; rooms in household spaces

Households with the following tenure and persons	TOTAL HOUSE-HOLDS	Households with the following rooms							TOTAL ROOMS
		1	2	3	4	5	6	7 or more	
a	b	c	d	e	f	g	h	i	j
				CUMBRIA - *continued*					
Rented with a job or business	**4,951**	**51**	**99**	**293**	**694**	**1,180**	**970**	**1,664**	**29,812**
1	997	45	65	155	223	224	131	154	4,772
2	1,472	6	30	92	281	363	290	410	8,455
3	941	-	3	30	108	241	202	357	5,971
4	1,012	-	1	13	69	248	228	453	6,837
5	397	-	-	1	9	83	91	213	2,833
6	106	-	-	2	3	17	26	58	746
7 or more	26	-	-	-	1	4	2	19	198
Total persons	**13,630**	**57**	**138**	**498**	**1,455**	**3,210**	**2,856**	**5,416**	
Rented from a housing association	**7,353**	**258**	**530**	**1,105**	**2,088**	**2,537**	**656**	**179**	**31,043**
1	3,252	249	441	819	1,017	570	133	23	11,504
2	2,140	6	88	256	763	821	162	44	9,416
3	913	1	1	26	200	507	143	35	4,544
4	652	1	-	4	76	419	115	37	3,421
5	285	1	-	-	27	164	71	22	1,517
6	80	-	-	-	3	44	22	11	443
7 or more	31	-	-	-	2	12	10	7	198
Total persons	**15,011**	**273**	**620**	**1,425**	**3,615**	**6,578**	**1,905**	**595**	
Rented from a local authority or new town	**31,992**	**488**	**2,097**	**4,094**	**8,756**	**11,522**	**4,215**	**820**	**140,870**
1	11,648	467	1,717	2,826	3,719	2,142	670	107	42,800
2	9,282	18	368	986	3,302	3,269	1,147	192	41,517
3	4,858	3	9	198	1,078	2,492	932	146	24,018
4	3,816	-	3	74	494	2,275	808	162	19,641
5	1,609	-	-	8	128	956	403	114	8,560
6	573	-	-	1	29	312	174	57	3,137
7 or more	206	-	-	1	6	76	81	42	1,197
Total persons	**73,045**	**512**	**2,492**	**5,741**	**16,391**	**32,460**	**12,644**	**2,805**	
				Allerdale					
ALL TENURES	**37,867**	**299**	**777**	**1,989**	**7,729**	**12,730**	**8,102**	**6,241**	**200,672**
1	9,656	278	622	1,280	3,021	2,477	1,326	652	42,919
2	12,668	15	133	548	3,182	4,268	2,734	1,788	66,475
3	6,595	4	17	117	957	2,662	1,588	1,250	37,050
4	6,330	-	2	37	472	2,456	1,791	1,572	37,473
5	2,030	1	2	5	84	715	503	720	12,822
6	467	-	1	1	12	128	121	204	3,111
7 or more	121	1	-	1	1	24	39	55	822
TOTAL PERSONS	**93,935**	**333**	**963**	**2,913**	**14,643**	**33,346**	**22,248**	**19,489**	
Owner occupied - owned outright	**10,903**	**9**	**93**	**304**	**2,238**	**3,264**	**2,699**	**2,296**	**60,954**
1	3,485	7	69	191	1,041	1,035	722	420	17,689
2	4,726	1	16	87	956	1,486	1,253	927	26,402
3	1,455	-	6	18	177	448	393	413	8,698
4	866	-	2	6	54	232	255	317	5,491
5	277	1	-	2	10	51	54	159	1,968
6	83	-	-	-	-	11	20	52	622
7 or more	11	-	-	-	-	1	2	8	84
Total persons	**22,731**	**14**	**127**	**453**	**3,750**	**6,611**	**5,832**	**5,944**	

22. Households with residents; residents in households; rooms in household spaces

Households with the following tenure and persons	TOTAL HOUSE-HOLDS	Households with the following rooms							TOTAL ROOMS
		1	2	3	4	5	6	7 or more	
a	b	c	d	e	f	g	h	i	j
				Allerdale - *continued*					
Owner occupied - buying	**14,160**	**11**	**67**	**286**	**2,082**	**4,865**	**3,646**	**3,203**	**80,986**
1	1,521	6	39	125	455	468	295	133	7,418
2	4,077	3	21	103	906	1,415	980	649	22,025
3	3,203	1	6	37	413	1,228	828	690	18,373
4	3,935	-	-	19	258	1,379	1,180	1,099	23,739
5	1,135	-	1	2	41	318	298	475	7,405
6	228	-	-	-	9	47	50	122	1,586
7 or more	61	1	-	-	-	10	15	35	440
Total persons	**42,507**	**23**	**104**	**528**	**4,797**	**14,443**	**11,356**	**11,256**	
Rented privately - furnished	**864**	**120**	**86**	**135**	**221**	**176**	**73**	**53**	**3,316**
1	469	107	63	90	105	68	24	12	1,508
2	245	10	20	36	88	55	22	14	1,022
3	91	3	1	8	19	35	15	10	454
4	46	-	-	1	8	13	12	12	259
5	11	-	1	-	1	4	-	5	66
6	2	-	1	-	-	1	-	-	7
7 or more	-	-	-	-	-	-	-	-	-
Total persons	**1,483**	**136**	**117**	**190**	**375**	**361**	**161**	**143**	
Rented privately - unfurnished	**1,421**	**24**	**60**	**157**	**412**	**363**	**227**	**178**	**6,836**
1	581	23	47	91	181	143	66	30	2,459
2	470	1	13	46	157	118	74	61	2,303
3	176	-	-	17	48	45	30	36	936
4	127	-	-	3	23	35	35	31	722
5	54	-	-	-	3	17	18	16	329
6	9	-	-	-	-	5	2	2	58
7 or more	4	-	-	-	-	-	2	2	29
Total persons	**2,916**	**25**	**73**	**246**	**746**	**769**	**562**	**495**	
Rented with a job or business	**818**	**8**	**14**	**44**	**127**	**199**	**172**	**254**	**4,843**
1	169	8	8	21	42	46	22	22	799
2	252	-	6	17	49	62	50	68	1,440
3	163	-	-	4	23	36	44	56	1,031
4	150	-	-	1	13	38	38	60	976
5	65	-	-	1	-	12	17	35	460
6	14	-	-	-	-	4	1	9	99
7 or more	5	-	-	-	-	1	-	4	38
Total persons	**2,206**	**8**	**20**	**76**	**261**	**521**	**497**	**823**	
Rented from a housing association	**2,994**	**43**	**99**	**298**	**862**	**1,257**	**350**	**85**	**13,588**
1	1,107	43	82	219	409	279	66	9	4,355
2	923	-	17	71	324	407	83	21	4,232
3	445	-	-	6	86	256	82	15	2,248
4	332	-	-	2	32	213	68	17	1,730
5	143	-	-	-	10	86	34	13	766
6	32	-	-	-	-	11	13	8	189
7 or more	12	-	-	-	1	5	4	2	68
Total persons	**6,608**	**43**	**116**	**387**	**1,500**	**3,245**	**1,026**	**291**	

22. Households with residents; residents in households; rooms in household spaces

Households with the following tenure and persons	TOTAL HOUSE-HOLDS	Households with the following rooms							TOTAL ROOMS
		1	2	3	4	5	6	7 or more	
a	b	c	d	e	f	g	h	i	j
				Allerdale - *continued*					
Rented from a local authority or new town	**6,707**	**84**	**358**	**765**	**1,787**	**2,606**	**935**	**172**	**30,149**
1	2,324	84	314	543	788	438	131	26	8,691
2	1,975	-	40	188	702	725	272	48	9,051
3	1,062	-	4	27	191	614	196	30	5,310
4	874	-	-	5	84	546	203	36	4,556
5	345	-	-	-	19	227	82	17	1,828
6	99	-	-	1	3	49	35	11	550
7 or more	28	-	-	1	-	7	16	4	163
Total persons	**15,484**	**84**	**406**	**1,033**	**3,214**	**7,396**	**2,814**	**537**	
				Barrow-in-Furness					
ALL TENURES	**29,627**	**203**	**922**	**1,846**	**7,042**	**9,467**	**7,068**	**3,079**	**148,864**
1	8,012	177	684	1,027	2,476	2,084	1,222	342	34,844
2	9,759	19	217	579	2,854	3,189	2,130	771	48,131
3	5,130	6	17	168	1,031	1,863	1,451	594	27,201
4	4,671	1	4	57	527	1,665	1,595	822	26,419
5	1,542	-	-	13	125	520	512	372	9,055
6	389	-	-	2	24	112	125	126	2,411
7 or more	124	-	-	-	5	34	33	52	803
TOTAL PERSONS	**72,564**	**237**	**1,185**	**2,994**	**14,189**	**24,228**	**19,768**	**9,963**	
Owner occupied - owned outright	**9,214**	**5**	**49**	**262**	**2,658**	**2,998**	**2,352**	**890**	**47,360**
1	3,472	3	33	126	1,204	1,146	747	213	17,075
2	3,929	2	15	111	1,176	1,295	976	354	20,056
3	1,100	-	1	16	197	359	373	154	6,042
4	540	-	-	9	63	156	196	116	3,129
5	139	-	-	-	16	34	49	40	835
6	28	-	-	-	2	6	9	11	186
7 or more	6	-	-	-	-	2	2	2	37
Total persons	**17,696**	**7**	**66**	**432**	**4,491**	**5,657**	**4,915**	**2,128**	
Owner occupied - buying	**14,010**	**3**	**43**	**364**	**2,828**	**4,868**	**3,950**	**1,954**	**75,383**
1	1,825	1	30	121	676	593	315	89	8,647
2	4,041	-	9	147	1,137	1,438	944	366	20,606
3	3,175	1	2	66	592	1,180	931	403	17,111
4	3,524	1	2	23	333	1,234	1,267	664	20,211
5	1,131	-	-	7	73	358	394	299	6,754
6	246	-	-	-	14	52	82	98	1,588
7 or more	68	-	-	-	3	13	17	35	466
Total persons	**41,163**	**8**	**62**	**740**	**6,528**	**14,142**	**12,651**	**7,032**	
Rented privately - furnished	**838**	**98**	**79**	**140**	**242**	**161**	**87**	**31**	**3,203**
1	430	82	64	79	111	56	27	11	1,413
2	245	12	13	45	87	59	22	7	1,003
3	99	4	2	12	29	28	19	5	450
4	42	-	-	3	10	12	13	4	215
5	15	-	-	-	4	4	4	3	85
6	7	-	-	1	1	2	2	1	37
7 or more	-	-	-	-	-	-	-	-	-
Total persons	**1,502**	**118**	**96**	**223**	**438**	**338**	**212**	**77**	

22. Households with residents; residents in households; rooms in household spaces

Households with the following tenure and persons	TOTAL HOUSE-HOLDS	Households with the following rooms							TOTAL ROOMS
		1	2	3	4	5	6	7 or more	
a	b	c	d	e	f	g	h	i	j
				Barrow-in-Furness - *continued*					
Rented privately - unfurnished	**1,107**	**17**	**175**	**293**	**314**	**189**	**96**	**23**	**4,205**
1	564	16	116	163	146	80	38	5	1,988
2	325	1	50	78	99	58	32	7	1,268
3	126	-	9	33	39	25	13	7	534
4	71	-	-	14	27	21	6	3	313
5	16	-	-	5	3	4	4	-	71
6	3	-	-	-	-	1	2	-	17
7 or more	2	-	-	-	-	-	1	1	14
Total persons	**1,992**	**18**	**243**	**499**	**584**	**381**	**207**	**60**	
Rented with a job or business	**269**	**1**	**6**	**36**	**45**	**78**	**51**	**52**	**1,430**
1	76	1	5	21	17	17	6	9	337
2	78	-	1	8	12	22	19	16	430
3	48	-	-	5	11	14	9	9	261
4	38	-	-	1	5	15	9	8	217
5	20	-	-	-	-	8	5	7	131
6	5	-	-	1	-	-	3	1	30
7 or more	4	-	-	-	-	2	-	2	24
Total persons	**688**	**1**	**7**	**62**	**94**	**217**	**150**	**157**	
Rented from a housing association	**348**	**60**	**67**	**102**	**64**	**36**	**11**	**8**	**1,068**
1	203	56	44	67	23	8	5	-	507
2	101	3	22	31	24	15	2	4	361
3	28	1	1	4	10	7	4	1	121
4	11	-	-	-	6	4	-	1	51
5	5	-	-	-	1	2	-	2	28
6	-	-	-	-	-	-	-	-	-
7 or more	-	-	-	-	-	-	-	-	-
Total persons	**558**	**65**	**91**	**141**	**130**	**85**	**21**	**25**	
Rented from a local authority or new town	**3,841**	**19**	**503**	**649**	**891**	**1,137**	**521**	**121**	**16,215**
1	1,442	18	392	450	299	184	84	15	4,877
2	1,040	1	107	159	319	302	135	17	4,407
3	554	-	2	32	153	250	102	15	2,682
4	445	-	2	7	83	223	104	26	2,283
5	216	-	-	1	28	110	56	21	1,151
6	100	-	-	-	7	51	27	15	553
7 or more	44	-	-	-	2	17	13	12	262
Total persons	**8,965**	**20**	**620**	**897**	**1,924**	**3,408**	**1,612**	**484**	
				Carlisle					
ALL TENURES	**40,883**	**510**	**1,108**	**2,975**	**9,794**	**12,310**	**8,408**	**5,778**	**208,487**
1	11,167	457	869	1,812	3,685	2,463	1,318	563	46,947
2	13,754	36	228	860	4,051	4,312	2,757	1,510	69,214
3	6,924	7	6	198	1,314	2,466	1,755	1,178	37,950
4	6,401	3	5	87	601	2,234	1,852	1,619	37,711
5	2,013	6	-	15	113	641	553	685	12,618
6	481	-	-	3	25	159	123	171	3,089
7 or more	143	1	-	-	5	35	50	52	958
TOTAL PERSONS	**99,059**	**599**	**1,363**	**4,567**	**18,885**	**31,831**	**23,379**	**18,435**	

22. Households with residents; residents in households; rooms in household spaces

Households with the following tenure and persons	TOTAL HOUSE-HOLDS	Households with the following rooms							TOTAL ROOMS
		1	2	3	4	5	6	7 or more	
a	b	c	d	e	f	g	h	i	j
				Carlisle - *continued*					
Owner occupied - owned outright	**9,922**	**13**	**58**	**388**	**2,412**	**2,922**	**2,438**	**1,691**	**53,754**
1	3,463	6	45	246	1,157	991	693	325	17,077
2	4,357	3	11	120	1,040	1,381	1,123	679	23,622
3	1,234	-	1	16	168	358	372	319	7,278
4	626	-	1	5	39	155	186	240	4,040
5	183	4	-	-	5	33	54	87	1,253
6	45	-	-	1	3	2	7	32	364
7 or more	14	-	-	-	-	2	3	9	120
Total persons	**19,674**	**32**	**74**	**560**	**3,940**	**5,638**	**5,133**	**4,297**	
Owner occupied - buying	**17,543**	**9**	**67**	**543**	**3,430**	**5,480**	**4,550**	**3,464**	**97,335**
1	2,290	3	46	202	909	644	352	134	10,714
2	5,454	1	19	218	1,481	1,792	1,248	695	28,412
3	3,834	4	-	80	644	1,293	1,075	738	21,447
4	4,371	1	2	35	332	1,375	1,398	1,228	26,265
5	1,277	-	-	7	56	310	385	519	8,300
6	250	-	-	1	6	55	67	121	1,717
7 or more	67	-	-	-	2	11	25	29	480
Total persons	**50,563**	**21**	**92**	**1,059**	**7,462**	**15,565**	**14,176**	**12,188**	
Rented privately - furnished	**1,157**	**316**	**112**	**157**	**232**	**170**	**102**	**68**	**3,932**
1	645	287	70	73	94	55	35	31	1,757
2	336	24	38	72	101	57	32	12	1,285
3	108	3	3	8	29	34	21	10	522
4	48	1	1	2	6	20	9	9	257
5	14	1	-	2	2	-	4	5	78
6	5	-	-	-	-	3	1	1	28
7 or more	1	-	-	-	-	1	-	-	5
Total persons	**1,940**	**353**	**159**	**259**	**417**	**376**	**224**	**152**	
Rented privately - unfurnished	**1,416**	**22**	**48**	**132**	**394**	**424**	**246**	**150**	**6,856**
1	546	19	24	88	179	130	75	31	2,389
2	471	1	23	32	139	160	69	47	2,262
3	172	-	1	10	41	55	45	20	899
4	168	-	-	1	31	67	41	28	932
5	44	1	-	-	2	8	16	17	285
6	12	-	-	1	2	4	-	5	71
7 or more	3	1	-	-	-	-	-	2	18
Total persons	**2,990**	**33**	**73**	**192**	**726**	**947**	**592**	**427**	
Rented with a job or business	**913**	**12**	**16**	**64**	**138**	**240**	**177**	**266**	**5,288**
1	169	8	13	29	38	31	23	27	774
2	263	4	3	19	57	80	46	54	1,423
3	192	-	-	11	26	47	41	67	1,188
4	203	-	-	5	9	60	49	80	1,313
5	67	-	-	-	7	16	13	31	474
6	17	-	-	-	1	6	4	6	102
7 or more	2	-	-	-	-	-	1	1	14
Total persons	**2,535**	**16**	**19**	**120**	**307**	**688**	**531**	**854**	

22. Households with residents; residents in households; rooms in household spaces

Households with the following tenure and persons	TOTAL HOUSE-HOLDS	Households with the following rooms							TOTAL ROOMS
		1	2	3	4	5	6	7 or more	
a	b	c	d	e	f	g	h	i	j
				Carlisle – *continued*					
Rented from a housing association	**839**	**73**	**71**	**212**	**298**	**137**	**39**	**9**	**3,034**
1	509	71	62	167	160	39	10	-	1,591
2	218	1	9	43	105	44	16	-	884
3	55	-	-	2	20	27	5	1	258
4	40	1	-	-	10	19	4	6	208
5	10	-	-	-	2	4	2	2	57
6	6	-	-	-	1	4	1	-	30
7 or more	1	-	-	-	-	-	1	-	6
Total persons	**1,365**	**77**	**80**	**259**	**486**	**328**	**98**	**37**	
Rented from a local authority or new town	**9,093**	**65**	**736**	**1,479**	**2,890**	**2,937**	**856**	**130**	**38,288**
1	3,545	63	609	1,007	1,148	573	130	15	12,645
2	2,655	2	125	356	1,128	798	223	23	11,326
3	1,329	-	1	71	386	652	196	23	6,358
4	945	-	1	39	174	538	165	28	4,696
5	418	-	-	6	39	270	79	24	2,171
6	146	-	-	-	12	85	43	6	777
7 or more	55	-	-	-	3	21	20	11	315
Total persons	**19,992**	**67**	**866**	**2,118**	**5,547**	**8,289**	**2,625**	**480**	
				Copeland					
ALL TENURES	**27,752**	**234**	**437**	**1,232**	**5,202**	**10,467**	**6,172**	**4,008**	**146,683**
1	6,903	211	347	747	2,146	1,987	1,017	448	31,243
2	8,941	17	78	337	1,956	3,444	1,940	1,169	47,142
3	4,928	3	7	90	666	2,126	1,277	759	27,139
4	4,746	2	5	52	339	2,049	1,315	984	27,402
5	1,633	1	-	3	76	654	452	447	9,905
6	487	-	-	3	17	175	132	160	3,112
7 or more	114	-	-	-	2	32	39	41	740
TOTAL PERSONS	**70,485**	**267**	**544**	**1,932**	**9,910**	**27,998**	**17,321**	**12,513**	
Owner occupied - owned outright	**6,384**	**7**	**40**	**194**	**1,184**	**2,130**	**1,611**	**1,218**	**35,519**
1	1,969	3	24	100	534	645	433	230	10,120
2	2,773	3	11	66	500	1,001	678	514	15,422
3	889	-	2	17	100	293	268	209	5,190
4	516	-	3	9	40	141	166	157	3,166
5	175	1	-	1	9	40	51	73	1,139
6	57	-	-	1	1	9	14	32	446
7 or more	5	-	-	-	-	1	1	3	36
Total persons	**13,501**	**14**	**64**	**330**	**2,045**	**4,351**	**3,604**	**3,093**	
Owner occupied - buying	**11,760**	**5**	**23**	**249**	**1,631**	**4,631**	**3,016**	**2,205**	**65,948**
1	1,432	3	13	98	435	501	255	127	7,069
2	3,365	1	9	82	625	1,321	835	492	18,248
3	2,607	-	-	40	325	1,120	698	424	14,478
4	3,130	1	1	27	207	1,264	898	732	18,358
5	950	-	-	2	31	354	256	307	5,929
6	233	-	-	-	8	63	62	100	1,559
7 or more	43	-	-	-	-	8	12	23	307
Total persons	**34,977**	**9**	**35**	**500**	**3,691**	**13,764**	**9,352**	**7,626**	

22. Households with residents; residents in households; rooms in household spaces

Households with the following tenure and persons	TOTAL HOUSE-HOLDS	Households with the following rooms							TOTAL ROOMS
		1	2	3	4	5	6	7 or more	
a	b	c	d	e	f	g	h	i	j
				Copeland – *continued*					
Rented privately - furnished	**541**	**95**	**57**	**89**	**103**	**102**	**50**	**45**	**2,047**
1	311	86	41	59	56	37	23	9	965
2	134	6	13	23	33	35	14	10	567
3	58	2	3	3	7	20	7	16	313
4	25	1	-	2	5	9	4	4	126
5	7	-	-	-	2	-	1	4	43
6	6	-	-	2	-	1	1	2	33
7 or more	-	-	-	-	-	-	-	-	-
Total persons	**924**	**108**	**76**	**134**	**173**	**209**	**99**	**125**	
Rented privately - unfurnished	**651**	**15**	**19**	**52**	**160**	**197**	**113**	**95**	**3,263**
1	259	13	11	32	81	74	32	16	1,135
2	227	2	6	16	54	63	48	38	1,189
3	76	-	1	3	15	25	14	18	425
4	54	-	1	1	6	23	11	12	303
5	20	-	-	-	3	8	5	4	111
6	14	-	-	-	1	4	3	6	92
7 or more	1	-	-	-	-	-	-	1	8
Total persons	**1,348**	**17**	**30**	**77**	**279**	**431**	**257**	**257**	
Rented with a job or business	**549**	**3**	**12**	**32**	**78**	**145**	**95**	**184**	**3,286**
1	112	3	5	15	20	35	10	24	573
2	167	-	6	13	41	33	31	43	953
3	115	-	1	2	11	44	20	37	684
4	91	-	-	2	5	23	17	44	598
5	41	-	-	-	-	8	7	26	311
6	17	-	-	-	1	1	9	6	117
7 or more	6	-	-	-	-	1	1	4	50
Total persons	**1,509**	**3**	**20**	**55**	**161**	**378**	**297**	**595**	
Rented from a housing association	**2,167**	**20**	**138**	**248**	**599**	**934**	**201**	**27**	**9,511**
1	884	19	123	177	305	217	39	4	3,363
2	635	1	15	61	201	303	46	8	2,865
3	296	-	-	9	60	176	42	9	1,472
4	198	-	-	1	19	145	31	2	1,004
5	106	-	-	-	11	62	31	2	554
6	35	-	-	-	2	24	8	1	183
7 or more	13	-	-	-	1	7	4	1	70
Total persons	**4,668**	**21**	**153**	**330**	**1,038**	**2,434**	**612**	**80**	
Rented from a local authority or new town	**5,700**	**89**	**148**	**368**	**1,447**	**2,328**	**1,086**	**234**	**27,109**
1	1,936	84	130	266	715	478	225	38	8,018
2	1,640	4	18	76	502	688	288	64	7,898
3	887	1	-	16	148	448	228	46	4,577
4	732	-	-	10	57	444	188	33	3,847
5	334	-	-	-	20	182	101	31	1,818
6	125	-	-	-	4	73	35	13	682
7 or more	46	-	-	-	1	15	21	9	269
Total persons	**13,558**	**95**	**166**	**506**	**2,523**	**6,431**	**3,100**	**737**	

22. Households with residents; residents in households; rooms in household spaces

Households with the following tenure and persons	TOTAL HOUSE-HOLDS	Households with the following rooms							TOTAL ROOMS
		1	2	3	4	5	6	7 or more	
a	b	c	d	e	f	g	h	i	j
				Eden					
ALL TENURES	**18,017**	**221**	**407**	**867**	**3,084**	**5,308**	**3,769**	**4,361**	**100,900**
1	4,502	199	293	498	1,284	1,117	627	484	20,729
2	6,268	16	90	286	1,297	1,930	1,345	1,304	34,518
3	2,961	4	16	53	304	1,012	733	839	17,691
4	3,034	1	6	29	159	950	769	1,120	19,292
5	943	1	1	-	34	227	235	445	6,426
6	254	-	-	1	6	63	48	136	1,842
7 or more	55	-	1	-	-	9	12	33	402
TOTAL PERSONS	**44,711**	**252**	**561**	**1,351**	**5,632**	**13,393**	**10,144**	**13,378**	
Owner occupied - owned outright	**6,321**	**16**	**59**	**186**	**1,080**	**1,727**	**1,500**	**1,753**	**36,904**
1	1,951	10	30	109	530	567	382	323	10,199
2	2,735	1	16	65	460	796	724	673	15,870
3	821	3	7	5	56	220	204	326	5,177
4	590	1	4	7	29	119	144	286	3,983
5	171	1	1	-	4	20	39	106	1,255
6	46	-	-	-	1	5	6	34	363
7 or more	7	-	1	-	-	-	1	5	57
Total persons	**13,433**	**30**	**115**	**282**	**1,760**	**3,425**	**3,258**	**4,563**	
Owner occupied - buying	**6,304**	**5**	**49**	**178**	**852**	**1,970**	**1,475**	**1,775**	**37,282**
1	773	3	33	80	239	209	127	82	3,726
2	1,844	2	12	67	385	614	372	392	10,204
3	1,355	-	3	19	136	488	356	353	8,087
4	1,686	-	1	12	73	515	471	614	10,707
5	495	-	-	-	15	113	120	247	3,412
6	124	-	-	-	4	28	23	69	943
7 or more	27	-	-	-	-	3	6	18	203
Total persons	**18,686**	**7**	**70**	**319**	**1,808**	**5,716**	**4,603**	**6,163**	
Rented privately - furnished	**478**	**46**	**43**	**57**	**126**	**88**	**60**	**58**	**2,065**
1	222	40	31	31	62	34	16	8	774
2	164	6	10	19	49	35	23	22	761
3	46	-	1	3	11	11	12	8	252
4	36	-	1	3	3	7	7	15	217
5	7	-	-	-	1	-	2	4	46
6	2	-	-	1	-	1	-	-	8
7 or more	1	-	-	-	-	-	-	1	7
Total persons	**886**	**52**	**58**	**96**	**210**	**171**	**136**	**163**	
Rented privately - unfurnished	**1,447**	**22**	**52**	**116**	**371**	**382**	**249**	**255**	**7,450**
1	473	17	38	64	164	116	45	29	2,063
2	512	5	10	43	135	146	91	82	2,620
3	200	-	4	7	47	53	46	43	1,101
4	180	-	-	2	22	51	45	60	1,105
5	60	-	-	-	3	14	18	25	400
6	19	-	-	-	-	2	4	13	136
7 or more	3	-	-	-	-	-	-	3	25
Total persons	**3,254**	**27**	**70**	**179**	**678**	**853**	**659**	**788**	

22. Households with residents; residents in households; rooms in household spaces

Households with the following tenure and persons	TOTAL HOUSE-HOLDS	Households with the following rooms							TOTAL ROOMS
		1	2	3	4	5	6	7 or more	
a	b	c	d	e	f	g	h	i	j
				Eden - *continued*					
Rented with a job or business	**1,061**	**5**	**19**	**31**	**96**	**227**	**214**	**469**	**6,982**
1	158	5	11	15	25	38	29	35	896
2	328	-	7	10	46	77	67	121	2,034
3	191	-	1	4	11	44	33	98	1,306
4	257	-	-	2	12	52	55	136	1,814
5	100	-	-	-	1	13	26	60	733
6	24	-	-	-	1	3	4	16	174
7 or more	3	-	-	-	-	-	-	3	25
Total persons	**3,082**	**5**	**28**	**55**	**209**	**615**	**636**	**1,534**	
Rented from a housing association	**410**	**22**	**91**	**92**	**97**	**81**	**13**	**14**	**1,462**
1	226	21	75	62	49	15	2	2	654
2	108	1	16	27	37	18	4	5	416
3	33	-	-	3	8	18	2	2	158
4	27	-	-	-	1	22	2	2	141
5	10	-	-	-	2	5	2	1	54
6	3	-	-	-	-	3	-	-	15
7 or more	3	-	-	-	-	-	1	2	24
Total persons	**740**	**23**	**107**	**125**	**161**	**236**	**41**	**47**	
Rented from a local authority or new town	**1,996**	**105**	**94**	**207**	**462**	**833**	**258**	**37**	**8,755**
1	699	103	75	137	215	138	26	5	2,417
2	577	1	19	55	185	244	64	9	2,613
3	315	1	-	12	35	178	80	9	1,610
4	258	-	-	3	19	184	45	7	1,325
5	100	-	-	-	8	62	28	2	526
6	36	-	-	-	-	21	11	4	203
7 or more	11	-	-	-	-	6	4	1	61
Total persons	**4,630**	**108**	**113**	**295**	**806**	**2,377**	**811**	**120**	
				South Lakeland					
ALL TENURES	**39,747**	**414**	**902**	**2,339**	**7,621**	**12,124**	**8,415**	**7,932**	**215,349**
1	10,929	353	646	1,453	3,139	2,853	1,558	927	49,685
2	14,643	57	237	695	3,244	4,676	3,144	2,590	78,527
3	5,949	3	14	139	806	2,099	1,501	1,387	34,380
4	5,818	-	3	42	364	1,896	1,586	1,927	36,426
5	1,877	1	1	7	57	492	510	809	12,506
6	436	-	1	2	9	88	97	239	3,120
7 or more	95	-	-	1	2	20	19	53	705
TOTAL PERSONS	**94,033**	**481**	**1,185**	**3,482**	**13,854**	**29,217**	**21,965**	**23,849**	
Owner occupied - owned outright	**13,913**	**24**	**134**	**540**	**2,854**	**4,265**	**3,149**	**2,947**	**77,460**
1	4,922	14	94	363	1,403	1,536	908	604	24,966
2	6,480	10	36	153	1,277	2,048	1,558	1,398	36,415
3	1,459	-	4	21	143	453	383	455	8,919
4	767	-	-	3	29	189	225	321	5,044
5	226	-	-	-	2	33	65	126	1,631
6	49	-	-	-	-	5	8	36	397
7 or more	10	-	-	-	-	1	2	7	88
Total persons	**26,824**	**34**	**178**	**744**	**4,512**	**7,949**	**6,460**	**6,947**	

22. Households with residents; residents in households; rooms in household spaces

Households with the following tenure and persons	TOTAL HOUSE-HOLDS	Households with the following rooms							TOTAL ROOMS
		1	2	3	4	5	6	7 or more	
a	b	c	d	e	f	g	h	i	j
				South Lakeland - *continued*					
Owner occupied - buying	**15,382**	**23**	**162**	**471**	**2,103**	**4,871**	**3,800**	**3,952**	**89,303**
1	2,068	19	97	217	573	620	349	193	9,859
2	4,830	4	57	184	955	1,610	1,103	917	26,496
3	3,074	-	4	42	368	1,099	831	730	17,905
4	3,871	-	2	23	176	1,192	1,122	1,356	24,442
5	1,226	-	1	3	27	302	332	561	8,278
6	262	-	1	1	3	39	56	162	1,936
7 or more	51	-	-	1	1	9	7	33	387
Total persons	**44,506**	**27**	**242**	**831**	**4,451**	**13,714**	**11,582**	**13,659**	
Rented privately - furnished	**1,416**	**145**	**136**	**213**	**345**	**289**	**175**	**113**	**5,840**
1	666	117	91	118	154	105	55	26	2,334
2	483	26	42	77	138	107	57	36	2,045
3	146	2	3	16	31	40	33	21	742
4	86	-	-	1	18	30	19	18	483
5	31	-	-	1	4	7	9	10	210
6	3	-	-	-	-	-	1	2	20
7 or more	1	-	-	-	-	-	1	-	6
Total persons	**2,596**	**175**	**184**	**329**	**615**	**594**	**404**	**295**	
Rented privately - unfurnished	**2,445**	**34**	**116**	**250**	**662**	**635**	**429**	**319**	**12,029**
1	935	29	89	151	303	192	120	51	3,947
2	916	5	27	81	260	276	173	94	4,516
3	271	-	-	14	57	78	61	61	1,545
4	215	-	-	2	31	69	47	66	1,317
5	83	-	-	2	8	14	22	37	539
6	22	-	-	-	3	6	4	9	145
7 or more	3	-	-	-	-	-	2	1	20
Total persons	**5,009**	**39**	**143**	**373**	**1,176**	**1,360**	**985**	**933**	
Rented with a job or business	**1,341**	**22**	**32**	**86**	**210**	**291**	**261**	**439**	**7,983**
1	313	20	23	54	81	57	41	37	1,393
2	384	2	7	25	76	89	77	108	2,175
3	232	-	1	4	26	56	55	90	1,501
4	273	-	1	2	25	60	60	125	1,919
5	104	-	-	-	1	26	23	54	724
6	29	-	-	1	-	3	5	20	224
7 or more	6	-	-	-	1	-	-	5	47
Total persons	**3,610**	**24**	**44**	**130**	**423**	**791**	**745**	**1,453**	
Rented from a housing association	**595**	**40**	**64**	**153**	**168**	**92**	**42**	**36**	**2,380**
1	323	39	55	127	71	12	11	8	1,034
2	155	-	9	23	72	34	11	6	658
3	56	-	-	2	16	23	8	7	287
4	44	-	-	1	8	16	10	9	287
5	11	1	-	-	1	5	2	2	58
6	4	-	-	-	-	2	-	2	26
7 or more	2	-	-	-	-	-	-	2	30
Total persons	**1,072**	**44**	**73**	**183**	**300**	**250**	**107**	**115**	

22. Households with residents; residents in households; rooms in household spaces

Households with the following tenure and persons	TOTAL HOUSE-HOLDS	Households with the following rooms							TOTAL ROOMS
		1	2	3	4	5	6	7 or more	
a	b	c	d	e	f	g	h	i	j
				South Lakeland - *continued*					
Rented from a local authority or new town	**4,655**	**126**	**258**	**626**	**1,279**	**1,681**	**559**	**126**	**20,354**
1	1,702	115	197	423	554	331	74	8	6,152
2	1,395	10	59	152	466	512	165	31	6,222
3	711	1	2	40	165	350	130	23	3,481
4	562	-	-	10	77	340	103	32	2,934
5	196	-	-	1	14	105	57	19	1,066
6	67	-	-	-	3	33	23	8	372
7 or more	22	-	-	-	-	10	7	5	127
Total persons	**10,416**	**138**	**321**	**892**	**2,377**	**4,559**	**1,682**	**447**	

23. Households with residents; residents in households

Tenure	TOTAL HOUSEHOLDS	Up to 0.5 persons per room	Over 0.5 and up to 1 person per room	Over 1 and up to 1.5 persons per room	Over 1.5 persons per room
a	b	c	d	e	f
	CUMBRIA				
TOTAL HOUSEHOLDS	**193,893**	**129,896**	**61,606**	**2,041**	**350**
All permanent buildings	**192,689**	**129,223**	**61,216**	**1,977**	**273**
Owner occupied - owned outright	55,995	47,865	7,979	137	14
- buying	79,000	43,581	34,502	850	67
Rented privately - furnished	5,084	3,230	1,717	43	94
- unfurnished	8,413	6,209	2,097	89	18
Rented with a job or business	4,887	3,164	1,658	54	11
Rented from a housing association	7,352	4,987	2,251	102	12
Rented from a local authority or new town	31,958	20,187	11,012	702	57
Non - permanent accommodation	**1,204**	**673**	**390**	**64**	**77**
TOTAL PERSONS IN HOUSEHOLDS	**474,787**	**234,280**	**227,725**	**11,381**	**1,401**
All permanent buildings	**472,505**	**233,350**	**226,888**	**11,138**	**1,129**
Owner occupied - owned outright	112,580	82,579	29,190	742	69
- buying	232,063	91,925	135,025	4,735	378
Rented privately - furnished	8,986	4,764	3,802	201	219
- unfurnished	17,371	9,855	7,001	446	69
Rented with a job or business	13,524	6,705	6,470	309	40
Rented from a housing association	15,010	7,190	7,170	603	47
Rented from a local authority or new town	72,971	30,332	38,230	4,102	307
Non - permanent accommodation	**2,282**	**930**	**837**	**243**	**272**
	Allerdale				
TOTAL HOUSEHOLDS	**37,867**	**25,070**	**12,416**	**339**	**42**
All permanent buildings	**37,644**	**24,949**	**12,334**	**327**	**34**
Owner occupied - owned outright	10,768	9,025	1,710	29	4
- buying	14,126	7,570	6,403	143	10
Rented privately - furnished	838	561	262	4	11
- unfurnished	1,406	1,045	347	13	1
Rented with a job or business	806	531	268	6	1
Rented from a housing association	2,994	2,000	961	31	2
Rented from a local authority or new town	6,706	4,217	2,383	101	5
Non - permanent accommodation	**223**	**121**	**82**	**12**	**8**
TOTAL PERSONS IN HOUSEHOLDS	**93,935**	**45,489**	**46,346**	**1,908**	**192**
All permanent buildings	**93,507**	**45,320**	**46,163**	**1,868**	**156**
Owner occupied - owned outright	22,478	15,869	6,430	154	25
- buying	42,430	16,436	25,140	806	48
Rented privately - furnished	1,434	803	590	18	23
- unfurnished	2,887	1,635	1,169	81	2
Rented with a job or business	2,187	1,108	1,039	35	5
Rented from a housing association	6,608	3,041	3,372	180	15
Rented from a local authority or new town	15,483	6,428	8,423	594	38
Non - permanent accommodation	**428**	**169**	**183**	**40**	**36**

23. Households with residents; residents in households

Tenure	TOTAL HOUSEHOLDS	Up to 0.5 persons per room	Over 0.5 and up to 1 person per room	Over 1 and up to 1.5 persons per room	Over 1.5 persons per room
a	b	c	d	e	f
	Barrow-in-Furness				
TOTAL HOUSEHOLDS	**29,627**	**19,145**	**10,018**	**404**	**60**
All permanent buildings	**29,342**	**18,922**	**9,965**	**399**	**56**
Owner occupied - owned outright	9,005	7,676	1,293	35	1
- buying	13,967	7,268	6,486	196	17
Rented privately - furnished	815	534	253	12	16
- unfurnished	1,100	761	305	27	7
Rented with a job or business	269	168	95	5	1
Rented from a housing association	348	197	145	2	4
Rented from a local authority or new town	3,838	2,318	1,388	122	10
Non - permanent accommodation	**285**	**223**	**53**	**5**	**4**
TOTAL PERSONS IN HOUSEHOLDS	**72,564**	**33,174**	**36,892**	**2,222**	**276**
All permanent buildings	**72,056**	**32,821**	**36,773**	**2,199**	**263**
Owner occupied - owned outright	17,325	12,589	4,550	184	2
- buying	41,080	14,594	25,282	1,099	105
Rented privately - furnished	1,466	756	615	56	39
- unfurnished	1,980	998	841	104	37
Rented with a job or business	688	293	355	34	6
Rented from a housing association	558	252	289	8	9
Rented from a local authority or new town	8,959	3,339	4,841	714	65
Non - permanent accommodation	**508**	**353**	**119**	**23**	**13**
	Carlisle				
TOTAL HOUSEHOLDS	**40,883**	**27,127**	**13,194**	**471**	**91**
All permanent buildings	**40,740**	**27,061**	**13,150**	**460**	**69**
Owner occupied - owned outright	9,856	8,496	1,342	16	2
- buying	17,526	9,922	7,405	183	16
Rented privately - furnished	1,119	575	508	10	26
- unfurnished	1,405	1,020	375	8	2
Rented with a job or business	907	561	323	19	4
Rented from a housing association	838	612	216	8	2
Rented from a local authority or new town	9,089	5,875	2,981	216	17
Non - permanent accommodation	**143**	**66**	**44**	**11**	**22**
TOTAL PERSONS IN HOUSEHOLDS	**99,059**	**48,303**	**47,756**	**2,619**	**381**
All permanent buildings	**98,771**	**48,225**	**47,673**	**2,572**	**301**
Owner occupied - owned outright	19,539	14,589	4,838	95	17
- buying	50,524	20,678	28,741	1,010	95
Rented privately - furnished	1,874	843	923	46	62
- unfurnished	2,963	1,624	1,285	46	8
Rented with a job or business	2,524	1,195	1,221	100	8
Rented from a housing association	1,364	802	507	49	6
Rented from a local authority or new town	19,983	8,494	10,158	1,226	105
Non - permanent accommodation	**288**	**78**	**83**	**47**	**80**

23. Households with residents; residents in households

Tenure	TOTAL HOUSEHOLDS	Up to 0.5 persons per room	Over 0.5 and up to 1 person per room	Over 1 and up to 1.5 persons per room	Over 1.5 persons per room
a	b	c	d	e	f
	Copeland				
TOTAL HOUSEHOLDS	**27,752**	**17,761**	**9,548**	**402**	**41**
All permanent buildings	**27,551**	**17,647**	**9,483**	**393**	**28**
Owner occupied - owned outright	6,284	5,176	1,077	29	2
- buying	11,731	6,187	5,391	148	5
Rented privately - furnished	489	308	166	6	9
- unfurnished	636	482	144	9	1
Rented with a job or business	546	346	193	7	-
Rented from a housing association	2,167	1,474	641	50	2
Rented from a local authority or new town	5,698	3,674	1,871	144	9
Non - permanent accommodation	**201**	**114**	**65**	**9**	**13**
TOTAL PERSONS IN HOUSEHOLDS	**70,485**	**32,000**	**36,004**	**2,307**	**174**
All permanent buildings	**70,111**	**31,854**	**35,857**	**2,275**	**125**
Owner occupied - owned outright	13,307	9,124	4,021	151	11
- buying	34,915	12,884	21,158	837	36
Rented privately - furnished	844	446	349	27	22
- unfurnished	1,322	767	504	49	2
Rented with a job or business	1,499	711	745	43	-
Rented from a housing association	4,668	2,134	2,223	301	10
Rented from a local authority or new town	13,556	5,788	6,857	867	44
Non - permanent accommodation	**374**	**146**	**147**	**32**	**49**
	Eden				
TOTAL HOUSEHOLDS	**18,017**	**12,497**	**5,314**	**171**	**35**
All permanent buildings	**17,827**	**12,414**	**5,245**	**152**	**16**
Owner occupied - owned outright	6,224	5,277	931	14	2
- buying	6,290	3,635	2,582	68	5
Rented privately - furnished	454	325	122	3	4
- unfurnished	1,429	1,028	388	12	1
Rented with a job or business	1,045	691	345	9	-
Rented from a housing association	410	274	128	7	1
Rented from a local authority or new town	1,975	1,184	749	39	3
Non - permanent accommodation	**190**	**83**	**69**	**19**	**19**
TOTAL PERSONS IN HOUSEHOLDS	**44,711**	**23,865**	**19,789**	**922**	**135**
All permanent buildings	**44,322**	**23,759**	**19,643**	**850**	**70**
Owner occupied - owned outright	13,216	9,590	3,540	78	8
- buying	18,656	8,073	10,184	372	27
Rented privately - furnished	847	515	305	15	12
- unfurnished	3,227	1,777	1,392	56	2
Rented with a job or business	3,058	1,590	1,420	48	-
Rented from a housing association	740	349	345	44	2
Rented from a local authority or new town	4,578	1,865	2,457	237	19
Non - permanent accommodation	**389**	**106**	**146**	**72**	**65**

23. Households with residents; residents in households

Tenure	TOTAL HOUSEHOLDS	Up to 0.5 persons per room	Over 0.5 and up to 1 person per room	Over 1 and up to 1.5 persons per room	Over 1.5 persons per room
a	b	c	d	e	f
	South Lakeland				
TOTAL HOUSEHOLDS	**39,747**	**28,296**	**11,116**	**254**	**81**
All permanent buildings	**39,585**	**28,230**	**11,039**	**246**	**70**
Owner occupied - owned outright	13,858	12,215	1,626	14	3
- buying	15,360	8,999	6,235	112	14
Rented privately - furnished	1,369	927	406	8	28
- unfurnished	2,437	1,873	538	20	6
Rented with a job or business	1,314	867	434	8	5
Rented from a housing association	595	430	160	4	1
Rented from a local authority or new town	4,652	2,919	1,640	80	13
Non - permanent accommodation	**162**	**66**	**77**	**8**	**11**
TOTAL PERSONS IN HOUSEHOLDS	**94,033**	**51,449**	**40,938**	**1,403**	**243**
All permanent buildings	**93,738**	**51,371**	**40,779**	**1,374**	**214**
Owner occupied - owned outright	26,715	20,818	5,811	80	6
- buying	44,458	19,260	24,520	611	67
Rented privately - furnished	2,521	1,401	1,020	39	61
- unfurnished	4,992	3,054	1,810	110	18
Rented with a job or business	3,568	1,808	1,690	49	21
Rented from a housing association	1,072	612	434	21	5
Rented from a local authority or new town	10,412	4,418	5,494	464	36
Non - permanent accommodation	**295**	**78**	**159**	**29**	**29**

Note: * May include a small number of households with no persons aged 18 and over

24. Households with residents; residents in households

Households with the following persons	TOTAL HOUSEHOLDS*	Households with the following persons aged 18 and over				TOTAL PERSONS AGED 18 AND OVER
		1	2	3	4 or more	
a	b	c	d	e	f	g
CUMBRIA						
TOTAL HOUSEHOLDS	**193,893**	**58,084**	**103,756**	**23,535**	**8,450**	**371,589**
1	51,169	51,127				51,127
2	66,033	3,429	62,584			128,597
3	32,487	2,444	14,162	15,877		78,399
4 or more	44,204	1,084	27,010	7,658	8,450	113,466
TOTAL PERSONS	**474,787**	**70,001**	**284,799**	**81,422**	**38,462**	
Allerdale						
TOTAL HOUSEHOLDS	**37,867**	**11,035**	**20,290**	**4,800**	**1,735**	**73,290**
1	9,656	9,651				9,651
2	12,668	714	11,952			24,618
3	6,595	470	2,889	3,236		15,956
4 or more	8,948	200	5,449	1,564	1,735	23,065
TOTAL PERSONS	**93,935**	**13,345**	**56,110**	**16,569**	**7,902**	
Barrow-in-Furness						
TOTAL HOUSEHOLDS	**29,627**	**9,321**	**15,582**	**3,529**	**1,185**	**56,000**
1	8,012	8,007				8,007
2	9,759	624	9,133			18,890
3	5,130	455	2,359	2,313		12,112
4 or more	6,726	235	4,090	1,216	1,185	16,991
TOTAL PERSONS	**72,564**	**11,632**	**43,225**	**12,278**	**5,411**	
Carlisle						
TOTAL HOUSEHOLDS	**40,883**	**12,812**	**21,557**	**4,864**	**1,623**	**77,305**
1	11,167	11,152				11,152
2	13,754	825	12,918			26,661
3	6,924	574	3,055	3,294		16,566
4 or more	9,038	261	5,584	1,570	1,623	22,926
TOTAL PERSONS	**99,059**	**15,669**	**59,187**	**16,820**	**7,343**	
Copeland						
TOTAL HOUSEHOLDS	**27,752**	**8,073**	**14,741**	**3,606**	**1,328**	**53,928**
1	6,903	6,900				6,900
2	8,941	562	8,378			17,318
3	4,928	408	2,166	2,354		11,802
4 or more	6,980	203	4,197	1,252	1,328	17,908
TOTAL PERSONS	**70,485**	**10,119**	**41,593**	**12,633**	**6,135**	

Note: * May include a small number of households with no persons aged 18 and over

24. Households with residents; residents in households

Households with the following persons	TOTAL HOUSEHOLDS*	Households with the following persons aged 18 and over				TOTAL PERSONS AGED 18 AND OVER
		1	2	3	4 or more	
a	b	c	d	e	f	g
			Eden			
TOTAL HOUSEHOLDS	**18,017**	**4,923**	**9,897**	**2,234**	**951**	**35,417**
1	4,502	4,494				4,494
2	6,268	209	6,057			12,323
3	2,961	161	1,233	1,567		7,328
4 or more	4,286	59	2,607	667	951	11,272
TOTAL PERSONS	**44,711**	**5,659**	**27,059**	**7,676**	**4,296**	
			South Lakeland			
TOTAL HOUSEHOLDS	**39,747**	**11,920**	**21,689**	**4,502**	**1,628**	**75,649**
1	10,929	10,923				10,923
2	14,643	495	14,146			28,787
3	5,949	376	2,460	3,113		14,635
4 or more	8,226	126	5,083	1,389	1,628	21,304
TOTAL PERSONS	**94,033**	**13,577**	**57,625**	**15,446**	**7,375**	

Table 25 Visitor households

Notes: (1) * Includes all students aged 18 and over, whether economically active or inactive
(2) ** Households with 3 or more cars are counted as having 3 cars

25. Households with persons present but no residents; persons present in such households; cars and rooms in such households

Households with no residents	TOTAL HOUSE-HOLDS	Lacking or sharing use of bath/ shower and/or inside WC	No central heating	Not self-contained accomm-odation	Tenure: Owner occupied	Tenure: Rented privately	Tenure: Rented from a housing assoc-iation	Tenure: Rented from a local authority or new town	TOTAL ROOMS	TOTAL CARS**	Total students* present
a	b	c	d	e	f	g	h	i	j	k	l
CUMBRIA											
TOTAL HOUSEHOLDS	**2,646**	**267**	**812**	**52**	**1,274**	**1,206**	**24**	**60**	**10,501**	**3,275**	**400**
Households with 1 or more students* aged 18 and over plus others	55	4	11	-	25	26	1	1	262	81	95
Households with student(s)* only	108	8	37	15	4	104	-	-	494	65	305
TOTAL PERSONS PRESENT	**6,118**	**519**	**1,707**	**70**	**2,748**	**3,051**	**53**	**110**			
Students* present	400	15	108	20	42	354	1	1			
Allerdale											
TOTAL HOUSEHOLDS	**503**	**55**	**178**	**5**	**209**	**254**	**11**	**21**	**1,967**	**624**	**16**
Households with 1 or more students* aged 18 and over plus others	4	-	1	-	1	2	-	1	24	5	6
Households with student(s)* only	5	-	2	-	-	5	-	-	19	7	10
TOTAL PERSONS PRESENT	**1,162**	**112**	**403**	**9**	**446**	**620**	**33**	**47**			
Students* present	16	-	5	-	1	14	-	1			
Barrow-in-Furness											
TOTAL HOUSEHOLDS	**107**	**5**	**46**	**2**	**36**	**61**	**-**	**3**	**446**	**113**	**1**
Households with 1 or more students* aged 18 and over plus others	1	-	-	-	-	-	-	-	3	1	1
Households with student(s)* only	-	-	-	-	-	-	-	-	-	-	-
TOTAL PERSONS PRESENT	**198**	**12**	**89**	**2**	**63**	**117**	**-**	**3**			
Students* present	1	-	-	-	-	-	-	-			
Carlisle											
TOTAL HOUSEHOLDS	**168**	**15**	**56**	**22**	**55**	**90**	**-**	**16**	**728**	**110**	**152**
Households with 1 or more students* aged 18 and over plus others	9	-	3	-	-	9	-	-	50	7	23
Households with student(s)* only	47	7	18	14	1	46	-	-	192	12	129
TOTAL PERSONS PRESENT	**359**	**17**	**101**	**25**	**91**	**229**	**-**	**24**			
Students* present	152	8	53	17	3	149	-	-			

Notes: (1) * Includes all students aged 18 and over, whether economically active or inactive
(2) ** Households with 3 or more cars are counted as having 3 cars

25. Households with persons present but no residents; persons present in such households; cars and rooms in such households

Households with no residents	TOTAL HOUSE-HOLDS	Lacking or sharing use of bath/ shower and/or inside WC	No central heating	Not self-contained accomm-odation	Tenure: Owner occupied	Tenure: Rented privately	Tenure: Rented from a housing assoc-iation	Tenure: Rented from a local authority or new town	TOTAL ROOMS	TOTAL CARS**	Total students* present
a	b	c	d	e	f	g	h	i	j	k	l
Copeland											
TOTAL HOUSEHOLDS	**167**	**19**	**47**	**10**	**65**	**89**	**2**	**5**	**690**	**193**	**3**
Households with 1 or more students* aged 18 and over plus others	1	-	-	-	-	1	-	-	4	2	1
Households with student(s)* only	1	-	-	-	-	1	-	-	4	1	2
TOTAL PERSONS PRESENT	**336**	**31**	**85**	**14**	**130**	**186**	**2**	**8**			
Students* present	3	-	-	-	-	3	-	-			
Eden											
TOTAL HOUSEHOLDS	**352**	**34**	**104**	**-**	**170**	**163**	**5**	**6**	**1,533**	**465**	**14**
Households with 1 or more students* aged 18 and over plus others	6	1	1	-	1	5	-	-	27	8	10
Households with student(s)* only	2	-	2	-	-	2	-	-	10	4	4
TOTAL PERSONS PRESENT	**828**	**60**	**197**	**-**	**360**	**432**	**9**	**12**			
Students* present	14	3	7	-	1	13	-	-			
South Lakeland											
TOTAL HOUSEHOLDS	**1,349**	**139**	**381**	**13**	**739**	**549**	**6**	**9**	**5,137**	**1,770**	**214**
Households with 1 or more students* aged 18 and over plus others	34	3	6	-	23	9	1	-	154	58	54
Households with student(s)* only	53	1	15	1	3	50	-	-	269	41	160
TOTAL PERSONS PRESENT	**3,235**	**287**	**832**	**20**	**1,658**	**1,467**	**9**	**16**			
Students* present	214	4	43	3	37	175	1	-			

Table 26 Students in households

Notes: (1) * Includes all students aged 18 and over whether economically active or inactive
(2) ** Households with 3 or more cars are counted as having 3 cars

26. Households with residents; residents in households; persons present in households; rooms in household spaces; cars in households

Households with residents enumerated with resident or visitor students aged 18 and over*	TOTAL HOUSE-HOLDS	Lacking or sharing use of bath/shower and/or inside WC	No central heating	Not self-contained accomm-odation	Tenure			
					Owner occupied	Rented privately	Rented from a housing association	Rented from a local authority or new town
a	b	c	d	e	f	g	h	i
CUMBRIA								
TOTAL HOUSEHOLDS	**193,893**	**2,494**	**50,633**	**1,177**	**135,816**	**13,781**	**7,353**	**31,992**
Households with students* (resident or visitor) only	163	16	53	20	45	101	5	11
Households with students* (resident or visitor) and non-students	6,064	19	781	13	5,166	248	96	369
Number of students in household (included above)*								
1	5,340	32	744	29	4,508	255	82	338
2	784	3	70	2	656	45	16	39
3 or more	103	-	20	2	47	49	3	3
TOTAL PERSONS RESIDENT OR PRESENT	**482,174**	**3,737**	**115,663**	**1,571**	**351,866**	**27,476**	**15,151**	**73,706**
Students* resident or present	7,276	38	959	41	5,964	545	124	427
Allerdale								
TOTAL HOUSEHOLDS	**37,867**	**460**	**8,789**	**182**	**25,063**	**2,285**	**2,994**	**6,707**
Households with students* (resident or visitor) only	31	4	9	1	9	18	-	4
Households with students* (resident or visitor) and non-students	1,221	2	167	1	1,006	37	54	94
Number of students in household (included above)*								
1	1,055	5	153	2	863	37	43	84
2	174	1	21	-	136	14	9	13
3 or more	23	-	2	-	16	4	2	1
TOTAL PERSONS RESIDENT OR PRESENT	**95,303**	**661**	**20,485**	**234**	**66,299**	**4,474**	**6,662**	**15,607**
Students* resident or present	1,475	7	201	2	1,183	77	68	115
Barrow-in-Furness								
TOTAL HOUSEHOLDS	**29,627**	**394**	**12,367**	**154**	**23,224**	**1,945**	**348**	**3,841**
Households with students* (resident or visitor) only	16	1	8	1	10	2	1	3
Households with students* (resident or visitor) and non-students	683	2	152	1	625	17	4	27
Number of students in household (included above)*								
1	644	3	149	2	583	19	5	28
2	49	-	9	-	46	-	-	2
3 or more	6	-	2	-	6	-	-	-
TOTAL PERSONS RESIDENT OR PRESENT	**73,373**	**585**	**28,329**	**188**	**59,507**	**3,558**	**566**	**9,043**
Students* resident or present	760	3	173	2	693	19	5	32

TOTAL ROOMS	TOTAL CARS**	Total student* visitors	Total student* residents	Households with the following persons present or resident					Households with residents enumerated with resident or visitor students aged 18 and over*
				1	2	3	4	5 or more	
j	k	l	m	n	o	p	q	r	a
1,020,955	**183,259**	**561**	**6,715**	**49,691**	**65,353**	**32,911**	**31,528**	**14,410**	**TOTAL HOUSEHOLDS**
747	126	50	277	90	28	16	17	12	Households with students* (resident or visitor) only
39,764	9,456	511	6,438	-	471	1,797	2,375	1,421	Households with students* (resident or visitor) and non-students
									Number of students in household (included above)*
34,236	8,121	369	4,971	90	471	1,734	1,967	1,078	1
5,588	1,316	117	1,451	-	28	63	395	298	2
687	145	75	293	-	-	16	30	57	3 or more
									TOTAL PERSONS RESIDENT OR PRESENT
				90	527	1,908	2,864	1,887	Students* resident or present
200,672	**36,130**	**78**	**1,397**	**9,423**	**12,487**	**6,698**	**6,400**	**2,859**	**TOTAL HOUSEHOLDS**
149	26	-	52	19	5	6	-	1	Households with students* (resident or visitor) only
7,849	1,912	78	1,345	-	95	338	472	316	Households with students* (resident or visitor) and non-students
									Number of students in household (included above)*
6,679	1,611	62	993	19	95	328	389	224	1
1,168	287	14	334	-	5	10	78	81	2
151	40	2	70	-	-	6	5	12	3 or more
									TOTAL PERSONS RESIDENT OR PRESENT
				19	105	366	560	425	Students* resident or present
148,864	**22,322**	**44**	**716**	**7,828**	**9,708**	**5,171**	**4,737**	**2,183**	**TOTAL HOUSEHOLDS**
68	8	-	17	15	1	-	-	-	Households with students* (resident or visitor) only
4,143	859	44	699	-	54	218	257	154	Households with students* (resident or visitor) and non-students
									Number of students in household (included above)*
3,846	793	36	608	15	54	215	235	125	1
321	65	7	91	-	1	3	22	23	2
44	9	1	17	-	-	-	-	6	3 or more
									TOTAL PERSONS RESIDENT OR PRESENT
				15	56	221	279	189	Students* resident or present

Table 26 Students in households - **continued**

Notes: (1) * Includes all students aged 18 and over whether economically active or inactive
(2) ** Households with 3 or more cars are counted as having 3 cars

26. Households with residents; residents in households; persons present in households; rooms in household spaces; cars in households

Households with residents enumerated with resident or visitor students aged 18 and over*	TOTAL HOUSE-HOLDS	Lacking or sharing use of bath/shower and/or inside WC	No central heating	Not self-contained accomm-odation	Tenure			
					Owner occupied	Rented privately	Rented from a housing association	Rented from a local authority or new town
a	b	c	d	e	f	g	h	i
			Carlisle					
TOTAL HOUSEHOLDS	**40,883**	**575**	**10,691**	**398**	**27,465**	**2,573**	**839**	**9,093**
Households with students* (resident or visitor) only	45	10	16	15	5	37	1	2
Households with students* (resident or visitor) and non-students	1,170	4	143	5	997	56	5	76
Number of students in household (included above)*								
1	1,062	14	138	20	884	63	6	77
2	128	-	16	-	110	14	-	-
3 or more	25	-	5	-	8	16	-	1
TOTAL PERSONS RESIDENT OR PRESENT	**100,420**	**823**	**23,659**	**484**	**71,254**	**5,035**	**1,381**	**20,162**
Students* resident or present	1,407	14	188	20	1,129	152	6	80
			Copeland					
TOTAL HOUSEHOLDS	**27,752**	**325**	**5,740**	**129**	**18,144**	**1,192**	**2,167**	**5,700**
Households with students* (resident or visitor) only	6	-	3	-	2	2	1	-
Households with students* (resident or visitor) and non-students	891	3	98	2	739	20	19	90
Number of students in household (included above)*								
1	762	2	89	1	636	20	16	72
2	128	1	11	1	100	2	3	17
3 or more	7	-	1	-	5	-	1	1
TOTAL PERSONS RESIDENT OR PRESENT	**71,358**	**519**	**13,490**	**183**	**49,078**	**2,329**	**4,704**	**13,695**
Students* resident or present	1,040	4	114	3	852	24	25	109
			Eden					
TOTAL HOUSEHOLDS	**18,017**	**331**	**4,081**	**82**	**12,625**	**1,925**	**410**	**1,996**
Households with students* (resident or visitor) only	17	-	2	1	9	7	-	1
Households with students* (resident or visitor) and non-students	595	2	71	2	503	28	4	25
Number of students in household (included above)*								
1	522	2	65	2	438	30	4	22
2	86	-	6	1	72	3	-	4
3 or more	4	-	2	-	2	2	-	-
TOTAL PERSONS RESIDENT OR PRESENT	**45,592**	**565**	**9,435**	**132**	**32,809**	**4,212**	**745**	**4,670**
Students* resident or present	708	2	84	4	588	44	4	30

TOTAL ROOMS	TOTAL CARS**	Total student* visitors	Total student* residents	Households with the following persons present or resident					Households with residents enumerated with resident or visitor students aged 18 and over*
				1	2	3	4	5 or more	
j	k	l	m	n	o	p	q	r	a
208,487	**36,306**	**144**	**1,263**	**10,884**	**13,633**	**7,018**	**6,499**	**2,849**	**TOTAL HOUSEHOLDS**
172	11	10	75	26	7	5	6	1	Households with students* (resident or visitor) only
7,575	1,718	134	1,188	-	112	365	445	248	Households with students* (resident or visitor) and non-students
									Number of students in household (included above)*
6,692	1,509	79	983	26	112	345	385	194	1
888	203	41	215	-	7	20	56	45	2
167	17	24	65	-	-	5	10	10	3 or more
									TOTAL PERSONS RESIDENT OR PRESENT
				26	126	400	533	322	Students* resident or present
146,683	**24,472**	**60**	**980**	**6,721**	**8,869**	**4,958**	**4,831**	**2,373**	**TOTAL HOUSEHOLDS**
26	2	-	7	5	1	-	-	-	Households with students* (resident or visitor) only
5,669	1,293	60	973	-	59	249	383	200	Households with students* (resident or visitor) and non-students
									Number of students in household (included above)*
4,775	1,097	47	715	5	59	238	307	153	1
873	191	10	246	-	1	11	73	43	2
47	7	3	19	-	-	-	3	4	3 or more
									TOTAL PERSONS RESIDENT OR PRESENT
				5	61	260	462	252	Students* resident or present
100,900	**20,926**	**55**	**653**	**4,357**	**6,168**	**2,994**	**3,077**	**1,421**	**TOTAL HOUSEHOLDS**
86	18	-	28	10	5	-	2	-	Households with students* (resident or visitor) only
4,159	1,077	55	625	-	34	171	251	139	Households with students* (resident or visitor) and non-students
									Number of students in household (included above)*
3,506	926	45	477	10	34	167	198	113	1
709	160	10	162	-	5	4	53	24	2
30	9	-	14	-	-	-	2	2	3 or more
									TOTAL PERSONS RESIDENT OR PRESENT
				10	44	175	312	167	Students* resident or present

Table 26 Students in households - continued

Notes: (1) * Includes all students aged 18 and over whether economically active or inactive
(2) ** Households with 3 or more cars are counted as having 3 cars

26. Households with residents; residents in households; persons present in households; rooms in household spaces; cars in households

Households with residents enumerated with resident or visitor students aged 18 and over*	TOTAL HOUSE-HOLDS	Lacking or sharing use of bath/shower and/or inside WC	No central heating	Not self-contained accomm-odation	Tenure			
					Owner occupied	Rented privately	Rented from a housing association	Rented from a local authority or new town
a	b	c	d	e	f	g	h	i
			South Lakeland					
TOTAL HOUSEHOLDS	**39,747**	**409**	**8,965**	**232**	**29,295**	**3,861**	**595**	**4,655**
Households with students* (resident or visitor) only	48	1	15	2	10	35	2	1
Households with students* (resident or visitor) and non-students	1,504	6	150	2	1,296	90	10	57
Number of students in household (included above)*								
1	1,295	6	150	2	1,104	86	8	55
2	219	1	7	-	192	12	4	3
3 or more	38	-	8	2	10	27	-	-
TOTAL PERSONS RESIDENT OR PRESENT	**96,128**	**584**	**20,265**	**350**	**72,919**	**7,868**	**1,093**	**10,529**
Students* resident or present	1,886	8	199	10	1,519	229	16	61

TOTAL ROOMS	TOTAL CARS**	Total student* visitors	Total student* residents	Households with the following persons present or resident					Households with residents enumerated with resident or visitor students aged 18 and over*
				1	2	3	4	5 or more	
j	k	l	m	n	o	p	q	r	a
215,349	**43,103**	**180**	**1,706**	**10,478**	**14,488**	**6,072**	**5,984**	**2,725**	**TOTAL HOUSEHOLDS**
246	61	40	98	15	9	5	9	10	Households with students* (resident or visitor) only
10,369	2,597	140	1,608	-	117	456	567	364	Households with students* (resident or visitor) and non-students
									Number of students in household (included above)*
8,738	2,185	100	1,195	15	117	441	453	269	1
1,629	410	35	403	-	9	15	113	82	2
248	63	45	108	-	-	5	10	23	3 or more
									TOTAL PERSONS RESIDENT OR PRESENT
				15	135	486	718	532	Students* resident or present

Note: * Private households with a visitor or visitors present but no usual residents ie a household with '0 persons'

27. Line 1: 1991 households with persons present (1971 population base): present residents and visitors; rooms
Line 2: 1991 households (1981 population base): present and absent residents; rooms
Line 3: 1991 households enumerated or absent (1991 population base): present and absent residents and imputed members of wholly absent households; rooms

	Households with the following persons								TOTAL HOUSE-HOLDS	TOTAL PERSONS (1991)	TOTAL ROOMS (1991)
	0*	1	2	3	4	5	6	7 or more			
a	b	c	d	e	f	g	h	i	j	k	l
CUMBRIA											
1. 1971 population base		48,947	65,752	32,569	30,002	10,005	2,651	770	190,696	469,831	1,002,607
2. 1981 population base	2,646	48,058	64,016	32,095	30,759	9,976	2,495	651	190,696	465,071	1,002,607
3. 1991 population base	2,646	51,169	66,033	32,487	31,000	10,038	2,514	652	196,539	474,787	1,031,456
Allerdale											
1. 1971 population base		9,278	12,636	6,623	6,157	2,046	491	148	37,379	93,323	197,873
2. 1981 population base	503	9,113	12,345	6,526	6,288	2,020	463	121	37,379	92,297	197,873
3. 1991 population base	503	9,656	12,668	6,595	6,330	2,030	467	121	38,370	93,935	202,639
Barrow-in-Furness											
1. 1971 population base		7,625	9,602	5,103	4,498	1,519	393	130	28,870	71,043	145,294
2. 1981 population base	107	7,530	9,499	5,059	4,630	1,533	388	124	28,870	71,134	145,294
3. 1991 population base	107	8,012	9,759	5,130	4,671	1,542	389	124	29,734	72,564	149,310
Carlisle											
1. 1971 population base		10,729	13,538	6,894	6,141	1,980	513	153	39,948	97,163	203,971
2. 1981 population base	168	10,569	13,403	6,850	6,342	1,998	476	142	39,948	97,189	203,971
3. 1991 population base	168	11,167	13,754	6,924	6,401	2,013	481	143	41,051	99,059	209,215
Copeland											
1. 1971 population base		6,627	8,828	4,931	4,576	1,633	474	122	27,191	69,299	143,674
2. 1981 population base	167	6,508	8,699	4,880	4,713	1,626	484	114	27,191	69,277	143,674
3. 1991 population base	167	6,903	8,941	4,928	4,746	1,633	487	114	27,919	70,485	147,373
Eden											
1. 1971 population base		4,292	6,265	3,003	2,920	953	301	73	17,807	44,630	99,442
2. 1981 population base	352	4,203	6,072	2,927	3,010	936	252	55	17,807	43,775	99,442
3. 1991 population base	352	4,502	6,268	2,961	3,034	943	254	55	18,369	44,711	102,433
South Lakeland											
1. 1971 population base		10,396	14,883	6,015	5,710	1,874	479	144	39,501	94,373	212,353
2. 1981 population base	1,349	10,135	13,998	5,853	5,776	1,863	432	95	39,501	91,399	212,353
3. 1991 population base	1,349	10,929	14,643	5,949	5,818	1,877	436	95	41,096	94,033	220,486

Table 28 Dependants in households

28. Households with residents; residents in households

Household composition	TOTAL HOUSE-HOLDS	No non-dependants	1 male non-dependant		1 female non-dependant		1 male and 1 female non-dependants		
			Not in employment	In employment	Not in employment	In employment	Neither in employment	1 in employment	Both in employment
a	b	c	d	e	f	g	h	i	j
			CUMBRIA						
TOTAL HOUSEHOLDS	**193,893**	**16,558**	**7,929**	**12,356**	**27,252**	**10,718**	**14,897**	**24,411**	**44,930**
Households with no dependants	105,528		5,622	9,578	17,445	6,234	12,638	9,948	21,773
Households with 1 dependant									
Age of dependant									
0 - 4	8,503	3	17	19	860	334	332	2,954	3,116
5 - 15	10,946	1	43	148	579	845	213	1,221	3,497
16 - 18	3,016	16	12	45	59	149	53	281	819
19 up to pensionable age	8,657	2,069	395	908	1,836	1,040	205	514	426
Pensionable age and over	18,904	10,201	1,573	864	4,049	528	173	473	266
Households with at least 2 dependants									
Age of youngest dependant 0 - 4 and age of oldest									
0 - 4	4,143	-	1	2	309	49	236	2,136	1,261
5 - 15	8,918	3	17	23	809	202	517	3,359	3,340
16 - 18	314	-	2	-	20	3	26	92	85
19 up to pensionable age	554	34	18	111	167	50	11	30	19
Pensionable age and over	135	2	3	1	11	10	9	25	27
Age of youngest dependant 5 - 15 and age of oldest									
5 - 15	14,239	1	41	115	606	729	364	2,635	8,307
16 - 18	3,037	1	5	30	66	146	66	511	1,620
19 up to pensionable age	1,150	112	66	225	178	201	23	59	70
Pensionable age and over	373	19	3	5	31	36	8	63	94
Age of youngest dependant 16 - 18 and age of oldest									
16 - 18	248	-	3	2	3	9	1	37	142
19 up to pensionable age	210	18	11	22	23	33	2	21	20
Pensionable age and over	70	7	2	3	7	6	3	4	10
Age of youngest dependant 19 up to pensionable age and age of oldest									
19 up to pensionable age	621	389	22	59	50	27	5	18	9
Pensionable age and over	941	638	33	70	87	35	7	15	13
Age of youngest dependant pensionable age and over	3,386	3,044	40	126	57	52	5	15	16
TOTAL PERSONS	**474,787**	**21,109**	**10,632**	**16,220**	**40,826**	**17,359**	**34,131**	**75,894**	**131,981**
Persons in households with dependants									
Non-dependants	137,654		2,307	2,778	9,807	4,484	4,518	28,926	46,314
Dependants	138,868	21,109	2,703	3,864	13,574	6,641	4,337	27,072	42,121

2 same sex non-dependants			3 or more non-dependants			Household composition
Neither in employment	1 in employment	Both in employment	None in employment	1 in employment	2 or more in employment	
k	l	m	n	o	p	a
997	**2,034**	**2,302**	**763**	**3,337**	**25,409**	**TOTAL HOUSEHOLDS**
673	1,147	1,502	536	2,250	16,182	Households with no dependants
						Households with 1 dependant
						Age of dependant
38	57	24	22	114	613	0 - 4
23	100	146	48	247	3,835	5 - 15
3	33	54	12	118	1,362	16 - 18
71	241	273	26	118	535	19 up to pensionable age
75	229	107	13	64	289	Pensionable age and over
						Households with at least 2 dependants
						Age of youngest dependant 0 - 4 and age of oldest
12	11	1	10	31	84	0 - 4
29	31	14	24	117	433	5 - 15
6	3	2	4	12	59	16 - 18
12	17	11	5	21	48	19 up to pensionable age
2	4	2	2	9	28	Pensionable age and over
						Age of youngest dependant 5 - 15 and age of oldest
23	52	50	34	120	1,162	5 - 15
2	13	17	13	58	489	16 - 18
16	43	47	7	24	79	19 up to pensionable age
-	14	3	1	8	88	Pensionable age and over
						Age of youngest dependant 16 - 18 and age of oldest
1	-	1	1	7	41	16 - 18
2	9	20	1	6	22	19 up to pensionable age
1	2	-	-	4	21	Pensionable age and over
						Age of youngest dependant 19 up to pensionable age and age of oldest
2	13	7	3	4	13	19 up to pensionable age
5	11	9	1	4	13	Pensionable age and over
1	4	12	-	1	13	Age of youngest dependant pensionable age and over
2,497	**5,271**	**5,649**	**2,817**	**12,105**	**98,296**	**TOTAL PERSONS**
						Persons in households with dependants
648	1,774	1,600	726	3,414	30,358	Non-dependants
503	1,203	1,045	404	1,700	12,592	Dependants

Table 28 Dependants in households - **continued**

28. Households with residents; residents in households

Household composition	TOTAL HOUSE-HOLDS	No non-dependants	1 male non-dependant		1 female non-dependant		1 male and 1 female non-dependants		
			Not in employment	In employment	Not in employment	In employment	Neither in employment	1 in employment	Both in employment
a	b	c	d	e	f	g	h	i	j
			Allerdale						
TOTAL HOUSEHOLDS	**37,867**	**3,272**	**1,638**	**2,161**	**5,559**	**1,866**	**3,066**	**5,083**	**8,426**
Households with no dependants	19,916		1,152	1,587	3,474	1,031	2,463	1,995	3,930
Households with 1 dependant									
Age of dependant									
0 - 4	1,660	1	4	2	209	52	82	603	560
5 - 15	2,338	-	7	42	132	154	50	272	744
16 - 18	595	3	-	8	15	25	13	70	161
19 up to pensionable age	1,861	429	83	182	404	213	55	133	93
Pensionable age and over	3,744	1,979	336	169	801	92	51	116	48
Households with at least 2 dependants									
Age of youngest dependant 0 - 4 and age of oldest									
0 - 4	783	-	-	-	42	7	57	424	221
5 - 15	1,690	-	2	3	154	27	144	682	581
16 - 18	76	-	-	-	4	1	6	26	19
19 up to pensionable age	126	8	4	34	41	10	-	11	1
Pensionable age and over	22	1	-	-	5	-	2	3	5
Age of youngest dependant 5 - 15 and age of oldest									
5 - 15	2,930	-	9	23	142	137	100	589	1,653
16 - 18	645	1	-	6	18	31	32	107	322
19 up to pensionable age	264	23	14	51	49	42	5	12	14
Pensionable age and over	77	2	1	1	5	7	3	15	20
Age of youngest dependant 16 - 18 and age of oldest									
16 - 18	57	-	1	-	-	1	-	6	37
19 up to pensionable age	42	2	4	2	5	4	-	5	7
Pensionable age and over	18	4	1	-	2	2	1	1	2
Age of youngest dependant 19 up to pensionable age and age of oldest									
19 up to pensionable age	143	92	8	13	13	5	1	3	1
Pensionable age and over	231	146	6	17	30	8	1	6	3
Age of youngest dependant pensionable age and over	649	581	6	21	14	17	-	4	4
TOTAL PERSONS	**93,935**	**4,191**	**2,202**	**2,975**	**8,452**	**3,094**	**7,273**	**15,871**	**24,951**
Persons in households with dependants									
Non-dependants	28,087		486	574	2,085	835	1,206	6,176	8,992
Dependants	28,059	4,191	564	814	2,893	1,228	1,141	5,705	8,099

2 same sex non-dependants: Neither in employment	2 same sex non-dependants: 1 in employment	2 same sex non-dependants: Both in employment	3 or more non-dependants: None in employment	3 or more non-dependants: 1 in employment	3 or more non-dependants: 2 or more in employment	Household composition
k	l	m	n	o	p	a
194	**382**	**354**	**156**	**766**	**4,944**	**TOTAL HOUSEHOLDS**
134	197	206	101	515	3,131	Households with no dependants
						Households with 1 dependant
						Age of dependant
6	6	5	6	20	104	0 - 4
4	19	21	17	65	811	5 - 15
-	8	9	2	15	266	16 - 18
13	60	57	3	31	105	19 up to pensionable age
14	41	15	5	13	64	Pensionable age and over
						Households with at least 2 dependants
						Age of youngest dependant 0 - 4 and age of oldest
3	1	-	3	9	16	0 - 4
7	5	1	3	19	62	5 - 15
1	2	-	1	4	12	16 - 18
1	4	3	-	4	5	19 up to pensionable age
-	-	-	-	1	5	Pensionable age and over
						Age of youngest dependant 5 - 15 and age of oldest
6	9	10	7	37	208	5 - 15
1	5	3	6	12	101	16 - 18
1	11	15	1	10	16	19 up to pensionable age
-	5	-	-	3	15	Pensionable age and over
						Age of youngest dependant 16 - 18 and age of oldest
-	-	1	1	1	9	16 - 18
-	1	4	-	3	5	19 up to pensionable age
1	-	-	-	-	4	Pensionable age and over
						Age of youngest dependant 19 up to pensionable age and age of oldest
1	2	1	-	2	1	19 up to pensionable age
1	6	1	-	2	4	Pensionable age and over
-	-	2	-	-	-	Age of youngest dependant pensionable age and over
478	**1,014**	**906**	**592**	**2,787**	**19,149**	**TOTAL PERSONS**
						Persons in households with dependants
120	370	296	180	790	5,977	Non-dependants
90	250	198	96	389	2,401	Dependants

Table 28 Dependants in households - continued

28. Households with residents; residents in households

Household composition	TOTAL HOUSE-HOLDS	No non-dependants	1 male non-dependant: Not in employment	1 male non-dependant: In employment	1 female non-dependant: Not in employment	1 female non-dependant: In employment	1 male and 1 female non-dependants: Neither in employment	1 male and 1 female non-dependants: 1 in employment	1 male and 1 female non-dependants: Both in employment
a	b	c	d	e	f	g	h	i	j
			Barrow-in-Furness						
TOTAL HOUSEHOLDS	**29,627**	**2,927**	**1,290**	**2,155**	**4,157**	**1,514**	**2,140**	**3,888**	**6,292**
Households with no dependants	15,374		886	1,630	2,493	839	1,725	1,515	3,009
Households with 1 dependant									
Age of dependant									
0 - 4	1,526	-	2	3	185	62	77	556	492
5 - 15	1,765	-	8	23	107	132	41	197	515
16 - 18	415	1	4	5	7	23	14	40	114
19 up to pensionable age	1,524	420	86	198	292	146	30	77	60
Pensionable age and over	2,971	1,743	253	138	556	57	16	62	31
Households with at least 2 dependants									
Age of youngest dependant 0 - 4 and age of oldest									
0 - 4	663	-	-	1	74	9	43	356	163
5 - 15	1,596	-	5	4	215	42	103	576	526
16 - 18	57	-	-	-	7	-	4	11	19
19 up to pensionable age	127	7	3	29	40	12	5	1	7
Pensionable age and over	19	-	1	-	1	2	1	4	3
Age of youngest dependant 5 - 15 and age of oldest									
5 - 15	1,980	-	8	13	98	106	63	374	1,107
16 - 18	389	-	2	3	11	18	9	82	196
19 up to pensionable age	222	24	12	52	34	33	6	10	17
Pensionable age and over	58	2	2	1	6	9	-	10	11
Age of youngest dependant 16 - 18 and age of oldest									
16 - 18	34	-	-	-	1	4	-	3	18
19 up to pensionable age	41	4	1	4	9	6	-	3	2
Pensionable age and over	9	1	-	1	2	1	-	2	-
Age of youngest dependant 19 up to pensionable age and age of oldest									
19 up to pensionable age	124	83	3	12	8	2	1	4	1
Pensionable age and over	164	129	7	12	4	6	1	2	1
Age of youngest dependant pensionable age and over	569	513	7	26	7	5	1	3	-
TOTAL PERSONS	**72,564**	**3,754**	**1,770**	**2,908**	**6,666**	**2,572**	**5,116**	**12,169**	**18,512**
Persons in households with dependants									
Non-dependants	21,456		404	525	1,664	675	830	4,746	6,566
Dependants	22,459	3,754	480	753	2,509	1,058	836	4,393	5,928

2 same sex non-dependants			3 or more non-dependants			Household composition
Neither in employment	1 in employment	Both in employment	None in employment	1 in employment	2 or more in employment	
k	l	m	n	o	p	a
139	**325**	**396**	**118**	**495**	**3,791**	**TOTAL HOUSEHOLDS**
81	178	257	74	319	2,368	Households with no dependants
						Households with 1 dependant
						Age of dependant
6	13	4	4	24	98	0 - 4
3	16	25	7	43	648	5 - 15
1	3	13	1	16	173	16 - 18
9	43	54	8	18	83	19 up to pensionable age
15	39	12	2	14	33	Pensionable age and over
						Households with at least 2 dependants
						Age of youngest dependant 0 - 4 and age of oldest
4	1	-	2	2	8	0 - 4
6	6	3	4	19	87	5 - 15
2	-	-	1	2	11	16 - 18
1	4	1	2	4	11	19 up to pensionable age
-	-	-	1	-	6	Pensionable age and over
						Age of youngest dependant 5 - 15 and age of oldest
3	9	7	9	18	165	5 - 15
-	-	1	2	8	57	16 - 18
5	7	6	1	1	14	19 up to pensionable age
-	2	1	-	1	13	Pensionable age and over
						Age of youngest dependant 16 - 18 and age of oldest
-	-	-	-	2	6	16 - 18
-	1	7	-	1	3	19 up to pensionable age
-	-	-	-	-	2	Pensionable age and over
						Age of youngest dependant 19 up to pensionable age and age of oldest
1	1	3	-	1	4	19 up to pensionable age
1	-	-	-	1	-	Pensionable age and over
1	2	2	-	1	1	Age of youngest dependant pensionable age and over
371	**849**	**973**	**450**	**1,809**	**14,645**	**TOTAL PERSONS**
						Persons in households with dependants
116	294	278	141	552	4,665	Non-dependants
93	199	181	80	264	1,931	Dependants

Table 28 Dependants in households – **continued**

28. Households with residents; residents in households

Household composition	TOTAL HOUSE-HOLDS	No non-dependants	1 male non-dependant		1 female non-dependant		1 male and 1 female non-dependants		
			Not in employment	In employment	Not in employment	In employment	Neither in employment	1 in employment	Both in employment
a	b	c	d	e	f	g	h	i	j
			Carlisle						
TOTAL HOUSEHOLDS	**40,883**	**3,709**	**1,650**	**2,629**	**5,738**	**2,500**	**2,795**	**4,668**	**9,876**
Households with no dependants	22,194		1,194	2,052	3,665	1,481	2,357	1,960	4,769
Households with 1 dependant									
Age of dependant									
0 - 4	1,841	-	6	4	216	75	66	558	742
5 - 15	2,421	1	11	32	139	208	49	249	784
16 - 18	605	6	4	12	13	37	11	53	160
19 up to pensionable age	1,786	501	66	184	350	219	27	101	88
Pensionable age and over	4,031	2,267	311	189	804	130	36	84	61
Households with at least 2 dependants									
Age of youngest dependant 0 - 4 and age of oldest									
0 - 4	900	-	-	-	89	13	61	408	298
5 - 15	1,878	-	4	5	190	48	88	638	759
16 - 18	51	-	1	-	3	-	6	12	17
19 up to pensionable age	113	9	6	19	28	8	3	5	6
Pensionable age and over	24	-	-	-	-	3	1	6	7
Age of youngest dependant 5 - 15 and age of oldest									
5 - 15	2,995	-	9	26	149	160	70	467	1,805
16 - 18	576	-	1	3	10	37	10	86	315
19 up to pensionable age	248	25	14	43	36	38	3	17	17
Pensionable age and over	69	5	-	3	4	6	1	11	17
Age of youngest dependant 16 - 18 and age of oldest									
16 - 18	26	-	-	-	-	2	-	4	16
19 up to pensionable age	36	3	5	5	1	9	-	3	2
Pensionable age and over	12	2	-	1	1	-	2	-	2
Age of youngest dependant 19 up to pensionable age and age of oldest									
19 up to pensionable age	122	83	3	8	9	7	-	-	4
Pensionable age and over	208	132	7	17	18	10	3	5	4
Age of youngest dependant pensionable age and over	747	675	8	26	13	9	1	1	3
TOTAL PERSONS	**99,059**	**4,708**	**2,196**	**3,418**	**8,671**	**3,988**	**6,438**	**14,416**	**28,902**
Persons in households with dependants									
Non-dependants	28,531		456	577	2,073	1,019	876	5,416	10,214
Dependants	29,200	4,708	546	789	2,933	1,488	848	5,080	9,150

2 same sex non-dependants			3 or more non-dependants			Household composition
Neither in employment	1 in employment	Both in employment	None in employment	1 in employment	2 or more in employment	
k	l	m	n	o	p	a
208	**491**	**536**	**171**	**645**	**5,267**	**TOTAL HOUSEHOLDS**
130	290	352	125	433	3,386	Households with no dependants
						Households with 1 dependant
						Age of dependant
7	11	7	4	24	121	0 - 4
11	31	39	11	56	800	5 - 15
-	5	12	3	21	268	16 - 18
19	48	55	6	20	102	19 up to pensionable age
7	51	23	-	12	56	Pensionable age and over
						Households with at least 2 dependants
						Age of youngest dependant 0 - 4 and age of oldest
2	4	-	1	5	19	0 - 4
9	8	4	5	24	96	5 - 15
1	-	-	1	2	8	16 - 18
4	4	2	3	4	12	19 up to pensionable age
-	-	-	-	2	5	Pensionable age and over
						Age of youngest dependant 5 - 15 and age of oldest
9	13	9	6	21	251	5 - 15
-	2	5	2	15	90	16 - 18
8	14	14	1	3	15	19 up to pensionable age
-	3	1	1	1	16	Pensionable age and over
						Age of youngest dependant 16 - 18 and age of oldest
-	-	-	-	-	4	16 - 18
-	2	3	-	-	3	19 up to pensionable age
-	-	-	-	-	4	Pensionable age and over
						Age of youngest dependant 19 up to pensionable age and age of oldest
-	3	1	2	1	1	19 up to pensionable age
1	2	3	-	1	5	Pensionable age and over
-	-	6	-	-	5	Age of youngest dependant pensionable age and over
557	**1,257**	**1,315**	**628**	**2,337**	**20,228**	**TOTAL PERSONS**
						Persons in households with dependants
156	402	368	144	672	6,158	Non-dependants
141	275	243	84	334	2,581	Dependants

28. Households with residents; residents in households

Household composition	TOTAL HOUSE-HOLDS	No non-dependants	1 male non-dependant		1 female non-dependant		1 male and 1 female non-dependants		
			Not in employment	In employment	Not in employment	In employment	Neither in employment	1 in employment	Both in employment
a	b	c	d	e	f	g	h	i	j
			Copeland						
TOTAL HOUSEHOLDS	**27,752**	**2,233**	**1,253**	**1,780**	**3,894**	**1,370**	**2,010**	**3,786**	**6,165**
Households with no dependants	14,196		910	1,343	2,292	703	1,535	1,421	2,828
Households with 1 dependant									
Age of dependant									
0 - 4	1,371	-	4	2	149	47	64	456	473
5 - 15	1,639	-	11	14	117	121	46	193	487
16 - 18	446	1	1	9	7	25	5	39	125
19 up to pensionable age	1,525	336	75	164	315	170	41	81	88
Pensionable age and over	2,493	1,318	193	127	530	72	24	68	34
Households with at least 2 dependants									
Age of youngest dependant 0 - 4 and age of oldest									
0 - 4	630	-	1	-	60	6	50	324	162
5 - 15	1,528	-	2	3	160	28	126	593	482
16 - 18	62	-	1	-	5	1	6	20	9
19 up to pensionable age	112	4	3	18	35	11	2	10	3
Pensionable age and over	26	-	1	-	4	1	2	3	5
Age of youngest dependant 5 - 15 and age of oldest									
5 - 15	2,208	-	9	12	124	100	90	477	1,142
16 - 18	467	-	2	5	18	16	10	70	265
19 up to pensionable age	194	19	13	31	28	35	6	9	12
Pensionable age and over	64	4	-	-	10	6	1	10	17
Age of youngest dependant 16 - 18 and age of oldest									
16 - 18	38	-	1	2	-	1	-	4	24
19 up to pensionable age	39	4	-	6	5	7	-	2	1
Pensionable age and over	13	-	1	1	1	1	-	-	3
Age of youngest dependant 19 up to pensionable age and age of oldest									
19 up to pensionable age	110	62	7	10	10	6	2	3	1
Pensionable age and over	161	109	7	12	17	5	-	-	2
Age of youngest dependant pensionable age and over	430	376	11	21	7	8	-	3	2
TOTAL PERSONS	**70,485**	**2,858**	**1,683**	**2,376**	**6,242**	**2,360**	**4,979**	**12,109**	**18,388**
Persons in households with dependants									
Non-dependants	21,852		343	437	1,602	667	950	4,730	6,674
Dependants	21,764	2,858	430	596	2,348	990	959	4,537	6,058

2 same sex non-dependants: Neither in employment	2 same sex non-dependants: 1 in employment	2 same sex non-dependants: Both in employment	3 or more non-dependants: None in employment	3 or more non-dependants: 1 in employment	3 or more non-dependants: 2 or more in employment	Household composition
k	l	m	n	o	p	a
153	**310**	**321**	**140**	**617**	**3,720**	**TOTAL HOUSEHOLDS**
97	161	197	81	372	2,256	Households with no dependants
						Households with 1 dependant
						Age of dependant
11	12	1	5	28	119	0 - 4
-	16	19	10	47	558	5 - 15
1	7	7	2	16	201	16 - 18
11	43	47	5	32	117	19 up to pensionable age
15	32	21	4	10	45	Pensionable age and over
						Households with at least 2 dependants
						Age of youngest dependant 0 - 4 and age of oldest
2	2	-	4	9	10	0 - 4
5	5	1	10	37	76	5 - 15
1	1	1	1	4	12	16 - 18
4	3	2	-	8	9	19 up to pensionable age
1	3	-	1	2	3	Pensionable age and over
						Age of youngest dependant 5 - 15 and age of oldest
3	9	4	9	26	203	5 - 15
-	3	3	2	11	62	16 - 18
-	3	9	4	8	17	19 up to pensionable age
-	-	1	-	2	13	Pensionable age and over
						Age of youngest dependant 16 - 18 and age of oldest
-	-	-	-	2	4	16 - 18
1	1	3	1	1	7	19 up to pensionable age
-	2	-	-	2	2	Pensionable age and over
						Age of youngest dependant 19 up to pensionable age and age of oldest
-	4	1	1	-	3	19 up to pensionable age
1	2	3	-	-	3	Pensionable age and over
-	1	1	-	-	-	Age of youngest dependant pensionable age and over
386	**822**	**802**	**550**	**2,352**	**14,578**	**TOTAL PERSONS**
						Persons in households with dependants
112	298	248	190	766	4,835	Non-dependants
80	202	160	110	417	2,019	Dependants

Table 28 Dependants in households – continued

28. Households with residents; residents in households

Household composition	TOTAL HOUSE-HOLDS	No non-dependants	1 male non-dependant		1 female non-dependant		1 male and 1 female non-dependants		
			Not in employment	In employment	Not in employment	In employment	Neither in employment	1 in employment	Both in employment
a	b	c	d	e	f	g	h	i	j
			Eden						
TOTAL HOUSEHOLDS	**18,017**	**1,182**	**658**	**1,159**	**2,269**	**1,019**	**1,370**	**2,478**	**4,422**
Households with no dependants	10,453		482	949	1,565	617	1,250	1,028	2,210
Households with 1 dependant									
Age of dependant									
0 - 4	723	1	1	4	26	37	19	287	279
5 - 15	891	-	4	10	22	54	11	117	295
16 - 18	298	2	1	2	8	9	4	29	79
19 up to pensionable age	633	123	29	47	153	102	19	47	28
Pensionable age and over	1,599	763	125	80	398	62	11	54	29
Households with at least 2 dependants									
Age of youngest dependant 0 - 4 and age of oldest									
0 - 4	412	-	-	-	14	5	12	225	136
5 - 15	710	3	1	3	27	20	15	311	279
16 - 18	19	-	-	-	-	-	2	6	6
19 up to pensionable age	24	1	2	4	7	3	-	-	2
Pensionable age and over	14	1	1	-	-	1	-	2	4
Age of youngest dependant 5 - 15 and age of oldest									
5 - 15	1,436	-	2	16	27	66	18	281	881
16 - 18	296	-	-	4	3	9	4	62	156
19 up to pensionable age	69	6	5	14	5	15	1	7	3
Pensionable age and over	38	3	-	-	3	3	-	7	9
Age of youngest dependant 16 - 18 and age of oldest									
16 - 18	31	-	1	-	-	1	1	4	19
19 up to pensionable age	19	-	-	2	-	4	1	5	1
Pensionable age and over	5	-	-	-	-	1	-	-	1
Age of youngest dependant 19 up to pensionable age and age of oldest									
19 up to pensionable age	33	15	1	5	1	5	-	4	-
Pensionable age and over	57	38	1	6	8	1	1	1	-
Age of youngest dependant pensionable age and over	257	226	2	13	2	4	1	1	5
TOTAL PERSONS	**44,711**	**1,491**	**864**	**1,458**	**3,119**	**1,601**	**2,941**	**7,656**	**12,966**
Persons in households with dependants									
Non-dependants	12,527		176	210	704	402	240	2,900	4,424
Dependants	12,029	1,491	206	299	850	582	201	2,700	4,122

2 same sex non-dependants			3 or more non-dependants			Household composition
Neither in employment	1 in employment	Both in employment	None in employment	1 in employment	2 or more in employment	
k	l	m	n	o	p	a
99	**169**	**196**	**42**	**276**	**2,678**	**TOTAL HOUSEHOLDS**
70	106	148	36	209	1,783	Households with no dependants
						Households with 1 dependant
						Age of dependant
3	1	2	-	6	57	0 - 4
2	5	10	2	13	346	5 - 15
-	3	3	2	11	145	16 - 18
8	13	8	-	10	46	19 up to pensionable age
12	20	8	-	5	32	Pensionable age and over
						Households with at least 2 dependants
						Age of youngest dependant 0 - 4 and age of oldest
-	2	1	-	2	15	0 - 4
1	6	1	-	2	41	5 - 15
-	-	-	-	-	5	16 - 18
1	1	1	-	-	2	19 up to pensionable age
1	1	-	-	2	1	Pensionable age and over
						Age of youngest dependant 5 - 15 and age of oldest
1	3	8	2	9	122	5 - 15
-	2	1	-	6	49	16 - 18
-	5	2	-	-	6	19 up to pensionable age
-	-	-	-	-	13	Pensionable age and over
						Age of youngest dependant 16 - 18 and age of oldest
-	-	-	-	-	5	16 - 18
-	1	2	-	1	2	19 up to pensionable age
-	-	-	-	-	3	Pensionable age and over
						Age of youngest dependant 19 up to pensionable age and age of oldest
-	-	-	-	-	2	19 up to pensionable age
-	-	1	-	-	-	Pensionable age and over
-	-	-	-	-	3	Age of youngest dependant pensionable age and over
234	**437**	**462**	**139**	**949**	**10,394**	**TOTAL PERSONS**
						Persons in households with dependants
58	126	96	19	208	2,964	Non-dependants
36	99	70	8	96	1,269	Dependants

Table 28 Dependants in households – **continued**

28. Households with residents; residents in households

Household composition	TOTAL HOUSE-HOLDS	No non-dependants	1 male non-dependant		1 female non-dependant		1 male and 1 female non-dependants		
			Not in employment	In employment	Not in employment	In employment	Neither in employment	1 in employment	Both in employment
a	b	c	d	e	f	g	h	i	j
			South Lakeland						
TOTAL HOUSEHOLDS	**39,747**	**3,235**	**1,440**	**2,472**	**5,635**	**2,449**	**3,516**	**4,508**	**9,749**
Households with no dependants	23,395		998	2,017	3,956	1,563	3,308	2,029	5,027
Households with 1 dependant									
Age of dependant									
0 - 4	1,382	1	-	4	75	61	24	494	570
5 - 15	1,892	-	2	27	62	176	16	193	672
16 - 18	657	3	2	9	9	30	6	50	180
19 up to pensionable age	1,328	260	56	133	322	190	33	75	69
Pensionable age and over	4,066	2,131	355	161	960	115	35	89	63
Households with at least 2 dependants									
Age of youngest dependant 0 - 4 and age of oldest									
0 - 4	755	-	-	1	30	9	13	399	281
5 - 15	1,516	-	3	5	63	37	41	559	713
16 - 18	49	-	-	-	1	1	2	17	15
19 up to pensionable age	52	5	-	7	16	6	1	3	-
Pensionable age and over	30	-	-	1	1	3	3	7	3
Age of youngest dependant 5 - 15 and age of oldest									
5 - 15	2,690	1	4	25	66	160	23	447	1,719
16 - 18	664	-	-	9	6	35	1	104	366
19 up to pensionable age	153	15	8	34	26	38	2	4	7
Pensionable age and over	67	3	-	-	3	5	3	10	20
Age of youngest dependant 16 - 18 and age of oldest									
16 - 18	62	-	-	-	2	-	-	16	28
19 up to pensionable age	33	5	1	3	3	3	1	3	7
Pensionable age and over	13	-	-	-	1	1	-	1	2
Age of youngest dependant 19 up to pensionable age and age of oldest									
19 up to pensionable age	89	54	-	11	9	2	1	4	2
Pensionable age and over	120	84	5	6	10	5	1	1	3
Age of youngest dependant pensionable age and over	734	673	6	19	14	9	2	3	2
TOTAL PERSONS	**94,033**	**4,107**	**1,917**	**3,085**	**7,676**	**3,744**	**7,384**	**13,673**	**28,262**
Persons in households with dependants									
Non-dependants	25,201		442	455	1,679	886	416	4,958	9,444
Dependants	25,357	4,107	477	613	2,041	1,295	352	4,657	8,764

2 same sex non-dependants			3 or more non-dependants			Household composition
Neither in employment	1 in employment	Both in employment	None in employment	1 in employment	2 or more in employment	
k	l	m	n	o	p	a
204	**357**	**499**	**136**	**538**	**5,009**	**TOTAL HOUSEHOLDS**
161	215	342	119	402	3,258	Households with no dependants
						Households with 1 dependant
						Age of dependant
5	14	5	3	12	114	0 - 4
3	13	32	1	23	672	5 - 15
1	7	10	2	39	309	16 - 18
11	34	52	4	7	82	19 up to pensionable age
12	46	28	2	10	59	Pensionable age and over
						Households with at least 2 dependants
						Age of youngest dependant 0 - 4 and age of oldest
1	1	-	-	4	16	0 - 4
1	1	4	2	16	71	5 - 15
1	-	1	-	-	11	16 - 18
1	1	2	-	1	9	19 up to pensionable age
-	-	2	-	2	8	Pensionable age and over
						Age of youngest dependant 5 - 15 and age of oldest
1	9	12	1	9	213	5 - 15
1	1	4	1	6	130	16 - 18
2	3	1	-	2	11	19 up to pensionable age
-	4	-	-	1	18	Pensionable age and over
						Age of youngest dependant 16 - 18 and age of oldest
1	-	-	-	2	13	16 - 18
1	3	1	-	-	2	19 up to pensionable age
-	-	-	-	2	6	Pensionable age and over
						Age of youngest dependant 19 up to pensionable age and age of oldest
-	3	1	-	-	2	19 up to pensionable age
1	1	1	1	-	1	Pensionable age and over
-	1	1	-	-	4	Age of youngest dependant pensionable age and over
471	**892**	**1,191**	**458**	**1,871**	**19,302**	**TOTAL PERSONS**
						Persons in households with dependants
86	284	314	52	426	5,759	Non-dependants
63	178	193	26	200	2,391	Dependants

29. Households with residents; dependants in households

Household composition	TOTAL HOUSEHOLDS	Dependants						
		TOTAL DEPENDANTS	Aged 0 - 15		Aged 16 - 18		Aged 19 up to pensionable age with long-term illness and permanently sick/retired	Pensionable age and over with long-term illness and permanently sick/retired
			With long-term illness	With no long-term illness	Single, in full-time education and economically inactive	With long-term illness and permanently sick/retired		
a	b	c	d	e	f	g	h	i
		CUMBRIA						
TOTAL HOUSEHOLDS	**193,893**	**138,868**	**1,814**	**89,225**	**7,452**	**59**	**12,981**	**27,337**
1 or more non-dependants, no dependants	105,528							
1 dependant, living alone	12,290	12,290	-	4	15	1	2,069	10,201
2 dependants, no non-dependants	4,049	8,098	5	76	14	1	1,393	6,609
3 or more dependants, no non-dependants	219	721	9	165	17	2	297	231
1 non-dependant with 1 or more dependant(s)	19,376	26,782	418	11,742	784	16	5,895	7,927
2 non-dependants with 1 or more dependant(s)	41,890	76,281	1,142	66,652	4,317	24	2,365	1,781
3 or more non-dependants with 1 or more dependant(s)	10,541	14,696	240	10,586	2,305	15	962	588
		Allerdale						
TOTAL HOUSEHOLDS	**37,867**	**28,059**	**371**	**17,834**	**1,569**	**11**	**2,859**	**5,415**
1 or more non-dependants, no dependants	19,916							
1 dependant, living alone	2,412	2,412	-	1	3	-	429	1,979
2 dependants, no non-dependants	813	1,626	-	13	5	-	324	1,284
3 or more dependants, no non-dependants	47	153	-	38	5	-	59	51
1 non-dependant with 1 or more dependant(s)	3,980	5,499	85	2,348	163	1	1,301	1,601
2 non-dependants with 1 or more dependant(s)	8,580	15,483	242	13,369	934	8	548	382
3 or more non-dependants with 1 or more dependant(s)	2,119	2,886	44	2,065	459	2	198	118
		Barrow-in-Furness						
TOTAL HOUSEHOLDS	**29,627**	**22,459**	**353**	**14,298**	**1,020**	**15**	**2,387**	**4,386**
1 or more non-dependants, no dependants	15,374							
1 dependant, living alone	2,164	2,164	-	-	1	-	420	1,743
2 dependants, no non-dependants	707	1,414	-	13	3	-	278	1,120
3 or more dependants, no non-dependants	56	176	2	31	2	1	82	58
1 non-dependant with 1 or more dependant(s)	3,268	4,800	101	2,348	141	6	1,051	1,153
2 non-dependants with 1 or more dependant(s)	6,415	11,630	205	10,209	581	5	396	234
3 or more non-dependants with 1 or more dependant(s)	1,643	2,275	45	1,697	292	3	160	78
		Carlisle						
TOTAL HOUSEHOLDS	**40,883**	**29,200**	**395**	**18,861**	**1,371**	**18**	**2,683**	**5,872**
1 or more non-dependants, no dependants	22,194							
1 dependant, living alone	2,775	2,775	-	1	6	-	501	2,267
2 dependants, no non-dependants	886	1,772	2	17	2	1	297	1,453
3 or more dependants, no non-dependants	48	161	4	33	3	-	64	57
1 non-dependant with 1 or more dependant(s)	4,125	5,756	84	2,733	156	6	1,156	1,621
2 non-dependants with 1 or more dependant(s)	8,716	15,737	259	13,853	779	7	481	358
3 or more non-dependants with 1 or more dependant(s)	2,139	2,999	46	2,224	425	4	184	116
		Copeland						
TOTAL HOUSEHOLDS	**27,752**	**21,764**	**302**	**14,376**	**1,155**	**8**	**2,288**	**3,635**
1 or more non-dependants, no dependants	14,196							
1 dependant, living alone	1,655	1,655	-	-	1	-	336	1,318
2 dependants, no non-dependants	549	1,098	2	8	3	-	235	850
3 or more dependants, no non-dependants	29	105	2	37	2	-	40	24
1 non-dependant with 1 or more dependant(s)	3,049	4,364	82	2,020	139	3	1,032	1,088
2 non-dependants with 1 or more dependant(s)	6,506	11,996	167	10,470	667	2	422	268
3 or more non-dependants with 1 or more dependant(s)	1,768	2,546	49	1,841	343	3	223	87

29. Households with residents; dependants in households

Household composition	TOTAL HOUSEHOLDS	Dependants						
		TOTAL DEPENDANTS	Aged 0 - 15		Aged 16 - 18		Aged 19 up to pensionable age with long-term illness and permanently sick/retired	Pensionable age and over with long-term illness and permanently sick/retired
			With long-term illness	With no long-term illness	Single, in full-time education and economically inactive	With long-term illness and permanently sick/retired		
a	b	c	d	e	f	g	h	i
		Eden						
TOTAL HOUSEHOLDS	**18,017**	**12,029**	**129**	**8,046**	**733**	**3**	**880**	**2,238**
1 or more non-dependants, no dependants	10,453							
1 dependant, living alone	889	889	-	1	1	1	123	763
2 dependants, no non-dependants	282	564	-	10	-	-	68	486
3 or more dependants, no non-dependants	11	38	1	11	1	-	13	12
1 non-dependant with 1 or more dependant(s)	1,492	1,937	28	689	52	-	434	734
2 non-dependants with 1 or more dependant(s)	3,922	7,228	84	6,357	436	1	170	180
3 or more non-dependants with 1 or more dependant(s)	968	1,373	16	978	243	1	72	63
		South Lakeland						
TOTAL HOUSEHOLDS	**39,747**	**25,357**	**264**	**15,810**	**1,604**	**4**	**1,884**	**5,791**
1 or more non-dependants, no dependants	23,395							
1 dependant, living alone	2,395	2,395	-	1	3	-	260	2,131
2 dependants, no non-dependants	812	1,624	1	15	1	-	191	1,416
3 or more dependants, no non-dependants	28	88	-	15	4	1	39	29
1 non-dependant with 1 or more dependant(s)	3,462	4,426	38	1,604	133	-	921	1,730
2 non-dependants with 1 or more dependant(s)	7,751	14,207	185	12,394	920	1	348	359
3 or more non-dependants with 1 or more dependant(s)	1,904	2,617	40	1,781	543	2	125	126

30. Households with residents; residents in households with dependants

Number, sex and age of non-dependants	TOTAL HOUSE-HOLDS	Households with no dependants	Households with 1 or more dependants: Age of youngest dependant 0 - 15 and age of oldest: 0 - 15	Households with 1 or more dependants: Age of youngest dependant 0 - 15 and age of oldest: 16 up to pension-able age	Households with 1 or more dependants: Age of youngest dependant 0 - 15 and age of oldest: Pension-able age and over	Households with 1 or more dependants: Age of youngest dependant 16 up to pensionable age and age of oldest: 16 up to pension-able age	Households with 1 or more dependants: Age of youngest dependant 16 up to pensionable age and age of oldest: Pension-able age and over	Households with 1 or more dependants: Age of youngest dependant pension-able age and over	Persons in households with dependants: Non-depen-dants	Persons in households with dependants: Depen-dants
a	b	c	d	e	f	g	h	i	j	k
				CUMBRIA						
TOTAL HOUSEHOLDS	**193,893**	**105,528**	**46,749**	**5,055**	**508**	**12,752**	**1,011**	**22,290**	**137,654**	**138,868**
No non-dependants	16,558		8	147	21	2,492	645	13,245		21,109
1 male	**20,285**	**15,200**	**426**	**457**	**12**	**1,479**	**108**	**2,603**	**5,085**	**6,567**
16 - 44	8,772	7,022	331	366	7	504	60	482	1,750	2,906
45 - 64	5,924	4,121	91	90	3	838	35	746	1,803	2,098
65 and over	5,589	4,057	4	1	2	137	13	1,375	1,532	1,563
1 female	**37,970**	**23,679**	**5,322**	**831**	**88**	**3,229**	**135**	**4,686**	**14,291**	**20,215**
16 - 44	9,898	3,474	5,056	695	63	390	26	194	6,424	11,758
45 - 59	5,505	2,981	249	129	15	1,643	42	446	2,524	2,941
60 and over	22,567	17,224	17	7	10	1,196	67	4,046	5,343	5,516
1 male and 1 female	**84,238**	**44,359**	**33,488**	**2,612**	**226**	**2,553**	**52**	**948**	**79,758**	**73,530**
Both of pensionable age	11,295	11,064	21	3	-	133	1	73	462	246
1 under, 1 of pensionable age	6,831	6,007	109	18	10	262	17	408	1,648	944
Both under pensionable age	66,112	27,288	33,358	2,591	216	2,158	34	467	77,648	72,340
2 of same sex	**5,333**	**3,322**	**611**	**189**	**25**	**730**	**28**	**428**	**4,022**	**2,751**
Both of pensionable age	483	439	-	-	1	15	-	28	88	45
1 under, 1 of pensionable age	1,333	880	78	14	15	109	8	229	906	539
Both under pensionable age	3,517	2,003	533	175	9	606	20	171	3,028	2,167
3 or more	**29,509**	**18,968**	**6,894**	**819**	**136**	**2,269**	**43**	**380**	**34,498**	**14,696**
All of pensionable age	122	116	-	-	-	1	-	5	18	6
1 or more under pensionable age	29,387	18,852	6,894	819	136	2,268	43	375	34,480	14,690
				Allerdale						
TOTAL HOUSEHOLDS	**37,867**	**19,916**	**9,401**	**1,111**	**99**	**2,698**	**249**	**4,393**	**28,087**	**28,059**
No non-dependants	3,272		1	32	3	526	150	2,560		4,191
1 male	**3,799**	**2,739**	**92**	**109**	**2**	**301**	**24**	**532**	**1,060**	**1,378**
16 - 44	1,535	1,161	70	88	-	104	16	96	374	618
45 - 64	1,160	789	21	21	1	165	8	155	371	441
65 and over	1,104	789	1	-	1	32	-	281	315	319
1 female	**7,425**	**4,505**	**1,056**	**196**	**17**	**685**	**42**	**924**	**2,920**	**4,121**
16 - 44	1,879	568	1,002	170	14	84	7	34	1,311	2,390
45 - 59	1,052	542	51	25	1	339	11	83	510	584
60 and over	4,494	3,395	3	1	2	262	24	807	1,099	1,147
1 male and 1 female	**16,575**	**8,388**	**6,762**	**555**	**48**	**585**	**14**	**223**	**16,374**	**14,945**
Both of pensionable age	2,090	2,030	5	1	-	32	-	22	120	62
1 under, 1 of pensionable age	1,309	1,119	23	5	2	57	2	101	380	215
Both under pensionable age	13,176	5,239	6,734	549	46	496	12	100	15,874	14,668
2 of same sex	**930**	**537**	**103**	**47**	**5**	**157**	**9**	**72**	**786**	**538**
Both of pensionable age	95	85	-	-	-	4	-	6	20	10
1 under, 1 of pensionable age	247	162	15	2	3	23	3	39	170	102
Both under pensionable age	588	290	88	45	2	130	6	27	596	426
3 or more	**5,866**	**3,747**	**1,387**	**172**	**24**	**444**	**10**	**82**	**6,947**	**2,886**
All of pensionable age	17	15	-	-	-	-	-	2	6	2
1 or more under pensionable age	5,849	3,732	1,387	172	24	444	10	80	6,941	2,884

30. Households with residents; residents in households with dependants

Number, sex and age of non-dependants	TOTAL HOUSE-HOLDS	Households with no dependants	Households with 1 or more dependants: Age of youngest dependant 0 - 15 and age of oldest: 0 - 15	16 up to pension-able age	Pension-able age and over	Age of youngest dependant 16 up to pensionable age and age of oldest: 16 up to pension-able age	Pension-able age and over	Age of youngest dependant pension-able age and over	Persons in households with dependants: Non-depen-dants	Depen-dants
a	b	c	d	e	f	g	h	i	j	k
				Barrow-in-Furness						
TOTAL HOUSEHOLDS	**29,627**	**15,374**	**7,530**	**795**	**77**	**2,138**	**173**	**3,540**	**21,456**	**22,459**
No non-dependants	2,927		-	31	2	508	130	2,256		3,754
1 male	**3,445**	**2,516**	**67**	**101**	**4**	**313**	**20**	**424**	**929**	**1,233**
16 - 44	1,570	1,221	51	84	3	125	7	79	349	594
45 - 64	1,042	713	16	17	-	162	9	125	329	381
65 and over	833	582	-	-	1	26	4	220	251	258
1 female	**5,671**	**3,332**	**1,030**	**155**	**18**	**498**	**13**	**625**	**2,339**	**3,567**
16 - 44	1,763	517	996	131	13	74	4	28	1,246	2,377
45 - 59	791	431	34	23	5	253	6	39	360	445
60 and over	3,117	2,384	-	1	-	171	3	558	733	745
1 male and 1 female	**12,320**	**6,249**	**5,189**	**367**	**29**	**367**	**6**	**113**	**12,142**	**11,157**
Both of pensionable age	1,492	1,464	2	1	-	15	-	10	56	32
1 under, 1 of pensionable age	885	796	7	3	1	32	3	43	178	106
Both under pensionable age	9,943	3,989	5,180	363	28	320	3	60	11,908	11,019
2 of same sex	**860**	**516**	**106**	**27**	**3**	**136**	**1**	**71**	**688**	**473**
Both of pensionable age	40	36	-	-	-	-	-	4	8	4
1 under, 1 of pensionable age	195	131	7	2	1	17	1	36	128	73
Both under pensionable age	625	349	99	25	2	119	-	31	552	396
3 or more	**4,404**	**2,761**	**1,138**	**114**	**21**	**316**	**3**	**51**	**5,358**	**2,275**
All of pensionable age	10	10	-	-	-	-	-	-	-	-
1 or more under pensionable age	4,394	2,751	1,138	114	21	316	3	51	5,358	2,275
				Carlisle						
TOTAL HOUSEHOLDS	**40,883**	**22,194**	**10,035**	**988**	**93**	**2,575**	**220**	**4,778**	**28,531**	**29,200**
No non-dependants	3,709		1	34	5	593	134	2,942		4,708
1 male	**4,279**	**3,246**	**97**	**87**	**3**	**287**	**25**	**534**	**1,033**	**1,335**
16 - 44	1,915	1,548	81	72	2	91	14	107	367	617
45 - 64	1,211	853	16	14	1	168	7	152	358	403
65 and over	1,153	845	-	1	-	28	4	275	308	315
1 female	**8,238**	**5,146**	**1,287**	**160**	**13**	**647**	**29**	**956**	**3,092**	**4,421**
16 - 44	2,373	862	1,229	134	9	88	7	44	1,511	2,730
45 - 59	1,189	680	55	23	2	319	8	102	509	579
60 and over	4,676	3,604	3	3	2	240	14	810	1,072	1,112
1 male and 1 female	**17,339**	**9,086**	**7,042**	**497**	**43**	**469**	**16**	**186**	**16,506**	**15,078**
Both of pensionable age	2,180	2,133	7	-	-	25	1	14	94	50
1 under, 1 of pensionable age	1,390	1,218	26	6	2	57	7	74	344	205
Both under pensionable age	13,769	5,735	7,009	491	41	387	8	98	16,068	14,823
2 of same sex	**1,235**	**772**	**164**	**54**	**4**	**148**	**6**	**87**	**926**	**659**
Both of pensionable age	83	76	-	-	-	4	-	3	14	7
1 under, 1 of pensionable age	293	196	21	5	3	23	-	45	194	120
Both under pensionable age	859	500	143	49	1	121	6	39	718	532
3 or more	**6,083**	**3,944**	**1,444**	**156**	**25**	**431**	**10**	**73**	**6,974**	**2,999**
All of pensionable age	23	23	-	-	-	-	-	-	-	-
1 or more under pensionable age	6,060	3,921	1,444	156	25	431	10	73	6,974	2,999

30. Households with residents; residents in households with dependants

Number, sex and age of non-dependants	TOTAL HOUSE-HOLDS	Households with no dependants	Households with 1 or more dependants: Age of youngest dependant 0 - 15 and age of oldest: 0 - 15	16 up to pension-able age	Pension-able age and over	Age of youngest dependant 16 up to pensionable age and age of oldest: 16 up to pension-able age	Pension-able age and over	Age of youngest dependant pension-able age and over	Persons in households with dependants: Non-depen-dants	Depen-dants
a	b	c	d	e	f	g	h	i	j	k
Copeland										
TOTAL HOUSEHOLDS	**27,752**	**14,196**	**7,376**	**835**	**90**	**2,158**	**174**	**2,923**	**21,852**	**21,764**
No non-dependants	2,233		-	23	4	403	109	1,694		2,858
1 male	**3,033**	**2,253**	**58**	**73**	**1**	**275**	**21**	**352**	**780**	**1,026**
16 - 44	1,435	1,134	46	59	-	93	13	90	301	482
45 - 64	857	552	11	14	1	164	7	108	305	364
65 and over	741	567	1	-	-	18	1	154	174	180
1 female	**5,264**	**2,995**	**912**	**149**	**21**	**546**	**24**	**617**	**2,269**	**3,338**
16 - 44	1,547	440	871	127	14	56	3	36	1,107	2,069
45 - 59	817	373	36	22	3	300	11	72	444	524
60 and over	2,900	2,182	5	-	4	190	10	509	718	745
1 male and 1 female	**11,961**	**5,784**	**5,165**	**422**	**38**	**416**	**5**	**131**	**12,354**	**11,554**
Both of pensionable age	1,253	1,227	1	-	-	17	-	8	52	27
1 under, 1 of pensionable age	934	797	25	2	1	46	1	62	274	153
Both under pensionable age	9,774	3,760	5,139	420	37	353	4	61	12,028	11,374
2 of same sex	**784**	**455**	**90**	**30**	**5**	**126**	**8**	**70**	**658**	**442**
Both of pensionable age	64	58	-	-	-	2	-	4	12	6
1 under, 1 of pensionable age	190	120	15	-	2	20	3	30	140	78
Both under pensionable age	530	277	75	30	3	104	5	36	506	358
3 or more	**4,477**	**2,709**	**1,151**	**138**	**21**	**392**	**7**	**59**	**5,791**	**2,546**
All of pensionable age	20	18	-	-	-	1	-	1	6	2
1 or more under pensionable age	4,457	2,691	1,151	138	21	391	7	58	5,785	2,544
Eden										
TOTAL HOUSEHOLDS	**18,017**	**10,453**	**4,172**	**408**	**52**	**1,014**	**62**	**1,856**	**12,527**	**12,029**
No non-dependants	1,182		4	7	4	140	38	989		1,491
1 male	**1,817**	**1,431**	**41**	**29**	**1**	**88**	**7**	**220**	**386**	**505**
16 - 44	731	601	32	22	1	28	6	41	130	227
45 - 64	549	420	8	7	-	51	1	62	129	150
65 and over	537	410	1	-	-	9	-	117	127	128
1 female	**3,288**	**2,182**	**298**	**42**	**7**	**283**	**10**	**466**	**1,106**	**1,432**
16 - 44	674	309	279	34	5	29	-	18	365	650
45 - 59	502	280	17	8	2	150	3	42	222	250
60 and over	2,112	1,593	2	-	-	104	7	406	519	532
1 male and 1 female	**8,270**	**4,488**	**3,166**	**249**	**22**	**241**	**3**	**101**	**7,564**	**7,023**
Both of pensionable age	1,159	1,137	1	1	-	14	-	6	44	24
1 under, 1 of pensionable age	748	654	14	1	2	29	2	46	188	109
Both under pensionable age	6,363	2,697	3,151	247	20	198	1	49	7,332	6,890
2 of same sex	**464**	**324**	**46**	**13**	**2**	**38**	**1**	**40**	**280**	**205**
Both of pensionable age	60	52	-	-	1	1	-	6	16	9
1 under, 1 of pensionable age	139	97	6	1	1	11	-	23	84	47
Both under pensionable age	265	175	40	12	-	26	1	11	180	149
3 or more	**2,996**	**2,028**	**617**	**68**	**16**	**224**	**3**	**40**	**3,191**	**1,373**
All of pensionable age	17	16	-	-	-	-	-	1	3	1
1 or more under pensionable age	2,979	2,012	617	68	16	224	3	39	3,188	1,372

30. Households with residents; residents in households with dependants

Number, sex and age of non-dependants	TOTAL HOUSE-HOLDS	Households with no dependants	Households with 1 or more dependants						Persons in households with dependants	
			Age of youngest dependant 0 - 15 and age of oldest			Age of youngest dependant 16 up to pensionable age and age of oldest		Age of youngest dependant pension-able age and over		
			0 - 15	16 up to pension-able age	Pension-able age and over	16 up to pension-able age	Pension-able age and over		Non-depen-dants	Depen-dants
a	b	c	d	e	f	g	h	i	j	k
			South Lakeland							
TOTAL HOUSEHOLDS	**39,747**	**23,395**	**8,235**	**918**	**97**	**2,169**	**133**	**4,800**	**25,201**	**25,357**
No non-dependants	3,235		2	20	3	322	84	2,804		4,107
1 male	**3,912**	**3,015**	**71**	**58**	**1**	**215**	**11**	**541**	**897**	**1,090**
16 - 44	1,586	1,357	51	41	1	63	4	69	229	368
45 - 64	1,105	794	19	17	-	128	3	144	311	359
65 and over	1,221	864	1	-	-	24	4	328	357	363
1 female	**8,084**	**5,519**	**739**	**129**	**12**	**570**	**17**	**1,098**	**2,565**	**3,336**
16 - 44	1,662	778	679	99	8	59	5	34	884	1,542
45 - 59	1,154	675	56	28	2	282	3	108	479	559
60 and over	5,268	4,066	4	2	2	229	9	956	1,202	1,235
1 male and 1 female	**17,773**	**10,364**	**6,164**	**522**	**46**	**475**	**8**	**194**	**14,818**	**13,773**
Both of pensionable age	3,121	3,073	5	-	-	30	-	13	96	51
1 under, 1 of pensionable age	1,565	1,423	14	1	2	41	2	82	284	156
Both under pensionable age	13,087	5,868	6,145	521	44	404	6	99	14,438	13,566
2 of same sex	**1,060**	**718**	**102**	**18**	**6**	**125**	**3**	**88**	**684**	**434**
Both of pensionable age	141	132	-	-	-	4	-	5	18	9
1 under, 1 of pensionable age	269	174	14	4	5	15	1	56	190	119
Both under pensionable age	650	412	88	14	1	106	2	27	476	306
3 or more	**5,683**	**3,779**	**1,157**	**171**	**29**	**462**	**10**	**75**	**6,237**	**2,617**
All of pensionable age	35	34	-	-	-	-	-	1	3	1
1 or more under pensionable age	5,648	3,745	1,157	171	29	462	10	74	6,234	2,616

Table 31 Dependent children in households

Note: * May include a small number of households with no adults

31. Households with residents; residents in households

Households with the following adults	Households with no dependent children	Households with dependent children						Persons in households				
		All households	With 1 dependent child		With 2 or more dependent children			With no dependent child(ren)		With dependent child(ren)		
			Aged 0 - 4	Aged 5 and over	All aged 0 - 4	All aged 5 and over	1 or more aged 0 - 4 and 1 or more aged 5 and over	All persons	Persons economically active	Dependent children	Adults	Persons economically active
a	b	c	d	e	f	g	h	i	j	k	l	m
CUMBRIA												
ALL HOUSEHOLDS*	**138,069**	**55,824**	**8,819**	**15,038**	**4,230**	**18,219**	**9,518**	**257,847**	**143,252**	**98,491**	**118,449**	**92,551**
1 male	19,169	556	37	263	3	211	42	19,169	10,999	893	556	421
1 female	31,981	5,869	1,209	1,679	360	1,581	1,040	31,981	6,802	10,061	5,869	2,732
2 (1 male and 1 female)	58,268	38,342	6,522	6,477	3,686	14,060	7,597	116,536	59,548	71,983	76,684	61,369
2 (same sex)	4,573	818	131	396	26	173	92	9,146	5,246	1,228	1,636	1,076
3 or more (male(s) and female(s))	23,457	10,122	901	6,154	152	2,185	730	79,023	59,187	14,166	33,418	26,751
3 or more (same sex)	621	93	16	53	3	7	14	1,992	1,470	129	286	202
Allerdale												
ALL HOUSEHOLDS*	**26,546**	**11,321**	**1,730**	**3,180**	**797**	**3,784**	**1,830**	**50,132**	**27,185**	**19,774**	**24,029**	**18,454**
1 male	3,556	116	7	62	-	42	5	3,556	1,925	173	116	89
1 female	6,096	1,170	263	334	49	335	189	6,096	1,152	1,970	1,170	501
2 (1 male and 1 female)	11,210	7,812	1,284	1,395	709	2,924	1,500	22,420	11,212	14,562	15,624	12,295
2 (same sex)	791	154	19	71	5	40	19	1,582	830	238	308	189
3 or more (male(s) and female(s))	4,791	2,040	150	1,301	34	439	116	16,153	11,831	2,795	6,737	5,325
3 or more (same sex)	102	24	6	14	-	3	1	325	235	30	74	55
Barrow-in-Furness												
ALL HOUSEHOLDS*	**20,736**	**8,891**	**1,583**	**2,370**	**685**	**2,533**	**1,720**	**38,234**	**21,363**	**15,671**	**18,659**	**14,210**
1 male	3,223	86	5	42	1	29	9	3,223	1,912	147	86	63
1 female	4,788	1,119	249	278	84	244	264	4,788	943	1,980	1,119	441
2 (1 male and 1 female)	8,480	5,937	1,148	999	575	1,928	1,287	16,960	8,590	11,097	11,874	9,249
2 (same sex)	705	137	26	66	5	22	18	1,410	894	205	274	180
3 or more (male(s) and female(s))	3,455	1,593	151	974	20	309	139	11,589	8,818	2,218	5,252	4,239
3 or more (same sex)	85	18	4	10	-	1	3	264	206	23	54	38

Note: * May include a small number of households with no adults

31. Households with residents; residents in households

Households with the following adults	Households with no dependent children	Households with dependent children						Persons in households				
		All households	With 1 dependent child		With 2 or more dependent children			With no dependent child(ren)		With dependent child(ren)		
			Aged 0 - 4	Aged 5 and over	All aged 0 - 4	All aged 5 and over	1 or more aged 0 - 4 and 1 or more aged 5 and over	All persons	Persons economically active	Dependent children	Adults	Persons economically active
a	b	c	d	e	f	g	h	i	j	k	l	m
Carlisle												
ALL HOUSEHOLDS*	**29,099**	**11,784**	**1,915**	**3,236**	**915**	**3,741**	**1,977**	**53,732**	**30,674**	**20,627**	**24,700**	**19,629**
1 male	4,135	124	10	63	-	41	10	4,135	2,375	188	124	89
1 female	7,025	1,410	296	405	102	363	244	7,025	1,620	2,421	1,410	641
2 (1 male and 1 female)	11,936	7,939	1,389	1,377	777	2,850	1,546	23,872	12,812	14,750	15,878	13,052
2 (same sex)	1,044	205	28	105	7	42	23	2,088	1,259	314	410	269
3 or more (male(s) and female(s))	4,796	2,079	191	1,268	27	443	150	16,091	12,235	2,918	6,815	5,532
3 or more (same sex)	163	20	1	11	2	2	4	521	373	29	63	46
Copeland												
ALL HOUSEHOLDS*	**18,920**	**8,832**	**1,430**	**2,279**	**644**	**2,824**	**1,655**	**35,857**	**20,115**	**15,833**	**18,795**	**14,199**
1 male	2,858	84	6	37	1	34	6	2,858	1,627	140	84	55
1 female	4,044	996	198	277	66	261	194	4,044	805	1,740	996	393
2 (1 male and 1 female)	7,776	5,949	1,009	974	549	2,140	1,277	15,552	8,041	11,342	11,898	9,255
2 (same sex)	647	127	26	57	4	25	15	1,294	745	183	254	156
3 or more (male(s) and female(s))	3,503	1,656	189	923	23	363	158	11,813	8,670	2,393	5,504	4,305
3 or more (same sex)	92	19	2	10	1	1	5	296	227	34	59	35
Eden												
ALL HOUSEHOLDS*	**13,033**	**4,984**	**736**	**1,264**	**421**	**1,818**	**745**	**25,002**	**14,374**	**8,908**	**10,801**	**8,597**
1 male	1,728	51	5	18	-	24	4	1,728	1,026	90	51	43
1 female	2,772	336	64	97	20	108	47	2,772	648	574	336	217
2 (1 male and 1 female)	5,667	3,601	589	560	378	1,448	626	11,334	5,898	6,795	7,202	5,784
2 (same sex)	415	59	6	26	3	15	9	830	477	101	118	84
3 or more (male(s) and female(s))	2,393	928	70	559	20	223	56	8,153	6,194	1,334	3,082	2,461
3 or more (same sex)	58	4	1	3	-	-	-	185	131	4	12	8

Table 31 Dependent children in households – **continued**

Note: * May include a small number of households with no adults

31. Households with residents; residents in households

Households with the following adults	Households with no dependent children	Households with dependent children						Persons in households				
		All households	With 1 dependent child		With 2 or more dependent children			With no dependent child(ren)		With dependent child(ren)		
			Aged 0 - 4	Aged 5 and over	All aged 0 - 4	All aged 5 and over	1 or more aged 0 - 4 and 1 or more aged 5 and over	All persons	Persons economically active	Dependent children	Adults	Persons economically active
a	b	c	d	e	f	g	h	i	j	k	l	m
South Lakeland												
ALL HOUSEHOLDS*	**29,735**	**10,012**	**1,425**	**2,709**	**768**	**3,519**	**1,591**	**54,890**	**29,541**	**17,678**	**21,465**	**17,462**
1 male	3,669	95	4	41	1	41	8	3,669	2,134	155	95	82
1 female	7,256	838	139	288	39	270	102	7,256	1,634	1,376	838	539
2 (1 male and 1 female)	13,199	7,104	1,103	1,172	698	2,770	1,361	26,398	12,995	13,437	14,208	11,734
2 (same sex)	971	136	26	71	2	29	8	1,942	1,041	187	272	198
3 or more (male(s) and female(s))	4,519	1,826	150	1,129	28	408	111	15,224	11,439	2,508	6,028	4,889
3 or more (same sex)	121	8	2	5	-	-	1	401	298	9	24	20

Note: * May include a small number of households with no persons aged 16 and over

32. Households with residents; residents in households

Households with the following persons aged 16 and over	Households with no person aged 0 - 15	Households with persons aged 0 - 15						Persons in households				
		All households	With one person aged 0 - 15		With two or more persons aged 0 - 15			With no person aged 0 - 15		With person(s) aged 0 - 15		
			Aged 0 - 4	Aged 5 - 15	All aged 0 - 4	All aged 5 - 15	1 or more aged 0 - 4 and 1 or more aged 5 - 15	All persons	Persons economically active	Persons aged 0 - 15	Persons aged 16 and over	Persons economically active
a	b	c	d	e	f	g	h	i	j	k	l	m
CUMBRIA												
ALL HOUSEHOLDS*	**141,581**	**52,312**	**8,915**	**14,117**	**4,245**	**15,628**	**9,407**	**270,397**	**150,311**	**91,039**	**113,351**	**85,492**
1 male	19,176	455	37	207	3	168	40	19,176	10,999	731	455	338
1 female	31,989	5,407	1,209	1,467	360	1,354	1,017	31,989	6,802	9,232	5,407	2,409
2 (1 male and 1 female)	58,390	34,561	6,526	5,323	3,688	11,638	7,386	116,780	59,644	64,413	69,122	54,871
2 (same sex)	4,720	821	135	394	26	176	90	9,440	5,357	1,226	1,642	955
3 or more (male(s) and female(s))	26,634	10,943	982	6,664	165	2,276	856	90,861	65,963	15,258	36,366	26,695
3 or more (same sex)	672	117	23	61	3	15	15	2,151	1,546	165	359	224
Allerdale												
ALL HOUSEHOLDS*	**27,256**	**10,611**	**1,752**	**3,029**	**800**	**3,225**	**1,805**	**52,671**	**28,601**	**18,205**	**23,059**	**17,038**
1 male	3,559	99	7	53	-	34	5	3,559	1,925	145	99	74
1 female	6,096	1,072	263	292	49	284	184	6,096	1,152	1,788	1,072	436
2 (1 male and 1 female)	11,234	7,004	1,284	1,153	710	2,410	1,447	22,468	11,228	12,942	14,008	10,939
2 (same sex)	819	155	19	74	5	38	19	1,638	852	233	310	162
3 or more (male(s) and female(s))	5,433	2,249	169	1,442	36	453	149	18,543	13,189	3,053	7,475	5,367
3 or more (same sex)	115	31	9	15	-	6	1	367	255	43	95	60
Barrow-in-Furness												
ALL HOUSEHOLDS*	**21,225**	**8,402**	**1,602**	**2,224**	**688**	**2,190**	**1,698**	**39,969**	**22,340**	**14,651**	**17,944**	**13,233**
1 male	3,223	72	5	33	1	24	9	3,223	1,912	125	72	50
1 female	4,789	1,047	249	248	84	209	257	4,789	943	1,845	1,047	395
2 (1 male and 1 female)	8,498	5,401	1,150	822	575	1,604	1,250	16,996	8,606	10,040	10,802	8,363
2 (same sex)	726	142	27	62	5	30	18	1,452	909	219	284	164
3 or more (male(s) and female(s))	3,893	1,722	166	1,050	23	322	161	13,211	9,748	2,400	5,684	4,227
3 or more (same sex)	96	18	5	9	-	1	3	298	222	22	55	34

Table 32 Children aged 0 - 15 in households – **continued**

Note: * May include a small number of households with no persons aged 16 and over

32. Households with residents; residents in households

Households with the following persons aged 16 and over	Households with no person aged 0 - 15	Households with persons aged 0 - 15						Persons in households				
		All households	With one person aged 0 - 15		With two or more persons aged 0 - 15			With no person aged 0 - 15		With person(s) aged 0 - 15		
			Aged 0 - 4	Aged 5 - 15	All aged 0 - 4	All aged 5 - 15	1 or more aged 0 - 4 and 1 or more aged 5 - 15	All persons	Persons economically active	Persons aged 0 - 15	Persons aged 16 and over	Persons economically active
a	b	c	d	e	f	g	h	i	j	k	l	m
Carlisle												
ALL HOUSEHOLDS*	**29,767**	**11,116**	**1,931**	**3,029**	**918**	**3,280**	**1,958**	**56,061**	**32,010**	**19,256**	**23,742**	**18,293**
1 male	4,136	105	10	49	-	37	9	4,136	2,375	162	105	76
1 female	7,030	1,307	296	355	102	313	241	7,030	1,620	2,235	1,307	564
2 (1 male and 1 female)	11,962	7,255	1,389	1,159	777	2,418	1,512	23,924	12,830	13,402	14,510	11,847
2 (same sex)	1,082	202	28	101	7	43	23	2,164	1,289	312	404	240
3 or more (male(s) and female(s))	5,388	2,222	207	1,350	30	466	169	18,268	13,512	3,110	7,341	5,515
3 or more (same sex)	169	24	1	14	2	3	4	539	384	34	75	51
Copeland												
ALL HOUSEHOLDS*	**19,451**	**8,301**	**1,456**	**2,140**	**644**	**2,432**	**1,629**	**37,750**	**21,181**	**14,678**	**18,057**	**13,133**
1 male	2,858	62	6	27	1	23	5	2,858	1,627	100	62	39
1 female	4,045	923	198	244	66	227	188	4,045	805	1,608	923	347
2 (1 male and 1 female)	7,798	5,352	1,011	796	549	1,756	1,240	15,596	8,060	10,112	10,704	8,227
2 (same sex)	668	130	28	58	4	25	15	1,336	761	192	260	134
3 or more (male(s) and female(s))	3,978	1,810	209	1,003	23	399	176	13,582	9,684	2,630	6,034	4,345
3 or more (same sex)	104	24	4	12	1	2	5	333	244	36	74	41
Eden												
ALL HOUSEHOLDS*	**13,385**	**4,632**	**740**	**1,174**	**422**	**1,556**	**740**	**26,290**	**15,100**	**8,175**	**10,246**	**7,871**
1 male	1,729	43	5	15	-	19	4	1,729	1,026	77	43	36
1 female	2,772	305	64	80	20	94	47	2,772	648	524	305	197
2 (1 male and 1 female)	5,676	3,222	589	444	378	1,200	611	11,352	5,904	6,043	6,444	5,137
2 (same sex)	426	63	6	30	3	15	9	852	484	101	126	81
3 or more (male(s) and female(s))	2,722	989	74	601	21	227	66	9,394	6,904	1,411	3,310	2,409
3 or more (same sex)	60	6	1	4	-	1	-	191	134	10	18	11

Note: * May include a small number of households with no persons aged 16 and over

32. Households with residents; residents in households

Households with the following persons aged 16 and over	Households with no person aged 0 - 15	Households with persons aged 0 - 15							Persons in households				
		All households	With one person aged 0 - 15		With two or more persons aged 0 - 15			With no person aged 0 - 15		With person(s) aged 0 - 15			
			Aged 0 - 4	Aged 5 - 15	All aged 0 - 4	All aged 5 - 15	1 or more aged 0 - 4 and 1 or more aged 5 - 15	All persons	Persons economically active	Persons aged 0 - 15	Persons aged 16 and over	Persons economically active
a	b	c	d	e	f	g	h	i	j	k	l	m
South Lakeland												
ALL HOUSEHOLDS*	**30,497**	**9,250**	**1,434**	**2,521**	**773**	**2,945**	**1,577**	**57,656**	**31,079**	**16,074**	**20,303**	**15,924**
1 male	3,671	74	4	30	1	31	8	3,671	2,134	122	74	63
1 female	7,257	753	139	248	39	227	100	7,257	1,634	1,232	753	470
2 (1 male and 1 female)	13,222	6,327	1,103	949	699	2,250	1,326	26,444	13,016	11,874	12,654	10,358
2 (same sex)	999	129	27	69	2	25	6	1,998	1,062	169	258	174
3 or more (male(s) and female(s))	5,220	1,951	157	1,218	32	409	135	17,863	12,926	2,654	6,522	4,832
3 or more (same sex)	128	14	3	7	-	2	2	423	307	20	42	27

33. Females resident in households of one male aged 16 or over and one female aged 16 or over with or without persons aged 0 - 15; number of persons aged 0 - 15 in such households

In households with:	TOTAL FEMALES	Economically active females: Employees: Full-time	Employees: Part-time	Self-employed	Other	Economically active students	Economically inactive females
a	b	c	d	e	f	g	h
CUMBRIA							
No persons aged 0 - 15	58,390	14,908	7,533	2,673	1,234	26	32,042
Person(s) aged 0 - 4 only	10,214	1,046	3,052	432	468	-	5,216
Person(s) aged 5 - 15 only	16,961	3,292	7,805	1,242	426	12	4,196
Persons aged 0 - 4 and 5 - 15	7,386	400	2,690	367	165	2	3,764
TOTAL PERSONS AGED 0 - 15	**64,413**	**7,827**	**25,225**	**3,869**	**1,759**	**24**	**25,733**
Persons aged 0 - 4	22,843	1,641	7,080	1,030	741	2	12,351
Allerdale							
No persons aged 0 - 15	11,234	2,679	1,365	520	314	3	6,356
Person(s) aged 0 - 4 only	1,994	240	496	87	121	-	1,050
Person(s) aged 5 - 15 only	3,563	754	1,487	260	89	2	973
Persons aged 0 - 4 and 5 - 15	1,447	89	442	70	40	-	806
TOTAL PERSONS AGED 0 - 15	**12,942**	**1,757**	**4,496**	**783**	**399**	**3**	**5,507**
Persons aged 0 - 4	4,453	372	1,156	203	184	-	2,538
Barrow-in-Furness							
No persons aged 0 - 15	8,498	2,113	1,107	209	264	5	4,805
Person(s) aged 0 - 4 only	1,725	142	495	42	89	-	957
Person(s) aged 5 - 15 only	2,426	380	1,199	109	85	4	653
Persons aged 0 - 4 and 5 - 15	1,250	50	452	47	29	2	672
TOTAL PERSONS AGED 0 - 15	**10,040**	**937**	**3,981**	**359**	**334**	**11**	**4,429**
Persons aged 0 - 4	3,827	218	1,145	111	137	2	2,216
Carlisle							
No persons aged 0 - 15	11,962	3,480	1,684	368	258	6	6,172
Person(s) aged 0 - 4 only	2,166	209	802	71	98	-	986
Person(s) aged 5 - 15 only	3,577	674	1,847	197	105	3	754
Persons aged 0 - 4 and 5 - 15	1,512	83	633	65	33	-	698
TOTAL PERSONS AGED 0 - 15	**13,402**	**1,590**	**5,992**	**619**	**398**	**4**	**4,803**
Persons aged 0 - 4	4,774	331	1,772	168	161	-	2,342
Copeland							
No persons aged 0 - 15	7,798	2,128	904	277	180	2	4,309
Person(s) aged 0 - 4 only	1,560	201	410	40	96	-	813
Person(s) aged 5 - 15 only	2,552	512	1,081	131	65	-	763
Persons aged 0 - 4 and 5 - 15	1,240	64	405	36	37	-	698
TOTAL PERSONS AGED 0 - 15	**10,112**	**1,268**	**3,542**	**406**	**330**	**-**	**4,566**
Persons aged 0 - 4	3,611	291	984	104	155	-	2,077
Eden							
No persons aged 0 - 15	5,676	1,337	767	442	71	3	3,059
Person(s) aged 0 - 4 only	967	74	258	88	22	-	525
Person(s) aged 5 - 15 only	1,644	305	711	197	33	1	398
Persons aged 0 - 4 and 5 - 15	611	32	213	46	10	-	310
TOTAL PERSONS AGED 0 - 15	**6,043**	**702**	**2,238**	**645**	**113**	**4**	**2,345**
Persons aged 0 - 4	2,083	117	591	178	36	-	1,161

33. Females resident in households of one male aged 16 or over and one female aged 16 or over with or without persons aged 0 - 15; number of persons aged 0 - 15 in such households

In households with:	TOTAL FEMALES	Economically active females					Economically inactive females
		Employees		Self-employed	Other	Economically active students	
		Full-time	Part-time				
a	b	c	d	e	f	g	h
South Lakeland							
No persons aged 0 - 15	13,222	3,171	1,706	857	147	7	7,341
Person(s) aged 0 - 4 only	1,802	180	591	104	42	-	885
Person(s) aged 5 - 15 only	3,199	667	1,480	348	49	2	655
Persons aged 0 - 4 and 5 - 15	1,326	82	545	103	16	-	580
TOTAL PERSONS AGED 0 - 15	**11,874**	**1,573**	**4,976**	**1,057**	**185**	**2**	**4,083**
Persons aged 0 - 4	4,095	312	1,432	266	68	-	2,017

Table 34 Economic position of household residents

34. Residents aged 16 and over in households

Economic position	TOTAL PERSONS	Males: Single, widowed or divorced	Males: Married	Females: Single, widowed or divorced	Females: Married	Students (economically active or inactive)
a	b	c	d	e	f	g
CUMBRIA						
TOTAL PERSONS AGED 16 AND OVER	**383,748**	**67,447**	**117,428**	**80,846**	**118,027**	**13,674**
Economically active	**235,803**	**49,550**	**86,669**	**35,837**	**63,747**	**1,730**
Employees - full time	141,613	33,793	62,343	22,255	23,222	180
- part time	42,430	1,661	2,135	7,482	31,152	1,496
Self-employed - with employees	12,621	1,502	7,480	577	3,062	5
- without employees	19,707	4,299	10,294	1,140	3,974	4
On a Government scheme	3,390	1,676	284	1,180	250	
Unemployed	16,042	6,619	4,133	3,203	2,087	45
Economically active students (included above)	*1,730*	*608*	*16*	*1,080*	*26*	
Economically inactive	**147,945**	**17,897**	**30,759**	**45,009**	**54,280**	**11,944**
Students	11,944	5,604	169	5,887	284	11,944
Permanently sick	13,911	2,833	5,505	2,585	2,988	
Retired	75,146	9,099	24,601	23,529	17,917	
Other inactive	46,944	361	484	13,008	33,091	
Allerdale						
TOTAL PERSONS AGED 16 AND OVER	**75,730**	**12,955**	**23,561**	**15,575**	**23,639**	**2,794**
Economically active	**45,639**	**9,296**	**17,408**	**6,560**	**12,375**	**275**
Employees - full time	26,989	6,094	12,329	3,947	4,619	29
- part time	7,579	272	354	1,273	5,680	235
Self-employed - with employees	2,641	294	1,595	114	638	1
- without employees	3,639	722	1,897	211	809	1
On a Government scheme	916	435	105	295	81	
Unemployed	3,875	1,479	1,128	720	548	9
Economically active students (included above)	*275*	*100*	-	*173*	*2*	
Economically inactive	**30,091**	**3,659**	**6,153**	**9,015**	**11,264**	**2,519**
Students	2,519	1,137	64	1,225	93	2,519
Permanently sick	3,109	623	1,271	541	674	
Retired	14,617	1,834	4,716	4,566	3,501	
Other inactive	9,846	65	102	2,683	6,996	
Barrow-in-Furness						
TOTAL PERSONS AGED 16 AND OVER	**57,913**	**10,740**	**17,270**	**12,537**	**17,366**	**1,707**
Economically active	**35,573**	**8,079**	**12,902**	**5,536**	**9,056**	**226**
Employees - full time	22,951	5,951	10,591	3,256	3,153	21
- part time	6,441	202	196	1,225	4,818	199
Self-employed - with employees	1,017	132	526	69	290	-
- without employees	1,577	325	820	107	325	-
On a Government scheme	582	263	39	243	37	
Unemployed	3,005	1,206	730	636	433	6
Economically active students (included above)	*226*	*70*	*2*	*148*	*6*	
Economically inactive	**22,340**	**2,661**	**4,368**	**7,001**	**8,310**	**1,481**
Students	1,481	702	14	726	39	1,481
Permanently sick	2,525	489	893	522	621	
Retired	10,848	1,406	3,385	3,387	2,670	
Other inactive	7,486	64	76	2,366	4,980	

34. Residents aged 16 and over in households

Economic position	TOTAL PERSONS	Males		Females		Students (economically active or inactive)
		Single, widowed or divorced	Married	Single, widowed or divorced	Married	
a	b	c	d	e	f	g
		Carlisle				
TOTAL PERSONS AGED 16 AND OVER	**79,803**	**14,196**	**23,923**	**17,574**	**24,110**	**2,619**
Economically active	**50,303**	**10,577**	**17,840**	**8,084**	**13,802**	**394**
Employees - full time	30,487	7,141	13,096	5,202	5,048	36
- part time	9,890	456	536	1,700	7,198	345
Self-employed - with employees	2,226	282	1,355	96	493	1
- without employees	3,522	808	1,955	172	587	-
On a Government scheme	658	332	48	228	50	
Unemployed	3,520	1,558	850	686	426	12
Economically active students (included above)	*394*	*141*	*4*	*244*	*5*	
Economically inactive	**29,500**	**3,619**	**6,083**	**9,490**	**10,308**	**2,225**
Students	2,225	1,041	11	1,140	33	2,225
Permanently sick	2,916	633	1,103	572	608	
Retired	15,646	1,867	4,870	5,220	3,689	
Other inactive	8,713	78	99	2,558	5,978	
		Copeland				
TOTAL PERSONS AGED 16 AND OVER	**55,807**	**10,269**	**17,016**	**11,441**	**17,081**	**2,014**
Economically active	**34,314**	**7,515**	**12,798**	**4,933**	**9,068**	**191**
Employees - full time	22,058	5,210	10,171	3,025	3,652	22
- part time	5,614	138	219	936	4,321	161
Self-employed - with employees	1,264	144	731	67	322	2
- without employees	1,734	384	849	113	388	-
On a Government scheme	575	305	45	201	24	
Unemployed	3,069	1,334	783	591	361	6
Economically active students (included above)	*191*	*54*	*3*	*131*	*3*	
Economically inactive	**21,493**	**2,754**	**4,218**	**6,508**	**8,013**	**1,823**
Students	1,823	804	37	925	57	1,823
Permanently sick	2,380	498	959	403	520	
Retired	9,746	1,387	3,154	2,979	2,226	
Other inactive	7,544	65	68	2,201	5,210	
		Eden				
TOTAL PERSONS AGED 16 AND OVER	**36,536**	**6,521**	**11,439**	**7,075**	**11,501**	**1,322**
Economically active	**22,971**	**4,870**	**8,566**	**3,370**	**6,165**	**173**
Employees - full time	12,093	3,063	4,915	2,114	2,001	19
- part time	3,991	163	244	719	2,865	152
Self-employed - with employees	2,088	268	1,271	81	468	-
- without employees	3,681	881	1,911	189	700	-
On a Government scheme	243	132	14	72	25	
Unemployed	875	363	211	195	106	2
Economically active students (included above)	*173*	*65*	*2*	*104*	*2*	
Economically inactive	**13,565**	**1,651**	**2,873**	**3,705**	**5,336**	**1,149**
Students	1,149	584	15	533	17	1,149
Permanently sick	926	186	405	171	164	
Retired	6,678	847	2,405	1,922	1,504	
Other inactive	4,812	34	48	1,079	3,651	

34. Residents aged 16 and over in households

Economic position	TOTAL PERSONS	Males		Females		Students (economically active or inactive)
		Single, widowed or divorced	Married	Single, widowed or divorced	Married	
a	b	c	d	e	f	g
		South Lakeland				
TOTAL PERSONS AGED 16 AND OVER	**77,959**	**12,766**	**24,219**	**16,644**	**24,330**	**3,218**
Economically active	**47,003**	**9,213**	**17,155**	**7,354**	**13,281**	**471**
Employees - full time	27,035	6,334	11,241	4,711	4,749	53
- part time	8,915	430	586	1,629	6,270	404
Self-employed - with employees	3,385	382	2,002	150	851	1
- without employees	5,554	1,179	2,862	348	1,165	3
On a Government scheme	416	209	33	141	33	
Unemployed	1,698	679	431	375	213	10
Economically active students (included above)	*471*	*178*	*5*	*280*	*8*	
Economically inactive	**30,956**	**3,553**	**7,064**	**9,290**	**11,049**	**2,747**
Students	2,747	1,336	28	1,338	45	2,747
Permanently sick	2,055	404	874	376	401	
Retired	17,611	1,758	6,071	5,455	4,327	
Other inactive	8,543	55	91	2,121	6,276	

35. Residents in households

Age	TOTAL PERSONS	Males					Females				
		Total	Single	Married	Widowed	Divorced	Total	Single	Married	Widowed	Divorced
a	b	c	d	e	f	g	h	i	j	k	l
					CUMBRIA						
ALL AGES	**474,787**	**231,591**	**96,963**	**117,428**	**7,482**	**9,718**	**243,196**	**84,293**	**118,027**	**28,552**	**12,324**
0 - 4	28,795	14,652	14,652				14,143	14,143			
5 - 9	28,858	14,901	14,901				13,957	13,957			
10 - 14	27,846	14,351	14,351				13,495	13,495			
15	5,540	2,812	2,812				2,728	2,728			
16 - 17	12,159	6,243	6,230	11	-	2	5,916	5,892	18	4	2
18 - 19	12,954	6,556	6,506	45	1	4	6,398	6,217	171	-	10
20 - 24	32,970	16,518	14,312	2,107	3	96	16,452	11,697	4,426	15	314
25 - 29	34,231	17,275	8,236	8,277	12	750	16,956	5,117	10,576	39	1,224
30 - 34	33,120	16,616	4,081	11,229	18	1,288	16,504	2,128	12,584	87	1,705
35 - 39	31,026	15,547	2,257	11,929	36	1,325	15,479	1,173	12,465	132	1,709
40 - 44	36,090	18,218	1,864	14,593	103	1,658	17,872	847	14,827	253	1,945
45 - 49	30,078	15,195	1,255	12,492	148	1,300	14,883	565	12,374	441	1,503
50 - 54	27,829	13,811	1,097	11,420	186	1,108	14,018	557	11,554	761	1,146
55 - 59	26,414	13,127	978	10,949	396	804	13,287	657	10,337	1,432	861
60 - 64	27,272	13,075	1,074	10,719	687	595	14,197	875	9,837	2,819	666
65 - 69	25,946	11,883	923	9,389	1,183	388	14,063	981	8,270	4,254	558
70 - 74	21,361	9,189	651	6,962	1,361	215	12,172	948	5,626	5,262	336
75 - 79	16,360	6,494	440	4,487	1,443	124	9,866	921	3,200	5,536	209
80 - 84	10,180	3,516	228	2,091	1,147	50	6,664	813	1,332	4,424	95
85 - 89	4,453	1,315	100	639	565	11	3,138	431	374	2,301	32
90 and over	1,305	297	15	89	193	-	1,008	151	56	792	9
					Allerdale						
ALL AGES	**93,935**	**45,949**	**19,028**	**23,561**	**1,554**	**1,806**	**47,986**	**16,290**	**23,639**	**5,736**	**2,321**
0 - 4	5,518	2,780	2,780				2,738	2,738			
5 - 9	5,769	3,024	3,024				2,745	2,745			
10 - 14	5,781	3,054	3,054				2,727	2,727			
15	1,137	575	575				562	562			
16 - 17	2,440	1,263	1,260	2	-	1	1,177	1,170	4	3	-
18 - 19	2,587	1,314	1,306	8	-	-	1,273	1,227	42	-	4
20 - 24	6,460	3,222	2,721	481	-	20	3,238	2,219	956	2	61
25 - 29	6,459	3,255	1,441	1,681	1	132	3,204	860	2,080	10	254
30 - 34	6,433	3,212	706	2,237	9	260	3,221	370	2,492	23	336
35 - 39	6,208	3,065	401	2,413	6	245	3,143	216	2,551	29	347
40 - 44	7,455	3,744	380	3,048	22	294	3,711	176	3,127	52	356
45 - 49	6,011	3,072	229	2,575	32	236	2,939	118	2,496	77	248
50 - 54	5,500	2,758	243	2,252	42	221	2,742	88	2,299	158	197
55 - 59	5,290	2,638	185	2,200	89	164	2,652	121	2,069	279	183
60 - 64	5,438	2,597	211	2,125	151	110	2,841	167	1,963	591	120
65 - 69	5,211	2,379	209	1,861	244	65	2,832	201	1,643	882	106
70 - 74	4,257	1,846	145	1,370	301	30	2,411	189	1,077	1,093	52
75 - 79	3,036	1,237	91	836	293	17	1,799	165	525	1,069	40
80 - 84	1,889	622	40	350	223	9	1,267	133	242	882	10
85 - 89	854	246	25	109	110	2	608	73	62	467	6
90 and over	202	46	2	13	31	-	156	25	11	119	1

35. Residents in households

Age	TOTAL PERSONS	Males					Females				
		Total	Single	Married	Widowed	Divorced	Total	Single	Married	Widowed	Divorced
a	b	c	d	e	f	g	h	i	j	k	l
					Barrow-in-Furness						
ALL AGES	**72,564**	**35,498**	**15,236**	**17,270**	**1,137**	**1,855**	**37,066**	**13,179**	**17,366**	**4,305**	**2,216**
0 - 4	5,058	2,600	2,600				2,458	2,458			
5 - 9	4,579	2,334	2,334				2,245	2,245			
10 - 14	4,132	2,096	2,096				2,036	2,036			
15	882	458	458				424	424			
16 - 17	1,913	979	976	3	-	-	934	931	3	-	-
18 - 19	2,103	1,053	1,046	7	-	-	1,050	1,027	22	-	1
20 - 24	5,631	2,797	2,363	420	-	14	2,834	1,960	818	1	55
25 - 29	5,763	2,905	1,303	1,449	5	148	2,858	768	1,840	4	246
30 - 34	5,075	2,591	593	1,776	-	222	2,484	306	1,880	11	287
35 - 39	4,584	2,299	316	1,743	2	238	2,285	146	1,808	16	315
40 - 44	5,305	2,685	234	2,126	17	308	2,620	104	2,130	32	354
45 - 49	4,614	2,359	176	1,872	32	279	2,255	82	1,811	65	297
50 - 54	4,222	2,118	142	1,718	38	220	2,104	65	1,704	108	227
55 - 59	3,704	1,880	137	1,528	63	152	1,824	90	1,369	229	136
60 - 64	3,704	1,778	135	1,424	95	124	1,926	91	1,332	407	96
65 - 69	3,571	1,626	134	1,227	190	75	1,945	102	1,115	637	91
70 - 74	3,327	1,369	88	1,028	210	43	1,958	107	895	901	55
75 - 79	2,327	909	66	610	216	17	1,418	106	420	864	28
80 - 84	1,363	466	24	267	162	13	897	71	170	634	22
85 - 89	538	157	11	64	80	2	381	45	42	290	4
90 and over	169	39	4	8	27	-	130	15	7	106	2
					Carlisle						
ALL AGES	**99,059**	**47,904**	**20,290**	**23,923**	**1,557**	**2,134**	**51,155**	**18,218**	**24,110**	**5,972**	**2,855**
0 - 4	6,153	3,147	3,147				3,006	3,006			
5 - 9	6,160	3,127	3,127				3,033	3,033			
10 - 14	5,801	2,934	2,934				2,867	2,867			
15	1,142	577	577				565	565			
16 - 17	2,498	1,254	1,253	1	-	-	1,244	1,239	5	-	-
18 - 19	2,844	1,433	1,417	12	1	3	1,411	1,370	37	-	4
20 - 24	6,875	3,391	2,923	438	1	29	3,484	2,504	900	4	76
25 - 29	7,293	3,633	1,720	1,731	3	179	3,660	1,181	2,197	8	274
30 - 34	7,293	3,647	907	2,423	3	314	3,646	499	2,728	20	399
35 - 39	6,594	3,295	484	2,502	6	303	3,299	280	2,584	26	409
40 - 44	7,320	3,699	393	2,936	29	341	3,621	186	2,948	55	432
45 - 49	5,969	2,962	243	2,417	30	272	3,007	122	2,451	108	326
50 - 54	5,602	2,731	216	2,267	33	215	2,871	137	2,306	158	270
55 - 59	5,538	2,716	215	2,233	87	181	2,822	164	2,149	301	208
60 - 64	5,632	2,700	267	2,172	141	120	2,932	200	1,962	606	164
65 - 69	5,474	2,490	188	1,983	236	83	2,984	214	1,721	914	135
70 - 74	4,168	1,767	121	1,347	245	54	2,401	183	1,074	1,059	85
75 - 79	3,411	1,350	90	889	341	30	2,061	198	688	1,126	49
80 - 84	2,115	749	45	444	252	8	1,366	157	284	907	18
85 - 89	889	239	18	112	107	2	650	81	69	494	6
90 and over	288	63	5	16	42	-	225	32	7	186	-

35. Residents in households

Age	TOTAL PERSONS	Males					Females				
		Total	Single	Married	Widowed	Divorced	Total	Single	Married	Widowed	Divorced
a	b	c	d	e	f	g	h	i	j	k	l
					Copeland						
ALL AGES	**70,485**	**34,865**	**15,352**	**17,016**	**1,077**	**1,420**	**35,620**	**12,796**	**17,081**	**4,011**	**1,732**
0 - 4	4,719	2,381	2,381				2,338	2,338			
5 - 9	4,735	2,504	2,504				2,231	2,231			
10 - 14	4,369	2,259	2,259				2,110	2,110			
15	855	436	436				419	419			
16 - 17	1,879	937	935	2	-	-	942	939	3	-	-
18 - 19	1,865	925	920	5	-	-	940	912	27	-	1
20 - 24	5,042	2,551	2,186	348	1	16	2,491	1,703	723	3	62
25 - 29	5,620	2,870	1,349	1,395	2	124	2,750	742	1,802	6	200
30 - 34	5,248	2,677	648	1,828	1	200	2,571	303	1,974	12	282
35 - 39	4,658	2,370	358	1,802	5	205	2,288	168	1,851	19	250
40 - 44	5,238	2,713	299	2,142	11	261	2,525	116	2,099	42	268
45 - 49	4,291	2,175	196	1,797	26	156	2,116	62	1,791	66	197
50 - 54	4,129	2,051	184	1,679	31	157	2,078	89	1,710	136	143
55 - 59	3,918	1,971	141	1,652	70	108	1,947	72	1,519	252	104
60 - 64	3,857	1,877	175	1,510	115	77	1,980	99	1,348	447	86
65 - 69	3,482	1,629	167	1,212	187	63	1,853	113	1,057	617	66
70 - 74	2,831	1,205	105	851	220	29	1,626	134	677	770	45
75 - 79	1,928	744	60	491	175	18	1,184	89	339	735	21
80 - 84	1,193	418	37	225	150	6	775	90	125	556	4
85 - 89	476	142	11	69	62	-	334	56	29	248	1
90 and over	152	30	1	8	21	-	122	11	7	102	2
					Eden						
ALL AGES	**44,711**	**22,102**	**9,226**	**11,439**	**665**	**772**	**22,609**	**7,661**	**11,501**	**2,524**	**923**
0 - 4	2,483	1,251	1,251				1,232	1,232			
5 - 9	2,584	1,298	1,298				1,286	1,286			
10 - 14	2,624	1,344	1,344				1,280	1,280			
15	484	249	249				235	235			
16 - 17	1,119	601	600	1	-	-	518	517	1	-	-
18 - 19	1,188	601	596	4	-	1	587	569	18	-	-
20 - 24	3,031	1,600	1,444	153	-	3	1,431	1,037	367	1	26
25 - 29	3,009	1,543	804	683	-	56	1,466	461	929	1	75
30 - 34	3,081	1,540	409	1,029	3	99	1,541	213	1,187	6	135
35 - 39	3,037	1,536	242	1,183	3	108	1,501	107	1,266	13	115
40 - 44	3,527	1,798	190	1,465	7	136	1,729	81	1,463	18	167
45 - 49	2,962	1,507	171	1,230	8	98	1,455	65	1,241	45	104
50 - 54	2,690	1,344	124	1,115	16	89	1,346	46	1,141	72	87
55 - 59	2,580	1,278	113	1,079	30	56	1,302	51	1,050	135	66
60 - 64	2,745	1,355	120	1,128	56	51	1,390	100	1,015	230	45
65 - 69	2,466	1,167	97	935	103	32	1,299	72	801	381	45
70 - 74	2,000	914	83	686	126	19	1,086	95	517	449	25
75 - 79	1,565	648	50	451	130	17	917	88	318	493	18
80 - 84	1,007	367	26	222	114	5	640	86	140	403	11
85 - 89	412	129	15	65	47	2	283	31	41	209	2
90 and over	117	32	-	10	22	-	85	9	6	68	2

35. Residents in households

Age	TOTAL PERSONS	Males					Females				
		Total	Single	Married	Widowed	Divorced	Total	Single	Married	Widowed	Divorced
a	b	c	d	e	f	g	h	i	j	k	l
					South Lakeland						
ALL AGES	**94,033**	**45,273**	**17,831**	**24,219**	**1,492**	**1,731**	**48,760**	**16,149**	**24,330**	**6,004**	**2,277**
0 - 4	4,864	2,493	2,493				2,371	2,371			
5 - 9	5,031	2,614	2,614				2,417	2,417			
10 - 14	5,139	2,664	2,664				2,475	2,475			
15	1,040	517	517				523	523			
16 - 17	2,310	1,209	1,206	2	-	1	1,101	1,096	2	1	2
18 - 19	2,367	1,230	1,221	9	-	-	1,137	1,112	25	-	-
20 - 24	5,931	2,957	2,675	267	1	14	2,974	2,274	662	4	34
25 - 29	6,087	3,069	1,619	1,338	1	111	3,018	1,105	1,728	10	175
30 - 34	5,990	2,949	818	1,936	2	193	3,041	437	2,323	15	266
35 - 39	5,945	2,982	456	2,286	14	226	2,963	256	2,405	29	273
40 - 44	7,245	3,579	368	2,876	17	318	3,666	184	3,060	54	368
45 - 49	6,231	3,120	240	2,601	20	259	3,111	116	2,584	80	331
50 - 54	5,686	2,809	188	2,389	26	206	2,877	132	2,394	129	222
55 - 59	5,384	2,644	187	2,257	57	143	2,740	159	2,181	236	164
60 - 64	5,896	2,768	166	2,360	129	113	3,128	218	2,217	538	155
65 - 69	5,742	2,592	128	2,171	223	70	3,150	279	1,933	823	115
70 - 74	4,778	2,088	109	1,680	259	40	2,690	240	1,386	990	74
75 - 79	4,093	1,606	83	1,210	288	25	2,487	275	910	1,249	53
80 - 84	2,613	894	56	583	246	9	1,719	276	371	1,042	30
85 - 89	1,284	402	20	220	159	3	882	145	131	593	13
90 and over	377	87	3	34	50	-	290	59	18	211	2

36. Households with residents; resident adults; dependent children

Households with the following adults			TOTAL HOUSEHOLDS	Households with the following dependent children				TOTAL DEPENDENT CHILDREN
Number	Economically active	In employment		0	1	2	3 or more	
a	b	c	d	e	f	g	h	i
CUMBRIA								
None	None	None	24		19	4	1	31
One	None	None	36,621	33,349	1,457	1,147	668	6,003
One	One	None	2,297	1,989	196	84	28	457
One	One	One	18,657	15,812	1,535	1,026	284	4,494
Two or more	None	None	25,344	24,464	403	268	209	1,670
Two or more	One	None	3,226	1,669	512	596	449	3,268
Two or more	One	One	29,351	15,809	4,685	6,064	2,793	25,951
Two or more	Two or more	None	884	526	160	122	76	663
Two or more	Two or more	One	4,848	2,984	1,014	627	223	2,982
Two or more	Two or more	Two or more	72,641	41,467	13,876	13,486	3,812	52,972
TOTAL HOUSEHOLDS			**193,893**	**138,069**	**23,857**	**23,424**	**8,543**	**98,491**
TOTAL ADULTS			**376,296**	**257,847**	**53,868**	**47,525**	**17,056**	
Economically active			235,803	143,252	42,647	37,764	12,140	
In employment			219,761	132,840	39,745	35,973	11,203	
Allerdale								
None	None	None	5		4	1	-	6
One	None	None	7,271	6,575	335	233	128	1,228
One	One	None	530	459	48	19	4	99
One	One	One	3,137	2,618	283	184	52	816
Two or more	None	None	5,026	4,799	99	76	52	425
Two or more	One	None	839	435	120	169	115	846
Two or more	One	One	5,959	3,154	974	1,265	566	5,354
Two or more	Two or more	None	214	129	40	25	20	158
Two or more	Two or more	One	1,162	710	251	164	37	695
Two or more	Two or more	Two or more	13,724	7,667	2,756	2,627	674	10,147
TOTAL HOUSEHOLDS			**37,867**	**26,546**	**4,910**	**4,763**	**1,648**	**19,774**
TOTAL ADULTS			**74,161**	**50,132**	**11,081**	**9,670**	**3,278**	
Economically active			45,639	27,185	8,657	7,544	2,253	
In employment			41,764	24,675	7,951	7,095	2,043	
Barrow-in-Furness								
None	None	None	1		1	-	-	1
One	None	None	5,857	5,156	287	251	163	1,336
One	One	None	443	386	40	12	5	80
One	One	One	2,916	2,469	247	147	53	711
Two or more	None	None	3,671	3,513	72	43	43	319
Two or more	One	None	632	305	124	109	94	687
Two or more	One	One	4,551	2,320	805	979	447	4,234
Two or more	Two or more	None	167	99	29	25	14	129
Two or more	Two or more	One	910	566	195	99	50	549
Two or more	Two or more	Two or more	10,479	5,922	2,153	1,849	555	7,625
TOTAL HOUSEHOLDS			**29,627**	**20,736**	**3,953**	**3,514**	**1,424**	**15,671**
TOTAL ADULTS			**56,893**	**38,234**	**8,825**	**7,056**	**2,778**	
Economically active			35,573	21,363	6,894	5,423	1,893	
In employment			32,568	19,430	6,323	5,114	1,701	

36. Households with residents; resident adults; dependent children

Households with the following adults			TOTAL HOUSEHOLDS	Households with the following dependent children				TOTAL DEPENDENT CHILDREN
Number	Economically active	In employment		0	1	2	3 or more	
a	b	c	d	e	f	g	h	i
Carlisle								
None	None	None	7		7	-	-	7
One	None	None	7,969	7,165	367	282	155	1,464
One	One	None	533	462	42	21	8	114
One	One	One	4,192	3,533	365	228	66	1,031
Two or more	None	None	4,908	4,741	76	44	47	328
Two or more	One	None	635	326	103	112	94	657
Two or more	One	One	5,687	3,167	910	1,079	531	4,814
Two or more	Two or more	None	219	128	41	33	17	164
Two or more	Two or more	One	1,054	651	213	137	53	658
Two or more	Two or more	Two or more	15,679	8,926	3,027	2,938	788	11,390
TOTAL HOUSEHOLDS			**40,883**	**29,099**	**5,151**	**4,874**	**1,759**	**20,627**
TOTAL ADULTS			**78,432**	**53,732**	**11,407**	**9,788**	**3,505**	
Economically active			50,303	30,674	9,145	7,975	2,509	
In employment			46,783	28,384	8,527	7,576	2,296	
Copeland								
None	None	None	1		1	-	-	1
One	None	None	5,102	4,470	264	225	143	1,189
One	One	None	443	386	37	14	6	84
One	One	One	2,437	2,046	217	139	35	607
Two or more	None	None	3,298	3,123	69	65	41	343
Two or more	One	None	639	305	101	130	103	713
Two or more	One	One	4,600	2,355	726	1,013	506	4,426
Two or more	Two or more	None	200	109	39	29	23	173
Two or more	Two or more	One	826	475	193	113	45	563
Two or more	Two or more	Two or more	10,206	5,651	2,062	1,924	569	7,734
TOTAL HOUSEHOLDS			**27,752**	**18,920**	**3,709**	**3,652**	**1,471**	**15,833**
TOTAL ADULTS			**54,652**	**35,857**	**8,419**	**7,433**	**2,943**	
Economically active			34,314	20,115	6,535	5,682	1,982	
In employment			31,245	18,213	5,945	5,321	1,766	
Eden								
None	None	None	5		2	2	1	10
One	None	None	2,953	2,826	57	50	20	231
One	One	None	128	108	11	7	2	31
One	One	One	1,806	1,566	116	94	30	402
Two or more	None	None	2,338	2,289	25	16	8	86
Two or more	One	None	168	100	29	23	16	129
Two or more	One	One	2,993	1,626	460	647	260	2,591
Two or more	Two or more	None	28	18	2	7	1	19
Two or more	Two or more	One	302	197	54	37	14	180
Two or more	Two or more	Two or more	7,296	4,303	1,244	1,346	403	5,229
TOTAL HOUSEHOLDS			**18,017**	**13,033**	**2,000**	**2,229**	**755**	**8,908**
TOTAL ADULTS			**35,803**	**25,002**	**4,657**	**4,592**	**1,552**	
Economically active			22,971	14,374	3,718	3,693	1,186	
In employment			22,096	13,775	3,577	3,601	1,143	

36. Households with residents; resident adults; dependent children

Households with the following adults			TOTAL HOUSEHOLDS	Households with the following dependent children				TOTAL DEPENDENT CHILDREN
Number	Economically active	In employment		0	1	2	3 or more	
a	b	c	d	e	f	g	h	i
				South Lakeland				
None	None	None	5		4	1	-	6
One	None	None	7,469	7,157	147	106	59	555
One	One	None	220	188	18	11	3	49
One	One	One	4,169	3,580	307	234	48	927
Two or more	None	None	6,103	5,999	62	24	18	169
Two or more	One	None	313	198	35	53	27	236
Two or more	One	One	5,561	3,187	810	1,081	483	4,532
Two or more	Two or more	None	56	43	9	3	1	20
Two or more	Two or more	One	594	385	108	77	24	337
Two or more	Two or more	Two or more	15,257	8,998	2,634	2,802	823	10,847
TOTAL HOUSEHOLDS			**39,747**	**29,735**	**4,134**	**4,392**	**1,486**	**17,678**
TOTAL ADULTS			**76,355**	**54,890**	**9,479**	**8,986**	**3,000**	
Economically active			47,003	29,541	7,698	7,447	2,317	
In employment			45,305	28,363	7,422	7,266	2,254	

37. Residents aged 16 - 24 in households

Age	TOTAL PERSONS		Married		Lone 'parent' aged 16 - 24 with child(ren) aged 0 - 15		Economically active		On a Government scheme		Unemployed		Students (including those economically active)	
	Males	Females	Males	Females	Males	Females	Males	Females	Males	Females	Males	Females	Males	Females
a	b	c	d	e	f	g	h	i	j	k	l	m	n	o
							CUMBRIA							
ALL AGES 16 - 24	**29,317**	**28,766**	**2,163**	**4,615**	**10**	**1,079**	**23,588**	**19,502**	**1,332**	**972**	**3,251**	**1,903**	**5,980**	**6,789**
16	3,128	2,878	1	5	1	1	1,084	903	241	172	203	110	2,193	2,273
17	3,115	3,038	10	13	-	15	2,218	1,800	546	423	210	173	1,036	1,457
18	3,246	3,116	8	40	-	32	2,583	2,109	278	192	373	258	766	1,025
19	3,310	3,282	37	131	-	92	2,758	2,384	87	64	425	287	563	666
20	3,421	3,352	83	296	-	128	2,903	2,477	48	34	427	280	514	529
21	3,212	3,274	183	571	4	147	2,787	2,392	35	29	418	236	400	430
22	3,345	3,306	340	873	1	213	3,042	2,514	36	19	438	191	273	231
23	3,193	3,166	598	1,169	2	220	3,020	2,404	37	19	373	195	135	128
24	3,347	3,354	903	1,517	2	231	3,193	2,519	24	20	384	173	100	50
							Allerdale							
ALL AGES 16 - 24	**5,799**	**5,688**	**491**	**1,002**	**2**	**213**	**4,627**	**3,790**	**342**	**246**	**747**	**440**	**1,191**	**1,359**
16	605	588	-	1	-	-	187	174	52	42	47	27	436	465
17	658	589	2	3	-	2	463	350	131	101	56	48	219	277
18	677	634	2	7	-	5	519	415	79	47	79	59	173	204
19	637	639	6	35	-	25	529	455	25	22	86	69	105	131
20	679	673	22	66	-	21	565	492	17	10	104	71	113	120
21	591	655	39	115	-	31	528	472	13	9	102	48	62	92
22	661	643	79	187	-	54	616	498	10	5	95	50	34	38
23	626	617	123	258	-	36	586	466	8	7	92	45	31	16
24	665	650	218	330	2	39	634	468	7	3	86	23	18	16
							Barrow-in-Furness							
ALL AGES 16 - 24	**4,829**	**4,818**	**430**	**843**	**3**	**268**	**4,082**	**3,301**	**197**	**219**	**596**	**405**	**742**	**850**
16	495	458	1	2	-	-	175	133	38	37	32	13	340	356
17	484	476	2	1	-	3	372	321	80	108	30	36	119	176
18	520	505	-	10	-	7	458	371	38	43	68	59	76	127
19	533	545	7	12	-	17	478	433	12	11	76	67	45	67
20	575	570	16	62	-	37	523	415	5	6	83	60	48	55
21	512	544	39	112	2	35	458	405	6	4	69	53	45	32
22	538	587	56	175	1	53	499	422	7	3	78	35	29	20
23	561	527	133	210	-	48	537	390	6	2	73	42	21	10
24	611	606	176	259	-	68	582	411	5	5	87	40	19	7
							Carlisle							
ALL AGES 16 - 24	**6,078**	**6,139**	**451**	**942**	**1**	**278**	**5,009**	**4,260**	**257**	**168**	**797**	**391**	**1,140**	**1,353**
16	657	595	-	1	-	1	267	210	49	32	57	34	425	448
17	597	649	1	4	-	8	448	408	101	59	59	41	188	295
18	685	674	3	6	-	9	573	489	44	34	113	55	139	189
19	748	737	9	31	-	30	616	521	17	12	118	53	137	150
20	716	695	15	67	-	32	618	502	10	7	87	58	95	107
21	658	702	36	130	1	34	585	514	10	5	93	38	67	93
22	684	706	74	170	-	48	623	533	10	6	95	35	54	40
23	649	681	128	242	-	63	626	516	12	6	94	35	16	24
24	684	700	185	291	-	53	653	567	4	7	81	42	19	7

37. Residents aged 16 - 24 in households

Age	TOTAL PERSONS		Married		Lone 'parent' aged 16 - 24 with child(ren) aged 0 - 15		Economically active		On a Government scheme		Unemployed		Students (including those economically active)	
	Males	Females	Males	Females	Males	Females	Males	Females	Males	Females	Males	Females	Males	Females
a	b	c	d	e	f	g	h	i	j	k	l	m	n	o
							Copeland							
ALL AGES 16 - 24	**4,413**	**4,373**	**355**	**753**	**3**	**191**	**3,600**	**2,830**	**254**	**175**	**635**	**378**	**825**	**1,024**
16	464	438	-	-	-	-	146	121	46	26	25	17	331	351
17	473	504	2	3	-	1	353	307	110	90	35	29	130	222
18	474	461	2	8	-	7	389	282	51	39	68	43	93	172
19	451	479	3	19	-	15	393	335	17	4	77	57	65	95
20	503	520	14	51	-	22	426	375	9	6	89	50	72	73
21	505	476	40	91	1	31	445	324	3	3	88	54	57	57
22	525	505	55	139	-	34	476	377	6	2	99	49	44	33
23	480	481	86	187	2	45	453	354	6	3	69	43	21	15
24	538	509	153	255	-	36	519	355	6	2	85	36	12	6
							Eden							
ALL AGES 16 - 24	**2,802**	**2,536**	**158**	**386**	**1**	**38**	**2,206**	**1,788**	**111**	**49**	**157**	**96**	**635**	**622**
16	310	260	-	1	1	-	110	90	21	11	19	6	217	205
17	291	258	1	-	-	-	205	131	47	18	9	4	105	142
18	313	298	1	3	-	1	241	203	22	10	14	12	85	113
19	288	289	3	15	-	1	227	221	12	6	20	13	63	53
20	333	278	4	11	-	5	275	226	2	3	17	13	61	41
21	330	284	9	39	-	3	276	230	1	1	27	15	52	35
22	316	306	28	77	-	12	285	252	1	-	20	9	31	21
23	317	278	47	112	-	9	295	215	3	-	17	12	14	8
24	304	285	65	128	-	7	292	220	2	-	14	12	7	4
							South Lakeland							
ALL AGES 16 - 24	**5,396**	**5,212**	**278**	**689**	**-**	**91**	**4,064**	**3,533**	**171**	**115**	**319**	**193**	**1,447**	**1,581**
16	597	539	-	-	-	-	199	175	35	24	23	13	444	448
17	612	562	2	2	-	1	377	283	77	47	21	15	275	345
18	577	544	-	6	-	3	403	349	44	19	31	30	200	220
19	653	593	9	19	-	4	515	419	4	9	48	28	148	170
20	615	616	12	39	-	11	496	467	5	2	47	28	125	133
21	616	613	20	84	-	13	495	447	2	7	39	28	117	121
22	621	559	48	125	-	12	543	432	2	3	51	13	81	79
23	560	582	81	160	-	19	523	463	2	1	28	18	32	55
24	545	604	106	254	-	28	513	498	-	3	31	20	25	10

38. Residents in households

Age	TOTAL PERSONS	Males	Females	Age	TOTAL PERSONS	Males	Females
a	b	c	d	a	b	c	d
	CUMBRIA				**CUMBRIA** - *continued*		
ALL AGES	**474,787**	**231,591**	**243,196**				
0	5,870	2,994	2,876	45	6,203	3,155	3,048
1	5,796	2,960	2,836	46	6,222	3,174	3,048
2	5,829	2,966	2,863	47	6,214	3,079	3,135
3	5,692	2,887	2,805	48	5,952	3,014	2,938
4	5,608	2,845	2,763	49	5,487	2,773	2,714
5	5,922	3,063	2,859	50	5,503	2,774	2,729
6	5,832	2,993	2,839	51	5,646	2,830	2,816
7	5,743	2,985	2,758	52	5,635	2,781	2,854
8	5,639	2,893	2,746	53	5,587	2,705	2,882
9	5,722	2,967	2,755	54	5,458	2,721	2,737
10	5,933	2,998	2,935	55	5,412	2,692	2,720
11	5,721	2,946	2,775	56	5,160	2,554	2,606
12	5,475	2,853	2,622	57	5,099	2,519	2,580
13	5,452	2,846	2,606	58	5,364	2,708	2,656
14	5,265	2,708	2,557	59	5,379	2,654	2,725
15	5,540	2,812	2,728	60	5,499	2,673	2,826
16	6,006	3,128	2,878	61	5,416	2,539	2,877
17	6,153	3,115	3,038	62	5,531	2,666	2,865
18	6,362	3,246	3,116	63	5,335	2,553	2,782
19	6,592	3,310	3,282	64	5,491	2,644	2,847
20	6,773	3,421	3,352	65	5,294	2,482	2,812
21	6,486	3,212	3,274	66	5,014	2,336	2,678
22	6,651	3,345	3,306	67	5,200	2,385	2,815
23	6,359	3,193	3,166	68	5,064	2,293	2,771
24	6,701	3,347	3,354	69	5,374	2,387	2,987
25	6,597	3,263	3,334	70	5,282	2,320	2,962
26	7,014	3,577	3,437	71	4,947	2,149	2,798
27	6,962	3,479	3,483	72	3,813	1,628	2,185
28	6,950	3,517	3,433	73	3,507	1,497	2,010
29	6,708	3,439	3,269	74	3,812	1,595	2,217
30	6,794	3,425	3,369	75	3,512	1,411	2,101
31	6,718	3,399	3,319	76	3,626	1,449	2,177
32	6,642	3,277	3,365	77	3,310	1,342	1,968
33	6,609	3,356	3,253	78	3,177	1,272	1,905
34	6,357	3,159	3,198	79	2,735	1,020	1,715
35	6,186	3,050	3,136	80	2,495	934	1,561
36	6,081	3,075	3,006	81	2,276	798	1,478
37	6,324	3,206	3,118	82	2,050	669	1,381
38	6,184	3,083	3,101	83	1,793	592	1,201
39	6,251	3,133	3,118	84	1,566	523	1,043
40	6,679	3,348	3,331	85	1,331	398	933
41	6,729	3,302	3,427	86	1,083	322	761
42	7,073	3,593	3,480	87	836	264	572
43	7,731	3,924	3,807	88	679	202	477
44	7,878	4,051	3,827	89	524	129	395
				90 and over	1,305	297	1,008

38. Residents in households

Age	TOTAL PERSONS	Males	Females	Age	TOTAL PERSONS	Males	Females
a	b	c	d	a	b	c	d
	Allerdale				**Allerdale** - *continued*		
ALL AGES	**93,935**	**45,949**	**47,986**				
0	1,128	580	548	45	1,236	640	596
1	1,118	527	591	46	1,215	639	576
2	1,096	559	537	47	1,248	617	631
3	1,082	547	535	48	1,190	609	581
4	1,094	567	527	49	1,122	567	555
5	1,201	646	555	50	1,046	555	491
6	1,110	586	524	51	1,164	596	568
7	1,151	598	553	52	1,148	550	598
8	1,148	606	542	53	1,059	514	545
9	1,159	588	571	54	1,083	543	540
10	1,260	655	605	55	1,112	562	550
11	1,209	617	592	56	1,037	510	527
12	1,097	554	543	57	971	476	495
13	1,129	644	485	58	1,075	557	518
14	1,086	584	502	59	1,095	533	562
15	1,137	575	562	60	1,098	554	544
16	1,193	605	588	61	1,091	513	578
17	1,247	658	589	62	1,067	507	560
18	1,311	677	634	63	1,083	501	582
19	1,276	637	639	64	1,099	522	577
20	1,352	679	673	65	1,122	513	609
21	1,246	591	655	66	982	476	506
22	1,304	661	643	67	1,022	454	568
23	1,243	626	617	68	1,005	470	535
24	1,315	665	650	69	1,080	466	614
25	1,244	636	608	70	1,053	488	565
26	1,298	673	625	71	1,010	429	581
27	1,300	659	641	72	721	299	422
28	1,318	628	690	73	704	320	384
29	1,299	659	640	74	769	310	459
30	1,257	623	634	75	625	237	388
31	1,307	650	657	76	718	310	408
32	1,255	624	631	77	593	250	343
33	1,345	665	680	78	564	230	334
34	1,269	650	619	79	536	210	326
35	1,237	577	660	80	504	179	325
36	1,186	619	567	81	385	128	257
37	1,256	612	644	82	375	118	257
38	1,304	625	679	83	327	109	218
39	1,225	632	593	84	298	88	210
40	1,367	701	666	85	263	76	187
41	1,369	649	720	86	207	54	153
42	1,470	727	743	87	158	52	106
43	1,649	833	816	88	118	39	79
44	1,600	834	766	89	108	25	83
				90 and over	202	46	156

38. Residents in households

Age	TOTAL PERSONS	Males	Females	Age	TOTAL PERSONS	Males	Females
a	b	c	d	a	b	c	d
	Barrow-in-Furness				**Barrow-in-Furness** – *continued*		
ALL AGES	**72,564**	**35,498**	**37,066**				
0	1,042	534	508	45	930	458	472
1	1,024	533	491	46	972	500	472
2	1,022	544	478	47	931	476	455
3	981	492	489	48	938	481	457
4	989	497	492	49	843	444	399
5	959	488	471	50	900	443	457
6	964	496	468	51	845	432	413
7	893	436	457	52	871	459	412
8	891	467	424	53	840	406	434
9	872	447	425	54	766	378	388
10	889	436	453	55	741	386	355
11	825	422	403	56	722	361	361
12	807	440	367	57	720	394	326
13	822	399	423	58	769	383	386
14	789	399	390	59	752	356	396
15	882	458	424	60	777	387	390
16	953	495	458	61	724	322	402
17	960	484	476	62	730	352	378
18	1,025	520	505	63	697	346	351
19	1,078	533	545	64	776	371	405
20	1,145	575	570	65	696	335	361
21	1,056	512	544	66	684	297	387
22	1,125	538	587	67	686	312	374
23	1,088	561	527	68	706	329	377
24	1,217	611	606	69	799	353	446
25	1,129	549	580	70	738	331	407
26	1,163	565	598	71	795	331	464
27	1,230	618	612	72	608	233	375
28	1,140	576	564	73	548	207	341
29	1,101	597	504	74	638	267	371
30	1,104	594	510	75	532	200	332
31	1,087	552	535	76	549	207	342
32	988	477	511	77	467	199	268
33	973	514	459	78	406	157	249
34	923	454	469	79	373	146	227
35	947	485	462	80	336	123	213
36	884	440	444	81	297	96	201
37	925	452	473	82	281	98	183
38	893	468	425	83	256	82	174
39	935	454	481	84	193	67	126
40	958	472	486	85	149	42	107
41	1,003	498	505	86	132	35	97
42	1,036	547	489	87	109	35	74
43	1,157	593	564	88	89	26	63
44	1,151	575	576	89	59	19	40
				90 and over	169	39	130

38. Residents in households

Age	TOTAL PERSONS	Males	Females	Age	TOTAL PERSONS	Males	Females
a	b	c	d	a	b	c	d
	Carlisle				**Carlisle** – *continued*		
ALL AGES	**99,059**	**47,904**	**51,155**				
0	1,308	692	616	45	1,268	634	634
1	1,256	646	610	46	1,183	583	600
2	1,191	596	595	47	1,219	601	618
3	1,220	600	620	48	1,221	619	602
4	1,178	613	565	49	1,078	525	553
5	1,229	642	587	50	1,160	578	582
6	1,272	654	618	51	1,103	531	572
7	1,270	651	619	52	1,079	538	541
8	1,220	597	623	53	1,135	550	585
9	1,169	583	586	54	1,125	534	591
10	1,245	630	615	55	1,142	546	596
11	1,191	576	615	56	1,045	509	536
12	1,140	595	545	57	1,113	542	571
13	1,144	590	554	58	1,112	555	557
14	1,081	543	538	59	1,126	564	562
15	1,142	577	565	60	1,150	572	578
16	1,252	657	595	61	1,126	546	580
17	1,246	597	649	62	1,149	541	608
18	1,359	685	674	63	1,079	511	568
19	1,485	748	737	64	1,128	530	598
20	1,411	716	695	65	1,135	530	605
21	1,360	658	702	66	1,013	470	543
22	1,390	684	706	67	1,101	499	602
23	1,330	649	681	68	1,060	466	594
24	1,384	684	700	69	1,165	525	640
25	1,387	686	701	70	1,058	439	619
26	1,494	753	741	71	959	428	531
27	1,467	739	728	72	787	337	450
28	1,524	755	769	73	680	295	385
29	1,421	700	721	74	684	268	416
30	1,522	774	748	75	771	315	456
31	1,426	717	709	76	763	320	443
32	1,530	773	757	77	690	270	420
33	1,456	735	721	78	634	246	388
34	1,359	648	711	79	553	199	354
35	1,311	648	663	80	515	195	320
36	1,293	643	650	81	459	171	288
37	1,363	693	670	82	415	140	275
38	1,313	671	642	83	368	120	248
39	1,314	640	674	84	358	123	235
40	1,354	687	667	85	248	77	171
41	1,435	716	719	86	193	58	135
42	1,408	721	687	87	175	43	132
43	1,507	743	764	88	153	41	112
44	1,616	832	784	89	120	20	100
				90 and over	288	63	225

38. Residents in households

Age	TOTAL PERSONS	Males	Females	Age	TOTAL PERSONS	Males	Females
a	b	c	d	a	b	c	d
	Copeland				**Copeland** – *continued*		
ALL AGES	**70,485**	**34,865**	**35,620**				
0	915	428	487	45	862	427	435
1	945	493	452	46	935	509	426
2	1,006	540	466	47	832	418	414
3	932	454	478	48	835	405	430
4	921	466	455	49	827	416	411
5	940	489	451	50	830	421	409
6	986	491	495	51	837	432	405
7	919	490	429	52	828	408	420
8	918	499	419	53	809	373	436
9	972	535	437	54	825	417	408
10	920	458	462	55	765	388	377
11	928	501	427	56	783	400	383
12	860	432	428	57	779	366	413
13	865	454	411	58	763	389	374
14	796	414	382	59	828	428	400
15	855	436	419	60	777	373	404
16	902	464	438	61	780	379	401
17	977	473	504	62	802	417	385
18	935	474	461	63	748	355	393
19	930	451	479	64	750	353	397
20	1,023	503	520	65	704	341	363
21	981	505	476	66	705	354	351
22	1,030	525	505	67	691	309	382
23	961	480	481	68	677	321	356
24	1,047	538	509	69	705	304	401
25	1,097	535	562	70	703	300	403
26	1,153	605	548	71	647	272	375
27	1,136	557	579	72	500	222	278
28	1,150	622	528	73	494	199	295
29	1,084	551	533	74	487	212	275
30	1,064	543	521	75	404	172	232
31	1,057	542	515	76	424	156	268
32	1,072	550	522	77	421	159	262
33	1,009	513	496	78	378	153	225
34	1,046	529	517	79	301	104	197
35	957	482	475	80	311	124	187
36	939	492	447	81	263	92	171
37	949	497	452	82	257	80	177
38	885	423	462	83	202	70	132
39	928	476	452	84	160	52	108
40	1,064	526	538	85	165	40	125
41	929	482	447	86	107	35	72
42	1,046	548	498	87	83	31	52
43	1,092	576	516	88	66	19	47
44	1,107	581	526	89	55	17	38
				90 and over	152	30	122

38. Residents in households

Age	TOTAL PERSONS	Males	Females	Age	TOTAL PERSONS	Males	Females
a	b	c	d	a	b	c	d
	Eden				**Eden** - *continued*		
ALL AGES	**44,711**	**22,102**	**22,609**				
0	517	246	271	45	608	328	280
1	511	253	258	46	626	305	321
2	488	245	243	47	620	310	310
3	503	265	238	48	575	295	280
4	464	242	222	49	533	269	264
5	544	268	276	50	504	255	249
6	517	251	266	51	554	278	276
7	500	260	240	52	581	272	309
8	492	242	250	53	529	260	269
9	531	277	254	54	522	279	243
10	555	288	267	55	544	258	286
11	564	298	266	56	515	260	255
12	538	289	249	57	506	252	254
13	499	241	258	58	516	264	252
14	468	228	240	59	499	244	255
15	484	249	235	60	544	258	286
16	570	310	260	61	542	261	281
17	549	291	258	62	564	287	277
18	611	313	298	63	537	262	275
19	577	288	289	64	558	287	271
20	611	333	278	65	512	249	263
21	614	330	284	66	479	238	241
22	622	316	306	67	530	258	272
23	595	317	278	68	490	217	273
24	589	304	285	69	455	205	250
25	578	267	311	70	530	255	275
26	664	341	323	71	425	191	234
27	602	319	283	72	352	167	185
28	572	309	263	73	319	144	175
29	593	307	286	74	374	157	217
30	638	306	332	75	347	153	194
31	612	331	281	76	314	128	186
32	630	286	344	77	310	125	185
33	625	333	292	78	343	144	199
34	576	284	292	79	251	98	153
35	563	275	288	80	241	90	151
36	591	302	289	81	240	90	150
37	624	335	289	82	209	75	134
38	614	291	323	83	174	60	114
39	645	333	312	84	143	52	91
40	689	361	328	85	117	35	82
41	626	320	306	86	98	29	69
42	688	335	353	87	88	35	53
43	753	374	379	88	62	14	48
44	771	408	363	89	47	16	31
				90 and over	117	32	85

38. Residents in households

Age	TOTAL PERSONS	Males	Females	Age	TOTAL PERSONS	Males	Females
a	b	c	d	a	b	c	d
	South Lakeland				**South Lakeland** – *continued*		
ALL AGES	**94,033**	**45,273**	**48,760**				
0	960	514	446	45	1,299	668	631
1	942	508	434	46	1,291	638	653
2	1,026	482	544	47	1,364	657	707
3	974	529	445	48	1,193	605	588
4	962	460	502	49	1,084	552	532
5	1,049	530	519	50	1,063	522	541
6	983	515	468	51	1,143	561	582
7	1,010	550	460	52	1,128	554	574
8	970	482	488	53	1,215	602	613
9	1,019	537	482	54	1,137	570	567
10	1,064	531	533	55	1,108	552	556
11	1,004	532	472	56	1,058	514	544
12	1,033	543	490	57	1,010	489	521
13	993	518	475	58	1,129	560	569
14	1,045	540	505	59	1,079	529	550
15	1,040	517	523	60	1,153	529	624
16	1,136	597	539	61	1,153	518	635
17	1,174	612	562	62	1,219	562	657
18	1,121	577	544	63	1,191	578	613
19	1,246	653	593	64	1,180	581	599
20	1,231	615	616	65	1,125	514	611
21	1,229	616	613	66	1,151	501	650
22	1,180	621	559	67	1,170	553	617
23	1,142	560	582	68	1,126	490	636
24	1,149	545	604	69	1,170	534	636
25	1,162	590	572	70	1,200	507	693
26	1,242	640	602	71	1,111	498	613
27	1,227	587	640	72	845	370	475
28	1,246	627	619	73	762	332	430
29	1,210	625	585	74	860	381	479
30	1,209	585	624	75	833	334	499
31	1,229	607	622	76	858	328	530
32	1,167	567	600	77	829	339	490
33	1,201	596	605	78	852	342	510
34	1,184	594	590	79	721	263	458
35	1,171	583	588	80	588	223	365
36	1,188	579	609	81	632	221	411
37	1,207	617	590	82	513	158	355
38	1,175	605	570	83	466	151	315
39	1,204	598	606	84	414	141	273
40	1,247	601	646	85	389	128	261
41	1,367	637	730	86	346	111	235
42	1,425	715	710	87	223	68	155
43	1,573	805	768	88	191	63	128
44	1,633	821	812	89	135	32	103
				90 and over	377	87	290

Notes: (1) * May include a small number of heads aged under 16
(2) ** May include a small number of persons in households with heads aged under 16

39. Residents in households

Age	TOTAL PERSONS	Males				Females			
		Total	Single	Married	Widowed or divorced	Total	Single	Married	Widowed or divorced
a	b	c	d	e	f	g	h	i	j
CUMBRIA									
Heads of households									
All ages 16 and over*	**193,893**	**137,392**	**14,053**	**109,496**	**13,843**	**56,501**	**11,532**	**9,102**	**35,867**
16 - 19*	754	255	223	30	2	499	469	18	12
20 - 24	6,953	4,113	2,337	1,736	40	2,840	2,129	523	188
25 - 29	14,713	10,754	3,068	7,269	417	3,959	1,864	1,226	869
30 - 44	51,628	41,557	3,807	34,688	3,062	10,071	1,967	3,558	4,546
45 - 59	46,663	38,157	1,972	32,993	3,192	8,506	1,057	2,061	5,388
60 - 64	16,494	12,143	774	10,217	1,152	4,351	636	471	3,244
65 - 74	31,714	19,769	1,246	15,675	2,848	11,945	1,516	720	9,709
75 - 84	20,409	9,252	541	6,221	2,490	11,157	1,414	424	9,319
85 and over	4,565	1,392	85	667	640	3,173	480	101	2,592
All persons in households by head's age, sex and marital status									
All ages 16 and over**	**474,787**	**375,035**	**22,005**	**331,538**	**21,492**	**99,752**	**18,641**	**25,431**	**55,680**
16 - 19**	1,517	518	424	90	4	999	923	50	26
20 - 24	15,355	9,074	4,291	4,704	79	6,281	4,345	1,454	482
25 - 29	37,885	28,027	5,237	22,055	735	9,858	3,721	3,730	2,407
30 - 44	170,071	142,165	5,966	130,006	6,193	27,906	3,450	11,997	12,459
45 - 59	125,897	109,438	2,695	101,245	5,498	16,459	1,391	5,150	9,918
60 - 64	33,142	26,956	999	24,351	1,606	6,186	768	927	4,491
65 - 74	54,995	39,837	1,587	34,630	3,620	15,158	1,796	1,333	12,029
75 - 84	29,837	16,709	697	13,056	2,956	13,128	1,676	650	10,802
85 and over	6,088	2,311	109	1,401	801	3,777	571	140	3,066
Allerdale									
Heads of households									
All ages 16 and over*	**37,867**	**27,224**	**2,396**	**22,141**	**2,687**	**10,643**	**1,969**	**1,555**	**7,119**
16 - 19*	126	37	33	4	-	89	80	4	5
20 - 24	1,253	781	373	400	8	472	348	88	36
25 - 29	2,757	2,083	495	1,515	73	674	277	213	184
30 - 44	10,162	8,301	566	7,162	573	1,861	342	610	909
45 - 59	9,241	7,722	375	6,721	626	1,519	185	317	1,017
60 - 64	3,297	2,419	153	2,028	238	878	117	99	662
65 - 74	6,373	3,938	276	3,082	580	2,435	296	138	2,001
75 - 84	3,811	1,693	104	1,115	474	2,118	237	66	1,815
85 and over	847	250	21	114	115	597	87	20	490
All persons in households by head's age, sex and marital status									
All ages 16 and over**	**93,935**	**75,438**	**3,695**	**67,623**	**4,120**	**18,497**	**3,162**	**4,321**	**11,014**
16 - 19**	247	69	58	11	-	178	158	10	10
20 - 24	2,833	1,807	694	1,099	14	1,026	697	242	87
25 - 29	7,329	5,626	850	4,640	136	1,703	547	656	500
30 - 44	34,038	28,902	865	26,912	1,125	5,136	626	2,017	2,493
45 - 59	25,038	22,168	512	20,616	1,040	2,870	240	807	1,823
60 - 64	6,683	5,425	198	4,875	352	1,258	154	193	911
65 - 74	11,024	7,949	363	6,862	724	3,075	348	261	2,466
75 - 84	5,602	3,070	134	2,360	576	2,532	289	108	2,135
85 and over	1,141	422	21	248	153	719	103	27	589

Notes: (1) * May include a small number of heads aged under 16
(2) ** May include a small number of persons in households with heads aged under 16

39. Residents in households

Age	TOTAL PERSONS	Males				Females			
		Total	Single	Married	Widowed or divorced	Total	Single	Married	Widowed or divorced
a	b	c	d	e	f	g	h	i	j
Barrow-in-Furness									
Heads of households									
All ages 16 and over*	**29,627**	**20,851**	**2,352**	**16,087**	**2,412**	**8,776**	**1,679**	**1,388**	**5,709**
16 - 19*	135	50	41	9	-	85	80	4	1
20 - 24	1,420	849	494	348	7	571	431	109	31
25 - 29	2,671	1,957	562	1,306	89	714	319	210	185
30 - 44	7,913	6,319	579	5,182	558	1,594	273	516	805
45 - 59	7,135	5,780	301	4,833	646	1,355	138	309	908
60 - 64	2,242	1,649	106	1,345	198	593	71	65	457
65 - 74	4,635	2,806	180	2,163	463	1,829	166	101	1,562
75 - 84	2,897	1,276	76	836	364	1,621	151	60	1,410
85 and over	579	165	13	65	87	414	50	14	350
All persons in households by head's age, sex and marital status									
All ages 16 and over**	**72,564**	**56,608**	**3,814**	**49,069**	**3,725**	**15,956**	**2,884**	**3,924**	**9,148**
16 - 19**	268	106	79	27	-	162	146	13	3
20 - 24	3,209	1,941	928	998	15	1,268	883	297	88
25 - 29	6,961	5,114	988	3,979	147	1,847	673	636	538
30 - 44	26,123	21,560	948	19,473	1,139	4,563	500	1,771	2,292
45 - 59	18,948	16,302	416	14,832	1,054	2,646	175	789	1,682
60 - 64	4,418	3,606	132	3,208	266	812	84	131	597
65 - 74	7,752	5,454	204	4,677	573	2,298	190	186	1,922
75 - 84	4,122	2,251	91	1,734	426	1,871	177	87	1,607
85 and over	763	274	28	141	105	489	56	14	419
Carlisle									
Heads of households									
All ages 16 and over*	**40,883**	**28,223**	**3,090**	**22,175**	**2,958**	**12,660**	**2,768**	**2,115**	**7,777**
16 - 19*	234	64	56	6	2	170	163	4	3
20 - 24	1,648	894	528	354	12	754	562	141	51
25 - 29	3,235	2,262	683	1,477	102	973	477	309	187
30 - 44	11,056	8,705	857	7,160	688	2,351	475	835	1,041
45 - 59	9,509	7,591	398	6,537	656	1,918	249	443	1,226
60 - 64	3,469	2,498	190	2,076	232	971	151	98	722
65 - 74	6,538	4,001	252	3,189	560	2,537	314	166	2,057
75 - 84	4,255	1,947	109	1,261	577	2,308	284	104	1,920
85 and over	939	261	17	115	129	678	93	15	570
All persons in households by head's age, sex and marital status									
All ages 16 and over**	**99,059**	**76,321**	**4,791**	**66,938**	**4,592**	**22,738**	**4,578**	**6,016**	**12,144**
16 - 19**	471	128	110	14	4	343	322	13	8
20 - 24	3,624	1,922	967	931	24	1,702	1,176	402	124
25 - 29	8,338	5,853	1,165	4,505	183	2,485	971	975	539
30 - 44	35,931	29,437	1,309	26,716	1,412	6,494	818	2,840	2,836
45 - 59	25,139	21,446	522	19,807	1,117	3,693	316	1,110	2,267
60 - 64	6,875	5,541	242	4,987	312	1,334	172	200	962
65 - 74	11,298	8,104	313	7,085	706	3,194	364	303	2,527
75 - 84	6,158	3,472	144	2,651	677	2,686	326	155	2,205
85 and over	1,225	418	19	242	157	807	113	18	676

Notes: (1) * May include a small number of heads aged under 16
(2) ** May include a small number of persons in households with heads aged under 16

39. Residents in households

Age	TOTAL PERSONS	Males				Females			
		Total	Single	Married	Widowed or divorced	Total	Single	Married	Widowed or divorced
a	b	c	d	e	f	g	h	i	j
Copeland									
Heads of households									
All ages 16 and over*	**27,752**	**19,957**	**2,177**	**15,767**	**2,013**	**7,795**	**1,469**	**1,329**	**4,997**
16 - 19*	89	33	31	2	-	56	53	2	1
20 - 24	1,046	614	337	272	5	432	293	100	39
25 - 29	2,431	1,801	517	1,221	63	630	275	214	141
30 - 44	7,790	6,332	579	5,282	471	1,458	270	515	673
45 - 59	6,797	5,597	289	4,851	457	1,200	128	283	789
60 - 64	2,330	1,712	119	1,430	163	618	65	57	496
65 - 74	4,324	2,643	215	1,968	460	1,681	185	104	1,392
75 - 84	2,450	1,078	82	675	321	1,372	149	46	1,177
85 and over	495	147	8	66	73	348	51	8	289
All persons in households by head's age, sex and marital status									
All ages 16 and over**	**70,485**	**55,870**	**3,411**	**49,218**	**3,241**	**14,615**	**2,512**	**3,924**	**8,179**
16 - 19**	192	71	66	5	-	121	114	4	3
20 - 24	2,372	1,368	639	719	10	1,004	608	290	106
25 - 29	6,357	4,717	846	3,760	111	1,640	565	687	388
30 - 44	26,217	22,012	909	20,154	949	4,205	496	1,809	1,900
45 - 59	18,711	16,324	403	15,094	827	2,387	169	741	1,477
60 - 64	4,774	3,824	153	3,433	238	950	85	114	751
65 - 74	7,547	5,334	279	4,448	607	2,213	232	191	1,790
75 - 84	3,631	1,962	108	1,460	394	1,669	182	75	1,412
85 and over	684	258	8	145	105	426	61	13	352
Eden									
Heads of households									
All ages 16 and over*	**18,017**	**13,272**	**1,363**	**10,736**	**1,173**	**4,745**	**935**	**799**	**3,011**
16 - 19*	58	25	21	4	-	33	32	1	-
20 - 24	494	322	186	136	-	172	132	27	13
25 - 29	1,146	893	253	604	36	253	129	76	48
30 - 44	4,870	4,055	380	3,426	249	815	173	304	338
45 - 59	4,449	3,704	234	3,233	237	745	90	202	453
60 - 64	1,644	1,269	83	1,086	100	375	71	51	253
65 - 74	2,989	1,950	142	1,553	255	1,039	130	72	837
75 - 84	1,959	922	57	624	241	1,037	147	53	837
85 and over	408	132	7	70	55	276	31	13	232
All persons in households by head's age, sex and marital status									
All ages 16 and over**	**44,711**	**36,560**	**2,158**	**32,558**	**1,844**	**8,151**	**1,411**	**2,133**	**4,607**
16 - 19**	114	55	40	15	-	59	57	2	-
20 - 24	1,041	679	326	353	-	362	254	74	34
25 - 29	2,839	2,283	427	1,791	65	556	231	207	118
30 - 44	16,201	13,982	621	12,834	527	2,219	284	1,024	911
45 - 59	12,248	10,797	336	10,044	417	1,451	125	479	847
60 - 64	3,446	2,855	120	2,595	140	591	84	109	398
65 - 74	5,358	4,014	200	3,474	340	1,344	158	132	1,054
75 - 84	2,914	1,677	79	1,314	284	1,237	179	83	975
85 and over	550	218	9	138	71	332	39	23	270

Notes: (1) * May include a small number of heads aged under 16
(2) ** May include a small number of persons in households with heads aged under 16

39. Residents in households

Age	TOTAL PERSONS	Males				Females			
		Total	Single	Married	Widowed or divorced	Total	Single	Married	Widowed or divorced
a	b	c	d	e	f	g	h	i	j
South Lakeland									
Heads of households									
All ages 16 and over*	**39,747**	**27,865**	**2,675**	**22,590**	**2,600**	**11,882**	**2,712**	**1,916**	**7,254**
16 - 19*	112	46	41	5	-	66	61	3	2
20 - 24	1,092	653	419	226	8	439	363	58	18
25 - 29	2,473	1,758	558	1,146	54	715	387	204	124
30 - 44	9,837	7,845	846	6,476	523	1,992	434	778	780
45 - 59	9,532	7,763	375	6,818	570	1,769	267	507	995
60 - 64	3,512	2,596	123	2,252	221	916	161	101	654
65 - 74	6,855	4,431	181	3,720	530	2,424	425	139	1,860
75 - 84	5,037	2,336	113	1,710	513	2,701	446	95	2,160
85 and over	1,297	437	19	237	181	860	168	31	661
All persons in households by head's age, sex and marital status									
All ages 16 and over**	**94,033**	**74,238**	**4,136**	**66,132**	**3,970**	**19,795**	**4,094**	**5,113**	**10,588**
16 - 19**	225	89	71	18	-	136	126	8	2
20 - 24	2,276	1,357	737	604	16	919	727	149	43
25 - 29	6,061	4,434	961	3,380	93	1,627	734	569	324
30 - 44	31,561	26,272	1,314	23,917	1,041	5,289	726	2,536	2,027
45 - 59	25,813	22,401	506	20,852	1,043	3,412	366	1,224	1,822
60 - 64	6,946	5,705	154	5,253	298	1,241	189	180	872
65 - 74	12,016	8,982	228	8,084	670	3,034	504	260	2,270
75 - 84	7,410	4,277	141	3,537	599	3,133	523	142	2,468
85 and over	1,725	721	24	487	210	1,004	199	45	760

40. Lone 'parents' aged 16 and over in households of one person aged 16 and over with person(s) aged 0 - 15; persons aged 0 - 15 in such households

Age of child(ren)	TOTAL LONE 'PARENTS'	Male lone 'parents'							Female lone 'parents'						
		Total male lone 'parents'	Economically active					Econom-ically inactive	Total female lone 'parents'	Economically active					Econom-ically inactive
			Employees		Self-employed	Other	Econom-ically active students			Employees		Self-employed	Other	Econom-ically active students	
			Full-time	Part-time						Full-time	Part-time				
a	b	c	d	e	f	g	h	i	j	k	l	m	n	o	p
CUMBRIA															
Total households	**5,862**	**455**	**206**	**16**	**83**	**33**	**1**	**117**	**5,407**	**693**	**1,294**	**130**	**292**	**7**	**2,998**
Child(ren) aged 0 - 4 only	1,609	40	15	3	3	6	-	13	1,569	108	253	13	85	1	1,110
Child(ren) aged 5 - 15 only	3,196	375	179	12	70	25	-	89	2,821	555	888	105	169	6	1,104
Child(ren) aged 0 - 4 and 5 - 15	1,057	40	12	1	10	2	1	15	1,017	30	153	12	38	-	784
TOTAL CHILDREN AGED 0 - 15	**9,963**	**731**	**318**	**26**	**134**	**47**	**2**	**206**	**9,232**	**1,003**	**2,087**	**217**	**450**	**11**	**5,475**
Children aged 0 - 4	3,271	89	29	4	15	9	1	32	3,182	149	459	31	137	1	2,406
Allerdale															
Total households	**1,171**	**99**	**42**	**2**	**25**	**5**	**-**	**25**	**1,072**	**136**	**202**	**28**	**70**	**-**	**636**
Child(ren) aged 0 - 4 only	319	7	1	1	-	1	-	4	312	17	37	4	24	-	230
Child(ren) aged 5 - 15 only	663	87	40	1	23	4	-	19	576	115	145	22	39	-	255
Child(ren) aged 0 - 4 and 5 - 15	189	5	1	-	2	-	-	2	184	4	20	2	7	-	151
TOTAL CHILDREN AGED 0 - 15	**1,933**	**145**	**58**	**2**	**39**	**6**	**-**	**40**	**1,788**	**197**	**321**	**51**	**104**	**-**	**1,115**
Children aged 0 - 4	591	12	2	1	2	1	-	6	579	22	62	8	35	-	452
Barrow-in-Furness															
Total households	**1,119**	**72**	**37**	**-**	**7**	**6**	**-**	**22**	**1,047**	**95**	**238**	**14**	**48**	**1**	**652**
Child(ren) aged 0 - 4 only	339	6	3	-	1	-	-	2	333	18	49	2	21	-	243
Child(ren) aged 5 - 15 only	514	57	32	-	4	6	-	15	457	73	154	9	21	1	200
Child(ren) aged 0 - 4 and 5 - 15	266	9	2	-	2	-	-	5	257	4	35	3	6	-	209
TOTAL CHILDREN AGED 0 - 15	**1,970**	**125**	**57**	**-**	**13**	**7**	**-**	**48**	**1,845**	**141**	**377**	**30**	**68**	**1**	**1,229**
Children aged 0 - 4	763	19	6	-	4	-	-	9	744	25	95	6	29	-	589

Table 40 Lone 'parents' – continued

40. Lone 'parents' aged 16 and over in households of one person aged 16 and over with person(s) aged 0 - 15; persons aged 0 - 15 in such households

Age of child(ren)	TOTAL LONE 'PARENTS'	Male lone 'parents'								Female lone 'parents'						
		Total male lone 'parents'	Economically active					Econom-ically inactive	Total female lone 'parents'	Economically active					Econom-ically inactive
			Employees		Self-employed	Other	Econom-ically active students			Employees		Self-employed	Other	Econom-ically active students	
			Full-time	Part-time						Full-time	Part-time				
a	b	c	d	e	f	g	h	i	j	k	l	m	n	o	p
Carlisle															
Total households	**1,412**	**105**	**45**	**2**	**20**	**9**	**-**	**29**	**1,307**	**162**	**305**	**23**	**74**	**-**	**743**
Child(ren) aged 0 - 4 only	408	10	4	-	-	3	-	3	398	22	62	2	18	-	294
Child(ren) aged 5 - 15 only	754	86	39	1	18	5	-	23	668	132	210	18	43	-	265
Child(ren) aged 0 - 4 and 5 - 15	250	9	2	1	2	1	-	3	241	8	33	3	13	-	184
TOTAL CHILDREN AGED 0 - 15	**2,397**	**162**	**68**	**4**	**29**	**13**	**-**	**48**	**2,235**	**232**	**488**	**38**	**125**	**-**	**1,352**
Children aged 0 - 4	824	21	7	1	2	5	-	6	803	31	111	5	37	-	619
Copeland															
Total households	**985**	**62**	**24**	**1**	**6**	**8**	**-**	**23**	**923**	**113**	**175**	**9**	**50**	**2**	**576**
Child(ren) aged 0 - 4 only	271	7	1	1	-	2	-	3	264	17	33	1	17	1	196
Child(ren) aged 5 - 15 only	521	50	21	-	5	5	-	19	471	88	125	7	24	1	227
Child(ren) aged 0 - 4 and 5 - 15	193	5	2	-	1	1	-	1	188	8	17	1	9	-	153
TOTAL CHILDREN AGED 0 - 15	**1,708**	**100**	**37**	**1**	**11**	**12**	**-**	**39**	**1,608**	**168**	**281**	**12**	**74**	**4**	**1,073**
Children aged 0 - 4	575	14	3	1	1	3	-	6	561	30	55	3	27	1	446
Eden															
Total households	**348**	**43**	**21**	**4**	**8**	**3**	**1**	**7**	**305**	**46**	**113**	**19**	**19**	**-**	**108**
Child(ren) aged 0 - 4 only	89	5	4	-	-	-	-	1	84	12	29	-	3	-	40
Child(ren) aged 5 - 15 only	208	34	15	4	7	3	-	5	174	31	67	19	15	-	42
Child(ren) aged 0 - 4 and 5 - 15	51	4	2	-	1	-	1	1	47	3	17	-	1	-	26
TOTAL CHILDREN AGED 0 - 15	**601**	**77**	**38**	**9**	**15**	**5**	**2**	**10**	**524**	**71**	**192**	**28**	**30**	**-**	**203**
Children aged 0 - 4	169	9	6	-	1	-	1	2	160	15	54	-	5	-	86

40. Lone 'parents' aged 16 and over in households of one person aged 16 and over with person(s) aged 0 - 15; persons aged 0 - 15 in such households

Age of child(ren)	TOTAL LONE 'PARENTS'	Male lone 'parents'							Female lone 'parents'						
		Total male lone 'parents'	Economically active					Econom-ically inactive	Total female lone 'parents'	Economically active					Econom-ically inactive
			Employees		Self-employed	Other	Econom-ically active students			Employees		Self-employed	Other	Econom-ically active students	
			Full-time	Part-time						Full-time	Part-time				
a	b	c	d	e	f	g	h	i	j	k	l	m	n	o	p
South Lakeland															
Total households	**827**	**74**	**37**	**7**	**17**	**2**	**-**	**11**	**753**	**141**	**261**	**37**	**31**	**4**	**283**
Child(ren) aged 0 - 4 only	183	5	2	1	2	-	-	-	178	22	43	4	2	-	107
Child(ren) aged 5 - 15 only	536	61	32	6	13	2	-	8	475	116	187	30	27	4	115
Child(ren) aged 0 - 4 and 5 - 15	108	8	3	-	2	-	-	3	100	3	31	3	2	-	61
TOTAL CHILDREN AGED 0 - 15	**1,354**	**122**	**60**	**10**	**27**	**4**	**-**	**21**	**1,232**	**194**	**428**	**58**	**49**	**6**	**503**
Children aged 0 - 4	349	14	5	1	5	-	-	3	335	26	82	9	4	-	214

Table 41 Shared accommodation

41. Households with residents not in self-contained accommodation; rooms in such households

Households with the following persons	TOTAL HOUSE-HOLDS	Over one person per room	Exclusive use of bath/shower			Shared use of bath/shower			No bath/shower			Central heating			No car	TOTAL ROOMS
			Exclusive use of inside WC	Shared use of inside WC	No inside WC	Exclusive use of inside WC	Shared use of inside WC	No inside WC	Exclusive use of inside WC	Shared use of inside WC	No inside WC	All rooms	Some rooms	No rooms		
a	b	c	d	e	f	g	h	i	j	k	l	m	n	o	p	q
CUMBRIA																
TOTAL HOUSEHOLDS	**1,177**	**76**	**589**	**5**	**1**	**16**	**550**	**2**	**7**	**1**	**6**	**449**	**116**	**612**	**788**	**2,382**
1 person	934		444	4	1	15	456	2	7	1	4	345	69	520	692	1,446
2 persons	171	63	94	1	-	-	74	-	-	-	2	70	28	73	82	533
3 or more persons	72	13	51	-	-	1	20	-	-	-	-	34	19	19	14	403
Allerdale																
TOTAL HOUSEHOLDS	**182**	**11**	**84**	**1**	**1**	**4**	**88**	**-**	**2**	**-**	**2**	**104**	**11**	**67**	**124**	**345**
1 person	151		62	1	1	4	79	-	2	-	2	87	9	55	115	229
2 persons	21	9	13	-	-	-	8	-	-	-	-	11	-	10	7	56
3 or more persons	10	2	9	-	-	-	1	-	-	-	-	6	2	2	2	60
Barrow-in-Furness																
TOTAL HOUSEHOLDS	**154**	**11**	**50**	**-**	**-**	**4**	**98**	**1**	**1**	**-**	**-**	**31**	**5**	**118**	**124**	**277**
1 person	126		42	-	-	4	78	1	1	-	-	22	2	102	106	202
2 persons	24	10	6	-	-	-	18	-	-	-	-	6	2	16	16	54
3 or more persons	4	1	2	-	-	-	2	-	-	-	-	3	1	-	2	21
Carlisle																
TOTAL HOUSEHOLDS	**398**	**20**	**217**	**2**	**-**	**5**	**174**	**-**	**-**	**-**	**-**	**147**	**38**	**213**	**301**	**695**
1 person	339		178	1	-	4	156	-	-	-	-	121	27	191	272	475
2 persons	46	18	30	1	-	-	15	-	-	-	-	19	7	20	25	143
3 or more persons	13	2	9	-	-	1	3	-	-	-	-	7	4	2	4	77
Copeland																
TOTAL HOUSEHOLDS	**129**	**8**	**47**	**2**	**-**	**2**	**76**	**-**	**1**	**-**	**1**	**34**	**24**	**71**	**81**	**255**
1 person	103		38	2	-	2	59	-	1	-	1	23	17	63	70	149
2 persons	13	4	3	-	-	-	10	-	-	-	-	5	5	3	8	35
3 or more persons	13	4	6	-	-	-	7	-	-	-	-	6	2	5	3	71

41. Households with residents not in self-contained accommodation; rooms in such households

Households with the following persons	TOTAL HOUSE-HOLDS	Over one person per room	Exclusive use of bath/shower			Shared use of bath/shower			No bath/shower			Central heating			No car	TOTAL ROOMS
			Exclusive use of inside WC	Shared use of inside WC	No inside WC	Exclusive use of inside WC	Shared use of inside WC	No inside WC	Exclusive use of inside WC	Shared use of inside WC	No inside WC	All rooms	Some rooms	No rooms		
a	b	c	d	e	f	g	h	i	j	k	l	m	n	o	p	q
							Eden									
TOTAL HOUSEHOLDS	**82**	**6**	**41**	**-**	**-**	**-**	**39**	**1**	**-**	**1**	**-**	**26**	**13**	**43**	**38**	**196**
1 person	54		27	-	-	-	25	1	-	1	-	19	4	31	33	70
2 persons	17	4	6	-	-	-	11	-	-	-	-	4	5	8	5	68
3 or more persons	11	2	8	-	-	-	3	-	-	-	-	3	4	4	-	58
							South Lakeland									
TOTAL HOUSEHOLDS	**232**	**20**	**150**	**-**	**-**	**1**	**75**	**-**	**3**	**-**	**3**	**107**	**25**	**100**	**120**	**614**
1 person	161		97	-	-	1	59	-	3	-	1	73	10	78	96	321
2 persons	50	18	36	-	-	-	12	-	-	-	2	25	9	16	21	177
3 or more persons	21	2	17	-	-	-	4	-	-	-	-	9	6	6	3	116

Table 42 Household composition and housing

Note: * May include a small number of households with no resident adults

42. Households with residents; dependent children in households

TOTAL HOUSE-HOLDS	Over 1 and up to 1.5 persons per room	Over 1.5 persons per room	Lacking or sharing use of bath/shower and/or inside WC	No central heating	Lacking or sharing use of bath/shower and/or inside WC and/or no central heating	Not self-contained accomm-odation	Household composition: Adults	Household composition: Dependent children
a	b	c	d	e	f	g	h	i
				CUMBRIA				
193,893	**2,041**	**350**	**2,494**	**50,633**	**51,333**	**1,177**	**ALL HOUSEHOLDS***	
31,482	-	-	957	10,345	10,651	109	1 adult of pensionable age	0
19,668	-	-	780	6,471	6,682	820	1 adult under pensionable age	0
6,425	62	38	53	1,993	2,011	41	1 adult any age	1 or more
58,268	-	119	400	14,266	14,361	111	2 adults (1 male and 1 female)	0
38,342	1,054	96	85	7,316	7,340	37		1 or more
4,573	-	14	66	1,541	1,554	25	2 adults (same sex)	0
818	26	4	7	238	239	1		1 or more
23,457	139	18	108	6,069	6,092	20	3 or more adults (male(s) and female(s))	0
10,122	743	58	27	2,168	2,176	6		1 or more
621	7	2	8	184	185	2	3 or more adults (same sex)	0
93	10	-	-	34	34	-		1 or more
98,491	**5,558**	**571**	**301**	**20,427**	**20,515**	**126**	**TOTAL DEPENDENT CHILDREN AGED 0 - 18**	
28,795	1,726	222	104	6,554	6,591	57	Dependent children aged 0 - 4	
62,244	3,582	335	178	12,620	12,665	55	Dependent children aged 5 - 15	
5,998	223	12	17	1,081	1,086	10	Dependent children aged 16 - 17	
				Allerdale				
37,867	**339**	**42**	**460**	**8,789**	**8,936**	**182**	**ALL HOUSEHOLDS***	
6,163	-	-	182	1,729	1,787	15	1 adult of pensionable age	0
3,489	-	-	149	967	1,024	136	1 adult under pensionable age	0
1,286	6	4	4	331	333	2	1 adult any age	1 or more
11,210	-	13	74	2,555	2,574	16	2 adults (1 male and 1 female)	0
7,812	174	15	15	1,269	1,273	2		1 or more
791	-	-	12	271	274	3	2 adults (same sex)	0
154	3	1	3	37	38	-		1 or more
4,791	29	1	17	1,191	1,194	5	3 or more adults (male(s) and female(s))	0
2,040	126	8	2	403	403	3		1 or more
102	-	-	2	28	28	-	3 or more adults (same sex)	0
24	1	-	-	8	8	-		1 or more
19,774	**922**	**91**	**43**	**3,508**	**3,520**	**11**	**TOTAL DEPENDENT CHILDREN AGED 0 - 18**	
5,518	267	39	10	1,047	1,052	3	Dependent children aged 0 - 4	
12,687	608	49	30	2,218	2,225	7	Dependent children aged 5 - 15	
1,242	41	2	3	204	204	1	Dependent children aged 16 - 17	
				Barrow-in-Furness				
29,627	**404**	**60**	**394**	**12,367**	**12,414**	**154**	**ALL HOUSEHOLDS***	
4,709	-	-	156	2,462	2,477	18	1 adult of pensionable age	0
3,302	-	-	112	1,786	1,800	108	1 adult under pensionable age	0
1,205	16	9	17	616	618	13	1 adult any age	1 or more
8,480	-	7	60	3,264	3,273	7	2 adults (1 male and 1 female)	0
5,937	232	24	11	2,012	2,014	2		1 or more
705	-	4	13	338	340	4	2 adults (same sex)	0
137	6	1	-	62	62	-		1 or more
3,455	16	2	17	1,225	1,227	2	3 or more adults (male(s) and female(s))	0
1,593	133	13	6	551	552	-		1 or more
85	-	-	2	41	41	-	3 or more adults (same sex)	0
18	1	-	-	9	9	-		1 or more
15,671	**1,145**	**132**	**49**	**5,748**	**5,753**	**15**	**TOTAL DEPENDENT CHILDREN AGED 0 - 18**	
5,058	390	51	21	2,035	2,039	11	Dependent children aged 0 - 4	
9,593	716	80	26	3,418	3,418	3	Dependent children aged 5 - 15	
868	34	1	1	266	267	1	Dependent children aged 16 - 17	

Tenure								
Owner occupied		Rented privately		Rented with a job or business	Rented from a housing association	Rented from a local authority or new town	No car	2 or more cars
Owned outright	Buying	Furnished	Unfurnished					
j	k	l	m	n	o	p	q	r
56,657	**79,159**	**5,294**	**8,487**	**4,951**	**7,353**	**31,992**	**59,653**	**41,742**
15,672	1,870	475	1,976	340	2,477	8,672	23,927	148
3,588	8,037	2,255	1,381	657	775	2,975	7,781	892
412	1,707	308	314	64	466	3,154	4,248	152
23,094	21,628	1,125	2,497	1,314	1,711	6,899	12,028	11,096
2,888	26,928	459	1,139	1,257	820	4,851	5,020	11,495
1,673	1,208	281	232	118	183	878	1,724	796
127	288	17	26	14	34	312	382	116
7,437	10,998	191	644	814	596	2,777	3,014	12,077
1,609	6,292	65	243	331	253	1,329	1,264	4,746
134	171	104	32	41	33	106	208	203
18	28	1	2	1	5	38	45	17
8,180	**62,051**	**1,328**	**2,946**	**3,093**	**2,800**	**18,093**	**19,400**	**28,851**
1,481	17,627	606	1,047	891	962	6,181	6,962	6,562
5,474	39,547	642	1,721	1,993	1,696	11,171	11,557	18,944
942	3,907	59	152	158	116	664	768	2,561
10,903	**14,160**	**864**	**1,421**	**818**	**2,994**	**6,707**	**11,668**	**8,427**
2,819	281	87	355	57	875	1,689	4,795	32
665	1,239	380	226	112	232	635	1,391	144
59	261	50	50	10	202	654	863	27
4,413	3,778	175	406	219	749	1,470	2,434	2,100
660	5,213	80	190	208	402	1,059	942	2,441
283	167	41	36	25	68	171	298	110
27	50	2	5	2	16	52	60	27
1,590	1,987	28	105	129	306	646	599	2,524
357	1,155	6	42	51	130	299	238	981
22	23	13	5	5	13	21	38	35
7	4	-	1	-	1	11	8	5
1,846	**11,675**	**223**	**500**	**494**	**1,323**	**3,713**	**3,659**	**6,099**
322	3,136	97	171	134	417	1,241	1,249	1,296
1,244	7,605	117	295	321	826	2,279	2,216	4,086
210	731	8	29	29	65	170	171	532
9,214	**14,010**	**838**	**1,107**	**269**	**348**	**3,841**	**11,705**	**3,830**
2,844	395	64	225	35	132	1,014	3,976	10
628	1,430	365	339	41	71	428	1,745	101
48	427	87	100	6	38	499	918	9
3,632	3,616	134	231	70	65	732	2,448	841
328	4,709	86	117	61	20	616	1,242	901
268	246	53	28	5	9	96	299	92
18	62	2	4	1	2	48	84	10
1,201	1,924	19	43	26	7	235	656	1,314
220	1,168	9	15	22	3	156	290	531
22	26	17	5	2	1	12	36	19
5	7	1	-	-	-	5	10	2
942	**11,170**	**291**	**358**	**164**	**89**	**2,657**	**4,575**	**2,399**
161	3,478	154	184	47	35	999	1,779	550
632	6,946	125	164	109	53	1,564	2,594	1,571
128	625	9	10	6	1	89	181	232

Table 42 Household composition and housing - continued

Note: * May include a small number of households with no resident adults

42. Households with residents; dependent children in households

TOTAL HOUSE-HOLDS	Over 1 and up to 1.5 persons per room	Over 1.5 persons per room	Lacking or sharing use of bath/shower and/or inside WC	No central heating	Lacking or sharing use of bath/shower and/or inside WC and/or no central heating	Not self-contained accomm-odation	Household composition: Adults	Household composition: Dependent children
a	b	c	d	e	f	g	h	i
				Carlisle				
40,883	**471**	**91**	**575**	**10,691**	**10,859**	**398**	**ALL HOUSEHOLDS***	
6,716	-	-	215	2,317	2,395	28	1 adult of pensionable age	0
4,444	-	-	217	1,404	1,463	308	1 adult under pensionable age	0
1,534	18	5	11	446	450	2	1 adult any age	1 or more
11,936	-	26	72	3,028	3,043	36	2 adults (1 male and 1 female)	0
7,939	233	28	27	1,413	1,423	8		1 or more
1,044	-	6	10	350	350	8	2 adults (same sex)	0
205	9	1	-	65	65	-		1 or more
4,796	38	7	18	1,225	1,225	2	3 or more adults (male(s) and female(s))	0
2,079	167	17	3	389	390	2		1 or more
163	2	1	2	43	44	1	3 or more adults (same sex)	0
20	4	-	-	9	9	-		1 or more
20,627	**1,282**	**154**	**81**	**3,995**	**4,027**	**18**	**TOTAL DEPENDENT CHILDREN AGED 0 - 18**	
6,153	402	63	28	1,258	1,273	5	Dependent children aged 0 - 4	
13,103	820	90	51	2,505	2,521	9	Dependent children aged 5 - 15	
1,127	55	1	2	205	206	2	Dependent children aged 16 - 17	
				Copeland				
27,752	**402**	**41**	**325**	**5,740**	**5,804**	**129**	**ALL HOUSEHOLDS***	
4,067	-	-	100	1,091	1,105	9	1 adult of pensionable age	0
2,835	-	-	108	725	748	94	1 adult under pensionable age	0
1,080	8	7	8	220	224	8	1 adult any age	1 or more
7,776	-	13	58	1,551	1,563	8	2 adults (1 male and 1 female)	0
5,949	184	13	10	874	876	7		1 or more
647	-	-	13	195	196	-	2 adults (same sex)	0
127	5	1	1	21	21	-		1 or more
3,503	25	-	21	743	749	3	3 or more adults (male(s) and female(s))	0
1,656	175	7	6	292	294	-		1 or more
92	1	-	-	21	21	-	3 or more adults (same sex)	0
19	4	-	-	6	6	-		1 or more
15,833	**1,106**	**86**	**44**	**2,472**	**2,486**	**26**	**TOTAL DEPENDENT CHILDREN AGED 0 - 18**	
4,719	327	33	19	797	802	12	Dependent children aged 0 - 4	
9,959	732	51	22	1,518	1,525	11	Dependent children aged 5 - 15	
925	41	2	3	131	133	3	Dependent children aged 16 - 17	
				Eden				
18,017	**171**	**35**	**331**	**4,081**	**4,197**	**82**	**ALL HOUSEHOLDS***	
2,766	-	-	117	793	853	7	1 adult of pensionable age	0
1,734	-	-	93	507	530	46	1 adult under pensionable age	0
387	7	5	10	81	85	5	1 adult any age	1 or more
5,667	-	12	56	1,233	1,247	10	2 adults (1 male and 1 female)	0
3,601	82	8	18	549	555	10		1 or more
415	-	1	9	115	117	3	2 adults (same sex)	0
59	2	-	-	13	13	-		1 or more
2,393	14	4	19	591	597	-	3 or more adults (male(s) and female(s))	0
928	64	4	5	179	180	-		1 or more
58	2	-	1	16	16	-	3 or more adults (same sex)	0
4	-	-	-	-	-	-		1 or more
8,908	**427**	**46**	**64**	**1,437**	**1,455**	**26**	**TOTAL DEPENDENT CHILDREN AGED 0 - 18**	
2,483	136	13	23	422	429	14	Dependent children aged 0 - 4	
5,692	267	29	37	889	898	9	Dependent children aged 5 - 15	
580	20	3	3	103	104	2	Dependent children aged 16 - 17	

Tenure							No car	2 or more cars
Owner occupied		Rented privately		Rented with a job or business	Rented from a housing association	Rented from a local authority or new town		
Owned outright	Buying	Furnished	Unfurnished					
j	k	l	m	n	o	p	q	r
9,922	**17,543**	**1,157**	**1,416**	**913**	**839**	**9,093**	**13,976**	**8,097**
2,803	418	79	327	85	358	2,646	5,342	24
660	1,871	562	218	84	151	898	1,984	171
97	338	49	54	15	32	949	1,087	25
3,991	4,964	236	399	228	180	1,938	2,792	2,054
428	5,718	81	206	239	45	1,222	1,144	2,334
310	318	67	34	24	24	267	440	143
26	68	3	5	1	3	99	108	19
1,294	2,455	37	115	163	31	701	706	2,352
283	1,342	11	43	65	10	325	285	932
28	43	28	14	9	5	36	69	41
2	7	-	-	-	-	11	12	2
1,324	**12,949**	**222**	**517**	**576**	**161**	**4,878**	**4,631**	**5,746**
234	3,677	100	170	186	69	1,717	1,670	1,362
892	8,337	103	326	358	87	3,000	2,769	3,804
166	759	12	16	20	5	149	161	462
6,384	**11,760**	**541**	**651**	**549**	**2,167**	**5,700**	**9,492**	**5,324**
1,547	241	47	153	38	657	1,384	3,310	12
422	1,191	263	106	74	227	552	1,213	101
49	227	43	16	10	156	579	795	15
2,546	3,097	87	195	149	503	1,199	1,893	1,305
406	4,131	37	78	141	251	905	996	1,488
203	167	21	21	15	55	165	286	116
13	32	1	3	2	11	65	75	13
936	1,662	20	49	78	208	550	589	1,615
246	981	8	26	35	85	275	293	625
13	28	13	3	6	10	19	29	33
3	3	-	1	1	4	7	12	1
1,151	**9,536**	**139**	**205**	**372**	**943**	**3,487**	**3,974**	**3,736**
220	2,792	63	67	94	347	1,136	1,366	855
754	6,003	69	124	253	558	2,198	2,429	2,434
128	594	6	11	19	32	135	158	331
6,321	**6,304**	**478**	**1,447**	**1,061**	**410**	**1,996**	**3,660**	**5,435**
1,525	135	46	306	39	181	534	1,853	31
426	638	174	167	119	45	165	458	126
52	114	24	41	7	15	134	166	24
2,502	1,727	125	455	301	87	470	683	1,471
466	2,199	52	251	289	42	302	185	1,495
200	76	22	39	22	11	45	109	102
11	26	2	2	2	1	15	17	15
915	895	17	133	202	15	216	130	1,548
199	474	8	52	78	10	107	46	590
22	19	6	1	2	3	5	10	30
-	1	-	-	-	-	3	2	2
1,270	**5,038**	**136**	**623**	**701**	**119**	**1,021**	**732**	**3,773**
256	1,376	57	222	208	40	324	259	869
860	3,242	70	357	443	72	648	439	2,480
116	330	7	39	39	5	44	28	320

Table 42 Household composition and housing - continued

Note: * May include a small number of households with no resident adults

42. Households with residents; dependent children in households

TOTAL HOUSE-HOLDS	Over 1 and up to 1.5 persons per room	Over 1.5 persons per room	Lacking or sharing use of bath/shower and/or inside WC	No central heating	Lacking or sharing use of bath/shower and/or inside WC and/or no central heating	Not self-contained accomm-odation	Household composition: Adults	Household composition: Dependent children
a	b	c	d	e	f	g	h	i
				South Lakeland				
39,747	**254**	**81**	**409**	**8,965**	**9,123**	**232**	**ALL HOUSEHOLDS***	
7,061	-	-	187	1,953	2,034	32	1 adult of pensionable age	0
3,864	-	-	101	1,082	1,117	128	1 adult under pensionable age	0
933	7	8	3	299	301	11	1 adult any age	1 or more
13,199	-	48	80	2,635	2,661	34	2 adults (1 male and 1 female)	0
7,104	149	8	4	1,199	1,199	8		1 or more
971	-	3	9	272	277	7	2 adults (same sex)	0
136	1	-	3	40	40	1		1 or more
4,519	17	4	16	1,094	1,100	8	3 or more adults (male(s) and female(s))	0
1,826	78	9	5	354	357	1		1 or more
121	2	1	1	35	35	1	3 or more adults (same sex)	0
8	-	-	-	2	2	-		1 or more
17,678	**676**	**62**	**20**	**3,267**	**3,274**	**30**	**TOTAL DEPENDENT CHILDREN AGED 0 - 18**	
4,864	204	23	3	995	996	12	Dependent children aged 0 - 4	
11,210	439	36	12	2,072	2,078	16	Dependent children aged 5 - 15	
1,256	32	3	5	172	172	1	Dependent children aged 16 - 17	

Tenure								
Owner occupied		Rented privately		Rented with a job or business	Rented from a housing association	Rented from a local authority or new town	No car	2 or more cars
Owned outright	Buying	Furnished	Unfurnished					
j	k	l	m	n	o	p	q	r
13,913	**15,382**	**1,416**	**2,445**	**1,341**	**595**	**4,655**	**9,152**	**10,629**
4,134	400	152	610	86	274	1,405	4,651	39
787	1,668	511	325	227	49	297	990	249
107	340	55	53	16	23	339	419	52
6,010	4,446	368	811	347	127	1,090	1,778	3,325
600	4,958	123	297	319	60	747	511	2,836
409	234	77	74	27	16	134	292	233
32	50	7	7	6	1	33	38	32
1,501	2,075	70	199	216	29	429	334	2,724
304	1,172	23	65	80	15	167	112	1,087
27	32	27	4	17	1	13	26	45
1	6	-	-	-	-	1	1	5
1,647	**11,683**	**317**	**743**	**786**	**165**	**2,337**	**1,829**	**7,098**
288	3,168	135	233	222	54	764	639	1,630
1,092	7,414	158	455	509	100	1,482	1,110	4,569
194	868	17	47	45	8	77	69	684

Table 43 Household composition and ethnic group

Note: * May include a small number of households with no resident adults

43. Households with residents; residents in households

Household composition: Adults	Household composition: Dependent children	TOTAL HOUSE-HOLDS	Ethnic group of head of household: White	Black Caribbean	Black African	Black other	Indian	Pakistani	Bangladeshi	Chinese	Other groups: Asian	Other groups: Other	Household head born in Ireland
a	b	c	d	e	f	g	h	i	j	k	l	m	n
					CUMBRIA								
ALL HOUSEHOLDS*		**193,893**	**193,268**	**40**	**23**	**89**	**95**	**32**	**31**	**115**	**47**	**153**	**1,967**
1 adult of pensionable age	0	31,482	31,464	5	-	2	4	-	-	-	-	7	320
1 adult under pensionable age	0	19,668	19,548	12	7	28	13	6	1	15	11	27	206
1 adult any age	1 or more	6,425	6,401	1	1	5	2	-	-	2	6	7	53
2 adults (1 male and 1 female)	0	58,268	58,170	9	4	14	19	5	3	12	9	23	598
	1 or more	38,342	38,117	9	5	22	42	14	13	44	13	63	299
2 adults (same sex)	0	4,573	4,558	-	-	2	1	-	-	3	1	8	67
	1 or more	818	813	-	1	2	-	-	-	1	-	1	8
3 or more adults (male(s) and female(s))	0	23,457	23,406	2	3	9	8	2	1	15	3	8	290
	1 or more	10,122	10,070	2	2	5	5	5	3	18	3	9	110
3 or more adults (same sex)	0	621	605	-	-	-	1	-	10	4	1	-	15
	1 or more	93	92	-	-	-	-	-	-	1	-	-	1
Households containing persons of pensionable age only (any number)		51,672	51,644	7	-	5	4	1	-	2	1	8	557
TOTAL PERSONS IN HOUSEHOLDS		**474,787**	**472,859**	**88**	**65**	**230**	**287**	**113**	**137**	**433**	**128**	**447**	**4,802**
All dependent children 0 - 18		98,491	97,855	21	18	69	94	43	48	145	40	158	858
Dependent children aged 0 - 4		28,795	28,590	5	4	28	23	16	17	45	11	56	213
Dependent children aged 5 - 15		62,244	61,862	15	13	37	62	23	30	85	21	96	571
Dependent children 0 - 17 included above		*97,037*	*96,416*	*21*	*18*	*67*	*90*	*42*	*48*	*142*	*37*	*156*	*842*
Persons pensionable age - 74		61,504	61,438	9	1	11	9	2	6	13	2	13	806
Persons aged 75 - 84		26,540	26,524	1	1	5	3	1	-	3	-	2	254
Persons aged 85 and over		5,758	5,753	1	-	-	-	1	-	-	2	1	44

Table 43 Household composition and ethnic group – continued

Note: * May include a small number of households with no resident adults

43. Households with residents; residents in households

Household composition: Adults	Dependent children	TOTAL HOUSE-HOLDS	White	Black Caribbean	Black African	Black other	Indian	Pakistani	Bangladeshi	Chinese	Other groups: Asian	Other groups: Other	Household head born in Ireland
a	b	c	d	e	f	g	h	i	j	k	l	m	n
Allerdale													
ALL HOUSEHOLDS*		**37,867**	**37,767**	**7**	**1**	**14**	**13**	**6**	**3**	**20**	**5**	**31**	**239**
1 adult of pensionable age	0	6,163	6,160	1	-	-	1	-	-	-	-	1	35
1 adult under pensionable age	0	3,489	3,471	3	-	4	-	2	-	2	-	7	25
1 adult any age	1 or more	1,286	1,284	-	-	-	-	-	-	-	1	1	5
2 adults (1 male and 1 female)	0	11,210	11,193	-	1	3	4	1	-	2	1	5	72
	1 or more	7,812	7,777	2	-	3	7	2	1	8	2	10	40
2 adults (same sex)	0	791	790	-	-	-	-	-	-	-	-	1	7
	1 or more	154	152	-	-	1	-	-	-	-	-	1	1
3 or more adults (male(s) and female(s))	0	4,791	4,780	1	-	2	1	-	-	4	1	2	42
	1 or more	2,040	2,032	-	-	1	-	1	-	3	-	3	11
3 or more adults (same sex)	0	102	100	-	-	-	-	-	2	-	-	-	1
	1 or more	24	23	-	-	-	-	-	-	1	-	-	-
Households containing persons of pensionable age only (any number)		9,992	9,989	1	-	-	1	-	-	-	-	1	59
TOTAL PERSONS IN HOUSEHOLDS		**93,935**	**93,624**	**17**	**2**	**38**	**40**	**20**	**13**	**81**	**14**	**86**	**592**
All dependent children 0 - 18		19,774	19,673	5	-	11	14	8	2	30	4	27	110
Dependent children aged 0 - 4		5,518	5,479	-	-	6	7	3	-	11	2	10	23
Dependent children aged 5 - 15		12,687	12,634	5	-	3	7	5	2	15	1	15	79
Dependent children 0 - 17 included above		*19,447*	*19,349*	*5*	-	*10*	*14*	*8*	*2*	*30*	*3*	*26*	*106*
Persons pensionable age - 74		12,309	12,302	1	-	1	1	-	-	2	-	2	108
Persons aged 75 - 84		4,925	4,924	-	-	-	1	-	-	-	-	-	17
Persons aged 85 and over		1,056	1,055	-	-	-	-	-	-	-	1	-	3

Table 43 Household composition and ethnic group – **continued**

Note: * May include a small number of households with no resident adults

43. Households with residents; residents in households

Household composition: Adults	Dependent children	TOTAL HOUSE-HOLDS	White	Black Caribbean	Black African	Black other	Indian	Pakistani	Bangladeshi	Chinese	Other groups: Asian	Other groups: Other	Household head born in Ireland
a	b	c	d	e	f	g	h	i	j	k	l	m	n
Barrow-in-Furness													
ALL HOUSEHOLDS*		**29,627**	**29,507**	**4**	**5**	**19**	**15**	**7**	**4**	**27**	**9**	**30**	**521**
1 adult of pensionable age	0	4,709	4,706	-	-	1	-	-	-	-	-	2	98
1 adult under pensionable age	0	3,302	3,284	1	2	5	1	2	-	3	1	3	44
1 adult any age	1 or more	1,205	1,199	-	1	1	-	-	-	1	1	2	15
2 adults (1 male and 1 female)	0	8,480	8,465	2	-	2	2	1	1	3	2	2	186
	1 or more	5,937	5,889	-	1	6	10	4	3	7	2	15	53
2 adults (same sex)	0	705	701	-	-	-	-	-	-	2	-	2	24
	1 or more	137	135	-	-	1	-	-	-	1	-	-	3
3 or more adults (male(s) and female(s))	0	3,455	3,444	1	1	2	1	-	-	5	-	1	72
	1 or more	1,593	1,581	-	-	1	1	-	-	4	3	3	23
3 or more adults (same sex)	0	85	84	-	-	-	-	-	-	1	-	-	3
	1 or more	18	18	-	-	-	-	-	-	-	-	-	-
Households containing persons of pensionable age only (any number)		7,524	7,518	1	-	1	-	-	-	1	-	3	178
TOTAL PERSONS IN HOUSEHOLDS		**72,564**	**72,171**	**8**	**14**	**55**	**55**	**18**	**16**	**100**	**32**	**95**	**1,198**
All dependent children 0 - 18		15,671	15,531	-	3	21	24	6	8	29	11	38	166
Dependent children aged 0 - 4		5,058	5,020	-	1	4	4	3	1	10	3	12	45
Dependent children aged 5 - 15		9,593	9,501	-	2	16	19	1	6	17	6	25	105
Dependent children 0 - 17 included above		*15,519*	*15,381*	-	*3*	*21*	*23*	*5*	*8*	*29*	*11*	*38*	*166*
Persons pensionable age - 74		8,824	8,808	4	-	2	2	-	-	3	-	5	228
Persons aged 75 - 84		3,690	3,684	-	1	-	1	-	-	3	-	1	88
Persons aged 85 and over		707	707	-	-	-	-	-	-	-	-	-	14

Table 43 Household composition and ethnic group – **continued**

Note: * May include a small number of households with no resident adults

43. Households with residents; residents in households

Household composition: Adults	Dependent children	TOTAL HOUSE-HOLDS	White	Black Caribbean	Black African	Black other	Indian	Pakistani	Bangladeshi	Chinese	Other groups: Asian	Other groups: Other	Household head born in Ireland
a	b	c	d	e	f	g	h	i	j	k	l	m	n
Carlisle													
ALL HOUSEHOLDS*		**40,883**	**40,707**	**12**	**6**	**23**	**33**	**7**	**16**	**31**	**14**	**34**	**485**
1 adult of pensionable age	0	6,716	6,713	1	-	1	1	-	-	-	-	-	81
1 adult under pensionable age	0	4,444	4,414	4	2	8	2	-	-	4	5	5	56
1 adult any age	1 or more	1,534	1,529	-	-	2	-	-	-	-	2	1	22
2 adults (1 male and 1 female)	0	11,936	11,912	2	1	2	9	1	-	3	1	5	118
	1 or more	7,939	7,869	4	1	7	14	4	5	14	3	18	74
2 adults (same sex)	0	1,044	1,040	-	-	-	1	-	-	-	1	2	18
	1 or more	205	205	-	-	-	-	-	-	-	-	-	2
3 or more adults (male(s) and female(s))	0	4,796	4,781	-	1	3	3	1	1	2	2	2	75
	1 or more	2,079	2,063	1	1	-	3	1	3	6	-	1	36
3 or more adults (same sex)	0	163	154	-	-	-	-	-	7	2	-	-	2
	1 or more	20	20	-	-	-	-	-	-	-	-	-	1
Households containing persons of pensionable age only (any number)		10,725	10,719	1	-	2	1	1	-	1	-	-	126
TOTAL PERSONS IN HOUSEHOLDS		**99,059**	**98,481**	**29**	**18**	**60**	**100**	**30**	**79**	**120**	**34**	**108**	**1,206**
All dependent children 0 - 18		20,627	20,437	9	5	18	27	12	25	42	10	42	233
Dependent children aged 0 - 4		6,153	6,092	4	1	10	4	4	10	10	3	15	49
Dependent children aged 5 - 15		13,103	12,986	5	4	8	18	8	15	27	5	27	168
Dependent children 0 - 17 included above		*20,383*	*20,198*	*9*	*5*	*18*	*25*	*12*	*25*	*40*	*9*	*42*	*228*
Persons pensionable age - 74		12,574	12,552	1	-	4	4	-	5	7	-	1	170
Persons aged 75 - 84		5,526	5,522	-	-	3	-	1	-	-	-	-	63
Persons aged 85 and over		1,177	1,175	-	-	-	-	1	-	-	1	-	11

Table 43 Household composition and ethnic group – **continued**

Note: * May include a small number of households with no resident adults

43. Households with residents; residents in households

Household composition: Adults	Dependent children	TOTAL HOUSE-HOLDS	White	Black Caribbean	Black African	Black other	Indian	Pakistani	Bangladeshi	Chinese	Other groups: Asian	Other groups: Other	Household head born in Ireland
a	b	c	d	e	f	g	h	i	j	k	l	m	n
Copeland													
ALL HOUSEHOLDS*		**27,752**	**27,662**	**8**	**3**	**14**	**12**	**6**	**2**	**15**	**10**	**20**	**253**
1 adult of pensionable age	0	4,067	4,067	-	-	-	-	-	-	-	-	-	36
1 adult under pensionable age	0	2,835	2,814	2	1	4	2	1	-	5	1	5	26
1 adult any age	1 or more	1,080	1,075	-	-	1	2	-	-	-	1	1	6
2 adults (1 male and 1 female)	0	7,776	7,758	3	1	3	2	1	1	1	3	3	67
	1 or more	5,949	5,920	2	1	2	4	2	1	6	4	7	49
2 adults (same sex)	0	647	643	-	-	2	-	-	-	-	-	2	6
	1 or more	127	127	-	-	-	-	-	-	-	-	-	1
3 or more adults (male(s) and female(s))	0	3,503	3,499	-	-	1	1	1	-	1	-	-	42
	1 or more	1,656	1,650	1	-	1	-	1	-	1	-	2	17
3 or more adults (same sex)	0	92	89	-	-	-	1	-	-	1	1	-	3
	1 or more	19	19	-	-	-	-	-	-	-	-	-	-
Households containing persons of pensionable age only (any number)		6,422	6,421	-	-	-	-	-	-	-	1	-	64
TOTAL PERSONS IN HOUSEHOLDS		**70,485**	**70,228**	**18**	**7**	**31**	**38**	**22**	**6**	**50**	**29**	**56**	**669**
All dependent children 0 - 18		15,833	15,748	3	2	6	15	8	2	20	9	20	138
Dependent children aged 0 - 4		4,719	4,688	1	-	4	2	3	2	8	2	9	43
Dependent children aged 5 - 15		9,959	9,911	1	2	1	13	5	-	10	7	9	84
Dependent children 0 - 17 included above		*15,603*	*15,520*	*3*	*2*	*5*	*15*	*8*	*2*	*20*	*9*	*19*	*136*
Persons pensionable age - 74		8,293	8,287	-	-	1	-	2	-	-	2	1	114
Persons aged 75 - 84		3,121	3,121	-	-	-	-	-	-	-	-	-	30
Persons aged 85 and over		628	628	-	-	-	-	-	-	-	-	-	4

Note: * May include a small number of households with no resident adults

43. Households with residents; residents in households

Household composition: Adults	Household composition: Dependent children	TOTAL HOUSE-HOLDS	Ethnic group of head of household: White	Black Caribbean	Black African	Black other	Indian	Pakistani	Bangladeshi	Chinese	Other groups: Asian	Other groups: Other	Household head born in Ireland
a	b	c	d	e	f	g	h	i	j	k	l	m	n
						Eden							
ALL HOUSEHOLDS*		**18,017**	**17,987**	**4**	**1**	**3**	**2**	**-**	**4**	**6**	**1**	**9**	**127**
1 adult of pensionable age	0	2,766	2,763	1	-	-	1	-	-	-	-	1	11
1 adult under pensionable age	0	1,734	1,729	1	-	1	1	-	1	-	-	1	10
1 adult any age	1 or more	387	384	1	-	-	-	-	-	1	-	1	1
2 adults (1 male and 1 female)	0	5,667	5,661	1	-	1	-	-	1	1	1	1	51
	1 or more	3,601	3,592	-	1	1	-	-	2	1	-	4	21
2 adults (same sex)	0	415	415	-	-	-	-	-	-	-	-	-	3
	1 or more	59	59	-	-	-	-	-	-	-	-	-	-
3 or more adults (male(s) and female(s))	0	2,393	2,392	-	-	-	-	-	-	-	-	1	19
	1 or more	928	925	-	-	-	-	-	-	3	-	-	10
3 or more adults (same sex)	0	58	58	-	-	-	-	-	-	-	-	-	1
	1 or more	4	4	-	-	-	-	-	-	-	-	-	-
Households containing persons of pensionable age only (any number)		4,733	4,730	1	-	-	1	-	-	-	-	1	27
TOTAL PERSONS IN HOUSEHOLDS		**44,711**	**44,618**	**7**	**4**	**8**	**2**	**-**	**13**	**27**	**2**	**30**	**333**
All dependent children 0 - 18		8,908	8,873	2	2	3	-	-	6	10	-	12	66
Dependent children aged 0 - 4		2,483	2,473	-	-	1	-	-	4	-	-	5	14
Dependent children aged 5 - 15		5,692	5,670	2	1	2	-	-	2	8	-	7	45
Dependent children 0 - 17 included above		*8,755*	*8,721*	*2*	*2*	*3*	-	-	*6*	*9*	-	*12*	*62*
Persons pensionable age - 74		5,856	5,853	-	-	-	1	-	1	-	-	1	50
Persons aged 75 - 84		2,572	2,571	-	-	-	-	-	-	-	-	1	13
Persons aged 85 and over		529	527	1	-	-	-	-	-	-	-	1	2

Table 43 Household composition and ethnic group – continued

Note: * May include a small number of households with no resident adults

43. Households with residents; residents in households

Household composition: Adults	Household composition: Dependent children	TOTAL HOUSE-HOLDS	Ethnic group of head of household: White	Black Caribbean	Black African	Black other	Indian	Pakistani	Bangladeshi	Chinese	Other groups: Asian	Other groups: Other	Household head born in Ireland
a	b	c	d	e	f	g	h	i	j	k	l	m	n
South Lakeland													
ALL HOUSEHOLDS*		**39,747**	**39,638**	**5**	**7**	**16**	**20**	**6**	**2**	**16**	**8**	**29**	**342**
1 adult of pensionable age	0	7,061	7,055	2	-	-	1	-	-	-	-	3	59
1 adult under pensionable age	0	3,864	3,836	1	2	6	7	1	-	1	4	6	45
1 adult any age	1 or more	933	930	-	-	1	-	-	-	-	1	1	4
2 adults (1 male and 1 female)	0	13,199	13,181	1	1	3	2	1	-	2	1	7	104
	1 or more	7,104	7,070	1	1	3	7	2	1	8	2	9	62
2 adults (same sex)	0	971	969	-	-	-	-	-	-	1	-	1	9
	1 or more	136	135	-	1	-	-	-	-	-	-	-	1
3 or more adults (male(s) and female(s))	0	4,519	4,510	-	1	1	2	-	-	3	-	2	40
	1 or more	1,826	1,819	-	1	2	1	2	-	1	-	-	13
3 or more adults (same sex)	0	121	120	-	-	-	-	-	1	-	-	-	5
	1 or more	8	8	-	-	-	-	-	-	-	-	-	-
Households containing persons of pensionable age only (any number)		12,276	12,267	3	-	2	1	-	-	-	-	3	103
TOTAL PERSONS IN HOUSEHOLDS		**94,033**	**93,737**	**9**	**20**	**38**	**52**	**23**	**10**	**55**	**17**	**72**	**804**
All dependent children 0 - 18		17,678	17,593	2	6	10	14	9	5	14	6	19	145
Dependent children aged 0 - 4		4,864	4,838	-	2	3	6	3	-	6	1	5	39
Dependent children aged 5 - 15		11,210	11,160	2	4	7	5	4	5	8	2	13	90
Dependent children 0 - 17 included above		*17,330*	*17,247*	*2*	*6*	*10*	*13*	*9*	*5*	*14*	*5*	*19*	*144*
Persons pensionable age - 74		13,648	13,636	3	1	3	1	-	-	1	-	3	136
Persons aged 75 - 84		6,706	6,702	1	-	2	1	-	-	-	-	-	43
Persons aged 85 and over		1,661	1,661	-	-	-	-	-	-	-	-	-	10

Table 44 Household composition and long-term illness

Note: * May include a small number of households with no resident adults

44. Households containing persons with limiting long-term illness; residents in such households

TOTAL HOUSE-HOLDS	TOTAL PERSONS		Total with limiting long-term illness		Persons with limiting long-term illness aged:				Household composition	
					0 - 4		5 - 15		Adults	Dependent children
	Males	Females	Males	Females	Males	Females	Males	Females		
a	b	c	d	e	f	g	h	i	j	k
						CUMBRIA				
48,199	**49,184**	**54,359**	**27,740**	**31,235**	**269**	**192**	**782**	**571**	**ALL HOUSEHOLDS***	
15,696	4,860	10,836	4,860	10,836					1 adult	0
570	614	987	251	429	55	45	127	94		1 or more
17,521	17,521	17,521	12,711	10,997					2 adults (1 male and 1 female)	0
3,506	6,986	6,682	2,424	1,866	185	137	497	359		1 or more
1,558	1,140	1,976	692	1,268					2 adults (same sex)	0
156	162	383	44	135	3	2	18	15		1 or more
6,973	12,626	10,685	5,219	4,284					3 or more adults (male(s) and female(s))	0
2,004	4,930	4,914	1,392	1,235	23	8	139	100		1 or more
192	308	308	134	160					3 or more adults (same sex)	0
23	37	67	13	25	3	-	1	3		1 or more
									Households with:	
28,116	18,373	25,840	14,901	19,579	47	43	122	90	0 persons economically active	
11,001	14,086	13,528	6,717	6,572	134	91	279	184	1 person economically active	
9,507	12,126	11,832	5,750	5,716	109	78	229	169	- in employment	
1,494	1,960	1,696	967	856	25	13	50	15	- unemployed	
9,082	16,725	14,991	6,122	5,084	88	58	381	297	2 or more persons economically active	
8,878	16,358	14,648	5,979	4,955	84	54	374	289	- 1 or more in employment	
204	367	343	143	129	4	4	7	8	- all unemployed	
	19,690	12,907	6,186	3,419					Persons economically active	
	17,162	11,889	5,258	3,016					Persons in employment	
						Allerdale				
9,757	**10,240**	**11,001**	**5,715**	**6,215**	**47**	**38**	**173**	**113**	**ALL HOUSEHOLDS***	
3,067	965	2,102	965	2,102					1 adult	0
115	123	201	52	77	8	11	29	13		1 or more
3,510	3,510	3,510	2,550	2,182					2 adults (1 male and 1 female)	0
748	1,495	1,420	527	387	37	25	114	78		1 or more
305	240	370	141	242					2 adults (same sex)	0
36	38	99	8	34	-	1	3	3		1 or more
1,531	2,786	2,303	1,143	945					3 or more adults (male(s) and female(s))	0
407	1,011	938	302	217	2	1	27	18		1 or more
34	66	46	26	24					3 or more adults (same sex)	0
4	6	12	1	5	-	-	-	1		1 or more
									Households with:	
5,694	3,843	5,261	3,100	3,885	7	9	28	14	0 persons economically active	
2,296	3,030	2,906	1,399	1,374	25	21	60	42	1 person economically active	
1,944	2,553	2,518	1,165	1,171	18	19	46	38	- in employment	
352	477	388	234	203	7	2	14	4	- unemployed	
1,767	3,367	2,834	1,216	956	15	8	85	57	2 or more persons economically active	
1,721	3,286	2,763	1,187	928	13	8	84	53	- 1 or more in employment	
46	81	71	29	28	2	-	1	4	- all unemployed	
	4,044	2,429	1,184	608					Persons economically active	
	3,434	2,202	969	512					Persons in employment	

Persons with limiting long-term illness aged: 16 - 29 Males	16 - 29 Females	30 - 44 Males	30 - 44 Females	45 - 54 Males	45 - 54 Females	55 - 59 Males	55 - 59 Females	60 - 64 Males	60 - 64 Females	65 - 74 Males	65 - 74 Females	75 - 84 Males	75 - 84 Females	85 and over Males	85 and over Females
l	m	n	o	p	q	r	s	t	u	v	w	x	y	z	aa
1,581	**1,443**	**2,821**	**2,536**	**3,116**	**3,202**	**2,726**	**2,361**	**4,147**	**3,036**	**7,079**	**7,706**	**4,300**	**7,568**	**919**	**2,620**
155	99	428	222	473	455	418	465	589	689	1,285	2,931	1,171	4,346	341	1,629
11	85	28	144	17	36	8	12	3	2	1	11	1	-	-	-
241	239	457	418	931	1,170	1,276	1,221	2,391	1,747	4,498	3,716	2,522	2,129	395	357
251	316	947	818	342	187	81	25	59	13	49	7	12	3	1	1
54	58	100	94	85	150	71	64	90	81	148	241	107	351	37	229
9	22	5	29	6	20	-	12	2	11	-	14	1	6	-	4
623	419	551	447	949	949	722	497	903	441	944	628	399	560	128	343
221	180	272	332	294	203	136	59	90	40	132	135	73	141	12	37
13	19	30	22	18	30	13	5	20	12	22	20	14	32	4	20
3	6	3	10	1	2	1	1	-	-	-	3	-	-	1	-
200	197	749	519	753	795	920	953	2,163	1,943	5,506	6,320	3,664	6,501	777	2,218
455	503	974	974	1,006	1,140	980	856	1,267	793	1,099	1,061	435	717	88	253
360	403	769	832	831	973	845	756	1,100	684	1,019	945	407	643	81	233
95	100	205	142	175	167	135	100	167	109	80	116	28	74	7	20
926	743	1,098	1,043	1,357	1,267	826	552	717	300	474	325	201	350	54	149
903	723	1,068	1,013	1,319	1,233	812	537	698	292	470	319	198	347	53	148
23	20	30	30	38	34	14	15	19	8	4	6	3	3	1	1
915	627	1,551	920	1,486	960	925	481	799	236	380	134	121	53	9	8
730	491	1,302	826	1,263	847	801	433	657	227	375	132	121	52	9	8
304	**293**	**581**	**504**	**650**	**642**	**596**	**519**	**905**	**643**	**1,480**	**1,579**	**815**	**1,409**	**164**	**475**
26	22	70	32	99	93	88	92	126	150	274	621	221	797	61	295
1	15	5	27	4	7	2	3	1	-	1	1	1	-	-	-
36	43	84	80	185	232	272	279	524	366	920	746	462	375	67	61
61	68	211	174	73	34	12	3	10	4	9	-	-	1	-	-
8	12	22	18	11	23	17	13	19	14	30	43	27	81	7	38
1	4	1	8	2	4	-	3	-	3	-	6	1	1	-	1
119	97	118	99	204	215	173	111	208	96	216	134	79	118	26	75
50	31	65	62	68	30	28	14	13	9	27	24	20	25	2	3
2	1	5	2	4	4	4	-	4	1	3	3	4	11	-	2
-	-	-	2	-	-	-	1	-	-	-	1	-	-	1	-
48	39	153	103	174	167	220	210	487	438	1,160	1,311	683	1,193	140	401
89	119	202	204	199	238	209	193	282	140	229	215	88	150	16	52
67	99	153	178	167	201	173	159	235	112	210	186	81	132	15	47
22	20	49	26	32	37	36	34	47	28	19	29	7	18	1	5
167	135	226	197	277	237	167	116	136	65	91	53	44	66	8	22
163	133	221	188	268	231	166	113	130	64	90	51	44	65	8	22
4	2	5	9	9	6	1	3	6	1	1	2	-	1	-	-
150	115	317	164	284	161	173	101	162	39	65	14	33	14	-	-
112	91	257	144	239	131	144	84	120	36	64	12	33	14	-	-

Table 44 Household composition and long-term illness – **continued**

Note: * May include a small number of households with no resident adults

44. Households containing persons with limiting long-term illness; residents in such households

TOTAL HOUSE-HOLDS	TOTAL PERSONS		Total with limiting long-term illness		Persons with limiting long-term illness aged:				Household composition	
					0 - 4		5 - 15		Adults	Dependent children
	Males	Females	Males	Females	Males	Females	Males	Females		
a	b	c	d	e	f	g	h	i	j	k
									Barrow-in-Furness	
8,018	**8,043**	**9,044**	**4,466**	**5,449**	**59**	**39**	**142**	**113**	**ALL HOUSEHOLDS***	
2,777	865	1,912	865	1,912					1 adult	0
106	110	193	51	84	15	7	23	22		1 or more
2,809	2,809	2,809	1,972	1,920					2 adults (1 male and 1 female)	0
638	1,278	1,240	430	373	40	29	91	65		1 or more
240	174	306	105	186					2 adults (same sex)	0
27	20	70	5	24	2	-	1	1		1 or more
1,041	1,867	1,604	780	682					3 or more adults (male(s) and female(s))	0
351	871	862	236	247	2	3	27	25		1 or more
24	43	31	21	15					3 or more adults (same sex)	0
5	6	17	1	6	-	-	-	-		1 or more
									Households with:	
4,762	3,052	4,364	2,460	3,432	16	9	28	20	0 persons economically active	
1,827	2,367	2,266	1,083	1,169	27	16	45	36	1 person economically active	
1,521	1,969	1,914	884	995	22	13	36	34	- in employment	
306	398	352	199	174	5	3	9	2	- unemployed	
1,429	2,624	2,414	923	848	16	14	69	57	2 or more persons economically active	
1,390	2,564	2,341	895	823	16	14	68	57	- 1 or more in employment	
39	60	73	28	25	-	-	1	-	- all unemployed	
	3,240	1,963	1,001	507					Persons economically active	
	2,778	1,745	827	430					Persons in employment	
									Carlisle	
10,115	**10,108**	**11,279**	**5,760**	**6,561**	**59**	**42**	**156**	**138**	**ALL HOUSEHOLDS***	
3,464	1,115	2,349	1,115	2,349					1 adult	0
143	149	246	54	118	10	13	28	25		1 or more
3,567	3,567	3,567	2,604	2,242					2 adults (1 male and 1 female)	0
705	1,404	1,356	467	386	43	27	94	87		1 or more
341	248	434	153	271					2 adults (same sex)	0
39	43	93	13	30	1	1	6	6		1 or more
1,404	2,537	2,164	1,054	851					3 or more adults (male(s) and female(s))	0
396	951	975	256	257	5	1	28	19		1 or more
51	85	80	42	49					3 or more adults (same sex)	0
5	9	15	2	8	-	-	-	1		1 or more
									Households with:	
5,916	3,801	5,379	3,125	4,125	8	12	28	27	0 persons economically active	
2,279	2,849	2,764	1,354	1,366	35	14	55	43	1 person economically active	
1,964	2,455	2,402	1,162	1,178	28	11	45	38	- in employment	
315	394	362	192	188	7	3	10	5	- unemployed	
1,920	3,458	3,136	1,281	1,070	16	16	73	68	2 or more persons economically active	
1,864	3,352	3,043	1,239	1,034	16	14	71	67	- 1 or more in employment	
56	106	93	42	36	-	2	2	1	- all unemployed	
	4,057	2,778	1,293	755					Persons economically active	
	3,483	2,554	1,071	657					Persons in employment	

Persons with limiting long-term illness aged:															
16 - 29		30 - 44		45 - 54		55 - 59		60 - 64		65 - 74		75 - 84		85 and over	
Males	Females	Males	Females	Males	Females	Males	Females	Males	Females	Males	Females	Males	Females	Males	Females
l	m	n	o	p	q	r	s	t	u	v	w	x	y	z	aa
286	**279**	**490**	**506**	**538**	**616**	**420**	**437**	**674**	**542**	**1,105**	**1,367**	**631**	**1,206**	**121**	**344**
32	23	87	45	102	94	72	83	102	126	234	569	185	742	51	230
2	20	5	30	5	4	1	-	-	-	-	1	-	-	-	-
42	55	85	93	153	238	202	219	393	324	691	633	369	312	37	46
56	74	163	162	52	34	12	4	10	4	5	1	1	-	-	-
10	9	13	13	17	37	11	7	19	8	24	41	7	47	4	24
2	3	-	6	-	3	-	3	-	2	-	3	-	2	-	1
95	60	75	79	163	160	100	107	127	71	137	93	60	79	23	33
44	31	55	74	42	43	21	12	19	7	14	24	7	21	5	7
2	3	7	1	4	2	1	2	4	-	-	1	2	3	1	3
1	1	-	3	-	1	-	-	-	-	-	1	-	-	-	-
34	49	147	114	165	172	149	188	366	361	902	1,168	558	1,049	95	302
101	100	167	195	173	233	150	151	199	141	160	155	47	114	14	28
79	79	126	169	140	194	123	130	159	118	145	136	41	98	13	24
22	21	41	26	33	39	27	21	40	23	15	19	6	16	1	4
151	130	176	197	200	211	121	98	109	40	43	44	26	43	12	14
146	127	169	190	192	204	117	93	106	38	43	44	26	42	12	14
5	3	7	7	8	7	4	5	3	2	-	-	-	1	-	-
168	108	253	139	226	153	159	60	141	28	42	10	12	9	-	-
136	78	210	124	188	136	134	48	106	26	41	10	12	8	-	-
336	**308**	**619**	**550**	**625**	**677**	**556**	**478**	**830**	**591**	**1,452**	**1,586**	**950**	**1,636**	**177**	**555**
36	24	118	60	110	114	105	103	143	153	242	598	289	943	72	354
2	24	7	41	4	9	2	4	1	-	-	2	-	-	-	-
60	49	89	89	194	242	252	242	461	323	938	761	529	477	81	59
38	66	199	161	57	33	13	7	12	2	10	2	1	1	-	-
14	12	26	21	19	37	13	16	15	13	29	49	30	64	7	59
3	4	2	6	1	6	-	2	-	2	-	2	-	-	-	1
140	80	116	90	186	178	138	91	171	83	205	142	82	111	16	76
38	38	52	71	48	49	31	11	21	9	18	21	14	35	1	3
5	7	8	9	6	9	2	2	6	6	10	8	5	5	-	3
-	4	2	2	-	-	-	-	-	-	-	1	-	-	-	-
40	47	168	120	151	167	193	197	433	380	1,134	1,290	811	1,419	159	466
80	110	212	210	203	233	194	172	257	155	208	237	96	138	14	54
67	75	166	171	160	199	168	157	231	136	195	214	89	127	13	50
13	35	46	39	43	34	26	15	26	19	13	23	7	11	1	4
216	151	239	220	271	277	169	109	140	56	110	59	43	79	4	35
204	141	226	210	265	268	163	107	137	55	110	59	43	78	4	35
12	10	13	10	6	9	6	2	3	1	-	-	-	1	-	-
214	146	346	209	310	218	181	106	144	39	68	28	28	8	2	1
161	105	282	182	258	195	153	100	119	38	68	28	28	8	2	1

Table 44 Household composition and long-term illness – continued

Note: * May include a small number of households with no resident adults

44. Households containing persons with limiting long-term illness; residents in such households

TOTAL HOUSE-HOLDS	TOTAL PERSONS		Total with limiting long-term illness		Persons with limiting long-term illness aged:				Household composition	
					0 - 4		5 - 15		Adults	Dependent children
	Males	Females	Males	Females	Males	Females	Males	Females		
a	b	c	d	e	f	g	h	i	j	k
						Copeland				
7,022	**7,626**	**8,109**	**4,235**	**4,428**	**41**	**36**	**139**	**86**	**ALL HOUSEHOLDS***	
2,123	711	1,412	711	1,412					1 adult	0
103	110	179	51	76	14	13	25	12		1 or more
2,467	2,467	2,467	1,785	1,553					2 adults (1 male and 1 female)	0
547	1,106	1,042	402	288	21	21	86	54		1 or more
241	212	270	129	177					2 adults (same sex)	0
23	25	54	4	20	-	-	2	2		1 or more
1,135	2,088	1,729	872	678					3 or more adults (male(s) and female(s))	0
347	858	879	261	199	4	2	25	17		1 or more
29	34	61	12	20					3 or more adults (same sex)	0
7	15	16	8	5	2	-	1	1		1 or more
									Households with:	
3,930	2,717	3,592	2,198	2,646	11	12	26	16	0 persons economically active	
1,734	2,320	2,190	1,097	1,015	20	17	56	29	1 person economically active	
1,454	1,936	1,866	915	853	16	13	45	27	- in employment	
280	384	324	182	162	4	4	11	2	- unemployed	
1,358	2,589	2,327	940	767	10	7	57	41	2 or more persons economically active	
1,313	2,498	2,249	907	740	8	6	55	38	- 1 or more in employment	
45	91	78	33	27	2	1	2	3	- all unemployed	
	3,045	1,932	865	442					Persons economically active	
	2,554	1,740	714	379					Persons in employment	
						Eden				
4,074	**4,302**	**4,582**	**2,439**	**2,506**	**20**	**9**	**56**	**44**	**ALL HOUSEHOLDS***	
1,227	393	834	393	834					1 adult	0
36	58	55	20	24	4	-	12	9		1 or more
1,571	1,571	1,571	1,156	905					2 adults (1 male and 1 female)	0
279	553	507	190	128	14	9	36	23		1 or more
126	86	166	52	110					2 adults (same sex)	0
11	12	24	4	12	-	-	2	1		1 or more
634	1,170	964	491	370					3 or more adults (male(s) and female(s))	0
169	424	430	116	107	2	-	6	11		1 or more
20	35	27	17	15					3 or more adults (same sex)	0
1	-	4	-	1	-	-	-	-		1 or more
									Households with:	
2,210	1,467	2,015	1,192	1,485	2	-	8	4	0 persons economically active	
1,005	1,256	1,157	636	561	11	4	17	12	1 person economically active	
917	1,146	1,064	578	517	10	3	17	11	- in employment	
88	110	93	58	44	1	1	-	1	- unemployed	
859	1,579	1,410	611	460	7	5	31	28	2 or more persons economically active	
854	1,571	1,404	607	459	7	5	31	28	- 1 or more in employment	
5	8	6	4	1	-	-	-	-	- all unemployed	
	1,837	1,241	665	346					Persons economically active	
	1,681	1,190	592	331					Persons in employment	

Persons with limiting long-term illness aged:															
16 - 29		30 - 44		45 - 54		55 - 59		60 - 64		65 - 74		75 - 84		85 and over	
Males	Females	Males	Females	Males	Females	Males	Females	Males	Females	Males	Females	Males	Females	Males	Females
l	m	n	o	p	q	r	s	t	u	v	w	x	y	z	aa
236	**212**	**472**	**381**	**536**	**521**	**475**	**382**	**659**	**470**	**1,053**	**1,118**	**525**	**914**	**99**	**308**
19	9	59	30	77	69	61	72	90	95	228	431	143	517	34	189
3	16	5	24	2	6	1	2	1	-	-	3	-	-	-	-
32	44	82	65	151	177	214	199	364	261	618	517	287	248	37	42
41	43	153	129	55	32	18	3	10	2	15	2	2	1	1	1
12	7	18	16	20	20	11	13	14	20	30	35	18	45	6	21
-	2	1	2	1	3	-	3	-	2	-	3	-	2	-	1
91	61	105	60	161	175	137	78	162	82	133	101	65	79	18	42
36	28	44	52	67	30	30	12	18	7	27	23	8	20	2	8
-	1	4	1	1	8	2	-	-	1	2	3	2	2	1	4
2	1	1	2	1	1	1	-	-	-	-	-	-	-	-	-
34	30	134	80	129	137	165	153	365	288	830	908	423	770	81	252
76	72	154	160	177	179	174	133	190	140	166	157	75	95	9	33
55	57	121	132	144	147	149	114	160	116	147	134	69	82	9	31
21	15	33	28	33	32	25	19	30	24	19	23	6	13	-	2
126	110	184	141	230	205	136	96	104	42	57	53	27	49	9	23
124	105	179	138	219	197	135	95	100	40	55	49	24	49	8	23
2	5	5	3	11	8	1	1	4	2	2	4	3	-	1	-
137	80	227	120	227	114	139	78	86	30	32	15	14	2	3	3
104	61	192	107	178	94	122	69	70	28	31	15	14	2	3	3
136	**91**	**214**	**204**	**267**	**251**	**238**	**173**	**362**	**238**	**667**	**624**	**391**	**662**	**88**	**210**
13	5	28	11	31	33	35	42	39	46	122	195	97	370	28	132
-	4	2	4	1	3	1	1	-	2	-	1	-	-	-	-
29	15	31	34	83	93	111	87	210	138	411	325	241	185	40	28
17	14	75	68	29	13	6	-	7	1	3	-	3	-	-	-
1	6	4	15	7	10	10	3	6	7	12	25	4	28	8	16
-	5	1	1	-	2	-	1	1	1	-	-	-	1	-	-
55	27	48	39	87	78	62	37	90	39	98	61	39	61	12	28
19	14	23	28	27	17	10	2	6	4	16	15	7	14	-	2
2	1	2	3	2	2	3	-	3	-	5	2	-	3	-	4
-	-	-	1	-	-	-	-	-	-	-	-	-	-	-	-
9	7	39	30	46	59	68	66	157	137	470	468	324	544	69	170
43	31	76	71	90	87	87	68	124	70	129	114	48	77	11	27
36	28	64	64	72	77	80	64	116	66	125	104	48	73	10	27
7	3	12	7	18	10	7	4	8	4	4	10	-	4	1	-
84	53	99	103	131	105	83	39	81	31	68	42	19	41	8	13
84	53	99	103	130	104	82	39	80	31	67	42	19	41	8	13
-	-	-	-	1	1	1	-	1	-	1	-	-	-	-	-
80	48	145	94	155	93	94	48	100	30	76	23	14	8	1	2
69	45	123	88	134	87	87	48	88	30	76	23	14	8	1	2

Table 44 Household composition and long-term illness - **continued**

Note: * May include a small number of households with no resident adults

44. Households containing persons with limiting long-term illness; residents in such households

TOTAL HOUSE-HOLDS	TOTAL PERSONS		Total with limiting long-term illness		Persons with limiting long-term illness aged:				Household composition	
					0 - 4		5 - 15		Adults	Dependent children
	Males	Females	Males	Females	Males	Females	Males	Females		
a	b	c	d	e	f	g	h	i	j	k
					South Lakeland					
9,213	**8,865**	**10,344**	**5,125**	**6,076**	**43**	**28**	**116**	**77**	**ALL HOUSEHOLDS***	
3,038	811	2,227	811	2,227					1 adult	0
67	64	113	23	50	4	1	10	13		1 or more
3,597	3,597	3,597	2,644	2,195					2 adults (1 male and 1 female)	0
589	1,150	1,117	408	304	30	26	76	52		1 or more
305	180	430	112	282					2 adults (same sex)	0
20	24	43	10	15	-	-	4	2		1 or more
1,228	2,178	1,921	879	758					3 or more adults (male(s) and female(s))	0
334	815	830	221	208	8	1	26	10		1 or more
34	45	63	16	37					3 or more adults (same sex)	0
1	1	3	1	-	1	-	-	-		1 or more
									Households with:	
5,604	3,493	5,229	2,826	4,006	3	1	4	9	0 persons economically active	
1,860	2,264	2,245	1,148	1,087	16	19	46	22	1 person economically active	
1,707	2,067	2,068	1,046	1,002	15	19	40	21	- in employment	
153	197	177	102	85	1	-	6	1	- unemployed	
1,749	3,108	2,870	1,151	983	24	8	66	46	2 or more persons economically active	
1,736	3,087	2,848	1,144	971	24	7	65	46	- 1 or more in employment	
13	21	22	7	12	-	1	1	-	- all unemployed	
	3,467	2,564	1,178	761					Persons economically active	
	3,232	2,458	1,085	707					Persons in employment	

Persons with limiting long-term illness aged:															
16 - 29		30 - 44		45 - 54		55 - 59		60 - 64		65 - 74		75 - 84		85 and over	
Males	Females	Males	Females	Males	Females	Males	Females	Males	Females	Males	Females	Males	Females	Males	Females
l	m	n	o	p	q	r	s	t	u	v	w	x	y	z	aa
283	**260**	**445**	**391**	**500**	**495**	**441**	**372**	**717**	**552**	**1,322**	**1,432**	**988**	**1,741**	**270**	**728**
29	16	66	44	54	52	57	73	89	119	185	517	236	977	95	429
3	6	4	18	1	7	1	2	-	-	-	3	-	-	-	-
42	33	86	57	165	188	225	195	439	335	920	734	634	532	133	121
38	51	146	124	76	41	20	8	10	-	7	2	5	-	-	-
9	12	17	11	11	23	9	12	17	19	23	48	21	86	5	71
3	4	-	6	2	2	-	-	1	1	-	-	-	-	-	-
123	94	89	80	148	143	112	73	145	70	155	97	74	112	33	89
34	38	33	45	42	34	16	8	13	4	30	28	17	26	2	14
2	6	4	6	1	5	1	1	3	4	2	3	1	8	2	4
-	-	-	-	-	-	-	-	-	-	-	-	-	-	-	-
35	25	108	72	88	93	125	139	355	339	1,010	1,175	865	1,526	233	627
66	71	163	134	164	170	166	139	215	147	207	183	81	143	24	59
56	65	139	118	148	155	152	132	199	136	197	171	79	131	21	54
10	6	24	16	16	15	14	7	16	11	10	12	2	12	3	5
182	164	174	185	248	232	150	94	147	66	105	74	42	72	13	42
182	164	174	184	245	229	149	90	145	64	105	74	42	72	13	41
-	-	-	1	3	3	1	4	2	2	-	-	-	-	-	1
166	130	263	194	284	221	179	88	166	70	97	44	20	12	3	2
148	111	238	181	266	204	161	84	154	69	95	44	20	12	3	2

Table 45 Migrant household heads

Note: * May include a small number of heads aged under 16

45. Households with residents

Tenure of household and economic activity of head	Households with head with different address one year before census: age and sex of head									
	Total migrant heads*		16 - 29*		30 - 44		45 up to pensionable age		Pensionable age and over	
	Males	Females	Males	Females	Males	Females	Males	Females	Males	Females
a	b	c	d	e	f	g	h	i	j	k
					CUMBRIA					
TOTAL HEADS	**11,403**	**5,094**	**4,360**	**2,314**	**3,949**	**1,249**	**2,185**	**522**	**909**	**1,009**
Owner occupied	**6,839**	**1,798**	**2,487**	**602**	**2,490**	**539**	**1,408**	**257**	**454**	**400**
Economically active	6,120	1,207	2,475	541	2,458	464	1,150	175	37	27
Unemployed	208	49	66	20	70	19	70	10	2	-
Economically active students (included above)	*1*	-	*1*	-	-	-	-	-	-	-
Economically inactive	719	591	12	61	32	75	258	82	417	373
Rented privately or with a job or business	**2,899**	**1,519**	**1,359**	**963**	**1,022**	**363**	**440**	**122**	**78**	**71**
Economically active	2,696	1,207	1,313	797	988	300	382	97	13	13
Unemployed	359	166	192	111	113	40	53	15	1	-
Economically active students (included above)	*5*	*10*	*5*	*10*	-	-	-	-	-	-
Economically inactive	203	312	46	166	34	63	58	25	65	58
Rented from a housing association	**343**	**340**	**94**	**129**	**88**	**53**	**70**	**38**	**91**	**120**
Economically active	216	95	86	53	79	28	47	7	4	7
Unemployed	58	18	27	10	16	5	15	2	-	1
Economically active students (included above)	*1*	-	*1*	-	-	-	-	-	-	-
Economically inactive	127	245	8	76	9	25	23	31	87	113
Rented from a local authority or new town	**1,322**	**1,437**	**420**	**620**	**349**	**294**	**267**	**105**	**286**	**418**
Economically active	880	388	402	195	310	132	160	50	8	11
Unemployed	281	96	146	57	89	27	46	11	-	1
Economically active students (included above)	*1*	*1*	*1*	-	-	*1*	-	-	-	-
Economically inactive	442	1,049	18	425	39	162	107	55	278	407
					Allerdale					
TOTAL HEADS	**2,130**	**947**	**799**	**422**	**733**	**230**	**415**	**107**	**183**	**188**
Owner occupied	**1,270**	**304**	**470**	**90**	**464**	**92**	**257**	**51**	**79**	**71**
Economically active	1,142	190	467	78	457	79	212	30	6	3
Unemployed	43	14	13	3	14	7	16	4	-	-
Economically active students (included above)	-	-	-	-	-	-	-	-	-	-
Economically inactive	128	114	3	12	7	13	45	21	73	68
Rented privately or with a job or business	**464**	**240**	**218**	**155**	**155**	**52**	**73**	**24**	**18**	**9**
Economically active	420	184	207	130	148	39	64	15	1	-
Unemployed	64	32	40	25	18	5	6	2	-	-
Economically active students (included above)	-	-	-	-	-	-	-	-	-	-
Economically inactive	44	56	11	25	7	13	9	9	17	9
Rented from a housing association	**98**	**109**	**20**	**40**	**31**	**23**	**22**	**12**	**25**	**34**
Economically active	66	22	19	8	28	10	17	2	2	2
Unemployed	12	4	5	2	2	2	5	-	-	-
Economically active students (included above)	-	-	-	-	-	-	-	-	-	-
Economically inactive	32	87	1	32	3	13	5	10	23	32
Rented from a local authority or new town	**298**	**294**	**91**	**137**	**83**	**63**	**63**	**20**	**61**	**74**
Economically active	210	67	84	36	80	19	44	8	2	4
Unemployed	64	20	23	11	24	6	17	2	-	1
Economically active students (included above)	-	-	-	-	-	-	-	-	-	-
Economically inactive	88	227	7	101	3	44	19	12	59	70

All households: age and sex of head										Tenure of household and economic activity of head
TOTAL HOUSEHOLD HEADS*		16 - 29*		30 - 44		45 up to pensionable age		Pensionable age and over		
Males	Females	Males	Females	Males	Females	Males	Females	Males	Females	
l	m	n	o	p	q	r	s	t	u	a
137,392	**56,501**	**15,122**	**7,298**	**41,557**	**10,071**	**50,300**	**8,506**	**30,413**	**30,626**	**TOTAL HEADS**
104,375	**31,441**	**10,437**	**2,476**	**33,291**	**5,773**	**39,849**	**5,498**	**20,798**	**17,694**	**Owner occupied**
78,108	11,949	10,344	2,070	32,836	4,887	33,048	3,924	1,880	1,068	Economically active
2,440	414	307	75	713	147	1,411	181	9	11	Unemployed
13	*18*	*3*	*9*	*9*	*8*	*1*	*1*	-	-	*Economically active students (included above)*
26,267	19,492	93	406	455	886	6,801	1,574	18,918	16,626	Economically inactive
12,679	**6,053**	**2,737**	**1,806**	**3,790**	**1,093**	**3,843**	**705**	**2,309**	**2,449**	**Rented privately or with a job or business**
9,968	3,051	2,644	1,453	3,677	903	3,330	527	317	168	Economically active
909	326	344	174	306	99	257	50	2	3	Unemployed
8	*16*	*7*	*14*	*1*	*2*	-	-	-	-	*Economically active students (included above)*
2,711	3,002	93	353	113	190	513	178	1,992	2,281	Economically inactive
3,827	**3,526**	**305**	**411**	**753**	**437**	**1,220**	**398**	**1,549**	**2,280**	**Rented from a housing association**
1,819	671	284	162	676	253	813	209	46	47	Economically active
400	113	78	34	141	37	179	39	2	3	Unemployed
1	*3*	*1*	*2*	-	*1*	-	-	-	-	*Economically active students (included above)*
2,008	2,855	21	249	77	184	407	189	1,503	2,233	Economically inactive
16,511	**15,481**	**1,643**	**2,605**	**3,723**	**2,768**	**5,388**	**1,905**	**5,757**	**8,203**	**Rented from a local authority or new town**
8,621	3,669	1,560	897	3,320	1,498	3,524	1,021	217	253	Economically active
1,938	601	445	201	753	217	732	173	8	10	Unemployed
6	*5*	*2*	*1*	*4*	*3*	-	*1*	-	-	*Economically active students (included above)*
7,890	11,812	83	1,708	403	1,270	1,864	884	5,540	7,950	Economically inactive

l	m	n	o	p	q	r	s	t	u	a
27,224	**10,643**	**2,901**	**1,235**	**8,301**	**1,861**	**10,141**	**1,519**	**5,881**	**6,028**	**TOTAL HEADS**
19,797	**5,266**	**1,962**	**343**	**6,523**	**923**	**7,634**	**856**	**3,678**	**3,144**	**Owner occupied**
15,023	1,828	1,940	286	6,423	784	6,321	577	339	181	Economically active
575	81	74	14	169	29	331	37	1	1	Unemployed
1	-	*1*	-	-	-	-	-	-	-	*Economically active students (included above)*
4,774	3,438	22	57	100	139	1,313	279	3,339	2,963	Economically inactive
2,098	**1,005**	**433**	**277**	**592**	**183**	**660**	**118**	**413**	**427**	**Rented privately or with a job or business**
1,587	475	411	225	569	146	562	85	45	19	Economically active
186	57	63	38	60	11	63	8	-	-	Unemployed
2	*1*	*2*	*1*	-	-	-	-	-	-	*Economically active students (included above)*
511	530	22	52	23	37	98	33	368	408	Economically inactive
1,690	**1,304**	**119**	**134**	**326**	**192**	**587**	**152**	**658**	**826**	**Rented from a housing association**
820	227	113	34	293	99	394	79	20	15	Economically active
191	38	31	9	70	11	89	16	1	2	Unemployed
-	-	-	-	-	-	-	-	-	-	*Economically active students (included above)*
870	1,077	6	100	33	93	193	73	638	811	Economically inactive
3,639	**3,068**	**387**	**481**	**860**	**563**	**1,260**	**393**	**1,132**	**1,631**	**Rented from a local authority or new town**
2,008	717	361	153	785	296	837	220	25	48	Economically active
508	149	86	45	199	51	221	47	2	6	Unemployed
-	-	-	-	-	-	-	-	-	-	*Economically active students (included above)*
1,631	2,351	26	328	75	267	423	173	1,107	1,583	Economically inactive

Table 45 Migrant household heads – **continued**

Note: * May include a small number of heads aged under 16

45. Households with residents

Tenure of household and economic activity of head	Households with head with different address one year before census: age and sex of head									
	Total migrant heads*		16 - 29*		30 - 44		45 up to pensionable age		Pensionable age and over	
	Males	Females	Males	Females	Males	Females	Males	Females	Males	Females
a	b	c	d	e	f	g	h	i	j	k
					Barrow-in-Furness					
TOTAL HEADS	**1,720**	**753**	**763**	**401**	**575**	**171**	**300**	**77**	**82**	**104**
Owner occupied	**1,117**	**297**	**490**	**128**	**382**	**82**	**207**	**41**	**38**	**46**
Economically active	1,046	199	489	106	376	65	178	26	3	2
Unemployed	37	9	12	6	14	2	11	1	-	-
Economically active students (included above)	-	-	-	-	-	-	-	-	-	-
Economically inactive	71	98	1	22	6	17	29	15	35	44
Rented privately or with a job or business	**383**	**240**	**195**	**178**	**133**	**43**	**51**	**9**	**4**	**10**
Economically active	371	162	193	124	128	31	49	6	1	1
Unemployed	67	32	35	24	23	6	9	2	-	-
Economically active students (included above)	-	*1*	-	*1*	-	-	-	-	-	-
Economically inactive	12	78	2	54	5	12	2	3	3	9
Rented from a housing association	**45**	**43**	**17**	**18**	**10**	**5**	**5**	**12**	**13**	**8**
Economically active	30	13	17	9	9	2	4	2	-	-
Unemployed	5	4	3	3	2	-	-	1	-	-
Economically active students (included above)	-	-	-	-	-	-	-	-	-	-
Economically inactive	15	30	-	9	1	3	1	10	13	8
Rented from a local authority or new town	**175**	**173**	**61**	**77**	**50**	**41**	**37**	**15**	**27**	**40**
Economically active	115	39	58	15	40	17	17	6	-	1
Unemployed	57	14	36	7	13	4	8	3	-	-
Economically active students (included above)	*1*	-	*1*	-	-	-	-	-	-	-
Economically inactive	60	134	3	62	10	24	20	9	27	39
					Carlisle					
TOTAL HEADS	**2,460**	**1,260**	**967**	**600**	**841**	**289**	**438**	**128**	**214**	**243**
Owner occupied	**1,413**	**394**	**534**	**150**	**529**	**124**	**265**	**59**	**85**	**61**
Economically active	1,280	302	532	138	524	111	219	48	5	5
Unemployed	48	9	13	6	16	-	19	3	-	-
Economically active students (included above)	-	-	-	-	-	-	-	-	-	-
Economically inactive	133	92	2	12	5	13	46	11	80	56
Rented privately or with a job or business	**612**	**338**	**299**	**232**	**216**	**72**	**81**	**23**	**16**	**11**
Economically active	568	277	285	193	209	61	71	19	3	4
Unemployed	103	41	63	32	25	5	14	4	1	-
Economically active students (included above)	-	*5*	-	*5*	-	-	-	-	-	-
Economically inactive	44	61	14	39	7	11	10	4	13	7
Rented from a housing association	**54**	**44**	**9**	**13**	**11**	**2**	**18**	**8**	**16**	**21**
Economically active	29	14	7	10	10	2	11	1	1	1
Unemployed	15	2	5	1	4	-	6	1	-	-
Economically active students (included above)	-	-	-	-	-	-	-	-	-	-
Economically inactive	25	30	2	3	1	-	7	7	15	20
Rented from a local authority or new town	**381**	**484**	**125**	**205**	**85**	**91**	**74**	**38**	**97**	**150**
Economically active	238	135	119	69	74	43	42	20	3	3
Unemployed	77	38	42	25	27	11	8	2	-	-
Economically active students (included above)	-	*1*	-	-	-	*1*	-	-	-	-
Economically inactive	143	349	6	136	11	48	32	18	94	147

All households: age and sex of head										
TOTAL HOUSEHOLD HEADS*		16 - 29*		30 - 44		45 up to pensionable age		Pensionable age and over		Tenure of household and economic activity of head
Males	Females	Males	Females	Males	Females	Males	Females	Males	Females	
l	m	n	o	p	q	r	s	t	u	a
20,851	**8,776**	**2,856**	**1,370**	**6,319**	**1,594**	**7,429**	**1,355**	**4,247**	**4,457**	**TOTAL HEADS**
17,478	**5,746**	**2,190**	**562**	**5,462**	**1,012**	**6,479**	**981**	**3,347**	**3,191**	**Owner occupied**
13,097	1,981	2,172	419	5,363	784	5,371	650	191	128	Economically active
566	95	79	19	162	32	322	41	3	3	Unemployed
4	*5*	*1*	*3*	*3*	*2*	-	-	-	-	*Economically active students (included above)*
4,381	3,765	18	143	99	228	1,108	331	3,156	3,063	Economically inactive
1,372	**842**	**435**	**347**	**377**	**153**	**361**	**87**	**199**	**255**	**Rented privately or with a job or business**
1,105	403	427	229	362	111	302	54	14	9	Economically active
206	71	95	42	63	18	48	11	-	-	Unemployed
-	*1*	-	*1*	-	-	-	-	-	-	*Economically active students (included above)*
267	439	8	118	15	42	59	33	185	246	Economically inactive
145	**203**	**26**	**39**	**25**	**25**	**28**	**31**	**66**	**108**	**Rented from a housing association**
70	43	24	19	24	14	20	10	2	-	Economically active
14	14	3	8	7	2	4	4	-	-	Unemployed
-	-	-	-	-	-	-	-	-	-	*Economically active students (included above)*
75	160	2	20	1	11	8	21	64	108	Economically inactive
1,856	**1,985**	**205**	**422**	**455**	**404**	**561**	**256**	**635**	**903**	**Rented from a local authority or new town**
891	397	187	95	377	175	312	107	15	20	Economically active
292	89	84	23	118	31	89	33	1	2	Unemployed
2	*1*	*1*	*1*	*1*	-	-	-	-	-	*Economically active students (included above)*
965	1,588	18	327	78	229	249	149	620	883	Economically inactive

28,223	**12,660**	**3,220**	**1,897**	**8,705**	**2,351**	**10,089**	**1,918**	**6,209**	**6,494**	**TOTAL HEADS**
21,078	**6,387**	**2,203**	**604**	**7,022**	**1,288**	**7,921**	**1,178**	**3,932**	**3,317**	**Owner occupied**
16,201	2,817	2,190	538	6,942	1,134	6,706	918	363	227	Economically active
467	93	51	22	126	24	289	45	1	2	Unemployed
1	*3*	-	*3*	*1*	-	-	-	-	-	*Economically active students (included above)*
4,877	3,570	13	66	80	154	1,215	260	3,569	3,090	Economically inactive
2,351	**1,135**	**555**	**391**	**723**	**199**	**652**	**116**	**421**	**429**	**Rented privately or with a job or business**
1,867	595	532	317	699	160	566	88	70	30	Economically active
217	71	96	40	72	20	48	11	1	-	Unemployed
-	*5*	-	*5*	-	-	-	-	-	-	*Economically active students (included above)*
484	540	23	74	24	39	86	28	351	399	Economically inactive
380	**459**	**33**	**44**	**64**	**42**	**108**	**46**	**175**	**327**	**Rented from a housing association**
154	85	30	26	52	26	68	26	4	7	Economically active
29	11	9	2	10	6	10	3	-	-	Unemployed
-	*1*	-	*1*	-	-	-	-	-	-	*Economically active students (included above)*
226	374	3	18	12	16	40	20	171	320	Economically inactive
4,414	**4,679**	**429**	**858**	**896**	**822**	**1,408**	**578**	**1,681**	**2,421**	**Rented from a local authority or new town**
2,183	1,147	411	312	792	477	924	306	56	52	Economically active
475	192	117	79	180	71	177	41	1	1	Unemployed
-	*2*	-	-	-	*2*	-	-	-	-	*Economically active students (included above)*
2,231	3,532	18	546	104	345	484	272	1,625	2,369	Economically inactive

Table 45 Migrant household heads - **continued**

Note: * May include a small number of heads aged under 16

45. Households with residents

Tenure of household and economic activity of head	Households with head with different address one year before census: age and sex of head									
	Total migrant heads*		16 - 29*		30 - 44		45 up to pensionable age		Pensionable age and over	
	Males	Females	Males	Females	Males	Females	Males	Females	Males	Females
a	b	c	d	e	f	g	h	i	j	k
					Copeland					
TOTAL HEADS	**1,558**	**603**	**664**	**288**	**556**	**154**	**233**	**53**	**105**	**108**
Owner occupied	**1,021**	**215**	**442**	**86**	**379**	**64**	**161**	**22**	**39**	**43**
Economically active	954	151	442	82	374	51	135	17	3	1
Unemployed	23	3	13	1	5	2	4	-	1	-
Economically active students (included above)	-	-	-	-	-	-	-	-	-	-
Economically inactive	67	64	-	4	5	13	26	5	36	42
Rented privately or with a job or business	**274**	**105**	**135**	**63**	**99**	**30**	**36**	**11**	**4**	**1**
Economically active	262	86	134	53	95	23	31	10	2	-
Unemployed	49	12	25	9	19	2	5	1	-	-
Economically active students (included above)	-	-	-	-	-	-	-	-	-	-
Economically inactive	12	19	1	10	4	7	5	1	2	1
Rented from a housing association	**77**	**82**	**26**	**40**	**19**	**14**	**12**	**4**	**20**	**24**
Economically active	50	21	25	12	18	9	7	-	-	-
Unemployed	20	6	12	3	5	3	3	-	-	-
Economically active students (included above)	-	-	-	-	-	-	-	-	-	-
Economically inactive	27	61	1	28	1	5	5	4	20	24
Rented from a local authority or new town	**186**	**201**	**61**	**99**	**59**	**46**	**24**	**16**	**42**	**40**
Economically active	127	52	61	30	53	14	12	7	1	1
Unemployed	59	14	33	10	19	2	7	2	-	-
Economically active students (included above)	-	-	-	-	-	-	-	-	-	-
Economically inactive	59	149	-	69	6	32	12	9	41	39
					Eden					
TOTAL HEADS	**1,154**	**423**	**389**	**172**	**421**	**115**	**252**	**50**	**92**	**86**
Owner occupied	**682**	**179**	**202**	**51**	**250**	**49**	**170**	**28**	**60**	**51**
Economically active	583	117	198	49	246	44	132	20	7	4
Unemployed	23	6	5	2	10	3	8	1	-	-
Economically active students (included above)	-	-	-	-	-	-	-	-	-	-
Economically inactive	99	62	4	2	4	5	38	8	53	47
Rented privately or with a job or business	**383**	**173**	**159**	**97**	**150**	**48**	**66**	**18**	**8**	**10**
Economically active	352	135	152	82	146	38	54	14	-	1
Unemployed	28	14	14	5	7	6	7	3	-	-
Economically active students (included above)	-	*1*	-	*1*	-	-	-	-	-	-
Economically inactive	31	38	7	15	4	10	12	4	8	9
Rented from a housing association	**14**	**5**	**6**	**1**	**3**	**2**	**1**	**-**	**4**	**2**
Economically active	7	1	5	1	2	-	-	-	-	-
Unemployed	-	-	-	-	-	-	-	-	-	-
Economically active students (included above)	-	-	-	-	-	-	-	-	-	-
Economically inactive	7	4	1	-	1	2	1	-	4	2
Rented from a local authority or new town	**75**	**66**	**22**	**23**	**18**	**16**	**15**	**4**	**20**	**23**
Economically active	50	28	22	14	16	12	11	2	1	-
Unemployed	6	1	5	1	1	-	-	-	-	-
Economically active students (included above)	-	-	-	-	-	-	-	-	-	-
Economically inactive	25	38	-	9	2	4	4	2	19	23

All households: age and sex of head										Tenure of household and economic activity of head
TOTAL HOUSEHOLD HEADS*		16 - 29*		30 - 44		45 up to pensionable age		Pensionable age and over		
Males	Females	Males	Females	Males	Females	Males	Females	Males	Females	
l	m	n	o	p	q	r	s	t	u	a
19,957	**7,795**	**2,448**	**1,118**	**6,332**	**1,458**	**7,309**	**1,200**	**3,868**	**4,019**	**TOTAL HEADS**
14,530	**3,614**	**1,785**	**370**	**4,988**	**735**	**5,527**	**692**	**2,230**	**1,817**	**Owner occupied**
11,383	1,503	1,777	314	4,932	609	4,492	473	182	107	Economically active
352	46	66	5	115	14	170	24	1	3	Unemployed
2	*1*	-	-	*1*	*1*	*1*	-	-	-	*Economically active students (included above)*
3,147	2,111	8	56	56	126	1,035	219	2,048	1,710	Economically inactive
1,210	**531**	**257**	**133**	**366**	**108**	**373**	**67**	**214**	**223**	**Rented privately or with a job or business**
935	248	253	104	352	85	309	47	21	12	Economically active
135	36	42	17	52	13	41	5	-	1	Unemployed
-	*1*	-	-	-	*1*	-	-	-	-	*Economically active students (included above)*
275	283	4	29	14	23	64	20	193	211	Economically inactive
1,142	**1,025**	**89**	**152**	**226**	**128**	**389**	**135**	**438**	**610**	**Rented from a housing association**
546	210	83	57	202	75	252	67	9	11	Economically active
144	45	30	13	46	17	68	15	-	-	Unemployed
-	*2*	-	*1*	-	*1*	-	-	-	-	*Economically active students (included above)*
596	815	6	95	24	53	137	68	429	599	Economically inactive
3,075	**2,625**	**317**	**463**	**752**	**487**	**1,020**	**306**	**986**	**1,369**	**Rented from a local authority or new town**
1,601	533	303	149	667	213	607	142	24	29	Economically active
478	113	121	40	190	40	164	32	3	1	Unemployed
2	-	*1*	-	*1*	-	-	-	-	-	*Economically active students (included above)*
1,474	2,092	14	314	85	274	413	164	962	1,340	Economically inactive
13,272	**4,745**	**1,240**	**458**	**4,055**	**815**	**4,973**	**745**	**3,004**	**2,727**	**TOTAL HEADS**
9,738	**2,887**	**759**	**164**	**3,059**	**499**	**3,792**	**509**	**2,128**	**1,715**	**Owner occupied**
7,179	1,058	746	142	3,022	432	3,110	346	301	138	Economically active
167	38	12	6	55	18	100	13	-	1	Unemployed
-	-	-	-	-	-	-	-	-	-	*Economically active students (included above)*
2,559	1,829	13	22	37	67	682	163	1,827	1,577	Economically inactive
2,214	**772**	**372**	**178**	**718**	**137**	**767**	**95**	**357**	**362**	**Rented privately or with a job or business**
1,824	370	362	147	705	118	679	72	78	33	Economically active
61	24	19	10	20	9	22	5	-	-	Unemployed
-	*1*	-	*1*	-	-	-	-	-	-	*Economically active students (included above)*
390	402	10	31	13	19	88	23	279	329	Economically inactive
205	**205**	**15**	**11**	**41**	**22**	**52**	**19**	**97**	**153**	**Rented from a housing association**
90	41	14	7	36	16	36	14	4	4	Economically active
11	2	1	-	5	1	4	1	1	-	Unemployed
-	-	-	-	-	-	-	-	-	-	*Economically active students (included above)*
115	164	1	4	5	6	16	5	93	149	Economically inactive
1,115	**881**	**94**	**105**	**237**	**157**	**362**	**122**	**422**	**497**	**Rented from a local authority or new town**
615	255	94	55	223	103	274	74	24	23	Economically active
64	21	9	4	24	7	31	10	-	-	Unemployed
1	-	-	-	*1*	-	-	-	-	-	*Economically active students (included above)*
500	626	-	50	14	54	88	48	398	474	Economically inactive

Table 45 Migrant household heads - continued

Note: * May include a small number of heads aged under 16

45. Households with residents

Tenure of household and economic activity of head	Households with head with different address one year before census: age and sex of head									
	Total migrant heads*		16 - 29*		30 - 44		45 up to pensionable age		Pensionable age and over	
	Males	Females	Males	Females	Males	Females	Males	Females	Males	Females
a	b	c	d	e	f	g	h	i	j	k
					South Lakeland					
TOTAL HEADS	**2,381**	**1,108**	**778**	**431**	**823**	**290**	**547**	**107**	**233**	**280**
Owner occupied	**1,336**	**409**	**349**	**97**	**486**	**128**	**348**	**56**	**153**	**128**
Economically active	1,115	248	347	88	481	114	274	34	13	12
Unemployed	34	8	10	2	11	5	12	1	1	-
Economically active students (included above)	*1*	-	*1*	-	-	-	-	-	-	-
Economically inactive	221	161	2	9	5	14	74	22	140	116
Rented privately or with a job or business	**783**	**423**	**353**	**238**	**269**	**118**	**133**	**37**	**28**	**30**
Economically active	723	363	342	215	262	108	113	33	6	7
Unemployed	48	35	15	16	21	16	12	3	-	-
Economically active students (included above)	*5*	*3*	*5*	*3*	-	-	-	-	-	-
Economically inactive	60	60	11	23	7	10	20	4	22	23
Rented from a housing association	**55**	**57**	**16**	**17**	**14**	**7**	**12**	**2**	**13**	**31**
Economically active	34	24	13	13	12	5	8	2	1	4
Unemployed	6	2	2	1	3	-	1	-	-	1
Economically active students (included above)	*1*	-	*1*	-	-	-	-	-	-	-
Economically inactive	21	33	3	4	2	2	4	-	12	27
Rented from a local authority or new town	**207**	**219**	**60**	**79**	**54**	**37**	**54**	**12**	**39**	**91**
Economically active	140	67	58	31	47	27	34	7	1	2
Unemployed	18	9	7	3	5	4	6	2	-	-
Economically active students (included above)	-	-	-	-	-	-	-	-	-	-
Economically inactive	67	152	2	48	7	10	20	5	38	89

All households: age and sex of head										Tenure of household and economic activity of head
TOTAL HOUSEHOLD HEADS*		16 - 29*		30 - 44		45 up to pensionable age		Pensionable age and over		
Males	Females	Males	Females	Males	Females	Males	Females	Males	Females	
l	m	n	o	p	q	r	s	t	u	a
27,865	**11,882**	**2,457**	**1,220**	**7,845**	**1,992**	**10,359**	**1,769**	**7,204**	**6,901**	**TOTAL HEADS**
21,754	**7,541**	**1,538**	**433**	**6,237**	**1,316**	**8,496**	**1,282**	**5,483**	**4,510**	**Owner occupied**
15,225	2,762	1,519	371	6,154	1,144	7,048	960	504	287	Economically active
313	61	25	9	86	30	199	21	3	1	Unemployed
5	*9*	*1*	*3*	*4*	*5*	-	*1*	-	-	*Economically active students (included above)*
6,529	4,779	19	62	83	172	1,448	322	4,979	4,223	Economically inactive
3,434	**1,768**	**685**	**480**	**1,014**	**313**	**1,030**	**222**	**705**	**753**	**Rented privately or with a job or business**
2,650	960	659	431	990	283	912	181	89	65	Economically active
104	67	29	27	39	28	35	10	1	2	Unemployed
6	*7*	*5*	*6*	*1*	*1*	-	-	-	-	*Economically active students (included above)*
784	808	26	49	24	30	118	41	616	688	Economically inactive
265	**330**	**23**	**31**	**71**	**28**	**56**	**15**	**115**	**256**	**Rented from a housing association**
139	65	20	19	69	23	43	13	7	10	Economically active
11	3	4	2	3	-	4	-	-	1	Unemployed
1	-	*1*	-	-	-	-	-	-	-	*Economically active students (included above)*
126	265	3	12	2	5	13	2	108	246	Economically inactive
2,412	**2,243**	**211**	**276**	**523**	**335**	**777**	**250**	**901**	**1,382**	**Rented from a local authority or new town**
1,323	620	204	133	476	234	570	172	73	81	Economically active
121	37	28	10	42	17	50	10	1	-	Unemployed
1	*2*	-	-	*1*	*1*	-	*1*	-	-	*Economically active students (included above)*
1,089	1,623	7	143	47	101	207	78	828	1,301	Economically inactive

Table 46 Households with dependent children: housing

46. Households with dependent children; residents in such households

Household composition	TOTAL HOUSE-HOLDS	Over 1 and up to 1.5 persons per room	Over 1.5 persons per room	Lacking or sharing use of bath/ shower and/or inside WC	No central heating	Not self-contained accomm-odation	Tenure: Owner occupied	Tenure: Rented privately	Tenure: Rented from a housing association	Tenure: Rented from a local authority or new town	No car	TOTAL PERSONS IN HOUSE-HOLDS
a	b	c	d	e	f	g	h	i	j	k	l	m
					CUMBRIA							
ALL HOUSEHOLDS WITH DEPENDENT CHILDREN	**55,824**	**1,895**	**197**	**175**	**11,757**	**90**	**40,306**	**2,588**	**1,578**	**9,685**	**10,971**	**216,940**
Households of 1 adult with 1 or more dependent children	**6,425**	**62**	**38**	**53**	**1,993**	**41**	**2,119**	**622**	**466**	**3,154**	**4,248**	**17,379**
Dependent child(ren) aged 0 - 4 only	1,609	2	24	27	525	28	277	222	149	949	1,286	3,612
Dependent child(ren) aged 5 and over only	3,734	18	10	24	1,128	13	1,603	327	249	1,507	2,121	9,785
Dependent children aged 0 - 4 and 5 and over	1,082	42	4	2	340	-	239	73	68	698	841	3,982
Dependent children in households of 1 adult with 1 or more dependent children												
All dependent children	10,954	257	68	72	3,300	47	3,569	909	764	5,616	7,283	
Dependent children aged 0 - 4	3,300	77	37	31	1,075	30	603	345	262	2,071	2,652	
Dependent children aged 5 - 15	7,063	175	28	36	2,055	12	2,626	525	473	3,368	4,351	
Dependent children aged 0 - 17	10,846	257	67	71	3,277	46	3,490	901	761	5,600	7,249	
Other households with dependent children	**49,399**	**1,833**	**159**	**122**	**9,764**	**49**	**38,187**	**1,966**	**1,112**	**6,531**	**6,723**	**199,561**
Dependent child(ren) aged 0 - 4 only	11,440	261	29	27	2,483	14	8,564	692	274	1,536	1,907	40,188
Dependent child(ren) aged 5 and over only	29,523	739	50	70	5,439	30	23,616	936	582	3,449	3,424	119,596
Dependent children aged 0 - 4 and 5 and over	8,436	833	80	25	1,842	5	6,007	338	256	1,546	1,392	39,777
Persons in other households with dependent children												
All adults	112,024	5,046	434	272	22,452	95	86,558	4,310	2,589	14,906	15,132	
All dependent children	87,537	5,301	503	229	17,127	79	66,662	3,365	2,036	12,477	12,117	
Dependent children aged 0 - 4	25,495	1,649	185	73	5,479	27	18,505	1,308	700	4,110	4,310	
Dependent children aged 5 - 15	55,181	3,407	307	142	10,565	43	42,395	1,838	1,223	7,803	7,206	
Dependent children aged 0 - 17	86,191	5,274	502	228	16,978	76	65,488	3,326	2,013	12,416	12,038	
Households with 3 or more dependent children	8,543	1,158	99	27	1,867	5	5,584	337	279	2,024	1,898	44,842
Households with 3 or more persons aged 0 - 15	7,603	1,087	98	27	1,699	4	4,867	302	258	1,892	1,789	39,991
Households with 4 or more dependent children	1,726	649	53	8	430	1	945	66	67	587	523	10,749
Households with 4 or more persons aged 0 - 15	1,485	588	52	8	374	-	776	63	59	538	480	9,276

46. Households with dependent children; residents in such households

Household composition	TOTAL HOUSE-HOLDS	Over 1 and up to 1.5 persons per room	Over 1.5 persons per room	Lacking or sharing use of bath/ shower and/or inside WC	No central heating	Not self-contained accomm-odation	Tenure: Owner occupied	Tenure: Rented privately	Tenure: Rented from a housing association	Tenure: Rented from a local authority or new town	No car	TOTAL PERSONS IN HOUSE-HOLDS
a	b	c	d	e	f	g	h	i	j	k	l	m
Allerdale												
ALL HOUSEHOLDS WITH DEPENDENT CHILDREN	**11,321**	**310**	**28**	**24**	**2,048**	**7**	**7,796**	**428**	**751**	**2,075**	**2,113**	**43,803**
Households of 1 adult with 1 or more dependent children	**1,286**	**6**	**4**	**4**	**331**	**2**	**320**	**100**	**202**	**654**	**863**	**3,429**
Dependent child(ren) aged 0 - 4 only	319	-	2	1	85	2	37	29	61	190	259	689
Dependent child(ren) aged 5 and over only	773	1	-	3	198	-	261	54	116	334	447	2,037
Dependent children aged 0 - 4 and 5 and over	194	5	2	-	48	-	22	17	25	130	157	703
Dependent children in households of 1 adult with 1 or more dependent children												
All dependent children	2,143	23	13	4	519	2	518	155	330	1,127	1,424	
Dependent children aged 0 - 4	597	7	7	1	150	2	67	48	100	380	489	
Dependent children aged 5 - 15	1,425	16	6	3	340	-	405	101	215	695	874	
Dependent children aged 0 - 17	2,126	23	13	4	517	2	506	155	329	1,123	1,419	
Other households with dependent children	**10,035**	**304**	**24**	**20**	**1,717**	**5**	**7,476**	**328**	**549**	**1,421**	**1,250**	**40,374**
Dependent child(ren) aged 0 - 4 only	2,208	41	5	4	398	1	1,571	107	122	349	327	7,737
Dependent child(ren) aged 5 and over only	6,191	128	8	13	1,009	4	4,802	155	311	765	668	24,966
Dependent children aged 0 - 4 and 5 and over	1,636	135	11	3	310	-	1,103	66	116	307	255	7,671
Persons in other households with dependent children												
All adults	22,743	841	66	42	3,992	14	16,906	711	1,274	3,263	2,809	
All dependent children	17,631	899	78	39	2,989	9	13,003	568	993	2,586	2,235	
Dependent children aged 0 - 4	4,921	260	32	9	897	1	3,391	220	317	861	760	
Dependent children aged 5 - 15	11,262	592	43	27	1,878	7	8,444	311	611	1,584	1,342	
Dependent children aged 0 - 17	17,321	893	77	39	2,952	9	12,742	562	979	2,567	2,217	
Households with 3 or more dependent children	1,648	196	17	5	297	1	1,029	67	130	370	333	8,616
Households with 3 or more persons aged 0 - 15	1,444	182	17	5	266	1	888	62	119	329	305	7,559
Households with 4 or more dependent children	317	112	11	1	70	1	184	11	25	91	93	1,972
Households with 4 or more persons aged 0 - 15	261	98	11	1	55	-	148	10	19	79	82	1,627

Table 46 Households with dependent children: housing – **continued**

46. Households with dependent children; residents in such households

Household composition	TOTAL HOUSE-HOLDS	Over 1 and up to 1.5 persons per room	Over 1.5 persons per room	Lacking or sharing use of bath/ shower and/or inside WC	No central heating	Not self-contained accomm-odation	Tenure: Owner occupied	Tenure: Rented privately	Tenure: Rented from a housing association	Tenure: Rented from a local authority or new town	No car	TOTAL PERSONS IN HOUSE-HOLDS
a	b	c	d	e	f	g	h	i	j	k	l	m
Barrow-in-Furness												
ALL HOUSEHOLDS WITH DEPENDENT CHILDREN	**8,891**	**388**	**47**	**34**	**3,251**	**15**	**6,992**	**422**	**63**	**1,324**	**2,545**	**34,330**
Households of 1 adult with 1 or more dependent children	**1,205**	**16**	**9**	**17**	**616**	**13**	**475**	**187**	**38**	**499**	**918**	**3,332**
Dependent child(ren) aged 0 - 4 only	339	1	6	12	189	10	82	89	15	151	292	769
Dependent child(ren) aged 5 and over only	593	5	2	3	283	3	302	73	21	194	399	1,549
Dependent children aged 0 - 4 and 5 and over	273	10	1	2	144	-	91	25	2	154	227	1,014
Dependent children in households of 1 adult with 1 or more dependent children												
All dependent children	2,127	65	15	23	1,063	13	838	269	55	954	1,633	
Dependent children aged 0 - 4	770	18	8	14	426	10	202	135	20	409	659	
Dependent children aged 5 - 15	1,263	45	7	9	593	2	572	129	34	522	914	
Dependent children aged 0 - 17	2,113	65	15	23	1,059	13	827	267	55	953	1,627	
Other households with dependent children	**7,686**	**372**	**38**	**17**	**2,635**	**2**	**6,517**	**235**	**25**	**825**	**1,627**	**30,998**
Dependent child(ren) aged 0 - 4 only	1,929	57	8	4	710	1	1,585	121	9	194	510	6,699
Dependent child(ren) aged 5 and over only	4,310	123	7	10	1,370	1	3,772	75	12	401	770	17,391
Dependent children aged 0 - 4 and 5 and over	1,447	192	23	3	555	-	1,160	39	4	230	347	6,908
Persons in other households with dependent children												
All adults	17,454	981	106	40	5,997	4	14,832	505	55	1,864	3,649	
All dependent children	13,544	1,080	117	26	4,685	2	11,274	380	34	1,703	2,942	
Dependent children aged 0 - 4	4,288	372	43	7	1,609	1	3,437	203	15	590	1,120	
Dependent children aged 5 - 15	8,330	671	73	17	2,825	1	7,006	160	19	1,042	1,680	
Dependent children aged 0 - 17	13,406	1,075	117	25	4,660	2	11,143	379	34	1,699	2,927	
Households with 3 or more dependent children	1,424	240	24	4	574	-	1,005	43	6	351	484	7,468
Households with 3 or more persons aged 0 - 15	1,293	231	23	4	533	-	898	40	5	331	451	6,807
Households with 4 or more dependent children	325	132	12	2	139	-	177	10	1	129	124	2,027
Households with 4 or more persons aged 0 - 15	294	122	12	2	126	-	157	10	1	119	115	1,840

46. Households with dependent children; residents in such households

Household composition	TOTAL HOUSE-HOLDS	Over 1 and up to 1.5 persons per room	Over 1.5 persons per room	Lacking or sharing use of bath/shower and/or inside WC	No central heating	Not self-contained accomm-odation	Tenure: Owner occupied	Tenure: Rented privately	Tenure: Rented from a housing association	Tenure: Rented from a local authority or new town	No car	TOTAL PERSONS IN HOUSE-HOLDS
a	b	c	d	e	f	g	h	i	j	k	l	m
Carlisle												
ALL HOUSEHOLDS WITH DEPENDENT CHILDREN	**11,784**	**431**	**51**	**41**	**2,324**	**15**	**8,310**	**457**	**90**	**2,607**	**2,643**	**45,327**
Households of 1 adult with 1 or more dependent children	**1,534**	**18**	**5**	**11**	**446**	**2**	**435**	**103**	**32**	**949**	**1,087**	**4,143**
Dependent child(ren) aged 0 - 4 only	408	-	3	5	102	2	53	33	10	308	336	927
Dependent child(ren) aged 5 and over only	872	5	1	6	279	-	353	61	15	433	544	2,265
Dependent children aged 0 - 4 and 5 and over	254	13	1	-	65	-	29	9	7	208	207	951
Dependent children in households of 1 adult with 1 or more dependent children												
All dependent children	2,609	83	11	16	731	2	692	143	62	1,692	1,870	
Dependent children aged 0 - 4	829	29	6	6	209	2	92	50	20	661	693	
Dependent children aged 5 - 15	1,654	52	5	10	484	-	524	85	41	991	1,112	
Dependent children aged 0 - 17	2,585	83	11	16	725	2	675	140	62	1,689	1,857	
Other households with dependent children	**10,250**	**413**	**46**	**30**	**1,878**	**13**	**7,875**	**354**	**58**	**1,658**	**1,556**	**41,184**
Dependent child(ren) aged 0 - 4 only	2,422	58	10	7	507	2	1,795	120	27	398	460	8,485
Dependent child(ren) aged 5 and over only	6,105	176	13	16	1,054	11	4,857	175	26	882	812	24,594
Dependent children aged 0 - 4 and 5 and over	1,723	179	23	7	317	-	1,223	59	5	378	284	8,105
Persons in other households with dependent children												
All adults	23,166	1,123	123	63	4,275	22	17,819	767	134	3,751	3,471	
All dependent children	18,018	1,199	143	65	3,264	16	13,581	596	99	3,186	2,761	
Dependent children aged 0 - 4	5,324	373	57	22	1,049	3	3,819	220	49	1,056	977	
Dependent children aged 5 - 15	11,449	768	85	41	2,021	9	8,705	344	46	2,009	1,657	
Dependent children aged 0 - 17	17,798	1,194	143	65	3,243	14	13,390	587	99	3,177	2,743	
Households with 3 or more dependent children	1,759	270	31	11	365	-	1,080	53	16	555	446	9,233
Households with 3 or more persons aged 0 - 15	1,589	255	31	11	333	-	947	48	14	531	424	8,364
Households with 4 or more dependent children	348	147	11	2	80	-	167	13	5	156	131	2,171
Households with 4 or more persons aged 0 - 15	306	132	11	2	73	-	139	13	5	143	122	1,913

Table 46 Households with dependent children: housing – **continued**

46. Households with dependent children; residents in such households

Household composition	TOTAL HOUSE-HOLDS	Over 1 and up to 1.5 persons per room	Over 1.5 persons per room	Lacking or sharing use of bath/ shower and/or inside WC	No central heating	Not self-contained accomm-odation	Tenure: Owner occupied	Tenure: Rented privately	Tenure: Rented from a housing association	Tenure: Rented from a local authority or new town	No car	TOTAL PERSONS IN HOUSE-HOLDS
a	b	c	d	e	f	g	h	i	j	k	l	m
Copeland												
ALL HOUSEHOLDS WITH DEPENDENT CHILDREN	**8,832**	**376**	**28**	**25**	**1,414**	**15**	**6,091**	**214**	**507**	**1,831**	**2,172**	**34,628**
Households of 1 adult with 1 or more dependent children	**1,080**	**8**	**7**	**8**	**220**	**8**	**276**	**59**	**156**	**579**	**795**	**2,960**
Dependent child(ren) aged 0 - 4 only	271	-	4	3	67	5	31	22	50	167	225	619
Dependent child(ren) aged 5 and over only	609	5	3	5	122	3	208	32	76	285	403	1,619
Dependent children aged 0 - 4 and 5 and over	200	3	-	-	31	-	37	5	30	127	167	722
Dependent children in households of 1 adult with 1 or more dependent children												
All dependent children	1,880	31	10	10	366	11	478	88	260	1,035	1,402	
Dependent children aged 0 - 4	583	3	6	4	125	7	81	34	103	362	489	
Dependent children aged 5 - 15	1,196	27	3	5	225	3	347	49	147	637	863	
Dependent children aged 0 - 17	1,864	31	10	10	362	11	466	87	259	1,033	1,400	
Other households with dependent children	**7,752**	**368**	**21**	**17**	**1,194**	**7**	**5,815**	**155**	**351**	**1,252**	**1,377**	**31,668**
Dependent child(ren) aged 0 - 4 only	1,803	46	3	4	280	2	1,365	60	75	266	338	6,377
Dependent child(ren) aged 5 and over only	4,494	148	7	8	665	4	3,485	78	165	656	709	18,349
Dependent children aged 0 - 4 and 5 and over	1,455	174	11	5	249	1	965	17	111	330	330	6,942
Persons in other households with dependent children												
All adults	17,715	1,067	55	41	2,785	14	13,204	359	831	2,909	3,160	
All dependent children	13,953	1,075	76	34	2,106	15	10,209	256	683	2,452	2,572	
Dependent children aged 0 - 4	4,136	324	27	15	672	5	2,931	96	244	774	877	
Dependent children aged 5 - 15	8,763	705	48	17	1,293	8	6,410	144	411	1,561	1,566	
Dependent children aged 0 - 17	13,739	1,069	76	34	2,084	15	10,025	253	678	2,436	2,553	
Households with 3 or more dependent children	1,471	231	11	4	232	2	872	29	106	417	419	7,763
Households with 3 or more persons aged 0 - 15	1,330	219	11	4	212	1	768	27	102	393	403	7,036
Households with 4 or more dependent children	330	133	8	1	50	-	157	6	31	126	118	2,052
Households with 4 or more persons aged 0 - 15	282	121	8	1	43	-	123	4	31	116	110	1,764

46. Households with dependent children; residents in such households

Household composition	TOTAL HOUSE-HOLDS	Over 1 and up to 1.5 persons per room	Over 1.5 persons per room	Lacking or sharing use of bath/ shower and/or inside WC	No central heating	Not self-contained accomm-odation	Tenure: Owner occupied	Tenure: Rented privately	Tenure: Rented from a housing association	Tenure: Rented from a local authority or new town	No car	TOTAL PERSONS IN HOUSE-HOLDS
a	b	c	d	e	f	g	h	i	j	k	l	m
Eden												
ALL HOUSEHOLDS WITH DEPENDENT CHILDREN	**4,984**	**155**	**18**	**36**	**826**	**16**	**3,545**	**434**	**68**	**561**	**417**	**19,709**
Households of 1 adult with 1 or more dependent children	**387**	**7**	**5**	**10**	**81**	**5**	**166**	**65**	**15**	**134**	**166**	**1,051**
Dependent child(ren) aged 0 - 4 only	89	1	2	5	19	3	16	27	5	39	52	198
Dependent child(ren) aged 5 and over only	247	2	3	5	50	2	131	27	9	75	86	662
Dependent children aged 0 - 4 and 5 and over	51	4	-	-	12	-	19	11	1	20	28	191
Dependent children in households of 1 adult with 1 or more dependent children												
All dependent children	664	24	9	15	138	6	291	102	21	240	283	
Dependent children aged 0 - 4	169	9	2	5	34	3	42	47	6	72	102	
Dependent children aged 5 - 15	454	15	5	7	92	1	223	51	13	160	169	
Dependent children aged 0 - 17	652	24	8	14	136	5	283	102	20	238	281	
Other households with dependent children	**4,597**	**148**	**13**	**26**	**745**	**11**	**3,379**	**369**	**53**	**427**	**251**	**18,658**
Dependent child(ren) aged 0 - 4 only	1,068	25	1	6	187	4	749	118	18	98	67	3,783
Dependent child(ren) aged 5 and over only	2,835	64	5	13	435	4	2,163	187	26	239	126	11,608
Dependent children aged 0 - 4 and 5 and over	694	59	7	7	123	3	467	64	9	90	58	3,267
Persons in other households with dependent children												
All adults	10,414	413	34	54	1,718	20	7,639	803	122	1,002	570	
All dependent children	8,244	403	37	49	1,299	20	6,017	657	98	781	449	
Dependent children aged 0 - 4	2,314	127	11	18	388	11	1,590	232	34	252	157	
Dependent children aged 5 - 15	5,238	252	24	30	797	8	3,879	376	59	488	270	
Dependent children aged 0 - 17	8,103	399	37	49	1,278	20	5,897	650	97	778	445	
Households with 3 or more dependent children	755	84	5	3	123	1	509	62	10	104	65	4,002
Households with 3 or more persons aged 0 - 15	669	78	5	3	105	1	453	54	9	95	62	3,547
Households with 4 or more dependent children	153	47	5	2	27	-	95	16	2	27	20	956
Households with 4 or more persons aged 0 - 15	131	42	5	2	22	-	82	16	1	25	19	819

46. Households with dependent children; residents in such households

Household composition	TOTAL HOUSE-HOLDS	Over 1 and up to 1.5 persons per room	Over 1.5 persons per room	Lacking or sharing use of bath/ shower and/or inside WC	No central heating	Not self-contained accomm-odation	Tenure: Owner occupied	Tenure: Rented privately	Tenure: Rented from a housing association	Tenure: Rented from a local authority or new town	No car	TOTAL PERSONS IN HOUSE-HOLDS
a	b	c	d	e	f	g	h	i	j	k	l	m
South Lakeland												
ALL HOUSEHOLDS WITH DEPENDENT CHILDREN	**10,012**	**235**	**25**	**15**	**1,894**	**22**	**7,572**	**633**	**99**	**1,287**	**1,081**	**39,143**
Households of 1 adult with 1 or more dependent children	**933**	**7**	**8**	**3**	**299**	**11**	**447**	**108**	**23**	**339**	**419**	**2,464**
Dependent child(ren) aged 0 - 4 only	183	-	7	1	63	6	58	22	8	94	122	410
Dependent child(ren) aged 5 and over only	640	-	1	2	196	5	348	80	12	186	242	1,653
Dependent children aged 0 - 4 and 5 and over	110	7	-	-	40	-	41	6	3	59	55	401
Dependent children in households of 1 adult with 1 or more dependent children												
All dependent children	1,531	31	10	4	483	13	752	152	36	568	671	
Dependent children aged 0 - 4	352	11	8	1	131	6	119	31	13	187	220	
Dependent children aged 5 - 15	1,071	20	2	2	321	6	555	110	23	363	419	
Dependent children aged 0 - 17	1,506	31	10	4	478	13	733	150	36	564	665	
Other households with dependent children	**9,079**	**228**	**17**	**12**	**1,595**	**11**	**7,125**	**525**	**76**	**948**	**662**	**36,679**
Dependent child(ren) aged 0 - 4 only	2,010	34	2	2	401	4	1,499	166	23	231	205	7,107
Dependent child(ren) aged 5 and over only	5,588	100	10	10	906	6	4,537	266	42	506	339	22,688
Dependent children aged 0 - 4 and 5 and over	1,481	94	5	-	288	1	1,089	93	11	211	118	6,884
Persons in other households with dependent children												
All adults	20,532	621	50	32	3,685	21	16,158	1,165	173	2,117	1,473	
All dependent children	16,147	645	52	16	2,784	17	12,578	908	129	1,769	1,158	
Dependent children aged 0 - 4	4,512	193	15	2	864	6	3,337	337	41	577	419	
Dependent children aged 5 - 15	10,139	419	34	10	1,751	10	7,951	503	77	1,119	691	
Dependent children aged 0 - 17	15,824	644	52	16	2,761	16	12,291	895	126	1,759	1,153	
Households with 3 or more dependent children	1,486	137	11	-	276	1	1,089	83	11	227	151	7,760
Households with 3 or more persons aged 0 - 15	1,278	122	11	-	250	1	913	71	9	213	144	6,678
Households with 4 or more dependent children	253	78	6	-	64	-	165	10	3	58	37	1,571
Households with 4 or more persons aged 0 - 15	211	73	5	-	55	-	127	10	2	56	32	1,313

Table 47 Households with pensioners: housing

47. Households with one or more residents of pensionable age; residents in such households

Household composition	TOTAL HOUSE-HOLDS	Up to 0.5 persons per room	Lacking or sharing use of bath/shower and/or inside WC	No central heating	Lacking or sharing use of bath/shower and/or inside WC and/or no central heating	Not self-contained accommodation
a	b	c	d	e	f	g
CUMBRIA						
TOTAL HOUSEHOLDS WITH 1 OR MORE PENSIONER(S)	**70,058**	**62,152**	**1,324**	**21,313**	**21,679**	**145**
Lone male 65 - 74	3,424	3,328	154	1,214	1,255	40
Lone male 75 - 84	2,687	2,594	112	1,025	1,054	14
Lone male 85 and over	639	621	48	265	275	2
Lone female 60 - 74	12,478	12,372	195	3,660	3,722	28
Lone female 75 - 84	9,559	9,323	287	3,151	3,254	19
Lone female 85 and over	2,695	2,561	161	1,030	1,091	6
2 or more, all pensioners, under 75	12,179	11,372	70	3,121	3,137	6
2 or more, all pensioners, any aged 75 and over	8,011	7,107	125	2,351	2,374	11
1 or more pensioner(s) with 1 non-pensioner	12,899	11,033	137	3,899	3,914	9
1 or more pensioner(s) with 2 or more non-pensioners	5,487	1,841	35	1,597	1,603	10
TOTAL PERSONS IN HOUSEHOLDS WITH PENSIONERS	**121,229**	**97,094**	**1,796**	**35,988**	**36,429**	**206**
Total persons of pensionable age	**93,802**	**81,982**	**1,569**	**28,003**	**28,414**	**168**
Pensionable age - 74	61,504	53,500	694	17,442	17,611	101
75 - 84	26,540	23,484	616	8,529	8,698	51
85 and over	5,758	4,998	259	2,032	2,105	16
Persons with limiting long-term illness						
Pensionable age - 74	17,821	15,050	238	5,198	5,272	42
75 - 84	11,868	10,230	288	3,737	3,835	23
85 and over	3,539	3,013	162	1,197	1,251	13
Allerdale						
TOTAL HOUSEHOLDS WITH 1 OR MORE PENSIONER(S)	**13,694**	**12,110**	**250**	**3,756**	**3,825**	**21**
Lone male 65 - 74	717	697	28	211	217	6
Lone male 75 - 84	495	477	20	178	186	2
Lone male 85 and over	117	115	10	46	46	-
Lone female 60 - 74	2,550	2,526	30	602	618	5
Lone female 75 - 84	1,778	1,739	62	521	539	2
Lone female 85 and over	506	490	32	171	181	-
2 or more, all pensioners, under 75	2,381	2,228	15	558	560	1
2 or more, all pensioners, any aged 75 and over	1,448	1,299	17	397	400	1
1 or more pensioner(s) with 1 non-pensioner	2,569	2,184	31	747	753	2
1 or more pensioner(s) with 2 or more non-pensioners	1,133	355	5	325	325	2
TOTAL PERSONS IN HOUSEHOLDS WITH PENSIONERS	**23,865**	**18,894**	**330**	**6,511**	**6,591**	**34**
Total persons of pensionable age	**18,290**	**15,924**	**288**	**4,938**	**5,012**	**24**
Pensionable age - 74	12,309	10,638	122	3,126	3,158	16
75 - 84	4,925	4,363	118	1,473	1,504	5
85 and over	1,056	923	48	339	350	3
Persons with limiting long-term illness						
Pensionable age - 74	3,702	3,134	45	909	925	11
75 - 84	2,224	1,922	54	633	650	4
85 and over	639	554	29	190	197	2

Owner occupied	Rented privately: Furnished	Rented privately: Unfurnished	Rented with a job or business	Rented from a housing association	Rented from a local authority or new town	No car	Persons with limiting long-term illness	Household composition
h	i	j	k	l	m	n	o	a
45,684	**671**	**3,604**	**1,059**	**4,068**	**14,972**	**34,716**	**37,699**	**TOTAL HOUSEHOLDS WITH 1 OR MORE PENSIONER(S)**
1,800	69	182	73	272	1,028	1,729	1,285	Lone male 65 - 74
1,446	51	194	43	187	766	1,639	1,171	Lone male 75 - 84
365	21	63	12	49	129	515	341	Lone male 85 and over
7,279	131	635	106	896	3,431	9,121	3,620	Lone female 60 - 74
5,266	150	687	79	826	2,551	8,378	4,346	Lone female 75 - 84
1,386	53	215	27	247	767	2,545	1,629	Lone female 85 and over
9,027	49	488	162	505	1,948	3,050	7,166	2 or more, all pensioners, under 75
5,598	60	480	110	406	1,357	3,543	6,689	2 or more, all pensioners, any aged 75 and over
9,417	55	482	273	493	2,179	3,242	7,621	1 or more pensioner(s) with 1 non-pensioner
4,100	32	178	174	187	816	954	3,831	1 or more pensioner(s) with 2 or more non-pensioners
83,351	**941**	**5,653**	**2,163**	**6,088**	**23,033**	**47,682**	**37,699**	**TOTAL PERSONS IN HOUSEHOLDS WITH PENSIONERS**
62,946	**800**	**4,699**	**1,428**	**5,128**	**18,801**	**42,072**	**33,228**	**Total persons of pensionable age**
42,578	399	2,598	1,007	3,050	11,872	22,270		Pensionable age - 74
16,821	308	1,687	347	1,693	5,684	15,679		75 - 84
3,547	93	414	74	385	1,245	4,123		85 and over
								Persons with limiting long-term illness
10,895	114	716	257	1,184	4,655	8,032		Pensionable age - 74
6,970	151	694	157	869	3,027	7,685		75 - 84
2,115	60	246	48	243	827	2,547		85 and over
8,183	**118**	**636**	**180**	**1,601**	**2,976**	**7,035**	**7,550**	**TOTAL HOUSEHOLDS WITH 1 OR MORE PENSIONER(S)**
334	14	33	9	117	210	391	274	Lone male 65 - 74
253	15	32	11	59	125	325	221	Lone male 75 - 84
56	4	12	4	18	23	97	61	Lone male 85 and over
1,314	27	113	11	360	725	1,909	771	Lone female 60 - 74
894	20	130	17	243	474	1,590	797	Lone female 75 - 84
249	7	35	5	78	132	483	295	Lone female 85 and over
1,617	11	92	30	228	403	670	1,458	2 or more, all pensioners, under 75
939	9	80	16	154	250	699	1,248	2 or more, all pensioners, any aged 75 and over
1,718	7	80	46	251	467	675	1,615	1 or more pensioner(s) with 1 non-pensioner
809	4	29	31	93	167	196	810	1 or more pensioner(s) with 2 or more non-pensioners
15,199	**154**	**998**	**368**	**2,538**	**4,608**	**9,719**	**7,550**	**TOTAL PERSONS IN HOUSEHOLDS WITH PENSIONERS**
11,274	**139**	**838**	**244**	**2,060**	**3,735**	**8,569**	**6,565**	**Total persons of pensionable age**
7,754	76	471	161	1,374	2,473	4,770		Pensionable age - 74
2,889	52	303	67	567	1,047	3,045		75 - 84
631	11	64	16	119	215	754		85 and over
								Persons with limiting long-term illness
2,024	23	128	45	538	944	1,768		Pensionable age - 74
1,211	27	138	28	283	537	1,460		75 - 84
362	7	43	8	75	144	459		85 and over

Table 47 Households with pensioners: housing - **continued**

47. Households with one or more residents of pensionable age; residents in such households

Household composition	TOTAL HOUSE-HOLDS	Up to 0.5 persons per room	Lacking or sharing use of bath/shower and/or inside WC	No central heating	Lacking or sharing use of bath/shower and/or inside WC and/or no central heating	Not self-contained accommodation
a	b	c	d	e	f	g
Barrow-in-Furness						
TOTAL HOUSEHOLDS WITH 1 OR MORE PENSIONER(S)	**9,991**	**8,858**	**227**	**4,730**	**4,753**	**20**
Lone male 65 - 74	553	537	28	281	286	12
Lone male 75 - 84	406	398	20	234	234	-
Lone male 85 and over	85	84	7	50	51	-
Lone female 60 - 74	1,894	1,876	37	900	903	3
Lone female 75 - 84	1,416	1,393	36	775	779	1
Lone female 85 and over	355	348	28	222	224	2
2 or more, all pensioners, under 75	1,759	1,615	8	706	707	-
2 or more, all pensioners, any aged 75 and over	1,056	921	33	535	539	1
1 or more pensioner(s) with 1 non-pensioner	1,770	1,485	21	743	745	1
1 or more pensioner(s) with 2 or more non-pensioners	697	201	9	284	285	-
TOTAL PERSONS IN HOUSEHOLDS WITH PENSIONERS	**16,868**	**13,445**	**315**	**7,655**	**7,688**	**22**
Total persons of pensionable age	**13,221**	**11,526**	**273**	**6,175**	**6,203**	**21**
Pensionable age - 74	8,824	7,639	115	3,827	3,840	16
75 - 84	3,690	3,266	106	1,946	1,958	3
85 and over	707	621	52	402	405	2
Persons with limiting long-term illness						
Pensionable age - 74	3,014	2,536	41	1,382	1,386	5
75 - 84	1,837	1,590	56	976	983	3
85 and over	465	397	42	268	271	2
Carlisle						
TOTAL HOUSEHOLDS WITH 1 OR MORE PENSIONER(S)	**14,533**	**12,710**	**275**	**4,691**	**4,778**	**35**
Lone male 65 - 74	686	672	27	252	259	6
Lone male 75 - 84	615	595	26	233	242	8
Lone male 85 and over	125	125	5	54	55	-
Lone female 60 - 74	2,724	2,705	57	853	875	7
Lone female 75 - 84	1,992	1,947	66	698	721	6
Lone female 85 and over	574	548	34	227	243	1
2 or more, all pensioners, under 75	2,409	2,184	15	694	699	1
2 or more, all pensioners, any aged 75 and over	1,600	1,338	19	507	510	2
1 or more pensioner(s) with 1 non-pensioner	2,665	2,242	21	848	849	2
1 or more pensioner(s) with 2 or more non-pensioners	1,143	354	5	325	325	2
TOTAL PERSONS IN HOUSEHOLDS WITH PENSIONERS	**24,918**	**19,505**	**350**	**7,777**	**7,873**	**44**
Total persons of pensionable age	**19,277**	**16,489**	**318**	**6,147**	**6,242**	**38**
Pensionable age - 74	12,574	10,691	144	3,842	3,884	19
75 - 84	5,526	4,794	130	1,865	1,901	17
85 and over	1,177	1,004	44	440	457	2
Persons with limiting long-term illness						
Pensionable age - 74	3,629	2,967	60	1,109	1,134	7
75 - 84	2,586	2,186	68	834	856	3
85 and over	732	612	24	263	275	2

Tenure: Owner occupied	Tenure: Rented privately: Furnished	Tenure: Rented privately: Unfurnished	Tenure: Rented with a job or business	Tenure: Rented from a housing association	Tenure: Rented from a local authority or new town	No car	Persons with limiting long-term illness	Household composition
h	i	j	k	l	m	n	o	a
7,702	**88**	**329**	**63**	**176**	**1,633**	**5,979**	**6,008**	**TOTAL HOUSEHOLDS WITH 1 OR MORE PENSIONER(S)**
343	17	34	13	13	133	346	234	Lone male 65 - 74
280	5	15	4	13	89	293	185	Lone male 75 - 84
64	-	5	1	3	12	79	51	Lone male 85 and over
1,320	14	73	8	40	439	1,567	695	Lone female 60 - 74
985	22	74	7	53	275	1,347	742	Lone female 75 - 84
247	6	24	2	10	66	344	230	Lone female 85 and over
1,489	6	37	8	14	205	613	1,182	2 or more, all pensioners, under 75
840	8	34	8	24	142	604	975	2 or more, all pensioners, any aged 75 and over
1,516	7	26	10	5	206	612	1,157	1 or more pensioner(s) with 1 non-pensioner
618	3	7	2	1	66	174	557	1 or more pensioner(s) with 2 or more non-pensioners
13,568	**116**	**453**	**98**	**223**	**2,410**	**8,417**	**6,008**	**TOTAL PERSONS IN HOUSEHOLDS WITH PENSIONERS**
10,393	**103**	**405**	**82**	**215**	**2,023**	**7,349**	**5,316**	**Total persons of pensionable age**
7,064	55	225	56	93	1,331	4,161		Pensionable age - 74
2,794	40	139	22	104	591	2,614		75 - 84
535	8	41	4	18	101	574		85 and over
								Persons with limiting long-term illness
2,208	21	86	29	48	622	1,658		Pensionable age - 74
1,306	24	64	18	64	361	1,372		75 - 84
350	5	28	4	14	64	377		85 and over
8,689	**105**	**611**	**233**	**527**	**4,368**	**7,746**	**7,848**	**TOTAL HOUSEHOLDS WITH 1 OR MORE PENSIONER(S)**
303	11	27	24	19	302	379	242	Lone male 65 - 74
266	8	35	8	30	268	396	289	Lone male 75 - 84
63	4	9	2	12	35	99	72	Lone male 85 and over
1,442	23	102	24	118	1,015	2,092	751	Lone female 60 - 74
916	24	115	20	133	784	1,823	943	Lone female 75 - 84
231	9	39	7	46	242	553	354	Lone female 85 and over
1,694	4	75	33	55	548	690	1,449	2 or more, all pensioners, under 75
1,017	7	80	29	64	403	751	1,404	2 or more, all pensioners, any aged 75 and over
1,915	9	90	46	40	565	741	1,533	1 or more pensioner(s) with 1 non-pensioner
842	6	39	40	10	206	222	811	1 or more pensioner(s) with 2 or more non-pensioners
16,085	**142**	**981**	**466**	**720**	**6,524**	**10,637**	**7,848**	**TOTAL PERSONS IN HOUSEHOLDS WITH PENSIONERS**
11,948	**119**	**791**	**317**	**654**	**5,448**	**9,354**	**6,947**	**Total persons of pensionable age**
8,215	58	433	225	317	3,326	5,019		Pensionable age - 74
3,114	47	297	74	265	1,729	3,460		75 - 84
619	14	61	18	72	393	875		85 and over
								Persons with limiting long-term illness
2,032	19	116	51	119	1,292	1,743		Pensionable age - 74
1,343	22	113	33	154	921	1,756		75 - 84
367	7	34	12	48	264	545		85 and over

Table 47 Households with pensioners: housing - continued

47. Households with one or more residents of pensionable age; residents in such households

Household composition	TOTAL HOUSE-HOLDS	Up to 0.5 persons per room	Lacking or sharing use of bath/shower and/or inside WC	No central heating	Lacking or sharing use of bath/shower and/or inside WC and/or no central heating	Not self-contained accommodation
a	b	c	d	e	f	g
Copeland						
TOTAL HOUSEHOLDS WITH 1 OR MORE PENSIONER(S)	**9,164**	**8,027**	**157**	**2,305**	**2,327**	**13**
Lone male 65 - 74	547	535	24	142	148	5
Lone male 75 - 84	345	328	14	109	110	1
Lone male 85 and over	68	63	7	29	29	-
Lone female 60 - 74	1,673	1,661	21	381	385	3
Lone female 75 - 84	1,145	1,121	24	335	338	-
Lone female 85 and over	289	267	10	95	95	-
2 or more, all pensioners, under 75	1,519	1,436	12	303	305	1
2 or more, all pensioners, any aged 75 and over	836	752	16	243	244	-
1 or more pensioner(s) with 1 non-pensioner	1,847	1,591	24	462	465	-
1 or more pensioner(s) with 2 or more non-pensioners	895	273	5	206	208	3
TOTAL PERSONS IN HOUSEHOLDS WITH PENSIONERS	**16,264**	**12,602**	**233**	**4,014**	**4,049**	**26**
Total persons of pensionable age	**12,042**	**10,408**	**196**	**3,008**	**3,036**	**17**
Pensionable age - 74	8,293	7,151	102	1,883	1,905	13
75 - 84	3,121	2,738	66	916	922	2
85 and over	628	519	28	209	209	2
Persons with limiting long-term illness						
Pensionable age - 74	2,641	2,240	24	542	547	7
75 - 84	1,439	1,218	22	366	369	1
85 and over	407	323	19	126	126	2
Eden						
TOTAL HOUSEHOLDS WITH 1 OR MORE PENSIONER(S)	**6,602**	**5,881**	**166**	**1,800**	**1,869**	**13**
Lone male 65 - 74	316	295	18	107	117	2
Lone male 75 - 84	261	245	15	83	91	1
Lone male 85 and over	58	55	7	29	32	-
Lone female 60 - 74	1,014	997	19	252	258	2
Lone female 75 - 84	884	853	40	243	264	2
Lone female 85 and over	233	216	18	79	91	-
2 or more, all pensioners, under 75	1,149	1,088	5	247	247	1
2 or more, all pensioners, any aged 75 and over	818	743	15	217	221	3
1 or more pensioner(s) with 1 non-pensioner	1,306	1,137	23	377	379	2
1 or more pensioner(s) with 2 or more non-pensioners	563	252	6	166	169	-
TOTAL PERSONS IN HOUSEHOLDS WITH PENSIONERS	**11,756**	**9,584**	**242**	**3,209**	**3,295**	**19**
Total persons of pensionable age	**8,957**	**7,887**	**199**	**2,409**	**2,485**	**17**
Pensionable age - 74	5,856	5,121	89	1,487	1,513	10
75 - 84	2,572	2,304	80	740	775	7
85 and over	529	462	30	182	197	-
Persons with limiting long-term illness						
Pensionable age - 74	1,529	1,284	29	415	427	4
75 - 84	1,053	907	42	279	304	3
85 and over	298	255	19	86	101	-

Tenure						No car	Persons with limiting long-term illness	Household composition
Owner occupied	Rented privately: Furnished	Rented privately: Unfurnished	Rented with a job or business	Rented from a housing association	Rented from a local authority or new town			
h	i	j	k	l	m	n	o	a
4,973	**68**	**303**	**137**	**1,129**	**2,554**	**5,074**	**5,195**	**TOTAL HOUSEHOLDS WITH 1 OR MORE PENSIONER(S)**
225	8	14	5	99	196	291	228	Lone male 65 - 74
149	5	13	5	49	124	244	143	Lone male 75 - 84
33	1	5	2	6	21	63	34	Lone male 85 and over
781	12	51	12	261	556	1,356	526	Lone female 60 - 74
476	20	57	8	199	385	1,076	517	Lone female 75 - 84
124	1	13	6	43	102	280	189	Lone female 85 and over
968	7	46	19	155	324	489	990	2 or more, all pensioners, under 75
492	1	43	16	79	205	463	738	2 or more, all pensioners, any aged 75 and over
1,147	6	40	36	165	453	605	1,187	1 or more pensioner(s) with 1 non-pensioner
578	7	21	28	73	188	207	643	1 or more pensioner(s) with 2 or more non-pensioners
9,470	**108**	**511**	**297**	**1,751**	**4,127**	**7,277**	**5,195**	**TOTAL PERSONS IN HOUSEHOLDS WITH PENSIONERS**
6,764	**81**	**405**	**186**	**1,410**	**3,196**	**6,164**	**4,487**	**Total persons of pensionable age**
4,845	46	231	131	940	2,100	3,595		Pensionable age - 74
1,602	30	141	43	397	908	2,085		75 - 84
317	5	33	12	73	188	484		85 and over
								Persons with limiting long-term illness
1,294	11	71	35	374	856	1,339		Pensionable age - 74
649	10	58	18	203	501	1,012		75 - 84
193	3	19	9	52	131	308		85 and over

h	i	j	k	l	m	n	o	a
4,514	**73**	**581**	**189**	**257**	**988**	**2,532**	**3,296**	**TOTAL HOUSEHOLDS WITH 1 OR MORE PENSIONER(S)**
194	5	30	10	13	64	110	122	Lone male 65 - 74
143	3	31	8	18	58	120	97	Lone male 75 - 84
29	2	11	1	6	9	47	28	Lone male 85 and over
667	14	103	17	45	168	648	241	Lone female 60 - 74
508	14	102	2	75	183	713	370	Lone female 75 - 84
119	8	29	1	24	52	215	132	Lone female 85 and over
880	6	73	33	19	138	171	627	2 or more, all pensioners, under 75
592	6	57	17	40	106	265	598	2 or more, all pensioners, any aged 75 and over
956	11	114	65	12	148	194	716	1 or more pensioner(s) with 1 non-pensioner
426	4	31	35	5	62	49	365	1 or more pensioner(s) with 2 or more non-pensioners
8,384	**115**	**915**	**416**	**353**	**1,573**	**3,325**	**3,296**	**TOTAL PERSONS IN HOUSEHOLDS WITH PENSIONERS**
6,291	**90**	**730**	**256**	**318**	**1,272**	**3,011**	**2,880**	**Total persons of pensionable age**
4,293	47	432	196	127	761	1,425		Pensionable age - 74
1,669	30	241	52	153	427	1,240		75 - 84
329	13	57	8	38	84	346		85 and over
								Persons with limiting long-term illness
1,002	12	121	51	49	294	486		Pensionable age - 74
640	15	93	17	78	210	574		75 - 84
171	9	35	4	21	58	203		85 and over

Table 47 Households with pensioners: housing **– continued**

47. Households with one or more residents of pensionable age; residents in such households

Household composition	TOTAL HOUSE-HOLDS	Up to 0.5 persons per room	Lacking or sharing use of bath/shower and/or inside WC	No central heating	Lacking or sharing use of bath/shower and/or inside WC and/or no central heating	Not self-contained accommodation
a	b	c	d	e	f	g
	South Lakeland					
TOTAL HOUSEHOLDS WITH 1 OR MORE PENSIONER(S)	**16,074**	**14,566**	**249**	**4,031**	**4,127**	**43**
Lone male 65 - 74	605	592	29	221	228	9
Lone male 75 - 84	565	551	17	188	191	2
Lone male 85 and over	186	179	12	57	62	2
Lone female 60 - 74	2,623	2,607	31	672	683	8
Lone female 75 - 84	2,344	2,270	59	579	613	8
Lone female 85 and over	738	692	39	236	257	3
2 or more, all pensioners, under 75	2,962	2,821	15	613	619	2
2 or more, all pensioners, any aged 75 and over	2,253	2,054	25	452	460	4
1 or more pensioner(s) with 1 non-pensioner	2,742	2,394	17	722	723	2
1 or more pensioner(s) with 2 or more non-pensioners	1,056	406	5	291	291	3
TOTAL PERSONS IN HOUSEHOLDS WITH PENSIONERS	**27,558**	**23,064**	**326**	**6,822**	**6,933**	**61**
Total persons of pensionable age	**22,015**	**19,748**	**295**	**5,326**	**5,436**	**51**
Pensionable age - 74	13,648	12,260	122	3,277	3,311	27
75 - 84	6,706	6,019	116	1,589	1,638	17
85 and over	1,661	1,469	57	460	487	7
Persons with limiting long-term illness						
Pensionable age - 74	3,306	2,889	39	841	853	8
75 - 84	2,729	2,407	46	649	673	9
85 and over	998	872	29	264	281	5

Owner occupied	Rented privately: Furnished	Rented privately: Unfurnished	Rented with a job or business	Rented from a housing association	Rented from a local authority or new town	No car	Persons with limiting long-term illness	Household composition
h	i	j	k	l	m	n	o	a
11,623	**219**	**1,144**	**257**	**378**	**2,453**	**6,350**	**7,802**	**TOTAL HOUSEHOLDS WITH 1 OR MORE PENSIONER(S)**
401	14	44	12	11	123	212	185	Lone male 65 - 74
355	15	68	7	18	102	261	236	Lone male 75 - 84
120	10	21	2	4	29	130	95	Lone male 85 and over
1,755	41	193	34	72	528	1,549	636	Lone female 60 - 74
1,487	50	209	25	123	450	1,829	977	Lone female 75 - 84
416	22	75	6	46	173	670	429	Lone female 85 and over
2,379	15	165	39	34	330	417	1,460	2 or more, all pensioners, under 75
1,718	29	186	24	45	251	761	1,726	2 or more, all pensioners, any aged 75 and over
2,165	15	132	70	20	340	415	1,413	1 or more pensioner(s) with 1 non-pensioner
827	8	51	38	5	127	106	645	1 or more pensioner(s) with 2 or more non-pensioners
20,645	**306**	**1,795**	**518**	**503**	**3,791**	**8,307**	**7,802**	**TOTAL PERSONS IN HOUSEHOLDS WITH PENSIONERS**
16,276	**268**	**1,530**	**343**	**471**	**3,127**	**7,625**	**7,033**	**Total persons of pensionable age**
10,407	117	806	238	199	1,881	3,300		Pensionable age - 74
4,753	109	566	89	207	982	3,235		75 - 84
1,116	42	158	16	65	264	1,090		85 and over
								Persons with limiting long-term illness
2,335	28	194	46	56	647	1,038		Pensionable age - 74
1,821	53	228	43	87	497	1,511		75 - 84
672	29	87	11	33	166	655		85 and over

48. Households with residents

Non-dependants, dependants and age of youngest or only dependant	Age of oldest dependant	ALL HOUSE-HOLDS	Over 1 person per room	Lacking or sharing use of bath/ shower and/or inside WC	No central heating	Not self-contained accomm-odation	No car
a	b	c	d	e	f	g	h
		CUMBRIA					
TOTAL HOUSEHOLDS		**193,893**	**2,391**	**2,494**	**50,633**	**1,177**	**59,653**
1 or more non-dependants, no dependants		105,528	245	1,664	28,999	936	31,823
1 dependent male living alone							
0 up to pensionable age		1,290		72	479	50	833
Pensionable age - 74		1,226		53	398	15	754
75 - 84		1,134		49	412	3	807
85 and over		333		27	130	2	296
1 dependent female living alone							
0 up to pensionable age		801		25	239	31	630
Pensionable age - 74		2,916		61	861	12	2,448
75 - 84		3,329		102	1,051	9	3,089
85 and over		1,261		84	468	5	1,219
2 or more persons dependant, no non-dependants							
0 up to pensionable age	0 up to pensionable age	621	9	6	158	5	286
	Pensionable age - 74	316	1	3	99	1	132
	75 - 84	105	-	2	36	-	52
	85 and over	41	-	2	19	-	24
Pensionable age - 74	Pensionable age - 74	1,530	2	7	416	2	604
	75 - 84	590	-	9	177	-	310
	85 and over	206	-	5	50	1	69
75 - 84	75 - 84	645	2	14	198	2	380
	85 and over	153	-	1	46	-	109
85 and over	85 and over	61	-	1	22	-	51
1 male non-dependant with 1 or more dependant(s)							
0 - 4	0 - 4	39	-	1	6	-	15
	5 - 15	40	-	1	11	-	15
	16 up to pensionable age	131	9	-	29	-	29
	Pensionable age and over	4	1	-	3	-	-
5 - 15	5 - 15	347	3	1	85	-	89
	16 up to pensionable age	326	10	2	72	2	60
	Pensionable age and over	8	-	-	3	-	5
16 up to pensionable age	16 up to pensionable age	1,485	6	10	443	5	393
	Pensionable age and over	90	-	1	26	-	33
Pensionable age and over	Pensionable age and over	2,615	1	33	833	1	915
1 female non-dependant with 1 or more dependant(s)							
0 - 4	0 - 4	1,552	25	26	513	28	1,260
	5 - 15	1,011	45	1	317	-	801
	16 up to pensionable age	240	34	3	76	-	105
	Pensionable age and over	21	4	-	6	-	9
5 - 15	5 - 15	2,759	16	17	868	7	1,717
	16 up to pensionable age	592	15	4	180	1	225
	Pensionable age and over	66	2	-	18	-	27
16 up to pensionable age	16 up to pensionable age	3,232	3	13	901	2	953
	Pensionable age and over	130	1	3	39	-	38
Pensionable age and over	Pensionable age and over	4,688	1	49	1,291	7	1,868
2 or more non-dependants with 1 or more dependant(s)							
0 - 4	0 - 4	11,052	258	26	2,372	14	1,789
	5 - 15	7,864	770	18	1,678	5	1,254
	16 up to pensionable age	463	103	2	136	-	107
	Pensionable age and over	108	22	-	27	-	21
5 - 15	5 - 15	22,077	556	53	4,127	20	2,576
	16 up to pensionable age	3,158	154	5	508	2	303
	Pensionable age and over	278	19	-	48	1	34
16 up to pensionable age	16 up to pensionable age	5,555	63	20	1,207	2	771
	Pensionable age and over	117	2	-	25	1	24
Pensionable age and over	Pensionable age and over	1,759	9	18	527	5	301

48. Households with residents

Non-dependants, dependants and age of youngest or only dependant	Age of oldest dependant	ALL HOUSE-HOLDS	Over 1 person per room	Lacking or sharing use of bath/ shower and/or inside WC	No central heating	Not self-contained accomm-odation	No car
a	b	c	d	e	f	g	h
		Allerdale					
TOTAL HOUSEHOLDS		**37,867**	**381**	**460**	**8,789**	**182**	**11,668**
1 or more non-dependants, no dependants		19,916	28	312	5,012	137	6,150
1 dependent male living alone							
0 up to pensionable age		281		13	76	15	177
Pensionable age - 74		268		5	61	3	172
75 - 84		211		11	67	1	164
85 and over		61		8	26	-	55
1 dependent female living alone							
0 up to pensionable age		152		6	22	6	120
Pensionable age - 74		618		11	133	5	516
75 - 84		601		21	155	2	555
85 and over		220		13	57	-	214
2 or more persons dependant, no non-dependants							
0 up to pensionable age	0 up to pensionable age	137	2	1	29	2	70
	Pensionable age - 74	72	-	1	18	-	32
	75 - 84	27	-	1	10	-	14
	85 and over	6	-	-	3	-	4
Pensionable age - 74	Pensionable age - 74	297	-	3	69	1	135
	75 - 84	126	-	2	40	-	70
	85 and over	49	-	-	13	-	11
75 - 84	75 - 84	102	-	1	22	-	56
	85 and over	34	-	-	8	-	21
85 and over	85 and over	10	-	-	3	-	8
1 male non-dependant with 1 or more dependant(s)							
0 - 4	0 - 4	6	-	-	-	-	3
	5 - 15	5	-	-	-	-	1
	16 up to pensionable age	38	1	-	8	-	8
	Pensionable age and over	-	-	-	-	-	-
5 - 15	5 - 15	81	-	-	12	-	16
	16 up to pensionable age	71	1	-	6	-	8
	Pensionable age and over	2	-	-	-	-	1
16 up to pensionable age	16 up to pensionable age	303	1	1	79	-	65
	Pensionable age and over	17	-	-	5	-	4
Pensionable age and over	Pensionable age and over	537	-	9	154	-	190
1 female non-dependant with 1 or more dependant(s)							
0 - 4	0 - 4	310	2	1	84	2	255
	5 - 15	181	7	-	44	-	150
	16 up to pensionable age	56	5	1	17	-	28
	Pensionable age and over	5	-	-	-	-	1
5 - 15	5 - 15	565	1	3	159	-	370
	16 up to pensionable age	140	-	1	29	-	45
	Pensionable age and over	12	-	-	2	-	4
16 up to pensionable age	16 up to pensionable age	687	-	3	173	1	206
	Pensionable age and over	39	1	1	13	-	6
Pensionable age and over	Pensionable age and over	925	-	8	229	1	407
2 or more non-dependants with 1 or more dependant(s)							
0 - 4	0 - 4	2,126	41	4	375	1	305
	5 - 15	1,504	120	1	279	-	220
	16 up to pensionable age	100	20	1	27	-	20
	Pensionable age and over	16	5	-	4	-	2
5 - 15	5 - 15	4,622	95	10	761	3	494
	16 up to pensionable age	675	29	-	98	-	65
	Pensionable age and over	60	3	-	10	1	8
16 up to pensionable age	16 up to pensionable age	1,188	14	6	270	-	164
	Pensionable age and over	31	1	-	9	-	7
Pensionable age and over	Pensionable age and over	377	4	1	118	1	71

48. Households with residents

Non-dependants, dependants and age of youngest or only dependant	Age of oldest dependant	ALL HOUSE-HOLDS	Over 1 person per room	Lacking or sharing use of bath/ shower and/or inside WC	No central heating	Not self-contained accomm-odation	No car
a	b	c	d	e	f	g	h
		Barrow-in-Furness					
TOTAL HOUSEHOLDS		**29,627**	**464**	**394**	**12,367**	**154**	**11,705**
1 or more non-dependants, no dependants		15,374	25	222	6,535	112	5,968
1 dependent male living alone							
0 up to pensionable age		245		13	146	6	168
Pensionable age - 74		228		11	107	3	155
75 - 84		184		10	105	-	139
85 and over		51		4	35	-	51
1 dependent female living alone							
0 up to pensionable age		176		11	84	11	150
Pensionable age - 74		551		14	273	1	506
75 - 84		562		10	305	1	543
85 and over		167		20	107	2	164
2 or more persons dependant, no non-dependants							
0 up to pensionable age	0 up to pensionable age	130	-	-	52	1	65
	Pensionable age - 74	65	-	1	29	-	31
	75 - 84	16	-	-	10	-	6
	85 and over	4	-	-	2	-	1
Pensionable age - 74	Pensionable age - 74	280	-	-	125	-	117
	75 - 84	101	-	3	49	-	66
	85 and over	44	-	1	12	-	11
75 - 84	75 - 84	101	-	5	55	1	63
	85 and over	16	-	1	8	-	12
85 and over	85 and over	6	-	1	5	-	6
1 male non-dependant with 1 or more dependant(s)							
0 - 4	0 - 4	6	-	1	4	-	2
	5 - 15	9	-	1	6	-	5
	16 up to pensionable age	32	6	-	9	-	5
	Pensionable age and over	1	-	-	1	-	-
5 - 15	5 - 15	52	-	-	22	-	17
	16 up to pensionable age	69	2	-	25	-	20
	Pensionable age and over	3	-	-	2	-	2
16 up to pensionable age	16 up to pensionable age	313	2	1	142	2	110
	Pensionable age and over	18	-	1	6	-	7
Pensionable age and over	Pensionable age and over	426	-	10	190	-	199
1 female non-dependant with 1 or more dependant(s)							
0 - 4	0 - 4	330	7	11	184	10	287
	5 - 15	257	11	1	133	-	215
	16 up to pensionable age	59	14	-	30	-	26
	Pensionable age and over	3	1	-	2	-	1
5 - 15	5 - 15	443	5	3	216	2	316
	16 up to pensionable age	96	8	-	45	-	46
	Pensionable age and over	15	2	-	8	-	12
16 up to pensionable age	16 up to pensionable age	498	-	2	210	-	170
	Pensionable age and over	13	-	-	7	-	7
Pensionable age and over	Pensionable age and over	625	-	12	288	-	319
2 or more non-dependants with 1 or more dependant(s)							
0 - 4	0 - 4	1,853	55	4	686	1	487
	5 - 15	1,330	179	3	495	-	312
	16 up to pensionable age	86	19	-	39	-	25
	Pensionable age and over	15	6	-	5	-	7
5 - 15	5 - 15	3,250	94	8	1,053	1	575
	16 up to pensionable age	422	21	1	116	-	65
	Pensionable age and over	38	1	-	8	-	6
16 up to pensionable age	16 up to pensionable age	819	6	3	289	-	175
	Pensionable age and over	10	-	-	3	-	5
Pensionable age and over	Pensionable age and over	235	-	5	99	-	60

48. Households with residents

Non-dependants, dependants and age of youngest or only dependant	Age of oldest dependant	ALL HOUSE-HOLDS	Over 1 person per room	Lacking or sharing use of bath/ shower and/or inside WC	No central heating	Not self-contained accomm-odation	No car
a	b	c	d	e	f	g	h
		Carlisle					
TOTAL HOUSEHOLDS		**40,883**	**562**	**575**	**10,691**	**398**	**13,976**
1 or more non-dependants, no dependants		22,194	64	394	6,219	347	7,448
1 dependent male living alone							
0 up to pensionable age		310		21	113	15	212
Pensionable age - 74		237		11	83	1	166
75 - 84		275		9	100	1	203
85 and over		69		1	28	-	61
1 dependent female living alone							
0 up to pensionable age		199		5	60	11	153
Pensionable age - 74		643		19	180	2	555
75 - 84		753		24	235	1	721
85 and over		289		17	105	1	282
2 or more persons dependant, no non-dependants							
0 up to pensionable age	0 up to pensionable age	134	2	1	24	1	61
	Pensionable age - 74	69	-	-	26	-	37
	75 - 84	24	-	-	6	-	10
	85 and over	12	-	1	4	-	8
Pensionable age - 74	Pensionable age - 74	327	1	3	100	-	144
	75 - 84	142	-	1	37	-	73
	85 and over	32	-	1	7	-	13
75 - 84	75 - 84	151	-	2	50	-	91
	85 and over	32	-	-	8	-	27
85 and over	85 and over	11	-	-	6	-	11
1 male non-dependant with 1 or more dependant(s)							
0 - 4	0 - 4	10	-	-	-	-	4
	5 - 15	9	-	-	2	-	4
	16 up to pensionable age	26	1	-	7	-	8
	Pensionable age and over	-	-	-	-	-	-
5 - 15	5 - 15	78	1	-	22	-	27
	16 up to pensionable age	61	2	1	10	-	15
	Pensionable age and over	3	-	-	1	-	2
16 up to pensionable age	16 up to pensionable age	288	2	2	82	2	81
	Pensionable age and over	21	-	-	7	-	8
Pensionable age and over	Pensionable age and over	537	-	4	192	1	194
1 female non-dependant with 1 or more dependant(s)							
0 - 4	0 - 4	393	3	5	100	2	330
	5 - 15	238	13	-	61	-	197
	16 up to pensionable age	39	7	1	11	-	18
	Pensionable age and over	3	-	-	1	-	1
5 - 15	5 - 15	656	3	5	220	-	444
	16 up to pensionable age	122	3	1	46	-	52
	Pensionable age and over	9	-	-	3	-	4
16 up to pensionable age	16 up to pensionable age	647	-	1	189	-	229
	Pensionable age and over	28	-	1	7	-	11
Pensionable age and over	Pensionable age and over	957	-	11	297	1	421
2 or more non-dependants with 1 or more dependant(s)							
0 - 4	0 - 4	2,338	61	7	479	2	432
	5 - 15	1,631	174	5	298	-	259
	16 up to pensionable age	90	25	1	27	-	26
	Pensionable age and over	21	2	-	2	-	3
5 - 15	5 - 15	4,681	136	13	801	7	609
	16 up to pensionable age	617	41	-	102	-	73
	Pensionable age and over	51	3	-	5	-	7
16 up to pensionable age	16 up to pensionable age	1,049	15	2	217	2	176
	Pensionable age and over	28	1	-	4	-	6
Pensionable age and over	Pensionable age and over	349	2	5	107	1	59

48. Households with residents

Non-dependants, dependants and age of youngest or only dependant	Age of oldest dependant	ALL HOUSE-HOLDS	Over 1 person per room	Lacking or sharing use of bath/ shower and/or inside WC	No central heating	Not self-contained accomm-odation	No car
a	b	c	d	e	f	g	h
		Copeland					
TOTAL HOUSEHOLDS		**27,752**	**443**	**325**	**5,740**	**129**	**9,492**
1 or more non-dependants, no dependants		14,196	30	239	3,262	98	4,769
1 dependent male living alone							
0 up to pensionable age		213		9	51	7	157
Pensionable age - 74		223		6	46	4	136
75 - 84		138		4	36	-	113
85 and over		32		3	11	-	30
1 dependent female living alone							
0 up to pensionable age		125		-	19	1	102
Pensionable age - 74		408		5	84	2	352
75 - 84		373		4	92	-	364
85 and over		143		6	45	-	140
2 or more persons dependant, no non-dependants							
0 up to pensionable age	0 up to pensionable age	101	4	1	18	1	47
	Pensionable age - 74	51	1	1	11	-	21
	75 - 84	16	-	-	3	-	11
	85 and over	10	-	1	4	-	7
Pensionable age - 74	Pensionable age - 74	219	-	-	31	-	107
	75 - 84	68	-	1	15	-	40
	85 and over	35	-	1	7	-	16
75 - 84	75 - 84	69	1	1	14	-	46
	85 and over	6	-	-	1	-	4
85 and over	85 and over	3	-	-	2	-	3
1 male non-dependant with 1 or more dependant(s)							
0 - 4	0 - 4	7	-	-	-	-	4
	5 - 15	5	-	-	1	-	2
	16 up to pensionable age	22	1	-	3	-	7
	Pensionable age and over	1	-	-	-	-	-
5 - 15	5 - 15	46	-	-	8	-	20
	16 up to pensionable age	51	3	1	7	1	12
	Pensionable age and over	-	-	-	-	-	-
16 up to pensionable age	16 up to pensionable age	276	-	1	63	-	80
	Pensionable age and over	19	-	-	2	-	11
Pensionable age and over	Pensionable age and over	353	-	4	74	-	144
1 female non-dependant with 1 or more dependant(s)							
0 - 4	0 - 4	262	3	3	67	5	219
	5 - 15	188	3	-	29	-	160
	16 up to pensionable age	52	6	-	7	-	23
	Pensionable age and over	5	1	-	2	-	4
5 - 15	5 - 15	462	5	3	99	1	328
	16 up to pensionable age	97	3	2	23	-	49
	Pensionable age and over	16	-	-	1	-	4
16 up to pensionable age	16 up to pensionable age	547	-	3	127	-	188
	Pensionable age and over	23	-	1	5	-	6
Pensionable age and over	Pensionable age and over	617	1	5	148	-	282
2 or more non-dependants with 1 or more dependant(s)							
0 - 4	0 - 4	1,732	45	4	265	2	306
	5 - 15	1,335	156	5	227	1	297
	16 up to pensionable age	96	21	-	22	-	30
	Pensionable age and over	20	3	-	4	-	5
5 - 15	5 - 15	3,339	107	4	501	2	529
	16 up to pensionable age	494	29	2	63	2	63
	Pensionable age and over	44	6	-	8	-	7
16 up to pensionable age	16 up to pensionable age	934	12	3	151	-	185
	Pensionable age and over	20	-	-	6	-	5
Pensionable age and over	Pensionable age and over	260	2	2	75	2	57

48. Households with residents

Non-dependants, dependants and age of youngest or only dependant	Age of oldest dependant	ALL HOUSE-HOLDS	Over 1 person per room	Lacking or sharing use of bath/ shower and/or inside WC	No central heating	Not self-contained accomm-odation	No car
a	b	c	d	e	f	g	h
		Eden					
TOTAL HOUSEHOLDS		**18,017**	**206**	**331**	**4,081**	**82**	**3,660**
1 or more non-dependants, no dependants		10,453	30	203	2,559	57	2,180
1 dependent male living alone							
0 up to pensionable age		74		10	29	4	37
Pensionable age - 74		102		9	36	1	47
75 - 84		95		5	31	-	60
85 and over		28		5	8	-	26
1 dependent female living alone							
0 up to pensionable age		52		3	19	-	38
Pensionable age - 74		176		7	44	-	138
75 - 84		269		23	71	-	240
85 and over		93		11	31	-	87
2 or more persons dependant, no non-dependants							
0 up to pensionable age	0 up to pensionable age	32	1	3	7	-	8
	Pensionable age - 74	17	-	-	5	-	3
	75 - 84	6	-	-	2	-	3
	85 and over	2	-	-	1	-	1
Pensionable age - 74	Pensionable age - 74	113	-	-	27	1	29
	75 - 84	43	-	-	8	-	15
	85 and over	16	-	1	4	1	6
75 - 84	75 - 84	46	-	2	10	-	20
	85 and over	13	-	-	4	-	7
85 and over	85 and over	5	-	-	1	-	4
1 male non-dependant with 1 or more dependant(s)							
0 - 4	0 - 4	5	-	-	-	-	1
	5 - 15	4	-	-	-	-	-
	16 up to pensionable age	6	-	-	1	-	-
	Pensionable age and over	1	1	-	1	-	-
5 - 15	5 - 15	32	2	1	4	-	4
	16 up to pensionable age	23	1	-	6	1	1
	Pensionable age and over	-	-	-	-	-	-
16 up to pensionable age	16 up to pensionable age	89	1	3	15	1	15
	Pensionable age and over	5	-	-	3	-	1
Pensionable age and over	Pensionable age and over	221	-	1	66	-	68
1 female non-dependant with 1 or more dependant(s)							
0 - 4	0 - 4	82	3	5	19	3	50
	5 - 15	47	4	-	12	-	28
	16 up to pensionable age	10	1	1	2	-	4
	Pensionable age and over	1	1	-	-	-	-
5 - 15	5 - 15	169	1	2	34	-	66
	16 up to pensionable age	32	1	-	5	1	10
	Pensionable age and over	6	-	-	2	-	1
16 up to pensionable age	16 up to pensionable age	283	1	3	72	-	51
	Pensionable age and over	10	-	-	3	-	2
Pensionable age and over	Pensionable age and over	466	-	7	117	3	139
2 or more non-dependants with 1 or more dependant(s)							
0 - 4	0 - 4	1,047	23	5	182	4	65
	5 - 15	656	54	4	112	3	54
	16 up to pensionable age	26	7	-	5	-	1
	Pensionable age and over	11	4	-	4	-	1
5 - 15	5 - 15	2,126	46	12	310	2	98
	16 up to pensionable age	304	12	1	50	-	8
	Pensionable age and over	29	5	-	9	-	1
16 up to pensionable age	16 up to pensionable age	503	7	1	105	-	23
	Pensionable age and over	7	-	-	1	-	-
Pensionable age and over	Pensionable age and over	181	-	3	44	-	19

48. Households with residents

Non-dependants, dependants and age of youngest or only dependant	Age of oldest dependant	ALL HOUSE-HOLDS	Over 1 person per room	Lacking or sharing use of bath/ shower and/or inside WC	No central heating	Not self-contained accomm-odation	No car
a	b	c	d	e	f	g	h
		South Lakeland					
TOTAL HOUSEHOLDS		**39,747**	**335**	**409**	**8,965**	**232**	**9,152**
1 or more non-dependants, no dependants		23,395	68	294	5,412	185	5,308
1 dependent male living alone							
0 up to pensionable age		167		6	64	3	82
Pensionable age - 74		168		11	65	3	78
75 - 84		231		10	73	1	128
85 and over		92		6	22	2	73
1 dependent female living alone							
0 up to pensionable age		97		-	35	2	67
Pensionable age - 74		520		5	147	2	381
75 - 84		771		20	193	5	666
85 and over		349		17	123	2	332
2 or more persons dependant, no non-dependants							
0 up to pensionable age	0 up to pensionable age	87	-	-	28	-	35
	Pensionable age - 74	42	-	-	10	1	8
	75 - 84	16	-	1	5	-	8
	85 and over	7	-	-	5	-	3
Pensionable age - 74	Pensionable age - 74	294	1	1	64	-	72
	75 - 84	110	-	2	28	-	46
	85 and over	30	-	1	7	-	12
75 - 84	75 - 84	176	1	3	47	1	104
	85 and over	52	-	-	17	-	38
85 and over	85 and over	26	-	-	5	-	19
1 male non-dependant with 1 or more dependant(s)							
0 - 4	0 - 4	5	-	-	2	-	1
	5 - 15	8	-	-	2	-	3
	16 up to pensionable age	7	-	-	1	-	1
	Pensionable age and over	1	-	-	1	-	-
5 - 15	5 - 15	58	-	-	17	-	5
	16 up to pensionable age	51	1	-	18	-	4
	Pensionable age and over	-	-	-	-	-	-
16 up to pensionable age	16 up to pensionable age	216	-	2	62	-	42
	Pensionable age and over	10	-	-	3	-	2
Pensionable age and over	Pensionable age and over	541	1	5	157	-	120
1 female non-dependant with 1 or more dependant(s)							
0 - 4	0 - 4	175	7	1	59	6	119
	5 - 15	100	7	-	38	-	51
	16 up to pensionable age	24	1	-	9	-	6
	Pensionable age and over	4	1	-	1	-	2
5 - 15	5 - 15	464	1	1	140	4	193
	16 up to pensionable age	105	-	-	32	-	23
	Pensionable age and over	8	-	-	2	-	2
16 up to pensionable age	16 up to pensionable age	570	2	1	130	1	109
	Pensionable age and over	17	-	-	4	-	6
Pensionable age and over	Pensionable age and over	1,098	-	6	212	2	300
2 or more non-dependants with 1 or more dependant(s)							
0 - 4	0 - 4	1,956	33	2	385	4	194
	5 - 15	1,408	87	-	267	1	112
	16 up to pensionable age	65	11	-	16	-	5
	Pensionable age and over	25	2	-	8	-	3
5 - 15	5 - 15	4,059	78	6	701	5	271
	16 up to pensionable age	646	22	1	79	-	29
	Pensionable age and over	56	1	-	8	-	5
16 up to pensionable age	16 up to pensionable age	1,062	9	5	175	-	48
	Pensionable age and over	21	-	-	2	1	1
Pensionable age and over	Pensionable age and over	357	1	2	84	1	35

49. Households with residents; residents in households

	TOTAL HOUSE-HOLDS	Ethnic group of household head										Household head born in:	
		White	Black Caribbean	Black African	Black other	Indian	Pakistani	Bangladeshi	Chinese	Other groups		New Common-wealth	Ireland
										Asian	Other		
a	b	c	d	e	f	g	h	i	j	k	l	m	n
					CUMBRIA								
ALL HOUSEHOLDS	**193,893**	**193,268**	**40**	**23**	**89**	**95**	**32**	**31**	**115**	**47**	**153**	**959**	**1,967**
Over 1 and up to 1.5 persons per room	2,041	2,000	-	-	3	4	4	3	16	3	8	38	18
Over 1.5 persons per room	350	342	-	-	-	-	-	3	2	-	3	4	5
Owner occupied - owned outright	56,657	56,578	4	4	9	13	3	1	24	4	17	201	512
- buying	79,159	78,834	17	9	40	54	19	19	64	25	78	505	793
Rented privately	13,781	13,694	10	5	18	6	7	6	8	7	20	115	163
Rented from a housing association	7,353	7,344	1	-	1	1	-	-	-	1	5	13	76
Rented from local authority or new town	31,992	31,924	7	3	20	5	1	-	6	5	21	74	380
Lacking or sharing use of bath/shower and/or inside WC	2,494	2,477	4	-	6	-	-	-	2	2	3	12	22
No central heating	50,633	50,485	7	7	37	8	7	9	28	10	35	178	557
Not self-contained accommodation	1,177	1,160	4	1	8	-	-	-	1	1	2	15	19
No car	59,653	59,480	13	9	36	19	6	13	23	13	41	195	750
Containing person(s) with limiting long-term illness	48,199	48,095	9	3	21	5	7	2	19	9	29	159	617
ALL RESIDENTS IN HOUSEHOLDS	**474,787**	**472,859**	**88**	**65**	**230**	**287**	**113**	**137**	**433**	**128**	**447**	**2,705**	**4,802**
Over 1 and up to 1.5 persons per room	11,381	11,164	-	-	16	18	21	14	96	13	39	211	112
Over 1.5 persons per room	1,401	1,349	-	-	-	-	-	24	14	-	14	26	22
Lacking or sharing use of bath/shower and/or inside WC	3,686	3,649	4	-	11	-	-	-	10	3	9	21	30
No central heating	114,326	113,917	9	15	89	21	17	32	110	24	92	478	1,259
Not self-contained accommodation	1,547	1,522	4	1	9	-	-	-	5	1	5	22	27
No car	108,592	108,198	20	21	72	44	19	52	57	25	84	412	1,433

Table 49 Ethnic group: housing – **continued**

49. Households with residents; residents in households

	TOTAL HOUSE-HOLDS	Ethnic group of household head										Household head born in:	
		White	Black Caribbean	Black African	Black other	Indian	Pakistani	Bangladeshi	Chinese	Other groups		New Common-wealth	Ireland
										Asian	Other		
a	b	c	d	e	f	g	h	i	j	k	l	m	n
Allerdale													
ALL HOUSEHOLDS	**37,867**	**37,767**	**7**	**1**	**14**	**13**	**6**	**3**	**20**	**5**	**31**	**149**	**239**
Over 1 and up to 1.5 persons per room	339	335	-	-	1	-	-	1	1	-	1	4	2
Over 1.5 persons per room	42	41	-	-	-	-	-	-	-	-	1	-	-
Owner occupied - owned outright	10,903	10,894	-	-	2	1	-	-	3	1	2	30	51
- buying	14,160	14,103	4	1	8	11	3	2	12	3	13	85	95
Rented privately	2,285	2,272	2	-	-	-	3	-	1	1	6	15	14
Rented from a housing association	2,994	2,989	-	-	-	1	-	-	-	-	4	4	24
Rented from local authority or new town	6,707	6,696	1	-	4	-	-	-	1	-	5	9	49
Lacking or sharing use of bath/shower and/or inside WC	460	457	1	-	-	-	-	-	-	-	2	1	2
No central heating	8,789	8,772	1	-	3	-	2	-	2	-	9	21	47
Not self-contained accommodation	182	180	1	-	-	-	-	-	-	-	1	1	3
No car	11,668	11,643	3	-	4	2	1	2	3	1	9	26	78
Containing person(s) with limiting long-term illness	9,757	9,742	2	-	2	1	-	-	2	2	6	21	63
ALL RESIDENTS IN HOUSEHOLDS	**93,935**	**93,624**	**17**	**2**	**38**	**40**	**20**	**13**	**81**	**14**	**86**	**434**	**592**
Over 1 and up to 1.5 persons per room	1,908	1,886	-	-	6	-	-	4	6	-	6	25	14
Over 1.5 persons per room	192	189	-	-	-	-	-	-	-	-	3	-	-
Lacking or sharing use of bath/shower and/or inside WC	651	646	1	-	-	-	-	-	-	-	4	1	2
No central heating	20,293	20,245	1	-	9	-	2	-	10	-	26	56	116
Not self-contained accommodation	234	232	1	-	-	-	-	-	-	-	1	1	7
No car	21,073	21,012	6	-	12	5	2	9	8	2	17	63	144

Table 49 Ethnic group: housing - **continued**

49. Households with residents; residents in households

	TOTAL HOUSE-HOLDS	Ethnic group of household head										Household head born in:	
		White	Black Caribbean	Black African	Black other	Indian	Pakistani	Bangladeshi	Chinese	Other groups		New Common-wealth	Ireland
										Asian	Other		
a	b	c	d	e	f	g	h	i	j	k	l	m	n
Barrow-in-Furness													
ALL HOUSEHOLDS	**29,627**	**29,507**	**4**	**5**	**19**	**15**	**7**	**4**	**27**	**9**	**30**	**146**	**521**
Over 1 and up to 1.5 persons per room	404	396	-	-	1	1	-	-	3	1	2	6	5
Over 1.5 persons per room	60	58	-	-	-	-	-	-	1	-	1	2	2
Owner occupied - owned outright	9,214	9,197	-	1	1	4	1	-	9	-	1	30	182
- buying	14,010	13,945	2	2	9	9	3	4	15	6	15	87	186
Rented privately	1,945	1,933	1	1	2	-	1	-	2	2	3	15	54
Rented from a housing association	348	348	-	-	-	-	-	-	-	-	-	-	7
Rented from local authority or new town	3,841	3,824	1	1	7	-	-	-	-	1	7	9	90
Lacking or sharing use of bath/shower and/or inside WC	394	392	-	-	2	-	-	-	-	-	-	2	4
No central heating	12,367	12,324	2	2	11	2	2	2	8	3	11	52	247
Not self-contained accommodation	154	154	-	-	-	-	-	-	-	-	-	1	5
No car	11,705	11,666	3	3	8	1	-	3	11	2	8	39	269
Containing person(s) with limiting long-term illness	8,018	7,997	2	1	6	1	-	-	5	1	5	20	196
ALL RESIDENTS IN HOUSEHOLDS	**72,564**	**72,171**	**8**	**14**	**55**	**55**	**18**	**16**	**100**	**32**	**95**	**440**	**1,198**
Over 1 and up to 1.5 persons per room	2,222	2,176	-	-	6	5	-	-	21	5	9	34	31
Over 1.5 persons per room	276	262	-	-	-	-	-	-	8	-	6	13	6
Lacking or sharing use of bath/shower and/or inside WC	582	575	-	-	7	-	-	-	-	-	-	2	4
No central heating	28,038	27,917	4	6	32	8	4	6	24	9	28	130	535
Not self-contained accommodation	187	187	-	-	-	-	-	-	-	-	-	1	8
No car	22,612	22,520	6	7	15	5	-	12	28	4	15	91	499

Table 49 Ethnic group: housing – **continued**

49. Households with residents; residents in households

	TOTAL HOUSE-HOLDS	Ethnic group of household head										Household head born in:	
		White	Black Caribbean	Black African	Black other	Indian	Pakistani	Bangladeshi	Chinese	Other groups		New Common-wealth	Ireland
										Asian	Other		
a	b	c	d	e	f	g	h	i	j	k	l	m	n
Carlisle													
ALL HOUSEHOLDS	**40,883**	**40,707**	**12**	**6**	**23**	**33**	**7**	**16**	**31**	**14**	**34**	**255**	**485**
Over 1 and up to 1.5 persons per room	471	461	-	-	-	-	-	1	6	1	2	10	3
Over 1.5 persons per room	91	87	-	-	-	-	-	2	1	-	1	1	3
Owner occupied - owned outright	9,922	9,906	-	1	1	3	1	-	7	-	3	35	91
- buying	17,543	17,445	6	4	8	21	5	9	16	10	19	148	222
Rented privately	2,573	2,545	3	1	8	1	-	6	2	2	5	28	31
Rented from a housing association	839	839	-	-	-	-	-	-	-	-	-	1	20
Rented from local authority or new town	9,093	9,074	3	-	5	3	1	-	2	2	3	33	108
Lacking or sharing use of bath/shower and/or inside WC	575	571	2	-	-	-	-	-	-	1	1	6	6
No central heating	10,691	10,656	2	3	9	1	-	6	6	4	4	45	135
Not self-contained accommodation	398	392	2	1	2	-	-	-	-	1	-	8	6
No car	13,976	13,917	5	2	13	4	1	7	8	6	13	61	188
Containing person(s) with limiting long-term illness	10,115	10,081	2	1	8	1	3	2	5	4	8	41	140
ALL RESIDENTS IN HOUSEHOLDS	**99,059**	**98,481**	**29**	**18**	**60**	**100**	**30**	**79**	**120**	**34**	**108**	**766**	**1,206**
Over 1 and up to 1.5 persons per room	2,619	2,567	-	-	-	-	-	4	32	4	12	56	18
Over 1.5 persons per room	381	353	-	-	-	-	-	17	6	-	5	6	16
Lacking or sharing use of bath/shower and/or inside WC	815	807	2	-	-	-	-	-	-	1	5	6	7
No central heating	23,414	23,320	2	4	21	2	-	23	24	7	11	115	316
Not self-contained accommodation	476	470	2	1	2	-	-	-	-	1	-	9	6
No car	25,555	25,413	6	5	28	6	5	27	18	10	37	137	371

Table 49 Ethnic group: housing – continued

49. Households with residents; residents in households

	TOTAL HOUSE-HOLDS	Ethnic group of household head										Household head born in:	
		White	Black Caribbean	Black African	Black other	Indian	Pakistani	Bangladeshi	Chinese	Other groups: Asian	Other groups: Other	New Common-wealth	Ireland
a	b	c	d	e	f	g	h	i	j	k	l	m	n
Copeland													
ALL HOUSEHOLDS	**27,752**	**27,662**	**8**	**3**	**14**	**12**	**6**	**2**	**15**	**10**	**20**	**104**	**253**
Over 1 and up to 1.5 persons per room	402	391	-	-	1	2	3	-	3	1	1	9	2
Over 1.5 persons per room	41	41	-	-	-	-	-	-	-	-	-	-	-
Owner occupied - owned outright	6,384	6,374	1	-	-	3	-	1	1	2	2	18	50
- buying	11,760	11,718	2	1	7	5	3	-	10	2	12	49	95
Rented privately	1,192	1,179	2	-	3	1	3	-	2	1	1	12	15
Rented from a housing association	2,167	2,165	1	-	1	-	-	-	-	-	-	5	21
Rented from local authority or new town	5,700	5,690	2	-	3	1	-	-	1	-	3	11	63
Lacking or sharing use of bath/shower and/or inside WC	325	322	1	-	1	-	-	-	1	-	-	2	3
No central heating	5,740	5,726	1	-	5	-	1	-	6	1	-	11	40
Not self-contained accommodation	129	126	1	-	2	-	-	-	-	-	-	1	2
No car	9,492	9,471	1	-	6	6	1	1	-	2	4	21	93
Containing person(s) with limiting long-term illness	7,022	7,010	1	-	2	-	-	-	3	2	4	14	87
ALL RESIDENTS IN HOUSEHOLDS	**70,485**	**70,228**	**18**	**7**	**31**	**38**	**22**	**6**	**50**	**29**	**56**	**289**	**669**
Over 1 and up to 1.5 persons per room	2,307	2,252	-	-	4	9	15	-	19	4	4	47	14
Over 1.5 persons per room	174	174	-	-	-	-	-	-	-	-	-	-	-
Lacking or sharing use of bath/shower and/or inside WC	516	506	1	-	1	-	-	-	8	-	-	10	7
No central heating	13,363	13,320	1	-	10	-	1	-	27	4	-	36	102
Not self-contained accommodation	182	179	1	-	2	-	-	-	-	-	-	2	2
No car	18,844	18,794	1	-	11	20	3	4	-	6	5	50	201

Table 49 Ethnic group: housing – continued

49. Households with residents; residents in households

	TOTAL HOUSE-HOLDS	Ethnic group of household head										Household head born in:	
		White	Black Caribbean	Black African	Black other	Indian	Pakistani	Bangladeshi	Chinese	Other groups		New Common-wealth	Ireland
										Asian	Other		
a	b	c	d	e	f	g	h	i	j	k	l	m	n
Eden													
ALL HOUSEHOLDS	**18,017**	**17,987**	**4**	**1**	**3**	**2**	**-**	**4**	**6**	**1**	**9**	**79**	**127**
Over 1 and up to 1.5 persons per room	171	166	-	-	-	-	-	1	2	-	2	3	3
Over 1.5 persons per room	35	35	-	-	-	-	-	-	-	-	-	-	-
Owner occupied - owned outright	6,321	6,314	-	-	1	1	-	-	2	-	3	23	43
- buying	6,304	6,289	2	-	2	-	-	3	3	1	4	37	51
Rented privately	1,925	1,920	2	-	-	1	-	-	1	-	1	14	17
Rented from a housing association	410	410	-	-	-	-	-	-	-	-	-	-	-
Rented from local authority or new town	1,996	1,994	-	1	-	-	-	-	-	-	1	2	14
Lacking or sharing use of bath/shower and/or inside WC	331	330	-	-	-	-	-	-	1	-	-	1	4
No central heating	4,081	4,075	-	1	-	1	-	-	1	-	3	9	25
Not self-contained accommodation	82	82	-	-	-	-	-	-	-	-	-	2	-
No car	3,660	3,655	1	1	-	1	-	-	-	-	2	11	25
Containing person(s) with limiting long-term illness	4,074	4,069	1	-	-	-	-	-	2	-	2	16	38
ALL RESIDENTS IN HOUSEHOLDS	**44,711**	**44,618**	**7**	**4**	**8**	**2**	**-**	**13**	**27**	**2**	**30**	**199**	**333**
Over 1 and up to 1.5 persons per room	922	895	-	-	-	-	-	6	13	-	8	15	16
Over 1.5 persons per room	135	135	-	-	-	-	-	-	-	-	-	-	-
Lacking or sharing use of bath/shower and/or inside WC	544	542	-	-	-	-	-	-	2	-	-	2	7
No central heating	9,283	9,263	-	4	-	1	-	-	6	-	9	23	61
Not self-contained accommodation	130	130	-	-	-	-	-	-	-	-	-	3	-
No car	5,810	5,800	1	4	-	1	-	-	-	-	4	16	45

49. Households with residents; residents in households

	TOTAL HOUSE-HOLDS	Ethnic group of household head										Household head born in:	
		White	Black Caribbean	Black African	Black other	Indian	Pakistani	Bangladeshi	Chinese	Other groups		New Common-wealth	Ireland
										Asian	Other		
a	b	c	d	e	f	g	h	i	j	k	l	m	n
South Lakeland													
ALL HOUSEHOLDS	**39,747**	**39,638**	**5**	**7**	**16**	**20**	**6**	**2**	**16**	**8**	**29**	**226**	**342**
Over 1 and up to 1.5 persons per room	254	251	-	-	-	1	1	-	1	-	-	6	3
Over 1.5 persons per room	81	80	-	-	-	-	-	1	-	-	-	1	-
Owner occupied - owned outright	13,913	13,893	3	2	4	1	1	-	2	1	6	65	95
- buying	15,382	15,334	1	1	6	8	5	1	8	3	15	99	144
Rented privately	3,861	3,845	-	3	5	3	-	-	-	1	4	31	32
Rented from a housing association	595	593	-	-	-	-	-	-	-	1	1	3	4
Rented from local authority or new town	4,655	4,646	-	1	1	1	-	-	2	2	2	10	56
Lacking or sharing use of bath/shower and/or inside WC	409	405	-	-	3	-	-	-	-	1	-	-	3
No central heating	8,965	8,932	1	1	9	4	2	1	5	2	8	40	63
Not self-contained accommodation	232	226	-	-	4	-	-	-	1	-	1	2	3
No car	9,152	9,128	-	3	5	5	3	-	1	2	5	37	97
Containing person(s) with limiting long-term illness	9,213	9,196	1	1	3	2	4	-	2	-	4	47	93
ALL RESIDENTS IN HOUSEHOLDS	**94,033**	**93,737**	**9**	**20**	**38**	**52**	**23**	**10**	**55**	**17**	**72**	**577**	**804**
Over 1 and up to 1.5 persons per room	1,403	1,388	-	-	-	4	6	-	5	-	-	34	19
Over 1.5 persons per room	243	236	-	-	-	-	-	7	-	-	-	7	-
Lacking or sharing use of bath/shower and/or inside WC	578	573	-	-	3	-	-	-	-	2	-	-	3
No central heating	19,935	19,852	1	1	17	10	10	3	19	4	18	118	129
Not self-contained accommodation	338	324	-	-	5	-	-	-	5	-	4	6	4
No car	14,698	14,659	-	5	6	7	9	-	3	3	6	55	173

Table 50 Country of birth: household heads and residents

Notes: (1) * Includes Channel Islands, the Isle of Man and United Kingdom (part not stated)
(2) ** Includes Ireland (part not stated)

50. Residents in households; household heads

Country of birth of household head	TOTAL PERSONS	Age and birthplace of persons							
		Total born		0 - 4		5 - 15		16 - 29	
		Inside UK	Outside UK	Inside UK	Outside UK	Inside UK	Outside UK	Inside UK	Outside UK
a	b	c	d	e	f	g	h	i	j
CUMBRIA									
ALL COUNTRIES OF BIRTH	**474,787**	**465,585**	**9,202**	**28,615**	**180**	**61,269**	**975**	**90,492**	**1,822**
United Kingdom*	**465,131**	**460,843**	**4,288**	**28,025**	**129**	**60,075**	**797**	**89,473**	**1,105**
England	438,040	434,278	3,762	26,552	117	56,700	716	84,574	979
Scotland	20,288	20,042	246	1,112	8	2,517	42	3,712	67
Wales	3,447	3,379	68	190	3	471	20	563	12
Northern Ireland	3,036	2,975	61	158	1	366	11	581	21
Irish Republic**	1,766	884	882	51	3	181	13	229	56
Old Commonwealth	949	474	475	60	5	87	13	105	94
New Commonwealth	**2,705**	**1,350**	**1,355**	**258**	**13**	**427**	**67**	**281**	**299**
Eastern Africa	363	196	167	46	3	67	11	33	42
Other Africa	182	98	84	22	1	33	8	11	19
Caribbean	167	85	82	13	1	15	3	22	7
Bangladesh	156	54	102	17	2	26	14	8	47
India	663	330	333	28	3	90	9	75	26
Pakistan	140	67	73	12	3	24	3	11	12
South East Asia	614	292	322	78	-	109	11	63	101
Cyprus	126	71	55	22	-	12	1	24	24
Other New Commonwealth	294	157	137	20	-	51	7	34	21
Other European Community	1,820	963	857	122	9	258	34	217	140
Other Europe	735	322	413	12	-	46	5	47	12
United States of America	412	136	276	17	12	24	20	24	30
China	109	36	73	5	1	12	3	6	12
Vietnam	14	1	13	1	-	-	-	-	7
Rest of the world	1,146	576	570	64	8	159	23	110	67
Allerdale									
ALL COUNTRIES OF BIRTH	**93,935**	**92,572**	**1,363**	**5,495**	**23**	**12,516**	**171**	**17,688**	**258**
United Kingdom*	**92,417**	**91,780**	**637**	**5,394**	**14**	**12,304**	**146**	**17,519**	**158**
England	88,389	87,822	567	5,154	12	11,796	130	16,796	146
Scotland	2,993	2,962	31	173	2	369	8	549	7
Wales	639	628	11	46	-	91	2	103	-
Northern Ireland	357	349	8	17	-	44	3	68	2
Irish Republic**	235	123	112	6	-	29	3	27	3
Old Commonwealth	157	84	73	10	2	13	1	20	15
New Commonwealth	**434**	**234**	**200**	**50**	**3**	**79**	**3**	**46**	**44**
Eastern Africa	92	59	33	15	2	22	-	10	7
Other Africa	26	17	9	6	-	4	-	-	2
Caribbean	23	12	11	1	-	2	-	5	-
Bangladesh	13	-	13	-	-	-	2	-	7
India	92	42	50	4	1	7	1	11	4
Pakistan	20	11	9	2	-	5	-	2	1
South East Asia	113	61	52	18	-	27	-	9	17
Cyprus	21	12	9	3	-	2	-	6	3
Other New Commonwealth	34	20	14	1	-	10	-	3	3
Other European Community	289	153	136	18	3	40	6	40	16
Other Europe	136	74	62	2	-	19	2	10	3
United States of America	46	16	30	1	-	4	4	3	2
China	36	12	24	3	1	2	-	5	5
Vietnam	3	1	2	1	-	-	-	-	-
Rest of the world	182	95	87	10	-	26	6	18	12

30 - 44		45 up to pensionable age		Pensionable age - 74		75 and over		TOTAL HOUSEHOLD HEADS	Country of birth of household head
Inside UK	Outside UK	Inside UK	Outside UK	Inside UK	Outside UK	Inside UK	Outside UK		
k	l	m	n	o	p	q	r	s	a
98,086	**2,150**	**95,539**	**1,857**	**59,886**	**1,618**	**31,698**	**600**	**193,893**	**ALL COUNTRIES OF BIRTH**
97,272	**906**	**94,986**	**625**	**59,412**	**596**	**31,600**	**130**	**189,977**	**United Kingdom***
91,751	797	89,260	529	55,565	521	29,876	103	178,801	England
4,193	69	4,313	26	2,873	28	1,322	6	8,402	Scotland
761	12	685	8	491	11	218	2	1,416	Wales
544	8	691	8	458	9	177	3	1,223	Northern Ireland
154	169	143	310	107	232	19	99	744	Irish Republic**
86	109	55	100	58	88	23	66	413	Old Commonwealth
202	**477**	**102**	**289**	**66**	**138**	**14**	**72**	**959**	**New Commonwealth**
34	74	10	21	5	6	1	10	120	Eastern Africa
27	41	4	10	1	3	-	2	68	Other Africa
17	25	10	26	7	12	1	8	66	Caribbean
2	27	-	5	1	7	-	-	37	Bangladesh
47	75	55	125	30	67	5	28	259	India
9	25	4	17	5	9	2	4	48	Pakistan
28	142	6	46	5	17	3	5	195	South East Asia
11	16	1	12	1	2	-	-	48	Cyprus
27	52	12	27	11	15	2	15	118	Other New Commonwealth
192	228	99	196	62	193	13	57	731	Other European Community
48	28	65	107	97	195	7	66	364	Other Europe
25	70	18	76	21	40	7	28	193	United States of America
3	16	4	25	6	12	-	4	38	China
-	3	-	2	-	-	-	1	6	Vietnam
104	144	67	127	57	124	15	77	468	Rest of the world

19,765	**331**	**19,128**	**270**	**12,074**	**235**	**5,906**	**75**	**37,867**	**ALL COUNTRIES OF BIRTH**
19,629	**127**	**19,039**	**86**	**12,004**	**90**	**5,891**	**16**	**37,282**	**United Kingdom***
18,786	112	18,182	72	11,411	81	5,697	14	35,654	England
619	8	649	2	454	4	149	-	1,219	Scotland
152	3	130	6	73	-	33	-	252	Wales
69	1	76	-	64	2	11	-	142	Northern Ireland
26	21	19	50	14	28	2	7	97	Irish Republic**
17	18	10	16	12	9	2	12	63	Old Commonwealth
28	**75**	**16**	**46**	**13**	**22**	**2**	**7**	**149**	**New Commonwealth**
9	19	2	5	1	-	-	-	27	Eastern Africa
4	4	3	3	-	-	-	-	9	Other Africa
2	4	1	4	1	3	-	-	9	Caribbean
-	4	-	-	-	-	-	-	3	Bangladesh
4	7	7	20	8	11	1	6	41	India
-	6	-	-	2	1	-	1	5	Pakistan
5	25	1	8	-	2	1	-	35	South East Asia
1	2	-	3	-	1	-	-	6	Cyprus
3	4	2	3	1	4	-	-	14	Other New Commonwealth
32	41	14	22	9	41	-	7	117	Other European Community
13	9	15	19	12	16	3	13	55	Other Europe
3	8	2	8	2	5	1	3	22	United States of America
-	6	1	10	1	2	-	-	11	China
-	2	-	-	-	-	-	-	1	Vietnam
17	24	12	13	7	22	5	10	70	Rest of the world

Table 50 Country of birth: household heads and residents - continued

Notes: (1) * Includes Channel Islands, the Isle of Man and United Kingdom (part not stated)
(2) ** Includes Ireland (part not stated)

50. Residents in households; household heads

Country of birth of household head	TOTAL PERSONS	Total born		0 - 4		5 - 15		16 - 29	
		Inside UK	Outside UK	Inside UK	Outside UK	Inside UK	Outside UK	Inside UK	Outside UK
a	b	c	d	e	f	g	h	i	j
Barrow-in-Furness									
ALL COUNTRIES OF BIRTH	**72,564**	**71,081**	**1,483**	**5,021**	**37**	**9,428**	**165**	**15,097**	**313**
United Kingdom*	**71,068**	**70,359**	**709**	**4,929**	**24**	**9,252**	**133**	**14,920**	**179**
England	66,574	65,962	612	4,648	20	8,696	121	13,994	160
Scotland	2,992	2,963	29	211	2	418	6	663	6
Wales	561	548	13	31	2	67	4	111	1
Northern Ireland	847	835	12	36	-	70	1	137	6
Irish Republic**	351	180	171	7	2	32	2	57	9
Old Commonwealth	121	62	59	9	-	10	-	11	11
New Commonwealth	**440**	**215**	**225**	**45**	**1**	**69**	**13**	**54**	**53**
Eastern Africa	33	18	15	5	-	8	-	3	5
Other Africa	33	18	15	1	-	10	1	2	3
Caribbean	15	8	7	1	-	2	-	2	-
Bangladesh	16	8	8	1	-	5	1	2	2
India	100	51	49	6	-	15	4	13	1
Pakistan	18	7	11	2	1	1	-	2	2
South East Asia	123	47	76	18	-	12	7	9	28
Cyprus	30	17	13	3	-	3	-	9	4
Other New Commonwealth	72	41	31	8	-	13	-	12	8
Other European Community	191	100	91	15	2	25	2	22	21
Other Europe	82	35	47	1	-	5	-	4	4
United States of America	111	30	81	3	6	5	6	5	13
China	15	2	13	-	-	2	2	-	3
Vietnam	3	-	3	-	-	-	-	-	2
Rest of the world	182	98	84	12	2	28	7	24	18
Carlisle									
ALL COUNTRIES OF BIRTH	**99,059**	**96,799**	**2,260**	**6,110**	**43**	**12,881**	**222**	**19,048**	**462**
United Kingdom*	**96,539**	**95,596**	**943**	**5,949**	**33**	**12,568**	**170**	**18,790**	**251**
England	87,041	86,238	803	5,503	29	11,397	151	17,171	216
Scotland	8,073	7,981	92	384	3	954	15	1,336	22
Wales	586	576	10	26	-	79	2	108	2
Northern Ireland	787	770	17	36	1	133	2	165	6
Irish Republic**	419	193	226	12	-	33	-	54	13
Old Commonwealth	224	105	119	14	2	26	6	20	27
New Commonwealth	**766**	**367**	**399**	**69**	**4**	**123**	**24**	**74**	**94**
Eastern Africa	89	42	47	6	-	14	5	8	10
Other Africa	35	17	18	2	1	4	3	4	3
Caribbean	55	33	22	9	-	4	2	9	1
Bangladesh	68	21	47	8	2	12	4	1	26
India	208	102	106	9	1	33	4	20	14
Pakistan	35	16	19	4	-	6	2	2	4
South East Asia	155	67	88	15	-	30	2	19	24
Cyprus	42	25	17	9	-	6	-	4	9
Other New Commonwealth	79	44	35	7	-	14	2	7	3
Other European Community	530	290	240	45	1	76	13	66	54
Other Europe	179	74	105	2	-	11	-	11	2
United States of America	53	20	33	2	-	4	3	5	2
China	30	13	17	-	-	6	-	-	-
Vietnam	5	-	5	-	-	-	-	-	2
Rest of the world	314	141	173	17	3	34	6	28	17

Age and birthplace of persons								TOTAL HOUSEHOLD HEADS	Country of birth of household head
30 - 44		45 up to pensionable age		Pensionable age - 74		75 and over			
Inside UK	Outside UK	Inside UK	Outside UK	Inside UK	Outside UK	Inside UK	Outside UK		
k	l	m	n	o	p	q	r	s	a
14,624	**340**	**13,993**	**325**	**8,605**	**219**	**4,313**	**84**	**29,627**	**ALL COUNTRIES OF BIRTH**
14,508	**136**	**13,905**	**117**	**8,547**	**106**	**4,298**	**14**	**29,043**	**United Kingdom***
13,613	123	13,006	90	7,949	88	4,056	10	27,193	England
641	8	581	3	327	3	122	1	1,204	Scotland
133	2	77	1	88	2	41	1	232	Wales
115	-	229	4	173	-	75	1	376	Northern Ireland
32	32	36	61	14	41	2	24	145	Irish Republic**
10	16	9	15	7	9	6	8	55	Old Commonwealth
24	**85**	**15**	**50**	**6**	**16**	**2**	**7**	**146**	**New Commonwealth**
2	8	-	1	-	1	-	-	12	Eastern Africa
3	8	1	3	1	-	-	-	13	Other Africa
1	4	1	1	1	2	-	-	5	Caribbean
-	4	-	1	-	-	-	-	4	Bangladesh
6	16	7	16	3	9	1	3	35	India
1	6	1	2	-	-	-	-	7	Pakistan
6	23	1	13	-	2	1	3	36	South East Asia
1	2	-	6	1	1	-	-	10	Cyprus
4	14	4	7	-	1	-	1	24	Other New Commonwealth
22	30	9	14	4	13	3	9	75	Other European Community
4	4	5	15	16	18	-	6	42	Other Europe
6	13	1	23	9	12	1	8	52	United States of America
-	1	-	5	-	1	-	1	4	China
-	1	-	-	-	-	-	-	2	Vietnam
18	22	13	25	2	3	1	7	63	Rest of the world

20,678	**529**	**19,377**	**432**	**12,152**	**422**	**6,553**	**150**	**40,883**	**ALL COUNTRIES OF BIRTH**
20,460	**211**	**19,245**	**123**	**12,049**	**125**	**6,535**	**30**	**39,867**	**United Kingdom***
18,550	171	17,179	102	10,651	108	5,787	26	35,858	England
1,635	28	1,763	12	1,232	8	677	4	3,449	Scotland
120	3	126	-	82	3	35	-	242	Wales
149	5	169	-	82	3	36	-	297	Northern Ireland
35	49	28	72	24	61	7	31	188	Irish Republic**
22	24	11	23	8	28	4	9	96	Old Commonwealth
62	**128**	**28**	**95**	**11**	**37**	**-**	**17**	**255**	**New Commonwealth**
11	19	3	7	-	3	-	3	31	Eastern Africa
7	8	-	2	-	1	-	-	14	Other Africa
7	9	3	8	1	2	-	-	18	Caribbean
-	7	-	3	-	5	-	-	14	Bangladesh
16	21	18	44	6	15	-	7	71	India
2	3	2	6	-	2	-	2	13	Pakistan
2	43	-	13	1	6	-	-	46	South East Asia
5	6	1	2	-	-	-	-	17	Cyprus
12	12	1	10	3	3	-	5	31	Other New Commonwealth
55	59	28	46	17	54	3	13	210	Other European Community
10	4	19	23	19	57	2	19	94	Other Europe
4	14	3	8	2	4	-	2	24	United States of America
3	4	2	6	2	5	-	2	12	China
-	-	-	2	-	-	-	1	2	Vietnam
27	36	13	34	20	51	2	26	135	Rest of the world

Table 50 Country of birth: household heads and residents – **continued**

Notes: (1) * Includes Channel Islands, the Isle of Man and United Kingdom (part not stated)
(2) ** Includes Ireland (part not stated)

50. Residents in households; household heads

Country of birth of household head	TOTAL PERSONS	Age and birthplace of persons							
		Total born		0 - 4		5 - 15		16 - 29	
		Inside UK	Outside UK	Inside UK	Outside UK	Inside UK	Outside UK	Inside UK	Outside UK
a	b	c	d	e	f	g	h	i	j
Copeland									
ALL COUNTRIES OF BIRTH	**70,485**	**69,326**	**1,159**	**4,694**	**25**	**9,822**	**137**	**14,171**	**235**
United Kingdom*	**69,316**	**68,760**	**556**	**4,619**	**19**	**9,691**	**113**	**14,048**	**148**
England	66,350	65,874	476	4,445	19	9,314	99	13,487	127
Scotland	2,051	2,019	32	123	-	269	5	386	11
Wales	436	425	11	18	-	54	4	78	3
Northern Ireland	426	419	7	33	-	53	3	91	1
Irish Republic**	243	119	124	10	-	24	4	25	12
Old Commonwealth	90	44	46	8	1	4	-	10	8
New Commonwealth	**289**	**131**	**158**	**19**	**3**	**45**	**14**	**24**	**40**
Eastern Africa	29	16	13	1	-	8	-	2	5
Other Africa	20	7	13	1	-	2	4	-	3
Caribbean	17	9	8	-	1	1	-	3	-
Bangladesh	30	9	21	4	-	4	4	-	10
India	59	30	29	1	-	7	-	11	3
Pakistan	23	9	14	2	2	5	-	-	4
South East Asia	67	33	34	9	-	13	1	6	12
Cyprus	3	1	2	-	-	-	-	1	1
Other New Commonwealth	41	17	24	1	-	5	5	1	2
Other European Community	261	148	113	19	1	36	2	43	19
Other Europe	107	44	63	3	-	4	-	7	-
United States of America	37	10	27	1	-	-	3	1	-
China	7	3	4	2	-	1	-	-	-
Vietnam	-	-	-	-	-	-	-	-	-
Rest of the world	135	67	68	13	1	17	1	13	8
Eden									
ALL COUNTRIES OF BIRTH	**44,711**	**43,944**	**767**	**2,469**	**14**	**5,604**	**88**	**8,219**	**128**
United Kingdom*	**43,907**	**43,530**	**377**	**2,429**	**12**	**5,493**	**81**	**8,149**	**81**
England	41,801	41,465	336	2,289	12	5,201	74	7,760	70
Scotland	1,564	1,550	14	104	-	210	3	292	4
Wales	297	290	7	21	-	45	2	48	2
Northern Ireland	213	208	5	12	-	33	-	44	2
Irish Republic**	120	63	57	2	-	12	-	15	6
Old Commonwealth	100	52	48	5	-	14	1	7	6
New Commonwealth	**199**	**111**	**88**	**18**	**-**	**40**	**2**	**18**	**16**
Eastern Africa	18	11	7	2	-	3	-	2	2
Other Africa	20	12	8	3	-	4	-	1	2
Caribbean	18	8	10	-	-	2	-	3	4
Bangladesh	13	8	5	4	-	2	-	2	2
India	58	35	23	2	-	16	-	4	-
Pakistan	11	5	6	1	-	1	1	-	-
South East Asia	37	21	16	4	-	8	-	5	3
Cyprus	6	1	5	1	-	-	1	-	3
Other New Commonwealth	18	10	8	1	-	4	-	1	-
Other European Community	164	81	83	9	1	21	3	13	9
Other Europe	58	23	35	-	-	1	-	5	2
United States of America	37	18	19	3	1	2	-	4	2
China	15	4	11	-	-	1	1	1	4
Vietnam	-	-	-	-	-	-	-	-	-
Rest of the world	111	62	49	3	-	20	-	7	2

30 - 44		45 up to pensionable age		Pensionable age - 74		75 and over		TOTAL HOUSEHOLD HEADS	Country of birth of household head
Inside UK	Outside UK	Inside UK	Outside UK	Inside UK	Outside UK	Inside UK	Outside UK		
k	l	m	n	o	p	q	r	s	a
14,901	**243**	**13,983**	**232**	**8,092**	**201**	**3,663**	**86**	**27,752**	**ALL COUNTRIES OF BIRTH**
14,805	**103**	**13,915**	**84**	**8,029**	**72**	**3,653**	**17**	**27,274**	**United Kingdom***
14,201	90	13,280	70	7,613	60	3,534	11	26,072	England
424	9	443	3	292	4	82	-	830	Scotland
90	1	106	-	60	3	19	-	189	Wales
89	-	78	1	58	1	17	1	156	Northern Ireland
22	24	12	39	23	32	3	13	97	Irish Republic**
9	6	9	14	3	6	1	11	43	Old Commonwealth
23	**56**	**9**	**24**	**10**	**15**	**1**	**6**	**104**	**New Commonwealth**
4	7	-	-	1	-	-	1	11	Eastern Africa
4	3	-	2	-	1	-	-	6	Other Africa
2	3	3	3	-	-	-	1	6	Caribbean
1	7	-	-	-	-	-	-	8	Bangladesh
5	8	4	9	2	7	-	2	25	India
1	5	-	1	1	1	-	1	7	Pakistan
3	14	1	6	1	1	-	-	22	South East Asia
-	1	-	-	-	-	-	-	2	Cyprus
3	8	1	3	5	5	1	1	17	Other New Commonwealth
24	22	17	35	6	28	3	6	100	Other European Community
5	2	11	11	14	39	-	11	53	Other Europe
3	5	3	12	2	3	-	4	20	United States of America
-	2	-	1	-	-	-	1	3	China
-	-	-	-	-	-	-	-	-	Vietnam
10	23	7	12	5	6	2	17	58	Rest of the world
9,462	**183**	**9,429**	**158**	**5,713**	**143**	**3,048**	**53**	**18,017**	**ALL COUNTRIES OF BIRTH**
9,379	**82**	**9,382**	**63**	**5,657**	**46**	**3,041**	**12**	**17,672**	**United Kingdom***
8,952	75	8,944	52	5,392	42	2,927	11	16,849	England
326	2	331	3	204	2	83	-	613	Scotland
62	1	59	1	34	-	21	1	121	Wales
38	-	44	3	27	-	10	-	77	Northern Ireland
11	8	13	25	9	14	1	4	50	Irish Republic**
11	14	4	7	10	11	1	9	45	Old Commonwealth
20	**35**	**9**	**14**	**5**	**14**	**1**	**7**	**79**	**New Commonwealth**
2	3	1	1	1	1	-	-	7	Eastern Africa
4	5	-	-	-	-	-	1	8	Other Africa
1	1	-	1	1	1	1	3	8	Caribbean
-	1	-	1	-	1	-	-	4	Bangladesh
7	10	4	6	2	7	-	-	21	India
2	-	1	2	-	3	-	-	5	Pakistan
3	9	1	3	-	1	-	-	14	South East Asia
-	1	-	-	-	-	-	-	4	Cyprus
1	5	2	-	1	-	-	3	8	Other New Commonwealth
19	26	9	20	10	19	-	5	72	Other European Community
5	-	6	11	6	17	-	5	30	Other Europe
5	4	2	3	1	5	1	4	18	United States of America
-	3	-	2	2	1	-	-	4	China
-	-	-	-	-	-	-	-	-	Vietnam
12	11	4	13	13	16	3	7	47	Rest of the world

Table 50 Country of birth: household heads and residents - continued

Notes: (1) * Includes Channel Islands, the Isle of Man and United Kingdom (part not stated)
(2) ** Includes Ireland (part not stated)

50. Residents in households; household heads

Country of birth of household head	TOTAL PERSONS	Total born		0 - 4		5 - 15		16 - 29	
		Inside UK	Outside UK	Inside UK	Outside UK	Inside UK	Outside UK	Inside UK	Outside UK
a	b	c	d	e	f	g	h	i	j
South Lakeland									
ALL COUNTRIES OF BIRTH	**94,033**	**91,863**	**2,170**	**4,826**	**38**	**11,018**	**192**	**16,269**	**426**
United Kingdom*	**91,884**	**90,818**	**1,066**	**4,705**	**27**	**10,767**	**154**	**16,047**	**288**
England	87,885	86,917	968	4,513	25	10,296	141	15,366	260
Scotland	2,615	2,567	48	117	1	297	5	486	17
Wales	928	912	16	48	1	135	6	115	4
Northern Ireland	406	394	12	24	-	33	2	76	4
Irish Republic**	398	206	192	14	1	51	4	51	13
Old Commonwealth	257	127	130	14	-	20	5	37	27
New Commonwealth	**577**	**292**	**285**	**57**	**2**	**71**	**11**	**65**	**52**
Eastern Africa	102	50	52	17	1	12	6	8	13
Other Africa	48	27	21	9	-	9	-	4	6
Caribbean	39	15	24	2	-	4	1	-	2
Bangladesh	16	8	8	-	-	3	3	3	-
India	146	70	76	6	1	12	-	16	4
Pakistan	33	19	14	1	-	6	-	5	1
South East Asia	119	63	56	14	-	19	1	15	17
Cyprus	24	15	9	6	-	1	-	4	4
Other New Commonwealth	50	25	25	2	-	5	-	10	5
Other European Community	385	191	194	16	1	60	8	33	21
Other Europe	173	72	101	4	-	6	3	10	1
United States of America	128	42	86	7	5	9	4	6	11
China	6	2	4	-	-	-	-	-	-
Vietnam	3	-	3	-	-	-	-	-	3
Rest of the world	222	113	109	9	2	34	3	20	10

Age and birthplace of persons								TOTAL HOUSEHOLD HEADS	Country of birth of household head
30 - 44		45 up to pensionable age		Pensionable age - 74		75 and over			
Inside UK	Outside UK	Inside UK	Outside UK	Inside UK	Outside UK	Inside UK	Outside UK		
k	l	m	n	o	p	q	r	s	a
18,656	**524**	**19,629**	**440**	**13,250**	**398**	**8,215**	**152**	**39,747**	**ALL COUNTRIES OF BIRTH**
18,491	**247**	**19,500**	**152**	**13,126**	**157**	**8,182**	**41**	**38,839**	**United Kingdom***
17,649	226	18,669	143	12,549	142	7,875	31	37,175	England
548	14	546	3	364	7	209	1	1,087	Scotland
204	2	187	-	154	3	69	-	380	Wales
84	2	95	-	54	3	28	1	175	Northern Ireland
28	35	35	63	23	56	4	20	167	Irish Republic**
17	31	12	25	18	25	9	17	111	Old Commonwealth
45	**98**	**25**	**60**	**21**	**34**	**8**	**28**	**226**	**New Commonwealth**
6	18	4	7	2	1	1	6	32	Eastern Africa
5	13	-	-	-	1	-	1	18	Other Africa
4	4	2	9	3	4	-	4	20	Caribbean
1	4	-	-	1	1	-	-	4	Bangladesh
9	13	15	30	9	18	3	10	66	India
3	5	-	6	2	2	2	-	11	Pakistan
9	28	2	3	3	5	1	2	42	South East Asia
4	4	-	1	-	-	-	-	9	Cyprus
4	9	2	4	1	2	1	5	24	Other New Commonwealth
40	50	22	59	16	38	4	17	157	Other European Community
11	9	9	28	30	48	2	12	90	Other Europe
4	26	7	22	5	11	4	7	57	United States of America
-	-	1	1	1	3	-	-	4	China
-	-	-	-	-	-	-	-	1	Vietnam
20	28	18	30	10	26	2	10	95	Rest of the world

Notes: (1) * Includes Channel Islands, the Isle of Man and United Kingdom (part not stated)
(2) ** Includes Ireland (part not stated)

51. Residents in households; household heads

Country of birth	TOTAL PERSONS	Ethnic group									
		White	Black Caribbean	Black African	Black other	Indian	Pakistani	Bangla-deshi	Chinese	Other groups	
										Asian	Other
a	b	c	d	e	f	g	h	i	j	k	l
					CUMBRIA						
TOTAL PERSONS	**474,787**	**472,742**	**99**	**78**	**254**	**253**	**89**	**135**	**449**	**169**	**519**
United Kingdom*	**465,869**	**464,891**	**60**	**37**	**217**	**71**	**43**	**52**	**157**	**26**	**315**
England	444,015	443,097	52	36	208	66	43	51	146	25	291
Scotland	16,514	16,466	7	-	8	5	-	-	10	1	17
Wales	2,775	2,766	1	1	1	-	-	-	-	-	6
Northern Ireland	2,270	2,269	-	-	-	-	-	-	1	-	-
Irish Republic**	1,338	1,333	-	-	3	-	1	-	-	-	1
Old Commonwealth	1,059	1,036	2	-	6	2	-	-	-	-	13
New Commonwealth	**2,221**	**1,475**	**35**	**31**	**18**	**179**	**45**	**83**	**226**	**54**	**75**
Eastern Africa	302	250	-	19	2	18	-	-	-	6	7
Other Africa	182	160	-	12	4	-	-	-	-	-	6
Caribbean	145	86	34	-	5	8	-	-	-	-	12
Bangladesh	113	6	-	-	1	11	-	83	-	9	3
India	442	278	-	-	-	135	4	-	-	-	25
Pakistan	92	40	-	-	-	1	41	-	-	5	5
South East Asia	523	275	-	-	2	3	-	-	226	8	9
Cyprus	146	143	-	-	1	-	-	-	-	-	2
Other New Commonwealth	276	237	1	-	3	3	-	-	-	26	6
Other European Community	2,011	2,005	1	-	2	-	-	-	-	2	1
Other Europe	614	612	-	-	-	-	-	-	-	-	2
United States of America	473	463	-	-	1	-	-	-	-	2	7
China	76	21	-	-	-	-	-	-	54	1	-
Vietnam	14	1	-	-	-	-	-	-	5	8	-
Rest of the world	1,112	905	1	10	7	1	-	-	7	76	105
Total household heads	**193,893**	**193,268**	**40**	**23**	**89**	**95**	**32**	**31**	**115**	**47**	**153**
United Kingdom*	**189,977**	**189,785**	**19**	**10**	**74**	**9**	**6**	**4**	**7**	**2**	**61**
England	178,801	178,628	14	9	67	9	6	4	7	2	55
Scotland	8,402	8,388	4	-	6	-	-	-	-	-	4
Wales	1,416	1,411	1	1	1	-	-	-	-	-	2
Northern Ireland	1,223	1,223	-	-	-	-	-	-	-	-	-
Irish Republic**	744	743	-	-	1	-	-	-	-	-	-
Old Commonwealth	413	406	1	-	2	-	-	-	-	-	4
New Commonwealth	**959**	**646**	**20**	**9**	**6**	**85**	**26**	**27**	**83**	**27**	**30**
Eastern Africa	120	102	-	4	1	8	-	-	-	5	-
Other Africa	68	61	-	5	-	-	-	-	-	-	2
Caribbean	66	39	19	-	4	1	-	-	-	-	3
Bangladesh	37	2	-	-	-	3	-	27	-	4	1
India	259	172	-	-	-	69	3	-	-	-	15
Pakistan	48	19	-	-	-	1	23	-	-	2	3
South East Asia	195	106	-	-	-	-	-	-	83	4	2
Cyprus	48	47	-	-	-	-	-	-	-	-	1
Other New Commonwealth	118	98	1	-	1	3	-	-	-	12	3
Other European Community	731	729	-	-	2	-	-	-	-	-	-
Other Europe	364	364	-	-	-	-	-	-	-	-	-
United States of America	193	192	-	-	-	-	-	-	-	-	1
China	38	15	-	-	-	-	-	-	23	-	-
Vietnam	6	1	-	-	-	-	-	-	2	3	-
Rest of the world	468	387	-	4	4	1	-	-	-	15	57

Notes: (1) * Includes Channel Islands, the Isle of Man and United Kingdom (part not stated)
(2) ** Includes Ireland (part not stated)

51. Residents in households; household heads

Country of birth	TOTAL PERSONS	Ethnic group									
		White	Black Caribbean	Black African	Black other	Indian	Pakistani	Bangla-deshi	Chinese	Other groups	
										Asian	Other
a	b	c	d	e	f	g	h	i	j	k	l
					CUMBRIA – *continued*						
TOTAL PERSONS	**474,787**	**472,742**	**99**	**78**	**254**	**253**	**89**	**135**	**449**	**169**	**519**
Country of birth of household head											
United Kingdom*	**465,131**	**464,262**	**76**	**53**	**212**	**48**	**18**	**25**	**47**	**73**	**317**
England	438,040	437,230	66	49	200	44	16	25	44	69	297
Scotland	20,288	20,243	9	3	11	3	2	-	2	3	12
Wales	3,447	3,433	1	1	1	1	-	-	1	1	8
Northern Ireland	3,036	3,036	-	-	-	-	-	-	-	-	-
Irish Republic**	1,766	1,759	-	-	1	1	-	-	-	5	-
Old Commonwealth	949	931	1	-	4	-	-	-	-	-	13
New Commonwealth	**2,705**	**1,794**	**22**	**21**	**22**	**200**	**71**	**110**	**321**	**61**	**83**
Eastern Africa	363	305	-	13	4	32	-	-	-	7	2
Other Africa	182	169	-	8	2	-	-	-	-	-	3
Caribbean	167	126	21	-	11	1	-	-	-	-	8
Bangladesh	156	12	-	-	3	13	-	110	-	12	6
India	663	470	-	-	-	147	12	-	-	2	32
Pakistan	140	60	-	-	-	4	59	-	-	7	10
South East Asia	614	279	-	-	-	-	-	-	321	6	8
Cyprus	126	125	-	-	-	-	-	-	-	-	1
Other New Commonwealth	294	248	1	-	2	3	-	-	-	27	13
Other European Community	1,820	1,812	-	-	4	2	-	-	-	1	1
Other Europe	735	734	-	-	-	-	-	-	1	-	-
United States of America	412	405	-	-	-	-	-	-	-	-	7
China	109	34	-	-	-	-	-	-	75	-	-
Vietnam	14	2	-	-	-	-	-	-	5	7	-
Rest of the world	1,146	1,009	-	4	11	2	-	-	-	22	98
					Allerdale						
TOTAL PERSONS	**93,935**	**93,622**	**12**	**7**	**41**	**28**	**17**	**13**	**85**	**19**	**91**
United Kingdom*	**92,617**	**92,463**	**4**	**2**	**33**	**8**	**12**	**-**	**34**	**4**	**57**
England	89,369	89,228	4	2	32	8	12	-	29	4	50
Scotland	2,451	2,443	-	-	-	-	-	-	5	-	3
Wales	483	478	-	-	1	-	-	-	-	-	4
Northern Ireland	269	269	-	-	-	-	-	-	-	-	-
Irish Republic**	174	174	-	-	-	-	-	-	-	-	-
Old Commonwealth	180	171	1	-	3	-	-	-	-	-	5
New Commonwealth	**327**	**234**	**7**	**2**	**1**	**20**	**5**	**13**	**32**	**6**	**7**
Eastern Africa	54	51	-	-	-	2	-	-	-	1	-
Other Africa	20	17	-	2	-	-	-	-	-	-	1
Caribbean	22	15	6	-	1	-	-	-	-	-	-
Bangladesh	13	-	-	-	-	-	-	13	-	-	-
India	67	44	-	-	-	17	-	-	-	-	6
Pakistan	10	3	-	-	-	-	5	-	-	2	-
South East Asia	86	51	-	-	-	1	-	-	32	2	-
Cyprus	23	23	-	-	-	-	-	-	-	-	-
Other New Commonwealth	32	30	1	-	-	-	-	-	-	1	-
Other European Community	300	299	-	-	1	-	-	-	-	-	-
Other Europe	90	90	-	-	-	-	-	-	-	-	-
United States of America	54	54	-	-	-	-	-	-	-	-	-
China	22	3	-	-	-	-	-	-	18	1	-
Vietnam	3	-	-	-	-	-	-	-	1	2	-
Rest of the world	168	134	-	3	3	-	-	-	-	6	22

Notes: (1) * Includes Channel Islands, the Isle of Man and United Kingdom (part not stated)
(2) ** Includes Ireland (part not stated)

51. Residents in households; household heads

Country of birth	TOTAL PERSONS	Ethnic group									
		White	Black Caribbean	Black African	Black other	Indian	Pakistani	Bangla-deshi	Chinese	Other groups	
										Asian	Other
a	b	c	d	e	f	g	h	i	j	k	l
				Allerdale – *continued*							
Total household heads	**37,867**	**37,767**	**7**	**1**	**14**	**13**	**6**	**3**	**20**	**5**	**31**
United Kingdom*	**37,282**	**37,246**	**2**	**-**	**12**	**2**	**4**	**-**	**1**	**-**	**15**
England	35,654	35,622	2	-	11	2	4	-	1	-	12
Scotland	1,219	1,218	-	-	-	-	-	-	-	-	1
Wales	252	249	-	-	1	-	-	-	-	-	2
Northern Ireland	142	142	-	-	-	-	-	-	-	-	-
Irish Republic**	97	97	-	-	-	-	-	-	-	-	-
Old Commonwealth	63	61	1	-	-	-	-	-	-	-	1
New Commonwealth	**149**	**109**	**4**	**1**	**-**	**11**	**2**	**3**	**10**	**4**	**5**
Eastern Africa	27	25	-	-	-	1	-	-	-	1	-
Other Africa	9	8	-	1	-	-	-	-	-	-	-
Caribbean	9	6	3	-	-	-	-	-	-	-	-
Bangladesh	3	-	-	-	-	-	-	3	-	-	-
India	41	26	-	-	-	10	-	-	-	-	5
Pakistan	5	2	-	-	-	-	2	-	-	1	-
South East Asia	35	24	-	-	-	-	-	-	10	1	-
Cyprus	6	6	-	-	-	-	-	-	-	-	-
Other New Commonwealth	14	12	1	-	-	-	-	-	-	1	-
Other European Community	117	116	-	-	1	-	-	-	-	-	-
Other Europe	55	55	-	-	-	-	-	-	-	-	-
United States of America	22	22	-	-	-	-	-	-	-	-	-
China	11	2	-	-	-	-	-	-	9	-	-
Vietnam	1	-	-	-	-	-	-	-	-	1	-
Rest of the world	70	59	-	-	1	-	-	-	-	-	10
TOTAL PERSONS	**93,935**	**93,622**	**12**	**7**	**41**	**28**	**17**	**13**	**85**	**19**	**91**
Country of birth of household head											
United Kingdom*	**92,417**	**92,281**	**7**	**6**	**38**	**7**	**7**	**-**	**7**	**9**	**55**
England	88,389	88,269	6	6	35	7	7	-	6	9	44
Scotland	2,993	2,987	1	-	2	-	-	-	-	-	3
Wales	639	629	-	-	1	-	-	-	1	-	8
Northern Ireland	357	357	-	-	-	-	-	-	-	-	-
Irish Republic**	235	235	-	-	-	-	-	-	-	-	-
Old Commonwealth	157	151	1	-	-	-	-	-	-	-	5
New Commonwealth	**434**	**319**	**4**	**1**	**-**	**21**	**10**	**13**	**47**	**8**	**11**
Eastern Africa	92	86	-	-	-	4	-	-	-	2	-
Other Africa	26	25	-	1	-	-	-	-	-	-	-
Caribbean	23	20	3	-	-	-	-	-	-	-	-
Bangladesh	13	-	-	-	-	-	-	13	-	-	-
India	92	65	-	-	-	17	-	-	-	-	10
Pakistan	20	5	-	-	-	-	10	-	-	4	1
South East Asia	113	65	-	-	-	-	-	-	47	1	-
Cyprus	21	21	-	-	-	-	-	-	-	-	-
Other New Commonwealth	34	32	1	-	-	-	-	-	-	1	-
Other European Community	289	287	-	-	2	-	-	-	-	-	-
Other Europe	136	136	-	-	-	-	-	-	-	-	-
United States of America	46	46	-	-	-	-	-	-	-	-	-
China	36	5	-	-	-	-	-	-	31	-	-
Vietnam	3	1	-	-	-	-	-	-	-	2	-
Rest of the world	182	161	-	-	1	-	-	-	-	-	20

Notes: (1) * Includes Channel Islands, the Isle of Man and United Kingdom (part not stated)
(2) ** Includes Ireland (part not stated)

51. Residents in households; household heads

Country of birth	TOTAL PERSONS	Ethnic group									
		White	Black Caribbean	Black African	Black other	Indian	Pakistani	Bangla-deshi	Chinese	Other groups: Asian	Other groups: Other
a	b	c	d	e	f	g	h	i	j	k	l
				Barrow-in-Furness							
TOTAL PERSONS	**72,564**	**72,171**	**12**	**11**	**43**	**43**	**17**	**13**	**108**	**35**	**111**
United Kingdom*	**71,148**	**70,986**	**9**	**4**	**40**	**11**	**5**	**5**	**27**	**5**	**56**
England	67,677	67,522	7	4	38	10	5	5	26	5	55
Scotland	2,375	2,369	2	-	2	1	-	-	-	-	1
Wales	416	416	-	-	-	-	-	-	-	-	-
Northern Ireland	612	611	-	-	-	-	-	-	1	-	-
Irish Republic**	262	260	-	-	-	-	1	-	-	-	1
Old Commonwealth	167	166	1	-	-	-	-	-	-	-	-
New Commonwealth	**358**	**205**	**2**	**6**	**1**	**32**	**11**	**8**	**63**	**10**	**20**
Eastern Africa	39	30	-	4	-	1	-	-	-	-	4
Other Africa	23	17	-	2	-	-	-	-	-	-	4
Caribbean	17	10	2	-	-	2	-	-	-	-	3
Bangladesh	8	-	-	-	-	-	-	8	-	-	-
India	60	27	-	-	-	28	-	-	-	-	5
Pakistan	12	1	-	-	-	-	11	-	-	-	-
South East Asia	111	44	-	-	1	-	-	-	63	1	2
Cyprus	27	27	-	-	-	-	-	-	-	-	-
Other New Commonwealth	61	49	-	-	-	1	-	-	-	9	2
Other European Community	251	251	-	-	-	-	-	-	-	-	-
Other Europe	66	64	-	-	-	-	-	-	-	-	2
United States of America	117	117	-	-	-	-	-	-	-	-	-
China	14	-	-	-	-	-	-	-	14	-	-
Vietnam	2	-	-	-	-	-	-	-	1	1	-
Rest of the world	179	122	-	1	2	-	-	-	3	19	32
Total household heads	**29,627**	**29,507**	**4**	**5**	**19**	**15**	**7**	**4**	**27**	**9**	**30**
United Kingdom*	**29,043**	**29,014**	**2**	**1**	**18**	**-**	**-**	**-**	**1**	**1**	**6**
England	27,193	27,168	-	1	16	-	-	-	1	1	6
Scotland	1,204	1,200	2	-	2	-	-	-	-	-	-
Wales	232	232	-	-	-	-	-	-	-	-	-
Northern Ireland	376	376	-	-	-	-	-	-	-	-	-
Irish Republic**	145	145	-	-	-	-	-	-	-	-	-
Old Commonwealth	55	55	-	-	-	-	-	-	-	-	-
New Commonwealth	**146**	**83**	**2**	**3**	**-**	**15**	**7**	**4**	**21**	**3**	**8**
Eastern Africa	12	9	-	2	-	1	-	-	-	-	-
Other Africa	13	11	-	1	-	-	-	-	-	-	1
Caribbean	5	2	2	-	-	-	-	-	-	-	1
Bangladesh	4	-	-	-	-	-	-	4	-	-	-
India	35	18	-	-	-	13	-	-	-	-	4
Pakistan	7	-	-	-	-	-	7	-	-	-	-
South East Asia	36	14	-	-	-	-	-	-	21	1	-
Cyprus	10	10	-	-	-	-	-	-	-	-	-
Other New Commonwealth	24	19	-	-	-	1	-	-	-	2	2
Other European Community	75	75	-	-	-	-	-	-	-	-	-
Other Europe	42	42	-	-	-	-	-	-	-	-	-
United States of America	52	52	-	-	-	-	-	-	-	-	-
China	4	-	-	-	-	-	-	-	4	-	-
Vietnam	2	-	-	-	-	-	-	-	1	1	-
Rest of the world	63	41	-	1	1	-	-	-	-	4	16

Notes: (1) * Includes Channel Islands, the Isle of Man and United Kingdom (part not stated)
(2) ** Includes Ireland (part not stated)

51. Residents in households; household heads

Country of birth	TOTAL PERSONS	Ethnic group									
		White	Black Caribbean	Black African	Black other	Indian	Pakistani	Bangla-deshi	Chinese	Other groups	
										Asian	Other
a	b	c	d	e	f	g	h	i	j	k	l
					Barrow-in-Furness - *continued*						
TOTAL PERSONS	**72,564**	**72,171**	**12**	**11**	**43**	**43**	**17**	**13**	**108**	**35**	**111**
Country of birth of household head											
United Kingdom*	**71,068**	**70,918**	**10**	**7**	**38**	**4**	**3**	**-**	**10**	**14**	**64**
England	66,574	66,432	8	5	36	4	1	-	10	14	64
Scotland	2,992	2,984	2	2	2	-	2	-	-	-	-
Wales	561	561	-	-	-	-	-	-	-	-	-
Northern Ireland	847	847	-	-	-	-	-	-	-	-	-
Irish Republic**	351	347	-	-	-	1	-	-	-	3	-
Old Commonwealth	121	121	-	-	-	-	-	-	-	-	-
New Commonwealth	**440**	**262**	**2**	**3**	**1**	**38**	**14**	**13**	**80**	**11**	**16**
Eastern Africa	33	24	-	2	1	6	-	-	-	-	-
Other Africa	33	31	-	1	-	-	-	-	-	-	1
Caribbean	15	12	2	-	-	-	-	-	-	-	1
Bangladesh	16	3	-	-	-	-	-	13	-	-	-
India	100	60	-	-	-	31	-	-	-	-	9
Pakistan	18	4	-	-	-	-	14	-	-	-	-
South East Asia	123	41	-	-	-	-	-	-	80	2	-
Cyprus	30	30	-	-	-	-	-	-	-	-	-
Other New Commonwealth	72	57	-	-	-	1	-	-	-	9	5
Other European Community	191	191	-	-	-	-	-	-	-	-	-
Other Europe	82	81	-	-	-	-	-	-	1	-	-
United States of America	111	111	-	-	-	-	-	-	-	-	-
China	15	-	-	-	-	-	-	-	15	-	-
Vietnam	3	-	-	-	-	-	-	-	2	1	-
Rest of the world	182	140	-	1	4	-	-	-	-	6	31
					Carlisle						
TOTAL PERSONS	**99,059**	**98,469**	**24**	**22**	**68**	**96**	**17**	**80**	**123**	**40**	**120**
United Kingdom*	**96,843**	**96,571**	**16**	**11**	**52**	**23**	**8**	**32**	**47**	**10**	**73**
England	89,249	89,004	11	10	48	19	8	31	43	9	66
Scotland	6,462	6,439	5	-	4	4	-	-	4	1	5
Wales	500	498	-	1	-	-	-	-	-	-	1
Northern Ireland	586	586	-	-	-	-	-	-	-	-	-
Irish Republic**	333	332	-	-	1	-	-	-	-	-	-
Old Commonwealth	204	191	-	-	3	2	-	-	-	-	8
New Commonwealth	**618**	**371**	**8**	**9**	**9**	**71**	**9**	**48**	**64**	**13**	**16**
Eastern Africa	67	50	-	6	-	9	-	-	-	2	-
Other Africa	36	29	-	3	3	-	-	-	-	-	1
Caribbean	30	18	8	-	2	2	-	-	-	-	-
Bangladesh	57	3	-	-	1	-	-	48	-	2	3
India	132	69	-	-	-	58	1	-	-	-	4
Pakistan	27	16	-	-	-	1	8	-	-	-	2
South East Asia	135	66	-	-	-	1	-	-	64	-	4
Cyprus	61	58	-	-	1	-	-	-	-	-	2
Other New Commonwealth	73	62	-	-	2	-	-	-	-	9	-
Other European Community	573	571	-	-	1	-	-	-	-	-	1
Other Europe	150	150	-	-	-	-	-	-	-	-	-
United States of America	61	53	-	-	-	-	-	-	-	2	6
China	18	7	-	-	-	-	-	-	11	-	-
Vietnam	6	1	-	-	-	-	-	-	-	5	-
Rest of the world	253	222	-	2	2	-	-	-	1	10	16

Notes: (1) * Includes Channel Islands, the Isle of Man and United Kingdom (part not stated)
(2) ** Includes Ireland (part not stated)

51. Residents in households; household heads

Country of birth	TOTAL PERSONS	Ethnic group									
		White	Black Caribbean	Black African	Black other	Indian	Pakistani	Bangla-deshi	Chinese	Other groups	
										Asian	Other
a	b	c	d	e	f	g	h	i	j	k	l
					Carlisle – *continued*						
Total household heads	**40,883**	**40,707**	**12**	**6**	**23**	**33**	**7**	**16**	**31**	**14**	**34**
United Kingdom*	**39,867**	**39,822**	**7**	**2**	**15**	**-**	**1**	**4**	**2**	**1**	**13**
England	35,858	35,820	5	1	12	-	1	4	2	1	12
Scotland	3,449	3,443	2	-	3	-	-	-	-	-	1
Wales	242	241	-	1	-	-	-	-	-	-	-
Northern Ireland	297	297	-	-	-	-	-	-	-	-	-
Irish Republic**	188	187	-	-	1	-	-	-	-	-	-
Old Commonwealth	96	91	-	-	2	-	-	-	-	-	3
New Commonwealth	**255**	**155**	**5**	**2**	**2**	**33**	**6**	**12**	**24**	**9**	**7**
Eastern Africa	31	26	-	-	-	3	-	-	-	2	-
Other Africa	14	11	-	2	-	-	-	-	-	-	1
Caribbean	18	10	5	-	2	1	-	-	-	-	-
Bangladesh	14	-	-	-	-	-	-	12	-	1	1
India	71	40	-	-	-	28	1	-	-	-	2
Pakistan	13	5	-	-	-	1	5	-	-	-	2
South East Asia	46	22	-	-	-	-	-	-	24	-	-
Cyprus	17	16	-	-	-	-	-	-	-	-	1
Other New Commonwealth	31	25	-	-	-	-	-	-	-	6	-
Other European Community	210	209	-	-	1	-	-	-	-	-	-
Other Europe	94	94	-	-	-	-	-	-	-	-	-
United States of America	24	23	-	-	-	-	-	-	-	-	1
China	12	7	-	-	-	-	-	-	5	-	-
Vietnam	2	1	-	-	-	-	-	-	-	1	-
Rest of the world	135	118	-	2	2	-	-	-	-	3	10
TOTAL PERSONS	**99,059**	**98,469**	**24**	**22**	**68**	**96**	**17**	**80**	**123**	**40**	**120**
Country of birth of household head											
United Kingdom*	**96,539**	**96,332**	**19**	**12**	**46**	**14**	**4**	**24**	**10**	**12**	**66**
England	87,041	86,857	14	10	42	11	4	24	9	10	60
Scotland	8,073	8,051	5	1	4	3	-	-	1	2	6
Wales	586	585	-	1	-	-	-	-	-	-	-
Northern Ireland	787	787	-	-	-	-	-	-	-	-	-
Irish Republic**	419	416	-	-	1	-	-	-	-	2	-
Old Commonwealth	224	213	-	-	3	-	-	-	-	-	8
New Commonwealth	**766**	**444**	**5**	**8**	**14**	**82**	**13**	**56**	**102**	**16**	**26**
Eastern Africa	89	72	-	4	-	11	-	-	-	2	-
Other Africa	35	27	-	4	2	-	-	-	-	-	2
Caribbean	55	40	5	-	9	1	-	-	-	-	-
Bangladesh	68	1	-	-	3	-	-	56	-	2	6
India	208	130	-	-	-	67	2	-	-	2	7
Pakistan	35	15	-	-	-	3	11	-	-	-	6
South East Asia	155	51	-	-	-	-	-	-	102	-	2
Cyprus	42	41	-	-	-	-	-	-	-	-	1
Other New Commonwealth	79	67	-	-	-	-	-	-	-	10	2
Other European Community	530	528	-	-	2	-	-	-	-	-	-
Other Europe	179	179	-	-	-	-	-	-	-	-	-
United States of America	53	50	-	-	-	-	-	-	-	-	3
China	30	19	-	-	-	-	-	-	11	-	-
Vietnam	5	1	-	-	-	-	-	-	-	4	-
Rest of the world	314	287	-	2	2	-	-	-	-	6	17

Notes: (1) * Includes Channel Islands, the Isle of Man and United Kingdom (part not stated)
(2) ** Includes Ireland (part not stated)

51. Residents in households; household heads

Country of birth	TOTAL PERSONS	Ethnic group									
		White	Black Caribbean	Black African	Black other	Indian	Pakistani	Bangla-deshi	Chinese	Other groups	
										Asian	Other
a	b	c	d	e	f	g	h	i	j	k	l
					Copeland						
TOTAL PERSONS	**70,485**	**70,216**	**24**	**10**	**42**	**32**	**18**	**7**	**48**	**39**	**49**
United Kingdom*	**69,379**	**69,240**	**17**	**5**	**39**	**11**	**7**	**4**	**21**	**3**	**32**
England	67,010	66,875	16	5	37	11	7	4	21	3	31
Scotland	1,675	1,672	-	-	2	-	-	-	-	-	1
Wales	345	344	1	-	-	-	-	-	-	-	-
Northern Ireland	294	294	-	-	-	-	-	-	-	-	-
Irish Republic**	170	170	-	-	-	-	-	-	-	-	-
Old Commonwealth	103	103	-	-	-	-	-	-	-	-	-
New Commonwealth	**253**	**158**	**7**	**2**	**3**	**20**	**11**	**3**	**22**	**19**	**8**
Eastern Africa	30	26	-	-	-	1	-	-	-	3	-
Other Africa	24	21	-	2	1	-	-	-	-	-	-
Caribbean	13	5	7	-	1	-	-	-	-	-	-
Bangladesh	19	-	-	-	-	10	-	3	-	6	-
India	41	27	-	-	-	8	2	-	-	-	4
Pakistan	16	4	-	-	-	-	9	-	-	3	-
South East Asia	56	30	-	-	1	1	-	-	22	2	-
Cyprus	13	13	-	-	-	-	-	-	-	-	-
Other New Commonwealth	41	32	-	-	-	-	-	-	-	5	4
Other European Community	289	287	-	-	-	-	-	-	-	2	-
Other Europe	96	96	-	-	-	-	-	-	-	-	-
United States of America	46	46	-	-	-	-	-	-	-	-	-
China	7	2	-	-	-	-	-	-	5	-	-
Vietnam	-	-	-	-	-	-	-	-	-	-	-
Rest of the world	142	114	-	3	-	1	-	-	-	15	9
Total household heads	**27,752**	**27,662**	**8**	**3**	**14**	**12**	**6**	**2**	**15**	**10**	**20**
United Kingdom*	**27,274**	**27,242**	**5**	**1**	**13**	**3**	**1**	**-**	**1**	**-**	**8**
England	26,072	26,042	4	1	12	3	1	-	1	-	8
Scotland	830	829	-	-	1	-	-	-	-	-	-
Wales	189	188	1	-	-	-	-	-	-	-	-
Northern Ireland	156	156	-	-	-	-	-	-	-	-	-
Irish Republic**	97	97	-	-	-	-	-	-	-	-	-
Old Commonwealth	43	43	-	-	-	-	-	-	-	-	-
New Commonwealth	**104**	**59**	**3**	**1**	**1**	**8**	**5**	**2**	**12**	**9**	**4**
Eastern Africa	11	8	-	-	-	1	-	-	-	2	-
Other Africa	6	5	-	1	-	-	-	-	-	-	-
Caribbean	6	2	3	-	1	-	-	-	-	-	-
Bangladesh	8	-	-	-	-	3	-	2	-	3	-
India	25	17	-	-	-	4	1	-	-	-	3
Pakistan	7	2	-	-	-	-	4	-	-	1	-
South East Asia	22	9	-	-	-	-	-	-	12	1	-
Cyprus	2	2	-	-	-	-	-	-	-	-	-
Other New Commonwealth	17	14	-	-	-	-	-	-	-	2	1
Other European Community	100	100	-	-	-	-	-	-	-	-	-
Other Europe	53	53	-	-	-	-	-	-	-	-	-
United States of America	20	20	-	-	-	-	-	-	-	-	-
China	3	1	-	-	-	-	-	-	2	-	-
Vietnam	-	-	-	-	-	-	-	-	-	-	-
Rest of the world	58	47	-	1	-	1	-	-	-	1	8

Notes: (1) * Includes Channel Islands, the Isle of Man and United Kingdom (part not stated)
(2) ** Includes Ireland (part not stated)

51. Residents in households; household heads

Country of birth	TOTAL PERSONS	Ethnic group									
		White	Black Caribbean	Black African	Black other	Indian	Pakistani	Bangla-deshi	Chinese	Other groups	
										Asian	Other
a	b	c	d	e	f	g	h	i	j	k	l
					Copeland – *continued*						
TOTAL PERSONS	**70,485**	**70,216**	**24**	**10**	**42**	**32**	**18**	**7**	**48**	**39**	**49**
Country of birth of household head											
United Kingdom*	**69,316**	**69,201**	**19**	**7**	**41**	**4**	**2**	**1**	**2**	**14**	**25**
England	66,350	66,238	18	7	40	4	2	1	2	13	25
Scotland	2,051	2,050	-	-	1	-	-	-	-	-	-
Wales	436	434	1	-	-	-	-	-	-	1	-
Northern Ireland	426	426	-	-	-	-	-	-	-	-	-
Irish Republic**	243	243	-	-	-	-	-	-	-	-	-
Old Commonwealth	90	90	-	-	-	-	-	-	-	-	-
New Commonwealth	**289**	**160**	**5**	**2**	**1**	**25**	**16**	**6**	**40**	**23**	**11**
Eastern Africa	29	25	-	-	-	1	-	-	-	3	-
Other Africa	20	18	-	2	-	-	-	-	-	-	-
Caribbean	17	9	5	-	1	-	-	-	-	-	2
Bangladesh	30	1	-	-	-	13	-	6	-	10	-
India	59	41	-	-	-	11	4	-	-	-	3
Pakistan	23	8	-	-	-	-	12	-	-	3	-
South East Asia	67	23	-	-	-	-	-	-	40	2	2
Cyprus	3	3	-	-	-	-	-	-	-	-	-
Other New Commonwealth	41	32	-	-	-	-	-	-	-	5	4
Other European Community	261	260	-	-	-	1	-	-	-	-	-
Other Europe	107	107	-	-	-	-	-	-	-	-	-
United States of America	37	37	-	-	-	-	-	-	-	-	-
China	7	1	-	-	-	-	-	-	6	-	-
Vietnam	-	-	-	-	-	-	-	-	-	-	-
Rest of the world	135	117	-	1	-	2	-	-	-	2	13
					Eden						
TOTAL PERSONS	**44,711**	**44,600**	**5**	**7**	**14**	**4**	**-**	**12**	**22**	**8**	**39**
United Kingdom*	**43,967**	**43,906**	**2**	**5**	**14**	**2**	**-**	**7**	**7**	**-**	**24**
England	42,216	42,159	2	5	14	2	-	7	6	-	21
Scotland	1,304	1,300	-	-	-	-	-	-	1	-	3
Wales	252	252	-	-	-	-	-	-	-	-	-
Northern Ireland	170	170	-	-	-	-	-	-	-	-	-
Irish Republic**	89	89	-	-	-	-	-	-	-	-	-
Old Commonwealth	103	103	-	-	-	-	-	-	-	-	-
New Commonwealth	**157**	**123**	**3**	**2**	**-**	**2**	**-**	**5**	**12**	**3**	**7**
Eastern Africa	19	19	-	-	-	-	-	-	-	-	-
Other Africa	17	15	-	2	-	-	-	-	-	-	-
Caribbean	14	9	3	-	-	-	-	-	-	-	2
Bangladesh	5	-	-	-	-	-	-	5	-	-	-
India	34	30	-	-	-	2	-	-	-	-	2
Pakistan	8	7	-	-	-	-	-	-	-	-	1
South East Asia	32	16	-	-	-	-	-	-	12	2	2
Cyprus	7	7	-	-	-	-	-	-	-	-	-
Other New Commonwealth	21	20	-	-	-	-	-	-	-	1	-
Other European Community	179	179	-	-	-	-	-	-	-	-	-
Other Europe	55	55	-	-	-	-	-	-	-	-	-
United States of America	51	51	-	-	-	-	-	-	-	-	-
China	6	3	-	-	-	-	-	-	3	-	-
Vietnam	-	-	-	-	-	-	-	-	-	-	-
Rest of the world	104	91	-	-	-	-	-	-	-	5	8

Notes: (1) * Includes Channel Islands, the Isle of Man and United Kingdom (part not stated)
(2) ** Includes Ireland (part not stated)

51. Residents in households; household heads

Country of birth	TOTAL PERSONS	Ethnic group									
		White	Black Caribbean	Black African	Black other	Indian	Pakistani	Bangla-deshi	Chinese	Other groups	
										Asian	Other
a	b	c	d	e	f	g	h	i	j	k	l
				Eden - *continued*							
Total household heads	**18,017**	**17,987**	**4**	**1**	**3**	**2**	**-**	**4**	**6**	**1**	**9**
United Kingdom*	**17,672**	**17,661**	**1**	**1**	**3**	**1**	**-**	**-**	**1**	**-**	**4**
England	16,849	16,839	1	1	3	1	-	-	1	-	3
Scotland	613	612	-	-	-	-	-	-	-	-	1
Wales	121	121	-	-	-	-	-	-	-	-	-
Northern Ireland	77	77	-	-	-	-	-	-	-	-	-
Irish Republic**	50	50	-	-	-	-	-	-	-	-	-
Old Commonwealth	45	45	-	-	-	-	-	-	-	-	-
New Commonwealth	**79**	**65**	**3**	**-**	**-**	**1**	**-**	**4**	**3**	**1**	**2**
Eastern Africa	7	7	-	-	-	-	-	-	-	-	-
Other Africa	8	8	-	-	-	-	-	-	-	-	-
Caribbean	8	4	3	-	-	-	-	-	-	-	1
Bangladesh	4	-	-	-	-	-	-	4	-	-	-
India	21	20	-	-	-	1	-	-	-	-	-
Pakistan	5	5	-	-	-	-	-	-	-	-	-
South East Asia	14	9	-	-	-	-	-	-	3	1	1
Cyprus	4	4	-	-	-	-	-	-	-	-	-
Other New Commonwealth	8	8	-	-	-	-	-	-	-	-	-
Other European Community	72	72	-	-	-	-	-	-	-	-	-
Other Europe	30	30	-	-	-	-	-	-	-	-	-
United States of America	18	18	-	-	-	-	-	-	-	-	-
China	4	2	-	-	-	-	-	-	2	-	-
Vietnam	-	-	-	-	-	-	-	-	-	-	-
Rest of the world	47	44	-	-	-	-	-	-	-	-	3
TOTAL PERSONS	**44,711**	**44,600**	**5**	**7**	**14**	**4**	**-**	**12**	**22**	**8**	**39**
Country of birth of household head											
United Kingdom*	**43,907**	**43,844**	**2**	**7**	**10**	**3**	**-**	**-**	**4**	**7**	**30**
England	41,801	41,741	2	7	10	2	-	-	4	7	28
Scotland	1,564	1,562	-	-	-	-	-	-	-	-	2
Wales	297	296	-	-	-	1	-	-	-	-	-
Northern Ireland	213	213	-	-	-	-	-	-	-	-	-
Irish Republic**	120	120	-	-	-	-	-	-	-	-	-
Old Commonwealth	100	100	-	-	-	-	-	-	-	-	-
New Commonwealth	**199**	**170**	**3**	**-**	**-**	**1**	**-**	**12**	**7**	**1**	**5**
Eastern Africa	18	18	-	-	-	-	-	-	-	-	-
Other Africa	20	20	-	-	-	-	-	-	-	-	-
Caribbean	18	11	3	-	-	-	-	-	-	-	4
Bangladesh	13	1	-	-	-	-	-	12	-	-	-
India	58	57	-	-	-	1	-	-	-	-	-
Pakistan	11	11	-	-	-	-	-	-	-	-	-
South East Asia	37	28	-	-	-	-	-	-	7	1	1
Cyprus	6	6	-	-	-	-	-	-	-	-	-
Other New Commonwealth	18	18	-	-	-	-	-	-	-	-	-
Other European Community	164	163	-	-	-	-	-	-	-	-	1
Other Europe	58	58	-	-	-	-	-	-	-	-	-
United States of America	37	37	-	-	-	-	-	-	-	-	-
China	15	4	-	-	-	-	-	-	11	-	-
Vietnam	-	-	-	-	-	-	-	-	-	-	-
Rest of the world	111	104	-	-	4	-	-	-	-	-	3

Notes: (1) * Includes Channel Islands, the Isle of Man and United Kingdom (part not stated)
(2) ** Includes Ireland (part not stated)

51. Residents in households; household heads

Country of birth	TOTAL PERSONS	Ethnic group: White	Black Caribbean	Black African	Black other	Indian	Pakistani	Bangla-deshi	Chinese	Other groups: Asian	Other groups: Other
a	b	c	d	e	f	g	h	i	j	k	l
					South Lakeland						
TOTAL PERSONS	**94,033**	**93,664**	**22**	**21**	**46**	**50**	**20**	**10**	**63**	**28**	**109**
United Kingdom*	**91,915**	**91,725**	**12**	**10**	**39**	**16**	**11**	**4**	**21**	**4**	**73**
England	88,494	88,309	12	10	39	16	11	4	21	4	68
Scotland	2,247	2,243	-	-	-	-	-	-	-	-	4
Wales	779	778	-	-	-	-	-	-	-	-	1
Northern Ireland	339	339	-	-	-	-	-	-	-	-	-
Irish Republic**	310	308	-	-	2	-	-	-	-	-	-
Old Commonwealth	302	302	-	-	-	-	-	-	-	-	-
New Commonwealth	**508**	**384**	**8**	**10**	**4**	**34**	**9**	**6**	**33**	**3**	**17**
Eastern Africa	93	74	-	9	2	5	-	-	-	-	3
Other Africa	62	61	-	1	-	-	-	-	-	-	-
Caribbean	49	29	8	-	1	4	-	-	-	-	7
Bangladesh	11	3	-	-	-	1	-	6	-	1	-
India	108	81	-	-	-	22	1	-	-	-	4
Pakistan	19	9	-	-	-	-	8	-	-	-	2
South East Asia	103	68	-	-	-	-	-	-	33	1	1
Cyprus	15	15	-	-	-	-	-	-	-	-	-
Other New Commonwealth	48	44	-	-	1	2	-	-	-	1	-
Other European Community	419	418	1	-	-	-	-	-	-	-	-
Other Europe	157	157	-	-	-	-	-	-	-	-	-
United States of America	144	142	-	-	1	-	-	-	-	-	1
China	9	6	-	-	-	-	-	-	3	-	-
Vietnam	3	-	-	-	-	-	-	-	3	-	-
Rest of the world	266	222	1	1	-	-	-	-	3	21	18
Total household heads	**39,747**	**39,638**	**5**	**7**	**16**	**20**	**6**	**2**	**16**	**8**	**29**
United Kingdom*	**38,839**	**38,800**	**2**	**5**	**13**	**3**	**-**	**-**	**1**	**-**	**15**
England	37,175	37,137	2	5	13	3	-	-	1	-	14
Scotland	1,087	1,086	-	-	-	-	-	-	-	-	1
Wales	380	380	-	-	-	-	-	-	-	-	-
Northern Ireland	175	175	-	-	-	-	-	-	-	-	-
Irish Republic**	167	167	-	-	-	-	-	-	-	-	-
Old Commonwealth	111	111	-	-	-	-	-	-	-	-	-
New Commonwealth	**226**	**175**	**3**	**2**	**3**	**17**	**6**	**2**	**13**	**1**	**4**
Eastern Africa	32	27	-	2	1	2	-	-	-	-	-
Other Africa	18	18	-	-	-	-	-	-	-	-	-
Caribbean	20	15	3	-	1	-	-	-	-	-	1
Bangladesh	4	2	-	-	-	-	-	2	-	-	-
India	66	51	-	-	-	13	1	-	-	-	1
Pakistan	11	5	-	-	-	-	5	-	-	-	1
South East Asia	42	28	-	-	-	-	-	-	13	-	1
Cyprus	9	9	-	-	-	-	-	-	-	-	-
Other New Commonwealth	24	20	-	-	1	2	-	-	-	1	-
Other European Community	157	157	-	-	-	-	-	-	-	-	-
Other Europe	90	90	-	-	-	-	-	-	-	-	-
United States of America	57	57	-	-	-	-	-	-	-	-	-
China	4	3	-	-	-	-	-	-	1	-	-
Vietnam	1	-	-	-	-	-	-	-	1	-	-
Rest of the world	95	78	-	-	-	-	-	-	-	7	10

Notes: (1) * Includes Channel Islands, the Isle of Man and United Kingdom (part not stated)
(2) ** Includes Ireland (part not stated)

51. Residents in households; household heads

Country of birth	TOTAL PERSONS	Ethnic group									
		White	Black Caribbean	Black African	Black other	Indian	Pakistani	Bangla-deshi	Chinese	Other groups	
										Asian	Other
a	b	c	d	e	f	g	h	i	j	k	l
					South Lakeland – *continued*						
TOTAL PERSONS	**94,033**	**93,664**	**22**	**21**	**46**	**50**	**20**	**10**	**63**	**28**	**109**
Country of birth of household head											
United Kingdom*	**91,884**	**91,686**	**19**	**14**	**39**	**16**	**2**	**-**	**14**	**17**	**77**
England	87,885	87,693	18	14	37	16	2	-	13	16	76
Scotland	2,615	2,609	1	-	2	-	-	-	1	1	1
Wales	928	928	-	-	-	-	-	-	-	-	-
Northern Ireland	406	406	-	-	-	-	-	-	-	-	-
Irish Republic**	398	398	-	-	-	-	-	-	-	-	-
Old Commonwealth	257	256	-	-	1	-	-	-	-	-	-
New Commonwealth	**577**	**439**	**3**	**7**	**6**	**33**	**18**	**10**	**45**	**2**	**14**
Eastern Africa	102	80	-	7	3	10	-	-	-	-	2
Other Africa	48	48	-	-	-	-	-	-	-	-	-
Caribbean	39	34	3	-	1	-	-	-	-	-	1
Bangladesh	16	6	-	-	-	-	-	10	-	-	-
India	146	117	-	-	-	20	6	-	-	-	3
Pakistan	33	17	-	-	-	1	12	-	-	-	3
South East Asia	119	71	-	-	-	-	-	-	45	-	3
Cyprus	24	24	-	-	-	-	-	-	-	-	-
Other New Commonwealth	50	42	-	-	2	2	-	-	-	2	2
Other European Community	385	383	-	-	-	1	-	-	-	1	-
Other Europe	173	173	-	-	-	-	-	-	-	-	-
United States of America	128	124	-	-	-	-	-	-	-	-	4
China	6	5	-	-	-	-	-	-	1	-	-
Vietnam	3	-	-	-	-	-	-	-	3	-	-
Rest of the world	222	200	-	-	-	-	-	-	-	8	14

52. Residents

Age	Country of birth: New Commonwealth	Country of birth: Outside of United Kingdom, Ireland, Old Commonwealth and United States of America	Age	Country of birth: New Commonwealth	Country of birth: Outside of United Kingdom, Ireland, Old Commonwealth and United States of America
a	b	c	a	b	c
	CUMBRIA			**Barrow-in-Furness**	
TOTAL PERSONS	**2,278**	**6,233**	**TOTAL PERSONS**	**364**	**888**
0 - 17	269	999	0 - 17	45	163
18 - 44	1,336	2,788	18 - 44	231	441
45 up to pensionable age	387	1,087	45 up to pensionable age	59	152
Pensionable age and over	286	1,359	Pensionable age and over	29	132
Persons in households	**2,221**	**6,048**	**Persons in households**	**358**	**870**
0 - 17	266	991	0 - 17	45	163
18 - 44	1,298	2,669	18 - 44	225	427
45 up to pensionable age	380	1,066	45 up to pensionable age	59	149
Pensionable age and over	277	1,322	Pensionable age and over	29	131
Persons in households by country of birth of head	**2,705**	**6,529**	**Persons in households by country of birth of head**	**440**	**913**
0 - 17	836	1,672	0 - 17	138	251
18 - 44	1,188	2,498	18 - 44	206	396
45 up to pensionable age	391	1,083	45 up to pensionable age	65	151
Pensionable age and over	290	1,276	Pensionable age and over	31	115
	Allerdale			**Carlisle**	
TOTAL PERSONS	**338**	**947**	**TOTAL PERSONS**	**628**	**1,659**
0 - 17	35	157	0 - 17	86	269
18 - 44	204	436	18 - 44	345	718
45 up to pensionable age	62	155	45 up to pensionable age	126	283
Pensionable age and over	37	199	Pensionable age and over	71	389
Persons in households	**327**	**910**	**Persons in households**	**618**	**1,618**
0 - 17	34	154	0 - 17	85	268
18 - 44	197	414	18 - 44	338	697
45 up to pensionable age	60	149	45 up to pensionable age	125	280
Pensionable age and over	36	193	Pensionable age and over	70	373
Persons in households by country of birth of head	**434**	**1,080**	**Persons in households by country of birth of head**	**766**	**1,824**
0 - 17	148	299	0 - 17	242	478
18 - 44	180	421	18 - 44	336	692
45 up to pensionable age	62	168	45 up to pensionable age	123	296
Pensionable age and over	44	192	Pensionable age and over	65	358

52. Residents

Age	Country of birth: New Commonwealth	Country of birth: Outside of United Kingdom, Ireland, Old Commonwealth and United States of America
a	b	c
Copeland		
TOTAL PERSONS	**259**	**802**
0 - 17	27	135
18 - 44	171	358
45 up to pensionable age	34	131
Pensionable age and over	27	178
Persons in households	**253**	**787**
0 - 17	27	134
18 - 44	166	349
45 up to pensionable age	33	129
Pensionable age and over	27	175
Persons in households by country of birth of head	**289**	**799**
0 - 17	90	200
18 - 44	134	302
45 up to pensionable age	33	127
Pensionable age and over	32	170
Eden		
TOTAL PERSONS	**164**	**514**
0 - 17	21	88
18 - 44	88	198
45 up to pensionable age	25	98
Pensionable age and over	30	130
Persons in households	**157**	**501**
0 - 17	21	87
18 - 44	84	189
45 up to pensionable age	25	98
Pensionable age and over	27	127
Persons in households by country of birth of head	**199**	**547**
0 - 17	63	131
18 - 44	86	197
45 up to pensionable age	23	88
Pensionable age and over	27	131
South Lakeland		
TOTAL PERSONS	**525**	**1,423**
0 - 17	55	187
18 - 44	297	637
45 up to pensionable age	81	268
Pensionable age and over	92	331
Persons in households	**508**	**1,362**
0 - 17	54	185
18 - 44	288	593
45 up to pensionable age	78	261
Pensionable age and over	88	323
Persons in households by country of birth of head	**577**	**1,366**
0 - 17	155	313
18 - 44	246	490
45 up to pensionable age	85	253
Pensionable age and over	91	310

53. Residents aged 16 and over in households

Lifestage category		ALL PERSONS		All household heads	
		In a 'couple' household	Not in a 'couple' household	In a 'couple' household	Not in a 'couple' household
a		b	c	d	e
CUMBRIA					
Aged 16 - 24	No children aged 0 - 15 in household	7,516	31,458	2,412	2,494
	Child(ren) aged 0 - 15 in household	4,669	14,440	1,590	1,203
Aged 25 - 34	No children aged 0 - 15 in household	14,698	15,035	7,220	5,917
	Child(ren) aged 0 - 4 in household	22,874	2,906	10,844	1,812
	Child(ren) in household, youngest aged 5 - 10	8,098	2,134	3,273	1,472
	Child(ren) in household, youngest aged 11 - 15	874	732	316	294
Aged 35 - 54	No children 0 - 15 in household	26,112	45,581	12,160	24,766
	Child(ren) aged 0 - 4 in household	8,217	3,051	5,203	1,633
	Child(ren) in household, youngest aged 5 - 10	14,934	6,170	8,267	3,480
	Child(ren) in household, youngest aged 11 - 15	8,643	12,315	4,465	6,606
Aged 55 - pensionable age	Working or retired	15,872	12,162	11,335	9,587
	Unemployed or economically inactive (but not retired)	6,118	5,337	3,098	3,399
Pensionable age - 74		35,244	26,260	15,425	20,640
Aged 75 and over		12,033	20,265	7,343	17,631
Allerdale					
Aged 16 - 24	No children aged 0 - 15 in household	1,449	6,101	447	368
	Child(ren) aged 0 - 15 in household	966	2,971	331	232
Aged 25 - 34	No children aged 0 - 15 in household	2,623	2,717	1,283	926
	Child(ren) aged 0 - 4 in household	4,449	538	2,121	349
	Child(ren) in household, youngest aged 5 - 10	1,761	453	724	306
	Child(ren) in household, youngest aged 11 - 15	200	151	66	68
Aged 35 - 54	No children 0 - 15 in household	5,137	9,091	2,365	4,822
	Child(ren) aged 0 - 4 in household	1,583	519	999	281
	Child(ren) in household, youngest aged 5 - 10	3,068	1,332	1,703	750
	Child(ren) in household, youngest aged 11 - 15	1,845	2,599	957	1,376
Aged 55 - pensionable age	Working or retired	2,973	2,228	2,109	1,762
	Unemployed or economically inactive (but not retired)	1,427	1,259	780	832
Pensionable age - 74		6,874	5,435	3,014	4,237
Aged 75 and over		2,121	3,860	1,339	3,319
Barrow-in-Furness					
Aged 16 - 24	No children aged 0 - 15 in household	1,309	4,904	438	468
	Child(ren) aged 0 - 15 in household	1,029	2,405	358	291
Aged 25 - 34	No children aged 0 - 15 in household	2,284	2,212	1,149	1,020
	Child(ren) aged 0 - 4 in household	3,889	526	1,875	371
	Child(ren) in household, youngest aged 5 - 10	1,284	366	521	253
	Child(ren) in household, youngest aged 11 - 15	145	132	52	58
Aged 35 - 54	No children 0 - 15 in household	3,857	7,142	1,818	4,004
	Child(ren) aged 0 - 4 in household	1,147	570	759	309
	Child(ren) in household, youngest aged 5 - 10	1,999	878	1,129	497
	Child(ren) in household, youngest aged 11 - 15	1,212	1,920	637	1,050
Aged 55 - pensionable age	Working or retired	2,023	1,646	1,470	1,338
	Unemployed or economically inactive (but not retired)	963	850	515	543
Pensionable age - 74		5,082	3,742	2,205	3,023
Aged 75 and over		1,575	2,822	973	2,503

53. Residents aged 16 and over in households

Lifestage category		ALL PERSONS: In a 'couple' household	ALL PERSONS: Not in a 'couple' household	All household heads: In a 'couple' household	All household heads: Not in a 'couple' household
a		b	c	d	e
	Carlisle				
Aged 16 - 24	No children aged 0 - 15 in household	1,748	6,504	594	626
	Child(ren) aged 0 - 15 in household	978	2,987	350	311
Aged 25 - 34	No children aged 0 - 15 in household	3,183	3,210	1,581	1,349
	Child(ren) aged 0 - 4 in household	4,850	684	2,295	435
	Child(ren) in household, youngest aged 5 - 10	1,808	497	768	368
	Child(ren) in household, youngest aged 11 - 15	197	157	72	71
Aged 35 - 54	No children 0 - 15 in household	5,272	9,328	2,475	5,141
	Child(ren) aged 0 - 4 in household	1,652	587	1,036	322
	Child(ren) in household, youngest aged 5 - 10	3,050	1,303	1,669	755
	Child(ren) in household, youngest aged 11 - 15	1,783	2,510	928	1,356
Aged 55 - pensionable age	Working or retired	3,289	2,688	2,297	2,075
	Unemployed or economically inactive (but not retired)	1,161	1,100	585	720
Pensionable age - 74		7,014	5,560	3,109	4,400
Aged 75 and over		2,449	4,254	1,458	3,736
	Copeland				
Aged 16 - 24	No children aged 0 - 15 in household	1,043	4,595	321	333
	Child(ren) aged 0 - 15 in household	771	2,377	267	214
Aged 25 - 34	No children aged 0 - 15 in household	2,181	2,352	1,070	906
	Child(ren) aged 0 - 4 in household	3,738	531	1,793	311
	Child(ren) in household, youngest aged 5 - 10	1,383	423	558	284
	Child(ren) in household, youngest aged 11 - 15	150	110	53	37
Aged 35 - 54	No children 0 - 15 in household	3,624	6,704	1,684	3,572
	Child(ren) aged 0 - 4 in household	1,175	633	749	331
	Child(ren) in household, youngest aged 5 - 10	2,140	984	1,204	551
	Child(ren) in household, youngest aged 11 - 15	1,206	1,850	624	985
Aged 55 - pensionable age	Working or retired	2,177	1,735	1,559	1,361
	Unemployed or economically inactive (but not retired)	977	906	505	593
Pensionable age - 74		4,471	3,822	1,969	2,973
Aged 75 and over		1,264	2,485	794	2,151
	Eden				
Aged 16 - 24	No children aged 0 - 15 in household	680	3,101	221	183
	Child(ren) aged 0 - 15 in household	325	1,232	99	45
Aged 25 - 34	No children aged 0 - 15 in household	1,408	1,463	681	500
	Child(ren) aged 0 - 4 in household	2,056	206	962	111
	Child(ren) in household, youngest aged 5 - 10	675	138	253	78
	Child(ren) in household, youngest aged 11 - 15	71	73	28	25
Aged 35 - 54	No children 0 - 15 in household	2,529	4,526	1,151	2,378
	Child(ren) aged 0 - 4 in household	806	243	514	130
	Child(ren) in household, youngest aged 5 - 10	1,584	597	876	323
	Child(ren) in household, youngest aged 11 - 15	852	1,079	437	568
Aged 55 - pensionable age	Working or retired	1,665	1,291	1,205	1,017
	Unemployed or economically inactive (but not retired)	526	453	237	260
Pensionable age - 74		3,413	2,443	1,502	1,862
Aged 75 and over		1,206	1,895	732	1,635

53. Residents aged 16 and over in households

Lifestage category		ALL PERSONS		All household heads	
		In a 'couple' household	Not in a 'couple' household	In a 'couple' household	Not in a 'couple' household
a		b	c	d	e
South Lakeland					
Aged 16 - 24	No children aged 0 - 15 in household	1,287	6,253	391	516
	Child(ren) aged 0 - 15 in household	600	2,468	185	110
Aged 25 - 34	No children aged 0 - 15 in household	3,019	3,081	1,456	1,216
	Child(ren) aged 0 - 4 in household	3,892	421	1,798	235
	Child(ren) in household, youngest aged 5 - 10	1,187	257	449	183
	Child(ren) in household, youngest aged 11 - 15	111	109	45	35
Aged 35 - 54	No children 0 - 15 in household	5,693	8,790	2,667	4,849
	Child(ren) aged 0 - 4 in household	1,854	499	1,146	260
	Child(ren) in household, youngest aged 5 - 10	3,093	1,076	1,686	604
	Child(ren) in household, youngest aged 11 - 15	1,745	2,357	882	1,271
Aged 55 - pensionable age	Working or retired	3,745	2,574	2,695	2,034
	Unemployed or economically inactive (but not retired)	1,064	769	476	451
Pensionable age - 74		8,390	5,258	3,626	4,145
Aged 75 and over		3,418	4,949	2,047	4,287

54. Household spaces; rooms in household spaces; rooms in hotels and boarding houses

Occupancy type	TOTAL HOUSEHOLD SPACES	TOTAL ROOMS	Occupancy type	TOTAL HOUSEHOLD SPACES	TOTAL ROOMS
a	b	c	a	b	c
CUMBRIA			**Barrow-in-Furness**		
ALL TYPES OF OCCUPANCY	**212,247**	**1,105,369**	**ALL TYPES OF OCCUPANCY**	**31,161**	**156,024**
Households with residents	**193,893**	**1,020,955**	**Households with residents**	**29,627**	**148,864**
Enumerated with person(s) present	188,050	992,106	Enumerated with person(s) present	28,763	144,848
Absent households (enumerated)	3,515	17,958	Absent households (enumerated)	406	1,981
Absent households (imputed)	2,328	10,891	Absent households (imputed)	458	2,035
Vacant accommodation	**9,767**	**46,611**	**Vacant accommodation**	**1,392**	**6,552**
New, never occupied	1,649	8,208	New, never occupied	214	1,130
Under improvement	2,093	10,079	Under improvement	256	1,150
Other	6,025	28,324	Other	922	4,272
Accommodation not used as main residence	**8,587**	**37,803**	**Accommodation not used as main residence**	**142**	**608**
No persons present	5,941	27,302	No persons present	35	162
Second residences	2,966	14,501	Second residences	20	101
Holiday accommodation	2,968	12,770	Holiday accommodation	15	61
Student accommodation	7	31	Student accommodation	-	-
Persons enumerated but no residents	2,646	10,501	Persons enumerated but no residents	107	446
Owner occupied	1,274	5,043	Owner occupied	36	155
Not owner occupied	1,372	5,458	Not owner occupied	71	291
Hotels and boarding houses		14,266	Hotels and boarding houses		510
Allerdale			**Carlisle**		
ALL TYPES OF OCCUPANCY	**41,397**	**216,917**	**ALL TYPES OF OCCUPANCY**	**43,132**	**218,517**
Households with residents	**37,867**	**200,672**	**Households with residents**	**40,883**	**208,487**
Enumerated with person(s) present	36,876	195,906	Enumerated with person(s) present	39,780	203,243
Absent households (enumerated)	603	2,993	Absent households (enumerated)	678	3,284
Absent households (imputed)	388	1,773	Absent households (imputed)	425	1,960
Vacant accommodation	**2,089**	**10,054**	**Vacant accommodation**	**1,935**	**8,555**
New, never occupied	374	1,799	New, never occupied	328	1,561
Under improvement	457	2,260	Under improvement	452	1,928
Other	1,258	5,995	Other	1,155	5,066
Accommodation not used as main residence	**1,441**	**6,191**	**Accommodation not used as main residence**	**314**	**1,475**
No persons present	938	4,224	No persons present	146	747
Second residences	333	1,686	Second residences	79	437
Holiday accommodation	603	2,532	Holiday accommodation	67	310
Student accommodation	2	6	Student accommodation	-	-
Persons enumerated but no residents	503	1,967	Persons enumerated but no residents	168	728
Owner occupied	209	846	Owner occupied	55	271
Not owner occupied	294	1,121	Not owner occupied	113	457
Hotels and boarding houses		3,211	Hotels and boarding houses		1,161

54. Household spaces; rooms in household spaces; rooms in hotels and boarding houses

Occupancy type	TOTAL HOUSEHOLD SPACES	TOTAL ROOMS
a	b	c
Copeland		
ALL TYPES OF OCCUPANCY	**29,620**	**155,552**
Households with residents	**27,752**	**146,683**
Enumerated with person(s) present	27,024	142,984
Absent households (enumerated)	434	2,267
Absent households (imputed)	294	1,432
Vacant accommodation	**1,211**	**5,864**
New, never occupied	186	950
Under improvement	270	1,378
Other	755	3,536
Accommodation not used as main residence	**657**	**3,005**
No persons present	490	2,315
Second residences	342	1,632
Holiday accommodation	148	683
Student accommodation	-	-
Persons enumerated but no residents	167	690
Owner occupied	65	270
Not owner occupied	102	420
Hotels and boarding houses		776
Eden		
ALL TYPES OF OCCUPANCY	**20,651**	**113,571**
Households with residents	**18,017**	**100,900**
Enumerated with person(s) present	17,455	97,909
Absent households (enumerated)	350	1,957
Absent households (imputed)	212	1,034
Vacant accommodation	**1,008**	**5,193**
New, never occupied	185	981
Under improvement	265	1,342
Other	558	2,870
Accommodation not used as main residence	**1,626**	**7,478**
No persons present	1,274	5,945
Second residences	611	3,046
Holiday accommodation	660	2,885
Student accommodation	3	14
Persons enumerated but no residents	352	1,533
Owner occupied	170	784
Not owner occupied	182	749
Hotels and boarding houses		1,723

Occupancy type	TOTAL HOUSEHOLD SPACES	TOTAL ROOMS
a	b	c
South Lakeland		
ALL TYPES OF OCCUPANCY	**46,286**	**244,788**
Households with residents	**39,747**	**215,349**
Enumerated with person(s) present	38,152	207,216
Absent households (enumerated)	1,044	5,476
Absent households (imputed)	551	2,657
Vacant accommodation	**2,132**	**10,393**
New, never occupied	362	1,787
Under improvement	393	2,021
Other	1,377	6,585
Accommodation not used as main residence	**4,407**	**19,046**
No persons present	3,058	13,909
Second residences	1,581	7,599
Holiday accommodation	1,475	6,299
Student accommodation	2	11
Persons enumerated but no residents	1,349	5,137
Owner occupied	739	2,717
Not owner occupied	610	2,420
Hotels and boarding houses		6,885

55. Household spaces in permanent buildings: dwellings

Occupancy type	TOTAL HOUSEHOLD SPACES	Household spaces in dwellings with the following number of household spaces			Unattached household spaces (not in a dwelling)
		1	2	3 or more	
a	b	c	d	e	f
	CUMBRIA				
ALL TYPES OF OCCUPANCY	**210,311**	**209,067**	**236**	**915**	**93**
Households with residents	**192,689**	**191,626**	**208**	**779**	**76**
Enumerated with person(s) present	186,923	185,975	195	680	73
Absent households (enumerated)	3,487	3,448	6	32	1
Absent households (imputed)	2,279	2,203	7	67	2
Vacant accommodation	**9,767**	**9,645**	**21**	**90**	**11**
New, never occupied	1,649	1,649	-	-	-
Under improvement	2,093	2,087	1	3	2
Other	6,025	5,909	20	87	9
Accommodation not used as main residence	**7,855**	**7,796**	**7**	**46**	**6**
No persons present	5,941	5,931	3	3	4
Second residences	2,966	2,962	-	3	1
Holiday accommodation	2,968	2,962	3	-	3
Student accommodation	7	7	-	-	-
Persons enumerated but no residents	1,914	1,865	4	43	2
Owner occupied	784	783	-	1	-
Not owner occupied	1,130	1,082	4	42	2
TOTAL DWELLINGS	**209,377**	**209,067**	**118**	**192**	
	Allerdale				
ALL TYPES OF OCCUPANCY	**41,011**	**40,823**	**32**	**142**	**14**
Households with residents	**37,644**	**37,483**	**27**	**123**	**11**
Enumerated with person(s) present	36,669	36,524	26	108	11
Absent households (enumerated)	599	591	1	7	-
Absent households (imputed)	376	368	-	8	-
Vacant accommodation	**2,089**	**2,067**	**5**	**16**	**1**
New, never occupied	374	374	-	-	-
Under improvement	457	456	1	-	-
Other	1,258	1,237	4	16	1
Accommodation not used as main residence	**1,278**	**1,273**	**-**	**3**	**2**
No persons present	938	937	-	-	1
Second residences	333	333	-	-	-
Holiday accommodation	603	602	-	-	1
Student accommodation	2	2	-	-	-
Persons enumerated but no residents	340	336	-	3	1
Owner occupied	126	126	-	-	-
Not owner occupied	214	210	-	3	1
TOTAL DWELLINGS	**40,868**	**40,823**	**16**	**29**	

55. Household spaces in permanent buildings: dwellings

Occupancy type	TOTAL HOUSEHOLD SPACES	Household spaces in dwellings with the following number of household spaces			Unattached household spaces (not in a dwelling)
		1	2	3 or more	
a	b	c	d	e	f
	Barrow-in-Furness				
ALL TYPES OF OCCUPANCY	**30,858**	**30,681**	**36**	**129**	**12**
Households with residents	**29,342**	**29,193**	**29**	**112**	**8**
Enumerated with person(s) present	28,495	28,371	28	89	7
Absent households (enumerated)	399	398	-	1	-
Absent households (imputed)	448	424	1	22	1
Vacant accommodation	**1,392**	**1,366**	**7**	**15**	**4**
New, never occupied	214	214	-	-	-
Under improvement	256	256	-	-	-
Other	922	896	7	15	4
Accommodation not used as main residence	**124**	**122**	**-**	**2**	**-**
No persons present	35	35	-	-	-
Second residences	20	20	-	-	-
Holiday accommodation	15	15	-	-	-
Student accommodation	-	-	-	-	-
Persons enumerated but no residents	89	87	-	2	-
Owner occupied	24	24	-	-	-
Not owner occupied	65	63	-	2	-
TOTAL DWELLINGS	**30,727**	**30,681**	**18**	**28**	
	Carlisle				
ALL TYPES OF OCCUPANCY	**42,978**	**42,545**	**60**	**351**	**22**
Households with residents	**40,740**	**40,364**	**53**	**303**	**20**
Enumerated with person(s) present	39,651	39,310	49	274	18
Absent households (enumerated)	676	659	1	15	1
Absent households (imputed)	413	395	3	14	1
Vacant accommodation	**1,935**	**1,901**	**5**	**27**	**2**
New, never occupied	328	328	-	-	-
Under improvement	452	452	-	-	-
Other	1,155	1,121	5	27	2
Accommodation not used as main residence	**303**	**280**	**2**	**21**	**-**
No persons present	146	145	-	1	-
Second residences	79	78	-	1	-
Holiday accommodation	67	67	-	-	-
Student accommodation	-	-	-	-	-
Persons enumerated but no residents	157	135	2	20	-
Owner occupied	50	50	-	-	-
Not owner occupied	107	85	2	20	-
TOTAL DWELLINGS	**42,649**	**42,545**	**30**	**74**	

55. Household spaces in permanent buildings: dwellings

Occupancy type	TOTAL HOUSEHOLD SPACES	Household spaces in dwellings with the following number of household spaces			Unattached household spaces (not in a dwelling)
		1	2	3 or more	
a	b	c	d	e	f
	Copeland				
ALL TYPES OF OCCUPANCY	**29,384**	**29,235**	**32**	**107**	**10**
Households with residents	**27,551**	**27,434**	**27**	**82**	**8**
Enumerated with person(s) present	26,831	26,722	27	74	8
Absent households (enumerated)	430	428	-	2	-
Absent households (imputed)	290	284	-	6	-
Vacant accommodation	**1,211**	**1,193**	**2**	**16**	**-**
New, never occupied	186	186	-	-	-
Under improvement	270	267	-	3	-
Other	755	740	2	13	-
Accommodation not used as main residence	**622**	**608**	**3**	**9**	**2**
No persons present	490	485	2	2	1
Second residences	342	339	-	2	1
Holiday accommodation	148	146	2	-	-
Student accommodation	-	-	-	-	-
Persons enumerated but no residents	132	123	1	7	1
Owner occupied	44	43	-	1	-
Not owner occupied	88	80	1	6	1
TOTAL DWELLINGS	**29,272**	**29,235**	**16**	**21**	
	Eden				
ALL TYPES OF OCCUPANCY	**20,365**	**20,291**	**26**	**45**	**3**
Households with residents	**17,827**	**17,756**	**25**	**43**	**3**
Enumerated with person(s) present	17,273	17,211	24	35	3
Absent households (enumerated)	345	342	-	3	-
Absent households (imputed)	209	203	1	5	-
Vacant accommodation	**1,008**	**1,006**	**-**	**2**	**-**
New, never occupied	185	185	-	-	-
Under improvement	265	265	-	-	-
Other	558	556	-	2	-
Accommodation not used as main residence	**1,530**	**1,529**	**1**	**-**	**-**
No persons present	1,274	1,273	1	-	-
Second residences	611	611	-	-	-
Holiday accommodation	660	659	1	-	-
Student accommodation	3	3	-	-	-
Persons enumerated but no residents	256	256	-	-	-
Owner occupied	111	111	-	-	-
Not owner occupied	145	145	-	-	-
TOTAL DWELLINGS	**20,313**	**20,291**	**13**	**9**	

55. Household spaces in permanent buildings: dwellings

Occupancy type	TOTAL HOUSEHOLD SPACES	Household spaces in dwellings with the following number of household spaces			Unattached household spaces (not in a dwelling)
		1	2	3 or more	
a	b	c	d	e	f
	South Lakeland				
ALL TYPES OF OCCUPANCY	**45,715**	**45,492**	**50**	**141**	**32**
Households with residents	**39,585**	**39,396**	**47**	**116**	**26**
Enumerated with person(s) present	38,004	37,837	41	100	26
Absent households (enumerated)	1,038	1,030	4	4	-
Absent households (imputed)	543	529	2	12	-
Vacant accommodation	**2,132**	**2,112**	**2**	**14**	**4**
New, never occupied	362	362	-	-	-
Under improvement	393	391	-	-	2
Other	1,377	1,359	2	14	2
Accommodation not used as main residence	**3,998**	**3,984**	**1**	**11**	**2**
No persons present	3,058	3,056	-	-	2
Second residences	1,581	1,581	-	-	-
Holiday accommodation	1,475	1,473	-	-	2
Student accommodation	2	2	-	-	-
Persons enumerated but no residents	940	928	1	11	-
Owner occupied	429	429	-	-	-
Not owner occupied	511	499	1	11	-
TOTAL DWELLINGS	**45,548**	**45,492**	**25**	**31**	

Table 56 Household space type and occupancy

56. Household spaces

Occupancy type	TOTAL HOUSEHOLD SPACES	Household space type in permanent buildings													Non-permanent accomm-odation
		Unshared dwellings - purpose-built					Unshared dwellings - converted		Unshared dwellings - not self-contained			Other household spaces - not self-contained			
		Detached	Semi-detached	Terraced	Purpose-built flat in: Residential building	Purpose-built flat in: Commercial building	Converted flat	Converted flatlet	Not self-contained flat	Not self-contained 'rooms'	Bedsit	Not self-contained flat	Not self-contained 'rooms'	Bedsit	
a	b	c	d	e	f	g	h	i	j	k	l	m	n	o	p
CUMBRIA															
ALL TYPES OF OCCUPANCY	**212,247**	**48,033**	**63,981**	**75,144**	**13,355**	**2,861**	**5,239**	**314**	**104**		**36**	**367**		**877**	**1,936**
Households with residents	**193,893**	**43,428**	**60,904**	**68,857**	**11,805**	**2,356**	**3,895**	**267**	**62**	**25**	**27**	**192**	**127**	**744**	**1,204**
Enumerated with person(s) present	188,050	41,995	59,518	66,946	11,288	2,255	3,627	239	61	24	22	178	119	651	1,127
Absent households	5,843	1,433	1,386	1,911	517	101	268	28	1	1	5	14	8	93	77
Vacant accommodation	**9,767**	**2,231**	**1,813**	**3,747**	**989**	**341**	**477**	**28**	**12**		**7**	**29**		**93**	
New, never occupied	1,649	587	266	306	415	30	38	-	7		-	-		-	
Other	8,118	1,644	1,547	3,441	574	311	439	28	5		7	29		93	
Accommodation not used as main residence	**8,587**	**2,374**	**1,264**	**2,540**	**561**	**164**	**867**	**19**	**5**		**2**	**19**		**40**	
No persons present	5,941	1,848	935	1,951	438	111	640	4	3		1	6		4	
Persons enumerated but no residents	2,646	526	329	589	123	53	227	15	2	-	1	11	2	36	732
Allerdale															
ALL TYPES OF OCCUPANCY	**41,397**	**9,339**	**12,879**	**14,846**	**2,249**	**662**	**784**	**38**	**13**		**13**	**57**		**131**	**386**
Households with residents	**37,867**	**8,507**	**12,281**	**13,538**	**1,962**	**521**	**625**	**28**	**10**	**1**	**10**	**25**	**23**	**113**	**223**
Enumerated with person(s) present	36,876	8,271	12,040	13,204	1,869	505	594	24	9	1	7	24	20	101	207
Absent households	991	236	241	334	93	16	31	4	1	-	3	1	3	12	16
Vacant accommodation	**2,089**	**497**	**353**	**841**	**197**	**103**	**65**	**8**	**-**		**3**	**8**		**14**	
New, never occupied	374	146	37	42	129	13	7	-	-		-	-		-	
Other	1,715	351	316	799	68	90	58	8	-		3	8		14	
Accommodation not used as main residence	**1,441**	**335**	**245**	**467**	**90**	**38**	**94**	**2**	**2**		**-**	**1**		**4**	
No persons present	938	247	178	351	71	25	64	-	1		-	1		-	
Persons enumerated but no residents	503	88	67	116	19	13	30	2	1	-	-	-	-	4	163

56. Household spaces

Occupancy type	TOTAL HOUSEHOLD SPACES	Household space type in permanent buildings													Non-permanent accommodation
		Unshared dwellings - purpose-built					Unshared dwellings - converted		Unshared dwellings - not self-contained			Other household spaces - not self-contained			
		Detached	Semi-detached	Terraced	Purpose-built flat in: Residential building	Purpose-built flat in: Commercial building	Converted flat	Converted flatlet	Not self-contained flat	Not self-contained 'rooms'	Bedsit	Not self-contained flat	Not self-contained 'rooms'	Bedsit	
a	b	c	d	e	f	g	h	i	j	k	l	m	n	o	p
Barrow-in-Furness															
ALL TYPES OF OCCUPANCY	**31,161**	**2,715**	**8,157**	**16,484**	**2,485**	**380**	**402**	**52**	**4**		**2**	**61**		**116**	**303**
Households with residents	**29,627**	**2,580**	**7,929**	**15,571**	**2,377**	**333**	**350**	**48**	**3**	**-**	**2**	**22**	**30**	**97**	**285**
Enumerated with person(s) present	28,763	2,498	7,747	15,148	2,280	322	330	42	3	-	1	19	30	75	268
Absent households	864	82	182	423	97	11	20	6	-	-	1	3	-	22	17
Vacant accommodation	**1,392**	**127**	**206**	**844**	**99**	**39**	**47**	**3**	**1**		**-**	**8**		**18**	
New, never occupied	214	74	56	55	25	-	4	-	-		-	-		-	
Other	1,178	53	150	789	74	39	43	3	1		-	8		18	
Accommodation not used as main residence	**142**	**8**	**22**	**69**	**9**	**8**	**5**	**1**	**-**		**-**	**1**		**1**	
No persons present	35	4	6	22	1	2	-	-	-		-	-		-	
Persons enumerated but no residents	107	4	16	47	8	6	5	1	-	-	-	-	1	1	18
Carlisle															
ALL TYPES OF OCCUPANCY	**43,132**	**8,615**	**14,654**	**14,794**	**3,385**	**414**	**594**	**65**	**16**		**8**	**99**		**334**	**154**
Households with residents	**40,883**	**8,173**	**14,204**	**13,999**	**3,046**	**353**	**509**	**58**	**11**	**3**	**8**	**61**	**27**	**288**	**143**
Enumerated with person(s) present	39,780	7,949	13,922	13,633	2,927	332	476	50	11	3	7	55	27	259	129
Absent households	1,103	224	282	366	119	21	33	8	-	-	1	6	-	29	14
Vacant accommodation	**1,935**	**353**	**391**	**707**	**329**	**50**	**65**	**4**	**2**		**-**	**6**		**28**	
New, never occupied	328	89	55	75	87	11	11	-	-		-	-		-	
Other	1,607	264	336	632	242	39	54	4	2		-	6		28	
Accommodation not used as main residence	**314**	**89**	**59**	**88**	**10**	**11**	**20**	**3**	**-**		**-**	**5**		**18**	
No persons present	146	71	32	23	3	3	12	1	-		-	-		1	
Persons enumerated but no residents	168	18	27	65	7	8	8	2	-	-	-	4	1	17	11

Table 56 Household space type and occupancy – **continued**

56. Household spaces

Occupancy type	TOTAL HOUSEHOLD SPACES	Household space type in permanent buildings													Non-permanent accomm-odation
		Unshared dwellings - purpose-built					Unshared dwellings - converted		Unshared dwellings - not self-contained			Other household spaces - not self-contained			
		Detached	Semi-detached	Terraced	Purpose-built flat in: Residential building	Purpose-built flat in: Commercial building	Converted flat	Converted flatlet	Not self-contained flat	Not self-contained 'rooms'	Bedsit	Not self-contained flat	Not self-contained 'rooms'	Bedsit	
a	b	c	d	e	f	g	h	i	j	k	l	m	n	o	p
Copeland															
ALL TYPES OF OCCUPANCY	**29,620**	**5,341**	**10,437**	**11,172**	**1,416**	**351**	**459**	**36**	**18**		**5**	**36**		**113**	**236**
Households with residents	**27,752**	**4,916**	**10,106**	**10,448**	**1,291**	**282**	**354**	**25**	**4**	**7**	**1**	**12**	**17**	**88**	**201**
Enumerated with person(s) present	27,024	4,765	9,887	10,209	1,231	270	326	22	4	7	1	12	17	80	193
Absent households	728	151	219	239	60	12	28	3	-	-	-	-	-	8	8
Vacant accommodation	**1,211**	**263**	**239**	**484**	**99**	**42**	**47**	**10**	**7**		**2**	**2**		**16**	
New, never occupied	186	85	33	19	41	1	-	-	7		-	-		-	
Other	1,025	178	206	465	58	41	47	10	-		2	2		16	
Accommodation not used as main residence	**657**	**162**	**92**	**240**	**26**	**27**	**58**	**1**	**-**		**2**	**5**		**9**	
No persons present	490	131	59	204	19	24	47	-	-		1	2		3	
Persons enumerated but no residents	167	31	33	36	7	3	11	1	-	-	1	3	-	6	35
Eden															
ALL TYPES OF OCCUPANCY	**20,651**	**7,786**	**5,633**	**5,101**	**995**	**300**	**435**	**29**	**11**		**1**	**22**		**52**	**286**
Households with residents	**18,017**	**6,761**	**5,065**	**4,431**	**895**	**261**	**304**	**28**	**4**	**6**	**1**	**12**	**9**	**50**	**190**
Enumerated with person(s) present	17,455	6,555	4,933	4,299	855	250	281	27	4	6	1	11	8	43	182
Absent households	562	206	132	132	40	11	23	1	-	-	-	1	1	7	8
Vacant accommodation	**1,008**	**425**	**238**	**236**	**44**	**24**	**38**	**-**	**1**		**-**	**-**		**2**	
New, never occupied	185	100	52	17	16	-	-	-	-		-	-		-	
Other	823	325	186	219	28	24	38	-	1		-	-		2	
Accommodation not used as main residence	**1,626**	**600**	**330**	**434**	**56**	**15**	**93**	**1**	**-**		**-**	**1**		**-**	
No persons present	1,274	502	281	363	49	11	67	-	-		-	1		-	
Persons enumerated but no residents	352	98	49	71	7	4	26	1	-	-	-	-	-	-	96

56. Household spaces

Occupancy type	TOTAL HOUSEHOLD SPACES	Household space type in permanent buildings														Non-permanent accommodation
		Unshared dwellings - purpose-built					Unshared dwellings - converted		Unshared dwellings - not self-contained			Other household spaces - not self-contained			
		Detached	Semi-detached	Terraced	Purpose-built flat in: Residential building	Purpose-built flat in: Commercial building	Converted flat	Converted flatlet	Not self-contained flat	Not self-contained 'rooms'	Bedsit	Not self-contained flat	Not self-contained 'rooms'	Bedsit	
a	b	c	d	e	f	g	h	i	j	k	l	m	n	o	p
					South Lakeland										
ALL TYPES OF OCCUPANCY	**46,286**	**14,237**	**12,221**	**12,747**	**2,825**	**754**	**2,565**	**94**	**42**		**7**	**92**		**131**	**571**
Households with residents	**39,747**	**12,491**	**11,319**	**10,870**	**2,234**	**606**	**1,753**	**80**	**30**	**8**	**5**	**60**	**21**	**108**	**162**
Enumerated with person(s) present	38,152	11,957	10,989	10,453	2,126	576	1,620	74	30	7	5	57	17	93	148
Absent households	1,595	534	330	417	108	30	133	6	-	1	-	3	4	15	14
Vacant accommodation	**2,132**	**566**	**386**	**635**	**221**	**83**	**215**	**3**	**1**		**2**	**5**		**15**	
New, never occupied	362	93	33	98	117	5	16	-	-		-	-		-	
Other	1,770	473	353	537	104	78	199	3	1		2	5		15	
Accommodation not used as main residence	**4,407**	**1,180**	**516**	**1,242**	**370**	**65**	**597**	**11**	**3**		**-**	**6**		**8**	
No persons present	3,058	893	379	988	295	46	450	3	2		-	2		-	
Persons enumerated but no residents	1,349	287	137	254	75	19	147	8	1	-	-	4	-	8	409

Table 57 Household space type: rooms and household size

Note: Maximum number of rooms in non-permanent accommodation is 5

57. Households with residents; residents in households; rooms in household spaces

	TOTAL HOUSE-HOLDS	Household space type in permanent buildings														Non-permanent accomm-odation	With migrant head
		Unshared dwellings - purpose-built					Unshared dwellings - converted		Unshared dwellings - not self-contained			Other household spaces - not self-contained				
		Detached	Semi-detached	Terraced	Purpose-built flat in: Residential building	Purpose-built flat in: Commercial building	Converted flat	Converted flatlet	Not self-contained flat	Not self-contained 'rooms'	Bedsit	Not self-contained flat	Not self-contained 'rooms'	Bedsit		
a	b	c	d	e	f	g	h	i	j	k	l	m	n	o	p	q
CUMBRIA																
Households with the following rooms																
TOTAL	**193,893**	**43,428**	**60,904**	**68,857**	**11,805**	**2,356**	**3,895**	**267**	**62**	**25**	**27**	**192**	**127**	**744**	**1,204**	**16,497**
1	1,881	10	6	25	632	40	-	267			27			744	130	668
2	4,553	178	305	645	2,286	169	585		6	9		45	59		266	858
3	11,248	580	1,603	3,386	3,847	334	1,055		12	3		60	32		336	1,650
4	40,472	4,746	10,734	18,831	4,123	596	1,009		11	1		37	12		372	4,209
5	62,406	10,723	23,997	25,620	791	611	522		10	4		13	15		100	4,470
6	41,934	10,706	17,214	13,264	99	323	300		6	3		14	5			2,669
7 or more	31,399	16,485	7,045	7,086	27	283	424		17	5		23	4			1,973
TOTAL ROOMS	**1,020,955**	**274,051**	**325,449**	**349,382**	**37,998**	**11,166**	**16,602**	**267**	**346**	**114**	**27**	**756**	**395**	**744**	**3,658**	**78,074**
Households with the following persons																
TOTAL	**193,893**	**43,428**	**60,904**	**68,857**	**11,805**	**2,356**	**3,895**	**267**	**62**	**25**	**27**	**192**	**127**	**744**	**1,204**	**16,497**
1	51,169	7,467	12,612	18,529	8,212	699	2,002	223	22	12	22	119	84	675	491	4,717
2	66,033	16,563	20,778	22,955	2,985	762	1,284	40	21	8	5	45	34	58	495	6,203
3	32,487	7,403	11,511	12,288	412	408	311	4	10	-	-	10	4	9	117	2,603
4	31,000	8,346	11,394	10,476	148	331	205	-	5	4	-	13	3	2	73	2,122
5	10,038	2,822	3,538	3,442	36	107	66	-	2	-	-	5	2	-	18	633
6	2,514	689	835	911	10	35	25	-	1	1	-	-	-	-	7	177
7 or more	652	138	236	256	2	14	2	-	1	-	-	-	-	-	3	42
TOTAL PERSONS	**474,787**	**115,464**	**158,696**	**167,781**	**16,265**	**5,618**	**6,819**	**315**	**137**	**50**	**32**	**316**	**186**	**826**	**2,282**	**37,954**
Households with the following persons per room																
TOTAL	**193,893**	**43,428**	**60,904**	**68,857**	**11,805**	**2,356**	**3,895**	**267**	**62**	**25**	**27**	**192**	**127**	**744**	**1,204**	**16,497**
Over 1.5	350	12	32	66	19	20	6	44	-	-	5	-	-	69	77	127
Over 1 and up to 1.5	2,041	147	710	993	46	56	23	-	2	-	-	-	-	-	64	194
Over 0.5 and up to 1	61,606	11,462	21,817	22,856	2,373	854	845	223	13	4	22	41	31	675	390	5,555
Up to 0.5	129,896	31,807	38,345	44,942	9,367	1,426	3,021	-	47	21	-	151	96	-	673	10,621

Note: Maximum number of rooms in non-permanent accommodation is 5

57. Households with residents; residents in households; rooms in household spaces

	TOTAL HOUSE-HOLDS	Household space type in permanent buildings: Unshared dwellings - purpose-built: Detached	Semi-detached	Terraced	Purpose-built flat in: Residential building	Commercial building	Unshared dwellings - converted: Converted flat	Converted flatlet	Unshared dwellings - not self-contained: Not self-contained flat	Not self-contained 'rooms'	Bedsit	Other household spaces - not self-contained: Not self-contained flat	Not self-contained 'rooms'	Bedsit	Non-permanent accomm-odation	With migrant head
a	b	c	d	e	f	g	h	i	j	k	l	m	n	o	p	q
							Allerdale									
Households with the following rooms																
TOTAL	**37,867**	**8,507**	**12,281**	**13,538**	**1,962**	**521**	**625**	**28**	**10**	**1**	**10**	**25**	**23**	**113**	**223**	**3,077**
1	299	1	3	-	113	7	-	28			10			113	24	95
2	777	19	50	133	377	33	100		1	1		6	10		47	156
3	1,989	86	311	630	606	62	218		1	-		6	6		63	276
4	7,729	1,005	2,265	3,376	709	158	140		-	-		8	2		66	773
5	12,730	2,026	4,968	5,360	137	143	61		3	-		4	5		23	884
6	8,102	2,143	3,372	2,451	16	73	47		-	-		-	-			499
7 or more	6,241	3,227	1,312	1,588	4	45	59		5	-		1	-			394
TOTAL ROOMS	**200,672**	**53,567**	**65,191**	**69,562**	**6,330**	**2,404**	**2,559**	**28**	**59**	**2**	**10**	**90**	**71**	**113**	**686**	**14,840**
Households with the following persons																
TOTAL	**37,867**	**8,507**	**12,281**	**13,538**	**1,962**	**521**	**625**	**28**	**10**	**1**	**10**	**25**	**23**	**113**	**223**	**3,077**
1	9,656	1,383	2,494	3,552	1,425	168	365	26	3	1	9	16	18	104	92	866
2	12,668	3,130	4,110	4,507	475	162	177	2	1	-	1	6	5	8	84	1,144
3	6,595	1,546	2,412	2,441	44	81	38	-	3	-	-	1	-	1	28	487
4	6,330	1,688	2,324	2,179	14	74	34	-	-	-	-	2	-	-	15	405
5	2,030	589	737	663	3	27	8	-	1	-	-	-	-	-	2	135
6	467	137	152	165	1	7	3	-	1	-	-	-	-	-	1	32
7 or more	121	34	52	31	-	2	-	-	1	-	-	-	-	-	1	8
TOTAL PERSONS	**93,935**	**23,051**	**32,220**	**33,138**	**2,584**	**1,223**	**1,027**	**30**	**32**	**1**	**11**	**39**	**28**	**123**	**428**	**7,160**
Households with the following persons per room																
TOTAL	**37,867**	**8,507**	**12,281**	**13,538**	**1,962**	**521**	**625**	**28**	**10**	**1**	**10**	**25**	**23**	**113**	**223**	**3,077**
Over 1.5	42	2	8	9	-	3	-	2	-	-	1	-	-	9	8	14
Over 1 and up to 1.5	339	32	128	152	2	10	2	-	1	-	-	-	-	-	12	25
Over 0.5 and up to 1	12,416	2,380	4,560	4,580	345	189	132	26	3	-	9	3	3	104	82	1,034
Up to 0.5	25,070	6,093	7,585	8,797	1,615	319	491	-	6	1	-	22	20	-	121	2,004

Table 57 Household space type: rooms and household size – continued

Note: Maximum number of rooms in non-permanent accommodation is 5

57. Households with residents; residents in households; rooms in household spaces

	TOTAL HOUSE-HOLDS	Household space type in permanent buildings													Non-permanent accomm-odation	With migrant head
		Unshared dwellings - purpose-built					Unshared dwellings - converted		Unshared dwellings - not self-contained			Other household spaces - not self-contained				
		Detached	Semi-detached	Terraced	Purpose-built flat in: Residential building	Purpose-built flat in: Commercial building	Converted flat	Converted flatlet	Not self-contained flat	Not self-contained 'rooms'	Bedsit	Not self-contained flat	Not self-contained 'rooms'	Bedsit		
a	b	c	d	e	f	g	h	i	j	k	l	m	n	o	p	q
Barrow-in-Furness																
Households with the following rooms																
TOTAL	**29,627**	**2,580**	**7,929**	**15,571**	**2,377**	**333**	**350**	**48**	**3**	**-**	**2**	**22**	**30**	**97**	**285**	**2,473**
1	203	-	-	1	49	1	-	48			2			97	5	67
2	922	1	12	79	671	23	92		-	-		7	17		20	150
3	1,846	13	108	567	901	43	137		1	-		8	6		62	297
4	7,042	295	1,288	4,555	585	73	68		1	-		2	4		171	677
5	9,467	843	3,021	5,298	141	101	34		1	-		-	1		27	680
6	7,068	702	2,586	3,683	28	52	14		-	-		2	1			430
7 or more	3,079	726	914	1,388	2	40	5		-	-		3	1			172
TOTAL ROOMS	**148,864**	**15,322**	**42,963**	**79,102**	**7,322**	**1,615**	**1,165**	**48**	**12**	**-**	**2**	**80**	**86**	**97**	**1,050**	**11,244**
Households with the following persons																
TOTAL	**29,627**	**2,580**	**7,929**	**15,571**	**2,377**	**333**	**350**	**48**	**3**	**-**	**2**	**22**	**30**	**97**	**285**	**2,473**
1	8,012	324	1,422	4,220	1,504	87	197	37	2	-	2	17	19	86	95	689
2	9,759	958	2,692	5,060	636	96	118	7	1	-	-	3	10	10	168	929
3	5,130	516	1,545	2,804	149	74	21	4	-	-	-	2	-	1	14	424
4	4,671	557	1,653	2,322	70	51	11	-	-	-	-	-	1	-	6	310
5	1,542	177	485	847	14	16	2	-	-	-	-	-	-	-	1	91
6	389	42	103	234	3	5	1	-	-	-	-	-	-	-	1	22
7 or more	124	6	29	84	1	4	-	-	-	-	-	-	-	-	-	8
TOTAL PERSONS	**72,564**	**7,198**	**21,306**	**38,304**	**3,598**	**844**	**556**	**63**	**4**	**-**	**2**	**29**	**43**	**109**	**508**	**5,704**
Households with the following persons per room																
TOTAL	**29,627**	**2,580**	**7,929**	**15,571**	**2,377**	**333**	**350**	**48**	**3**	**-**	**2**	**22**	**30**	**97**	**285**	**2,473**
Over 1.5	60	-	2	22	6	3	1	11	-	-	-	-	-	11	4	14
Over 1 and up to 1.5	404	10	72	270	33	8	6	-	-	-	-	-	-	-	5	38
Over 0.5 and up to 1	10,018	862	3,012	5,125	602	135	94	37	-	-	2	1	9	86	53	912
Up to 0.5	19,145	1,708	4,843	10,154	1,736	187	249	-	3	-	-	21	21	-	223	1,509

Note: Maximum number of rooms in non-permanent accommodation is 5

57. Households with residents; residents in households; rooms in household spaces

	TOTAL HOUSE-HOLDS	Household space type in permanent buildings: Unshared dwellings - purpose-built: Detached	Semi-detached	Terraced	Purpose-built flat in: Residential building	Commercial building	Unshared dwellings - converted: Converted flat	Converted flatlet	Unshared dwellings - not self-contained: Not self-contained flat	Not self-contained 'rooms'	Bedsit	Other household spaces - not self-contained: Not self-contained flat	Not self-contained 'rooms'	Bedsit	Non-permanent accomm-odation	With migrant head
a	b	c	d	e	f	g	h	i	j	k	l	m	n	o	p	q
							Carlisle									
Households with the following rooms																
TOTAL	**40,883**	**8,173**	**14,204**	**13,999**	**3,046**	**353**	**509**	**58**	**11**	**3**	**8**	**61**	**27**	**288**	**143**	**3,720**
1	510	-	-	6	101	12	-	58			8			288	37	228
2	1,108	114	116	199	500	31	85		1	1		15	16		30	196
3	2,975	192	504	938	1,015	76	176		4	-		20	7		43	401
4	9,794	821	2,891	4,591	1,235	89	122		2	-		15	-		28	1,015
5	12,310	1,942	5,233	4,802	182	89	51		1	-		2	3		5	943
6	8,408	2,005	4,048	2,284	12	32	25		-	1		1	-			554
7 or more	5,778	3,099	1,412	1,179	1	24	50		3	1		8	1			383
TOTAL ROOMS	**208,487**	**50,902**	**74,418**	**68,429**	**10,079**	**1,492**	**2,051**	**58**	**76**	**17**	**8**	**231**	**75**	**288**	**363**	**16,909**
Households with the following persons																
TOTAL	**40,883**	**8,173**	**14,204**	**13,999**	**3,046**	**353**	**509**	**58**	**11**	**3**	**8**	**61**	**27**	**288**	**143**	**3,720**
1	11,167	1,398	2,970	3,726	2,229	118	263	53	3	1	7	40	19	269	71	1,158
2	13,754	2,891	4,921	4,813	746	119	179	5	6	1	1	15	6	17	34	1,334
3	6,924	1,476	2,689	2,598	50	52	33	-	2	-	-	3	2	1	18	567
4	6,401	1,734	2,590	1,985	17	43	20	-	-	1	-	2	-	1	8	474
5	2,013	539	789	645	3	15	11	-	-	-	-	1	-	-	10	133
6	481	109	190	173	1	5	2	-	-	-	-	-	-	-	1	45
7 or more	143	26	55	59	-	1	1	-	-	-	-	-	-	-	1	9
TOTAL PERSONS	**99,059**	**22,086**	**36,724**	**33,792**	**3,960**	**796**	**874**	**63**	**21**	**7**	**9**	**92**	**37**	**310**	**288**	**8,422**
Households with the following persons per room																
TOTAL	**40,883**	**8,173**	**14,204**	**13,999**	**3,046**	**353**	**509**	**58**	**11**	**3**	**8**	**61**	**27**	**288**	**143**	**3,720**
Over 1.5	91	1	13	21	1	7	1	5	-	-	1	-	-	19	22	29
Over 1 and up to 1.5	471	30	184	233	1	8	4	-	-	-	-	-	-	-	11	45
Over 0.5 and up to 1	13,194	2,310	5,043	4,756	428	127	133	53	3	-	7	14	7	269	44	1,319
Up to 0.5	27,127	5,832	8,964	8,989	2,616	211	371	-	8	3	-	47	20	-	66	2,327

Table 57 Household space type: rooms and household size – continued

Note: Maximum number of rooms in non-permanent accommodation is 5

57. Households with residents; residents in households; rooms in household spaces

	TOTAL HOUSE-HOLDS	Household space type in permanent buildings													Non-permanent accomm-odation	With migrant head
		Unshared dwellings - purpose-built					Unshared dwellings - converted		Unshared dwellings - not self-contained			Other household spaces - not self-contained				
		Detached	Semi-detached	Terraced	Purpose-built flat in: Residential building	Purpose-built flat in: Commercial building	Converted flat	Converted flatlet	Not self-contained flat	Not self-contained 'rooms'	Bedsit	Not self-contained flat	Not self-contained 'rooms'	Bedsit		
a	b	c	d	e	f	g	h	i	j	k	l	m	n	o	p	q
Copeland																
Households with the following rooms																
TOTAL	**27,752**	**4,916**	**10,106**	**10,448**	**1,291**	**282**	**354**	**25**	**4**	**7**	**1**	**12**	**17**	**88**	**201**	**2,161**
1	234	1	-	1	102	2	-	25			1			88	14	82
2	437	7	16	26	258	15	55		1	4		1	4		50	84
3	1,232	54	184	350	428	36	107		1	2		3	7		60	149
4	5,202	466	1,565	2,536	420	68	90		2	-		2	1		52	522
5	10,467	1,200	4,205	4,838	76	71	50		-	-		-	2		25	715
6	6,172	1,220	3,050	1,821	6	46	23		-	-		4	2			356
7 or more	4,008	1,968	1,086	876	1	44	29		-	1		2	1			253
TOTAL ROOMS	**146,683**	**31,437**	**54,329**	**53,188**	**4,009**	**1,384**	**1,429**	**25**	**13**	**27**	**1**	**64**	**62**	**88**	**627**	**10,462**
Households with the following persons																
TOTAL	**27,752**	**4,916**	**10,106**	**10,448**	**1,291**	**282**	**354**	**25**	**4**	**7**	**1**	**12**	**17**	**88**	**201**	**2,161**
1	6,903	717	2,035	2,640	1,005	76	217	20	1	5	1	7	9	80	90	590
2	8,941	1,813	3,247	3,349	252	100	88	5	2	1	-	1	5	4	74	767
3	4,928	884	2,006	1,912	28	54	23	-	1	-	-	-	-	3	17	369
4	4,746	1,025	1,909	1,735	4	33	18	-	-	-	-	3	1	1	17	291
5	1,633	357	661	597	-	9	5	-	-	-	-	1	2	-	1	107
6	487	103	192	178	2	6	3	-	-	1	-	-	-	-	2	29
7 or more	114	17	56	37	-	4	-	-	-	-	-	-	-	-	-	8
TOTAL PERSONS	**70,485**	**13,635**	**27,051**	**26,334**	**1,621**	**681**	**577**	**30**	**8**	**13**	**1**	**26**	**33**	**101**	**374**	**5,163**
Households with the following persons per room																
TOTAL	**27,752**	**4,916**	**10,106**	**10,448**	**1,291**	**282**	**354**	**25**	**4**	**7**	**1**	**12**	**17**	**88**	**201**	**2,161**
Over 1.5	41	2	4	5	4	-	-	5	-	-	-	-	-	8	13	20
Over 1 and up to 1.5	402	16	163	199	2	10	3	-	-	-	-	-	-	-	9	27
Over 0.5 and up to 1	9,548	1,438	3,754	3,790	234	91	62	20	2	1	1	3	7	80	65	727
Up to 0.5	17,761	3,460	6,185	6,454	1,051	181	289	-	2	6	-	9	10	-	114	1,387

Table 57 Household space type: rooms and household size – **continued**

Note: Maximum number of rooms in non-permanent accommodation is 5

57. Households with residents; residents in households; rooms in household spaces

	TOTAL HOUSE-HOLDS	Household space type in permanent buildings													Non-permanent accomm-odation	With migrant head
		Unshared dwellings - purpose-built					Unshared dwellings - converted		Unshared dwellings - not self-contained			Other household spaces - not self-contained				
		Detached	Semi-detached	Terraced	Purpose-built flat in: Residential building	Purpose-built flat in: Commercial building	Converted flat	Converted flatlet	Not self-contained flat	Not self-contained 'rooms'	Bedsit	Not self-contained flat	Not self-contained 'rooms'	Bedsit		
a	b	c	d	e	f	g	h	i	j	k	l	m	n	o	p	q
							Eden									
Households with the following rooms																
TOTAL	**18,017**	**6,761**	**5,065**	**4,431**	**895**	**261**	**304**	**28**	**4**	**6**	**1**	**12**	**9**	**50**	**190**	**1,577**
1	221	2	1	4	101	6	-	28			1			50	28	59
2	407	9	40	70	151	30	41		-	1		2	3		60	68
3	867	70	149	300	210	25	55		1	1		1	1		54	118
4	3,084	616	812	1,114	367	54	83		-	-		1	3		34	378
5	5,308	1,466	2,177	1,465	59	69	47		1	3		5	2		14	391
6	3,769	1,679	1,142	873	5	30	39		1	-		-	-			274
7 or more	4,361	2,919	744	605	2	47	39		1	1		3	-			289
TOTAL ROOMS	**100,900**	**44,477**	**27,315**	**22,775**	**2,842**	**1,354**	**1,397**	**28**	**22**	**27**	**1**	**65**	**31**	**50**	**516**	**7,969**
Households with the following persons																
TOTAL	**18,017**	**6,761**	**5,065**	**4,431**	**895**	**261**	**304**	**28**	**4**	**6**	**1**	**12**	**9**	**50**	**190**	**1,577**
1	4,502	1,156	1,085	1,302	595	70	138	26	-	2	1	4	2	45	76	410
2	6,268	2,502	1,765	1,463	254	94	107	2	2	2	-	3	6	4	64	630
3	2,961	1,157	928	737	36	42	33	-	1	-	-	1	-	1	25	234
4	3,034	1,320	942	679	6	40	19	-	1	2	-	3	1	-	21	225
5	943	472	264	187	3	8	5	-	-	-	-	1	-	-	3	56
6	254	130	69	47	1	5	2	-	-	-	-	-	-	-	-	18
7 or more	55	24	12	16	-	2	-	-	-	-	-	-	-	-	1	4
TOTAL PERSONS	**44,711**	**18,230**	**12,989**	**10,495**	**1,256**	**628**	**564**	**30**	**11**	**14**	**1**	**30**	**18**	**56**	**389**	**3,691**
Households with the following persons per room																
TOTAL	**18,017**	**6,761**	**5,065**	**4,431**	**895**	**261**	**304**	**28**	**4**	**6**	**1**	**12**	**9**	**50**	**190**	**1,577**
Over 1.5	35	1	-	4	2	1	1	2	-	-	-	-	-	5	19	11
Over 1 and up to 1.5	171	32	56	49	3	9	2	-	1	-	-	-	-	-	19	30
Over 0.5 and up to 1	5,314	1,692	1,754	1,330	230	93	64	26	-	2	1	4	4	45	69	465
Up to 0.5	12,497	5,036	3,255	3,048	660	158	237	-	3	4	-	8	5	-	83	1,071

Table 57 Household space type: rooms and household size – **continued**

Note: Maximum number of rooms in non-permanent accommodation is 5

57. Households with residents; residents in households; rooms in household spaces

	TOTAL HOUSE-HOLDS	Household space type in permanent buildings														Non-permanent accomm-odation	With migrant head
		Unshared dwellings - purpose-built					Unshared dwellings - converted		Unshared dwellings - not self-contained			Other household spaces - not self-contained					
		Detached	Semi-detached	Terraced	Purpose-built flat in: Residential building	Purpose-built flat in: Commercial building	Converted flat	Converted flatlet	Not self-contained flat	Not self-contained 'rooms'	Bedsit	Not self-contained flat	Not self-contained 'rooms'	Bedsit			
a	b	c	d	e	f	g	h	i	j	k	l	m	n	o		p	q
South Lakeland																	
Households with the following rooms																	
TOTAL	**39,747**	**12,491**	**11,319**	**10,870**	**2,234**	**606**	**1,753**	**80**	**30**	**8**	**5**	**60**	**21**	**108**		**162**	**3,489**
1	414	6	2	13	166	12	-	80			5			108		22	137
2	902	28	71	138	329	37	212		3	2		14	9			59	204
3	2,339	165	347	601	687	92	362		4	-		22	5			54	409
4	7,621	1,543	1,913	2,659	807	154	506		6	1		9	2			21	844
5	12,124	3,246	4,393	3,857	196	138	279		4	1		2	2			6	857
6	8,415	2,957	3,016	2,152	32	90	152		5	2		7	2				556
7 or more	7,932	4,546	1,577	1,450	17	83	242		8	2		6	1				482
TOTAL ROOMS	**215,349**	**78,346**	**61,233**	**56,326**	**7,416**	**2,917**	**8,001**	**80**	**164**	**41**	**5**	**226**	**70**	**108**		**416**	**16,650**
Households with the following persons																	
TOTAL	**39,747**	**12,491**	**11,319**	**10,870**	**2,234**	**606**	**1,753**	**80**	**30**	**8**	**5**	**60**	**21**	**108**		**162**	**3,489**
1	10,929	2,489	2,606	3,089	1,454	180	822	61	13	3	2	35	17	91		67	1,004
2	14,643	5,269	4,043	3,763	622	191	615	19	9	4	3	17	2	15		71	1,399
3	5,949	1,824	1,931	1,796	105	105	163	-	3	-	-	3	2	2		15	522
4	5,818	2,022	1,976	1,576	37	90	103	-	4	1	-	3	-	-		6	417
5	1,877	688	602	503	13	32	35	-	1	-	-	2	-	-		1	111
6	436	168	129	114	2	7	14	-	-	-	-	-	-	-		2	31
7 or more	95	31	32	29	1	1	1	-	-	-	-	-	-	-		-	5
TOTAL PERSONS	**94,033**	**31,264**	**28,406**	**25,718**	**3,246**	**1,446**	**3,221**	**99**	**61**	**15**	**8**	**100**	**27**	**127**		**295**	**7,814**
Households with the following persons per room																	
TOTAL	**39,747**	**12,491**	**11,319**	**10,870**	**2,234**	**606**	**1,753**	**80**	**30**	**8**	**5**	**60**	**21**	**108**		**162**	**3,489**
Over 1.5	81	6	5	5	6	6	3	19	-	-	3	-	-	17		11	39
Over 1 and up to 1.5	254	27	107	90	5	11	6	-	-	-	-	-	-	-		8	29
Over 0.5 and up to 1	11,116	2,780	3,694	3,275	534	219	360	61	5	1	2	16	1	91		77	1,098
Up to 0.5	28,296	9,678	7,513	7,500	1,689	370	1,384	-	25	7	-	44	20	-		66	2,323

58. Households with residents

Tenure and amenities	TOTAL HOUSE-HOLDS	Household space type in permanent buildings: Unshared dwellings - purpose-built: Detached	Semi-detached	Terraced	Purpose-built flat in: Residential building	Commercial building	Unshared dwellings - converted: Converted flat	Converted flatlet	Unshared dwellings - not self-contained: Not self-contained flat	Not self-contained 'rooms'	Bedsit	Other household spaces - not self-contained: Not self-contained flat	Not self-contained 'rooms'	Bedsit	Non-permanent accomm-odation
a	b	c	d	e	f	g	h	i	j	k	l	m	n	o	p
					CUMBRIA										
TOTAL HOUSEHOLDS	**193,893**	**43,428**	**60,904**	**68,857**	**11,805**	**2,356**	**3,895**	**267**	**62**	**25**	**27**	**192**	**127**	**744**	**1,204**
Owner occupied - owned outright	56,657	19,499	16,258	17,626	1,262	362	921	5	12	4	1	25	15	5	662
- buying	79,159	18,789	27,356	30,068	1,193	642	868	19	17	3	1	30	9	5	159
Rented privately - furnished	5,294	606	675	1,563	270	344	700	124	15	7	14	90	78	598	210
- unfurnished	8,487	1,769	1,629	2,905	869	406	678	37	12	8	3	31	13	53	74
Rented with a job or business	4,951	2,240	1,070	697	178	520	144	4	2	3	2	7	-	20	64
Rented from a housing association	7,353	127	2,568	2,708	1,612	14	248	25	2	-	2	3	10	33	1
Rented from a local authority or new town	31,992	398	11,348	13,290	6,421	68	336	53	2	-	4	6	2	30	34
Exclusive use of bath/shower and inside WC	**191,399**	**43,192**	**60,687**	**67,957**	**11,551**	**2,314**	**3,895**	**267**	**62**		**18**	**192**		**317**	**947**
With central heating - all rooms	110,986	32,422	36,927	29,306	7,767	1,306	2,343	134	29		12	80		141	519
- some rooms	31,574	6,420	10,283	12,245	1,509	338	604	14	17		1	26		37	80
No central heating	48,839	4,350	13,477	26,406	2,275	670	948	119	16		5	86		139	348
Exclusive use of bath/shower, shared or no inside WC	**614**	**93**	**117**	**334**	**15**	**6**	**-**	**-**		**1**	**-**		**2**	**3**	**43**
With central heating - all rooms	72	18	11	19	10	2	-	-		-	-		-	1	11
- some rooms	68	14	21	26	-	1	-	-		-	-		1	-	5
No central heating	474	61	85	289	5	3	-	-		1	-		1	2	27
Exclusive use of inside WC, shared or no bath/shower	**532**	**32**	**42**	**142**	**224**	**5**	**-**	**-**		**4**	**-**		**8**	**11**	**64**
With central heating - all rooms	251	1	11	14	210	1	-	-		3	-		2	2	7
- some rooms	32	4	5	13	8	-	-	-		1	-		-	-	1
No central heating	249	27	26	115	6	4	-	-		-	-		6	9	56
Lacking or sharing use of bath/shower and inside WC	**1,348**	**111**	**58**	**424**	**15**	**31**	**-**	**-**		**20**	**9**		**117**	**413**	**150**
With central heating - all rooms	217	3	2	6	9	8	-	-		5	2		36	136	10
- some rooms	60	1	1	16	1	4	-	-		4	-		12	17	4
No central heating	1,071	107	55	402	5	19	-	-		11	7		69	260	136

Table 58 Household space type: tenure and amenities – continued

58. Households with residents

Tenure and amenities	TOTAL HOUSE-HOLDS	Household space type in permanent buildings														Non-permanent accomm-odation
		Unshared dwellings - purpose-built					Unshared dwellings - converted		Unshared dwellings - not self-contained			Other household spaces - not self-contained			
		Detached	Semi-detached	Terraced	Purpose-built flat in: Residential building	Purpose-built flat in: Commercial building	Converted flat	Converted flatlet	Not self-contained flat	Not self-contained 'rooms'	Bedsit	Not self-contained flat	Not self-contained 'rooms'	Bedsit	
a	b	c	d	e	f	g	h	i	j	k	l	m	n	o	p
					Allerdale										
TOTAL HOUSEHOLDS	**37,867**	**8,507**	**12,281**	**13,538**	**1,962**	**521**	**625**	**28**	**10**	**1**	**10**	**25**	**23**	**113**	**223**
Owner occupied - owned outright	10,903	3,934	2,827	3,609	217	78	98	-	1	-	-	2	1	1	135
- buying	14,160	3,725	4,711	5,256	169	144	102	-	5	-	-	6	4	4	34
Rented privately - furnished	864	105	105	251	44	87	124	15	1	-	7	11	9	79	26
- unfurnished	1,421	277	272	592	38	85	115	4	1	1	1	3	4	13	15
Rented with a job or business	818	384	159	113	16	108	21	2	-	-	1	1	-	1	12
Rented from a housing association	2,994	31	1,518	1,092	278	4	54	3	-	-	1	1	5	7	-
Rented from a local authority or new town	6,707	51	2,689	2,625	1,200	15	111	4	2	-	-	1	-	8	1
Exclusive use of bath/shower and inside WC	**37,407**	**8,473**	**12,226**	**13,355**	**1,918**	**514**	**625**	**28**	**10**		**4**	**25**		**45**	**184**
With central heating - all rooms	23,553	6,413	7,691	6,951	1,627	299	412	10	5		3	15		28	99
- some rooms	5,378	1,179	1,914	1,983	120	76	72	5	3		-	1		5	20
No central heating	8,476	881	2,621	4,421	171	139	141	13	2		1	9		12	65
Exclusive use of bath/shower, shared or no inside WC	**125**	**13**	**23**	**74**	**4**	**1**	**-**	**-**		**-**	**-**		**-**	**2**	**8**
With central heating - all rooms	20	4	3	5	4	1	-	-		-	-		-	1	2
- some rooms	9	-	3	4	-	-	-	-		-	-		-	-	2
No central heating	96	9	17	65	-	-	-	-		-	-		-	1	4
Exclusive use of inside WC, shared or no bath/shower	**106**	**5**	**17**	**31**	**38**	**1**	**-**	**-**		**1**	**-**		**2**	**3**	**8**
With central heating - all rooms	47	-	5	3	37	-	-	-		1	-		-	-	1
- some rooms	7	2	2	2	1	-	-	-		-	-		-	-	-
No central heating	52	3	10	26	-	1	-	-		-	-		2	3	7
Lacking or sharing use of bath/shower and inside WC	**229**	**16**	**15**	**78**	**2**	**5**	**-**	**-**		**-**	**6**		**21**	**63**	**23**
With central heating - all rooms	58	-	1	-	-	2	-	-		-	2		13	36	4
- some rooms	6	-	-	3	1	-	-	-		-	-		-	2	-
No central heating	165	16	14	75	1	3	-	-		-	4		8	25	19

Table 58 Household space type: tenure and amenities – **continued**

58. Households with residents

Tenure and amenities	TOTAL HOUSE-HOLDS	Household space type in permanent buildings														Non-permanent accomm-odation
		Unshared dwellings - purpose-built					Unshared dwellings - converted		Unshared dwellings - not self-contained			Other household spaces - not self-contained			
		Detached	Semi-detached	Terraced	Purpose-built flat in: Residential building	Purpose-built flat in: Commercial building	Converted flat	Converted flatlet	Not self-contained flat	Not self-contained 'rooms'	Bedsit	Not self-contained flat	Not self-contained 'rooms'	Bedsit	
a	b	c	d	e	f	g	h	i	j	k	l	m	n	o	p
Barrow-in-Furness															
TOTAL HOUSEHOLDS	**29,627**	**2,580**	**7,929**	**15,571**	**2,377**	**333**	**350**	**48**	**3**	**-**	**2**	**22**	**30**	**97**	**285**
Owner occupied - owned outright	9,214	959	2,785	5,069	81	42	63	2	-	-	-	2	1	1	209
- buying	14,010	1,511	4,453	7,777	80	104	34	2	1	-	-	2	3	-	43
Rented privately - furnished	838	24	57	385	49	62	110	23	-	-	1	15	19	70	23
- unfurnished	1,107	22	36	280	668	35	39	2	2	-	1	1	2	12	7
Rented with a job or business	269	46	45	67	34	73	2	-	-	-	-	1	-	1	-
Rented from a housing association	348	3	16	92	188	-	25	6	-	-	-	1	4	13	-
Rented from a local authority or new town	3,841	15	537	1,901	1,277	17	77	13	-	-	-	-	1	-	3
Exclusive use of bath/shower and inside WC	**29,233**	**2,573**	**7,917**	**15,324**	**2,368**	**330**	**350**	**48**	**3**		**-**	**22**		**25**	**273**
With central heating - all rooms	13,010	2,191	4,960	4,427	912	153	110	21	-		-	6		5	225
- some rooms	4,203	224	1,171	2,313	398	42	41	1	-		-	-		3	10
No central heating	12,020	158	1,786	8,584	1,058	135	199	26	3		-	16		17	38
Exclusive use of bath/shower, shared or no inside WC	**104**	**1**	**8**	**88**	**2**	**-**	**-**	**-**		**-**	**-**		**-**	**-**	**5**
With central heating - all rooms	6	-	1	5	-	-	-	-		-	-		-	-	-
- some rooms	6	-	1	4	-	-	-	-		-	-		-	-	1
No central heating	92	1	6	79	2	-	-	-		-	-		-	-	4
Exclusive use of inside WC, shared or no bath/shower	**32**	**1**	**2**	**20**	**4**	**-**	**-**	**-**		**-**	**-**		**2**	**3**	**-**
With central heating - all rooms	3	-	1	1	1	-	-	-		-	-		-	-	-
- some rooms	2	-	-	2	-	-	-	-		-	-		-	-	-
No central heating	27	1	1	17	3	-	-	-		-	-		2	3	-
Lacking or sharing use of bath/shower and inside WC	**258**	**5**	**2**	**139**	**3**	**3**	**-**	**-**		**-**	**2**		**28**	**69**	**7**
With central heating - all rooms	20	-	-	-	-	-	-	-		-	-		3	17	-
- some rooms	10	-	-	7	-	1	-	-		-	-		2	-	-
No central heating	228	5	2	132	3	2	-	-		-	2		23	52	7

Table 58 Household space type: tenure and amenities – **continued**

58. Households with residents

Tenure and amenities	TOTAL HOUSE-HOLDS	Household space type in permanent buildings: Unshared dwellings - purpose-built: Detached	Semi-detached	Terraced	Purpose-built flat in: Residential building	Commercial building	Unshared dwellings - converted: Converted flat	Converted flatlet	Unshared dwellings - not self-contained: Not self-contained flat	Not self-contained 'rooms'	Bedsit	Other household spaces - not self-contained: Not self-contained flat	Not self-contained 'rooms'	Bedsit	Non-permanent accomm-odation
a	b	c	d	e	f	g	h	i	j	k	l	m	n	o	p
Carlisle															
TOTAL HOUSEHOLDS	**40,883**	**8,173**	**14,204**	**13,999**	**3,046**	**353**	**509**	**58**	**11**	**3**	**8**	**61**	**27**	**288**	**143**
Owner occupied - owned outright	9,922	3,155	3,617	2,576	374	43	78	1	1	-	-	8	2	1	66
- buying	17,543	4,027	6,715	6,188	409	86	90	1	2	1	-	6	1	-	17
Rented privately - furnished	1,157	83	144	296	44	58	141	30	5	2	4	34	19	259	38
- unfurnished	1,416	307	314	551	41	71	90	4	1	-	-	8	4	14	11
Rented with a job or business	913	373	249	148	39	78	16	1	1	-	-	-	-	2	6
Rented from a housing association	839	5	154	208	398	-	54	5	1	-	1	1	1	10	1
Rented from a local authority or new town	9,093	223	3,011	4,032	1,741	17	40	16	-	-	3	4	-	2	4
Exclusive use of bath/shower and inside WC	**40,308**	**8,131**	**14,142**	**13,849**	**2,978**	**343**	**509**	**58**	**11**		**8**	**61**		**137**	**81**
With central heating - all rooms	23,560	6,397	8,544	5,992	1,978	188	287	37	5		5	23		62	42
- some rooms	6,464	1,032	2,270	2,532	470	37	85	3	2		1	12		16	4
No central heating	10,284	702	3,328	5,325	530	118	137	18	4		2	26		59	35
Exclusive use of bath/shower, shared or no inside WC	**159**	**12**	**49**	**78**	**3**	**1**	**-**	**-**		**-**	**-**		**2**	**-**	**14**
With central heating - all rooms	13	3	2	4	1	-	-	-		-	-		-	-	3
- some rooms	15	1	6	6	-	-	-	-		-	-		1	-	1
No central heating	131	8	41	68	2	1	-	-		-	-		1	-	10
Exclusive use of inside WC, shared or no bath/shower	**103**	**9**	**7**	**16**	**58**	**-**	**-**	**-**		**1**	**-**		**2**	**2**	**8**
With central heating - all rooms	63	1	2	2	52	-	-	-		1	-		1	1	3
- some rooms	4	-	-	-	4	-	-	-		-	-		-	-	-
No central heating	36	8	5	14	2	-	-	-		-	-		1	1	5
Lacking or sharing use of bath/shower and inside WC	**313**	**21**	**6**	**56**	**7**	**9**	**-**	**-**		**2**	**-**		**23**	**149**	**40**
With central heating - all rooms	61	3	-	1	6	1	-	-		1	-		4	44	1
- some rooms	12	1	-	2	-	2	-	-		1	-		2	3	1
No central heating	240	17	6	53	1	6	-	-		-	-		17	102	38

Table 58 Household space type: tenure and amenities – continued

58. Households with residents

Tenure and amenities	TOTAL HOUSE-HOLDS	Household space type in permanent buildings													Non-permanent accomm-odation
		Unshared dwellings - purpose-built					Unshared dwellings - converted		Unshared dwellings - not self-contained			Other household spaces - not self-contained			
		Detached	Semi-detached	Terraced	Purpose-built flat in: Residential building	Purpose-built flat in: Commercial building	Converted flat	Converted flatlet	Not self-contained flat	Not self-contained 'rooms'	Bedsit	Not self-contained flat	Not self-contained 'rooms'	Bedsit	
a	b	c	d	e	f	g	h	i	j	k	l	m	n	o	p
Copeland															
TOTAL HOUSEHOLDS	27,752	4,916	10,106	10,448	1,291	282	354	25	4	7	1	12	17	88	201
Owner occupied - owned outright	6,384	1,955	1,789	2,342	80	60	49	-	1	1	-	2	4	1	100
- buying	11,760	2,530	4,544	4,400	87	76	85	4	-	-	-	5	-	-	29
Rented privately - furnished	541	61	64	144	12	26	76	12	2	2	-	4	10	76	52
- unfurnished	651	120	119	297	8	35	39	6	1	4	1	1	2	3	15
Rented with a job or business	549	195	146	90	28	73	14	-	-	-	-	-	-	-	3
Rented from a housing association	2,167	16	739	987	358	2	59	3	-	-	-	-	-	3	-
Rented from a local authority or new town	5,700	39	2,705	2,188	718	10	32	-	-	-	-	-	1	5	2
Exclusive use of bath/shower and inside WC	**27,427**	**4,887**	**10,079**	**10,310**	**1,288**	**272**	**354**	**25**	**4**		**1**	**12**		**30**	**165**
With central heating - all rooms	17,526	3,748	6,882	5,294	1,093	169	237	11	2		-	6		12	72
- some rooms	4,422	699	1,583	1,895	136	41	35	1	2		-	3		6	21
No central heating	5,479	440	1,614	3,121	59	62	82	13	-		1	3		12	72
Exclusive use of bath/shower, shared or no inside WC	**76**	**11**	**9**	**50**	**1**	**-**	**-**	**-**		**1**	**-**		**-**	**1**	**3**
With central heating - all rooms	8	2	1	3	1	-	-	-		-	-		-	-	1
- some rooms	7	1	2	4	-	-	-	-		-	-		-	-	-
No central heating	61	8	6	43	-	-	-	-		1	-		-	1	2
Exclusive use of inside WC, shared or no bath/shower	**69**	**5**	**6**	**26**	**2**	**3**	**-**	**-**		**1**	**-**		**-**	**2**	**24**
With central heating - all rooms	12	-	2	4	2	1	-	-		-	-		-	1	2
- some rooms	7	-	1	4	-	-	-	-		1	-		-	-	1
No central heating	50	5	3	18	-	2	-	-		-	-		-	1	21
Lacking or sharing use of bath/shower and inside WC	**180**	**13**	**12**	**62**	**-**	**7**	**-**	**-**		**5**	**-**		**17**	**55**	**9**
With central heating - all rooms	18	-	-	1	-	3	-	-		-	-		4	9	1
- some rooms	12	-	-	-	-	-	-	-		1	-		6	5	-
No central heating	150	13	12	61	-	4	-	-		4	-		7	41	8

58. Households with residents

Tenure and amenities	TOTAL HOUSE-HOLDS	Household space type in permanent buildings													Non-permanent accomm-odation
		Unshared dwellings - purpose-built					Unshared dwellings - converted		Unshared dwellings - not self-contained			Other household spaces - not self-contained			
		Detached	Semi-detached	Terraced	Purpose-built flat in: Residential building	Purpose-built flat in: Commercial building	Converted flat	Converted flatlet	Not self-contained flat	Not self-contained 'rooms'	Bedsit	Not self-contained flat	Not self-contained 'rooms'	Bedsit	
a	b	c	d	e	f	g	h	i	j	k	l	m	n	o	p
					Eden										
TOTAL HOUSEHOLDS	**18,017**	**6,761**	**5,065**	**4,431**	**895**	**261**	**304**	**28**	**4**	**6**	**1**	**12**	**9**	**50**	**190**
Owner occupied - owned outright	6,321	3,237	1,532	1,223	119	35	67	1	1	-	-	4	4	1	97
- buying	6,304	2,252	1,999	1,705	181	66	77	3	1	2	-	2	1	1	14
Rented privately - furnished	478	110	83	111	22	45	43	2	-	1	-	1	4	32	24
- unfurnished	1,447	477	369	392	53	49	71	6	2	-	-	2	-	8	18
Rented with a job or business	1,061	651	210	77	15	63	22	-	-	3	-	2	-	2	16
Rented from a housing association	410	14	41	148	204	1	2	-	-	-	-	-	-	-	-
Rented from a local authority or new town	1,996	20	831	775	301	2	22	16	-	-	1	1	-	6	21
Exclusive use of bath/shower and inside WC	**17,686**	**6,698**	**5,039**	**4,365**	**839**	**256**	**304**	**28**	**4**		**1**	**12**		**24**	**116**
With central heating - all rooms	9,607	4,199	2,527	1,793	697	151	158	24	2		1	6		3	46
- some rooms	4,213	1,454	1,271	1,253	88	41	80	-	1		-	5		3	17
No central heating	3,866	1,045	1,241	1,319	54	64	66	4	1		-	1		18	53
Exclusive use of bath/shower, shared or no inside WC	**67**	**26**	**12**	**19**	**1**	**2**	**-**	**-**		**-**	**-**		**-**	**-**	**7**
With central heating - all rooms	13	6	2	-	1	1	-	-		-	-		-	-	3
- some rooms	16	6	3	5	-	1	-	-		-	-		-	-	1
No central heating	38	14	7	14	-	-	-	-		-	-		-	-	3
Exclusive use of inside WC, shared or no bath/shower	**93**	**5**	**4**	**15**	**53**	**-**	**-**	**-**		**-**	**-**		**-**	**-**	**16**
With central heating - all rooms	55	-	1	2	52	-	-	-		-	-		-	-	-
- some rooms	2	-	-	1	1	-	-	-		-	-		-	-	-
No central heating	36	5	3	12	-	-	-	-		-	-		-	-	16
Lacking or sharing use of bath/shower and inside WC	**171**	**32**	**10**	**32**	**2**	**3**	**-**	**-**		**6**	**-**		**9**	**26**	**51**
With central heating - all rooms	20	-	-	1	2	1	-	-		1	-		4	9	2
- some rooms	10	-	1	2	-	-	-	-		1	-		1	2	3
No central heating	141	32	9	29	-	2	-	-		4	-		4	15	46

58. Households with residents

Tenure and amenities	TOTAL HOUSE-HOLDS	Household space type in permanent buildings														Non-permanent accomm-odation
		Unshared dwellings - purpose-built					Unshared dwellings - converted		Unshared dwellings - not self-contained			Other household spaces - not self-contained			
		Detached	Semi-detached	Terraced	Purpose-built flat in: Residential building	Commercial building	Converted flat	Converted flatlet	Not self-contained flat	Not self-contained 'rooms'	Bedsit	Not self-contained flat	Not self-contained 'rooms'	Bedsit	
a	b	c	d	e	f	g	h	i	j	k	l	m	n	o	p
South Lakeland															
TOTAL HOUSEHOLDS	**39,747**	**12,491**	**11,319**	**10,870**	**2,234**	**606**	**1,753**	**80**	**30**	**8**	**5**	**60**	**21**	**108**	**162**
Owner occupied - owned outright	13,913	6,259	3,708	2,807	391	104	566	1	8	3	1	7	3	-	55
- buying	15,382	4,744	4,934	4,742	267	166	480	9	8	-	1	9	-	-	22
Rented privately - furnished	1,416	223	222	376	99	66	206	42	7	2	2	25	17	82	47
- unfurnished	2,445	566	519	793	61	131	324	15	5	3	-	16	1	3	8
Rented with a job or business	1,341	591	261	202	46	125	69	1	1	-	1	3	-	14	27
Rented from a housing association	595	58	100	181	186	7	54	8	1	-	-	-	-	-	-
Rented from a local authority or new town	4,655	50	1,575	1,769	1,184	7	54	4	-	-	-	-	-	9	3
Exclusive use of bath/shower and inside WC	**39,338**	**12,430**	**11,284**	**10,754**	**2,160**	**599**	**1,753**	**80**	**30**		**4**	**60**		**56**	**128**
With central heating - all rooms	23,730	9,474	6,323	4,849	1,460	346	1,139	31	15		3	24		31	35
- some rooms	6,894	1,832	2,074	2,269	297	101	291	4	9		-	5		4	8
No central heating	8,714	1,124	2,887	3,636	403	152	323	45	6		1	31		21	85
Exclusive use of bath/shower, shared or no inside WC	**83**	**30**	**16**	**25**	**4**	**2**	**-**	**-**		**-**	**-**		**-**	**-**	**6**
With central heating - all rooms	12	3	2	2	3	-	-	-		-	-		-	-	2
- some rooms	15	6	6	3	-	-	-	-		-	-		-	-	-
No central heating	56	21	8	20	1	2	-	-		-	-		-	-	4
Exclusive use of inside WC, shared or no bath/shower	**129**	**7**	**6**	**34**	**69**	**1**	**-**	**-**		**1**	**-**		**2**	**1**	**8**
With central heating - all rooms	71	-	-	2	66	-	-	-		1	-		1	-	1
- some rooms	10	2	2	4	2	-	-	-		-	-		-	-	-
No central heating	48	5	4	28	1	1	-	-		-	-		1	1	7
Lacking or sharing use of bath/shower and inside WC	**197**	**24**	**13**	**57**	**1**	**4**	**-**	**-**		**7**	**1**		**19**	**51**	**20**
With central heating - all rooms	40	-	1	3	1	1	-	-		3	-		8	21	2
- some rooms	10	-	-	2	-	1	-	-		1	-		1	5	-
No central heating	147	24	12	52	-	2	-	-		3	1		10	25	18

Table 59 Household space type: household composition

Note: * May include a small number of households with no resident adults

59. Households with residents; residents in households

Household composition		TOTAL HOUSE-HOLDS	Household space type in permanent buildings						
			Unshared dwellings - purpose-built					Unshared dwellings - converted	
						Purpose-built flat in:			
Adults	Dependent children		Detached	Semi-detached	Terraced	Residential building	Commercial building	Converted flat	Converted flatlet
a	b	c	d	e	f	g	h	i	j
			CUMBRIA						
All households*		**193,893**	**43,428**	**60,904**	**68,857**	**11,805**	**2,356**	**3,895**	**267**
1 adult of pensionable age	0	31,482	5,004	8,375	10,908	5,806	180	912	60
1 adult under pensionable age	0	19,668	2,460	4,234	7,617	2,406	516	1,090	162
1 adult any age	1 or more	6,425	479	2,156	3,227	302	73	97	3
2 adults (1 male and 1 female)	0	58,268	15,541	18,454	19,485	2,486	628	1,093	33
	1 or more	38,342	9,533	13,766	13,865	297	405	304	3
2 adults (same sex)	0	4,573	803	1,367	1,867	270	84	127	4
	1 or more	818	125	281	377	18	6	6	-
3 or more adults (male(s) and female(s))	0	23,457	6,487	8,412	7,840	180	294	179	1
	1 or more	10,122	2,868	3,624	3,361	31	141	73	-
3 or more adults (same sex)	0	621	112	195	261	9	26	14	-
	1 or more	93	11	37	45	-	-	-	-
Households containing persons of pensionable age only (any number)		51,672	10,905	14,924	16,718	7,156	253	1,248	61
Households containing persons aged 75 and over only (any number)		19,479	3,602	5,052	6,359	3,659	87	582	28
All dependent children		98,491	23,564	35,360	36,356	914	1,051	781	7
Dependent children aged 0 - 4		28,795	5,220	10,164	12,232	461	261	268	5
Dependent children aged 5 - 15		62,244	15,704	22,736	22,004	422	684	443	1
Persons pensionable age - 74		61,504	15,665	19,964	19,391	4,583	326	1,020	34
Persons aged 75 - 84		26,540	6,025	7,605	8,423	3,547	136	635	21
Persons aged 85 and over		5,758	1,334	1,521	1,768	926	26	148	7
			Allerdale						
All households*		**37,867**	**8,507**	**12,281**	**13,538**	**1,962**	**521**	**625**	**28**
1 adult of pensionable age	0	6,163	939	1,689	2,245	1,054	44	146	3
1 adult under pensionable age	0	3,489	444	802	1,307	371	123	219	23
1 adult any age	1 or more	1,286	94	546	577	30	13	18	-
2 adults (1 male and 1 female)	0	11,210	2,961	3,544	3,900	420	140	150	2
	1 or more	7,812	1,969	2,900	2,757	27	85	43	-
2 adults (same sex)	0	791	125	292	304	33	14	15	-
	1 or more	154	26	60	65	1	1	-	-
3 or more adults (male(s) and female(s))	0	4,791	1,331	1,690	1,644	22	68	20	-
	1 or more	2,040	591	703	696	2	31	13	-
3 or more adults (same sex)	0	102	22	42	33	2	1	1	-
	1 or more	24	4	10	10	-	-	-	-
Households containing persons of pensionable age only (any number)		9,992	1,996	2,953	3,430	1,296	63	181	3
Households containing persons aged 75 and over only (any number)		3,549	601	948	1,273	607	19	82	-
All dependent children		19,774	4,853	7,424	6,991	85	231	115	-
Dependent children aged 0 - 4		5,518	1,052	2,163	2,160	39	38	39	-
Dependent children aged 5 - 15		12,687	3,271	4,735	4,360	42	169	66	-
Persons pensionable age - 74		12,309	3,030	4,055	4,045	871	76	137	3
Persons aged 75 - 84		4,925	1,061	1,422	1,686	605	37	90	-
Persons aged 85 and over		1,056	231	302	356	145	2	16	-

Household space type in permanent buildings: Unshared dwellings - not self-contained: Not self-contained flat	Not self-contained 'rooms'	Bedsit	Other household spaces - not self-contained: Not self-contained flat	Not self-contained 'rooms'	Bedsit	Non-permanent accommodation	Households with migrant head	Persons in households with migrant head	Household composition: Adults	Dependent children
k	l	m	n	o	p	q	r	s	a	b
62	**25**	**27**	**192**	**127**	**744**	**1,204**	**16,497**	**37,954**	**All households***	
11	3	4	31	25	35	128	1,100	1,100	1 adult of pensionable age	0
11	9	18	86	59	637	363	3,609	3,609	1 adult under pensionable age	0
2	-	-	4	9	26	47	1,139	2,916	1 adult any age	1 or more
17	7	4	29	22	32	437	5,100	10,200	2 adults (1 male and 1 female)	0
10	2	-	18	3	4	132	3,695	13,912		1 or more
3	1	1	12	3	5	26	422	844	2 adults (same sex)	0
-	-	-	-	1	-	4	78	273		1 or more
4	2	-	8	4	2	44	791	2,625	3 or more adults (male(s) and female(s))	0
3	1	-	2	-	-	18	443	2,087		1 or more
1	-	-	-	1	-	2	107	359	3 or more adults (same sex)	0
-	-	-	-	-	-	-	5	21		1 or more
13	7	6	37	28	35	281	1,713	2,332	Households containing persons of pensionable age only (any number)	
6	2	5	15	12	8	62	541	648	Households containing persons aged 75 and over only (any number)	
23	5	-	43	16	39	332	9,078		All dependent children	
7	1	-	10	13	26	127	4,121		Dependent children aged 0 - 4	
15	4	-	26	3	7	195	4,609		Dependent children aged 5 - 15	
13	9	1	27	23	28	420	2,100		Persons pensionable age - 74	
7	3	7	16	10	8	97	751		Persons aged 75 - 84	
3	1	-	5	7	-	12	128		Persons aged 85 and over	
10	**1**	**10**	**25**	**23**	**113**	**223**	**3,077**	**7,160**	**All households***	
-	-	1	4	4	6	28	219	219	1 adult of pensionable age	0
3	1	8	12	14	98	64	646	646	1 adult under pensionable age	0
-	-	-	-	-	2	6	248	631	1 adult any age	1 or more
1	-	1	4	4	6	77	941	1,882	2 adults (1 male and 1 female)	0
-	-	-	1	-	1	29	732	2,781		1 or more
-	-	-	2	1	-	5	48	96	2 adults (same sex)	0
-	-	-	-	-	-	1	12	44		1 or more
4	-	-	1	-	-	11	145	474	3 or more adults (male(s) and female(s))	0
2	-	-	1	-	-	1	77	361		1 or more
-	-	-	-	-	-	1	8	25	3 or more adults (same sex)	0
-	-	-	-	-	-	-	-	-		1 or more
-	-	1	6	4	6	53	335	453	Households containing persons of pensionable age only (any number)	
-	-	-	3	-	2	14	84	103	Households containing persons aged 75 and over only (any number)	
5	-	-	3	-	3	64	1,832		All dependent children	
-	-	-	-	-	3	24	806		Dependent children aged 0 - 4	
4	-	-	3	-	-	37	959		Dependent children aged 5 - 15	
2	-	1	5	4	4	76	427		Persons pensionable age - 74	
-	-	-	3	-	2	19	128		Persons aged 75 - 84	
2	-	-	1	-	-	1	22		Persons aged 85 and over	

Table 59 Household space type: household composition – **continued**

Note: * May include a small number of households with no resident adults

59. Households with residents; residents in households

Household composition: Adults	Dependent children	TOTAL HOUSE-HOLDS	Household space type in permanent buildings: Unshared dwellings - purpose-built: Detached	Semi-detached	Terraced	Purpose-built flat in: Residential building	Commercial building	Unshared dwellings - converted: Converted flat	Converted flatlet
a	b	c	d	e	f	g	h	i	j
				Barrow-in-Furness					
All households*		**29,627**	**2,580**	**7,929**	**15,571**	**2,377**	**333**	**350**	**48**
1 adult of pensionable age	0	4,709	203	995	2,493	841	17	80	14
1 adult under pensionable age	0	3,302	121	427	1,727	663	69	117	23
1 adult any age	1 or more	1,205	36	176	777	160	12	26	2
2 adults (1 male and 1 female)	0	8,480	904	2,508	4,284	454	73	88	4
	1 or more	5,937	629	1,922	3,146	129	80	19	3
2 adults (same sex)	0	705	39	133	432	63	15	11	1
	1 or more	137	10	25	91	9	-	1	-
3 or more adults (male(s) and female(s))	0	3,455	431	1,178	1,741	45	42	5	1
	1 or more	1,593	202	535	817	10	22	3	-
3 or more adults (same sex)	0	85	5	23	52	3	2	-	-
	1 or more	18	-	7	11	-	-	-	-
Households containing persons of pensionable age only (any number)		7,524	492	1,865	3,860	1,018	20	111	15
Households containing persons aged 75 and over only (any number)		2,739	138	628	1,451	441	6	46	4
All dependent children		15,671	1,545	4,732	8,652	442	190	70	5
Dependent children aged 0 - 4		5,058	343	1,322	3,023	245	61	40	4
Dependent children aged 5 - 15		9,593	1,034	3,042	5,176	186	112	29	1
Persons pensionable age - 74		8,824	795	2,436	4,490	753	25	99	12
Persons aged 75 - 84		3,690	260	961	1,922	443	10	47	4
Persons aged 85 and over		707	39	172	385	96	1	9	-
				Carlisle					
All households*		**40,883**	**8,173**	**14,204**	**13,999**	**3,046**	**353**	**509**	**58**
1 adult of pensionable age	0	6,716	921	1,966	1,966	1,673	28	96	16
1 adult under pensionable age	0	4,444	477	1,004	1,758	556	89	167	36
1 adult any age	1 or more	1,534	91	519	867	25	11	12	-
2 adults (1 male and 1 female)	0	11,936	2,695	4,329	3,951	648	97	150	3
	1 or more	7,939	1,944	3,135	2,716	31	44	35	-
2 adults (same sex)	0	1,044	148	353	423	75	14	20	2
	1 or more	205	21	79	102	1	2	-	-
3 or more adults (male(s) and female(s))	0	4,796	1,267	1,940	1,499	31	32	18	-
	1 or more	2,079	590	831	615	4	24	9	-
3 or more adults (same sex)	0	163	17	40	90	2	11	2	-
	1 or more	20	2	8	10	-	-	-	-
Households containing persons of pensionable age only (any number)		10,725	1,874	3,492	3,010	2,099	43	129	16
Households containing persons aged 75 and over only (any number)		4,107	651	1,167	1,080	1,093	15	64	9
All dependent children		20,627	4,702	8,109	7,429	82	129	89	1
Dependent children aged 0 - 4		6,153	1,030	2,380	2,617	32	36	34	-
Dependent children aged 5 - 15		13,103	3,189	5,267	4,417	45	83	48	-
Persons pensionable age - 74		12,574	2,679	4,694	3,666	1,321	58	99	7
Persons aged 75 - 84		5,526	1,081	1,785	1,457	1,082	19	68	5
Persons aged 85 and over		1,177	227	346	306	265	6	19	4

Household space type in permanent buildings						Non-perm-anent accomm-odation	Households with migrant head	Persons in households with migrant head	Household composition	
Unshared dwellings - not self-contained			Other household spaces - not self-contained							
Not self-contained flat	Not self-contained 'rooms'	Bedsit	Not self-contained flat	Not self-contained 'rooms'	Bedsit				Adults	Dependent children
k	l	m	n	o	p	q	r	s	a	b
3	**-**	**2**	**22**	**30**	**97**	**285**	**2,473**	**5,704**	**All households***	
1	-	-	2	6	9	48	109	109	1 adult of pensionable age	0
1	-	2	15	13	77	47	579	579	1 adult under pensionable age	0
-	-	-	1	6	6	3	213	538	1 adult any age	1 or more
1	-	-	1	3	2	158	728	1,456	2 adults (1 male and 1 female)	0
-	-	-	1	-	1	7	567	2,122		1 or more
-	-	-	1	1	2	7	71	142	2 adults (same sex)	0
-	-	-	-	-	-	1	14	47		1 or more
-	-	-	1	1	-	10	114	368	3 or more adults (male(s) and female(s))	0
-	-	-	-	-	-	4	63	293		1 or more
-	-	-	-	-	-	-	11	36	3 or more adults (same sex)	0
-	-	-	-	-	-	-	3	13		1 or more
1	-	-	2	7	9	124	161	214	Households containing persons of pensionable age only (any number)	
-	-	-	-	4	-	21	44	51	Households containing persons aged 75 and over only (any number)	
-	-	-	2	6	7	20	1,424		All dependent children	
-	-	-	-	5	6	9	707		Dependent children aged 0 - 4	
-	-	-	1	1	1	10	668		Dependent children aged 5 - 15	
1	-	-	2	3	10	198	215		Persons pensionable age - 74	
-	-	-	-	3	-	40	62		Persons aged 75 - 84	
-	-	-	-	2	-	3	12		Persons aged 85 and over	
11	**3**	**8**	**61**	**27**	**288**	**143**	**3,720**	**8,422**	**All households***	
-	-	3	8	5	12	22	285	285	1 adult of pensionable age	0
3	1	4	31	14	255	49	868	868	1 adult under pensionable age	0
-	-	-	-	-	2	7	281	708	1 adult any age	1 or more
4	1	1	11	6	13	27	1,042	2,084	2 adults (1 male and 1 female)	0
2	-	-	4	1	1	26	803	3,025		1 or more
2	-	-	4	-	2	1	120	240	2 adults (same sex)	0
-	-	-	-	-	-	-	19	69		1 or more
-	-	-	1	-	1	7	157	519	3 or more adults (male(s) and female(s))	0
-	1	-	1	-	-	4	106	508		1 or more
-	-	-	-	1	-	-	33	107	3 or more adults (same sex)	0
-	-	-	-	-	-	-	1	4		1 or more
-	1	4	9	5	12	31	415	546	Households containing persons of pensionable age only (any number)	
-	-	4	4	2	6	12	140	163	Households containing persons aged 75 and over only (any number)	
2	1	-	9	1	5	68	2,039		All dependent children	
-	-	-	2	-	3	19	913		Dependent children aged 0 - 4	
2	1	-	5	1	-	45	1,055		Dependent children aged 5 - 15	
2	2	-	5	4	6	31	467		Persons pensionable age - 74	
-	-	5	5	1	6	12	187		Persons aged 75 - 84	
-	-	-	1	1	-	2	31		Persons aged 85 and over	

Table 59 Household space type: household composition – continued

Note: * May include a small number of households with no resident adults

59. Households with residents; residents in households

Household composition: Adults	Dependent children	TOTAL HOUSE-HOLDS	Unshared dwellings - purpose-built: Detached	Semi-detached	Terraced	Purpose-built flat in: Residential building	Commercial building	Unshared dwellings - converted: Converted flat	Converted flatlet
a	b	c	d	e	f	g	h	i	j
			Copeland						
All households*		**27,752**	**4,916**	**10,106**	**10,448**	**1,291**	**282**	**354**	**25**
1 adult of pensionable age	0	4,067	424	1,264	1,559	708	18	71	-
1 adult under pensionable age	0	2,835	293	771	1,080	297	58	146	20
1 adult any age	1 or more	1,080	53	482	498	6	12	10	1
2 adults (1 male and 1 female)	0	7,776	1,695	2,822	2,817	220	78	72	4
	1 or more	5,949	1,293	2,317	2,231	7	44	26	-
2 adults (same sex)	0	647	95	209	288	26	12	9	-
	1 or more	127	10	61	53	1	1	-	-
3 or more adults (male(s) and female(s))	0	3,503	702	1,441	1,281	22	37	12	-
	1 or more	1,656	331	697	595	4	19	7	-
3 or more adults (same sex)	0	92	19	34	35	-	3	1	-
	1 or more	19	1	8	10	-	-	-	-
Households containing persons of pensionable age only (any number)		6,422	913	2,148	2,359	841	27	90	-
Households containing persons aged 75 and over only (any number)		2,233	261	652	869	397	8	37	-
All dependent children		15,833	3,118	6,433	5,973	22	128	71	1
Dependent children aged 0 - 4		4,719	716	1,920	1,987	10	32	22	1
Dependent children aged 5 - 15		9,959	2,056	4,085	3,632	9	84	41	-
Persons pensionable age - 74		8,293	1,489	3,160	2,879	582	44	82	-
Persons aged 75 - 84		3,121	458	1,024	1,206	368	12	37	-
Persons aged 85 and over		628	102	192	219	99	3	8	-
			Eden						
All households*		**18,017**	**6,761**	**5,065**	**4,431**	**895**	**261**	**304**	**28**
1 adult of pensionable age	0	2,766	749	715	790	395	22	64	14
1 adult under pensionable age	0	1,734	406	370	512	200	48	74	12
1 adult any age	1 or more	387	64	140	132	13	11	4	-
2 adults (1 male and 1 female)	0	5,667	2,326	1,597	1,295	223	77	90	2
	1 or more	3,601	1,481	1,103	868	29	49	29	-
2 adults (same sex)	0	415	148	107	108	21	10	14	-
	1 or more	59	21	17	16	2	1	1	-
3 or more adults (male(s) and female(s))	0	2,393	1,110	714	505	11	29	19	-
	1 or more	928	433	280	190	1	13	8	-
3 or more adults (same sex)	0	58	22	20	13	-	1	1	-
	1 or more	4	-	2	2	-	-	-	-
Households containing persons of pensionable age only (any number)		4,733	1,625	1,263	1,190	486	34	88	14
Households containing persons aged 75 and over only (any number)		1,803	498	461	500	280	8	42	6
All dependent children		8,908	3,705	2,722	2,114	61	125	63	-
Dependent children aged 0 - 4		2,483	905	753	684	33	30	21	-
Dependent children aged 5 - 15		5,692	2,436	1,759	1,299	27	82	32	-
Persons pensionable age - 74		5,856	2,481	1,650	1,278	276	46	67	8
Persons aged 75 - 84		2,572	884	706	631	265	13	55	5
Persons aged 85 and over		529	189	121	125	77	4	11	1

Household space type in permanent buildings						Non-permanent accommodation	Households with migrant head	Persons in households with migrant head	Household composition	
Unshared dwellings - not self-contained			Other household spaces - not self-contained						Adults	Dependent children
Not self-contained flat	Not self-contained 'rooms'	Bedsit	Not self-contained flat	Not self-contained 'rooms'	Bedsit					
k	l	m	n	o	p	q	r	s	a	b
4	**7**	**1**	**12**	**17**	**88**	**201**	**2,161**	**5,163**	**All households***	
1	-	-	2	2	4	14	129	129	1 adult of pensionable age	0
-	5	1	5	7	76	76	461	461	1 adult under pensionable age	0
1	-	-	-	1	6	10	174	459	1 adult any age	1 or more
1	1	-	1	4	1	60	628	1,256	2 adults (1 male and 1 female)	0
1	-	-	4	1	1	24	549	2,068		1 or more
-	-	-	-	-	-	8	42	84	2 adults (same sex)	0
-	-	-	-	-	-	1	9	33		1 or more
-	1	-	-	2	-	5	85	297	3 or more adults (male(s) and female(s))	0
-	-	-	-	-	-	3	67	322		1 or more
-	-	-	-	-	-	-	17	54	3 or more adults (same sex)	0
-	-	-	-	-	-	-	-	-		1 or more
1	-	-	3	2	4	34	192	256	Households containing persons of pensionable age only (any number)	
-	-	-	-	1	-	8	56	62	Households containing persons aged 75 and over only (any number)	
2	-	-	9	4	11	61	1,377		All dependent children	
2	-	-	-	3	7	19	640		Dependent children aged 0 - 4	
-	-	-	7	1	3	41	689		Dependent children aged 5 - 15	
1	1	-	4	3	4	44	240		Persons pensionable age - 74	
-	-	-	-	2	-	14	68		Persons aged 75 - 84	
-	-	-	-	2	-	3	11		Persons aged 85 and over	
4	**6**	**1**	**12**	**9**	**50**	**190**	**1,577**	**3,691**	**All households***	
-	1	-	4	1	1	10	80	80	1 adult of pensionable age	0
-	1	1	-	1	43	66	329	329	1 adult under pensionable age	0
-	-	-	-	2	3	18	69	193	1 adult any age	1 or more
2	2	-	2	3	1	47	559	1,118	2 adults (1 male and 1 female)	0
2	2	-	5	1	-	32	373	1,404		1 or more
-	-	-	1	1	1	4	35	70	2 adults (same sex)	0
-	-	-	-	-	-	1	4	16		1 or more
-	-	-	-	-	-	5	78	258	3 or more adults (male(s) and female(s))	0
-	-	-	-	-	-	3	38	183		1 or more
-	-	-	-	-	-	1	11	39	3 or more adults (same sex)	0
-	-	-	-	-	-	-	-	-		1 or more
1	2	-	5	2	1	22	155	230	Households containing persons of pensionable age only (any number)	
1	-	-	2	1	-	4	49	63	Households containing persons aged 75 and over only (any number)	
3	4	-	10	4	5	92	855		All dependent children	
2	1	-	6	4	1	43	372		Dependent children aged 0 - 4	
1	3	-	4	-	1	48	445		Dependent children aged 5 - 15	
-	3	-	4	2	1	40	215		Persons pensionable age - 74	
2	1	-	2	2	-	6	76		Persons aged 75 - 84	
-	-	-	-	-	-	1	13		Persons aged 85 and over	

Table 59 Household space type: household composition - **continued**

Note: * May include a small number of households with no resident adults

59. Households with residents; residents in households

Household composition: Adults	Dependent children	TOTAL HOUSE-HOLDS	Unshared dwellings - purpose-built: Detached	Semi-detached	Terraced	Purpose-built flat in: Residential building	Commercial building	Unshared dwellings - converted: Converted flat	Converted flatlet
a	b	c	d	e	f	g	h	i	j
			South Lakeland						
All households*		**39,747**	**12,491**	**11,319**	**10,870**	**2,234**	**606**	**1,753**	**80**
1 adult of pensionable age	0	7,061	1,768	1,746	1,855	1,135	51	455	13
1 adult under pensionable age	0	3,864	719	860	1,233	319	129	367	48
1 adult any age	1 or more	933	141	293	376	68	14	27	-
2 adults (1 male and 1 female)	0	13,199	4,960	3,654	3,238	521	163	543	18
	1 or more	7,104	2,217	2,389	2,147	74	103	152	-
2 adults (same sex)	0	971	248	273	312	52	19	58	1
	1 or more	136	37	39	50	4	1	4	-
3 or more adults (male(s) and female(s))	0	4,519	1,646	1,449	1,170	49	86	105	-
	1 or more	1,826	721	578	448	10	32	33	-
3 or more adults (same sex)	0	121	27	36	38	2	8	9	-
	1 or more	8	4	2	2	-	-	-	-
Households containing persons of pensionable age only (any number)		12,276	4,005	3,203	2,869	1,416	66	649	13
Households containing persons aged 75 and over only (any number)		5,048	1,453	1,196	1,186	841	31	311	9
All dependent children		17,678	5,641	5,940	5,197	222	248	373	-
Dependent children aged 0 - 4		4,864	1,174	1,626	1,761	102	64	112	-
Dependent children aged 5 - 15		11,210	3,718	3,848	3,120	113	154	227	-
Persons pensionable age - 74		13,648	5,191	3,969	3,033	780	77	536	4
Persons aged 75 - 84		6,706	2,281	1,707	1,521	784	45	338	7
Persons aged 85 and over		1,661	546	388	377	244	10	85	2

All columns d–j are Household space type in permanent buildings.

Household space type in permanent buildings: Unshared dwellings - not self-contained: Not self-contained flat	Unshared dwellings - not self-contained: Not self-contained 'rooms'	Unshared dwellings - not self-contained: Bedsit	Other household spaces - not self-contained: Not self-contained flat	Other household spaces - not self-contained: Not self-contained 'rooms'	Other household spaces - not self-contained: Bedsit	Non-permanent accommodation	Households with migrant head	Persons in households with migrant head	Household composition: Adults	Household composition: Dependent children
k	l	m	n	o	p	q	r	s	a	b
30	**8**	**5**	**60**	**21**	**108**	**162**	**3,489**	**7,814**	**All households***	
9	2	-	11	7	3	6	278	278	1 adult of pensionable age	0
4	1	2	23	10	88	61	726	726	1 adult under pensionable age	0
1	-	-	3	-	7	3	154	387	1 adult any age	1 or more
8	3	2	10	2	9	68	1,202	2,404	2 adults (1 male and 1 female)	0
5	-	-	3	-	-	14	671	2,512		1 or more
1	1	1	4	-	-	1	106	212	2 adults (same sex)	0
-	-	-	-	1	-	-	20	64		1 or more
-	1	-	5	1	1	6	212	709	3 or more adults (male(s) and female(s))	0
1	-	-	-	-	-	3	92	420		1 or more
1	-	-	-	-	-	-	27	98	3 or more adults (same sex)	0
-	-	-	-	-	-	-	1	4		1 or more
10	4	1	12	8	3	17	455	633	Households containing persons of pensionable age only (any number)	
5	2	1	6	4	-	3	168	206	Households containing persons aged 75 and over only (any number)	
11	-	-	10	1	8	27	1,551		All dependent children	
3	-	-	2	1	6	13	683		Dependent children aged 0 - 4	
8	-	-	6	-	2	14	793		Dependent children aged 5 - 15	
7	3	-	7	7	3	31	536		Persons pensionable age - 74	
5	2	2	6	2	-	6	230		Persons aged 75 - 84	
1	1	-	3	2	-	2	39		Persons aged 85 and over	

Table 60 Dwellings and household spaces

Note: * Includes unshared dwelling(s) plus an unattached household space (not in a dwelling)

60. Converted or shared accommodation; dwellings; household spaces; rooms in such accommodation

Type of dwelling(s) in converted or shared accommodation	TOTAL CONVERTED OR SHARED ACCOMM-ODATION	TOTAL DWELLINGS	Total shared dwellings	Shared dwellings with the following household spaces				Un-attached spaces	TOTAL HOUSE-HOLD SPACES	Household space type						TOTAL ROOMS
				2	3	4	5 or more			Converted flat	Converted flatlet	Not self-contained flat	Not self-contained 'rooms'	Bedsit	Not self-contained unocc-upied	
a	b	c	d	e	f	g	h	i	j	k	l	m	n	o	p	q
CUMBRIA																
TOTAL CONVERTED OR SHARED ACCOMMODATION	**2,109**	**6,003**	**310**	**118**	**54**	**51**	**87**	**93**	**6,937**	**5,239**	**314**	**267**	**154**	**913**	**50**	**24,935**
Unconverted accommodation																
1 shared dwelling	188	188	188	78	37	24	49		666			96	79	471	20	1,231
Partly converted accommodation																
1 shared, 1 unshared dwelling*	117	198	81	23	11	20	27	36	490	99	14	56	32	282	7	1,031
1 shared, 2 unshared dwellings*	47	114	20	8	4	3	5	27	190	75	19	26	11	57	2	439
1 shared, 3 or more unshared dwellings*	51	295	21	9	2	4	6	30	383	229	42	26	9	71	6	948
Converted accommodation																
2 unshared dwellings	982	1,964							1,964	1,835	54	38	16	14	7	9,062
3 unshared dwellings	343	1,029							1,029	973	36	11	3	5	1	4,477
4 or more unshared dwellings	381	2,215							2,215	2,028	149	14	4	13	7	7,747
Allerdale																
TOTAL CONVERTED OR SHARED ACCOMMODATION	**312**	**893**	**45**	**16**	**5**	**9**	**15**	**14**	**1,036**	**784**	**38**	**36**	**24**	**144**	**10**	**3,621**
Unconverted accommodation																
1 shared dwelling	34	34	34	12	4	5	13		134			13	19	95	7	231
Partly converted accommodation																
1 shared, 1 unshared dwelling*	8	12	4	2	1	1	-	4	23	7	-	5	-	11	-	58
1 shared, 2 unshared dwellings*	7	16	2	1	-	1	-	5	25	12	2	3	1	6	1	59
1 shared, 3 or more unshared dwellings*	10	60	5	1	-	2	2	5	83	45	9	4	4	20	1	204
Converted accommodation																
2 unshared dwellings	143	286							286	264	7	7	-	8	-	1,309
3 unshared dwellings	49	147							147	139	6	1	-	-	1	558
4 or more unshared dwellings	61	338							338	317	14	3	-	4	-	1,202

Note: * Includes unshared dwelling(s) plus an unattached household space (not in a dwelling)

60. Converted or shared accommodation; dwellings; household spaces; rooms in such accommodation

Type of dwelling(s) in converted or shared accommodation	TOTAL CONVERTED OR SHARED ACCOMMODATION	TOTAL DWELLINGS	Total shared dwellings	Shared dwellings with the following household spaces				Un-attached spaces	TOTAL HOUSEHOLD SPACES	Household space type						TOTAL ROOMS
				2	3	4	5 or more			Converted flat	Converted flatlet	Not self-contained flat	Not self-contained 'rooms'	Bedsit	Not self-contained unoccupied	
a	b	c	d	e	f	g	h	i	j	k	l	m	n	o	p	q
Barrow-in-Furness																
TOTAL CONVERTED OR SHARED ACCOMMODATION	**193**	**506**	**46**	**18**	**7**	**8**	**13**	**12**	**637**	**402**	**52**	**25**	**31**	**118**	**9**	**1,761**
Unconverted accommodation																
1 shared dwelling	29	29	29	12	5	4	8		103			12	16	71	4	196
Partly converted accommodation																
1 shared, 1 unshared dwelling*	13	24	11	3	2	2	4	2	58	12	1	2	13	29	1	112
1 shared, 2 unshared dwellings*	8	19	3	1	-	1	1	5	32	15	1	5	-	10	1	76
1 shared, 3 or more unshared dwellings*	8	42	3	2	-	1	-	5	52	36	3	3	2	6	2	147
Converted accommodation																
2 unshared dwellings	91	182							182	170	8	1	-	2	1	667
3 unshared dwellings	22	66							66	59	7	-	-	-	-	186
4 or more unshared dwellings	22	144							144	110	32	2	-	-	-	377
Carlisle																
TOTAL CONVERTED OR SHARED ACCOMMODATION	**319**	**787**	**104**	**30**	**26**	**15**	**33**	**22**	**1,116**	**594**	**65**	**76**	**31**	**342**	**8**	**3,206**
Unconverted accommodation																
1 shared dwelling	58	58	58	19	16	8	15		208			30	12	161	5	341
Partly converted accommodation																
1 shared, 1 unshared dwelling*	43	74	31	5	5	7	14	12	205	36	5	25	8	131	-	408
1 shared, 2 unshared dwellings*	12	33	9	3	3	-	3	3	61	18	6	4	7	26	-	115
1 shared, 3 or more unshared dwellings*	13	57	6	3	2	-	1	7	77	36	13	7	2	18	1	174
Converted accommodation																
2 unshared dwellings	120	240							240	225	7	4	2	-	2	1,014
3 unshared dwellings	35	105							105	95	5	3	-	2	-	439
4 or more unshared dwellings	38	220							220	184	29	3	-	4	-	715

Table 60 Dwellings and household spaces – **continued**

Note: * Includes unshared dwelling(s) plus an unattached household space (not in a dwelling)

60. Converted or shared accommodation; dwellings; household spaces; rooms in such accommodation

Type of dwelling(s) in converted or shared accommodation	TOTAL CONVERTED OR SHARED ACCOMM-ODATION	TOTAL DWELLINGS	Total shared dwellings	Shared dwellings with the following household spaces				Un-attached spaces	TOTAL HOUSE-HOLD SPACES	Household space type						TOTAL ROOMS
				2	3	4	5 or more			Converted flat	Converted flatlet	Not self-contained flat	Not self-contained 'rooms'	Bedsit	Not self-contained unocc-upied	
a	b	c	d	e	f	g	h	i	j	k	l	m	n	o	p	q
Copeland																
TOTAL CONVERTED OR SHARED ACCOMMODATION	**192**	**555**	**37**	**16**	**4**	**4**	**13**	**10**	**667**	**459**	**36**	**19**	**24**	**118**	**11**	**2,156**
Unconverted accommodation																
1 shared dwelling	21	21	21	8	3	2	8		85			10	13	60	2	164
Partly converted accommodation																
1 shared, 1 unshared dwelling*	15	27	12	6	1	2	3	3	56	11	4	3	3	33	2	125
1 shared, 2 unshared dwellings*	4	8	-	-	-	-	-	4	12	3	5	1	1	2	-	27
1 shared, 3 or more unshared dwellings*	7	39	4	2	-	-	2	3	54	30	5	1	-	18	-	109
Converted accommodation																
2 unshared dwellings	78	156							156	146	2	3	3	2	-	685
3 unshared dwellings	32	96							96	87	8	-	1	-	-	404
4 or more unshared dwellings	35	208							208	182	12	1	3	3	7	642
Eden																
TOTAL CONVERTED OR SHARED ACCOMMODATION	**184**	**498**	**22**	**13**	**1**	**4**	**4**	**3**	**550**	**435**	**29**	**16**	**15**	**53**	**2**	**2,198**
Unconverted accommodation																
1 shared dwelling	17	17	17	12	1	3	1		45			9	8	27	1	110
Partly converted accommodation																
1 shared, 1 unshared dwelling*	4	7	3	1	-	1	1	1	19	4	-	2	1	12	-	40
1 shared, 2 unshared dwellings*	3	7	1	-	-	-	1	2	13	6	-	1	-	6	-	29
1 shared, 3 or more unshared dwellings*	1	4	1	-	-	-	1	-	10	3	-	-	-	7	-	14
Converted accommodation																
2 unshared dwellings	107	214							214	195	8	4	6	-	1	1,013
3 unshared dwellings	26	78							78	77	1	-	-	-	-	415
4 or more unshared dwellings	26	171							171	150	20	-	-	1	-	577

Table 60 Dwellings and household spaces – **continued**

Note: * Includes unshared dwelling(s) plus an unattached household space (not in a dwelling)

60. Converted or shared accommodation; dwellings; household spaces; rooms in such accommodation

Type of dwelling(s) in converted or shared accommodation	TOTAL CONVERTED OR SHARED ACCOMM-ODATION	TOTAL DWELLINGS	Total shared dwellings	Shared dwellings with the following household spaces: 2	3	4	5 or more	Un-attached spaces	TOTAL HOUSE-HOLD SPACES	Household space type: Converted flat	Converted flatlet	Not self-contained flat	Not self-contained 'rooms'	Bedsit	Not self-contained unocc-upied	TOTAL ROOMS
a	b	c	d	e	f	g	h	i	j	k	l	m	n	o	p	q
South Lakeland																
TOTAL CONVERTED OR SHARED ACCOMMODATION	**909**	**2,764**	**56**	**25**	**11**	**11**	**9**	**32**	**2,931**	**2,565**	**94**	**95**	**29**	**138**	**10**	**11,993**
Unconverted accommodation																
1 shared dwelling	29	29	29	15	8	2	4		91			22	11	57	1	189
Partly converted accommodation																
1 shared, 1 unshared dwelling*	34	54	20	6	2	7	5	14	129	29	4	19	7	66	4	288
1 shared, 2 unshared dwellings*	13	31	5	3	1	1	-	8	47	21	5	12	2	7	-	133
1 shared, 3 or more unshared dwellings*	12	93	2	1	-	1	-	10	107	79	12	11	1	2	2	300
Converted accommodation																
2 unshared dwellings	443	886							886	835	22	19	5	2	3	4,374
3 unshared dwellings	179	537							537	516	9	7	2	3	-	2,475
4 or more unshared dwellings	199	1,134							1,134	1,085	42	5	1	1	-	4,234

61. Dwellings; non-permanent accommodation

Occupancy type	TOTAL DWELLINGS	Unshared dwellings											Shared dwellings	TOTAL NON-PERM-ANENT ACCOMM-ODATION
		Total unshared dwellings	Unshared dwellings - purpose-built					Unshared dwellings - converted		Unshared dwellings - not self-contained				
			Detached	Semi-detached	Terraced	Purpose-built flat in:								
						Residential building	Commercial building	Converted flat	Converted flatlet	Not self-contained flat	Not self-contained 'rooms'	Bedsit		
a	b	c	d	e	f	g	h	i	j	k	l	m	n	o
CUMBRIA														
ALL TYPES OF OCCUPANCY	**209,377**	**209,067**	**48,033**	**63,981**	**75,144**	**13,355**	**2,861**	**5,239**	**314**	**104**		**36**	**310**	**1,936**
Dwellings with residents	**191,926**	**191,626**	**43,428**	**60,904**	**68,857**	**11,805**	**2,356**	**3,895**	**267**	**62**	**25**	**27**	**300**	**1,204**
Dwellings with person(s) present	186,271	185,975	41,995	59,518	66,946	11,288	2,255	3,627	239	61	24	22	296	1,127
Dwellings with no person(s) present	5,655	5,651	1,433	1,386	1,911	517	101	268	28	1	1	5	4	77
Vacant accommodation	**9,654**	**9,645**	**2,231**	**1,813**	**3,747**	**989**	**341**	**477**	**28**	**12**		**7**	**9**	
New, never occupied	1,649	1,649	587	266	306	415	30	38	-	7		-	-	
Under improvement	2,087	2,087	398	357	1,030	127	50	124	1	-		-	-	
Other	5,918	5,909	1,246	1,190	2,411	447	261	315	27	5		7	9	
Accommodation not used as main residence	**7,797**	**7,796**	**2,374**	**1,264**	**2,540**	**561**	**164**	**867**	**19**	**5**		**2**	**1**	**732**
No persons present	5,932	5,931	1,848	935	1,951	438	111	640	4	3		1	1	
Second residences	2,962	2,962	1,065	404	956	205	46	282	1	2		1	-	
Holiday accommodation	2,963	2,962	779	531	994	233	63	358	3	1		-	1	
Student accommodation	7	7	4	-	1	-	2	-	-	-		-	-	
Persons enumerated but no residents	1,865	1,865	526	329	589	123	53	227	15	2	-	1	-	732
Owner occupied	783	783	270	127	258	62	13	52	1	-	-	-	-	490
Not owner occupied	1,082	1,082	256	202	331	61	40	175	14	2	-	1	-	242
Allerdale														
ALL TYPES OF OCCUPANCY	**40,868**	**40,823**	**9,339**	**12,879**	**14,846**	**2,249**	**662**	**784**	**38**	**13**		**13**	**45**	**386**
Dwellings with residents	**37,526**	**37,483**	**8,507**	**12,281**	**13,538**	**1,962**	**521**	**625**	**28**	**10**	**1**	**10**	**43**	**223**
Dwellings with person(s) present	36,567	36,524	8,271	12,040	13,204	1,869	505	594	24	9	1	7	43	207
Dwellings with no person(s) present	959	959	236	241	334	93	16	31	4	1	-	3	-	16
Vacant accommodation	**2,069**	**2,067**	**497**	**353**	**841**	**197**	**103**	**65**	**8**	**-**		**3**	**2**	
New, never occupied	374	374	146	37	42	129	13	7	-	-		-	-	
Under improvement	456	456	67	74	283	3	14	15	-	-		-	-	
Other	1,239	1,237	284	242	516	65	76	43	8	-		3	2	
Accommodation not used as main residence	**1,273**	**1,273**	**335**	**245**	**467**	**90**	**38**	**94**	**2**	**2**		**-**	**-**	**163**
No persons present	937	937	247	178	351	71	25	64	-	1		-	-	
Second residences	333	333	126	52	122	12	5	15	-	1		-	-	
Holiday accommodation	602	602	121	126	229	59	18	49	-	-		-	-	
Student accommodation	2	2	-	-	-	-	2	-	-	-		-	-	
Persons enumerated but no residents	336	336	88	67	116	19	13	30	2	1	-	-	-	163
Owner occupied	126	126	33	22	51	8	4	8	-	-	-	-	-	83
Not owner occupied	210	210	55	45	65	11	9	22	2	1	-	-	-	80

61. Dwellings; non-permanent accommodation

Occupancy type	TOTAL DWELLINGS	Unshared dwellings												Shared dwellings	TOTAL NON-PERM-ANENT ACCOMM-ODATION
		Total unshared dwellings	Unshared dwellings - purpose-built					Unshared dwellings - converted		Unshared dwellings - not self-contained				
			Detached	Semi-detached	Terraced	Purpose-built flat in:								
						Residential building	Commercial building	Converted flat	Converted flatlet	Not self-contained flat	Not self-contained 'rooms'	Bedsit		
a	b	c	d	e	f	g	h	i	j	k	l	m	n	o
Barrow-in-Furness														
ALL TYPES OF OCCUPANCY	**30,727**	**30,681**	**2,715**	**8,157**	**16,484**	**2,485**	**380**	**402**	**52**		**4**	**2**	**46**	**303**
Dwellings with residents	**29,237**	**29,193**	**2,580**	**7,929**	**15,571**	**2,377**	**333**	**350**	**48**	**3**	-	**2**	**44**	**285**
Dwellings with person(s) present	28,414	28,371	2,498	7,747	15,148	2,280	322	330	42	3	-	1	43	268
Dwellings with no person(s) present	823	822	82	182	423	97	11	20	6	-	-	1	1	17
Vacant accommodation	**1,368**	**1,366**	**127**	**206**	**844**	**99**	**39**	**47**	**3**		**1**	-	**2**	
New, never occupied	214	214	74	56	55	25	-	4	-		-	-	-	
Under improvement	256	256	10	22	195	15	5	9	-		-	-	-	
Other	898	896	43	128	594	59	34	34	3		1	-	2	
Accommodation not used as main residence	**122**	**122**	**8**	**22**	**69**	**9**	**8**	**5**	**1**		-	-	-	**18**
No persons present	35	35	4	6	22	1	2	-	-		-	-	-	
Second residences	20	20	1	4	12	1	2	-	-		-	-	-	
Holiday accommodation	15	15	3	2	10	-	-	-	-		-	-	-	
Student accommodation	-	-	-	-	-	-	-	-	-		-	-	-	
Persons enumerated but no residents	87	87	4	16	47	8	6	5	1	-	-	-	-	18
Owner occupied	24	24	4	2	17	1	-	-	-	-	-	-	-	12
Not owner occupied	63	63	-	14	30	7	6	5	1	-	-	-	-	6
Carlisle														
ALL TYPES OF OCCUPANCY	**42,649**	**42,545**	**8,615**	**14,654**	**14,794**	**3,385**	**414**	**594**	**65**		**16**	**8**	**104**	**154**
Dwellings with residents	**40,464**	**40,364**	**8,173**	**14,204**	**13,999**	**3,046**	**353**	**509**	**58**	**11**	**3**	**8**	**100**	**143**
Dwellings with person(s) present	39,408	39,310	7,949	13,922	13,633	2,927	332	476	50	11	3	7	98	129
Dwellings with no person(s) present	1,056	1,054	224	282	366	119	21	33	8	-	-	1	2	14
Vacant accommodation	**1,905**	**1,901**	**353**	**391**	**707**	**329**	**50**	**65**	**4**		**2**	-	**4**	
New, never occupied	328	328	89	55	75	87	11	11	-		-	-	-	
Under improvement	452	452	57	91	209	80	2	13	-		-	-	-	
Other	1,125	1,121	207	245	423	162	37	41	4		2	-	4	
Accommodation not used as main residence	**280**	**280**	**89**	**59**	**88**	**10**	**11**	**20**	**3**		-	-	-	**11**
No persons present	145	145	71	32	23	3	3	12	1		-	-	-	
Second residences	78	78	41	15	13	3	2	4	-		-	-	-	
Holiday accommodation	67	67	30	17	10	-	1	8	1		-	-	-	
Student accommodation	-	-	-	-	-	-	-	-	-		-	-	-	
Persons enumerated but no residents	135	135	18	27	65	7	8	8	2	-	-	-	-	11
Owner occupied	50	50	11	11	22	3	1	2	-	-	-	-	-	5
Not owner occupied	85	85	7	16	43	4	7	6	2	-	-	-	-	6

Table 61 Dwelling type and occupancy – **continued**

61. Dwellings; non-permanent accommodation

Occupancy type	TOTAL DWELLINGS	Unshared dwellings											Shared dwellings	TOTAL NON-PERM-ANENT ACCOMM-ODATION
		Total unshared dwellings	Unshared dwellings - purpose-built					Unshared dwellings - converted		Unshared dwellings - not self-contained				
			Detached	Semi-detached	Terraced	Purpose-built flat in: Residential building	Purpose-built flat in: Commercial building	Converted flat	Converted flatlet	Not self-contained flat	Not self-contained 'rooms'	Bedsit		
a	b	c	d	e	f	g	h	i	j	k	l	m	n	o
Copeland														
ALL TYPES OF OCCUPANCY	**29,272**	**29,235**	**5,341**	**10,437**	**11,172**	**1,416**	**351**	**459**	**36**		**18**	**5**	**37**	**236**
Dwellings with residents	**27,469**	**27,434**	**4,916**	**10,106**	**10,448**	**1,291**	**282**	**354**	**25**	**4**	**7**	**1**	**35**	**201**
Dwellings with person(s) present	26,757	26,722	4,765	9,887	10,209	1,231	270	326	22	4	7	1	35	193
Dwellings with no person(s) present	712	712	151	219	239	60	12	28	3	-	-	-	-	8
Vacant accommodation	**1,194**	**1,193**	**263**	**239**	**484**	**99**	**42**	**47**	**10**		**7**	**2**	**1**	
New, never occupied	186	186	85	33	19	41	1	-	-		7	-	-	
Under improvement	267	267	58	44	140	7	9	9	-		-	-	-	
Other	741	740	120	162	325	51	32	38	10		-	2	1	
Accommodation not used as main residence	**609**	**608**	**162**	**92**	**240**	**26**	**27**	**58**	**1**		**-**	**2**	**1**	**35**
No persons present	486	485	131	59	204	19	24	47	-		-	1	1	
Second residences	339	339	72	38	163	10	22	33	-		-	1	-	
Holiday accommodation	147	146	59	21	41	9	2	14	-		-	-	1	
Student accommodation	-	-	-	-	-	-	-	-	-		-	-	-	
Persons enumerated but no residents	123	123	31	33	36	7	3	11	1	-	-	1	-	35
Owner occupied	43	43	13	10	15	-	1	4	-	-	-	-	-	21
Not owner occupied	80	80	18	23	21	7	2	7	1	-	-	1	-	14
Eden														
ALL TYPES OF OCCUPANCY	**20,313**	**20,291**	**7,786**	**5,633**	**5,101**	**995**	**300**	**435**	**29**		**11**	**1**	**22**	**286**
Dwellings with residents	**17,778**	**17,756**	**6,761**	**5,065**	**4,431**	**895**	**261**	**304**	**28**	**4**	**6**	**1**	**22**	**190**
Dwellings with person(s) present	17,233	17,211	6,555	4,933	4,299	855	250	281	27	4	6	1	22	182
Dwellings with no person(s) present	545	545	206	132	132	40	11	23	1	-	-	-	-	8
Vacant accommodation	**1,006**	**1,006**	**425**	**238**	**236**	**44**	**24**	**38**	**-**		**1**	**-**	**-**	
New, never occupied	185	185	100	52	17	16	-	-	-		-	-	-	
Under improvement	265	265	101	51	74	8	8	23	-		-	-	-	
Other	556	556	224	135	145	20	16	15	-		1	-	-	
Accommodation not used as main residence	**1,529**	**1,529**	**600**	**330**	**434**	**56**	**15**	**93**	**1**		**-**	**-**	**-**	**96**
No persons present	1,273	1,273	502	281	363	49	11	67	-		-	-	-	
Second residences	611	611	289	107	172	24	1	18	-		-	-	-	
Holiday accommodation	659	659	210	174	191	25	10	49	-		-	-	-	
Student accommodation	3	3	3	-	-	-	-	-	-		-	-	-	
Persons enumerated but no residents	256	256	98	49	71	7	4	26	1	-	-	-	-	96
Owner occupied	111	111	46	22	36	3	2	2	-	-	-	-	-	59
Not owner occupied	145	145	52	27	35	4	2	24	1	-	-	-	-	37

61. Dwellings; non-permanent accommodation

Occupancy type	TOTAL DWELLINGS	Unshared dwellings											Shared dwellings	TOTAL NON-PERM-ANENT ACCOMM-ODATION
		Total unshared dwellings	Unshared dwellings - purpose-built					Unshared dwellings - converted		Unshared dwellings - not self-contained				
			Detached	Semi-detached	Terraced	Purpose-built flat in:								
						Residential building	Commercial building	Converted flat	Converted flatlet	Not self-contained flat	Not self-contained 'rooms'	Bedsit		
a	b	c	d	e	f	g	h	i	j	k	l	m	n	o
South Lakeland														
ALL TYPES OF OCCUPANCY	**45,548**	**45,492**	**14,237**	**12,221**	**12,747**	**2,825**	**754**	**2,565**	**94**	**42**		**7**	**56**	**571**
Dwellings with residents	**39,452**	**39,396**	**12,491**	**11,319**	**10,870**	**2,234**	**606**	**1,753**	**80**	**30**	**8**	**5**	**56**	**162**
Dwellings with person(s) present	37,892	37,837	11,957	10,989	10,453	2,126	576	1,620	74	30	7	5	55	148
Dwellings with no person(s) present	1,560	1,559	534	330	417	108	30	133	6	-	1	-	1	14
Vacant accommodation	**2,112**	**2,112**	**566**	**386**	**635**	**221**	**83**	**215**	**3**	**1**		**2**	**-**	
New, never occupied	362	362	93	33	98	117	5	16	-	-		-	-	
Under improvement	391	391	105	75	129	14	12	55	1	-		-	-	
Other	1,359	1,359	368	278	408	90	66	144	2	1		2	-	
Accommodation not used as main residence	**3,984**	**3,984**	**1,180**	**516**	**1,242**	**370**	**65**	**597**	**11**	**3**		**-**	**-**	**409**
No persons present	3,056	3,056	893	379	988	295	46	450	3	2		-	-	
Second residences	1,581	1,581	536	188	474	155	14	212	1	1		-	-	
Holiday accommodation	1,473	1,473	356	191	513	140	32	238	2	1		-	-	
Student accommodation	2	2	1	-	1	-	-	-	-	-		-	-	
Persons enumerated but no residents	928	928	287	137	254	75	19	147	8	1	-	-	-	409
Owner occupied	429	429	163	60	117	47	5	36	1	-	-	-	-	310
Not owner occupied	499	499	124	77	137	28	14	111	7	1	-	-	-	99

Table 62 Occupancy and tenure of dwellings

62. Dwellings with persons present or resident

Occupancy type	TOTAL DWELLINGS	Owner occupied		Rented privately		Rented with a job or business	Rented from a housing association	Rented from a local authority or new town
		Owned outright	Buying	Furnished	Unfurnished			
a	b	c	d	e	f	g	h	i
CUMBRIA								
ALL TYPES OF OCCUPANCY	**193,791**	**56,402**	**79,345**	**5,403**	**8,401**	**4,918**	**7,344**	**31,978**
Dwellings with residents	**191,926**	**55,983**	**78,981**	**4,484**	**8,355**	**4,866**	**7,326**	**31,931**
Dwellings with person(s) present	186,271	53,725	77,066	4,206	8,088	4,758	7,125	31,303
Dwellings with no person(s) present	5,655	2,258	1,915	278	267	108	201	628
Dwellings with persons enumerated but no residents	**1,865**	**419**	**364**	**919**	**46**	**52**	**18**	**47**
Allerdale								
ALL TYPES OF OCCUPANCY	**37,862**	**10,823**	**14,191**	**925**	**1,407**	**810**	**2,994**	**6,712**
Dwellings with residents	**37,526**	**10,767**	**14,121**	**756**	**1,395**	**804**	**2,985**	**6,698**
Dwellings with person(s) present	36,567	10,418	13,829	697	1,360	783	2,921	6,559
Dwellings with no person(s) present	959	349	292	59	35	21	64	139
Dwellings with persons enumerated but no residents	**336**	**56**	**70**	**169**	**12**	**6**	**9**	**14**
Barrow-in-Furness								
ALL TYPES OF OCCUPANCY	**29,324**	**9,012**	**13,982**	**786**	**1,091**	**273**	**339**	**3,841**
Dwellings with residents	**29,237**	**9,004**	**13,966**	**735**	**1,088**	**267**	**339**	**3,838**
Dwellings with person(s) present	28,414	8,671	13,682	693	1,054	257	316	3,741
Dwellings with no person(s) present	823	333	284	42	34	10	23	97
Dwellings with persons enumerated but no residents	**87**	**8**	**16**	**51**	**3**	**6**	**-**	**3**
Carlisle								
ALL TYPES OF OCCUPANCY	**40,599**	**9,880**	**17,549**	**929**	**1,398**	**910**	**831**	**9,102**
Dwellings with residents	**40,464**	**9,855**	**17,524**	**872**	**1,391**	**905**	**831**	**9,086**
Dwellings with person(s) present	39,408	9,512	17,104	827	1,342	890	810	8,923
Dwellings with no person(s) present	1,056	343	420	45	49	15	21	163
Dwellings with persons enumerated but no residents	**135**	**25**	**25**	**57**	**7**	**5**	**-**	**16**
Copeland								
ALL TYPES OF OCCUPANCY	**27,592**	**6,307**	**11,747**	**482**	**637**	**551**	**2,168**	**5,700**
Dwellings with residents	**27,469**	**6,283**	**11,728**	**418**	**633**	**546**	**2,166**	**5,695**
Dwellings with person(s) present	26,757	6,019	11,481	401	615	534	2,111	5,596
Dwellings with no person(s) present	712	264	247	17	18	12	55	99
Dwellings with persons enumerated but no residents	**123**	**24**	**19**	**64**	**4**	**5**	**2**	**5**
Eden								
ALL TYPES OF OCCUPANCY	**18,034**	**6,291**	**6,329**	**557**	**1,427**	**1,045**	**412**	**1,973**
Dwellings with residents	**17,778**	**6,221**	**6,288**	**423**	**1,425**	**1,042**	**410**	**1,969**
Dwellings with person(s) present	17,233	5,980	6,104	398	1,391	1,024	398	1,938
Dwellings with no person(s) present	545	241	184	25	34	18	12	31
Dwellings with persons enumerated but no residents	**256**	**70**	**41**	**134**	**2**	**3**	**2**	**4**

62. Dwellings with persons present or resident

Occupancy type	TOTAL DWELLINGS	Owner occupied		Rented privately		Rented with a job or business	Rented from a housing association	Rented from a local authority or new town
		Owned outright	Buying	Furnished	Unfurnished			
a	b	c	d	e	f	g	h	i
		South Lakeland						
ALL TYPES OF OCCUPANCY	**40,380**	**14,089**	**15,547**	**1,724**	**2,441**	**1,329**	**600**	**4,650**
Dwellings with residents	**39,452**	**13,853**	**15,354**	**1,280**	**2,423**	**1,302**	**595**	**4,645**
Dwellings with person(s) present	37,892	13,125	14,866	1,190	2,326	1,270	569	4,546
Dwellings with no person(s) present	1,560	728	488	90	97	32	26	99
Dwellings with persons enumerated but no residents	**928**	**236**	**193**	**444**	**18**	**27**	**5**	**5**

Table 63 Dwelling type and tenure

63. Dwellings with residents; non-permanent accommodation

Tenure	TOTAL DWELLINGS	Unshared dwellings											Shared dwellings	TOTAL NON-PERMANENT ACCOMMODATION
		Total unshared dwellings	Unshared dwellings - purpose-built					Unshared dwellings - converted		Unshared dwellings - not self-contained				
			Detached	Semi-detached	Terraced	Purpose-built flat in: Residential building	Purpose-built flat in: Commercial building	Converted flat	Converted flatlet	Not self-contained flat	Not self-contained 'rooms'	Bedsit		
a	b	c	d	e	f	g	h	i	j	k	l	m	n	o
CUMBRIA														
ALL TENURES	**191,926**	**191,626**	**43,428**	**60,904**	**68,857**	**11,805**	**2,356**	**3,895**	**267**	**62**	**25**	**27**	**300**	**1,204**
Owner occupied - owned outright	55,983	55,950	19,499	16,258	17,626	1,262	362	921	5	12	4	1	33	662
- buying	78,981	78,956	18,789	27,356	30,068	1,193	642	868	19	17	3	1	25	159
Rented privately - furnished	4,484	4,318	606	675	1,563	270	344	700	124	15	7	14	166	210
- unfurnished	8,355	8,316	1,769	1,629	2,905	869	406	678	37	12	8	3	39	74
Rented with a job or business	4,866	4,860	2,240	1,070	697	178	520	144	4	2	3	2	6	64
Rented from a housing association	7,326	7,306	127	2,568	2,708	1,612	14	248	25	2	-	2	20	1
Rented from a local authority or new town	31,931	31,920	398	11,348	13,290	6,421	68	336	53	2	-	4	11	34
Allerdale														
ALL TENURES	**37,526**	**37,483**	**8,507**	**12,281**	**13,538**	**1,962**	**521**	**625**	**28**	**10**	**1**	**10**	**43**	**223**
Owner occupied - owned outright	10,767	10,764	3,934	2,827	3,609	217	78	98	-	1	-	-	3	135
- buying	14,121	14,112	3,725	4,711	5,256	169	144	102	-	5	-	-	9	34
Rented privately - furnished	756	739	105	105	251	44	87	124	15	1	-	7	17	26
- unfurnished	1,395	1,386	277	272	592	38	85	115	4	1	1	1	9	15
Rented with a job or business	804	804	384	159	113	16	108	21	2	-	-	1	-	12
Rented from a housing association	2,985	2,981	31	1,518	1,092	278	4	54	3	-	-	1	4	-
Rented from a local authority or new town	6,698	6,697	51	2,689	2,625	1,200	15	111	4	2	-	-	1	1
Barrow-in-Furness														
ALL TENURES	**29,237**	**29,193**	**2,580**	**7,929**	**15,571**	**2,377**	**333**	**350**	**48**	**3**	**-**	**2**	**44**	**285**
Owner occupied - owned outright	9,004	9,001	959	2,785	5,069	81	42	63	2	-	-	-	3	209
- buying	13,966	13,962	1,511	4,453	7,777	80	104	34	2	1	-	-	4	43
Rented privately - furnished	735	711	24	57	385	49	62	110	23	-	-	1	24	23
- unfurnished	1,088	1,085	22	36	280	668	35	39	2	2	-	1	3	7
Rented with a job or business	267	267	46	45	67	34	73	2	-	-	-	-	-	-
Rented from a housing association	339	330	3	16	92	188	-	25	6	-	-	-	9	-
Rented from a local authority or new town	3,838	3,837	15	537	1,901	1,277	17	77	13	-	-	-	1	3

63. Dwellings with residents; non-permanent accommodation

Tenure	TOTAL DWELLINGS	Unshared dwellings											Shared dwellings	TOTAL NON-PERM-ANENT ACCOMM-ODATION
		Total unshared dwellings	Unshared dwellings - purpose-built					Unshared dwellings - converted		Unshared dwellings - not self-contained				
			Detached	Semi-detached	Terraced	Purpose-built flat in: Residential building	Purpose-built flat in: Commercial building	Converted flat	Converted flatlet	Not self-contained flat	Not self-contained 'rooms'	Bedsit		
a	b	c	d	e	f	g	h	i	j	k	l	m	n	o
Carlisle														
ALL TENURES	**40,464**	**40,364**	**8,173**	**14,204**	**13,999**	**3,046**	**353**	**509**	**58**	**11**	**3**	**8**	**100**	**143**
Owner occupied - owned outright	9,855	9,845	3,155	3,617	2,576	374	43	78	1	1	-	-	10	66
- buying	17,524	17,519	4,027	6,715	6,188	409	86	90	1	2	1	-	5	17
Rented privately - furnished	872	807	83	144	296	44	58	141	30	5	2	4	65	38
- unfurnished	1,391	1,379	307	314	551	41	71	90	4	1	-	-	12	11
Rented with a job or business	905	905	373	249	148	39	78	16	1	1	-	-	-	6
Rented from a housing association	831	826	5	154	208	398	-	54	5	1	-	1	5	1
Rented from a local authority or new town	9,086	9,083	223	3,011	4,032	1,741	17	40	16	-	-	3	3	4
Copeland														
ALL TENURES	**27,469**	**27,434**	**4,916**	**10,106**	**10,448**	**1,291**	**282**	**354**	**25**	**4**	**7**	**1**	**35**	**201**
Owner occupied - owned outright	6,283	6,277	1,955	1,789	2,342	80	60	49	-	1	1	-	6	100
- buying	11,728	11,726	2,530	4,544	4,400	87	76	85	4	-	-	-	2	29
Rented privately - furnished	418	399	61	64	144	12	26	76	12	2	2	-	19	52
- unfurnished	633	630	120	119	297	8	35	39	6	1	4	1	3	15
Rented with a job or business	546	546	195	146	90	28	73	14	-	-	-	-	-	3
Rented from a housing association	2,166	2,164	16	739	987	358	2	59	3	-	-	-	2	-
Rented from a local authority or new town	5,695	5,692	39	2,705	2,188	718	10	32	-	-	-	-	3	2
Eden														
ALL TENURES	**17,778**	**17,756**	**6,761**	**5,065**	**4,431**	**895**	**261**	**304**	**28**	**4**	**6**	**1**	**22**	**190**
Owner occupied - owned outright	6,221	6,215	3,237	1,532	1,223	119	35	67	1	1	-	-	6	97
- buying	6,288	6,286	2,252	1,999	1,705	181	66	77	3	1	2	-	2	14
Rented privately - furnished	423	417	110	83	111	22	45	43	2	-	1	-	6	24
- unfurnished	1,425	1,419	477	369	392	53	49	71	6	2	-	-	6	18
Rented with a job or business	1,042	1,041	651	210	77	15	63	22	-	-	3	-	1	16
Rented from a housing association	410	410	14	41	148	204	1	2	-	-	-	-	-	-
Rented from a local authority or new town	1,969	1,968	20	831	775	301	2	22	16	-	-	1	1	21

63. Dwellings with residents; non-permanent accommodation

Tenure	TOTAL DWELLINGS	Unshared dwellings											Shared dwellings	TOTAL NON-PERM-ANENT ACCOMM-ODATION
		Total unshared dwellings	Unshared dwellings - purpose-built					Unshared dwellings - converted		Unshared dwellings - not self-contained				
			Detached	Semi-detached	Terraced	Purpose-built flat in:								
						Residential building	Commercial building	Converted flat	Converted flatlet	Not self-contained flat	Not self-contained 'rooms'	Bedsit		
a	b	c	d	e	f	g	h	i	j	k	l	m	n	o
South Lakeland														
ALL TENURES	**39,452**	**39,396**	**12,491**	**11,319**	**10,870**	**2,234**	**606**	**1,753**	**80**	**30**	**8**	**5**	**56**	**162**
Owner occupied - owned outright	13,853	13,848	6,259	3,708	2,807	391	104	566	1	8	3	1	5	55
- buying	15,354	15,351	4,744	4,934	4,742	267	166	480	9	8	-	1	3	22
Rented privately - furnished	1,280	1,245	223	222	376	99	66	206	42	7	2	2	35	47
- unfurnished	2,423	2,417	566	519	793	61	131	324	15	5	3	-	6	8
Rented with a job or business	1,302	1,297	591	261	202	46	125	69	1	1	-	1	5	27
Rented from a housing association	595	595	58	100	181	186	7	54	8	1	-	-	-	-
Rented from a local authority or new town	4,645	4,643	50	1,575	1,769	1,184	7	54	4	-	-	-	2	3

64. Dwellings; household spaces in dwellings

Tenure or occupancy type of dwelling	TOTAL DWELLINGS	Unshared dwellings	Shared dwellings	TOTAL HOUSE-HOLD SPACES	Tenure or occupancy type of household spaces: Owner occupied		Rented privately		Rented with a job or business	Rented from a housing assoc-iation	Rented from a local authority or new town	Vacant accomm-odation	Accommodation not used as main residence - no persons present		
					Owned outright	Buying	Furnished	Un-furnished					Second residences	Holiday accomm-odation	Student accomm-odation
a	b	c	d	e	f	g	h	i	j	k	l	m	n	o	p
CUMBRIA															
ALL TENURES OR OCCUPANCY TYPES	**209,377**	**209,067**	**310**	**210,218**	**56,408**	**79,357**	**6,005**	**8,446**	**4,944**	**7,365**	**32,000**	**9,756**	**2,965**	**2,965**	**7**
Dwellings with residents	**191,926**	**191,626**	**300**	**192,755**	**55,989**	**78,993**	**5,086**	**8,400**	**4,892**	**7,347**	**31,953**	**91**	**3**	**1**	**-**
Owner occupied - owned outright	55,983	55,950	33	56,045	55,989	4	43	5	1	1	-	2	-	-	-
- buying	78,981	78,956	25	79,015		78,989	17	6	1	-	-	2	-	-	-
Rented privately - furnished	4,484	4,318	166	4,972			4,898		10			62	2	-	-
- unfurnished	8,355	8,316	39	8,477			84	8,378	1			14	-	-	-
Rented with a job or business	4,866	4,860	6	4,880					4,879			-	-	1	-
Rented from a housing association	7,326	7,306	20	7,397			34	11	-	7,346	-	6	-	-	-
Rented from a local authority or new town	31,931	31,920	11	31,969			10	-	-		31,953	5	1	-	-
Persons enumerated but no residents	**1,865**	**1,865**	**-**	**1,865**	**419**	**364**	**919**	**46**	**52**	**18**	**47**		**-**	**-**	**-**
Owner occupied	783	783	-	783	419	364	-	-	-	-	-		-	-	-
Not owner occupied	1,082	1,082	-	1,082			919	46	52	18	47			-	-
Vacant accommodation	9,654	9,645	9	9,665	-	-	-	-	-	-	-	9,665	-	-	-
Other unoccupied accommodation	5,932	5,931	1	5,933			-	-	-	-	-		2,962	2,964	7
Allerdale															
ALL TENURES OR OCCUPANCY TYPES	**40,868**	**40,823**	**45**	**40,997**	**10,824**	**14,196**	**1,004**	**1,417**	**811**	**3,002**	**6,718**	**2,088**	**333**	**602**	**2**
Dwellings with residents	**37,526**	**37,483**	**43**	**37,653**	**10,768**	**14,126**	**835**	**1,405**	**805**	**2,993**	**6,704**	**17**	**-**	**-**	**-**
Owner occupied - owned outright	10,767	10,764	3	10,779	10,768	-	10	1	-	-	-	-	-	-	-
- buying	14,121	14,112	9	14,137		14,126	9	1	-	-	-	1	-	-	-
Rented privately - furnished	756	739	17	813			802		1			10	-	-	-
- unfurnished	1,395	1,386	9	1,416			8	1,403	-			5	-	-	-
Rented with a job or business	804	804	-	804					804			-	-	-	-
Rented from a housing association	2,985	2,981	4	3,000			6	-	-	2,993	-	1	-	-	-
Rented from a local authority or new town	6,698	6,697	1	6,704			-	-	-		6,704	-	-	-	-
Persons enumerated but no residents	**336**	**336**	**-**	**336**	**56**	**70**	**169**	**12**	**6**	**9**	**14**		**-**	**-**	**-**
Owner occupied	126	126	-	126	56	70	-	-	-	-	-		-	-	-
Not owner occupied	210	210	-	210			169	12	6	9	14			-	-
Vacant accommodation	2,069	2,067	2	2,071	-	-	-	-	-	-	-	2,071	-	-	-
Other unoccupied accommodation	937	937	-	937			-	-	-	-	-		333	602	2

Table 64 Tenure of dwellings and household spaces – **continued**

64. Dwellings; household spaces in dwellings

Tenure or occupancy type of dwelling	TOTAL DWELLINGS	Unshared dwellings	Shared dwellings	TOTAL HOUSE-HOLD SPACES	Tenure or occupancy type of household spaces										
					Owner occupied		Rented privately		Rented with a job or business	Rented from a housing assoc-iation	Rented from a local authority or new town	Vacant accomm-odation	Accommodation not used as main residence - no persons present		
					Owned outright	Buying	Furnished	Un-furnished					Second residences	Holiday accomm-odation	Student accomm-odation
a	b	c	d	e	f	g	h	i	j	k	l	m	n	o	p
Barrow-in-Furness															
ALL TENURES OR OCCUPANCY TYPES	**30,727**	**30,681**	**46**	**30,846**	**9,012**	**13,983**	**863**	**1,102**	**275**	**347**	**3,841**	**1,388**	**20**	**15**	**-**
Dwellings with residents	**29,237**	**29,193**	**44**	**29,354**	**9,004**	**13,967**	**812**	**1,099**	**269**	**347**	**3,838**	**18**	**-**	**-**	**-**
Owner occupied - owned outright	9,004	9,001	3	9,007	9,004	-	3	-	-	-	-	-	-	-	-
- buying	13,966	13,962	4	13,970		13,967	1	1	-	-	-	1	-	-	-
Rented privately - furnished	735	711	24	801			784		2			15	-	-	-
- unfurnished	1,088	1,085	3	1,097			7	1,090	-			-	-	-	-
Rented with a job or business	267	267	-	267					267			-	-	-	-
Rented from a housing association	339	330	9	373			16	8	-	347	-	2	-	-	-
Rented from a local authority or new town	3,838	3,837	1	3,839			1	-	-		3,838	-	-	-	-
Persons enumerated but no residents	**87**	**87**	**-**	**87**	**8**	**16**	**51**	**3**	**6**	**-**	**3**		**-**	**-**	**-**
Owner occupied	24	24	-	24	8	16	-	-	-	-	-		-	-	-
Not owner occupied	63	63	-	63			51	3	6	-	3			-	-
Vacant accommodation	1,368	1,366	2	1,370	-	-	-	-	-	-	-	1,370	-	-	-
Other unoccupied accommodation	35	35	-	35			-	-	-	-	-		20	15	-
Carlisle															
ALL TENURES OR OCCUPANCY TYPES	**42,649**	**42,545**	**104**	**42,956**	**9,881**	**17,550**	**1,186**	**1,408**	**913**	**836**	**9,103**	**1,933**	**79**	**67**	**-**
Dwellings with residents	**40,464**	**40,364**	**100**	**40,765**	**9,856**	**17,525**	**1,129**	**1,401**	**908**	**836**	**9,087**	**22**	**1**	**-**	**-**
Owner occupied - owned outright	9,855	9,845	10	9,874	9,856	1	12	4	-	1	-	-	-	-	-
- buying	17,524	17,519	5	17,530		17,524	4	2	-	-	-	-	-	-	-
Rented privately - furnished	872	807	65	1,077			1,057		3			16	1	-	-
- unfurnished	1,391	1,379	12	1,440			43	1,393	-			4	-	-	-
Rented with a job or business	905	905	-	905					905			-	-	-	-
Rented from a housing association	831	826	5	847			8	2	-	835	-	2	-	-	-
Rented from a local authority or new town	9,086	9,083	3	9,092			5	-	-		9,087	-	-	-	-
Persons enumerated but no residents	**135**	**135**	**-**	**135**	**25**	**25**	**57**	**7**	**5**	**-**	**16**		**-**	**-**	**-**
Owner occupied	50	50	-	50	25	25	-	-	-	-	-		-	-	-
Not owner occupied	85	85	-	85			57	7	5	-	16			-	-
Vacant accommodation	1,905	1,901	4	1,911	-	-	-	-	-	-	-	1,911	-	-	-
Other unoccupied accommodation	145	145	-	145			-	-	-	-	-		78	67	-

Table 64 Tenure of dwellings and household spaces – **continued**

64. Dwellings; household spaces in dwellings

Tenure or occupancy type of dwelling	TOTAL DWELLINGS	Unshared dwellings	Shared dwellings	TOTAL HOUSE-HOLD SPACES	Tenure or occupancy type of household spaces: Owner occupied - Owned outright	Owner occupied - Buying	Rented privately - Furnished	Rented privately - Un-furnished	Rented with a job or business	Rented from a housing assoc-iation	Rented from a local authority or new town	Vacant accomm-odation	Accommodation not used as main residence - no persons present: Second residences	Holiday accomm-odation	Student accomm-odation
a	b	c	d	e	f	g	h	i	j	k	l	m	n	o	p
					Copeland										
ALL TENURES OR OCCUPANCY TYPES	**29,272**	**29,235**	**37**	**29,374**	**6,308**	**11,749**	**557**	**639**	**551**	**2,168**	**5,702**	**1,211**	**341**	**148**	**-**
Dwellings with residents	**27,469**	**27,434**	**35**	**27,569**	**6,284**	**11,730**	**493**	**635**	**546**	**2,166**	**5,697**	**16**	**2**	**-**	**-**
Owner occupied - owned outright	6,283	6,277	6	6,299	6,284	1	12	-	-	-	-	2	-	-	-
- buying	11,728	11,726	2	11,730		11,729	1	-	-	-	-	-	-	-	-
Rented privately - furnished	418	399	19	476			466		-			9	1	-	-
- unfurnished	633	630	3	644			7	634	-			3	-	-	-
Rented with a job or business	546	546	-	546					546			-	-	-	-
Rented from a housing association	2,166	2,164	2	2,172			4	1	-	2,166	-	1	-	-	-
Rented from a local authority or new town	5,695	5,692	3	5,702			3	-	-		5,697	1	1	-	-
Persons enumerated but no residents	**123**	**123**	**-**	**123**	**24**	**19**	**64**	**4**	**5**	**2**	**5**		**-**	**-**	**-**
Owner occupied	43	43	-	43	24	19	-	-	-	-	-		-		-
Not owner occupied	80	80	-	80			64	4	5	2	5			-	-
Vacant accommodation	1,194	1,193	1	1,195	-	-	-	-	-	-	-	1,195	-	-	-
Other unoccupied accommodation	486	485	1	487			-	-	-	-	-		339	148	-
					Eden										
ALL TENURES OR OCCUPANCY TYPES	**20,313**	**20,291**	**22**	**20,362**	**6,293**	**6,331**	**587**	**1,430**	**1,048**	**412**	**1,979**	**1,008**	**611**	**660**	**3**
Dwellings with residents	**17,778**	**17,756**	**22**	**17,827**	**6,223**	**6,290**	**453**	**1,428**	**1,045**	**410**	**1,975**	**2**	**-**	**1**	**-**
Owner occupied - owned outright	6,221	6,215	6	6,227	6,223	2	1	-	1	-	-	-	-	-	-
- buying	6,288	6,286	2	6,291		6,288	2	-	1	-	-	-	-	-	-
Rented privately - furnished	423	417	6	433			433		-			-	-	-	-
- unfurnished	1,425	1,419	6	1,447			16	1,428	1			2	-	-	-
Rented with a job or business	1,042	1,041	1	1,043					1,042			-	-	1	-
Rented from a housing association	410	410	-	410			-	-	-	410	-	-	-	-	-
Rented from a local authority or new town	1,969	1,968	1	1,976			1	-	-		1,975	-	-	-	-
Persons enumerated but no residents	**256**	**256**	**-**	**256**	**70**	**41**	**134**	**2**	**3**	**2**	**4**		**-**	**-**	**-**
Owner occupied	111	111	-	111	70	41	-	-	-	-	-		-		-
Not owner occupied	145	145	-	145			134	2	3	2	4			-	-
Vacant accommodation	1,006	1,006	-	1,006	-	-	-	-	-	-	-	1,006	-	-	-
Other unoccupied accommodation	1,273	1,273	-	1,273			-	-	-	-	-		611	659	3

Table 64 Tenure of dwellings and household spaces – **continued**

64. Dwellings; household spaces in dwellings

Tenure or occupancy type of dwelling	TOTAL DWELLINGS	Unshared dwellings	Shared dwellings	TOTAL HOUSE-HOLD SPACES	Tenure or occupancy type of household spaces										
					Owner occupied		Rented privately		Rented with a job or business	Rented from a housing assoc-iation	Rented from a local authority or new town	Vacant accomm-odation	Accommodation not used as main residence - no persons present		
					Owned outright	Buying	Furnished	Un-furnished					Second residences	Holiday accomm-odation	Student accomm-odation
a	b	c	d	e	f	g	h	i	j	k	l	m	n	o	p
					South Lakeland										
ALL TENURES OR OCCUPANCY TYPES	**45,548**	**45,492**	**56**	**45,683**	**14,090**	**15,548**	**1,808**	**2,450**	**1,346**	**600**	**4,657**	**2,128**	**1,581**	**1,473**	**2**
Dwellings with residents	**39,452**	**39,396**	**56**	**39,587**	**13,854**	**15,355**	**1,364**	**2,432**	**1,319**	**595**	**4,652**	**16**	**-**	**-**	**-**
Owner occupied - owned outright	13,853	13,848	5	13,859	13,854	-	5	-	-	-	-	-	-	-	-
- buying	15,354	15,351	3	15,357		15,355	-	2	-	-	-	-	-	-	-
Rented privately - furnished	1,280	1,245	35	1,372			1,356		4			12	-	-	-
- unfurnished	2,423	2,417	6	2,433			3	2,430	-			-	-	-	-
Rented with a job or business	1,302	1,297	5	1,315					1,315			-	-	-	-
Rented from a housing association	595	595	-	595			-	-	-	595	-	-	-	-	-
Rented from a local authority or new town	4,645	4,643	2	4,656			-	-	-		4,652	4	-	-	-
Persons enumerated but no residents	**928**	**928**	**-**	**928**	**236**	**193**	**444**	**18**	**27**	**5**	**5**		**-**	**-**	**-**
Owner occupied	429	429	-	429	236	193	-	-	-	-	-		-	-	-
Not owner occupied	499	499	-	499			444	18	27	5	5			-	-
Vacant accommodation	2,112	2,112	-	2,112	-	-	-	-	-	-	-	2,112	-	-	-
Other unoccupied accommodation	3,056	3,056	-	3,056			-	-	-	-	-		1,581	1,473	2

Table 65 Occupancy of dwellings and household spaces

65. Dwellings; household spaces in dwellings

Occupancy type of dwelling	TOTAL DWELLINGS	Unshared dwellings	Shared dwellings	TOTAL HOUSE-HOLD SPACES	Occupancy type of household spaces									
					Households with residents		Vacant accommodation			Accommodation not used as main residence				
										No persons present			Persons enumerated but no residents	
					Persons present	Absent household	New	Under improve-ment	Other	Second residences	Holiday accomm-odation	Student accomm-odation	Owner occupied	Not owner occupied
a	b	c	d	e	f	g	h	i	j	k	l	m	n	o
CUMBRIA														
ALL TYPES OF OCCUPANCY	**209,377**	**209,067**	**310**	**210,218**	**186,850**	**5,763**	**1,649**	**2,091**	**6,016**	**2,965**	**2,965**	**7**	**784**	**1,128**
Dwellings with residents	**191,926**	**191,626**	**300**	**192,755**	**186,850**	**5,763**	**-**	**4**	**87**	**3**	**1**	**-**	**1**	**46**
Dwellings with person(s) present	186,271	185,975	296	187,092	186,850	100	-	4	87	3	1	-	1	46
Dwellings with no person(s) present	5,655	5,651	4	5,663		5,663	-	-	-	-	-	-	-	-
Vacant accommodation	**9,654**	**9,645**	**9**	**9,665**			**1,649**	**2,087**	**5,929**	**-**	**-**	**-**	**-**	**-**
New, never occupied	1,649	1,649	-	1,649			1,649							
Under improvement	2,087	2,087	-	2,087			-	2,087	-	-	-	-	-	-
Other	5,918	5,909	9	5,929			-		5,929	-	-	-	-	-
Accommodation not used as main residence	**7,797**	**7,796**	**1**	**7,798**			**-**			**2,962**	**2,964**	**7**	**783**	**1,082**
No persons present	5,932	5,931	1	5,933			-			2,962	2,964	7		-
Second residences	2,962	2,962	-	2,962			-			2,962	-	-		-
Holiday accommodation	2,963	2,962	1	2,964			-				2,964	-		
Student accommodation	7	7	-	7			-					7		
Persons enumerated but no residents	1,865	1,865	-	1,865			-			-	-	-	783	1,082
Owner occupied	783	783	-	783			-			-	-	-	783	-
Not owner occupied	1,082	1,082	-	1,082			-				-	-		1,082

Table 65 Occupancy of dwellings and household spaces – **continued**

65. Dwellings; household spaces in dwellings

Occupancy type of dwelling	TOTAL DWELLINGS	Unshared dwellings	Shared dwellings	TOTAL HOUSE-HOLD SPACES	Occupancy type of household spaces									
					Households with residents		Vacant accommodation			Accommodation not used as main residence				
										No persons present			Persons enumerated but no residents	
					Persons present	Absent household	New	Under improve-ment	Other	Second residences	Holiday accomm-odation	Student accomm-odation	Owner occupied	Not owner occupied
a	b	c	d	e	f	g	h	i	j	k	l	m	n	o
					Allerdale									
ALL TYPES OF OCCUPANCY	**40,868**	**40,823**	**45**	**40,997**	**36,658**	**975**	**374**	**457**	**1,257**	**333**	**602**	**2**	**126**	**213**
Dwellings with residents	**37,526**	**37,483**	**43**	**37,653**	**36,658**	**975**	**-**	**1**	**16**	**-**	**-**	**-**	**-**	**3**
Dwellings with person(s) present	36,567	36,524	43	36,694	36,658	16	-	1	16	-	-	-	-	3
Dwellings with no person(s) present	959	959	-	959		959	-	-	-	-	-	-	-	-
Vacant accommodation	**2,069**	**2,067**	**2**	**2,071**			**374**	**456**	**1,241**	**-**	**-**	**-**	**-**	**-**
New, never occupied	374	374	-	374			374							
Under improvement	456	456	-	456			-	456	-	-	-	-	-	-
Other	1,239	1,237	2	1,241			-		1,241	-	-	-	-	-
Accommodation not used as main residence	**1,273**	**1,273**	**-**	**1,273**			**-**			**333**	**602**	**2**	**126**	**210**
No persons present	937	937	-	937			-			333	602	2		-
Second residences	333	333	-	333			-			333	-	-		-
Holiday accommodation	602	602	-	602			-				602	-		
Student accommodation	2	2	-	2			-					2		
Persons enumerated but no residents	336	336	-	336			-			-	-	-	126	210
Owner occupied	126	126	-	126			-			-	-	-	126	-
Not owner occupied	210	210	-	210			-				-	-		210

65. Dwellings; household spaces in dwellings

Occupancy type of dwelling	TOTAL DWELLINGS	Unshared dwellings	Shared dwellings	TOTAL HOUSE-HOLD SPACES	Occupancy type of household spaces									
					Households with residents		Vacant accommodation			Accommodation not used as main residence				
										No persons present			Persons enumerated but no residents	
					Persons present	Absent household	New	Under improve-ment	Other	Second residences	Holiday accomm-odation	Student accomm-odation	Owner occupied	Not owner occupied
a	b	c	d	e	f	g	h	i	j	k	l	m	n	o
					Barrow-in-Furness									
ALL TYPES OF OCCUPANCY	**30,727**	**30,681**	**46**	**30,846**	**28,488**	**846**	**214**	**256**	**918**	**20**	**15**	**-**	**24**	**65**
Dwellings with residents	**29,237**	**29,193**	**44**	**29,354**	**28,488**	**846**	**-**	**-**	**18**	**-**	**-**	**-**	**-**	**2**
Dwellings with person(s) present	28,414	28,371	43	28,526	28,488	18	-	-	18	-	-	-	-	2
Dwellings with no person(s) present	823	822	1	828		828	-	-	-	-	-	-	-	-
Vacant accommodation	**1,368**	**1,366**	**2**	**1,370**			**214**	**256**	**900**	**-**	**-**	**-**	**-**	**-**
New, never occupied	214	214	-	214			214							
Under improvement	256	256	-	256			-	256	-	-	-	-	-	-
Other	898	896	2	900			-		900	-	-	-	-	-
Accommodation not used as main residence	**122**	**122**	**-**	**122**			**-**			**20**	**15**	**-**	**24**	**63**
No persons present	35	35	-	35			-			20	15	-		-
Second residences	20	20	-	20			-			20	-	-		-
Holiday accommodation	15	15	-	15			-				15	-		
Student accommodation	-	-	-	-			-					-		
Persons enumerated but no residents	87	87	-	87			-			-	-	-	24	63
Owner occupied	24	24	-	24			-			-	-	-	24	-
Not owner occupied	63	63	-	63			-				-	-		63

Table 65 Occupancy of dwellings and household spaces – **continued**

65. Dwellings; household spaces in dwellings

Occupancy type of dwelling	TOTAL DWELLINGS	Unshared dwellings	Shared dwellings	TOTAL HOUSE-HOLD SPACES	Occupancy type of household spaces: Households with residents: Persons present	Households with residents: Absent household	Vacant accommodation: New	Vacant accommodation: Under improve-ment	Vacant accommodation: Other	Accommodation not used as main residence: No persons present: Second residences	No persons present: Holiday accomm-odation	No persons present: Student accomm-odation	Persons enumerated but no residents: Owner occupied	Persons enumerated but no residents: Not owner occupied
a	b	c	d	e	f	g	h	i	j	k	l	m	n	o
					Carlisle									
ALL TYPES OF OCCUPANCY	**42,649**	**42,545**	**104**	**42,956**	**39,633**	**1,087**	**328**	**452**	**1,153**	**79**	**67**	**-**	**50**	**107**
Dwellings with residents	**40,464**	**40,364**	**100**	**40,765**	**39,633**	**1,087**	**-**	**-**	**22**	**1**	**-**	**-**	**-**	**22**
Dwellings with person(s) present	39,408	39,310	98	39,707	39,633	29	-	-	22	1	-	-	-	22
Dwellings with no person(s) present	1,056	1,054	2	1,058		1,058	-	-	-	-	-	-	-	-
Vacant accommodation	**1,905**	**1,901**	**4**	**1,911**			**328**	**452**	**1,131**	**-**	**-**	**-**	**-**	**-**
New, never occupied	328	328	-	328			328							
Under improvement	452	452	-	452			-	452	-	-	-	-	-	-
Other	1,125	1,121	4	1,131			-		1,131	-	-	-	-	-
Accommodation not used as main residence	**280**	**280**	**-**	**280**			**-**			**78**	**67**	**-**	**50**	**85**
No persons present	145	145	-	145			-			78	67	-		-
Second residences	78	78	-	78			-			78	-	-		-
Holiday accommodation	67	67	-	67			-				67	-		
Student accommodation	-	-	-	-			-					-		
Persons enumerated but no residents	135	135	-	135			-			-	-	-	50	85
Owner occupied	50	50	-	50			-			-	-	-	50	-
Not owner occupied	85	85	-	85			-				-	-		85

65. Dwellings; household spaces in dwellings

Occupancy type of dwelling	TOTAL DWELLINGS	Unshared dwellings	Shared dwellings	TOTAL HOUSE-HOLD SPACES	Occupancy type of household spaces									
					Households with residents		Vacant accommodation			Accommodation not used as main residence				
										No persons present			Persons enumerated but no residents	
					Persons present	Absent household	New	Under improve-ment	Other	Second residences	Holiday accomm-odation	Student accomm-odation	Owner occupied	Not owner occupied
a	b	c	d	e	f	g	h	i	j	k	l	m	n	o
					Copeland									
ALL TYPES OF OCCUPANCY	**29,272**	**29,235**	**37**	**29,374**	**26,823**	**720**	**186**	**270**	**755**	**341**	**148**	**-**	**44**	**87**
Dwellings with residents	**27,469**	**27,434**	**35**	**27,569**	**26,823**	**720**	**-**	**3**	**13**	**2**	**-**	**-**	**1**	**7**
Dwellings with person(s) present	26,757	26,722	35	26,857	26,823	8	-	3	13	2	-	-	1	7
Dwellings with no person(s) present	712	712	-	712		712	-	-	-	-	-	-	-	-
Vacant accommodation	**1,194**	**1,193**	**1**	**1,195**			**186**	**267**	**742**	**-**	**-**	**-**	**-**	**-**
New, never occupied	186	186	-	186			186							
Under improvement	267	267	-	267			-	267	-	-	-	-	-	-
Other	741	740	1	742			-		742	-	-	-	-	-
Accommodation not used as main residence	**609**	**608**	**1**	**610**			**-**			**339**	**148**	**-**	**43**	**80**
No persons present	486	485	1	487			-			339	148	-		-
Second residences	339	339	-	339			-			339	-	-		-
Holiday accommodation	147	146	1	148			-				148	-		
Student accommodation	-	-	-	-			-					-		
Persons enumerated but no residents	123	123	-	123			-			-	-	-	43	80
Owner occupied	43	43	-	43			-			-	-	-	43	-
Not owner occupied	80	80	-	80			-				-	-		80

Table 65 Occupancy of dwellings and household spaces – **continued**

65. Dwellings; household spaces in dwellings

Occupancy type of dwelling	TOTAL DWELLINGS	Unshared dwellings	Shared dwellings	TOTAL HOUSE-HOLD SPACES	Occupancy type of household spaces: Households with residents: Persons present	Households with residents: Absent household	Vacant accommodation: New	Vacant accommodation: Under improve-ment	Vacant accommodation: Other	Accommodation not used as main residence: No persons present: Second residences	No persons present: Holiday accomm-odation	No persons present: Student accomm-odation	Persons enumerated but no residents: Owner occupied	Persons enumerated but no residents: Not owner occupied
a	b	c	d	e	f	g	h	i	j	k	l	m	n	o
					Eden									
ALL TYPES OF OCCUPANCY	**20,313**	**20,291**	**22**	**20,362**	**17,270**	**554**	**185**	**265**	**558**	**611**	**660**	**3**	**111**	**145**
Dwellings with residents	**17,778**	**17,756**	**22**	**17,827**	**17,270**	**554**	**-**	**-**	**2**	**-**	**1**	**-**	**-**	**-**
Dwellings with person(s) present	17,233	17,211	22	17,282	17,270	9	-	-	2	-	1	-	-	-
Dwellings with no person(s) present	545	545	-	545		545	-	-	-	-	-	-	-	-
Vacant accommodation	**1,006**	**1,006**	**-**	**1,006**			**185**	**265**	**556**	**-**	**-**	**-**	**-**	**-**
New, never occupied	185	185	-	185			185							
Under improvement	265	265	-	265			-	265	-	-	-	-	-	-
Other	556	556	-	556			-		556	-	-	-	-	-
Accommodation not used as main residence	**1,529**	**1,529**	**-**	**1,529**			**-**			**611**	**659**	**3**	**111**	**145**
No persons present	1,273	1,273	-	1,273			-			611	659	3		-
Second residences	611	611	-	611			-			611	-	-		-
Holiday accommodation	659	659	-	659			-				659	-		
Student accommodation	3	3	-	3			-					3		
Persons enumerated but no residents	256	256	-	256			-			-	-	-	111	145
Owner occupied	111	111	-	111			-			-	-	-	111	-
Not owner occupied	145	145	-	145			-				-	-		145

65. Dwellings; household spaces in dwellings

Occupancy type of dwelling	TOTAL DWELLINGS	Unshared dwellings	Shared dwellings	TOTAL HOUSE-HOLD SPACES	Occupancy type of household spaces									
					Households with residents		Vacant accommodation			Accommodation not used as main residence				
										No persons present			Persons enumerated but no residents	
					Persons present	Absent household	New	Under improve-ment	Other	Second residences	Holiday accomm-odation	Student accomm-odation	Owner occupied	Not owner occupied
a	b	c	d	e	f	g	h	i	j	k	l	m	n	o
					South Lakeland									
ALL TYPES OF OCCUPANCY	**45,548**	**45,492**	**56**	**45,683**	**37,978**	**1,581**	**362**	**391**	**1,375**	**1,581**	**1,473**	**2**	**429**	**511**
Dwellings with residents	**39,452**	**39,396**	**56**	**39,587**	**37,978**	**1,581**	**-**	**-**	**16**	**-**	**-**	**-**	**-**	**12**
Dwellings with person(s) present	37,892	37,837	55	38,026	37,978	20	-	-	16	-	-	-	-	12
Dwellings with no person(s) present	1,560	1,559	1	1,561		1,561	-	-	-	-	-	-	-	-
Vacant accommodation	**2,112**	**2,112**	**-**	**2,112**			**362**	**391**	**1,359**	**-**	**-**	**-**	**-**	**-**
New, never occupied	362	362	-	362			362							
Under improvement	391	391	-	391			-	391	-	-	-	-	-	-
Other	1,359	1,359	-	1,359			-		1,359	-	-	-	-	-
Accommodation not used as main residence	**3,984**	**3,984**	**-**	**3,984**			**-**			**1,581**	**1,473**	**2**	**429**	**499**
No persons present	3,056	3,056	-	3,056			-			1,581	1,473	2		-
Second residences	1,581	1,581	-	1,581			-			1,581	-	-		-
Holiday accommodation	1,473	1,473	-	1,473			-				1,473	-		
Student accommodation	2	2	-	2			-					2		
Persons enumerated but no residents	928	928	-	928			-			-	-	-	429	499
Owner occupied	429	429	-	429			-			-	-	-	429	-
Not owner occupied	499	499	-	499			-				-	-		499

66. Shared dwellings; household spaces in shared dwellings

Number of household spaces within dwelling	TOTAL HOUSEHOLD SPACES	Type of not self-contained household space in shared dwellings				TOTAL SHARED DWELLINGS
		Not self-contained flat	Not self-contained 'rooms'	Bedsit	Not self-contained unoccupied	
a	b	c	d	e	f	g
CUMBRIA						
TOTAL SHARED DWELLINGS	**1,151**	**153**	**119**	**855**	**24**	**310**
2	236	81	52	87	16	118
3	162	35	18	105	4	54
4	204	19	17	166	2	51
5	145	1	11	133	-	29
6	180	5	12	161	2	30
7	91	5	4	82	-	13
8 or more	133	7	5	121	-	15
Allerdale						
TOTAL SHARED DWELLINGS	**174**	**19**	**20**	**128**	**7**	**45**
2	32	12	6	11	3	16
3	15	4	4	6	1	5
4	36	2	3	30	1	9
5	40	-	6	34	-	8
6	18	1	1	14	2	3
7	14	-	-	14	-	2
8 or more	19	-	-	19	-	2
Barrow-in-Furness						
TOTAL SHARED DWELLINGS	**165**	**17**	**30**	**113**	**5**	**46**
2	36	11	15	5	5	18
3	21	3	2	16	-	7
4	32	1	3	28	-	8
5	15	-	-	15	-	3
6	54	1	9	44	-	9
7	7	1	1	5	-	1
8 or more	-	-	-	-	-	-
Carlisle						
TOTAL SHARED DWELLINGS	**411**	**53**	**26**	**327**	**5**	**104**
2	60	24	9	25	2	30
3	78	14	5	56	3	26
4	60	6	3	51	-	15
5	60	1	4	55	-	12
6	48	1	-	47	-	8
7	42	2	1	39	-	6
8 or more	63	5	4	54	-	7
Copeland						
TOTAL SHARED DWELLINGS	**139**	**11**	**16**	**108**	**4**	**37**
2	32	6	5	18	3	16
3	12	1	4	7	-	4
4	16	2	3	10	1	4
5	20	-	1	19	-	4
6	36	1	1	34	-	6
7	14	1	2	11	-	2
8 or more	9	-	-	9	-	1
Eden						
TOTAL SHARED DWELLINGS	**71**	**10**	**9**	**51**	**1**	**22**
2	26	9	6	10	1	13
3	3	-	1	2	-	1
4	16	-	1	15	-	4
5	5	-	-	5	-	1
6	6	-	-	6	-	1
7	7	-	-	7	-	1
8 or more	8	1	1	6	-	1

66. Shared dwellings; household spaces in shared dwellings

Number of household spaces within dwelling	TOTAL HOUSEHOLD SPACES	Type of not self-contained household space in shared dwellings				TOTAL SHARED DWELLINGS
		Not self-contained flat	Not self-contained 'rooms'	Bedsit	Not self-contained unoccupied	
a	b	c	d	e	f	g
		South Lakeland				
TOTAL SHARED DWELLINGS	**191**	**43**	**18**	**128**	**2**	**56**
2	50	19	11	18	2	25
3	33	13	2	18	-	11
4	44	8	4	32	-	11
5	5	-	-	5	-	1
6	18	1	1	16	-	3
7	7	1	-	6	-	1
8 or more	34	1	-	33	-	4

Annex A Changes of boundary (between 5th April 1981 and 21st April 1991)

Date of change	Authority for change	Existing area i.e. as constituted at 21st April 1991 (names or descriptions not existing on 5th April 1981 are marked *)	Composition of existing area in terms of areas as constituted at 5th April 1981 (names or descriptions of counties/districts which have now ceased to exist are marked #)	Present population 1981	Existing areas in which the balance (if any) of the area named in col d is now situated
a	b	c	d	e	f
1st April 1989	The Cumbria and Lancashire (County Boundaries) Order 1988	CUMBRIA		487,036	
			Cumbria	487,038	
			except:		
			South Lakeland (pt)		†Lancashire
			Burton and Holme Ward (pt)	-5	
			Kirkby Lonsdale Ward (pt)	-	
			Lancashire (pt)		
			viz:		
			Lancaster (pt)		†Lancashire
			Arkholme Ward (pt)	-	
1st April 1990	The Cumbria, Northumberland and North Yorkshire (County Boundaries) Order 1989		Cumbria		
			except:		
			Carlisle (pt)		†Northumberland
			No 15 Ward (pt)	-	
			Eden (pt)		†North Yorkshire
			Kirkby Stephen Ward (pt)	-	
			Northumberland (pt)		
			viz:		
			Tynedale (pt)		†Northumberland
			West Tynedale Ward (pt)	+3	
1st April 1984	The Allerdale and Carlisle (Areas) Order 1983	Allerdale		97,121	
			Allerdale	97,121	Carlisle
			except:		
			Wampool Ward (pt)	-	
			Warnell Ward (pt)	-	
1st April 1984	The Allerdale and Carlisle (Areas) Order 1983	Carlisle		101,095	
			Carlisle	101,092	
			Allerdale (pt)		Allerdale
			viz:		
			Wampool Ward (pt)	-	
			Warnell Ward (pt)	-	
1st April 1990	The Cumbria, Northumberland and North Yorkshire (County Boundaries) Order 1989		Carlisle		Tynedale †(Northumberland)
			except:		
			No 15 Ward (pt)	-	
			Tynedale (pt)		Tynedale †(Northumberland)
			viz:		
			West Tynedale Ward (pt)	+3	
1st April 1990	The Cumbria, Northumberland and North Yorkshire (County Boundaries) Order 1989	Eden		44,191	
			Eden	44,191	Richmondshire †(North Yorkshire)
			except:		
			Kirkby Stephen Ward (pt)	-	
1st April 1989	The Cumbria and Lancashire (County Boundaries) Order 1988	South Lakeland		98,300	
			South Lakeland	98,305	Lancaster †(Lancashire)
			except:		
			Burton and Holme Ward (pt)	-5	
			Kirkby Lonsdale Ward (pt)	-	
			Lancaster (pt)		Lancaster †(Lancashire)
			viz:		
			Arkholme Ward (pt)	-	

†See relevant County Report

Notes:- Hectare measurements for those areas affected by boundary changes have not been included because the figures are not routinely available.
Changes of boundaries may involve areas of land with no population present in 1981, this is shown by a dash in Column e.
Where changes have affected ward or parish boundaries and/or names, details can be obtained from the Office of Population Censuses and Surveys, Census Customer Services, Titchfield, Fareham, Hants. PO15 5RR.

Annex B How to obtain 1991 Census results

The products described in this Annex become available in the period May 1992 until mid-1994. Dates of availability are not given, to avoid any confusion as this Report continues to be used during and after the period 1992-94. All products are described as if available, but, in any case of doubt, a check should be made with OPCS Census Customer Services at the address given at the end of this Annex.

The form of results

The statistical results of the Census are made available in two ways:

(a) in printed *reports* sold by HMSO bookshops (or, in a few cases, directly from the Census Offices); or

(b) in *statistical abstracts* available, on request and for a charge, from the Census offices.

The *reports* take three general forms:

- volumes - such as this Report - containing substantial and detailed tables;
- *key statistics*, which give around 200 summary statistics for particular types of areas throughout the country, with national and regional figures, laid out for easy comparison between areas; and
- *Monitors*, pamphlets which either give between 20 and 60 summary statistics for particular types of area in parts of the country, sometimes issued before main reports to give early results, or provide summaries for the country as a whole.

Statistical abstracts are supplied mainly in machine-readable form, although small quantities can be supplied as hard copies, and are generally either:

- in a standard form, commissioned by a number of customers sharing costs, particularly to provide results for areas and populations smaller than those covered in reports; or
- specially designed output commissioned by individual customers.

The Census Offices also supply supplementary products, for example to provide information on the geographical base of the Census, and documentation in a series of OPCS/GRO(S) *1991 Census User Guides*.

There are two broad types of results:

(a) *local statistics*, which cover the full range of census topics - such as this Report; and

(b) *topic statistics*, which focus on particular census topics in more detail, mainly at national and regional level.

All the main statistical results and products are described in *Prospectuses* in the *User Guides* series, available from the addresses given in section 13 and at the end of this Annex. Prospectuses for reports and abstracts contain complete outlines of the tables which will become available.

All areas for which results are provided in reports and abstracts are as at the time of the 1991 Census (unless otherwise indicated).

Local statistics

Local authorities

Results for smaller areas within the local authorities covered in this Report, or within local authorities elsewhere, are available as:

Ward and Civil Parish Monitors (England) or *Ward and Community Monitors* (Wales): pamphlets for each county in England and Wales which give some 30 statistics for each ward and civil parish/community, with figures for counties and districts/boroughs for comparison (see *Prospectus/User Guide 32)*.

Local and Small Area Statistics are standard abstracts available from a variety of areas throughout Britain from the smallest - the Census Enumeration District - upwards. They are introduced in section 3 of this Report, and further information is available in *Prospectus/User Guide 3*. Further *User Guides* give: the file specification (number 21); the cell numbering system (24 and 25); and explanatory notes (38).

Results for local authorities in other parts of the country are available, with full comparability, as:

County Reports (England and Wales) and *Region Reports* (Scotland): issued separately in two parts for each County in England and Wales and for each Region in Scotland.

Key Statistics (Great Britain): a single report giving around 200 summary statistics, with some 1981/91 comparisons, for each local authority (see *Prospectus/User Guide 20*).

County Monitors (England and Wales) and *Region Monitors* (Scotland): pamphlets issued separately for each County or Region in advance of the main *Reports*, with contents as section 15 of this Report. Welsh County Monitors will be produced in bi-lingual format (Welsh and English).

Local and Small Area Statistics are also available at local authority level.

Results for other types of area, in forms comparable with those for local authorities listed above, are available for:

Health authority areas

Health Regions Report: a single report, in the form of a County Report, for Regional Health Authorities in England (elsewhere in Britain health authority boundaries coincided with those of local authorities at the time of the 1991 Census).

Key Statistics: a single report giving some 200 summary statistics for each Regional and District Health Authority in England (see *Prospectus/User Guide 30*).

Health Authority Monitors: pamphlets, in the form of County Monitors, for Regional and District Health Authorities.

Local and Small Area Statistics are also available at health authority level.

Urban and Rural Areas

Key Statistics: a single report for the larger urban areas and the rural areas in Great Britain, giving some 200 summary statistics for each area, with six 'regional' reports covering urban areas of all sizes and the rural areas in various parts of England and, separately, for Wales and Scotland (see *User Guide/Prospectus 31*).

Urban and rural areas have been specially defined for both the 1981 and 1991 Censuses, and a further report will give figures on change over the decade. 'Urban areas' cover conurbations, cities and towns of all sizes defined on a land use ('bricks and mortar') basis, so, for example, Census results are available for smaller towns *within* the larger local authority areas.

Small Area Statistics are also available for each urban and rural area.

Parliamentary and European Constituencies

Parliamentary Constituency Monitors: pamphlets, in the form of County Monitors, but with some additional '10 per cent' statistics, with results for each Parliamentary Constituency (and with figures for Britain for comparison). There are separate Monitors for each standard statistical region in England, and for Wales and Scotland (see *User Guide/ Prospectus 34*). A single pamphlet in the same form is available for the European Parliamentary Constituencies in Great Britain.

Postcode areas

Postcode Sector Monitors: pamphlets for counties or groups of counties in England and Wales, giving some 30 '100 per cent' and '10 per cent' summary statistics at postcode sector level (see *Prospectus/User Guide 33*).

Small Area Statistics are also available for postcode sectors.

The 1991 Census records for England and Wales are re-sorted to give exact counts for postcode sectors. Results for a wide range of postcode based areas are available in Scotland.

National versions of local results

Results for Great Britain, regions in England, and Wales and Scotland, for these areas as a whole in forms comparable with those for local authorities and other types of area listed above, are available as:

National Reports: issued in two parts, on the lines of this Report, for Great Britain as a whole, including results for standard statistical regions in England and for Wales and Scotland; there is also a *Report for Wales*, bi-lingual in Welsh and English, and a *Report for Scotland*.

National and Regional Summary Monitor: pamphlet for Great Britain, including results for standard statistical regions in England and for Wales and Scotland, with contents as section 15 of this Report. Similar summary Monitors will be issued for Wales (bi-lingual) and Scotland, including summary results at County/Region level.

Topic statistics

Results for particular census topics are available in a series of reports summarised in the table on the following page. The reports present results mainly at the national level, but the following table shows those which have results at regional level, or at a county or district (or equivalent) level. Prospectuses should be checked for detailed information. The Regional Migration Reports comprise separate volumes for each standard statistical region of England, and for Wales and for Scotland.

Workplace and migration statistics

The analysis of the Census questions on 'address of workplace' and 'usual address' one year before the Census give results on journeys from residences to workplaces and on migration moves, together with figures on people with workplaces in an area and out-migrants from an area, not only for the larger areas covered by the Reports listed above but also for smaller local areas. The latter are:

Special Migration Statistics: which provide information (in machine-readable form only) on migrants within and between local areas (see *Prospectus/User Guide 35)*.

Special Workplace Statistics: which provide information (in machine-readable form only) on workforces in areas of workplace and residence for customer defined zones, and on journeys from residence to workplace between the zones (see *Prospectus/User Guide 36*).

Other products

Commissioned tables

In addition to the standard tables prepared for the local and topic statistics, the Census Offices also supply tables, on request, to a customer's own specification, at a charge which meets the marginal cost of production. *Prospectus/User Guide 14* explains how customers may specify and order commissioned tables, and provides guidance on estimation of costs.

Topic	Processing level (per cent)	Prospectus (number)	With some results for:		
			Standard Statistical Regions*	Counties/ regions	Districts
Sex, Age and Marital Status (GB)	100	2	yes	yes	no
Historical Tables (GB)	100	4	yes	yes	no
Usual Residence (GB)	100	7	yes	yes	yes
Persons Aged 60 and Over (GB)	100	6	yes	no	no
Housing and Availability of Cars (GB and S)	100	12	yes	yes	yes
Communal Establishments (GB)	100	15	yes	no	no
Household Composition (GB)	100	11	yes	no	no
Limiting Long-term Illness (GB)	100	5	yes	no	no
Ethnic Group and Country of Birth (GB)	100/10	9	yes	yes	yes
Welsh Language in Wales	100/10	10	n/a	yes	yes
Gaelic Language in Scotland	100/10	18	n/a	yes	yes
National Migration (Part 1) (GB)	100	17	yes**	no	no
National Migration (Part 2) (GB)	10	17	yes**	no	no
Regional Migration (Part 1)	100	22	yes**	yes	yes
Regional Migration (Part 2)	10	22	yes**	no	no
Report for Health Areas (GB)	100	39	n/a	n/a	n/a
Economic Activity (GB and S)	10	16	yes	no	no
Workplace and Transport to Work (GB and S)	10	20	yes	yes	yes***
Household and Family Composition (GB)	10	23	no	no	no
Qualified Manpower (GB)	10	8	yes	no	no
Children and Young Adults (GB)	100/10	13	yes	no	no

GB Volumes for Great Britain
GB and S Volumes for Great Britain together with additional volumes for Scotland

* includes Metropolitan Counties in England
** includes main urban areas
*** includes city centres

Enumeration District/Postcode Directory

This Directory provides a means of associating enumeration districts to postcodes to enable users to undertake their own linkage between census and other datasets. It is available, on magnetic media only, separately for each county. Alternatively, customers may purchase a National Directory. Further details of the file specification, information on availability, cost and ordering are provided in *Prospectus 26*.

User Guide Catalogue

This catalogue is available from the Census Customer Services at the address given below. The catalogue is regularly revised to provide up-to-date information on all Prospectuses/User Guides.

Census Newsletter

The Newsletter is published several times a year to provide a link with users. It gives information on many aspects of the 1991 Census, including details of relevant publications and census-related activities. The Newsletter is a major source of information about the availability of census results and also reports on the main findings from evaluations of coverage and quality. Customers wishing to be included on the mailing list for future copies of the Newsletter should contact Census Customer Services.

Information on all products described in this Annex may be obtained from

Census Customer Services
OPCS
Segensworth Road
Titchfield
Fareham
Hampshire
PO15 5RR

Telephone 0329 81 3800

Please mention this Report when making an enquiry.

Annex C Explanatory notes on the summary and main (part 1) tables

Summary tables

References to the '*Definitions* volume' are to the publication described in section 7.

Tables A and B

Tables A and B are the only summary tables which refer to the present population. In Tables A and B, and in the accompanying diagram, *preliminary counts of the population present* for 1981 have been used because they are felt to be generally more accurate than the final 1981 counts of the population present which were inflated by a processing error (see *1981 Census Monitor CEN 82/3*). The 1981 preliminary counts have been corrected for a few errors (also reported in *1981 Census Monitor CEN 82/3*), and for boundary changes between 1981 and 1991. Because of the preliminary nature of these figures, they have been rounded to the nearest hundred before presentation.

Tables C, E, F, G, I, K, L, and M

Tables C, E, F, G, I, K and L (also M - Wales only) include comparisons between the numbers of residents, and households with residents, in 1981 and 1991. These comparisons are made using the 1981 resident population base (that is, the 1991 statistics used in the comparisons exclude wholly absent households in the same way that the 1981 statistics do) to give a valid picture of intercensal changes.

Tables F and K

The 1981-91 comparisons in Tables F and K use the 1981 definition of students, in which all students are categorised as economically inactive. The remaining sections of these tables use the 1991 definition, in which students who were in employment or seeking work in the week before the Census are categorised as economically active and are included in the relevant economically active categories.

The 1981-91 comparisons of residents and households with residents in section 15 also use the 1981 population base. Some intercensal changes are expressed in terms of *'percentage points'*. This is the arithmetic difference between the 1991 percentage and the 1981 percentage.

All Tables

The following terms appear in the *Summary* tables - see the *Definitions* volume for full details:

(i) A 'hectare' is equivalent to 2.471 acres.

(ii) A 'household' is either one person living alone; or a group of people (who may or may not be related), living, or staying temporarily, at the same address with common housekeeping - that is, sharing at least one meal a day or sharing a living room or sitting room.

(iii) 'Communal establishments' comprise:

- NHS and non-NHS hospitals,
- local authority homes,
- housing association homes and hostels,
- nursing homes,
- residential homes,
- children's homes,
- prison service establishments,
- defence establishments,
- educational establishments,
- hotels and boarding houses,
- hostels and lodging houses,
- other miscellaneous establishments,
- campers and people sleeping rough, and
- civilian ships, boats, and barges.

(iv) A 'person of pensionable age' is a man aged 65 or over or a woman aged 60 or over.

(v) 'Economically inactive' includes:

- students without a job in the week before the Census,
- permanently sick people,
- retired people, and
- people looking after the home or family and not in paid employment.

(vi) A 'dwelling' consists of one or more household spaces, which may be occupied or unoccupied. A *shared dwelling* consists of two or more household spaces in a multi-occupied building which share access and are not self-contained.

(vii) A 'lone parent' in the Summary tables is a person who is the only adult (person aged 16 or over) in a household with children aged 15 or under.

(viii) A 'dependant' is either a dependent child, or a person with limiting long-term illness *and* permanently sick or retired.

(ix) A 'dependent child' is defined as either a person aged 0-15 in a household; or one aged 16-18, never married, in full-time education, *and* economically inactive.

Percentages in the tables do not necessarily add up to exactly 100 per cent, because each is individually rounded.

Vertical lines in the tables separate different analyses. Percentages or counts should only be summed *within* vertical lines.

In the tables a count or percentage of zero is shown by a dash (-). In Tables A and B percentages of less than 0.005 per cent are shown as 0.00 per cent. In other tables percentages of less than 0.05 per cent are shown as 0.0 per cent.

In Tables E, F, I, K, and L a blank means that no relevant 1981 Census data exist.

In Table G the 1981 percentages for household amenities straddle two columns because no information on central heating was collected in the 1981 Census.

Main tables

References to the '*Definitions* volume' are to the publication described in section 7.

I Demographic and economic characteristics

Table 1

Definitions of populations counted on rows 1 to 5 are:

1. Present residents - residents and persons of no fixed abode or no usual residence who were present on Census night (that is, for whom the response to Question 6, whereabouts, was 'at this address').

2. Absent residents (part of household present) - residents for whom the response to Question 6, whereabouts, was not 'at this address' in households where one or more persons were enumerated as present 'at that address' on Census night.

3. Absent residents (wholly absent household - enumerated) - residents in households where nobody was enumerated as present at that address on Census night (wholly absent households), where a Census form was returned under the voluntary arrangements for the enumeration of such wholly absent households.

4. Absent residents (wholly absent household - imputed) - residents in households where nobody was enumerated as present at that address on Census night (wholly absent households), but where no Census form was returned. Details for the households and residents have been imputed - see the *Definitions* volume paragraphs 1.48-1.54. This category also includes imputed residents of households reported to have residents but where no contact could be made, and also imputed residents in households that refused to complete a Census form.

5. Visitors - persons present at an address for whom the response to Question 7, usual address, was 'elsewhere'.

   The components in rows 1 to 5 are used to compile counts on three population bases - those used in the 1971, 1981, and 1991 Censuses. This allows comparison with Small Area Statistics (SAS) results from previous censuses:

   PERSONS PRESENT 1991: 1971 BASE (1+5) - this is the sum of lines 1 and 5; that is all present residents plus all visitors. This is equivalent to the count 'Total population present' in 1971 SAS Table 1, from which other sub-populations of persons were drawn for the 1971 SAS.

   RESIDENTS 1991: 1981 BASE (1+2) - this is the sum of lines 1 and 2; that is all present residents plus all absent residents in households where someone was enumerated as present on Census night. This is equivalent to the count ALL RESIDENT 1981: 1981 BASE in 1981 SAS Table 1, which formed the base for most 1981 SAS Tables, most tables in the 1981 Reports, and many other 1981 Census Tables.

   RESIDENTS 1991: 1991 BASE (1+2+3+4) - this is the sum of lines 1, 2, 3, and 4; that is all present and absent residents. This is the count which forms the base for most 1991 100 per cent tables in the Reports/LBS, SAS, and most other 100 per cent tables.

Table 3

(i) 'Persons present not in households' are all persons enumerated in communal establishments, plus persons sleeping rough and campers.

(ii) 'Number of establishments' is the total number of each type of establishment in the area at which persons were enumerated on Census night. No counts of 'establishments' are given for persons sleeping rough or for campers.

(iii) 'Residents: Staff' includes residents returned on the Census form as relatives of the manager or other staff, and other people who are not guests (in hotels, etc) or inmates. It should be noted that staff **on duty** in an establishment on Census night whose usual addresses were elsewhere were **not** enumerated in the establishment unless they were temporarily residing in the establishment.

(iv) 'Residents: Other' will, in general, include only those persons who were resident guests (in hotels, etc) or resident inmates. However, **all** persons resident on ships and all persons resident in defence establishments are included in this category.

(v) 'Non-NHS/LA/HA' means that the establishments are not under the management of the National Health Service, a local authority, or a housing association. 'Non-HA' means not under the management of a housing association.

(vi) For the full definition and classification of communal establishments see Chapter 4 of the *Definitions* volume.

Table 4

(i) 'Residents (non-staff) present not in households' will, in general, include only those persons who were resident guests (in hotels, etc) or resident inmates. However, **all** persons resident on ships and all persons resident in defence establishments are included in this category.

(ii) 'Non-NHS/LA/HA' means that the establishments are not under the management of the National Health Service, a local authority, or a housing association.

Table 5

(i) See note (i) to Table 4.

(ii) 'Non-HA' means not under the management of a housing association.

Table 7

(i) The 'Europe' sub-total comprises UK, Channel Islands, Isle of Man, Irish Republic, Ireland (part not stated), and all countries under 'Remainder of Europe'.

(ii) The 'European Community' sub-total comprises UK and all countries listed under 'European Community'.

Table 10

Because the County Reports are published for each county soon after processing of the Census data for each is completed, this table counts only those students who are resident in the area and those who are not residents but were present on Census night. Students who normally live in the area during term-time but are not residents of the area and were not present in the area on Census night are excluded from the table. A complete matrix of area of residence and area of term-time address for students is being prepared by the Census Offices when processing all areas of Great Britain is complete. More information on the availability of statistics from this matrix can be obtained from the Census Offices at the addresses shown in section 13.

Table 11

(i) 'Residents: Staff' includes residents returned on the Census form as relatives of the manager or other staff, and other people who are not guests (in hotels, etc) or inmates. It should be noted that staff **on duty** in an establishment on Census night whose usual addresses were elsewhere were **not** enumerated in the establishment unless they were temporarily residing in the establishment.

(ii) 'Residents: Other' will, in general, include only those persons who were resident guests (in hotels, etc) or resident inmates. However, **all** persons resident on ships and all persons resident in defence establishments are included in this category.

Table 13

(i) 'Other' establishments comprises 'Detention, defence, and education' establishments, and 'Other groups' including persons sleeping rough and campers.

(ii) For the full definition and classification of communal establishments see Chapter 4 of the *Definitions* volume.

Table 15

'Neighbouring counties/neighbouring districts' are areas with common boundaries. This concept is used in tables counting 'migrants' (usual residents of an area with a different usual address one year before the Census). The counts in these columns represent the number of migrants resident in an area who lived in neighbouring areas one year before Census night. For each local government district the counts represent those migrants who formerly lived in the counties/Scottish regions neighbouring the county containing the area in question, or those formerly living in the local government districts neighbouring the district in question. For the county as a whole the counts will represent the sum of all migrants who moved from neighbouring counties/ Scottish regions and neighbouring districts. (All areas/ boundaries are as on 21 April 1991.)

All areas which share a section of land boundary, including those which touch at a point, are included as neighbours. Areas which are separated by water (a river, or larger body of water) are included as neighbours if there is a transport link (rail or road bridge, or tunnel, or vehicle ferry) between the two areas. Areas which are separated by land belonging to a third area are not included as neighbours, no matter how close together the areas are. The lists of neighbouring areas were compiled in consultation with the local authorities.

The full lists of neighbouring counties/Scottish regions and neighbouring districts are shown in a *User Guide* available from the Census Offices.

Table 16

(i) See note to Table 15.

(ii) Counts of persons and households in the section for 'Wholly moving households with dependent children' may include a small number of households with no adults.

Table 18

(i) This table includes counts of all imputed residents in wholly absent households which did not return a form under the voluntary arrangements for the enumeration of wholly absent households, plus imputed residents in households where people were reported to live, but where no contact could be made, plus imputed residents of households which refused to complete a Census form.

(ii) 'Other ethnic groups' comprises Black-Caribbean, Black-African, Black-Other, Indian, Pakistani, Bangladeshi, Chinese, and Other groups.

(iii) See paragraphs 1.48-1.54 of the *Definitions* volume for details of the imputation of wholly absent households.

II Housing

Table 19

(i) This table gives imputed counts of all wholly absent households which did not return a form under the voluntary arrangements for the enumeration of such wholly absent households, plus households where people were reported to live, but where no contact could be made, plus households which refused to complete a Census form.

(ii) See paragraphs 1.48-1.54 of the *Definitions* volume for details of the imputation of wholly absent households.

(iii) The range of tenure categories in this table is incomplete; the category 'rented with a job or business' is omitted because it would contain only very small numbers. The counts can be derived by subtracting the sum of the given tenure categories from the table total.

Table 21

(i) 'Number of persons aged 17 and over (with and without others)' is a classification of residents aged 17 and over in households regardless of whether any other residents in the household are aged under 17.

(ii) The rows 'ALL HOUSEHOLDS' and 'TOTAL PERSONS (ALL AGES)' may include a small number of households with no person aged 17 and over, and residents in such households. Such households and residents are not included elsewhere in the table.

Table 22

(i) 'Households with the following rooms' counts the number of households with the stated number of rooms.

(ii) 'Households with the following . . . persons' counts the number of households with the stated number of residents.

Table 24

(i) 'Households with the following persons' and 'Households with the following number of persons aged 18 and over' count the number of households with the stated number of residents, and residents aged 18 and over respectively.

(ii) The column 'TOTAL HOUSEHOLDS' may include a small number of households with no person aged 18 and over, and residents in such households. Such households and residents are not included elsewhere in the table.

Table 25

(i) This table counts households which were enumerated with persons present but which had no residents, whether present or absent; that is households consisting entirely of visitors. The table will include occupied second homes, holiday accommodation, and student residences (excluding halls of residence and other communal student accommodation).

(ii) 'Students' in this table are defined as those aged 18 and over to exclude schoolchildren enumerated with their parents.

(iii) The range of tenure categories in this table is incomplete; the category 'rented with a job or business' is omitted because it would contain only very small numbers. The counts can be derived by subtracting the sum of the given tenure categories from the table total.

Table 26

(i) This table counts households enumerated with residents (whether present or absent) in which at least one student (aged 18 or over) was resident (whether present or absent) or a visitor.

(ii) 'Students' in this table are defined as those aged 18 and over, to exclude schoolchildren enumerated with their parents.

(iii) The range of tenure categories in this table is incomplete; the category 'rented with a job or business' is omitted because it would contain only very small numbers. The counts can be derived by subtracting the sum of the given tenure categories from the table total.

Table 27

(i) This table counts households, persons in households, and rooms, according to the population bases used in the 1971, 1981, and 1991 Censuses.

(ii) Row 1 counts households with at least one person present on Census night 1991, whether a resident or not, sub-divided by the number of persons present on Census night. The 'TOTAL PERSONS' column counts the total number of persons present in households.

(iii) Row 2 counts households with at least one person present on Census night 1991, whether a resident or not, sub-divided by the number of residents, whether present or absent on Census night. The entry in the column headed '0' counts households with no residents but at least one person present on Census night. The 'TOTAL PERSONS' column counts the total number of residents present in households, and absent residents in households where at least one person was present.

(iv) Row 3 counts households with at least one person present (whether a resident or not), plus wholly absent households (enumerated and imputed), plus imputed counts for households where people were reported to live, but where no contact could be made, or which refused to complete a Census form, sub-divided by the number of residents, whether present or absent on Census night. The entry in the column headed '0' counts households with no residents but at least one person present on Census night. The 'TOTAL PERSONS' column counts the total number of residents in households, whether present or absent.

III Households and household composition

Table 30

In the columns classifying households by the age of the youngest and oldest dependant, households with only one dependant are classified by taking the dependant as both the youngest and the oldest in the household.

Table 31

The row 'ALL HOUSEHOLDS' may include a small number of households with no adults, and residents in such households. Such households and residents are not included elsewhere in the table.

Table 32

(i) This table is given alongside Table 31 to provide comparative statistics with 1981 County Report Table 34.

(ii) The row 'ALL HOUSEHOLDS' may include a small number of households with no persons aged 16 and over, and residents in such households. Such households and residents are not included elsewhere in the table.

Table 33

(i) A 'couple' is a male aged 16 and over and a female aged 16 and over, whether or not both were returned as 'married' (whether to each other or not), resident in a household with no other residents aged 16 and over.

(ii) 'Other' economically active females comprise females on a Government scheme, and those unemployed.

Table 36

'Households with the following adults' and 'Households with the following dependent children' count respectively households with the stated number of resident adults, and resident dependent children.

Table 37

(i) Lone 'parents' are the sole *residents* aged 16-24 (with no residents aged 25 or over) in households with a child or children aged 0-15 in the household. The 'lone parent' is not necessarily a parent of the child, for example, a woman aged 21 living alone with her 15 year old sister will be included in the counts. The counts will not include all lone parent families; those in households with other adults will be excluded - see Table 87 in Part 2 of the County Report for 10 per cent sample counts of *lone parent families*.

(ii) The range of employment position categories in this table is incomplete; the category 'self-employed' is omitted because it contains only very small numbers. The counts can be derived by subtracting the sum of the given economic position categories from the table total.

Table 39

The two total rows 'All ages 16 and over' may include a small number of heads and residents in households where the head is aged under 16. Such households and residents are also included in the rows for ages 16-19.

Table 40

(i) Lone 'parents' are the sole *residents* aged 16 or over in households with a child or children aged 0-15 in the household. The 'lone parent' is not necessarily a parent of the child, for example, a woman aged 21 living alone with her 15 year old sister will be included in the counts. The counts will not include all lone parent families; those in households with other adults will be excluded (see Table 87 in Part 2 of the County Report for 10 per cent sample counts of all *lone parent* families).

(ii) 'Other' economically active comprises those on a Government scheme, and those unemployed.

Table 42

(i) The range of 'persons per room' categories in this table is incomplete; the categories 'up to 0.5 persons per room' and 'over 0.5 and up to 1 person per room' are omitted. A total for these two counts can be derived by subtracting the sum of the given 'persons per room' categories from the table total.

(ii) The range of categories of dependent children by age in this table is incomplete; the category 'dependent children aged 18' is omitted. The counts can be derived by subtracting the sum of the given categories from the total for all dependent children.

(iii) The range of categories of cars in this table is incomplete; the categories '1 car' and '2 cars' are omitted. A total for these counts can be derived by subtracting the sum of the given categories from the table total.

(iv) The total row 'ALL HOUSEHOLDS' may include a small number of households with no resident adults. Such households are not included in the other household composition categories.

Table 43

(i) The total row 'ALL HOUSEHOLDS' may include a small number of households with no resident adults. Such households are not included in the other household composition categories.

(ii) The range of categories of residents by age in this table is incomplete; ages 19 up to pensionable age are omitted. A total for these ages can be derived by subtracting the sum of the given categories from the total. (**Note**: the age categories 0-4, 5-15 and 0-17 are all sub-categories of 'All dependent children aged 0-18' and therefore should be omitted from any calculation of the number of residents aged 19 up to pensionable age.)

Table 44

The total row 'ALL HOUSEHOLDS' may include a small number of households with no resident adults. Such households are not included in the other household composition categories.

Table 45

The columns 'Total migrant heads' and 'TOTAL HOUSEHOLD HEADS' may include a small number of households where the head is aged under 16. Such households are also included in the age 16-19 columns.

Table 46

(i) The range of 'persons per room' categories in this table is incomplete; the categories 'up to 0.5 persons per room' and 'over 0.5 and up to 1 person per room' are omitted. A total for these two counts can be derived by subtracting the sum of the given 'persons per room' categories from the table total.

(ii) The range of tenure categories in this table is incomplete; the category 'rented with a job or business' is omitted because it would contain only very small numbers. The counts can be derived by subtracting the sum of the given tenure categories from the table total.

Table 47

The final six cells in the last column of this table are blank to avoid needless repetition of the counts in the last three cells of the first column.

Table 49

(i) The range of 'persons per room' categories in this table is incomplete; the categories 'up to 0.5 persons per room' and 'over 0.5 and up to 1 person per room' are omitted. A total for these two counts can be derived by subtracting the sum of the given 'persons per room' categories from the table total.

(ii) The range of tenure categories in this table is incomplete; the category 'rented with a job or business' is omitted because it would contain only very small counts for most ethnic groups. The counts can be derived by subtracting the sum of the given tenure categories from the table total.

(iii) Counts for households with head born in the New Commonwealth are included to provide some statistics to compare with 1981 Report Table 33.

Table 50

In the columns, 'Inside UK' **does not** include Channel Islands and the Isle of Man.

Table 52

This table is included as a proxy measure of the population not having English as a first language.

Table 53

A 'couple' household is a household with one male resident aged 16 and over and one female resident aged 16 and over, whether or not both were returned as 'married' (whether to each other or not), with no other residents aged 16 and over in the household.

IV Household spaces and dwellings

Table 54

(i) 'TOTAL HOUSEHOLD SPACES' for households with residents, and with persons enumerated but no residents, include as 'household spaces' the accommodation of any households living in non-permanent accommodation. The other occupancy types shown comprise only accommodation in permanent buildings.

(ii) 'TOTAL ROOMS' in 'Hotels and boarding houses' include only those rooms used by guests or staff for living, eating or sleeping.

(iii) 'TOTAL ROOMS' in absent households (imputed), in vacant accommodation, and in accommodation not used as main residence in which no persons were present (that is, second residences, holiday accommodation, and student accommodation), are totals of estimates made in each such case by the enumerator.

Table 56

(i) 'Absent households' includes both enumerated and imputed absent households.

(ii) 'Other' vacant accommodation includes vacant accommodation 'under improvement'.

(iii) The distinction between 'not self-contained flat' and 'not self-contained 'rooms'' in columns j and k, and columns m and n is made with reference to whether basic household amenities are shared. For household spaces where nobody was enumerated (vacant accommodation etc), this distinction is not possible, and only a single count can be given to cover 'not self-contained flat' and 'not self-contained 'rooms''. This also affects any totals which incorporate unoccupied accommodation. Some counts in this table therefore straddle columns.

Table 57

'Households with the following rooms', 'Households with the following persons', and 'Households with the following persons per room' count the number of households with the stated number of rooms, residents, and residents per room respectively.

Table 59

(i) The range of categories of residents by age in this table is incomplete; adults up to pensionable age are omitted. A total for this group can be derived by subtracting the sum of the given categories from the total. (**Note**: the age categories 0-4 and 5-15 are all sub-categories of 'All dependent children' and therefore should be omitted from any calculation of the number of resident adults up to pensionable age.)

(ii) The total row 'ALL HOUSEHOLDS' may include a small number of households with no resident adults. Such households are not included in the other household composition categories.

Table 60

'TOTAL CONVERTED OR SHARED ACCOMMODATION' is a count of buildings containing converted or shared household spaces; that is, a count of multi-occupied buildings.

Table 61

The distinction between 'not self-contained flat' and 'not self-contained 'rooms'' in columns k and l is made with reference to whether basic household amenities are shared. For dwellings where nobody was enumerated (vacant accommodation, etc), this distinction is not possible, and only a single count can be given to cover 'not self-contained flat' and 'not self-contained 'rooms''. This also affects any totals which incorporate unoccupied accommodation. Some counts in this table therefore straddle columns.

Table 64

(i) The tenure of a dwelling is chosen with reference to the tenure(s) of the household space(s) making up the dwelling. For a dwelling of one household space the tenure will be the same for both the dwelling and the household space. For a multi-household space dwelling the tenure is chosen according to a priority order:

1 Owner occupied - owned outright
2 Owner occupied - buying
3 Rented from a housing association
4 Rented from a new town
5 Rented from a local authority
6 Rented privately - unfurnished
7 Rented privately - furnished
8 Rented with a job or business

(Items 4 and 5 are always taken together in England and Wales.)

The highest ranked tenure among the household spaces becomes the tenure for the dwelling. For example, a dwelling consisting of one 'owner occupied - buying' household space and one 'rented privately - furnished' household space will be classified as an 'owner occupied - buying' dwelling.

Impossible combinations of dwelling and household space tenures (where the dwelling would have a lower priority tenure than a household space) are shown in the table as blank cells.

(ii) 'Other unoccupied accommodation' comprises second residences, holiday accommodation and student accommodation.

Table 65

The occupancy type of a dwelling is chosen with reference to the occupancy type(s) of the household space(s) making up the dwelling. For a dwelling of one household space the occupancy type will be the same for both the dwelling and the household space. For a multi-household space dwelling the occupancy type is chosen according to a priority order:

1 With residents - persons present
2 With residents - absent household (no persons present)
3 Vacant - under improvement
4 Vacant - other
5 Persons enumerated but no residents - owner occupied
6 Second residences
7 Persons enumerated but no residents - not owner occupied
8 Holiday accommodation
9 Student accommodation
10 Vacant - new, never occupied

The highest ranked occupancy type among the household spaces becomes the occupancy type for the dwelling. For example, a dwelling consisting of one 'second residence' household space and one household space 'with residents - persons present' will be classified as a dwelling 'with residents - persons present'.

Impossible combinations of dwelling and household space occupancy types (where the dwelling would have a lower priority occupancy type than a household space) are shown in the table as blank cells.

V Wales only table

Table 67

The question on the Welsh language is asked only of persons aged 3 and over.

Imputed data

A Tables 18 and 19 show counts of residents in imputed households, and imputed households for a selection of key variables (these tables include imputed wholly absent households and the other categories of imputed households and residents described in section 5). Table 71 in part 2 of the Report shows a comparison of the numbers of households processed at 100 per cent, and the number included in the 10 per cent sample.

B These counts will aid any comparison of grossed-up estimates from 10 per cent sample tables with 100 per cent processed tables, and to calculate percentage distributions of 10 per cent items based on an estimate of the total population. The imputed households and imputed residents form, in effect, 'not stated' cases for each census topic in the 10 per cent sample tables.

Printed in the United Kingdom for HMSO
Dd294994 10/92 C6 G3397 10170